FAUST

A *Tragedy*

A NEW TRANSLATION
BACKGROUNDS AND SOURCES
THE AUTHOR ON THE DRAMA
CONTEMPORARY REACTIONS
MODERN CRITICISM

JOHANN WOLFGANG VON GOETHE

FAUST

A Tragedy

BACKGROUNDS AND SOURCES

THE AUTHOR ON THE DRAMA

CONTEMPORARY REACTIONS

MODERN CRITICISM

➤➤◄◄

Translated by WALTER ARNDT

DARTMOUTH COLLEGE

Edited by CYRUS HAMLIN

VICTORIA COLLEGE, UNIVERSITY OF TORONTO

W · W · NORTON & COMPANY · INC · *New York*

Library of Congress Cataloging in Publication Data

Goethe, Johann Wolfgang von, 1749–1832.
  Faust: backgrounds, criticism.
  (A Norton critical edition)
  Bibliography: p.
  I. Arndt, Walter W., 1916–   II. Hamlin, Cyrus.   III. Title.
PT2026.F2A75   1976   831'.6   75-37791✓
ISBN 0-393-04424-6
ISBN 0-393-09208-9 pbk.

Contents

Contemporary Reactions   433

Modern Criticism   445

Preface

A critical edition of Goethe's *Faust* in a new verse translation is a formidable undertaking. Both the translator and the editor hope that this book may testify, without further comment from them, to the seriousness with which they have approached their respective labors. The entire project has been a cooperative venture, though the translation was already well underway before the editor was introduced to it through the mediating influence of the publisher. Advice and suggestions have been exchanged liberally in both directions between Hanover and Toronto over a four-year period. The result, despite the clear division of labor indicated on the title page, may be regarded as the product of genuine cooperation. Some of the essential presuppositions with which the translator and the editor have approached their respective tasks are outlined in the essays entitled "Translating *Faust*" and "Reading *Faust*," below. Remarks may thus be limited here to mechanical matters.

The translation presents the entire text of Goethe's drama, both *Parts I* and *II*, with strict adherence to the form of the original in all its varied meters and rhyme patterns, and generally maintaining a strict line-by-line correspondence. The traditional procedure of numbering the whole of *Faust* (with the single exception of the prose scene "Dreary Day. Field") through marginal notation has also been retained. The spatial arrangement of the text on the page, which Goethe himself determined with some care in the original published versions, has been followed as closely as possible. Annotation by the editor, in accord with the general policy of the Norton Critical Editions, consists of glosses, located at the bottom of the page, addressed to particular points of complexity and obscurity in the text of the drama. These have been kept to a minimum, but the question of adequacy for so difficult and wide-ranging a work of the imagination has not been easy to resolve. The editor, who always tended to comment beyond need, wishes to express his gratitude for patience and for practical advice on many, many details from both Walter Arndt and John Francis. In recognition of the unique problems of interpreting the multifarious riches of Goethe's play, the publishers have also approved the inclusion of selected interpretive footnotes in a separate section following the text, where various problems which face a reader of *Faust* are considered in greater detail than the format of the footnotes allowed. (The symbol † has been used to alert the reader to these interpretive notes, which begin on p. 309.) For such generosity the editor, who takes sole responsibility for the critical perspective there presented, wishes to express special thanks.

The critical material represents the broadest range of perspectives possible within a format limited by expediency. Two considerations were applied above all in the choice of particular texts: 1) that Goethe's *Faust* is the representative masterpiece of that era in European literature and culture which is usually referred to as Romanticism and that Goethe, however universal in his poetic vision, was also created by, and a creator of, his age; and 2) that few discussions of *Faust* from the perspective of the entire work could provide practical assistance for the study of the particular problems which arise for any reading of it. A few comments in regard to these considerations may clarify the selection of material.

Although the popular legend of Faust played an important role in the composition of Goethe's work and still provides a sense of the general tradition within which this unique drama came to be, the most important material for any study of *Faust* in its own time must be found among Goethe's own remarks and among those of his contemporaries. Selections from the earlier tradition have been included—from the initial English translation of the original chapbook and from the almost sub-literary puppet play (first published in the mid-nineteenth century)—as well as an essay by Hans Mayer which offers a broad assessment of this tradition. Also included (for the first time in English) is the seventeenth "Literary Letter" by Lessing, which marked a turning point in taste that led directly to Goethe's drama. Yet the material which should prove of special value for the general student, much of it unavailable in English up to now, is contained in the sections entitled "The Author on the Drama" and "Contemporary Reactions." Most of the items by Goethe on *Faust* were translated especially for this volume. The same holds true for the critical comments by August Wilhelm and Friedrich Schlegel and by the philosopher Schelling. The texts by Hegel, Mme. de Stael, and Heine had appeared in English at one time or another, but for various reasons they remain largely unknown to all but the specialized *Faust* scholar.

Most of the headings in the section "Essays in Criticism" are self-explanatory. The valuable survey of *Faust* in the essay by Hermann Weigand was undertaken, as the subtitle indicates, for just such an audience as may presumably find occasion to use this book. The essays by Eudo C. Mason and Emil Staiger concerning Goethe's use of the traditional pact and his adaptation of the Faust legend to his own poetic purposes complement each other regarding the most crucial issue for any study of *Faust*. The selections from two essays on the Gretchen tragedy by Barker Fairley and Georg Lukacs approach the same subject with apparent differences of method and point of view, though the arguments which result do not necessarily exclude each other. The two sections entitled "The

Dramatic Structure of *Faust*" and "The Problematics of *Part II*" are concerned with important critical issues which will provide the student with a glimpse into the workshop of criticism, so to speak, where all questions are still wide open and authority is difficult to find. The essays by Wolfgang Binder and Herman Meyer, especially, provide a sense of what may be called frontiers of Goethe scholarship. The method of morphological and structural interpretation offered by L. A. Willoughby and Harold Jantz constitutes a distinct contribution to *Faust* studies by Anglo-Saxon criticism and has become increasingly important even among German readers in recent years. The essay by Wilhelm Emrich, author of the most comprehensive study of *Part II* yet attempted, provides a helpful outline of an approach to the vexing complexities of that vast poetic structure. The brief study by Hans Eichner, finally, provides a perspective on the continuity of an ethical concern pertaining to the final passage in *Faust* which extends throughout Goethe's work. In a number of the essays, notably those by Mason and Jantz, comments with reference to other scholars on *Faust* have been deleted. All quotations from the drama throughout the critical essays have been given in Arndt's translation. Occasional explanatory footnotes have been added by the editor. In addition to the critical essays the editor has provided an analytical table of contents for *Faust* which attempts to correlate the dates of composition for the individual scenes and the various metrical forms, insofar as these data may be conveniently summarized in a table. The selected bibliography, which includes information on editions in German as well as other English translations of *Faust*, various scholarly aids to the study of the drama, and a brief survey of works on *Faust* in English, is intended to indicate how further research into this great drama should proceed. Ultimately there is, of course, no ideal substitute for access to Goethe's original German.

The labor of the editor of this Critical Edition has been, appropriately, more modest than that of the translator, who faced no less a task than measuring his English against the full range of Goethe's poetry. But scholarship and criticism impose their own burdens, accompanied by a necessary loss of innocence. All responsibility for errors, omissions, and idiosyncracies of judgment and perspective resides exclusively, of course, with the editor. I wish to express particular thanks for assistance in the reading of the drama to students in several graduate seminars in Comparative Literature during the past five years, and especially to Dolores Signori, who undertook preliminary versions of much of the translated material in the critical essays and who devoted patient effort to the preparation of the typescript of it all at various stages along the way. The translator and the editor are both grateful to Emily Garlin for patient and meticulous copy editing and consultation beyond the call of duty.

CYRUS HAMLIN

The Text of
Faust

A Tragedy

Dedication[1]†

Once more you near me, wavering apparitions
That early showed before the turbid gaze.
Will now I seek to grant you definition,
My heart essay again the former daze?
You press me! Well, I yield to your petition,   5
As all around, you rise from mist and haze;
What wafts about your train with magic glamor
Is quickening my breast to youthful tremor.

You conjure up delightful days and places,
And there ascends so many a cherished shade;   10
Like an old legend's half-forgotten graces,
First love's and friendship's echoes are replayed;
Old grief revives, a mournful plaint retraces
Life's labyrinthine and erratic gait,
And names the dear ones who, by fortune cheated   15
Of blissful hours, before me have retreated.

They do not listen to the later cantos,
The souls to whom I once intoned the first;
Long waned those early echoes and mementos,
The friendly multitude, alas, dispersed.   20
Indifferent ears my song of sorrow[2] enters,
Their very praises weigh upon my heart,
And those my lyre might still have pleased and flattered,
If living yet, are swept abroad and scattered.

And I am seized by long-unwonted yearning   25
For that domain of spirits calm and grave,
To tenuous notes my lisping song is turning,
Like Aeol's harp[3] it fitfully would wave,
A shudder grips me, tear on tear is burning,
With softening balm the somber heart they lave;   30
What I possess I see as from a distance,
And what has passed, to me becomes existence.

Prelude in the Theater[1]†

DIRECTOR. DRAMATIC POET. MERRY PERSON.
DIRECTOR. Let's hear, you two, who have so long
  Here by my side endured and suffered,

1. As he resumes work on his drama
after an interruption of several decades,
the poet addresses the half-formed figures and ideas out of his past which
crave full embodiment.
2. The first edition of *Part I* contained a
misprint here (*Leid*, "Sorrow," for *Lied*,
"Song"), which Goethe subsequently retained. Arndt's phrase retains the ambiguity.
3. The wind harp, which produces musical tones in response to the play of the
wind, was often associated during the
Romantic era with poetry generally.

1. The three figures here belong to a
troupe of itinerant players, preparing a
production of the *Faust* which follows
for an unspecified German theater. Such
ironic juxtaposition of opposing attitudes
toward the theater is derived from traditional prologues in Renaissance drama
and techniques of improvisation in popular comedy. A specific source is found in
Śakuntalā by the fourth-century Indian
poet Kālidāsa, which attracted Goethe's
interest, in a German translation by
Georg Forster (published 1791).

1

What might be hoped for from this effort 35
In countries of the German tongue?
I would prepare the crowd a special revel,
For they believe in living, letting live.
The posts are raised, the boards laid down and level,
All are in hopes we have a feast to give. 40
With eyebrows raised they sit in the enclosure
And long to be amazed, with due composure.
I know how people's taste may be caressed;
And yet I am in direr straits than ever;
While they are not accustomed to the best, 45
Still they are frightfully well-read and clever.
How can we see that all is fresh and new
And, with significance, engaging too?
Of course I find a crowd of people pleasing,
Delight in throngs at our pavilion queued, 50
In pulsing pangs of mighty labor squeezing
Through the tight portals of beatitude,
When in bright daylight, well before it's four,[2]
They fight their way up to the cashier's slot
And, as in time of famine by the baker's door, 55
For tickets break their necks, as like as not.
Upon such diverse folk can work this wondrous sway
None but the poet; friend, do it today!

POET. Invoke me not the motley crowd unsteady,
Whose very aspect puts the mind to flight! 60
Oh, shroud from me the swirling human eddy
That draws us downward, struggle as we might.
Find me that nook of heaven's stillness, heady
With blossom of the poet's pure delight,
Where for the heart both love and friendship flourish, 65
With godly hands create its bliss and nourish.
Ah, what broke forth where deeply it lay buried,
What lip has shyly lisped in private hours,
Accomplished now, at other times miscarried,
The savage moment's vehemence devours. 70
It often is through years of waiting ferried
Before it issues in its ripened powers.
What shines is for the moment born, must perish;
The genuine, posterity will cherish.

MERRY PERSON. That talk about posterity won't sell me; 75
If I talked of posterity, just tell me
Who would supply the fun for Now?
Now claims its time and wants it pleasant.
I find an honest fellow's present

---

2. The normal starting time for theater   5:30 or 6:00 in the evening.
performances in Goethe's Weimar was

Is always something, anyhow.   80
Him who with comfort can convey his sense,
The people's mood will not embitter, surely;
He wants a broader audience
To grip their hearts the more securely.
So do be good and act in model fashion,   85
Show Fancy in her fullest panoply:
Sense, understanding, sentiment, and passion,
And mind you, last not least, some foolery.

DIRECTOR. Above all, let there be sufficient plot!
They like to look, so let them see a lot.   90
You give the audience a solid eyeful,
So they can gasp and marvel all the time,
You'll grip them by sheer quantity of trifle,
Your popularity will climb.
Mass calls for mass in order to be won,   95
Each ends up choosing something for his own;
Who brings a lot, brings bits for everyone,
And they will all be happy going home.
You stage a piece—serve it in pieces, do!
Why, it's a snap to make this kind of stew;   100
It's served as fast as cooked up in your head.
What use is it to bring your whole instead,
The public shreds it anyway for you.

POET. You do not sense how cheap this is, how tawdry,
How shamefully true art is thus maligned!   105
The charlatan's ragout of tricks and bawdry,
I see, is now an axiom in your mind.

DIRECTOR. Such reprobation leaves me cool:
To do a proper job you choose the tool
That is adapted to your timber.   110
The wood you are to split is soft, remember,
Just look for whom you will have striven!
This one may be by boredom driven,
That one is comatose from overfeeding,
And, what is most reluctantly forgiven,   115
A lot arrive here fresh from journal-reading.
Mere curiosity will spur their paces,
They come with scattered wits as for a masquerade,
The ladies show their get-ups and their faces,
Each plays an extra, though unpaid.   120
Why daydream on your poet's eminence?
Why should a full house gladden you?
Look closely at your patrons, do!
One half is cold, the other dense.
One, when the show ends, looks to cards and booze,   125
Another to a wild night with a trollop;
Would you spur Pegasus to gallop

For this, poor fools, and plague the Muse?
I tell you, just give more, and ever, ever more,
And you will never stray off-target.   130
Endeavor to confuse your human market,
To sate it truly is a chore—
What's come upon you? Ecstasy or ache?
POET. Begone and find yourself another minion!
The poet should forgo, in your opinion,   135
The loftiest human right of which he may partake
By nature's gift, profane it grossly for your sake?
How does he kindle every heart?
How conquer every elemental part?
Not by the chords that from his bosom waft   140
And snare the universe back by his craft?
The while indifferent nature helter-skelter
Twists the eternal thread upon her spindle,
When all created things' discordant welter
Would coalesce into a graceless brindle,   145
Who parts the sequence, changeless and perpetual,
Enliveningly into rhythmic ease,
Who calls the single to the common ritual,
Where it resounds in glorious harmonies?
Who lets the tempest's passions rage their maddest,   150
Imparts grave meaning to the sunset glow?
Who strews the bloom of springtime at its gladdest
Where the beloved is wont to go?
Who braids the insignificant green laurels
To every merit's honorific wreaths?   155
Who firms Olympus? unifies Immortals?
The might of man, which in the poet breathes.
MERRY PERSON. So draw on them, those fine perfections,
And ply your lyrical transactions
As one conducts an amorous intrigue.   160
One happens in, feels, lingers, is in league
And more and more drawn in and interested;
Enchantment grows, and then it is contested,
As you rejoice, now pain receives its chance,
Before you know it, presto! there is your romance.   165
Such is the spectacle we should be giving!
Just reach into the wealth of human living!
Each lives it, those who know it are but few,
And grip it where you will, it's gripping too.
In colorful show less light than dark,   170
Much error, and of truth a spark,
Thus is the headiest mixture brewed
To slake and edify the multitude.
Then flocks to you the finest youthful splendor
And listens as to revelation holy,   175
To every soul of sentiment you tender

The suck and sustenance of melancholy.
There is stirred up now this, now that soft part,
Each sees what is sequestered in his heart.
Their gift for laughter, tears, is undiminished,   180
Illusion yet delights, élan still ranks;
There is no pleasing someone who is finished;
He who still grows will ever render thanks.

POET. Then to me, too, return those times
When I myself was growing still,   185
When a clear fount surcharged with rhymes
Sprang self-renewing from the well,
The time the world was swathed in veils,
When yet the bud held wondrous bowers,
When I would pluck the thousand flowers   190
That richly covered all the dales.
Nothing I had, and yet enough for youth,
Delight in fictions, and the thirst for truth.
Return untamed to me those surges,
That agonizing blissful ruth,   195
The strength of hate, love's mighty urges,
Alas, return to me my youth!

MERRY PERSON. Your youth, good friend, you need at best
When enemies in battle press you,
When, falling on your neck with zest,   200
A throng of lovely girls caress you,
When, racing hard, you stole a glance
Where goal and distant laurels beckoned,
When after reckless whirling dance
You drink the night through, time unreckoned.   205
But on the long-familiar lyre
To sound a chord with pluck and grace,
To self-appointed goal aspire
At charmingly erratic pace—
Old fellows, that's your proper game,   210
And we shall not revere you less for it.
Old age does not make childish, as they claim,
It merely finds us genuine children yet.

DIRECTOR. Sufficient speeches have been bandied,
Now let me see some deeds at last;   215
While mutual compliments are candied,
The time might usefully be passed.
What use to prate of inspiration?
The laggard it will ever flee.
Call yourselves poets by vocation?   220
Then order up your poetry.[3]
What we require is known to you,
We want to sip a potent brew;

3. See Goethe's use of these lines in his letter to Wilhelm von Humboldt of December 1, 1831, below.

Start brewing it without delay!
Tomorrow's late for what's not done today.   225
There's not a day to lose, and so,
Whatever's possible, resolve robust
Should take it by the forelock fast,[4]
Then it is loath to let it go
And labors on because it must.   230
You know, upon our German stages
Each man puts on just what he may;
So spare me not upon this day
Machinery and cartonnages.
The great and little light of heaven[5] employ,   235
The stars you may as freely squander;
Cliff-drops and water, fire and thunder,
Birds, animals, are in supply.
So in this narrow house of boarded space
Creation's fullest circle[6] go to pace,   240
And walk with leisured speed your spell
From Heaven through the World to Hell.[7]

Prologue in Heaven†

THE LORD. THE HEAVENLY HOST. *Later* MEPHISTOPHELES.

[*The* THREE ARCHANGELS *step forward.*]
RAPHAEL. The sun contends in age-old fashion
    With brother spheres in hymnic sound,
    And in far-thundering progression   245
    Discharges his appointed round.[1]
    His aspect lends the angels power,
    While none may gauge his secret way;
    Sublime past understanding tower
    Those works as on the primal day.   250
GABRIEL. The earth's resplendence spins and ranges
    Past understanding swift in flight,
    And paradisiac lucence changes
    With awe-inspiring depths of night;
    The ocean's foaming seas run shoreward,   255
    On rocky depths rebound and rear,
    And rock and ocean hurtle forward,
    Sped by the ever-hurrying sphere.

4. In an adaptation of a popular adage, "resolve" (personified) is urged to seize opportunity ("whatever's possible") by the forelock.
5. The sun and the moon, traditionally represented on the canopy above the platform stage.
6. A traditional metaphor of the theater as the world, *theatrum mundi* (see Shakespeare's "wooden O" in the Chorus of *Henry V*, Prologue, line 13).

7. Applied to *Faust*, this progression extends from the "Prologue in Heaven" to the Hell-mouth of the scene following Faust's death (see stage direction preceding line 11644).
1. The sun's path is associated with the musical harmony of the heavenly spheres. See also Job 38:7, "When the morning stars sang together, and all the sons of God shouted for joy."

MICHAEL. And tempest roars, with tempest vying,
From sea to land, from land to sea, 260
In their alternate[2] furies tying
A chain of deepest potency.
A flash of fiery disaster
Precedes the thunder on its way;
Thy envoys,[3] though, revere, o Master, 265
The gentle progress of Thy day.
THE THREE. [*in unison*] This aspect lends the angels power,
As none may gauge Thy secret way,
And all Thy sovereign works still tower
Sublime as on the primal day. 270

MEPHISTOPHELES.[4] Since once again, o Lord, I find you
deigning
To walk amongst us, asking how we do,
And in the past you thought me entertaining,
You see me too here with your retinue.
Fine speeches are, beg pardon, not my forte, 275
Though all this round may mock me; but I know,
My rhetoric, you'd laugh it out of court,
Had you not cast off laughter long ago.
On suns and worlds I can shed little light,
I see but humans, and their piteous plight. 280
Earth's little god runs true to his old way
And is as weird as on the primal day.[5]
He might be living somewhat better
Had you not given him of Heaven's light a glitter;
He calls it reason and, ordained its priest, 285
Becomes more bestial than any beast.
He seems to me, begging your Honor's pardon,
Like one of those grasshoppers in the garden
That leg it skip-a-skimming all day long
And in the grass chirp out the same old song. 290
If only he'd just lie in the grass at that!
But no, he sticks his nose in every pat.
THE LORD. And do you have no other news?
Do you come always only to accuse?
Does nothing please you ever on the earth? 295
MEPHISTOPHELES. No, Lord! I find it still of precious little worth.
I feel for mankind in their wretchedness,
It almost makes me want to plague them less.

---

2. Observe the adjectival stress: *altér-nate*.
3. A translation of the Greek for "messengers" (*angeloi*), from which the word *angels* is derived.
4. The origin of the name is uncertain (*Mephostophiles* in the chapbook of 1587; *Mephostophilis* in Marlowe's *Dr. Faustus*), though possibly derived from the Hebrew *Mephistoph*, "destroyer of the good." Here in the court of the Lord, as later in the court of the Emperor (*Part II*, Act I), Mephistopheles plays the role of jester, "rogue" (line 339).
5. A parody of the refrain in the Archangels' song (lines 269–70).

THE LORD. Do you know Faust?

MEPHISTOPHELES.   The doctor?

THE LORD.   Yes, my serf![6]

MEPHISTOPHELES. Forsooth! He serves you in a curious
    fashion.   300
Not of this earth the madman's drink or ration,
He's driven far afield by some strange leaven,
He's half aware of his demented quest,
He claims the most resplendent stars from heaven,
And from the earth each pleasure's highest zest,   305
Yet near or far, he finds no haven
Of solace for his deeply troubled breast.

THE LORD. Though now he serve me but in clouded ways,
Soon I shall guide him so his spirit clears.
The gardener knows by the young tree's green haze   310
That bloom and fruit will grace it down the years.

MEPHISTOPHELES. You'll lose him yet! I offer bet and tally,
Provided that your Honor gives
Me leave to lead him gently up my alley!

THE LORD. As long as on the earth he lives,   315
So long it shall not be forbidden.
Man ever errs the while he strives.[7]

MEPHISTOPHELES. My thanks to you; I've never hidden
An old distaste for dealing with the dead.
Give me a full-cheeked, fresh-faced lad!   320
A corpse with me is just no dice,
In this way I am like a cat with mice.

THE LORD. So be it; I shall not forbid it!
Estrange this spirit from its primal source,
Have licence, if you can but win it,   325
To lead it down your path by shrewd resource;
And stand ashamed when you must own perforce:
A worthy soul through the dark urge within it
Is well aware of the appointed course.

MEPHISTOPHELES. May be—but it has never lasted yet;   330
I am by no means worried for my bet.
And if I do achieve my stated perpent,
You grant me the full triumph that I covet.
Dust shall he swallow, aye, and love it,
Like my old cousin, the illustrious serpent.[8]   335

THE LORD. Then, too, enjoy free visitation;
I never did abominate your kind.
Of all the spirits of negation
The rogue has been least onerous to my mind.

---

6. See the Lord's question to Satan concerning Job, 1:8.
7. This wager between the Lord and Mephistopheles concerning the salvation of Faust should be compared to the wager between Faust and Mephistopheles in the pact scene (lines 1692–1706).
8. See the judgment on the serpent for the fall of man in Genesis 3:14, "Upon thy belly shalt thou go, and dust shalt thou eat all the days of thy life."

Man all too easily grows lax and mellow,   340
He soon elects repose at any price;
And so I like to pair him with a fellow
To play the deuce, to stir, and to entice.
But you, true scions of the godly race,[9]
Rejoice you in the font of living grace!   345
By ever active, ever live creation
In love's enchanting fetters be you caught,
And that which sways in wavering revelation,
May you compact it with enduring thought.
　　　[*Heaven closes; the* ARCHANGELS *disperse.*]
MEPHISTOPHELES. [*alone*][1] At times I don't mind seeing the
　　　old gent,   350
And try to keep relations smooth and level.
Say what you like, it's quite a compliment:
A swell like him so man-to-man with the Devil!

1. Following the tradition of the comic actor in popular theater, Mephistopheles often addresses himself directly to the audience.

9. The sons of God, the angels, represented in this scene by the Archangels of the opening hymn.

The Tragedy's First Part

NIGHT[1]†

In a narrow, high-vaulted Gothic chamber, FAUST, *restless in his armchair by the desk.*

FAUST. I have pursued, alas, philosophy,
Jurisprudence, and medicine,   355
And, help me God, theology,[2]
With fervent zeal through thick and thin.
And here, poor fool, I stand once more,
No wiser than I was before.
They call me Magister, Doctor,[3] no less,   360
And for some ten years, I would guess,
Through ups and downs and tos and fros
I have led my pupils by the nose—
And see there is nothing we can know!
It fair sears my heart to find it so.   365
True, I know more than those imposters,
Those parsons and scribes, doctors and masters;
No doubt can plague me or conscience cavil,
I stand not in fear of hell or devil—
But then, all delight for me is shattered;   370
I do not pretend to worthwhile knowledge,
Don't flatter myself I can teach in college
How men might be converted or bettered.
Nor have I estate or moneyed worth,
Nor honor or splendor of this earth;   375
No dog would live out such wretched part!
So I resorted to Magic's art,
To see if by spirit mouth and might
Many a secret may come to light;
So I need toil no longer so,   380
Propounding what I do not know;
So I perceive the inmost force
That bonds the very universe,
View all enactment's seed and spring,
And quit my verbiage-mongering.   385

1. The first half of this scene (to line 605, excluding 598–601) was one of the earliest composed by Goethe (see the essay by Eudo Mason, below). The opening part of the monologue, in archaic popular meter (*Knittelvers*), adopts the satirical tone of the puppet plays (see below), which began—following Marlowe's *Dr. Faustus*—with Faust alone in his study.
2. Faust mentions the four traditional faculties of the medieval university.
3. The two advanced degrees beyond the baccalaureate.

Oh full moon radiant, would that you,
Who many a midnight vigil through
Have found me wakeful in this chair,
Might look your last on my despair!
As over books I used to bend,   390
You would appear to me, sad friend;[4]
Ah, would that on high mountain ways
I wandered by your lovely rays,
Might haunt with sprites a cavern rift,
On meadows in your twilight drift,   395
And rid of learning's fetid fume,
Bathe whole my spirit in your spume!
Woe! stuck within this dungeon yet?
Curse this dank frowsty cabinet,
Where even Heaven's dear ray can pass   400
But murkily through tinted glass!
Entombed within this book-lined tower,
Which dust envelops, worms devour,
By fumigated charts unrolled
As high up as this vault can hold;   405
In instruments all choked and furled,
Hemmed in by flagon, jar, and trunk,
Stuffed tightly with ancestral junk—
This is your world! Call this a world!

And still you wonder what constrained   410
Your thwarted spirit's anxious surge,
Still ask what torment unexplained
Will cramp your every vital urge?
Shut out from Nature's teeming throng,
Which God made man to dwell among,   415
You skulk in reek and mold alone
'Mid ribs of beast and human bone.

Flee! Up! Escape to open fields!
Full-armed with that mysterious script
Which Nostradamus'[5] wisdom yields,   420
Why ask for more companionship?
In Nature's proper school enrolled,
You learn the course of stars and moons,
Then will your power of soul unfold
How spirit with its like communes.   425
In vain to hope reflection dry
Could make the sacred tokens clear—

4. Goethe employs in the following lines
the language of the sentimental sublime
from eighteenth-century nature poetry,
popular especially from the *Songs of Os-
sian* in the 1760s and also used by
Goethe in his novel *The Sorrows of
Young Werther* (1774).
5. Michael Notredame (1503–66), known
for a collection of prophecies concerning
future events. The interaction of spirits
and heavenly bodies described in the
lines following is thought to derive from
Emmanuel von Swedenborg (1688–1772),
especially his theosophical treatise *Ar-
cana Coelestia* (1749).

You spirits, you who float nearby,
Give me an answer, if you hear!
   [*He opens the book and perceives the sign of the Macro-
   cosm.*]
Ah—what enchantment at the sight of this   430
Suffuses every sense, what lovely verve!
I feel new-burgeoning life, with sacred bliss
Reincandescent, course through vein and nerve.
Was it a god that fashioned this design
Which calms the tumult in my breast,   435
Floods my poor heart with happiness,
And with a secret thrust divine
Makes Nature's powers about me manifest?
Am I a god? I feel such light in me!
Within these tracings pure and whole   440
There lies creative Nature open to my soul.
At last I comprehend the sage's plea:
"The world of spirits is not barred,
Your sense is shut, your heart is dead!
Go, bathe, disciple, undeterred   445
Your mortal breast in sunrise red!"
   [*He scrutinizes the sign.*]
How all one common weft contrives,
Each in the other works and thrives!
How heavenly forces rising and descending
Pass golden ewers in exchange unending,   450
On wings with blessing fragrant
From Heaven the earth pervading,
Fill all the world with harmonies vagrant!

What glorious show! Yet but a show, alas!
How, boundless Nature, seize you in my clasp?   455
You breasts where, all life's sources twain,
Both heaven and earth are pressed,
Where thrusts itself my shriveled breast,
You brim, you quench, yet I must thirst in vain?
   [*Moodily he turns up another page and perceives the sign
   of the* EARTH SPIRIT.[6]]
Not so this sign affects my soul, not so!   460
You, Spirit of the Earth, are nigher,
I sense my powers rising higher,
Already with new wine I am aglow,
I feel emboldened now to venture forth,
To bear the bliss, the sorrow of this earth,   465
Do battle with its tempests breaking,
Brave crunching shipwreck without quaking.

6. Primarily Goethe's own conception, despite esoteric sources in the *archeus terrae* of Paracelsus or *anima terrae* of Giordano Bruno, sixteenth-century natu- ral philosophers. See, below, the essay by Eudo Mason, as well as the *"Faust* Plan of 1800" and the discussion of it by Wolfgang Binder.

Above me vapors swirl—
The moon conceals her rays—
The lamplight wanes!   470
It steams, and scarlet lightning plays
About my head—there wafts
A tremor down the vaulting
And seizes me!
I feel you float about me, spirit I adjured.   475
Reveal yourself! Ah—how it wrenches at my soul!
All senses reeling
And rooting darkly toward new feeling!
I feel my very soul is yours to take!
You must! You must! And were my life at stake!   480

[*He seizes the book and mysteriously pronounces the sign of
the* SPIRIT. *A reddish flame flashes; the* SPIRIT *appears in
the flame.*[7]]

SPIRIT. Who calls for me?
FAUST. [*face averted*] Appalling vision!
SPIRIT. Long have you drawn me here,
  With potent summons sucking at my sphere,
  And now—
FAUST. I cannot bear you! Woe!   485
SPIRIT. With bated breath you yearn to meet me,
  To hear my voice, to gaze upon my face;
  Swayed as your mighty soul-pleadings entreat me,
  I yield, am here! What horrors base
  Now seize you superman! Where's the soul's
      call you hurled?   490
  Where is the breast that wrought in it a world,
  That bore and nursed it, that with joyous tremble
  Swelled up to soar, us spirits to resemble?
  Where is the Faust whose voice rang out to me,
  Who urged himself on me with utmost energy?   495
  Could you be he, who at my wafting breath
  Is shaken even unto death,
  Shrinking aside, a fearful writhing worm?
FAUST. Am I to yield to you, semblance of flame?
  No, I am Faust, your match, I am the same!   500
SPIRIT. In tides of living, in doing's storm,
  Up, down, I wave,
  Waft to and fro,
  Birth and grave,
  An endless flow,   505
  A changeful plaiting,
  Fiery begetting,

7. A drawing by Goethe survives, showing the Earth Spirit as a gigantic head
hovering over the stage. In a letter of
June 2, 1819, to Count Brühl, theater
director in Berlin, Goethe stated that he
envisioned the projection of a transpar-
ency which would show a head resembling the Zeus of Otricoli in the Vatican
Museum, Rome.

Thus at Time's scurrying loom I weave and warp
And broider at the Godhead's living garb.
FAUST. You who bestride the world from end to end,   510
  Spirit of deeds, how close I feel to thee!
SPIRIT. Close to the wraith you comprehend,
  Not me!
      [*Vanishes.*]
FAUST. Not thee?
  Whom, then? What, I,   515
  Made in God's likeness,
  Yet like—not even thee?
      [*A knock at the door.*]
  Death! It's my famulus[8]—I know that knock;
  My fairest hour of luck is spoiled.
  Oh, must this wealth of visions then be foiled   520
  By that dry sneaking cluck?
      [WAGNER *in dressing-gown and night-cap, a lamp in his
      hand.* FAUST *turns around with distaste.*]
WAGNER. Your leave! I heard declaiming—in this art[9]
  I stand to profit from your kind directive.
  You read, I think, a Greek dramatic part?
  Such nowadays is most effective.   525
  I've often heard the claim at least
  That a comedian could instruct a priest.
FAUST. Yes, if the priest is a comedian, I suggest;
  As I am told from time to time befalls.
WAGNER. Ah me, thus pent within one's study walls,   530
  Seeing the world on holidays at best,
  By spyglass from afar, on rare occasion,
  How can one influence it by persuasion?
FAUST. What you don't feel, you won't hunt down by art,
  Unless it wells from your own inward source,   535
  And with contentment's elemental force
  Takes sway of every hearer's heart.
  Just sit there, pasting joints to members,
  Concoct from others' feasts your hash,
  And blow a puny glow of embers   540
  Up from your little heap of ash!
  From minds of babes and apes you may be coining
  Tribute of awe, if this be what you seek;
  But never heart to heart will you be joining
  Unless you let your own heart speak.   545
WAGNER. Delivery, though, commends a speaker's mind;
  I feel it well, I still am far behind.
FAUST. Seek you but honest recompense!

8. Faust's academic assistant. The name
"Wagner" derives from the chapbooks,
and in the puppet plays Faust's assistant
provided a comic foil to the magus. In
the "*Faust* Plan of 1800" (see below),
Goethe referred to Wagner as "bright,
clear scientific striving."
9. An allusion to Rhetoric, one of the
three disciplines in the medieval Trivium,
part of the liberal arts.

Be not a fool with jangling bells!
For solid reason and good sense   550
With little art commend themselves.
If you're in earnest to be heard,
Should there be need to chase the word?
That edge of rhetoric that glints and cleaves
By which you curl the shavings of mankind   555
Is idle as the fog-wind to my mind
That rustles through the dry autumnal leaves!

WAGNER. Dear me! how long is art!
  And short is our life![1]
  I often know amid the scholar's strife   560
  A sinking feeling in my mind and heart.
  How difficult the means are to be found
  By which the primal sources may be breached;
  And long before the halfway point is reached,
  They bury a poor devil in the ground.   565
FAUST. Of parchment then is made the sacred spring,
  A draught of which forever slakes all thirst?
  From naught can you refreshment wring
  Unless from your own inmost soul it burst.
WAGNER. Your pardon! yet the joy is unsurpassed   570
  Of insight into eras long ago,
  To see how wise men then thought thus and so,
  And how we reached our splendid heights at last.
FAUST. Oh, starry heights, indeed!
  To us the times of yore, it is decreed,   575
  Are like a book by seven seals protected;[2]
  The so-called spirit of the age, you'll find,
  In truth is but the gentlemen's own mind
  In which the ages are reflected.
  And there you're apt to face a scene of gloom!   580
  One glance is quite enough to make you stagger:
  A refuse barrel or a lumber-room,
  At best a stiff bombastic masque aswagger
  With such sagaciously pragmatic saws
  As might come fitly from a puppet's jaws.   585
WAGNER. But take the world of man—his heart and mind!
  We all seek some perception of the same.
FAUST. Ah, yes—perception of a kind . . .
  Who dares to call the child by its right name?
  Those few who were vouchsafed of it one whit,   590
  And rashly failed to curb their full heart's throb,
  Bared what they felt and witnessed to the mob,
  Were ever burnt and crucified for it.

1. An adaptation of the familiar Latin aphorism derived from the ancient Greek doctor Hippocrates, *"Ars longa, vita brevis."*

2. Revelations 5:1, "And I saw in the right hand of him who was seated on the throne a scroll written within and on the back, sealed with seven seals."

I beg you, friend, the night is halfway gone,
For now we must break off discussion.   595

WAGNER. I should have willingly stayed on and on,
Disputing with you in this learned fashion.
Tomorrow, though, it being Easter Day,[3]
Indulge me for some further questioning.
I've studied with a will and worked away;   600
Though I know much, I would know everything.
    [*Exit.*]

FAUST. [*alone*] How does the mind sustain some hope and pleasure
That's stuck forever to the same old terms,
With greedy fingers grubbing after treasure,
And gratified to dig up worms![4]   605

May such a human accent here resound,
Where all about was spirit wealth and worth?
Alas, this once, though, I am bound
To thank you, poorest of the sons of earth.
You banished the despair that held me fast,   610
That was about to overthrow my mind.
Alas! the apparition was so vast,
It showed me all too well my dwarfish kind.

I, godhead's likeness, who had soared in mind
Close to the mirror of eternal verity,   615
Self-relishing in heaven's radiant clarity,
The son of earth quite left behind;
I, more than cherub, whose free energy
Foreboding dared through Nature's veins to flow,
And, through creation, joyously to know   620
Godlike estate—must I now rue it so!
A thunder word rang out and withered me.

No, I may not presume to be your equal:
While I had strength to draw you here, the sequel,
The strength to hold you, was denied to me.   625
That fleeting moment of high bliss,
I felt myself so small, so great;
Until you thrust me, merciless,
Back to uncertain human fate.
Who teaches me? What should I shun?   630
That urge I feel—should I obey?
Both what we do and what we suffer to be done,
Alas, impedes us on life's way.

The greatest glory ever mind received,

---

3. This reference to Easter, added
around 1800, provides the first indication
of the time of year in which this scene
takes place.
4. The so-called great lacuna in *Faust*,
which Goethe filled ca. 1800–1801, begins
here and extends to line 1770. See, below, the essays by Emil Staiger and Wolfgang Binder.

By alien stuff becloyed, is choked and flawed,   635
When what this earth calls good has been achieved,
The better is accounted dream or fraud.
Those feelings, which were glorious rebirth,
Congeal amidst the welter of this earth.

Where fancy in audacious flight expanded   640
To the Eternal once its buoyant hope,
Now it contents itself with little scope,
As ship on ship in whirls of time is stranded.
Deep in the heart, gray Care[5] anon will settle,
In secret plant her stinging nettle,   645
With restless rocking spoil repose and joy,
Ever new masks for her disguise employ;
And be it wife and child or land and corn,
Be it knife, poison, fire or water,
At blows that never fall you falter,   650
And what you never lose, you must forever mourn.

Not like the gods am I—profoundly it is rued!
I'm of the earthworm's dust-engendered brood,
Which, blindly burrowing, by dust is fed,
And crushed and buried by the wanderer's tread.   655

These hundred shelves, is it not dust that bent
Their lofty wall into a cell which stifles,
A universe of moths where I am pent
Into a dustbin with a thousand trifles?
Here would I find the thing I lack?   660
Am I to plow a thousand books to read
Of man at all times stretched upon a rack,
And, here and there, one happy one, indeed?—
Ho, grinning hollow skull,[6] well you may leer,
To think that once your brain, like this one here,   665
In murky bondage sought the easeful day,
And parched with thirst for truth went grievously astray.
You instruments, you mock me, I can see,
With wheel and pulley, cylinder and cords:[7]
I faced the gate, you were to be the key,   670
But cannot lift the bolts, however shrewd your wards.[8]
Mysterious in bright daylight, never
Will Nature be defrauded of her veil,
What to your spirit she reveal not, that you fail

5. See the aged crone of *Part II*, Act V (lines 11384 ff.). The scene called "Midnight," in which she appears, was drafted ca. 1800, about the same time as the passage here.
6. The skull indicates the ancient theme of *momento mori*, "remember (you must) die," for which see Hamlet with the skull of Yorick in Act V of Shakespeare's play.
7. The instrument described here is probably an electrostatic machine containing a rotating disk and comblike collectors (invented in the mid-seventeenth century).
8. Metaphorical reference to the instrument as if it were the key to a lock where "wards" and "bolts" did not fit.

To torture out of her with screw or lever. 675
You ancient gear I never used, you loom
About here just because my father worked you.
You ancient scroll, you have been cured with fume
While at this desk the feeble lamp bemurked you.
Far better to have squandered free of care 680
My pittance than to sweat withal and scoff it!
What you received but as your father's heir,
Make it your own to gain possession of it!
What is unused is ballast hard to bear:
Alone what moment has begot can yield it profit. 685

Why is that spot there riveting my glances?
Is that small flask a magnet to my sight?
A sudden lovely gleam my soul entrances
Like moonlight wafting through the woods at night!

I bid you greeting, vial unique! 690
Which now with veneration I fetch down,
In you I reverence of human wit the peak,
Of gracious slumber saps the inmost flower,
Quintessence of all subtly lethal power,
Prove to your lord your favor and renown! 695
I see you, and the agony decreases,
I grasp you, and the striving half-releases
Its hold, the spirit's floodtide ebbs betimes.
Out to the open sea am I directed,
Its mirror flood bright at my feet reflected, 700
And day new-dawning lures me to new climes.

A fiery chariot wings on pinions light,
Approaches![9] I am ready, I feel free
To cleave the ether on a novel flight,
To novel spheres of pure activity. 705
Such lofty life, such godly benison!
You, but a worm as yet, deserve it, you?
With firm resolve, then, turn your back upon
This lovely sun of earth, the sun you knew.
Embold yourself to fling apart the gate 710
Past which all other men would crawl weak-kneed!
That manhood does not yield to gods' high state,
Now is the moment to affirm by deed.
To tremble not before the somber hollow
Wherein our fancy on itself but preys, 715
And gird oneself that passageway to follow
About whose narrow mouth all Hell's ablaze;
Resolve serenely to essay no less—

9. Faust may refer here to the sun as it rises (which has clearly happened by line 736). The image of the fiery chariot is both Biblical (see Elijah's ascent to heaven, 2 Kings 2:11) and Classical (the chariot of Apollo, god of the sun).

Be it on pain of ebbing into nothingness.

Now then, o flawless crystal shell,[1] descend!   720
Forth from your ancient casing, friend,
Of whom I have not thought in many a year!
You gleamed at fathers' festival of spring,
Helped turn their gravity to cheer,
When to their mutual pledges you would ring.   725
Your many splendid pictures' opulent craft,
The drinker's task to rhyme upon their truth,
To drain your hollow in a single draught,
Puts me in mind of many a night of youth.
I shall not pass you to a neighbor now,   730
I shall not hone my wits against your graven brow;
Here is a juice whose punch is swift and thorough!
With flood of brown it fills your hollow bowl.
I brewed it, and I choose it, so
With this for my last drink, from all my soul,   735
With festive high salute, I hail Tomorrow!
    [*He raises the bowl to his lips.*]
    [*Sound of bells and choral song.*[2]†]
CHORUS OF ANGELS. Christ is arisen!
        Joy to the mortal,
        Him whom invidious,
        Subtle, insidious   740
        Blemishes prisoned.
FAUST. What solemn droning, what melodious fluting
Perforce arrests the goblet in mid-way?
Are you already, deep-toned bells, saluting
The festive breaking hour of Easter Day?   745
You choirs, do you the solace-hymn resume
That angels lips intoned in the Sepulchre's gloom,
New covenant's sure warranty?
CHORUS OF WOMEN.[3] We stayed to tend Him
        With spices rare,   750
        Last to befriend Him,
        We laid Him there,
        His body binding
        In wrappings sheer;
        Lo, now we find Him   755.
        No longer here.

1. A ceremonial drinking chalice with carved scenes on the outside. Such a chalice used at a banquet may be associated with the cup of Christ's Last Supper, symbolized in the Eucharist of Holy Communion, about to be celebrated in the Easter Mass.
2. According to traditions of medieval liturgy, the Easter Mass is celebrated by a dramatic representation of the discovery of Christ's empty tomb (see Matthew 28; Mark 16; Luke 24; John 20). Three choruses are heard singing from a nearby cathedral in an antiphonal cantata adapted from the style of medieval Latin hymns.
3. Mary Magdalene and Mary the mother of James and Salome (see Mark 16:1), who have brought spices with which to anoint the body of Christ.

CHORUS OF ANGELS. Christ is arisen!
　　　　　　　　Blest the love spirit
　　　　　　　　Whose suffering merit
　　　　　　　　Earned grace from flesh's prison　　760
　　　　　　　　For us to inherit.
FAUST. Why, o celestial music, strong and gentle,
　　Pursue me here where in the dust I grieve?
　　Ring out your notes where men are sentimental:
　　I hear the message, but I can't believe;　　765
　　Belief's beloved child is Miracle.
　　To yonder spheres I venture not to strive
　　Whence issues the enchanting spell;
　　And yet, inured from childhood to this knell,
　　Now also to its summons I revive.　　770
　　Time was, the kiss of heavenly love
　　Sank down on me in earnest sabbath calm,
　　So bodefully the bell-notes throbbed above,
　　And praying was voluptuous balm;
　　A lovely longing no one understands　　775
　　Drove me to roam in woods and meadowlands,
　　Of scalding tears I paid a generous toll
　　As a new world unfolded in my soul.
　　The merry games of youth this song is pealing,
　　The spring rite's happy grace;　　780
　　And now remembrance rouses childlike feeling
　　To bar the path that none retrace.
　　Resound, sound on, o sweet celestial chord!
　　The tear wells up, to Earth I am restored!
CHORUS OF DISCIPLES. While the Envaulted　　785
　　　　　　　　From the tomb's prison,
　　　　　　　　Revives exalted,
　　　　　　　　In splendor risen,
　　　　　　　　In rapt gestation
　　　　　　　　Nears joyous creation:　　790
　　　　　　　　Woe! in earth's furrow
　　　　　　　　We know but sorrow.
　　　　　　　　Who once were his,
　　　　　　　　He left to languish;
　　　　　　　　We mourn in anguish,　　795
　　　　　　　　Master, Thy bliss!
CHORUS OF ANGELS.　　Risen is Christ
　　　　　　　　Out of corruption's trough;
　　　　　　　　You too arise,
　　　　　　　　Your bonds cast off!　　800
　　　　　　　　Who praise him in action
　　　　　　　　Practice affection,
　　　　　　　　Nourishing brothers,
　　　　　　　　Preaching to others
　　　　　　　　Glad resurrection—　　805

For you, the Lord is near,
For you, is here!

OUTSIDE THE CITY GATE†

People of all sorts coming out for walks.

SOME APPRENTICES. Why there? Where are you bound?
OTHERS. We're heading for the Stag-and-Hound.
THE FORMER. We meant to strike out for the Mill.   810
ONE APPRENTICE. Let's make it Lakeside Hostel if you will.
ANOTHER. The road down there is not the best.
THE OTHERS. What will you do?
A THIRD. I'm going with the rest.
A FOURTH. Come up to Burgdorf, there you'll find it true
    They have the prettiest girls, the finest brew.   815
    And there'll be first-rate hassles for us.
A FIFTH. An over-lusty lad, I swear!
    You're itching to be tanned a third time there?
    No, not for me, that place gives me the horrors.
SERVANT GIRL. No, no! I'm going back to town, just see.   820
ANOTHER. I'm sure he's waiting by the poplars there.
THE FIRST. That's precious little fun for me;
    You'll have a lark, two make a pair;
    Sure, arm in arm with you he'll go
    And dance with no one else, I know.   825
THE OTHER. But there'll be two today, you're wrong:
    He said that curlyhead would be along.
STUDENT. Gad, how those sturdy wenches sail!
    My word, we mustn't let them go to waste.
    A pungent smoke, a hearty mug of ale,   830
    A dolled-up maid—such, brother, is my taste.
GIRL OF THE BURGHER CLASS. Look, will you, at those handsome
        lads!
    That really seems a shame to me;
    Here they could have the choicest company,
    And who do they run after? Maids!   835
SECOND STUDENT. [*to the first*] No, wait—here comes a turnout to
        explore,
    Both very pretty and well-dressed;
    One is a girl who lives next door
    In whom I take warm interest.
    They trip along there, all demure,   840
    Yet would not mind our company, I'm sure.
FIRST STUDENT. No, friend! No parlor tricks for me, I say.
    Be quick, or we may lose that other game.
    The hand that plies the broom on Saturday
    Will best caress you Sunday, all the same.   845
CITIZEN. No, I don't like him, the new burgomaster!

Now that he's in, he just gets bolder faster.
And for the town what is he doing, pray?
Are we not worse off every day?
It's Do-what-you-are-told as never,   850
And fork out taxes more than ever.

BEGGAR. [*singing*]¹ Fair ladies, kindly sirs, for pity,
                So red of cheek and fine of dress,
                Be pleased to heed my poor entreaty,
                And see and lighten my distress!   855
                Let me not vainly grind my barrel:
                He who can give, alone is gay.
                A day on which all men make merry,
                Be it for me a harvest day!

ANOTHER CITIZEN. On holidays I know of nothing cozier, neigh-
        bor,   860
Than a good chat of war and war's alarms,
When far away, in Turkey,² tribes in arms
Whack one another and belabor;
While you stand by the window, down your glass,
Watch the bright-colored ships glide down the breeze,   865
And in the evening amble home at last
With blessings upon peace and peacetime ease.

A THIRD CITIZEN. Well spoken, friend, just what I always say!
Let them crack noggins freely, sir,
Let things go every which-a-way,   870
If just at home they stay as they were.

OLD WOMAN. [*to the burgher girls*] What stately finery, my!
        What pretty faces!
Who would not fall for such a dainty dish?
Never you mind those airs and graces!
I might just find a way to what you wish.   875

FIRST YOUNG GIRL. Quick, Agatha, it really wouldn't do
To walk in public with a witch like her;
Though on St. Andrew's Eve³ she let me view
My future love in person, I prefer . . .

THE OTHER. She showed me mine, too, in the crystal's face,   880
A soldier, like, with others bold and trim;
I've looked about, been searching every place,
But cannot seem to meet with him.

SOLDIERS. Castles with frowning
                Battlements rude,   885
                Maidens in haughty
                Mettlesome mood,
                These I would savor,

---

1. Presumably onstage from the outset, the beggar accompanies his song with a barrel-organ.
2. No specific historical allusion is intended. Wars with the Turks were often fought during the sixteenth and seven-teenth centuries.
3. According to popular tradition, on the eve of this saint (November 29) young girls by incanting magical verses could see their future husbands in their dreams.

Keen is the labor,
Splendid the prize.   890

Trumpets blaring
Do our wooing,
For love's delight,
For foe's undoing.
Boisterous onslaught   895
Cruel or tender,
Maidens and castles,
Both must surrender!
Keen is the labor
Sweet the reward!   900
After the contest,
Soldiers depart.

[*Enter* FAUST *and* WAGNER.]

FAUST. Freed from the ice are brooks and rivers
By spring's enchanting, enlivening gaze;
The valley is blithe with hope's green haze;   905
Hoary winter with senile shivers
Back to his mountain lair withdrew.
Thence he flings, shorn of his powers,
Granules of ice in spiteful showers
Streaking over the verdant site;   910
The sun, however, allows no white,
All is astir with shaping and striving,
All he would dower with hues and enliven;
The flower season still lies ahead:
Folk in their finery do instead.   915
Turn around with me, look down
From these lofty hillsides back toward town,
See how the gate's dark cave exudes
Teeming colorful multitudes.
All seek the sun with glad accord,   920
They exult in the rising of the Lord;
For they are resurrected themselves,
Freed from the shackles of shops and crafts,
From stuffy dwellings like narrow shelves,
From smothering roofs and gable lofts,   925
From the city streets with their smothering press,
From out the churches' reverend night,
They have all been raised to light.
Look, look, how nimbly the human crest
Breaks and surges through field and park,   930
How the length and width of the river's breast
Cradles many a pleasure bark;
Yonder, laden full to sinking,
The last of the fragile craft unties;
From the very hilltops far off winking   935
Bright-colored dresses strike our eyes.

I hear the village buzz already,
True people's heaven, crowded, heady;
And young and old exult in glee:
"Here I am Man, am free to be!"   940
WAGNER. To stroll with you, Sir Doctor, never
But profits and exalts the mind;
But on my own I would not stray here ever,
Because I shun all that is unrefined.
How I abominate these vulgar revels,   945
The fiddling, roaring, clash of the bowling-run!
They rave as if pursued by a thousand devils,
And call it singing, call it fun.
PEASANTS. [*under the linden tree*]
      [*Dance and song.*][4]
            The shepherd dressed him for the jig,
            With ribbon and wreath, a colorful rig,   950
            He made a handsome show.
            The throng around the linden pressed
            And whirled about as if possessed.
            Heigh-ho! Heigh-ho!
            Heigh nonny nonny ho!   955
            Went fiddle and flying bow.

            In clumsy haste he crowded hard,
            And straightway with his elbow jarred
            A maiden dancing near.
            The pert young wench, she turned about   960
            And said: "Be off, you stupid lout!"
            Heigh-ho! Heigh-ho!
            Heigh nonny nonny ho!
            "You mind your manners here!"

            But round and round in whisking flight,   965
            In circles left, in circles right,
            Spun skirts and furbelow.
            They grew so flushed, they grew so warm,
            Encircled breathless arm in arm,
            Heigh-ho! Heigh-ho!   970
            Heigh nonny nonny ho!
            His hand, her waist, just so.

            Don't you make up to me, my lad!
            I know of many a maiden sad,
            Forsaken and betrayed!   975
            Aside he coaxed her anyhow,
            And far off from the linden now,
            Heigh-ho! Heigh-ho!
            Heigh nonny nonny ho!
            Rose shouts and fiddles played.   980

4. This folk song (mentioned in the first draft of Goethe's novel *Wilhelm Meister*, Book IV, chatper 13) was probably composed by Goethe in the early 1780s, not intended for *Faust* at all.

OLD PEASANT. Sir, Doctor, it is kind of you
  On this our day to be not proud,
  But, full of learning though you are,
  To mingle with the jostling crowd.
  So I present the finest jug,   985
  Which we have freshly filled with beer,
  And pledging you, pronounce the wish
  That it not just refresh you here,
  But that your span of days have gained
  One for each drop that it contained.   990
FAUST. I take the cooling potion here
  And bid you all a grateful cheer.
      [*The people gather in a circle.*]
OLD PEASANT. It is well done, and fit indeed,
  That this glad day you pay us call,
  Who formerly in days of need   995
  Have done so kindly by us all.
  For many a man here drawing breath,
  Caught in the fever's parching grasp,
  Was by your father snatched from death,
  The time he stemmed the plague at last.[5]   1000
  You also did, a young man then,
  Attend each sick-bed without fail,
  And many a corpse was carried hence,
  But you did issue safe and hale.
  You passed through many a hard ordeal;   1005
  The Healer helped his helpmeet heal.
ALL. May health attend this man of worth,
  Long to help others on this earth!
FAUST. Obeisance make to Him on high,
  Who teaches help, whose help is nigh!   1010
      [*He walks on with* WAGNER.]
WAGNER. What sentiments, great man, must swell your breast
  Upon the homage of this multitude!
  Ah, he who can derive such good
  From his own gifts indeed is blessed!
  Fathers lift boys up as you go,   1015
  All push and run and ask the cause,
  The fiddle rests, the dancers pause.
  You pass, they stand there, row on row,
  And all the caps go flying high:
  They all but genuflect and bend down low   1020
  As if the Sacrament came by.[6]
FAUST. A few steps further up yet to that stone—
  Here we may rest us from our expedition.
  Here I sat often, thoughtful and alone,
  And plagued myself with prayer and inanition.   1025

5. The story that Faust's father had been a doctor of medicine who treated peasants during an epidemic of the plague is Goethe's own invention.

6. An allusion to the custom of kneeling before the Host as it passed in religious processions.

Steadfast in faith and rich in confidence,
I wrung my hands with many a tear and sigh
To wrest the lifting of that pestilence
From the Almighty Lord on high.
Now people's cheers to me ring jeering fun.   1030
Could you but read within my soul the story
How little father and son
Were truly worthy of such glory!
My father, man of honor though unsung,
Brooded on Nature with a crotchety passion,   1035
And—in all probity yet in his fashion—
Upon her sacred circles raptly hung;
By secret recipes unending,
Locked up in the Black Kitchen[7] with retorts,
He brewed away with adepts, blending   1040
Contrariness of every sort.
There was a Scarlet Lion, intrepid wooer,
Wed to the Lily in a tepid ewer,
And then by open flames the two were vexed
From one new bridal chamber to the next.   1045
And when at last, with rainbow colors vying,
The Young Queen glistened in the yield,
There was your dose, the patients went on dying,
And nobody enquired: who was healed?
And thus with our infernal tonic   1050
Upon these hills, these dales we visited
A plague far worse than the bubonic.
Why, with this poison I myself defrauded
Men by the thousands, leaving them for dead;
Now I must hear the brazen killers lauded.   1055

WAGNER. Why feel so bitterly disgusted?
Come, does an honest man do ill
Pursuing with good faith and will
The art with which he was entrusted?
If you revere your father as a youth,   1060
You will accept from him with pleasure;
If as a man you swell the store of truth,
Your son may grow to yet more lofty measure.

FAUST.† Oh! Lucky who can still aspire
To surface from this sea of aberration!   1065
What we know not, of that our need is dire,
And what we know lacks application.
However, this bright hour's fair benison
Let such low spirits not embitter!

7. Faust refers to the alchemical laboratory and experiments in black magic. He
describes the creation of an elixir used
as a medicine against the plague. With
imagery of a marriage, a union occurs
between the masculine "Scarlet Lion"
(reddish mercuric oxide) and the feminine "Lily" (hydrochloric acid), which
are heated over a flame to yield as
offspring the "Young Queen," the subli-
mate that served as the specific.

Observe how in the flaming evening sun 1070
Those green-embowered cabins glitter.
He yields and sinks, the day is lived and done,
He hastes beyond, new life to breed and nourish.
Oh, that I have no buoyant wings to flourish,
To strive and follow, on and on! 1075
I'd see in endless vesper rays
The silent world beneath me glowing,
The valleys all appeased, each hill ablaze,
The silver brooks to golden rivers flowing.
No more would then this rugged bluff deny 1080
With cliff and precipice the godlike motion;
Already with its sun-warmed bays the ocean
Reveals itself to the astonished eye.
At last, it seems, the god is downward sinking;
Yet to new urge awakes the mind, 1085
I hasten on, his ceaseless radiance drinking,
The day ahead of me, night left behind,
The waves below, and overhead the sky.
A happy fancy—meanwhile he must pass.
To spirit wings will scarce be joined, alas, 1090
Corporeal wings wherewith to fly.
Yet is is innate in us all
That feeling ever upward, forward presses
When, lost above in heaven's azure spaces,
The skylark trills his jubilant call, 1095
When over craggy fir-clad highlands
On outspread wings the eagle rides,
And striving over plains and islands,
The crane toward his homeland glides.

WAGNER. I too have been to moody crotchets given, 1100
By such an urge, though, I was never driven.
The charm in watching woods and fields is brief,
I never shall begrudge the bird its soaring.
Compare the mind's delights which wing us poring
From book to book, from leaf to leaf! 1105
Then nights of winter bloom with grace and zest,
Your limbs glow with a blissful warming leaven,
And, ah! should you unroll a worthy palimpsest,
Then there descends on you the whole of heaven.

FAUST.† You are by just a single urge possessed; 1110
Oh may you never know the other!
Two souls, alas, are dwelling in my breast,
And either would be severed from its brother;
The one holds fast with joyous earthy lust
Onto the world of man with organs clinging; 1115
The other soars impassioned from the dust,
To realms of lofty forebears winging.
Oh, be there spirits in the air

Who 'twixt the earth and heaven reigning hover,
Descend ye from the golden fragrance there,   1120
To new and changeful living lead me over!
Why, if a magic cape were only mine
And were to bear me over alien borders,
I'd trade it not for choicest robes and orders,
Not for the royal cloak incarnadine!   1125

WAGNER. Forbear to call on the notorious clan
Which, all abroad in misty concourse faring,
In thousandfold disguise imperils man,
Hazards from every side preparing.
From North with arrow-tapered tongues that threaten   1130
The ghostly razor fang is thrust at you;
From Orient with withering breath they drew
Upon your parching lungs to batten;
While Noon sends those who from the desert burst
And glow on searing glow amass around you,   1135
West brings the swarm who will, refreshing first,
Pour floods on fields and pasturelands and drown you.
They gladly listen, being glad to grieve,
To cheat us keen, hence eagerly complying,
As if from Heaven sent, they make believe   1140
With angel lisps as they are lying.[8]
But let us go; the world about has paled,
The air grown chill, in vapors veiled.
At dusk the home we doubly prize.
Why do you stand and peer in moot surmise?
What can engage you so here in the gloaming?

FAUST. See that black dog through seed and fallow roaming?[9]

WAGNER. I saw it long before and paid it little heed.

FAUST. Look at it well! What would you call its breed?

WAGNER. A poodle, I should say, with canine snooping   1150
At pains upon its master's trail.

FAUST. Do you observe him near and nearer, looping
A narrowing spiral like the convolute snail?
Unless I err, there rises in his track
A swirling fiery effusion.   1155

WAGNER. I see a poodle, and I see it's black;
Yours must have been some optical illusion.

FAUST. He seems to snare our feet with magic, weaving
Some future bondage, thread by stealthy thread.

WAGNER. He's circling us in wonder or misgiving   1160
To see two strangers in his master's stead.

FAUST. The ring grows tight, already he is near!

---

8. In the preceding lines Wagner has described spirits of the weather associated in popular belief with the four directions of the compass.
9. There is no precedent in the popular legend of Faust for the appearance of Mephistopheles in the guise of a dog. In one of the chapbooks which Goethe knew Faustus was said to have owned a black dog named Praestigiar which had demonic powers.

WAGNER. You see? A dog—there is no specter here.
   He gives a growl, he wonders, lies down flat,
   He wags his tail—all canine conduct, that.   1165
FAUST. Come here and join us! Come to me!
WAGNER. A skittish fool of a poodle, see?
   You stop, he sits and begs;
   You speak to him, he rears on his hind legs;
   Lose something and he will retrieve it,   1170
   Swim out for sticks you throw, believe it.
FAUST. You must be right; for watch him as I will,
   I find no trace of spirit; all is drill.
WAGNER. A dog, if ably trained and clever,
   Will even gain a wise man's favor.   1175
   Yes, he deserves your good will without scruple,
   The undergraduate's accomplished pupil.
      [*They pass under the city gate.*]

STUDY†

FAUST. [*entering with the poodle*]
               I have forsaken field and meadow,
               Now sunken deep in darkness, when
               To boding sacred awe night's shadow   1180
               Awakes the better self in men.
               Now lie aslumber savage urges
               With every vehemence of deed;
               Now love of man for man resurges,
               The love of God is stirred and freed.   1185
   Where are you running, poodle? Cease your riot!
   Why snuffle at the threshold for outdoors?[1]
   Go lie behind the stove in quiet,
   My finest cushion shall be yours.
   As you amused us on our hillside ramble,   1190
   Running and jumping without rest,
   Accept my care in here with never a gambol,
   Be welcome as a silent guest.
               Ah, when in our restricted cell
               The lamp resumes its kindly blaze,   1195
               It lights the inner self as well,
               The heart aware of its own ways.
               Then reason reasserts its forces,
               New hope begins to stir and flow;
               One yearns again to trace life's courses, 1200
               Alas—life's springs one yearns to know.
   Stop growling, poodle! Poorly suited
   To the sacred tones that gently clasp
   My soul entire, is that animal rasp.

1. The poodle, in trying to leave the study, discovers that the "Druid's claw" prevents him from going (see lines 1259 and 1395).

We know that men have always hooted   1205
At what they cannot grasp,
And that the beautiful and good
Is often hissed as irksome to boor and varlet;
For dogs, then, too, is it fit to snarl at?†

But oh! though my resolve grows even stronger,   1210
I feel contentment welling from my soul no longer.
Yet why must the flood so soon run dry,
And we be left again in thirst to lie?
I have had proof of it in such full measure.
Still, for this lack there's compensation: 1215
The supernatural we learn to treasure,
We come to long for revelation,
Which nowhere burns so finely, so unflawed,
As in the Gospel of our Lord.
I feel an urge to reach   1220
For the original, the sacred text, appealing
To simple honesty of feeling
To render it in my dear German speech.
          [*He opens a tome and sets forth.*]
"In the beginning was the Word"—thus runs the text.[2]
Who helps me on? Already I'm perplexed!   1225
I cannot grant the word such sovereign merit,
I must translate it in a different way
If I'm indeed illumined by the Spirit.
"In the beginning was the Sense." But stay!
Reflect on this first sentence well and truly   1230
Lest the light pen be hurrying unduly!
Is sense in fact all action's spur and source?
It should read: "In the beginning was the Force!"
Yet as I write it down, some warning sense
Alerts me that it, too, will give offense.   1235
The spirit speaks! And lo, the way is freed,
I calmly write: "In the beginning was the Deed!"

Poodle, stop your barking,
If you wish to go on sharing
This room with me, not a growl or yap!   1240
Such a noisy larking chap
Near my person I find past bearing.
One of us, I can tell,
Must quit this cell.
It pains me to cancel the guest-right—still: 1245
The door is open, run where you will.
But what is this, I say?
Could this occur in the natural way?
Is it real or some shadow-fraud?
How my poodle grows long and broad!   1250

2. The opening line of the Gospel of John.

See him hugely swell and rise—
This is not canine shape or size!
What have I brought to the house, an incubus?
By now it's like a hippopotamus,
With fiery eyes and fearsome tooth. 1255
Ah, I'll make sure of you, forsooth!
For such half-hellish brood
Solomon's key is good.[3]

SPIRITS. [*in the hallway*][4] One is caught in there, you hear?
No one follow, all keep clear! 1260
Like a trapped fox there shrinks
Some wily old hell's lynx.
But pay heed!
Upward soar, downward flow,
To and fro, 1265
Soon he'll be freed.
There's tricks to show him,
Aid to be tendered,
We all here owe him
For favors rendered. 1270

FAUST. First the brute I score
With the Spell of the Four:[5]
Let Salamander flare,
Undine coil,
Sylph thin to air, 1275
Hobgoblin toil.
Who knows not the lore
Of the elements four,
Each one's merits
And dower, 1280
Has no power
Over spirits.

Shrink in fiery flashing,
Salamander!
Curb thy waters rushing, 1285
Undine!
Glow with meteor sheen,
Sylph!
Bring domestic help,
Incubus! Incubus! 1290
Be the last, step forth for us.
None of these four
Is the brute's core.
He lounges there with a careless grin;

3. Faust turns to a book of magic well known in the sixteenth century, *Clavicula Salomonis*, falsely attributed to Solomon, which contained chants and spells for controlling spirits.
4. Of uncertain origin and without explanation, these spirits, who appear subject to Mephistopheles' command, try to come to his aid.
5. The following spells, read from the book, are addressed to the spirits of the four elements: Salamander for fire, Undine for water, Sylph for air, Incubus (or Hobgoblin) for earth.

As yet I've left no mark on him.   1295
I'll be at your shell
With a stronger spell!
        Might you be, tell,
        A truant from Hell?
        Then see this sign![6]   1300
        Before whose power
        The black hosts cower.
There, it swells up with bristling spine.
        Monster degraded,
        Dare you see him,   1305
        The never-created
        Ineffable being,
        Through all the heavens poured,
        Heinously gored?
In the stove-nook's gloom,   1310
Swelled to elephant size,
It fair crowds the room,
Into vapor would blur;
To the ceiling do not rise!
Down, to your master's heel, cur!   1315
You see, mine are no idle threats.
I sear you with sacred fire jets!
Dare not bide
The thrice-glowing light![7]
Dare not bide   1320
The strongest art within my sway!
    [MEPHISTOPHELES, *clothed like a medieval traveling stu-
    dent, steps forth from behind the stove as the vapor clears.*]
MEPHISTOPHELES. Why all the fuss? What's milord's pleasure,
    pray?
FAUST. So this was at the poodle's core!
    A traveling scholar? Most amusing case!
MEPHISTOPHELES. Allow me to salute you, learned sir!   1325
    You really had me sweating for a space.
FAUST. What are you called?
MEPHISTOPHELES.   For one so down on the word,
    Who, so remote from everything external,
    Past all appearance seeks the inmost kernel,
    This question seems a bit absurd.   1330
FAUST. With gentry such as you, their nature
    Is aptly gathered from the nomenclature,
    Whence all too clearly it transpires
    When you are labeled Lord of Flies,[8] corrupters, liars.

---

6. Surmising that the spirit is a demon from Hell, Faust confronts it with the sign of Christ, the title which was inscribed on the cross at the crucifixion (see John 19:19): *INRI, Jesus Nazareneus Rex Judaeorum* ("Jesus of Naza- reth, King of the Jews").

7. Faust holds up the sign of the Trinity, a triangle with the eye of God in the center.

8. A literal translation of the Hebrew *Baal-zebub* (see 2 Kings 1:2).

All right—who are you, then?
MEPHISTOPHELES.   Part of that force which would 1335
     Do ever evil, and does ever good.[9]
FAUST. And that conundrum of a phrase implies?
MEPHISTOPHELES. The spirit which eternally denies![1]
     And justly so; for all that which is wrought
     Deserves that it should come to naught;   1340
     Hence it were best if nothing were engendered.
     Which is why all things you have rendered
     By terms like sin, destruction—evil, in brief
     Are my true element-in-chief.
FAUST. You call yourself a part, yet whole you stand in view?   1345
MEPHISTOPHELES. I speak a modest truth for you.
     Whereas your Man, that microcosmic fool,
     Regards himself an integer as a rule,
     I am but part of the part that was the whole at first,
     Part of the dark which bore itself the light,   1350
     That supercilious light which lately durst
     Dispute her ancient rank and realm to Mother Night;
     And yet to no avail, for strive as it may,
     It cleaves in bondage to corporeal clay.
     It streams from bodies, bodies it lends sheen,   1355
     A body can impede its thrust,
     And so it should not be too long, I trust,
     Before with bodies it departs the scene.[2]
FAUST. Now I perceive your worthy role!
     Unable to destroy on the scale of the whole,   1360
     You now attempt it in the little way.
MEPHISTOPHELES. It does not come to much, I'm bound to say.
     What bids defiance to the Naught,
     The clumsy lumber of the Aught,
     Endeavor what I would against it,   1365
     I never have discountenanced it
     By waves or tempests, quake or firebrand—
     Sedately rest at last both sea and land!
     As for that scum of beast- and humanhood,
     There's just no curbing it, no quelling,   1370
     I've buried them in droves past telling,
     Yet ever newly circulates fresh blood.
     And so it goes, it drives one to distraction!
     From air, from water, as from soil
     A thousand germinating seeds uncoil,   1375
     In warm or cold, in moist or dry-as-bone!

9. See Milton, *Paradise Lost*: "His providence/Out of our evil seek[s] to bring forth good" (I.162–63, Satan speaks of God) and "all his malice served but to bring forth goodness, grace, and mercy" (I.217–18, the poet speaking of Satan).
1. This is a paraphrase of the meaning of the name Satan (literally, "adversary"). See also line 338.
2. Mephistopheles applies the distinction of darkness and light to the doctrine that light derives from physical bodies and can manifest itself only against physical bodies.

Had I not fire for my preserve of action,
I should not have a place to call my own.
FAUST. And so against the ever sanely,
 Benignantly creative might   1380
 You clench your devil's fist, inanely
 Upraising it in frigid spite!
 Come, seek another occupation,
 Hoar Chaos's fantastic son!
MEPHISTOPHELES. It merits earnest contemplation; 1385
 We shall talk more of this anon!
 For now, though, would you let me quit you?
FAUST. Can I forbid you or permit you?
 Now we have met, feel free to pay
 Your further calls in any way.   1390
 Here is the window, there the door,
 The chimney, too, may be conceded.
MEPHISTOPHELES. I might as well own up! I am impeded
 Of egress by a minor flaw,
 That Druid's claw[3] at the threshold's center— 1395
FAUST. The pentagram can make you wince?
 Confide to me, Gehenna's[4] prince,
 If that confines you, how then did you enter?
 How was a mind like yours betrayed?
MEPHISTOPHELES. Look at it closely: it is not well made; 1400
 One of the corners of it, as you see,
 That faces outward, is a little split.
FAUST. Then I have chance to thank for it!
 So you are now a prisoner to me?
 That was a windfall, quite unearned!   1405
MEPHISTOPHELES. The poodle scampered in quite unconcerned;
 Now we are on a different tack,
 The Devil can't get back.
FAUST. Why not out through the window, then?
MEPHISTOPHELES. Devils and ghosts obey a regimen; 1410
 They must slip in and out by the same track.
 Entry is of our choice, for exit we're enslaved.
FAUST. Is even Hell with statutes paved?
 I am intrigued—then with you gentlemen
 A compact could, and safely too, be entered? 1415
MEPHISTOPHELES. That which is promised shall be neatly
   rendered,
 And nothing stinted or subtracted.
 But this cannot be hastily transacted,
 We may consider it when next we meet.
 But now I urge you and entreat   1420
 That for the nonce I might be gone.

---

3. The "Druid's claw," or pentagram, is a sign like a five-pointed star, one point of which is here split open (line 1402).
4. Another name for Hell.

FAUST. A moment more let me insist upon,
  Perhaps you have glad tidings to present.
MEPHISTOPHELES. Now let me go! I shall be back anon.
  Then you may question to your heart's content.   1425
FAUST. I used no trap or stratagem,
  All on your own you walked into my pen.
  Who holds Old Nick had best hang on to him!
  He will not capture him so soon again.
MEPHISTOPHELES. I am quite willing, if such be your pleasure,   1430
  To stay in company with a man of parts;
  Provided I may while away your leisure
  In some rewarding fashion by my arts.
FAUST. By all means do, you may feel free,
  But mind the art appeals to me.   1435
MEPHISTOPHELES. In this one hour, my friend, your senses
  Will garner in more recompenses
  Than in the year's monotony.
  What songs the delicate spirits sing you,
  The pleasing pictures they will bring you,   1440
  They are no idle magic game.
  Smell will be set to rapt enjoyment,
  The palate to superb employment,
  Your touch not least be set aflame.
  No preparation needs our art;   1445
  We are forgathered, let us start!
SPIRITS.† Melt, ye confining
       Vaults up yonder!
       Yield to the shining
       Ether's fonder   1450
       Cerulean gaze!
       Cloudbanks darkling
       Dwindle for sparkling
       Starlets winking,
       Milder sun-rays   1455
       Drinking the haze!
       Heavenly offspring's
       Graces uplifting,
       Swaying and turning,
       Drifting they wander,   1460
       Lovelorn yearning
       Follows them yonder.
       And their garments'
       Fluttering garlands
       Cover the far lands,   1465
       Cover the arbor
       Where thought-rapt lover
       Lifelong trusting
       Pledges to lover.
       Arbor on arbor!   1470

Tendrils thrusting!
Plump grape clusters
Plunging in masses
To groaning presses,
With froth and rumble   1475
Wine floods tumble
Down craggy tunnels,
Crystalline runnels
Through pure gem funnels
Downward heading,   1480
To lakes outspreading,
Embedding, embanking,
Calm hills' green flanking.
And winged creation
Imbibes elation   1485
Sunward streaming
Soars on to dreaming
Islands skimming
On wavelets gleaming,
Sinking and lifting;   1490
Where we hear choiring
In jubilant chorus,
See dancers gyring
On meadows before us,
Dispersing at pleasure   1495
In airy leisure.
Some go scaling
The mountain quarters,
Others trailing
The lake's slow waters,   1500
Others sailing
The air; all to living,
All to afars
Of stars love-giving,
Of blessed requital.   1505

MEPHISTOPHELES. Asleep! Well done, my airy cherubim!
    You found the proper lullaby for him!
    I am obliged to you for this recital.
    You are not yet the man to hold on to the Devil!
    In welters of sweet fancy make him revel,   1510
    Plunge him into an ocean of deceit;
    Meanwhile, the spell cast at this threshold level
    Demands a rat's tooth to defeat.
    No need to conjure—one is near me,
    Close-by he rustles, and will forthwith hear me.[5] 1515

    The lord of rats and mice,
    Of flies, frogs, bedbugs, lice,

5. Mephistopheles calls forth a rat to   enough for him to squeeze through.
nibble a hole in the pentagram big

Hither bids you dare!
Gnaw the threshold there,
Where the oil I rub—   1520
There you come scampering up!
To work, fall to! The gap that needs enlarging,
You'll find it at the outmost margin.
Another bite, and it is done.—

Now, Faust, until we meet again, dream on!   1525
FAUST. [*awakening*] Am I then once again deluded?
    Thus fades for me the spirits' rich array,
    That in a cheating dream the Devil had intruded,
    And that a poodle slipped away!

STUDY†

FAUST. MEPHISTOPHELES.

FAUST. A knock? Come in! Who now will try my patience?   1530
MEPHISTOPHELES. It's me.
FAUST.   Come in!
MEPHISTOPHELES.   It takes three invitations.
FAUST. Come in, then!
MEPHISTOPHELES.   Now you know the cue.
    We two, I trust, will have no altercations!
    For to chase off your lucubrations,
    I'm here as a young nobleman for you,   1535
    In scarlet suit with golden braiding,
    A mantlet stiff with silk brocading,
    Cock-feather perched on beret brim,
    A rapier, long and pointed nicely:[1]
    And I advise you now, concisely,   1540
    To throw yourself in similar trim,
    So that, emancipated, free,
    You may explore what life can be.
FAUST. I greatly fear, regardless of attire,
    I'll walk in pain the narrow earthly way.[2]   1545
    I am too old to be content with play,
    To young to be without desire.
    What does the world hold out by way of gain?
    Abstain! it calls, You shall abstain!
    Thus goes the sempiternal song   1550
    That every mortal creature hears,
    That our entire existence long
    Each hour comes rasping to our ears.
    Each morning I awake in desperation,

---

1. Mephistopheles wears the conventional theatrical costume of a Spanish cavalier.
2. Faust's drastic change of mood to pessimism and despair is unmotivated as the drama now stands. Goethe intended to write a disputation scene between the study scenes which would have explained the change.

Sick unto tears to see begun   1555
Yet one more day that in its ambulation
Will grant me not a single wish, not one,
That with its stubborn carping tempers
Each mere presentiment of joy,
With thousand shams of living hampers   1560
My live creative mind's employ.
When night descends and I would seek for slumber,
Then, too, I am not granted rest;
I dread to bed me down—wild visions cumber
My dreams and make repose unblessed.   1565
The lord within my bosom bowered
Can stir me to the inmost kernel;
The one past all my powers empowered,
He cannot alter anything external.
Existence seems a burden to detest,   1570
Death to be wished for, life a hateful jest.

MEPHISTOPHELES. And yet death never is a wholly welcome guest.
FAUST. O, blessèd he about whose brow he winds
    The bloodstained laurels of victorious war,
    Or whom, spun breathless off the ballroom floor,   1575
    Locked in a maiden's arms he finds!
    Oh, had I sunken lifeless, wasted
    Of bliss before the lofty Spirit's might![3]
MEPHISTOPHELES. And yet a certain person left untasted
    A certain brownish elixir that night.[4]   1580
FAUST. In spying, it would seem, you have a special touch.
MEPHISTOPHELES. All-knowing I am not; albeit aware of much.
FAUST. What if a sweet familiar pealing
    Recalled me from that fearsome maze,
    Lured what remained of childlike feeling   1585
    With echoings of happier days?[5]
    My curse† I hurl on all that spangles
    The mind with dazzling make-belief,
    With lures and blandishments entangles
    The soul within this cave of grief!   1590
    Accursed, to start, the smug delusion
    Whereby the mind itself ensnares!
    Cursed, brash phenomenal intrusion
    That blinds the senses unawares!
    Cursed, what in lying dreams assures us   1595
    Of name and glory past the grave!
    Cursed, pride of ownership that lures us
    Through wife and children, plow and slave!
    Accursed be Mammon, when his treasure
    To deeds of daring eggs us on,   1600
    For idle self-indulgent leisure

3. An allusion to the Earth Spirit (see lines 482–513).
4. An allusion to Faust's temptation to suicide (see lines 720–36).
5. An allusion to Faust's recovery in response to the Easter Chorus (see lines 762–84).

Spreads a luxurious divan!
Cursed be the balsam of the grape!
Cursed, highest prize of lovers' thrall!
A curse on faith! A curse on hope!   1605
A curse on patience, above all!
CHORUS OF SPIRITS. [*invisible*] Woe! Woe!
             You have destroyed it,
             The beautiful world,
             With mighty fist;[6]   1610
             It crumbles scattered,
             By a demigod shattered.
             Forlorn,
             We bear the ruins into the void,
             And mourn   1615
             For beauty destroyed.
             Mighty one
             Of the earth's sons,
             In splendor perfected
             See it rewon,   1620
             In your own breast re-erect it!
             Set forth
             Upon rebirth
             With freshened sense;
             And new-sung mirth   1625
             Re-echo thence!
MEPHISTOPHELES.   Hear the smallest of all
             Who are at my call,
             Precociously suing
             For joyous doing!
             To the world entire,
             From this lonesome plot
             Where thought and juices clot,
             They bid you aspire.
Be done with nursing your despair,   1635
Which, like a vulture, feeds upon your mind;
The very meanest company bids fair
To let you feel a man among mankind.
It's not that we propose
To toss you in among the rabble.   1640
I am no ranking devil;
But let us say you chose
To fall in step with me for life's adventure,
I'd gladly, forthwith, go into indenture,
Be yours, as well as I know how.   1645
I'm your companion now,
And if this meets with your desire,
Will be your servitor, your squire!
FAUST. And for my part—what is it you require?

6. In German, the term *Faust* introduces an intentional pun on the protagonist's
name.

MEPHISTOPHELES. Never you mind, it's much too soon to
    worry.   1650
FAUST. No, no! Old Nick's an egoist—it's hard
    To picture him in any special hurry
    To be of service for the love of God.[7]
    Spell out just what the bargain turns upon;
    Not safely is such servant taken on.   1655
MEPHISTOPHELES. I shall be at your service by this bond
    Without relief or respite here on earth;
    And if or when we meet again beyond,
    You are to give me equal worth.
FAUST. Beyond to me makes little matter;   1660
    If once this earthly world you shatter,
    The next may rise when this has passed.
    It is from out this earth my pleasures spring,
    It is this sun shines on my suffering;
    If once from these I draw asunder,   1665
    Then come to pass what will and must.
    I do not further choose to wonder
    If hate may then be felt or love,
    Or whether in those regions yonder
    They still know nether or above.   1670
MEPHISTOPHELES. So minded, you may dare with fitness.
    Engage yourself; these days you are to witness
    Examples of my pleasing arts galore.
    I'll give you what no man has seen before.
FAUST. What is, poor devil, in your giving?   1675
    Has ever human mind in its high striving
    Been comprehended by the likes of you?
    What's yours but food unsating, the red hue
    Of gold which, shifting and untrue,
    Quicksilverlike will through the fingers run,   1680
    A game which always stays unwon,
    A girl who at my very breast
    Trades winks already with another's eyes,
    But honor's fair and godly zest
    Which like a meteor flares and dies?   1685
    Show me the fruit which, still unplucked, will rot,
    Trees freshly green with every day's renewal!
MEPHISTOPHELES. Such a commission daunts me not,
    I can provide that sort of jewel.
    But nonetheless, there comes a time, my friend,   1690
    When good things savored at our ease give pleasure.
FAUST. Should ever I take ease upon a bed of leisure,
    May that same moment mark my end!
    When first by flattery you lull me
    Into a smug complacency,   1695
    When with indulgence you can gull me,

7. This colloquial phrase means "without payment."

Let that day be the last for me!
This is my wager![8]

MEPHISTOPHELES.   Done!

FAUST.   And beat for beat!
If the swift moment† I entreat:
Tarry a while! you are so fair!   1700
Then forge the shackles to my feet,
Then I will gladly perish there!
Then let them toll the passing-bell,
Then of your servitude be free,
The clock may stop, its hands fall still,   1705
And time be over then for me!

MEPHISTOPHELES. Reflect upon this—we shall not forget it.

FAUST. That is your right, by no means to be waived!
My stake was in no wanton spirit betted.
Once come to rest, I am enslaved—   1710
To you, whomever—why regret it?

MEPHISTOPHELES. This very evening, at the doctoral feast,
Watch me my servant's duty plying.
Just one more thing—for living or for dying,
I'd like a line or two at least.   1715

FAUST. Cannot you pedant do without a screed?
Have you not met a man, not found his word his deed?
What, is it not enough my spoken word should force
My days into eternal peonage?
Does not the world rush on with brimming course,   1720
And I am to be prisoned by a pledge?
Yet this conceit is lodged within our breast,
And who would gladly see it leave him?
Who bears good faith in his pure soul is blessed,
No sacrifice will ever grieve him!   1725
A square of parchment, though, all writ and stamped,
Becomes a specter that repels all men.
Still in the pen, the word is cramped,
And wax and leather lord it then.
What, evil spirit, say your rules?   1730
Parchment or paper? Marble? Brass? What tools,
The stylus, chisel, pen? How shall I write it?
You are at liberty to choose.

MEPHISTOPHELES. How can you with so puny a fuse
Get such hot rhetoric ignited?   1735
Just any slip will do, it's all the same.
You draw a drop of blood and sign your name.

FAUST. On with the hocus-pocus—I am game,
If this is all you need to be requited.

MEPHISTOPHELES. Blood is a very special juice.   1740

8. In addition to the traditional pact
Faust offers a wager (lines 1699–1706),
which Mephistopheles accepts. Compare
the earlier wager between Mephistopheles and the Lord in the "Prologue in
Heaven" (lines 312–17).

FAUST. Oh, never fear my promise might be broken!
　My utmost striving's fullest use
　Is just the part I have bespoken.
　I sought to puff myself too high,
　Your rank is all I may attain.　　　　　　　　　　1745
　The lofty Spirit spurned me, and I pry
　At Nature's bolted doors in vain.[9]
　The web of thought is all in slashes,
　All knowledge long turned dust and ashes.
　Let in the depths of sensual life　　　　　　　　1750
　The blaze of passions be abated!
　May magic shrouds unpenetrated
　With every miracle be rife!
　Let's hurl ourselves in time's on-rushing tide,
　Occurrence's on-rolling stride!　　　　　　　　　1755
　So may then pleasure and distress,
　Failure and success,
　Follow each other as they please;
　Man's active only when he's never at ease.
MEPHISTOPHELES. No bars or bounds are set for you.　1760
　If anywhere you feel like snatching
　Chance relish, sweets of passage catching,
　May what delights prove wholesome too.
　Just help yourself and don't be coy.
FAUST. You heard me, there can be no thought of joy.　1765
　Frenzy I choose, most agonizing lust,
　Enamored enmity, restorative disgust.
　Henceforth my soul, for knowledge sick no more,
　Against no kind of suffering shall be cautioned,
　And[1] what to all of mankind is apportioned　　1770
　I mean to savor in my own self's core,
　Grasp with my mind both highest and most low,
　Weigh down my spirit with their weal and woe,
　And thus my selfhood to their own distend,
　And be, as they are, shattered in the end.　　　1775
MEPHISTOPHELES. Oh, take my word, who for millennia past
　Has had this rocky fare to chomp,
　That from his first breath to his last
　No man digests that ancient sourdough lump!
　Believe the likes of us: the whole　　　　　　　1780
　Is made but for a god's delight!
　He dwells in an eternal aureole,
　Us he committed to the depth of night,
　And you make do with dark and light.

---

9. Faust here recalls his meeting with the Earth Spirit in the opening scene. Goethe may have intended, in composing this ca. 1800–1801, to make a transition to the text of the *Fragment* published in 1790, which recommences at line 1770.

1. Lines 1770–1867 were published in the *Fragment* of 1790. Since line 1770 begins in mid-sentence and lines 1770–71 rhyme with the two lines preceding, it may be that some of what immediately precedes had already been written before 1790.

FAUST. And yet I choose it!

MEPHISTOPHELES.   Worthily decided!   1785
  I fear just one thing, for my part:
  Short is the time, and long is art.[2]
  In this, I trust, you will be guided.
  Associate yourself with a poetaster,
  And let that sportsman brood and roam   1790
  And all the noble virtues cluster
  Upon your venerable dome,
  The lion's audacity,
  The stag's swift surge,
  The Italian's fiery urge,   1795
  The North's tenacity;
  Let him reveal the arcane style
  Of joining generosity and guile,
  Whereby, youth's ardor freshly fanning,
  One falls in love with proper planning.   1800
  I should myself be glad to meet him,
  "Sir Microcosm" I would greet him.

FAUST. What am I, if it is past human power
  To conquer mankind's loftiest plane,
  The crown toward which all senses strain?   1805

MEPHISTOPHELES. You are, all told—just what you are.
  Put wigs on of a million powdered rolls,
  Increase your height with ell-high actors' soles,
  You still remain just what you are.

FAUST. In vain all treasures of the human mind,   1810
  I feel it, have I raked to me; at length,
  When I sit down to marshal them, I find
  There wells within no fresh resource of strength;
  Not by a hairsbreadth am I grown,
  No nearer to the limitless unknown.   1815

MEPHISTOPHELES. Dear Sir, you look on things as crudely
  As men are apt to do; instead,
  We must conduct ourselves more shrewdly,
  Before the joys of life have fled.
  Bah! Hands and feet belong to you,   1820
  And head and arse too, if you please,
  But what I freely taste and view,
  Is that less mine than these?
  If I can pay for half-a-dozen horse,
  Have I not bought their sixfold thew?   1825
  I run and show off with the force
  Of four-and-twenty legs, not two.
  Cheer up! Throw over all reflection,
  And off into the world post-haste!
  Take it from me: the slave of introspection   1830

2. Adapted from the aphorism of Hippocrates earlier cited by Wagner (lines 558–59).

Is like a beast on arid waste
By some foul fiend led round and round,
While, all about, green meadowlands abound.

FAUST. How do we set about it?

MEPHISTOPHELES.   We set off, that's all.
    What is this place, a penitents' hive?   1835
    What sort of life is this, to drive
    Both self and students up the wall?
    Let that be neighbor Potbelly's concern!
    Why thresh that straw in the sweat of your brow?
    The best you can expect to learn   1840
    You cannot tell the youngsters anyhow.
    There—I can hear one now outside.

FAUST. I cannot bring myself to face him.

MEPHISTOPHELES. The poor boy, he has long been pacing,
    He must not go unsatisfied.   1845
    Come, let me have your cap and gown;
    A priceless mask they should provide
        [*He changes into* FAUST's *garb.*]
    No fear, my wits won't let me down!
    I only need a quarter-hour's delay;
    Meanwhile prepare to start upon our merry way!   1850
        [*Exit* FAUST.]

MEPHISTOPHELES. [*in Faust's long robe*] Go, spurn intelligence and
    science,
    Man's lodestar and supreme reliance,
    Be furthered by the liar-in-chief[3]
    In works of fraud and make-believe,
    And I shall have you dead to rights.   1855
    Fate has endowed him with a forward-driving
    Impetuousness that reaches past all sights,
    And which, precipitately striving,
    Would overleap the earth's delights.
    Through dissipation I will drag him,   1860
    Through shallow insignificance,
    I'll have him sticking, writhing, flagging,
    And for his parched incontinence
    Have food and drink suspended at lip level;
    In vain will he be yearning for relief,   1865
    And had he not surrendered to the devil,
    He still must needs have come to grief!
        [*Enter a* STUDENT.][4]

STUDENT. I have been here but a short span,

---

3. Scholars generally agree that this refers not to Mephistopheles but to the self-deceiving aspect of Faust's own mind.

4. The student scene (to line 2050) derives with some revisions from the *Urfaust* and was published in its present form in the *Fragment.* Goethe omitted discussion of the Student's living quarters from the original version and expanded the satirical attack on the university faculties, with lines 1964–2000 added. See Goethe's comment on the Student in the "*Faust* Plan of 1800," below.

And come with reverent emotion
To wait upon and know a man   1870
Whom all regard with deep devotion.
MEPHISTOPHELES. I am much pleased by your polite address!
You see a man like others, more or less.
Have you had time to look about elsewhere?
STUDENT. I beg of you, receive me in your care!   1875
With every good intention I am here,
In tolerable funds and best of cheer,
My mother would scarce hear about my going,
I'd truly like to learn a thing worth knowing.
MEPHISTOPHELES. You've found the very place, forsooth.   1880
STUDENT. I feel like pushing on, to tell the truth:
These vaults, this maze of brick and wall
Will not agree with me at all.
It's such a close, constricted place,
No tree, no green thing—when I face   1885
These halls, these benches, tier on tier,
I cannot think or see or hear.
MEPHISTOPHELES. It all depends on what you're used to.
Thus many a child has first refused to
Take nourishment at mother's breast,   1890
And soon begun to nurse with zest.
So you will suck the breasts of learning
With rising appetite and yearning.
STUDENT. I will hang on with joyful clasp;
But tell me how to bring them within grasp!   1895
MEPHISTOPHELES. Tell me, before we come to that,
What Faculty are you aiming at?
STUDENT. I want to get a power of learning,
Fill up with everything concerning
The earth and heaven you could mention,   1900
Science and nature, at the source.
MEPHISTOPHELES. Then you are on the proper course;
But do not spare your full attention.
STUDENT. I will go to it with a will;
Of course, time-off and relaxation   1905
Might sometimes take my fancy still,
Like when it's summer and vacation.
MEPHISTOPHELES. Husband your time, it flies so swiftly past;
Yet order teaches you to make time last.
So first, dear friend, you should make room   1910
For the Collegium Logicum.
This leaves the mind all trained and dressed,
In Spanish trusses[5] tightly pressed,
So that it, slow and undistraught,
Will potter down the train of thought,   1915

5. An instrument of torture which was   on like iron boots.
fastened to the victim's legs and screwed

Not like a will o' the wisp cavort
Hither and yon, aside, athwart.
They teach you for a year or so
That what you did all at one go,
Like eating and drinking, fancy-free,   1920
Needs stages one, and two, and three.
What though the thought-assembly shop
Is like a master-weaver's job,
Where one tread stirs a thousand points,
The shuttles back and forward fly,   1925
Threads flow too swiftly for the eye,
One downbeat strikes a thousand joints:
Enter: Philosopher, and lo!
He proves to you it must be so;
The first being thus, the second thus,   1930
The third and fourth must needs be thus,
And were it not for one and two,
The three and four could not be true.
His pupils laud him, busy as beavers,
And somehow never turn into weavers.   1935
Who would know and describe a living thing,
Seeks first to expel the spirit within,
Then he stands there, the parts held in his grasp,
Lost just the spiritual bond, alas!
Encheiresis naturae,[6] chemistry declares,   1940
Mocking itself all unawares.

STUDENT. I don't quite follow you, I fear.

MEPHISTOPHELES. It soon will grow more nearly clear,
    When you learn how to analyze,
    And properly categorize.   1945

STUDENT. All this leaves me as limp and dull
    As if millstones were grinding in my skull.

MEPHISTOPHELES. Next, Metaphysics I should mention
    As the foremost study for your attention!
    There make your deepest insight strain   1950
    For things out of scale with the human brain;
    For whatever fits into it and what doesn't
    Some wondrous word is always present.
    This first semester, though, have patience,
    Minutely observe the regulations,   1955
    Five lecture hours is your daily spell,
    Be there at the very stroke of the bell,
    Having prepared yourself well before,
    Cramming *paragraphos,* what's more,

6. This phrase, a mixture of Greek and Latin meaning "handholds of nature," derives from a book by a professor of chemistry at the University of Strassburg whom Goethe heard lecture when he was a student there (J. R. Spielmann, *Institutiones chemiae*, 1763).

To make quite sure with no further look   1960
The man says nothing that's not in the book.[7]
Yet by all means take it down in writing,
As though it were the Holy Ghost reciting.
STUDENT. You shall not have to tell me twice!
I sense that it is good advice.   1965
What one has black on white recorded
May safely be borne home and hoarded.
MEPHISTOPHELES. Select a Faculty, however.
STUDENT. For Jurisprudence I feel no special bent.
MEPHISTOPHELES. I scarcely blame you for the sentiment.   1970
I know about the state of this endeavor.
We drag prerogatives and laws
From place to place by slow degrees,
Age handing age ancestral flaws
Like an inherited disease.   1975
Sense turns to nonsense, boon to plague,
Woe to the grandson that you are!
Our human birthright prior to the bar,
On that, alas! the gentlemen are vague.
STUDENT. You make my own revulsion rise.   1980
Lucky the man whom you advise!
Theology looks more like my profession.
MEPHISTOPHELES. I would not give the wrong impression
As it concerns this discipline.
It's all too easy to get sidetracked in,   1985
So much of poison lies concealed within
That's scarce distinguishable from the medicine.
Here too the risk is least when just one voice is heard;
Swear only by the master's word.
In sum—have words to lean upon,   1990
And through that trusty gateway, lexicon,
You pass into the shrine of certainty.[8]
STUDENT. Yet with each word there must a concept be.
MEPHISTOPHELES. Oh, quite—no need, though, to be racking
One's brain, for just where concept's lacking   1995
A word in time supplies the remedy.
Words are good things to be debated,
With words are systems generated,
In words belief is safely vested,
From words no jot or tittle can be wrested.†   2000
STUDENT. I dare not waste your time with many questions,
But there is one more discipline;
I wonder if concerning Medicine

<hr>

7. Mephistopheles refers to the practice at German universities in the eighteenth century of lecturing from a textbook, where the subject matter was defined by numbered paragraphs (*paragraphos*, a Greek term) to be studied ahead of time by the students.

8. Preference for the word over the sense or spirit agrees with Wagner's trust of rhetoric (lines 546–47) and opposes Faust's rejection of "word" as a translation of *logos* (lines 1224–37).

You might not have some down-to-earth suggestions?
Three years are very quickly past, 2005
And Lord! the field is far too vast.[9]
With just a hint on what is right or wrong
It's easier to feel one's way along.

MEPHISTOPHELES. [*aside*] I've had enough of the didactic vein,
I must go back and play the Deuce again. 2010
[*aloud*] The gist of Medicine is grasped with ease.
You study up on macro-, microcosm, just so
That in the end you let things go
As God may please.
It's vain to roam afield the scientific way, 2015
For everyone learns only what he can;
He who will seize the moment when he may,
He is the proper man.
You're fairly well-built, to my mind,
I'd say there is some spunk in you; 2020
If you just trust yourself, you'll find
The other folk will trust you too.
Especially the women learn to guide;
Their everlasting ahs and ohs,
Their myriad woes, 2025
Can all be cured at one divide.
If you adopt a halfway decent air,
You'll lure them all into your lair.
First win their trust, by some well-chosen title,
That your art puts all other arts to shame; 2030
Then for a start you grope for portions vital
That cost another many a year's campaign;
You squeeze her pulse a little harder,
Then lay with cunning looks of ardor
Your arm about the slender waist 2035
To see how tightly she is laced.

STUDENT. Now that sounds better! Much less guesswork or surmising.

MEPHISTOPHELES. Gray, dear young fellow, is all theorizing,
And green, life's golden tree.

STUDENT. I swear, this all seems like a dream to me. 2040
Might I another time entreat your leisure
To draw more fully on your deep sagacity?

MEPHISTOPHELES. What I can do I'll do with pleasure.

STUDENT. I find I cannot bear to see
My way to go until I have bespoken 2045
Into my album of your grace some token![1]

MEPHISTOPHELES. Oh yes, indeed.
[*He writes, and returns the book.*]

---

9. An unintentional allusion by the Student to the aphorism of Hippocrates earlier cited by Wagner (lines 558–59) and
Mephistopheles (line 1787).

1. University students in Goethe's time
often collected signatures in an album
from friends and teachers, with words or
verses of advice.

STUDENT. [*reads*] *Eritis sicut Deus, scientes bonum et malum.*[2]
    [*Closes the album reverently and takes his leave*]
MEPHISTOPHELES. Go on, heed the old saying, and my cousin,
    the Snake;
    There'll come a time your godlike state will make you
        quake!   2050
    [*Enter* FAUST.]
FAUST. Where are we off to now?
MEPHISTOPHELES.   Wherever you choose.
    The small world, then the great we shall peruse.
    Ah, with what profit, with what glee
    You'll take this seminar for free!
FAUST. My long gray beard, though, spoils my chance,   2055
    It cramps the proper nonchalance.
    This venture won't be a success;
    I never had a vein for worldliness.
    In company I feel so small;
    I'll never be at ease at all.   2060
MEPHISTOPHELES. Acquiring confidence, good friend, the more
    you try,
    You'll get the hang of living by and by.
FAUST. But tell me, how are we to ride?
    Where are your groom and coach and horses?
MEPHISTOPHELES. We simply spread my mantle wide,   2065
    It shall convey us on our airy courses.
    Embarking on this daring flight,
    You will do best to travel light.
    Some fiery air which I shall fashion here
    Will buoy us up from earth quick as you please.   2070
    Light as we'll be, we should soar up with ease.
    Congratulations on your new career!

AUERBACH'S TAVERN IN LEIPZIG

JOLLY FELLOWS *carousing.*

FROSCH. Nobody drinking? No guffaws, grimaces?
    I'll teach you not to make long faces!
    Like crackers you used to fizz and pop,   2075
    And now you're gay as a sodden mop.
BRANDER. It's all your fault; you brought no pig in your poke,
    No bit of nonsense, not a dirty joke.
FROSCH. [*pours a glass of wine over his head*]
    There's both in one!
BRANDER.   You double pig! Nitwit!
FROSCH. That's what you wanted, wasn't it?   2080
SIEBEL. Who starts a quarrel here, goes out!
    A rollicking round-song, come now, swill and shout!
    Hey! Holler! Ho!

2. "You will be like God, knowing good and evil" (Genesis 3:5), the words with which the serpent tempts Eve to eat the forbidden fruit.

ALTMAYER.   That does for me, my God!
  Bring cotton, or he'll burst my ears, the sod.
SIEBEL. When hall and vault reverberate,   2085
  That's when you feel the bass's might and weight.
FROSCH. That's right, out with the boob that takes offense!
  A, tralala, trala!
ALTMAYER. A, tralala, trala!
FROSCH.   Our throats are tuned, I sense.
    [*Sings.*]
              Oh Holy Roman Empire dear,   2090
              What holds you still together?[1]
BRANDER. A nasty song! Phew! a political song,
  A wretched song. Praise God for each day's bliss
  That the old Empire's not your business!
  For I at least account it ample profit   2095
  That I'm not emperor or chancellor of it.
  Still, we shan't lack a chief, I hope:
  Let us elect a tippling pope.
  You know what qualities avail
  To mark the man and turn the scale.   2100
FROSCH. [*sings*] Miss Nightingale, o soar above,
              Take ten thousand greetings to my love.
SIEBEL. No love to females! I'll have none of this!
FROSCH. Don't interfere—I still say love and a kiss!
    [*Sings.*]
              Unbolt the door, in dark of night;   2105
              Unbolt the door, the lover cries;
              Bolt up the door, at dawn's first light.
SIEBEL. Oh yes, go on and yodel, praise her to the skies![2]
  I'll have the last laugh, time will tell.
  She's pulled my leg, and she'll pull your as well.   2110
  She'd haunt the crossroads if she had her merit,
  To bill and coo there with some evil spirit;
  A rank old buck, from Hallowe'en returning,
  Should bleat goodnights to her with tender yearning,
  A regular lad of flesh and blood   2115
  Is thrown away upon that slut.
  For compliments that really mattered
  I'd like to see her windows shattered!
BRANDER. [*slamming his fist on the table*]
  Look here! Attention! Listen, you!
  Confess, I know a thing or two;   2120
  I see some swains among us sitting,
  To them I offer, as is fitting,
  A piece that should be right on cue.

---

1. The political satire of Frosch's song reflects an eighteenth-century attitude toward the Empire, at that time little more than a medieval remnant.
2. Frosch has stolen a girl away from Siebel, and the latter abuses her from spite as a witch haunting a crossroads or joining in the "Hallowe'en" orgies of the Walpurgis Night.

Attend! A song in latest vein!
Chime in with vigorous refrain! 2125
    [*He sings.*]
        In a cellar nest there lived a rat,
        Had butter and lard to suit her,
        She wore a belly-bag of fat,
        A pouch like Dr. Luther.[3]
        The cook had poison scattered out; 2130
        That drove her hither and about,
        As if the love-bug bit her.
CHORUS. [*cheering*]
        As if the love-bug bit her.
BRANDER. She hurried, scurried, pawed and clawed,
        And swilled from every puddle, 2135
        The house was all scratched up and gnawed,
        To soothe her frantic muddle;
        Tried many a leap in fear and pain,
        But all she tried was tried in vain,
        As if the love-bug bit her. 2140
CHORUS. As if the love-bug bit her.
BRANDER. In fright she sought the light of day,
        Came running in the kitchen,
        Fell at the stove and there she lay,
        With piteous gasp and twitching. 2145
        The poisoner only laughed, she knew
        She'd bit off more than she could chew,
        As if the love-bug bit her.
CHORUS. As if the love-bug bit her.
SIEBEL. Guffaws! That shows these dolts' horizon! 2150
  A worthy pastime, it would seem,
  To prey on helpless rats with poison!
BRANDER. They must stand high in your esteem?
ALTMAYER. That greasepot with his shining pate!
  He takes the ballad much to heart; 2155
  He honors in the swollen rat
  His natural kin and counterpart.
    [*Enter* FAUST *and* MEPHISTOPHELES.]
MEPHISTOPHELES. My foremost duty is, you see,
  To show you merry company,
  How one may idle best and worry least; 2160
  The people here make every day a feast.
  With comfort ample, humor stale,
  Each spins in his constricted round,
  Like kittens chasing their own tail.
  Provided that their heads are sound, 2165
  And while the landlord's credit holds,
  They are right merry and carefree souls.

3. Martin Luther, a contemporary of the historical Faustus, visited Leipzig in 1525, the year following the supposed visit by the magus.

BRANDER. I bet these two have come wayfaring,
    You look at their outlandish bearing;
    They haven't been an hour in town. 2170

FROSCH. I think you're right! That's Leipzig's new renown!
    A lesser Paris, and it polishes its people.[4]

SIEBEL. Who are these strangers, would you guess?

FROSCH. Let us accost them—over a toast, forsooth,
    I'll pull their secret like a baby tooth; 2175
    Trust me to pump them with finesse
    They seem to be of notable descent,
    They both look arrogant and ill-content.

BRANDER. They're quacks, I bet, that on the market holler.

ALTMAYER. Perhaps. 2180

FROSCH.   I'll squeeze 'em—watch them twist!

MEPHISTOPHELES. [*to* FAUST] They never recognize the devil's fist
    Though he may have them by the collar!

FAUST. Our greetings, gentlemen!

SIEBEL.   Our thanks for quit-salute.
    [*under his breath, looking sideways at* MEPHISTOPHELES]
    I say, the fellow limps upon one foot![5]

MEPHISTOPHELES. May we sit down here and in lieu 2185
    Of decent drink one cannot find,
    Enjoy good company with you?

ALTMAYER. You seem a most fastidious kind.

FROSCH. You must have left your Cattlebury late—
    Did you have supper with Sir Bumpkin first?[6] 2190

MEPHISTOPHELES. This trip, we bypassed his estate;
    We saw him last time, though; he was immersed
    In memories of many a country cousin,
    And charged us greetings by the dozen.
    [*He bows in* FROSCH's *direction.*]

ALTMAYER. [*under his breath*] My word! No flies on him!

SIEBEL.   He got you, mate! 2195

FROSCH. I'll have him squirming yet, you wait!

MEPHISTOPHELES. Just now, did we not hear the sound
    Of voices trained in part-song pealing?
    For sure, good singing must resound
    Right smartly from this vaulted ceiling! 2200

FROSCH. Why—might you be a professional?

MEPHISTOPHELES. Oh no! My talent's small, though there is
        much good will.

ALTMAYER Give us a song!

MEPHISTOPHELES.   As many as you choose.

SIEBEL. But only of most recent date!

---

4. In the eighteenth century, Leipzig prided itself on being "a lesser Paris," Paris being regarded as the center of European taste and culture.

5. A reference to the devil's traditional cloven hoof, also attributed to Mephi-

stopheles in lines 2490, 4065, and 6335–39.

6. A local joke in Leipzig concerning a village named Rippach ("Cattlebury") where a certain Hans Arse resided.

MEPHISTOPHELES. We're back from sunny Spain of late, 2205
  The land of wine and of the tuneful Muse.
     [*Sings.*]
          There ruled a king among us,
          Who had a mighty big flea—[7]
FROSCH. Hark! Had a flea! A flea, you catch the jest?
  A flea must be a savory guest. 2210
MEPHISTOPHELES. [*sings*]
          There ruled a king among us,
          Who had a mighty big flea,
          He paid him princely honors,
          So fond of him was he.
          He called his tailor mincing, 2215
          Who bowed and scraped and rose:
          A doublet for the princeling,
          Here, measure him for hose!
BRANDER. Be sure now to impress upon the tailor
  To ply the tape with bated breath, 2220
  So that no wrinkle shows, for failure
  Will bring about his instant death!
MEPHISTOPHELES. In silk with velvet lining
          He now was fitly dressed,
          Wore atlas sashes shining, 2225
          A ribbon and a crest,
          At once he was a minister
          And had a glittering star;
          His kin at court, oh sinister,
          Advanced almost as far. 2230

          The lords and maids-in-waiting
          At court were sorely plagued,
          And titled fleas were baiting
          The Queen and her chambermaid.
          Nor could they like us others, 2235
          Rub, itch and scratch what ails,
          We pinch and crunch what bothers
          With pouncing fingernails.
CHORUS. [*cheering*]
          We pinch and crunch what bothers
          With pouncing fingernails. 2240
FROSCH. Bravo! Bravo! That was good fun!
SIEBEL. Thus shall to every flea be done!
BRANDER. Stalk 'em, snip 'em with fingertips fine!
ALTMAYER. And long live freedom! Long live wine!
MEPHISTOPHELES. I'd gladly raise my glass to freedom,
  let it clink, 2245

7. The source of the song of the flea, a satire against court dandies, is thought to be a fable, "The Rooster and the Eagle," by C. F. D. Schubart (1739–91), first published in 1774, which suggests that the final version of this scene in the *Urfaust* must have been written after that time.

If just your wines were halfway fit to drink.

SIEBEL. You've said this once too much, I think.

MEPHISTOPHELES. I only fear the landlord might protest,
Or I'd provide each honored guest
From my own cellar a fine drop.[8]   2250

SIEBEL. I'll square the landlord—let it pop!

FROSCH. Bring us good drink, you'll hear our praise ring out.
But see you make the portions ample,
For if I am to judge a sample,
I do it on a well-filled snout.   2255

ALTMAYER. [*under his breath*] They're from the Rhineland,
doubt it not.

MEPHISTOPHELES. Find me a drill!

BRANDER.   What for? Why do you ask it?
You have your barrels just outdoors, or what?

ALTMAYER. Back there, the landlord keeps some tools in a
basket.

MEPHISTOPHELES. [*takes the drill; to* FROSCH] Now say what wine
you wish from me.   2260

FROSCH. How do you mean? You've many a vintage then?

MEPHISTOPHELES. To each his chosen specimen.

ALTMAYER. [*to* FROSCH] Aha! One here already licks his chops, I
see.

FROSCH. Good! If I am to choose, I choose the Rhine wine's
flower.
One's native land bestows the finest dower.   2265

MEPHISTOPHELES. [*drilling a hole in the table's edge at* FROSCH's
place]
Find us some wax to make the stoppers from!

ALTMAYER. Oh, these are parlor tricks, come on!

MEPHISTOPHELES. [*to* BRANDER] And you?

BRANDER. I want to drink champagne,
And it should foam with might and main!
        [MEPHISTOPHELES *drills; someone has by now made the wax
        stoppers and does the plugging.*]

BRANDER. One can't become one country's henchman,   2270
Much good hails from a distant spot;
Your proper German can't abide a Frenchman,
But likes French vintages a lot.

SIEBEL. [*while* MEPHISTOPHELES *is approaching his place*]
I own I do not like the sour stuff,
Tap me the true, the honeyed juice!   2275

MEPHISTOPHELES. [*drilling*] You'll have Tokay[9] to sample
soon enough.

ALTMAYER. Oh come, own up, Sirs, what's the use?

---

8. The wine trick, part of the popular
Faust legend, derives from the original
chapbook of 1587 (chapter 55).

9. A sweet wine from Hungary, grown
near the town for which it is named.

I know full well you lead us up the garden.

MEPHISTOPHELES. With guests of rank, I beg your pardon,
  I would be bold indeed to try.   2280
  Quick, place your order, don't be shy!
  What kind of vintage may I serve you?

ALTMAYER. Stop asking—anything will satisfy.
      [*when the holes have all been drilled and plugged*]

MEPHISTOPHELES. [*with weird gestures*][1]
           Grapes on the vinestock,
           Horns on the goat-buck;   2285
           Juice is the wine, wood is the vine,
           A wooden table can flow with wine.
           A singular gaze up Nature's sleeve—
           Here is a miracle—believe!
Now draw the plug, hold out your cup!   2290

ALL [*as they draw the stoppers and each has the chosen wine
    run into his glass*] Oh joyous fountain bubbling up!

MEPHISTOPHELES. Be careful, though, let no one spill a drop!
    [*They drink repeatedly*]

ALL [*singing*] Carouse like aborigines,
        Five hundred wallowing swine!

MEPHISTOPHELES. Free men, you see, at play in nature's state! 2295

FAUST. I'd like to quit their playing-field.

MEPHISTOPHELES. You wait a while—their bestial estate
  Will soon be splendidly revealed.

SIEBEL. [*drinks carelessly, spilling some wine on the floor,
    where it turns to flame*] Help! Hell's afire! Help, a curse!

MEPHISTOPHELES. [*adjuring the flame*] Down, friendly element,
    be quiet   2300
  [*to the fellow*] A purgatory drop—as yet no worse.

SIEBEL. Next time think twice before you try it,
  Or else get measured for a hearse!

FROSCH. You do not know us yet, I fear!

ALTMAYER. I think we ought to lead him gently hence.   2305

SIEBEL. I say, Sir! Damn your impudence,
  To work your hocus-pocus here!

MEPHISTOPHELES. Dry up, old wine tub!

SIEBEL.   Broomstick you!
  What next? He would insult us, too!

BRANDER. Just wait, we'll tan your hide for you!   2310

ALTMAYER. [*draws a plug from the table; fire leaps out at
  him*] I'm burning!

SIEBEL.   Sorcery, I vow!
  Stab home, the cad's an outlaw now!
    [*They draw their knives and lunge at* MEPHISTOPHELES.]

---

1. The following incantation begins with   erates into nonsense.
lines from a children's rhyme and degen-

MEPHISTOPHELES. [*with a solemn gesture*]
　　　　　Double-face, pretense,
　　　　　Alter place and sense!
　　　　　Be here and hence![2]　　　　　　　　　2315
　　[*They stand in amazement, looking at each other.*]
ALTMAYER. Where am I? What a lovely land!
FROSCH. They're vineyards, are they not?
SIEBEL.　　　　　　　　And grapes, right close at hand!
BRANDER. In this green arbor, what a cluster
　Of swelling grapes! What size! What luster!
　　[*He seizes* SIEBEL *by the nose; the others do the same in
　　pairs and raise their knives.*]
MEPHISTOPHELES. [*as above*] Now mark the devil's pranking!
　Error,　　　　　　　　　　　　　　　　　2320
　Release their vision from thy throes!
　　[*He vanishes with* FAUST; *the fellows leap apart.*]
SIEBEL. What happened?
ALTMAYER.　　　　　How . . . ?
FROSCH.　　　　　　　　　Was that your nose?
BRANDER. [*to* SIEBEL] And I am clutching yours!
ALTMAYER.　　　　　　　　　　Oh terror!
　I felt a shock go through me like a dagger!
　Get me a chair, someone, I stagger!　　　　　2325
FROSCH. No, fellows, say, what was all this?
SIEBEL. One sniff of where the bastard's hiding,
　And he won't leave here in one piece!
ALTMAYER. He's gone, I saw him, he was riding
　Outdoor upon a keg . . . I couldn't miss . . .　　2330
　I've leaden weights in legs and toes.
　　[*turning toward the table*] My! Is the wine still running, you
　suppose?
SIEBEL. It was all lies and fraud, a juggler's game.
FROSCH. I tasted wine, I tell you, all the same.
BRANDER. What of those grapes, those sights that stunned us?　2335
ALTMAYER. And then they tell you, don't believe in wonders!

WITCH'S KITCHEN†

*On a low stove a large caldron stands over the fire. In the
steam rising up from it appear various figures. A* FEMALE MAR-
MOSET *is sitting by the caldron, skimming it and keeping it from
running over. The* MARMOSET TOM *with the young ones are sitting nearby, warming themselves.[1] Walls and ceiling are decorated with the quaintest witches' furnishings.*

　FAUST. MEPHISTOPHELES.
FAUST. I find this magic-mongery abhorrent;

---

2. The hypnotizing of the four drunk-
ards, so that they imagine themselves
transported to a beautiful vineyard, is
derived from the popular Faust legend
(in the historical account by Philipp Ca-
merarius, 1591).

1. The Marmosets were apparently a gift
to the Witch by Mephistopheles, and
their main duty is to tend the brew
cooking in the Witch's cauldron.

And I am to be cured, you warrant,
In this hotchpotch of lunacy?
Do I seek counsel from some skirted quack?   2340
Will this absurd swill-cookery
Charm thirty winters off my back?
If that's your best, then woe is me!
My hopes already seem confounded.
Might there not be some balm, some remedy   2345
By nature or a noble mind compounded?

MEPHISTOPHELES. The know-it-all, as always! Look—
True, nature's way to youth is apter;
However, that comes in a different book,
And it's a curious chapter.   2350

FAUST. I want to know it.

MEPHISTOPHELES.   Very well; it comes your way
Without physician, gold, or magic-rigging:
Go out into the fields, today,
Fall to a-hoeing, digging,
Contain yourself, your mind and mood,   2355
Within the narrowest of spheres,
Subsist on uncommingled food,
Live as a beast with beasts and spurn not chores unsung,
In person spread your crop-fields with manure;
This is the best resource, you may be sure,   2360
Through eighty years to stay forever young!

FAUST. I am not used to that, it goes against my marrow
To put my hand to hoe or harrow.
A narrow life would suit me not at all.

MEPHISTOPHELES. So back to witching after all.   2365

FAUST.[2] What need have we of that old bat?
Why cannot you yourself concoct it?

MEPHISTOPHELES. I can just see myself at that!
A thousand bridges I could have constructed
Meanwhile; not merely craft and art,   2370
Patience is needed for the part.
This takes a quiet sprite a year or longer;
It's time that makes the subtle ferment stronger.
And what all goes into the brew!
A power of wondrous things, you take it   2375
From me; the Devil taught it, true,
And yet the Devil cannot make it.
[*catching sight of the animals*] Look—is it not a graceful clan?
This is the maid! That is the serving man!
[*to the animals*] It seems the lady's not about?   2380

ANIMALS. Gone out,
            To gad about,
            Up the chimney spout!

---

2. Lines 2366–77 were added to the text of Part I (1808) to explain why Mephistopheles could not himself transform Faust into a young man.

MEPHISTOPHELES. Does she stay out long when she gads?
ANIMALS. Long as it takes to warm our pads.   2385
MEPHISTOPHELES. The dainty darlings—aren't they striking?
FAUST. In quite the worst of taste, I find.
MEPHISTOPHELES. Why, chat like this is just the kind
  That is most truly to my liking!
  [*to the animals*] Tell me, confounded puppet troupe,   2390
  What do you stir that porridge for?
ANIMALS. We're cooking a broad beggar's soup.
MEPHISTOPHELES. You'll have a crowd to forage for.
MARMOSET TOM. [*sidles up and fawns on* MEPHISTOPHELES].
          Come sir, be nice
          And throw the dice,   2395
          Things have been vile, sir,
          Win me a pile, sir,
          And rich in pence
          Is rich in sense.
MEPHISTOPHELES. How happy would the monkey be   2400
  Could he, too, play the lottery![3]
    [*Meanwhile, the* YOUNG MARMOSETS *have been playing
    with a large sphere, which they now roll forward.*]
MARMOSET TOM. The world's a ball,
          Will rise and fall,
          Roll far and wide;
          Like glass its tune,   2405
          Can break as soon!
          It's hollow inside.
          Here it gleams fair,
          More brightly there,
          I am alive!   2410
          Son, use your wit,
          Stay clear of it,
          Death's in the matter,
          It's clay from the pit,
          It may shatter.   2415
MEPHISTOPHELES. Why the sieve?
MARMOSET TOM. [*taking it down*]
          Were you a thief,
          I'd know it and proclaim.[4]
    [*He runs to the female and has her look through it.*]
          Look through the sieve,
          You see the thief,   2420
          Yet may not tell his name?
MEPHISTOPHELES. [*approaching the fire*] And this pot?
BOTH MARMOSETS. The silly sot!
          Knows not the pot,
          Knows not the kettle!   2425

3. The lottery, popular in the eighteenth century (especially in Italy), would provide even a monkey with the means of getting rich.

4. According to popular superstition, a thief could be recognized if observed through a sieve.

MEPHISTOPHELES. Ill-mannered clod!
MARMOSET TOM. Here, take this rod
And sit in the settle![5]
[*He makes* MEPHISTOPHELES *sit down.*]
FAUST. [*who during this time has stood before a mirror, now
approaching it, now standing off*] What do I see? A form
from heaven above
    Appears to me within this magic mirror![6]   2430
    Lend me the swiftest of your wings, o love,
    And lead me nearer to her, nearer!
    Alas! but when I fail to keep my distance,
    And venture closer up to gaze,
    I see her image dimmed as through a haze!   2435
    The loveliest woman in existence!
    Can earthly beauty so amaze?
    What lies there in recumbent grace and glistens
    Must be quintessence of all heaven's rays!
    Or could its like on earth be found?   2440
MEPHISTOPHELES. You know, a god can't strain six days, my
friend,
    And vote himself a bravo at the end,
    Unless the job was pretty sound.
    This once, keep gazing at your leisure;
    I may just sniff you out a peach like this,   2445
    And lucky he whom fate allots the pleasure
    To lodge her at his hearth in wedded bliss.
        [FAUST *keeps looking into the mirror.* MEPHISTOPHELES,
        *lounging in the armchair and playing with the feather
        duster, goes on speaking.*]
    Here is my scepter, this my royal seat,
    Now for a crown, and I'll be all complete.
ANIMALS. [*who up to now have been going through various
weird movements and evolutions, bring* MEPHISTOPHELES *a
crown, with much shouting*]
               Please be so good   2450
               With sweat and blood
               The crown to glue!
    [*They handle the crown clumsily and break it into two
    pieces, with which they scamper about.*]
               There, that's done it!
               We rhyme and pun it,
               We hark and view;   2455
FAUST. [*facing the mirror*] Alas! My mind becomes disjoint.
MEPHISTOPHELES. [*pointing at the animals*] By now this fairly has
my own head spinning.
ANIMALS.   If haply point

5. Mephistopheles now presides over the
scene, holding the feather duster as a
scepter and seated upon the settle as a
throne, a Lord of Misrule.
6. The magic mirror is presumably there

from the start. What causes the image of
the Feminine (presumably resembling
Italian Renaissance paintings of the nude
Venus) to appear is not stated.

Is joined to point
With luck it's meaning!   2460

FAUST. [*as above*] A blaze is kindled in my bosom!
Let us escape from here and flee!

MEPHISTOPHELES. [*in previous posture*] At least we've seen in
microcosm
The workings of true poesy.

[*The caldron, neglected by the* FEMALE MARMOSET *in
the interim, starts running over; a great flame arises and
flares up the chimney. The* WITCH *comes down through
the flames with horrendous screaming.*]

WITCH. Ouch! Ow! Ow! Ouch!   2465
Infernal sow! Confounded slouch!
Forget the kettle and singe my pouch!
A curse on you!

[*catching sight of* FAUST *and* MEPHISTOPHELES]

                    And who is new?
                    Who are you two?   2470
                    Strangers rude?
                    Come to intrude?
                    A fiery splash
                    At you trash!

[*She plunges the skimming ladle into the caldron and
splashes flames at* FAUST, MEPHISTOPHELES, *and the* ANI-
MALS. *The* ANIMALS *whimper.*]

MEPHISTOPHELES.[*turning around the duster in his hand and
striking at the pots and glassware with it*]

                    In two! In two!   2475
                    There goes the stew!
                    There goes the glass!
                    Just fun, my lass,
                    To your tune, foul shrew,
                    A gay tattoo.   2480

[*while the witch recoils in wrath and terror*] You recognize me?
Bag of bones! Vile trash!
You know me now, your lord and master?
What odds I lay about and smash
Hellcat and cattery with joint disaster?
When did the scarlet doublet fall from grace?   2485
Is the cock-feather hard to recognize?
Did I perhaps conceal my face?
You need my name to know my guise?

WITCH. My rudeness, Sir, deserves reproof!
I missed, for one, the cloven hoof,   2490
And your two ravens, for another![7]

MEPHISTOPHELES. For this time I will let you off;
It's been some little time now, true enough,

---

7. The cloven hoof (see line 2184) and
the ravens (thought to derive from the
companions of the pagan war god
Wotan; see lines 10664 ff.) are traditional attributes of the devil.

Since last we ran into each other.
Civilization, glossing all we knew, 2495
Has rubbed off on the Devil, too.
That Nordic spook has nowadays been banished;
Those talons, horns, and tail—all vanished!
As for the foot I cannot be without,
It would impair my social chances; 2500
So for some years now I have eked it out,
Like many young men, with false appurtenances.[8]

WITCH. [*dancing*] My senses reel with joy and fear
To see young Esquire Satan here!

MEPHISTOPHELES. That name's forbidden, hag, you hear? 2505

WITCH. Why of a sudden is it bad?

MEPHISTOPHELES. It's been consigned to storybooks for young-
sters;
Mind you, men are no better off for that.
The Fiend is gone, the fiends are still amongst us.
Call me Sir Knight, the rest we can forgo; 2510
I am a gentleman like other gentry.
My noble blood is not in doubt, I know;
Look, here's the coat of arms that gives me entry!
[*He makes an indecent gesture.[9]*]

WITCH. [*laughing immoderately*] Ha, ha! That's in your former
vogue!
You are as you have ever been, a rogue. 2515

MEPHISTOPHELES. [*to* FAUST] Friend, mark it well for your own
sake:
With witches that's the tone to take.

WITCH. Now tell me, Sirs, what brought you here.

MEPHISTOPHELES. A good glass of the well-known elixir,
But I would have the oldest vintage; 2520
It's strength increases year by year.

WITCH. A pleasure! Here's a flagon from my shelf
From which I like to steal a nip myself;
What's more, it has completely lost its stink;
I'll let you have a sample of its power. 2525
[*drops her voice*] But if this man, unprimed, should take a
drink,
You know it well, he won't live out the hour.

MEPHISTOPHELES. He's a good friend of mine, he'll come out
whole;
He's welcome to the finest of your kitchen.
Now draw your circle, do your witching, 2530
And let him have a bowl.
[*The* WITCH *with strange gestures draws a circle and
places peculiar objects in it; meanwhile the glassware be-*

---

8. An allusion to the eighteenth-century
practice among men of padding their
stockings to make their calves appear
more muscular.

9. Goethe later instructed an actor to
represent this "indecent gesture" by
turning his back on the audience, raising
one leg, and slapping his thigh.

gins to ring, the caldrons to drone, making music. Finally
she brings a great tome and within the circle arranges the
MARMOSETS, *who must serve her for a pulpit and hold the*
torch. She beckons FAUST *to join her.*]

FAUST. [*to* MEPHISTOPHELES] No, tell me what is here intended?
  This mummery, this gesturing demented,
  I've seen preposterous low-grade mime
  Enough to gag on in my time.   2535

MEPHISTOPHELES. Oh, stuff! You don't know what a joke is.
  Come, don't be such a solemn stick!
  She must work up some doctor's hocus-pocus
  Or else the juice might make you sick.
    [*He makes* FAUST *step into the circle.*]

WITCH. [*beginning to recite from the book with great emphasis*]
                    Now mind me, son,   2540
                    Make ten of one,
                    With two have done,
                    Make even three,
                    And rich you'll be.
                    Let four go free!   2545
                    The five and six
                    Contrive and hex
                    To seven and eight,
                    That does the trick;
                    And nine is one,   2550
                    And ten is none,
                    And there's your witch-arithmetic![1]

FAUST. I think the crone speaks in a fever fit.

MEPHISTOPHELES. You haven't heard the half of it;
  I know the tenor of that kind of fiction,   2555
  I've lost much time exploring it for rules;
  You see, a perfect contradiction
  Is equally occult to sages as to fools.
  My friend, this art is new and old.
  It has at all times been the custom   2560
  By Three in One and One threefold[2]
  To propagate not truth but fustian.
  That's how they teach and prattle undisturbed;
  Who wants to argue color with the blinded?
  For people by and large, just given a word,   2565
  Believe there needs must be some sense behind it.

WITCH. [*continuing*] The potent core
                    Of nature lore
                    From all that seek it shrinking!
                    Who's never thought   2570
                    Finds it unsought,
                    Possesses it unthinking.

---

1. All speculation concerning the possible significance of this number sequence,
despite ingenious attempts by many

scholars, seems fruitless.
2. An allusion to the Christian doctrine
of the Trinity.

FAUST. What babble does she mouth before us?
I am about to lose my mind.
She sounds to me just like a chorus   2575
Of hundred thousand fools combined.
MEPHISTOPHELES. Enough, oh excellent sybil, say no more,
Bring up your elixir and quickly pour
The bowl brimful, he'll drain it to the lees;
My friend here will withstand it well enough: 2580
He is a man of multiple degrees,
Who's downed some strong libations in his puff.
[*With much ceremony, the* WITCH *pours the potion into a
bowl; as* FAUST *raises it to his lips, a faint flame forms.*]
MEPHISTOPHELES. Well, down with it, and no excuse!
Soon you will have your heart's desire.
As thick as you are with the deuce,   2585
Why fuss about a lick of fire?
[*The* WITCH *dissolves the circle.* FAUST *steps forth.*]
MEPHISTOPHELES. Out, with a will! No time to lose.
WITCH. I hope my draught will soothe your vitals!
MEPHISTOPHELES. As for a favor in return, just choose,
And on Walpurgis night we'll have requitals.[3]   2590
WITCH. Here is a song to sing, and when you do,
You will perceive an added virtue.[4]
MEPHISTOPHELES. Quick, for a walk now, let me urge you,
You must work up a sweat to purge you,
So that the power may permeate through and through.   2595
Later I'll teach you noble sloth's employment,
And soon you'll feel with exquisite enjoyment
Young Cupid[5] stir and skip about in you.
FAUST. Just one more glance before into that mirror!
That beauty was so fair, so fresh!   2600
MEPHISTOPHELES. No, no! That paragon of women, sirrah,
Shall soon confront you in the flesh.
[*aside*] No fear—with this behind your shirt
You'll soon see Helen of Troy in every skirt![†]

STREET[1]

FAUST. MARGARETE *walking past.*[2][†]

3. At the witches' sabbath on Walpurgis
Night (see the later scene of that title)
the devil was supposed to render his
thanks to the witches who had served
him.
4. The Witch gives Faust a lewd song
printed on a broadsheet, intended to
arouse his sexual desires.
5. The god of love, here associated by
Mephistopheles with sexual desire.
1. The sequence of scenes from here to
the end of *Part I*, excepting the "Walpurgis Night" and "Dream," constitutes
the so-called Gretchen tragedy and was

composed for the most part in early
1775 as part of the *Urfaust*. The text
through the cathedral scene (to line
3834) was published as it stands in the
Fragment of 1790. See the critical essays
by Barker Fairley and Georg Lukacs,
below.
2. As indicated in a draft, Goethe originally intended Gretchen to appear at the
end of a procession coming from the cathedral. Mephistopheles later acknowledges (lines 2621–26) that the girl has
just received confession.

FAUST. My fair young lady, may I make free   2605
  To offer you my arm and company?
MARGARETE. I'm neither fair nor lady, pray,
  Can unescorted find my way.
      [*She frees herself and exits.*]
FAUST. God, what a lovely child! I swear
  I've never seen the like of her.   2610
  She is so dutiful and pure,
  Yet not without a pert allure.
  Her rosy lip, her cheek aglow
  I never shall forget, I know!
  Her glance's timid downward dart   2615
  Is graven deeply in my heart!
  But how she was so short with me—
  That was consummate ecstasy!
      [MEPHISTOPHELES *enters.*]
FAUST. Here get me that young wench—for certain!
MEPHISTOPHELES. Which one?
FAUST.   The one that just walked past. 2620
MEPHISTOPHELES. Her? I just happened by the curtain
  At her confession; she's just been
  Pronounced absolved of any sin;
  She's a right innocent young lass
  Who brought mere nothings to confess;   2625
  On her I have no hold at all!
FAUST. She's over fourteen, after all.
MEPHISTOPHELES. You're like a loose Lothario
  Who thinks that all dear blossoms blow
  For him, can see no honest name   2630
  Nor favor that is not fair game;
  It does not always work, I fear.
FAUST. Your pious Worship, spare my ear
  Your wise proprieties and charters!
  Let me be plain, and hear me right,   2635
  Unless I have that sweet delight
  Nestling in my embrace, tonight,
  The selfsame midnight hour will part us.
MEPHISTOPHELES. Come, think what can be and what can't!
  A fortnight even will be scant   2640
  To spy out chances, scheme ahead.
FAUST. If I were granted seven hours,
  I should not need the devil's powers
  To lure a fledgling to my bed.
MEPHISTOPHELES. That sounded like a Frenchman's boast.   2645
  Don't wolf your pleasures like a glutton,
  Who would gulp down a quail like mutton!
  This thing is half the treat at most
  Unless you knead, by guile and art
  And flummery of every sort,   2650

Your sweetmeat to the proper turn,
As from the Gallic tales we learn.
FAUST. My appetite is keen enough.
MEPHISTOPHELES. Once and for all, a laugh's a laugh,
But you just cannot have your way   2655
With that young cherub in a day.
Assault head-on will net us bruises.
We must bethink ourselves of ruses.
FAUST. Get me some thing of hers for keeps!
Lead me to where my angel sleeps!   2660
Bring me a bosom-cloth, a garter!
Some token for my love to barter!
MEPHISTOPHELES. To show you how I strive and strain
To serve and soothe your amorous pain,
I will not waste another minute: 2665
I know her room—tonight you shall be in it.
FAUST. And shall I see her, have her?
MEPHISTOPHELES.   No.
She will be at a neighbor's, though,
And, sensing future joys, you may at will   2670
Of her ethereal aura breathe your fill.
FAUST. Can we go now?
MEPHISTOPHELES.   No, it is early yet.
FAUST. I need a gift for her—you see to that.
    [*Exit.*]
MEPHISTOPHELES. Well! He'll go far. A gift right off, no loitering!
I know no end of likely spots,   2675
Sequestered treasure-burying plots;
I'll do a little reconnoitering.
    [*Exit.*]

EVENING[1]

A *Clean Little Room*

MARGARETE. [*braiding her hair and putting it up*] I'd give a
    deal if I could say
Who was that gentleman today.
I liked his looks and how he spoke;   2680
He must be born of noble folk,
That I could tell from brow and eyes—
Would he have been so forward otherwise?
    [*Exit.*]
MEPHISTOPHELES *and* FAUST.
MEPHISTOPHELES. Go on, come in, on silent feet!
FAUST. [*after a brief silence*] Leave me alone now, I
    entreat.   2685

---

1. This scene invites comparison with   Jachimo observes the sleeping Imogen in
Shakespeare's *Cymbeline* (II.ii), where   her bed.

MEPHISTOPHELES. [*snooping around*] Not every maiden is so neat.
    [*Exit.*]

FAUST. [*gazing up and about*] Ah, welcome, blessèd twilight haze
  That hovers in this sanctuary's scope!
  Ignite my heart, love's sweet and searing blaze,
  Soothed but to languish by the dew ot hope!   2690
  How all here breathes a sense of stillness,
  Of order and of calm content!
  Within this penury, what fullness!
  What bliss in this imprisonment!
     [*He throws himself into the leather armchair by the
     bed.*]
  Receive me, who for generations flown,   2695
  Have welcomed many a glad or mournful pilgrim!
  To think, about this patriarchal throne
  Time and again has swarmed a throng of children!
  I seem to see my little darling stand
  As she, round-cheeked, with joys of Christmas thrilling,   2700
  Devoutly kissed her grandsire's withered hand.
  I sense, dear girl, your very spirit
  Of plenitude and order all about,
  Benignly counseling domestic merit,
  Seeing the tablecloth all tidily spread out,   2705
  Even the sanded floor in patterns fine.
  Oh dearest hand! so near divine!
  Through you this cabin turns into a shrine.
  And here!
     [*He lifts a bed-curtain.*]
  What thrill of ecstasy! Forlorn,
  Here I would linger many hours.   2710
  Here, Nature did you nurse, with gentle showers
  Of dreams, this angel native-born;
  Here came, its bosom gently heaving
  With tender life, the child in bloom,
  And here in chaste and sacred weaving   2715
  God's image ripened in the loom!

  And you? Do you recall your quest?
  How deeply all my soul's astir!
  What do you want? Why is your heart oppressed?
  Ah, wretched Faust—no longer what you were!   2720
  Am I in thrall to fairy fragrance here?
  Impelled to dally at my ease,
  In dream of love I melt and disappear;
  Are we but sport to any passing breeze?

  If she this very instant were to come,   2725
  How you would expiate your desecration!
  Big Thomas, woe, would shrink into Tom Thumb,
  Swept to her feet in adoration.
     [MEPHISTOPHELES *enters.*]

MEPHISTOPHELES. Quick! I can see her by the gate.

FAUST. Off, never to return! I'm gone. 2730

MEPHISTOPHELES. Here is a box of middling weight
    That somewhere else I came upon.
    Just leave it in this cabinet,
    I warrant it will drive her silly;
    I've baited it with this and that, 2735
    Enough for quite another filly.
    A child's a child, a toy's a toy.

FAUST. I wonder—should I?

MEPHISTOPHELES.   Why so coy?
    You mean perhaps to keep the hoard?
    Then I advise my greedy Lord 2740
    To save the precious time of day
    And spare me further trouble. Say,
    I trust you're not the grasping sort!
    I scratch my head, I fret and scurry—
    *[He places the box in the cabinet and presses the lock
    back in.]*
    Away now, hurry! 2745
    Take all this trouble just to bend
    That sweet young thing to your heart's wish and end;
    And you look glum,
    As if you faced an auditorium
    And looming in it, in the flesh, all gray, 2750
    Physics and Metaphysica![2]
    Away!
    [Exeunt.]

MARGARETE. *[holding a lamp]* It is so sultry here, so hot—
    [Opens the window.]
    And yet outdoors it's not uncommon warm.
    There's something here, I don't know what— 2755
    If only my mother were coming home.
    I'm all of a shudder, I declare—
    What a timid little goose, for fair!
    [She starts singing as she undresses.]
        There was a king in Thule,[3]
        Right faithful unto death, 2760
        Whom she who loved him truly
        Gave a cup with her dying breath.

        Naught dearer in his keeping,
        He drained it at every sup;
        And never could help weeping 2765
        Each time he raised the cup.

2. Allusion to academic disciplines and Faust's former life as a scholar. For the contrast of gray learning and the "green of life's golden tree" see lines 2038f.

3. The ballad of the King of Thule, an imitation of a medieval Scandinavian folk song, was probably composed by the young Goethe independently of *Faust* and then incorporated into the text of this scene in 1775. *Ultima Thule* was the mythological name given by ancient geographers to the northernmost habitable region of the world.

And when it came to dying,
His cities all he told,
Naught to his heir denying
Save for the cup of gold.   2770

He held a banquet royal
In his sea-girt castle tall,
Filled with his vassals loyal
The high ancestral hall.

There stood the hoary drinker   2775
And sipped of life's last glow,
Then flung the holy trinket
Into the brine below.

He saw it plunging, winking
And sinking deep at sea,   2780
His lids grew heavy, sinking,
No other drop drank he.

[*She opens the cabinet to put away her clothes and notices the jewel-box.*]

How did this handsome casket get in there?
I surely locked the closet, I could swear.
What might be in it? What a strange affair!   2785
Did someone bring it here to pawn,
And Mother took it for security?
A little key is fastened on,
I think I'll open it and see!
What is this? Look at it! God bless—   2790
I never saw such jewels! What rich array—
Why, such a set a noble baroness
Could wear on a high holiday.
How would this necklace look on me?
Who calls this gorgeousness her own?   2795

[*She tricks herself out with it and steps before the mirror.*]

Were these fine ear-bobs mine alone!
They give one quite another air.
What use are simple looks and youth?
Oh, they are well and good in truth;
That's all folk mean, though—pretty fair.   2800
The praise you get is half good-natured fuss.
For gold contend,
On gold depend
All things and men. . . . Poor us!

ON A WALK[1]

FAUST, *walking to and fro in thought.* MEPHISTOPHELES *joins him.*

MEPHISTOPHELES. By love disdained and spurned! By hellfire in-
      finite!   2805

1. *Allee,* "avenue" (as the scene is titled in the *Urfaust*), a public pathway outside the city walls.

I wish I knew of something worse so I could swear by it!

FAUST. What irks you? You're all out of level!
    I never saw quite such a phiz!

MEPHISTOPHELES. I swear I'd send myself straight to the devil
    If I were not a devil as it is!   2810

FAUST. Have you been struck in the upper story?
    You really look the part, all grim and gory!

MEPHISTOPHELES. Just think, the hoard for Gretchen fetched
    A meddling priest has gone and snatched.
    Her mother had scarce laid eyes on it   2815
    And straightway threw a shivering fit:
    That woman's nose is mighty clever,
    It's stuck in the prayer-book forever,
    And with each mortal thing can tell
    Profane from sacred by the smell;   2820
    This finery had, she never doubted,
    No odor of sanctity about it.
    My child, she cried, ill-gotten wealth
    Ensnares the soul, beshrews one's health,
    Let's give it into the Virgin's keeping,   2825
    Manna from Heaven to be reaping![2]
    Little Meg made a long face, of course,
    Thought: after all, it's a gift horse,
    He surely did not lack God's fear
    Who had so cleverly brought it here.   2830
    The mother, though, had a priest come in
    Who, the moment the trick was explained to him,
    Cast a well-pleased eye upon the lot
    And called it a truly pious thought:
    He who abstains is he who gains!   2835
    The Church has a superb digestion,
    Has swallowed whole countries without question
    And never suffered from stomach pains;
    She, ladies, can alone digest
    Ill-gotten goods along with the rest.   2840

FAUST. I'd say the trick was trite enough,
    Both Jews and princes bring it off.

MEPHISTOPHELES. With this he slipped into his pocket
    Ring, clasp, and bracelet, chain and locket,
    With no more thanks or ifs and buts   2845
    Than if he were given a bag of nuts,
    Promised them heavenly wage beside,
    And they were greatly edified.

FAUST. And Gretchen?

MEPHISTOPHELES.   Sits there all distraught
    And knows not what she would or ought,   2850
    Thinks day and night of that display,
    Still more of him by whom it came her way.

2. See Revelations 2:17, "To him that overcometh will I give to eat of the hidden manna." Manna was the food sent by God to nourish Israel in the wilderness (Exodus 16).

FAUST. I hate to have the darling fret.
Get her at once another set!
The first was really no great hoard. 2855
MEPHISTOPHELES. Oh yes, it's all just child's play to Milord!
FAUST. Come on, arrange things as I say,
Involve her neighbor in some way!
You're like cold porridge, Devil, stir your bones
And bring a new array of stones! 2860
MEPHISTOPHELES. I'm proud to serve you, gracious Sir.
[*Exit* FAUST.]
Your lovestruck fool thinks nothing of
Puffing sun, moon, and stars into the air
Like fireworks to please his lady love.
[*Exit.*]

THE NEIGHBOR'S HOUSE

MARTHE.[1] [*alone*] God pardon my husband if He can, 2865
He has done ill by me, dear man.
Left for the wide world, just like that,
And me a grass widow on the mat.
Yet never did I grieve him or oppose
But loved him tenderly, God knows. 2870
[*She cries.*]
For all I know he's dead—oh grief!
Had I at least a Coroner's brief![2]
[*Margarete enters.*]
MARGARETE. Frau Marthe!
MARTHE   Gretchen! What, my pet?
MARGARETE. My knees are shaking, I declare!
I've found another casket there, 2875
Of ebony, in my cabinet,
And full of jewels, star on star,
More precious than the first by far.
MARTHE. You must keep mum about it to your mother;
She'd take it to confession, like the other. 2880
MARGARETE. Just look and see! Oh, just look here!
MARTHE. [*does her up with the jewelry*] Aren't you the luckiest girl!
My dear!
MARGARETE. Just that I dare not wear it in the street,
Nor yet at church be seen in it.
MARTHE. Come over oftener, don't look sour, 2885
And give the things a secret try,
Parade before the mirror for an hour,
And we'll enjoy them on the sly.
On some occasion then, a feast or such,
We'll show them one by one, so folk won't notice much. 2890

1. The traditional role, in domestic drama, of the gossip or matchmaker (see the Nurse in *Romeo and Juliet*).

2. The Coroner's brief would prove Marthe to be a widow and free her to look for a new husband.

The chain will keep a while, we'll try an ear-bob first;
Your Ma may never see; we'll hookwink her at worst.
MARGARETE. Whoever left these chests for me to find?
Here's something quite uncanny, to my mind.
    [*A knock at the door.*]
Could this be Mother? Oh my sin!   2895
MARTHE. [*peering through the little curtain*] It's a strange gentle-
    man. Come in.
    [*Enter* MEPHISTOPHELES.]
MEPHISTOPHELES. I step straight in—my forthright venture
I hope the ladies will not censure.
    [*Respectfully steps back before* MARGARETE.]
It's for Frau Marthe Schwerdtlein I inquire!
MARTHE. I'm she, Sir—what is your desire?   2900
MEPHISTOPHELES. [*under his breath to her*] I know you now;
    that is enough for me;
I see you have distinguished company.
I took a liberty, excuse me, pray.
I'll wait till later in the day.
MARTHE. [*aloud*] God help us, child, by all that's human!   2905
He takes you for a gentlewoman.
MARGARETE. I'm nothing but a poor young maid.
My lord's too kind. I am afraid.
These gems and chains are not my own.
MEPHISTOPHELES. Oh, it is not the gems alone;   2910
You have a way, a look so *distingué*,
How glad I am that I may stay!
MARTHE. You bring . . . ? I'm eager, you'll excuse . . .
MEPHISTOPHELES. I wish I had more cheerful news!
Please not to blame it on your guest: 2915
Your husband's dead and sends his best.
MARTHE. He's dead? The faithful heart! Oh no!
My husband dead! I won't survive the blow!
MARGARETE. My poor dear Madam, don't despair!
MEPHISTOPHELES. Let me relate the sad affair.   2920
MARGARETE. God spare me loving and its cost!
I could not bear it if I lost.
MEPHISTOPHELES. Joy must with grief, and grief with joy be stirred.
MARTHE. Recount me how his passing came!
MEPHISTOPHELES. He lies at Padua interred,   2925
Of Saint Antonius' fame,[3]
Upon a grave-site duly blessed,
Bedded for cool eternal rest.
MARTHE. And have you nothing more along from him?
MEPHISTOPHELES. Oh yes, a large and grave request: 2930
Be sure to have three hundred masses sung for him!
My pocket's empty, for the rest.

3. The basilica of St. Anthony in Padua   in love, brides, and wives.
was sacred to the patron saint of women

MARTHE. What! Not a gift, a prize to cheer the heart with,
What any journeyman saves in his satchel's deeps,   2935
To carry home for keeps,
Would sooner beg or starve than part with?
MEPHISTOPHELES. Madam, your troubles truly grieve me;
He did not waste his substance, though, he swore.
He rued his errors much, believe me,
Oh yes, and his ill fortune even more.   2940
MARGARETE. Alas, that people are so sorely tried!
Sure, many a requiem for him I'll pray.
MEPHISTOPHELES. You're worthy to be married any day:
You are an amiable child.
MARGARETE. Oh no, it's long before I can.   2945
MEPHISTOPHELES. If not a husband, take a fancy-man.
It's boon of Heaven's highest grace,
A peach like you in one's embrace.
MARGARETE. That's not the custom with us, Sir.
MEPHISTOPHELES. Custom or no, it will occur.   2950
MARTHE. Do tell!
MEPHISTOPHELES. I stood beside his bed at his last breath,
It was of something better than manure,
Half-rotten straw; and yet, he died a Christian death,
And mourned his dying more in debt than merely poor.
"Alas," he cried, "with what self-hate it fills me,   2955
Thus to forsake my calling, thus my wife!
Ah, it's this consciousness that kills me.
Had I but her forgiveness in this life!"
MARTHE. [*crying*] The poor dear man! I've long forgiven him.
MEPHISTOPHELES. "But she, God knows, was more to blame
than I."   2960
MARTHE. He lied! With one foot in the grave, to lie!
MEPHISTOPHELES. He doubtless raved in a delirious dream,
Or I'm no judge at all—a dying trance.
"There was," he said, "no idling for a second,
To get first children and then bread for her; bread reckoned   2965
In the most all-inclusive sense;
And I could never eat my share in peace, what's more."
MARTHE. Oh! could he so forget all love, all vows he swore,
The drudgery by day and night?
MEPHISTOPHELES. No—he was warmly mindful of your
plight;   2970
Said: "As I sailed from Malta on my trip,
I prayed for wife and child with fervor rare;
And Heaven duly heard my prayer,
In that our vessel caught a Turkish ship
Which bore a cargo of the Sultan's treasure.   2975
Then valor reaped its just reward,
And I received my well-earned measure
Out of the Ottoman hoard."

MARTHE. Oh yes? Oh where? Perhaps he buried it?

MEPHISTOPHELES. Who knows where the four winds have
  carried it?   2980
 A fine young Neapolitan took pity
 On him, astray in a strange city;
 She proved to him a dear and faithful friend,
 Of which he felt the blessings to the end.[4]

MARTHE. The thief! Defrauder of his child and wife!   2985
 That neither grief nor misery
 Could wean him from his shameful life!

MEPHISTOPHELES. Well, now he's dead for it, you see.
 If I were in your place,
 I'd mourn him for a decorous year   2990
 Meanwhile discreetly look for some new face.

MARTHE. The kind my first one was, oh dear!
 I'd not find easily another such.
 There never was more winsome scamp than mine!
 He only liked the roving life too much,   2995
 And foreign women, and foreign wine
 And those confounded dice.

MEPHISTOPHELES. Well, tit for tat, and give and take,
 If he made light of, for your sake,
 An equal pinch of harmless vice.   3000
 I swear, were this proviso true,
 I might myself change rings with you!

MARTHE. Oh now, my Lord is pleased to jest.

MEPHISTOPHELES. [*aside*] I'd best be off before this gets
  absurd!
 She'd hold the very devil to his word.   3005
 [*to* GRETCHEN] Where lies your own heart's interest?

MARGARETE. What is your meaning, Sir?

MEPHISTOPHELES. [*aside*]   Dear artless innocence you!
 [*aloud*] Good ladies, my farewell!

MARGARETE.   Farewell!

MARTHE.   Before you go!
 I should be thankful for a witness,
 Where, how, and when my spouse found rest eternal.   3010
 I've always liked propriety and fitness,
 Would want to read his passing in the journal.

MEPHISTOPHELES. Yes, Ma'am—by what two witnesses attest
 Truth's always rendered manifest.[5]
 I have a mate, a quite superior sort,   3015
 That I can call upon before your court,
 I'll bring him here.

MARTHE.   Be sure you do!

MEPHISTOPHELES. And will our Miss be present too?

---

4. These blessings from the Neapolitan lady, presumably a prostitute, would be the *mal de Naples*, euphemism for syphilis.

5. Testimony by two witnesses would qualify as legal proof of an undocumented event.

A gallant lad, been everywhere,
Speaks all young ladies passing fair.   3020
MARGARETE. I'd have to blush for my low birth.
MEPHISTOPHELES. Before no sovereign on earth!
MARTHE. Behind the house there, in my garden, then,
Tonight we shall await the gentlemen.

STREET

FAUST. MEPHISTOPHELES.

FAUST. How now? Soon ready? Are things nearly right?   3025
MEPHISTOPHELES. Bravo! Stoked up and going strong!
You'll have your Gretchen before long.
You'll see her at Frau Marthe's house tonight.
Oh, there's a woman needs no jogging
For pander's work and pettifogging!   3030
FAUST. Good work!
MEPHISTOPHELES.   But first we're asked—no bother—
FAUST. Done—one good turn deserves another.
MEPHISTOPHELES. We merely testify, just for the docket,
That her late husband kicked the bucket
And rests at Padua in hallowed ground.   3035
FAUST. So we must make the trip first! That was smart!
MEPHISTOPHELES. Sancta Simplicitas![1] You are not bound
To know much, you just speak your part.
FAUST. If that's the best you know, the deal is off.
MEPHISTOPHELES. A saint! Just hear him huff and puff!   3040
Is it unheard of, a new start,
For you to deal in perjured witness?
Of God, the world, its every moving part,
Of Man, the stirrings in his head and heart,
Have you not judged with utmost force and glibness?   3045
With bold assertion, fluent breath?
And yet, confess it, if you searched your soul,
You knew of all this, on the whole,
About as much as of Herr Schwerdtlein's death!
FAUST. You are a liar, a sophist, and were ever so.   3050
MEPHISTOPHELES. Yes—if one weren't more deeply in the know!
Tomorrow won't you try, in honorable guise,
To pull the wool about poor Gretchen's eyes,
And pledge her soul-love as you go?
FAUST. Yes—and sincerely!
MEPHISTOPHELES.   I can tell!   3055
Then deathless faith and love, a generous surge
About that single, all-o'erpowering urge . . .
Will that be so sincere as well?
FAUST. Have done! It will! For when I feel, all blinded,

1. "Sacred Simplicity."

And for that well, that teeming wealth   3060
Search for a name and cannot find it,
Then through the world send all my senses casting,
For most sublime expression grasping,
And call this blaze that leaves me breathless
Eternal, infinite—yes! deathless!   3065
Is that a trick of devilish stealth?
MEPHISTOPHELES. Still I am right!
FAUST.   Here, take this in,
I beg of you, and spare my lung:
Who wants the last word, using but his tongue,
Is sure to win.   3070
Let's go, I'm weary of your voice,
You're right, the more so since I have no choice.

GARDEN

MARGARETE *on* FAUST'S *arm,* MARTHE *with* MEPHISTOPHELES,
strolling to and fro.

MARGARETE. I feel quite well Your Honor deigns to spare
And shame me with the kind intention.
A voyager is used to common fare   3075
And takes pot-luck with condescension.
I know too well, a traveled man of parts
Can't be diverted by my homely arts.
FAUST. One glance from you, one word holds more dear mirth
Than all the wisdom of this earth.   3080
[*He kisses her hand.*]
MARGARETE. Oh, don't—how can you kiss my hand? You shouldn't!
It is so coarse, so rough to touch!
The work I have been set to, would or wouldn't!
My mother asks so much.
[*They pass on.*]
MARTHE. And you, dear Sir, are always on the road?   3085
MEPHISTOPHELES. Would bounden duty were not always stronger!
How hard to leave is many a dear abode,
Yet one just cannot tarry longer!
MARTHE. It's fine to roam one's flighty years,
Enjoy the wide world to the fullest,   3090
But when that ill time nears,
To drag oneself unto the grave unsolaced
Brings but regrets and tears.
MEPHISTOPHELES. I see it from afar and dread it.
MARTHE. Take thought in time, dear Sir, mind where you're
headed.   3095
[*They pass on.*]
MARGARETE. You have such ready courtesy—

But out of sight is out of mind!
You must have friends of every kind,
All folk much cleverer than me.

FAUST. Dear heart—believe me, what most men call clever   3100
  Is oftener vain and shallow.

MARGARETE.   How on earth?

FAUST. That artlessness, that innocence should never
  Respect itself and know its holy worth!
  That meekness, modesty, the gifts most true
  Of fondly lavish Nature can—   3105

MARGARETE. If you but think of me a little span,
  I shall have time enough to think of you.

FAUST. You must be much alone?

MARGARETE. Oh yes; our household is a modest one,
  Yet it's no little thing to run.   3110
  We have no maid; I cook and sweep and knit
  And launder, late abed, early to rise,
  And Mother has on all of it
  Such watchful eyes!
  Not that we are so pressed to keep expenses down,   3115
  We could spread out far more than many another:
  There's quite a tidy sum left us by Father,
  A little house and garden out of town.
  But now my days go by more calmly rather;
  My brother's soldiering,   3120
  My little sister's dead.
  I had a deal of trouble with the little thing,
  But I would have it all again, twice more instead,
  She was so dear to me.

FAUST.   An angel, if like you.

MARGARETE. I brought her up, and how she loved me too!   3125
  She wasn't born yet when we lost our father.
  We'd all but given up my mother,
  So weakly did she lie.
  And she got well but slowly by and by.
  She could not dream, such was her plight,   3130
  Herself to nurse the little mite,
  And so I reared it all alone
  With milk and water; thus it grew my own,
  And in my arms and on my lap
  It kicked its legs, turned cheerful, and grew up.   3135

FAUST. That must have been the purest bliss for you.

MARGARETE. But with it came long hours of hardship, too.
  At night the little one would sleep
  Beside my bed; it uttered hardly a peep
  And I was up;   3140
  I'd lay it down beside me, get it fed,
  Or if it didn't stop, get out of bed
  And jog it on my shoulder, on and off,

Then at first light stand by the laundering-trough,
Then mind the stove, then do the marketing,   3145
And so day in, day out, the same old thing.
It's hard at times to keep in cheerful mood;
But rest tastes sweeter then, and so does food.
    [*They pass on.*]
MARTHE. Ah, women's lot is wretched—to subdue
    A crusty bachelor is vain exertion.   3150
MEPHISTOPHELES. It's surely up to ladies such as you
    To give me reason for conversion.
MARTHE. You have not found it yet? Speak frankly, Sir,
    Your heart has not yet chosen anywhere?
MEPHISTOPHELES. An honest wife, a home and hearth,   3155
    They say, is more than gold and jewels worth.[2]
MARTHE. I meant to say, you've never really wooed?
MEPHISTOPHELES. I've always met with kind solicitude.
MARTHE. I mean, was it in earnest ever, on your part?
MEPHISTOPHELES. A knave who trifles with a lady's heart. 3160
MARTHE.   Oh, you mistake my words!
MEPHISTOPHELES.   I'm pained to be remiss!
    But this I know—you are all kindliness.
    [*They pass on.*]
FAUST. You knew me then, dear little elf,
    Right as I came into the garden?
MARGARETE. I dropped my eyes, you must have seen yourself. 3165
FAUST. And did my liberty then win your pardon?
    What impudence presumed to do and say,
    By the cathedral steps the other day?
MARGARETE. I was dismayed, I'd never known this pass,
    Could think of no good reason to be slandered.   3170
    Has he in my deportment seen, I wondered,
    Something unseemly, forward, crass?
    Here is a wench, he seemed impelled to say,
    You'd come to business with right away.
    Yet to be frank—something, I hardly knew,   3175
    Stirred in my heart at once to plead for you;
    I know I felt quite angry that I could
    Not get as angry with you as I should.
FAUST. Sweet love!
MARGARETE.   No, wait a bit!
    [*She breaks a star-flower and plucks the petals off, one
    by one.*]
FAUST.   What is this, a nosegay?
MARGARETE. No, just a game.
FAUST.   What game?
MARGARETE.   You'll laugh, just stay away. 3180
FAUST. What are you whispering?

---

2. A combination of a folk saying, "One's own hearth is gold's worth," and Proverbs 31:10, "Who can find a virtuous woman? for her price is far above rubies."

MARGARETE. [*under her breath*] He loves me—loves me not.

FAUST. Oh, bless your innocent heart!

MARGARETE. [*continuing*] He loves me—not, he loves me—not
[*plucking off the last petal, in a touching tone of exultation*]
He loves me!

FAUST.   Yes, my child! Yes, let this flower-word
Be godly oracle to you. He loves you!   3185
Ah, know you what this means? He loves you!
[*He takes both her hands.*]

MARGARETE. I'm shuddering!

FAUST. Oh do not shudder! Let this gaze,
This pressure of my hands express to you
What is ineffable: 3190
To give one's whole self, and to feel
An ecstasy that must endure forever!
Forever!—For its end would be despair,
No, without end! No end!
[MARGARETE *presses his hands, frees herself and runs
away. He stands there, pensive, for a while, then follows
her.*]

MARTHE. [*entering*] It is near night.

MEPHISTOPHELES.   Yes, and we would be gone.   3195

MARTHE. I should have gladly asked you to stay on,
But this is such a wicked neighborhood.
You'd say no one had anything he should
Or wants to think upon,
But snoop upon his neighbor, fuss and buzz,   3200
And gossip sticks to one, no matter what one does.
And our young pair?

MEPHISTOPHELES.   Flown down the alley there.
Frolicking butterflies!

MARTHE.   I'd say he's fond of her.

MEPHISTOPHELES. And she of him. That's how it ever was.

A GARDEN PAVILION[1]

MARGARETE *slips inside, hides behind the door, fingertip to her
lips, and peeks through the crack.*

MARGARETE. He's coming!

FAUST. [*enters*]   Scamp, you're teasing me!   3205
Now you'll see!
[*He kisses her.*]

MARGARETE. [*seizing him and returning the kiss*]
Dearest man, I love you with all my heart.
[MEPHISTOPHELES *knocks.*]

FAUST. [*stamping his foot*] Who's there?

MEPHISTOPHELES.   A friend!

FAUST.   A brute!

1. This brief scene immediately follows the preceding one.

MEPHISTOPHELES. It must be time to part.

MARTHE. [*entering*] Yes, it is late, good sir.

FAUST. Might I escort . . . ?

MARGARETE. My mother would—Farewell!

FAUST. Must I leave then?
Farewell!

MARTHE. Adieu!

MARGARETE. To see you soon again! 3210
  [*Exeunt* FAUST *and* MEPHISTOPHELES.]

MARGARETE. The things and things a man like he
 Can think of in his mind—dear me!
 I stand and gape in shy distress,
 And all I find to say is Yes.
 I'm such a poor young goose, and he— 3215
 The Lord knows what he sees in me.
  [*Exit.*]

FOREST AND CAVE†

FAUST, *alone.*

FAUST. You gave me, lofty spirit,[1] gave me all
 I pleaded for. Not vainly did you turn
 Your countenance to me amid the fire.
 You gave me splendored Nature for my kingdom, 3220
 And strength to feel her, relish her. Not merely
 A coldly wondering visit did you grant,
 But suffered me into her inner depth
 To gaze as in the bosom of a friend.
 You lead the varied muster of the living 3225
 Before me, teaching me to know my brothers
 In leafy stillness, in the air and water.
 When in the wood the tempest roars and crunches,
 The giant fir shears down its neighbor boughs,
 Its brother columns in its bruising fall, 3230
 The hill reechoing its thunderous thud,
 You lead me to the cavern refuge, show
 My own self to me, and of my own breast
 The secret deep-laid miracles unfold.[2]
 And when before my gaze the limpid moon 3335
 Ascends and, soothing, wafts across, there rise
 From rocky cliffs, from out the moisty foliage
 The silver shapes of some anterior age
 And milden contemplation's joy austere.

 Ah, nothing perfect is vouchsafed to man, 3240
 I sense it now. Unto this ecstasy
 That takes me near and nearer to the gods,

1. An allusion to the Earth Spirit.
2. Recall the Ossianic vision of landscape in the opening monologue (lines
762–84).

You joined me that companion,[3] whom already
I cannot miss, though, chill and insolent,
He does debase me to myself, makes naught   3245
Your gifts with but the vapor of a word.
He fans within my breast a raging fire
For that fair image with his busy spite.
Thus reel I from desire to fulfillment,
And in fulfillment languish for desire.[4]   3250
    [*Enter* MEPHISTOPHELES.]
MEPHISTOPHELES. Well, had your fill yet, living in the rough?
    It may be pleasant for some innings;
    But come, a single sampling is enough,
    Then it is time for new beginnings!
FAUST. I wish you'd find yourself some other use   3255
    Than spoil a good day with your riot.
MEPHISTOPHELES. Well, well! Stew on in your own juice,
    I'm glad to let you rest in quiet.
    One has a precious lot to lose
    In one like you, all quirks and quills and dudgeon!   3260
    One wears out patience, wears out shoes,
    But what to shun for him and what to choose,
    You try to tell it by my Lord Curmudgeon!
FAUST. That was a speech in proper vein!
    He pesters me and wants a thank-you too.   3265
MEPHISTOPHELES. Without my help, how would you fain
    Have led your life, poor earthling you?
    I've cured you from the crochety throng
    Of vague imaginings for years;
    But for my coming you would long   3270
    Have tiptoed from this vale of tears.
    Why make your perch in caverns foul
    And rock-cracks like a moulting owl?
    Why slurp from dripping cliff and oozing root
    Your slimy diet like a newt?   3275
    A pretty path to health and wisdom!
    There's still the doctor in your system.
FAUST. You know with what new zest I am imbued
    By every ramble in this solitude?
    Yes—could you share this revelation,   3280
    You would be fiend enough to grudge me my elation.
MEPHISTOPHELES. A truly transcendental binge!
    By night and dew lie on a mountain range,
    Of earth and sky essay ecstatic capture,
    Swell up to girth divine with mystic rapture,   3285
    Root up earth's core with urgent divination,
    Feel in one's breast six day's worth of creation,
    In pride of potency I don't know what bestowing,
    Soon maudlin-lovingly all borders overflowing,

3. Mephistopheles.
4. See Binder's discussion of "desire" and "fulfillment" in relation to Faust's striving in his essay "Goethe's Classical Conception of *Faust*," below.

Those earthly coils completely rend— 3290
Then the transcendent act of knowing
[*with a gesture*] I won't say how to end.

FAUST. Fie, fie on you!

MEPHISTOPHELES.   You find this hard to swallow;
Outraged decorum's fie rings sadly hollow!
One mustn't to the modest ear blurt out 3295
What modest heart yet cannot do without.
There, there, I will not grudge you on occasion
The luxuries of innocent evasion.
But soon you'll tire of dissembling;
You are already all at sea, 3300
And, driven farther, you will be
Worn out in madness, fear and trembling.
Enough of this! Your lovebird sits and feels
Downcast in spirit and confined,
She is in love head over heels 3305
And cannot drive you from her mind.[5]
First your love-craze brimmed over in a torrent,
Just as a freshet floods its banks when swelled by thaw;
You poured into her heart the raging current,
And now your brook is shallow as before. 3310
Instead of haunting forests, on reflection
It would behoove his lordship to requite
The poor young monkey with a mite
Of your reciprocal affection.
She has been waiting pitifully long; 3315
Stands by the window, sees the clouds, so free,
Across the city ramparts flee,
Were I a little bird, thus goes her song,[6]
Day after day, and half the night.
Now she will be serene, more often blue, 3320
Sometimes shed tear on tear,
Then be in fair good cheer,
And always loving you.

FAUST. Ah, serpent! Venomous wretch you![7]

MEPHISTOPHELES. [*aside*] I thought that this might fetch you! 3325

FAUST. Vile profligate, betake thee hence![8]
Name not her sweetness that enslaves me!
Make not my lust for her who craves me,
Enflame again the exacerbated sense!

MEPHISTOPHELES. No need to fret! She thinks you flown afar; 3330
And in a way, I think you are.

FAUST. However far, I'm near to her and crave her,
She never is forgotten, never spent,

5. See "Gretchen's Chamber," immediately following.
6. An allusion to a popular folk song:
"If I were a little bird/and also had two
wings,/I would fly to you. . . ."
7. An allusion to the Biblical myth of

the fall, identifying Mephistopheles with
the serpent.
8. An allusion to Christ's rejection of
Satan's temptation in the wilderness
(Matthew 4:10).

I grudge the very body of the Savior
Her lips that touch it at the Sacrament.   3335
MEPHISTOPHELES. Well said! I've often envied you, my friend,
That pair of twins beneath the roses pent.[9]
FAUST. Off, pimp!
MEPHISTOPHELES. You tickle me, all bark and fizz!
The god who lads and lassies made
Discerned at once the noblest trade: 3340
Himself to see to opportunities.
Cheer up, o effigy of dread!
You're going to your lady's bed,
Not to the tomb!
FAUST. What use her love's celestial graces?   3345
As I grow warm in her embraces
Do I not always sense her doom?
Am I not fugitive, the homeless rover,
The man-beast void of goal or bliss,
Who roars in cataracts from cliff to boulder   3350
In avid frenzy for the precipice?
And to one side, she, still in childhood's shadow,
All in domestic cares enfurled,
In a small cabin on an alpine meadow,
Encompassed by the little world?   3355
And I, the God-forsaken,
Was not content
With cliffsides shaken
And granite crushed and rent,
No, she, her sweet composure, must be shattered too!   3360
This victim, Hell, must needs be proffered you!
Make shorter, fiend, my time of dread contrition!
Let it be now, what needs must be!
May then her destiny collapse on me
And she be joined in my perdition.   3365
MEPHISTOPHELES. Aboil again, all hiss and spout!
Go in and comfort her, you dunce!
Where such a birdbrain finds no quick way out
He sees the end of things at once.
He prospers who stands undeterred!   3370
You're surely well tradeuced to our affairs;
To me there's nothing more insipid in the world
Than a devil who despairs.

GRETCHEN'S CHAMBER[1]

GRETCHEN *by the spinning-wheel, alone.*

GRETCHEN. My peace is gone,
My heart is sore;   3375

9. An allusion to the Song of Songs 4:5, "Your two breasts are like two fawns, twins of a gazelle, that feed among the lilies." (Luther's German Bible substitutes "roses" for "lilies.")
1. Despite frequent musical settings for Gretchen's monologue at the spinning wheel (notably by Schubert), she apparently speaks the lines of this scene, the short, rhymed lines of which intensify and formalize her emotions.

Can find it never
And never more.

When he is fled,
My soul is dead,
My world is all   3380
As bitter gall.

My wretched head
Is all askew,
My bit of sense
All come in two.   3385

My peace is gone,
My heart is sore;
Can find it never
And never more.

Just him I spy   3390
At the window for,
Just him I fly
To meet outdoor.

His noble frame,
Tall gait and stand,   3395
The smile of his lips,
His eye's command,

And then his speech
Of magic bliss,
His hand on mine,   3400
And oh, his kiss!

My peace is gone,
My heart is sore;
Can find it never
And never more.   3405

My bosom strains
Unto his clasp,
Ah, could I gather
And hold him fast,

And kiss him, oh,   3410
The way I felt,
Under his kisses
Would swoon and melt!

MARTHE'S GARDEN[1]

MARGARETE, FAUST.

MARGARETE. Oh, Heinrich,[2] promise!
FAUST.   Anything I can.

1. An uncertain length of time passes
between each scene in the latter half of
the Gretchen tragedy. This scene per-
pares the consummation of Faust's love
through the administering of a sleeping
potion to Gretchen's mother.

MARGARETE. What is your way about religion, pray?   3415
  You are a dear and kindly man,
  And yet you pay it little heed, I'd say.
FAUST. No matter, dear! I'm fond of you, you feel,
  And this my love with my life's blood would seal;
  Nobody's church and creed would I presume to slight.   3420
MARGARETE. One must have faith, though; it just isn't right.
FAUST. Must one?
MARGARETE. O that I could prevail on you!
  You pay the Sacraments scant honor, too.
FAUST. I honor them.
MARGARETE. But from no inner need.
  How long since you were shriven, been to Mass, indeed?   3425
  Do you believe in God?
FAUST.   My dear one, who may say:
  I believe in God?
  Ask all your sages, clerical or lay,
  And their reply appears but sport
  Made of the questioner.
MARGARETE.   So you don't believe?   3430
FAUST.† Do not mishear me, dear my heart,
  For who may name Him
  And go proclaiming:
  Yes, I believe in him?
  Who search his heart   3435
  And dare say for his part:
  No, I believe him not?
  The All-comprising,
  The All-sustaining,
  Does he comprise, sustain not   3440
  You, me, himself?
  Are not the vaulted heavens hung on high?
  Is earth not anchored here below?
  And do with kindly gaze
  Eternal stars not rise aloft?   3445
  Join I not eye to eye with thee,
  Does all not surge
  Into thy head and heart,
  And in perpetual mystery
  Unseenly visible weave beside thee?   3450
  Fill full your heart, all it will hold, with this,
  And when you're all suffused and lost in bliss,
  Then call it what you will,
  Call it fulfillment! Heart! Love! God!
  I have no name for it!   3455

2. In the traditional legend, Faust is named "Johann." Goethe may have chosen this name because it occurs side by side with "Margareta" in the Catholic calendar (July 12 and 13).

Feeling is all;
Name is but sound and fume
Befogging heaven's blaze.
MARGARETE. All well and good; the turn of phrase
Is something different, but I presume   3460
What Parson says means much the same.
FAUST. It's what all hearts proclaim,
All places in the light of heaven's day,
Each in its language;
Why not I in my own?   3465
MARGARETE. Put in this way, it has a likely tone.
And yet it's all askew to me;
For you have no Christianity.
FAUST. Dear child!
MARGARETE.   It's long been grieving me
To see you in that company.   3470
FAUST. How so?
MARGARETE.   That man from whom you never part
Is hateful to me in my inmost heart;
Nothing in all my life
Has stabbed me to my soul as with a knife,
Like that man's horrid leer.   3475
FAUST. Dear baby, have no fear!
MARGARETE. His presence rouses up my blood.
I find most every person good;
But, as I long to see you night and morning,
He makes my hackles rise in secret warning.   3480
What's more, I take him for a knave, as well!
God pardon me if I should judge him ill!
FAUST. It takes all kinds of folk, you'll find.
MARGARETE. I would not mingle with his kind!
He's hardly through the door to me,   3485
And he puts on that face, half mockery,
And half grim;
One knows there's nothing rouses sympathy in him;
You read on his brow as on a scroll
That he cannot love a single soul.   3490
I come to feel so blissful in your arm,
So warmly yielding, free and calm,
But his presence chills my heart with loathing.
FAUST. Ah, tender angel of foreboding!
MARGARETE. I am so overcome,   3495
Let him just enter and survey us,
I fancy all my love for you grows numb,
Nor could I in his presence say my prayers,
And that just cuts my heart in two;
O, Heinrich, you must feel it too!   3500
FAUST. You simply have this prejudice.

MARGARETE. I must be gone.

FAUST.   Must I forgo the bliss
  Of knowing at your bosom an hour's rest,
  Thrusting together soul to soul and breast to breast?

MARGARETE. Oh, if I only slept alone!   3505
  I'd gladly leave my door unlocked tonight;
  But any little thing will wake my mother,
  And if she found us with each other
  I would just perish at her sight!

FAUST. You angel, this is no sore plight.   3510
  Here is a flask—three drops to take,
  Mixed with her drink, will steep
  Her nature in profoundest sleep.

MARGARETE. What would I not do for your sake?
  And she will take no harm from it?   3515

FAUST. Would I advise it, darling, if she did?

MARGARETE. Just looking at you, dearest man,
  What drives me to your will—I wish I knew;
  With all I have already done,
  I've precious little left to do for you.   3520
  [*Exit.*]

MEPHISTOPHELES. [*enters*] The mama-doll! Gone yet?

FAUST.   What, spying still?

MEPHISTOPHELES. Well, I took in a pretty earful;
  Herr Doctor went through catechism drill;
  I hope it left you fairly cheerful.
  Girls long to know if one will follow still   3525
  The plain old ways and pieties; they know
  If he's in go-strings there, they'll keep him on the go.

FAUST. You monster, cannot you conceive
  How this pure faithful dear,
  Bred to implicit trust   3530
  In faith, and to believe
  It sole salvation, writhes in holy fear
  To see him she holds dearest damned and lost?

MEPHISTOPHELES. Oh you transsensually sensuous squire!
  A lassie has you by the nose!   3535

FAUST. Miscarriage you of filth and fire!

MEPHISTOPHELES. And Physiognomy[3] she truly knows,
  Behind my mask divines some hidden truth,
  In my poor presence feels I don't know how;
  I am some sort of genius, she would vow,   3540
  Perhaps the Devil himself, forsooth.
  Well, and tonight—?

FAUST.   What's it to you?

MEPHISTOPHELES. I take my pleasure in it too!

---

3. The eighteenth-century pseudo-science   of the face and head.
of deducing character from the features

AT THE WELL[1]

GRETCHEN *and* LIESCHEN *with jars.*

LIESCHEN. You heard about dear Barbara?
GRETCHEN. Not a word. I don't see much of people.   3545
LIESCHEN. It's so, I just heard it from Sybil!
    She has at long last gone too far.
    That comes from stuck-up airs!
GRETCHEN.   What does?
LIESCHEN.   It stinks!
    She's feeding two now when she eats and drinks.
GRETCHEN. Oh!   3550
LIESCHEN. At last she's getting her comeuppance.
    How long she's hung upon the fellow's neck!
    I would like tuppence
    For each stroll, each tryst on common and dancing-deck,
    Everywhere had to be first in line,   3555
    He making up to her, pastries and wine,
    Always flaunting her so-called beauty,
    And yet so lost to honor and duty
    As to take gifts from him. Oh, fine!
    The billing and cooing that went on;   3560
    So now the wee cherry-blossom is gone!
GRETCHEN. The poor thing!
LIESCHEN.   What, you pity her still?
    When our sort sat at the spinning-wheel,
    And our mothers wouldn't let us go out,
    She'd be with her sweetheart, mooning about   3565
    On the door-bench, in a dark alleyway,
    Not a dull moment they had, I'd say.
    Now she might as well keep her stiff neck bowed,
    Doing penitence in the sinner's shroud![2]
GRETCHEN. He'll take her for his wife, I'm sure.   3570
LIESCHEN. He'd be a fool! His kind of night-flier
    Has more than one iron in the fire.
    Besides, he's gone.
GRETCHEN.   That is not fair!
LIESCHEN. If she gets him, we'll make it hot for her.
    The lads will tear off her wreath, and we,   3575
    We'll scatter chaff at her door, you'll see![3]
    [*Exit.*]
GRETCHEN. [*on her way home*] How readily I used to blame
    Some poor young soul that came to shame!

1. A public well where girls in the small town fetch water. Gretchen is apparently already pregnant by Faust and knows it.
2. It had been customary in the eighteenth century for unwed mothers to appear in church wearing a sinner's smock, where they were subject to the abuse of both the preacher and their neighbors.

3. A woman who had borne an illegitimate child was forbidden to wear a bridal wreath if she married. If she did so, her neighbors were free to grab it and tear it apart. Chaff or sawdust was scattered instead of the traditional flowers before the door of such a girl on her wedding day.

Never found sharp enough words like pins
To stick into other people's sins! 3580
Black as it seemed, I tarred it to boot,
And still never black enough to suit,
Would cross myself, exclaim and preen—
Now I myself am bared to sin!
Yet all of it that drove me here, 3585
God! was so innocent, was so dear!

BY THE CITY WALL

A niche in the masonry contains a shrine depicting the Sorrowing Mother of Christ, with flower jars before it.[1]

GRETCHEN. *[putting fresh flowers into the jars]*
    Incline,
    Thou rich in grief, oh shine
    Thy grace upon my wretchedness!

    Pierced to the heart 3590
    With thousandfold dart,
    Thou gazest up to thy dead son's face.

    To Him in the highest
    Thou gazest, sighest
    For thine and thy son's distress. 3595

    Who gauges
    How rages
    Pain in my marrow and bone?
    My poor heart's reaching,
    Quaking, beseeching, 3600
    Thou knowest, thou alone!

    Wherever I go,
    Woe, woe, oh woe
    Rends my bosom apart!
    Scarce left alone, 3605
    I moan, moan, moan,
    And weep to break my heart.

    At morn I plucked thee flowers,
    My bitter tears did rain,
    Bedewed the shards with showers 3610
    Outside my window pane.

1. Gretchen prays before a statue of the *Mater Dolorosa* in a niche of the city wall. Mary is represented as sorrowing for the dead Christ, with her visible heart pierced by a sword (following Luke 2:35). The first three stanzas of Gretchen's prayer are adapted from a thirteenth-century Latin hymn attributed to Jacopone da Todi and set to music by Palestrina and Pergolesi, among others. An adaptation of this prayer is later directed to the *Mater Gloriosa* by the spirit of Gretchen as *Una Poenitentium* in gratitude for the salvation of Faust in the final scene of *Part II* (lines 12069–75).

When in my room at dawning
The sun its brightness shed,
I sat in wakeful mourning
Already up in bed.   3615

Mercy! Save me from shame and death!
Incline,
Thou rich in grief, oh shine
Thy grace upon my wretchedness!

NIGHT†

Street in Front of Gretchen's Door

VALENTINE, *a soldier*, GRETCHEN'S *brother*.[1]

VALENTINE. When I would sit at a drinking bout,   3620
  Where many a lad might brag and shout,
  Commending the flower of maidenhood
  To my face as loudly as they could,
  Bloating their praise with a flowing cup,
  I'd sit there with my head propped up,   3625
  Secure and snugly as you please,
  Let all the bombast roll at ease,
  I'd chuckle, pass my beard through my hand,
  Reach for my well-filled mug and say:
  All this is fair enough in its way!   3630
  But is there one in all the land
  Who with my Gretel can compare?
  One that can hold a candle to her?
  Hear! Hear! Clink, clank! rang cup to cup,
  And some would shout with flashing eyes: 3635
  He's right! She is the maidens' prize!
  That shut the noisy champions up.
  And now? I feel like tearing my hair,
  Running up walls from sheer despair!
  With needling speeches, sly mockery,   3640
  Any scoundrel may wipe his mouth on me!
  I sit like a sponger long in debt,
  Whom any chance remark can sweat!
  And if I mangled the whole damned crew,
  I never could call them liars, too!   3645
  What's coming there? What sneaks along?
  There's two of them, unless I'm wrong.
  If it is he I'll have his fleece,
  He shall not leave here in one piece!
    [*Enter* FAUST, MEPHISTOPHELES.]

1. Valentine has learned of Gretchen's affair with Faust, though it has not yet become public knowledge. He apparently has come to confront her lover.

FAUST. How from the vestry's narrow window-cleft   3650
  The everlasting flame does upward glimmer
  And filter sideways, dim and dimmer,
  And darkness throngs it right and left!
  So night does in my bosom writhe.

MEPHISTOPHELES. I feel more like a tomcat, slim and lithe   3655
  About the fire ladders[2] sneaking,
  Past masonry and gutters streaking;
  I feel quite virtuous and blithe,
  A dram of thievery, a pinch of buck in heat.
  My blood runs hot already for the treat   3660
  Of great Walpurgis Night ahead—
  Two nights to go. Ah, on that beat
  One knows why one is not in bed.

FAUST. Will these two nights avail to raise the treasure
  Which I see shimmer thereabout?[3]   3665

MEPHISTOPHELES. Yes, you may soon enjoy the pleasure
  Of lifting the container out.
  I took a squint from out-of-bounds,
  It's full of splendid lion crowns.[4]

FAUST. But not a gem set, not a ring   3670
  Wherewith I might adorn my lover?

MEPHISTOPHELES. I think I saw beneath the cover
  A string of pearl or some such thing.

FAUST. I'm glad of that. It pains me so
  To go to her with nothing to show.   3675

MEPHISTOPHELES. For once it should not be unpleasant
  To have the prize without the present.
  Now that the sky is all with stars aglitter,
  Here is a *tour de force*—surprise!
  I'll sing a moral song, the better   3680
  To throw the stardust in her eyes.
    [*Sings to the zither.*][5]
        Why do you wait,
        Sweet Kate,

2. Reference to the ladders kept by the side of houses, especially those with thatched roofs, to facilitate swift extinguishing of fires.
3. Faust apparently has agreed to accompany Mephistopheles to the Walpurgis Night to secure additional buried treasure (see lines 2675 ff.). According to popular superstition, such treasure would shine by night (see lines 3916 ff.).
4. Lion crowns were silver coins of considerable value used for trade in the Levant and in Bohemia.
5. As Goethe later acknowledged to Eckermann (January 18, 1825; see below), this song derives from Shakespeare's *Hamlet* (IV.v.48–55), where it is sung by the deranged Ophelia for St. Valentine's day:

To-morrow is Saint Valentine's day,
  All in a morning betime,
And I a maid at your window,
  To be your Valentine.

Then up he rose and donn'd his clo'es,
  And dupp'd the chamber-door,
Let in the maid, that out a maid
  Never departed more.

Goethe's use of the name "Kate" (line 3683), which is not in Shakespeare, indicates that the translation by A. W. Schlegel (published 1797), where the name appears, was Goethe's source. The second stanza of the song, its ironic "moral," has no parallel in the Shakespearian source.

At lover's gate
At early light of day?   3685
Do not begin!
He'll let you in,
A maiden in,
A maiden not away.

Take heed, take flight!   3690
Once out of sight,
It is good night.
Good night, poor piteous thing!
For your own sake
Have with a rake   3695
No give and take,
But with a wedding ring.

VALENTINE. [*steps forward*] Whom would you lure here? Ah,
  the pox!
  Ratcatcher,[6] damm you to perdition!
  To hell first with the music-box!   3700
  To hell then with the foul musician!
MEPHISTOPHELES. The zither's done for—nothing left worth hit-
  ting.
VALENTINE. Now for a merry noggin-splitting!
MEPHISTOPHELES. [*to* FAUST] No yielding, doctor, there's no need!
  Keep close to me, quick, do not tarry!   3705
  Out with your duster! Mark my lead,
  You do the lunging! I will parry.
VALENTINE. Here, parry this then!
MEPHISTOPHELES.   Dead to rights.
VALENTINE. And this.
MEPHISTOPHELES.   Of course.
VALENTINE.   Methinks the devil fights!
  What can this be? My arm's already lame.   3710
MEPHISTOPHELES. [*to* FAUST] Now lunge!
VALENTINE. [*falling*]   O Jesus!
MEPHISTOPHELES.   There, the lout is tame.
  Now off post-haste, though! Things are getting ugly,
  The hue and cry is up, and not in vain.
  I cope with the police extremely snugly,
  Not quite so smoothly with the murder bane.[7]   3715
MARTHE. [*at her window*] Out, people, out!
GRETCHEN. [*at her window*] A light, bring light!
MARTHE. [*as above*] They swear and scuffle, shout and fight.
PEOPLE. One lies already dead!

6. An allusion to the Pied Piper of Ha-
melin, who was the subject of a ballad
by Goethe entitled "Ratcatcher" (published 1803). Also an echo of Shakespeare's *Romeo and Juliet* (III.i.75),
where Mercutio draws his sword to fight
with Tybalt, who subsequently kills him:

"Tybalt, you ratcatcher, will you
walk?"
7. The court of law concerned with matters of life and death pronounced sentence in God's name, which explains
why Mephistopheles could not control
such judgments.

MARTHE. [*stepping out*] The murderers—where did they run?
GRETCHEN. [*stepping out*] Who's lying there?
PEOPLE.   Your mother's son. 3720
GRETCHEN. What grief, oh God! upon my head!
VALENTINE. I'm dying. It is simply said,
　More simply brought about.
　Why stand there, cry and moan? Instead
　Come up and hear me out!   3725
　　　[*All surround him.*]
　Dear Gretchen—you are young, my pet,
　And not half wise enough as yet,
　You're in a sorry way.
　I tell you, just for you and me,
　You are a whore, what's there to say?   3730
　It can't be helped, you see.
GRETCHEN. My brother! God! What cruel shame!
VALENTINE. Call not on the Almighty's name.
　What's done is done, alas, and past,
　Now it will go the way it must.   3735
　With one in stealth it was begun,
　Soon there'll be some in place of one,
　And when a dozen's been with you,
　Then all the town has had you too.

　Where once Disgrace[8] has made its entry,   3740
　It is in deep concealment born,
　And veils of night are diligently
　About its head and shoulders drawn.
　Aye, they would smother it and murther;
　But as it grows, it breaks away,   3745
　Walks naked in the light of day,
　And grows no fairer as it goes further.
　The keener light shines on disgrace,
　The more repulsive grows its face.

　Indeed, I see the time upon you   3750
　When, harlot, all good folk will shun you
　And step around you, lifting their feet,
　As at infected carrion-meat.
　When people look into your eyes,
　The very heart in you shall quail,   3755
　You shall no more wear chain or prize,
　Step up no more to the altar rail,
　In handsome collars of lace no more
　Make merry on the dancing floor!
　No, you shall hide, a wretched mourner,   3760
　Midst cripples and beggars in a dark corner,
　And if God at last your sin forgive—

---

8. The allegorical personification of Dis-
grace may derive from Milton's *Paradise*
Lost (Book II), where Satan meets
Death and Sin outside the gates of Hell.

On earth be cursed as long as you live!
MARTHE. Seek for your soul God's merciful ease!
 Why burden it more with blasphemies?   3765
VALENTINE. If I could fly at your shriveled throat,
 You shameless, pandering nanny-goat,
 Forgiveness I might hope to win
 In heaping measure for every sin.
GRETCHEN. My brother! Brother! What agony!   3770
VALENTINE. I tell you, don't waste tears on me.
 When you renounced your honor first,
 Then was my heart most sorely pierced.
 I pass through death's brief slumber-span
 To God, a soldier and an honest man.   3775
  [*Dies.*]

CATHEDRAL

Mass, Organ and Singing[1]

GRETCHEN, *among many people,* EVIL SPIRIT *behind* GRETCHEN.

EVIL SPIRIT.[2] How changed, Gretchen, you feel
 Since full of innocence
 You would approach this altar,
 From the well-thumbed booklet
 Prattling prayers,   3780
 Half childish games,
 Half God in your heart!
 Gretchen!
 Where now your mind?
 Within your heart   3785
 What misdeed?
 Do you pray for your mother's soul, through you
 Sent in her sleep to long, long agony?
 Whose blood upon your threshold?
 And here beneath your heart   3790
 Is it not swellingly astir already,
 Alarming you, itself,
 With its foreboding presence?
GRETCHEN. Oh! Oh!
 Would I were rid of thoughts   3795
 That course my mind along, athwart,
 To spite me!

1. In the *Urfaust* a stage direction indicates that this scene occurs at a Requiem Mass for Gretchen's mother, who may have died from an overdose of the sleeping potion (see 3787–88 and 4570 ff.). In the present context it may be surmised that the Mass is for Valentine. 2. This spirit, of uncertain status, is apparently unrelated to those in attendance on Mephistopheles and may be associated with Gretchen's own conscience (analogous with the spirit of Care, which appears to Faust in *Part II*, Act V). A possible source is I Samuel 16:14, where King Saul is troubled by an evil spirit.

CHOIR. *Dies irae, dies illa*
　Solvet saeclum in favilla.[3]
　　[*Organ chords.*]
EVIL SPIRIT. Wrath clutches you!　　　　　　　　　3800
　The trumpet sounds!
　The graves are quaking!
　And your heart,
　From ashen stillness
　To flaming torment　　　　　　　　　　　　　3805
　Raised again,
　Starts with quailing![4]
GRETCHEN. Would I were far!
　I feel as though the organ here
　Stifled my breath,　　　　　　　　　　　　　3810
　The singing severed
　My very soul.
CHOIR. *Iudex ergo cum sedebit,*
　quidquid latet adparebit,
　Nil inultum remanebit.[5]　　　　　　　　　3815
GRETCHEN. I feel pent in!
　The stony pillars
　Confine me!
　The vaulted heights
　Press in on me! Air!　　　　　　　　　　　3820
EVIL SPIRIT. Go hide! Yet sin and shame
　Will not stay hidden.
　Air? Light?
　Woe unto you!
CHOIR. *Quid sum miser tunc dicturus?*　　　　　　3825
　Quem patronem rogaturus?
　Cum vix iustus sit securus.[6]
EVIL SPIRIT. Transfigured spirits
　Avert their countenance,
　Shrinking, the pure ones,　　　　　　　　　3830
　From your hand's touch.
　Woe!
CHOIR. *Quid sum miser tunc dicturus?*
GRETCHEN. Neighbor! Your salts![7]
　　[*She faints.*]

3. "Day of wrath, that day/will dissolve
the world into cinders." The Choir sings
from the medieval Latin sequence concerning the Last Judgment traditionally
used as part of the Requiem Mass for
the dead.
4. The Evil Spirit paraphrases several
stanzas in the Latin from the Requiem
and applies them directly to Gretchen.
The Biblical source for this passage is
St. Paul, I Corinthians 15:52, "For the
trumpet will sound, and the dead will be
raised imperishable, and we shall be

changed."
5. "Thus when the judge holds
court,/whatever is hidden will appear,/nothing will remain unavenged."
6. "What am I, wretched one, then to
say?/ whom for patron to implore?/
when scarcely the just man is secure."
7. As Gretchen falls unconscious, she
asks her neighbor in the pew for her
smelling salts, the small flask often carried by women in the eighteenth and
nineteenth centuries to sniff if they felt
faint.

⤳ WALPURGIS NIGHT†

The Harz Mountains; the Country Around Schierke and Elend[1]

FAUST. MEPHISTOPHELES.

MEPHISTOPHELES. Would you not have a broomstick rather? 3835
  I wish I rode a buck, however tough.
  Our route will take us yet a good way farther.
FAUST. While I'm still fresh upon my legs and gay,
  I find this knotted stick enough.
  What good is shortening one's way? 3840
  To trudge along the winding valley's shoulder,
  Then to climb up this rugged boulder,
  Whence ever plunging torrent hurls its spray,
  This is what lends such paths their zest and charm!
  Spring is already weaving in the birches, 3845
  The fir begins to sense its balm;
  Shall not our limbs, too, feel its livening purchase?
MEPHISTOPHELES. Forsooth, it leaves me numb and calm.
  I'm in the proper tune for winter,
  I wish my path were still in frost and snow. 3850
  How drearily the moon-disk's ragged cinder
  Swims up with its belated reddish glow,
  And shines so poorly that one risks collision
  At every step with crag or rooted snare!
  I'll call a will-o'-the-wisp,[2] with your permission! 3855
  I see one yonder that's in merry flare.
  Hey you, my friend, may we enlist your service?
  Why blaze away there to no purpose?
  Please be so kind and light us up that way!
WILL-O'-THE-WISP. My reverence for you, I hope, will force 3860
  My flighty temper to your course;
  Our usual path is zigzag and astray.
MEPHISTOPHELES. Well, well! He looks to men and does the same.
  Just you go straight, in devil's name!
  Or with one puff I'll end your flickering spell. 3865
WILL-O'-THE-WISP. You are the master here, that I can tell,
  I'll gladly straighten for your vision.
  Tonight the mountain's mad with magic, though,
  And if a will-o'-the-wisp shall show you where to go
  You mustn't ask too much precision. 3870
FAUST, MEPHISTOPHELES, WILL-O'-THE-WISP. [*chanting by turns*]
        Here, it seems, we pass the gateway
        Into magic dreams and mazes.
        Guide us well and earn our praises,
        Speed us on our courses straightway

---

1. The names of two villages along the road which leads to the Brocken.
2. *Ignis fatuus*, associated in folklore with the devil, a spirit that leads travelers astray into marshes and bogs.

Through the vast deserted spaces.   3875

See how tree with tree enlaces,
Past each other swiftly scudding,
And the cliffsides squatly nodding,
And the rocky noses goring,
Roaring in the gale and snoring![3]   3880

Down through sward and pebbles pouring,
Rill and rivulet are springing.
Are they bubbling? Are they singing?
Lament sweet of lovelorn maidens,
Voices of celestial cadence?   3885
Hope and love anew imagined!
And the echo like a legend
Conjures bygone ages back.

Oo-hoo! Shoo-hoo! hear them call,
Screech-owl, plover, jaybird all,   3890
Did they all remain awake?
Newts among the rootwork crouching,
Lanky legs and bellies pouching,
Serpent roots, their reptile creepers
Up through rock and bracken wending,   3895
Weirdly writhing loops extending,
Bent to scare us, snare us, keep us,
From their sturdy tendrils sloping
Sending mollusk fringes groping
For the wanderer. Mice are teeming,   3900
Thousand-hued battalions streaming
Through the moss and heath in millions.
Fireflies in squadrons gather,
Add their mind-bedazzling brilliance
To the turmoil high and nether.   3905

Tell me, someone, are we halting
Or advancing? All is vaulting,
All revolves and swirls and races,
Crags and trees' distorted faces,
And the jack-o'-lanterns floating,   3910
Breeding as they spin and bloating.[4]

MEPHISTOPHELES. Hold my coat-tail, clutch it tight!
   Here we reach a middling height
   Whence you glimpse a sight astounding,
   Mammon glistening through the mountain.[5]   3915

3. An intentional transformation of the natural landscape into the animated forces of a fairy realm. The "snoring cliffs" are two large rocks which actually exist on the road between Schierke and Elend.
4. Intentional confusion of all spatial relations results from the chant, as the will-o'-the-wisp also disappears among the other "jack-o'-lanterns."
5. An open pit reveals buried treasure glowing within the mountain (see lines 3664–65). Mammon is a personification of these metals (see Matthew 6:24, "You cannot serve God and Mammon"; also, Milton's *Paradise Lost*, Book I, where Mammon takes charge of building the infernal city of Pandemonium).

FAUST. How strangely in the vales it glimmers,
  As of a lurid sunrise sheen,
  And probes with summer-lightning shimmers
  The deepest clefts of the ravine!
  There vapor wells, in billows sweeping,   3920
  There mist and haze with embers glow,
  Now like the finest webwork seeping,
  Now breaking forth in bubbling flow.
  Here it will thread in disalignment
  Downhill, a hundred veins of light,   3925
  And cornered there in close confinement,
  All of a sudden reunite.
  Close by us, points of fire are sparkling
  Like golden sand-grains scattered low,
  But watch! The entire rock-face darkling   3930
  Is kindled now from top to toe.
MEPHISTOPHELES. How splendidly Lord Mammon is contriving
  To light his palace for the feast!
  I'm glad you caught a glimpse at least;
  I sense the boisterous company arriving.   3935
FAUST. Ah, how the stormwind roars and hisses!
  What blows it rains upon my neck!⁶
MEPHISTOPHELES. Cleave to the ribwork of the ancient rock,
  Or it will hurl you down these deadly precipices.
  Fog thickens the nocturnal dark;   3940
  Hark, all the forests clatter,
  Owls flutter up and scatter,
  Hear it shatter the stanchions
  Of evergreen mansions,
  Boughs whirring and snapping,   3945
  Trunks thunderclapping,
  Roots creaking and gaping,
  Fearfully tangled all
  Crashes in smashing fall,
  And over the trammeled vales   3950
  Whistle and howl the gales.
  Hear the voices on high,
  Far off and nigh?
  Yes, all the mountain long
  Surges maniacal magical song!   3955
WITCHES IN CHORUS. The witches to the Brocken fare
              By acres green and stubble bare,
              There to assemble, host on host,
              Sir Urian⁷ sitting uppermost,

6. The procession of witches riding upwards on the air is described as a stormwind. Mephistopheles' description of it
in the speech following conjures up the
wild troop from Germanic folklore, the
spirit army of Wotan, which manifested
itself as a storm roaring through the forest.
7. Not a traditional name for the devil,
but rather a title for anyone of uncertain
name who appears unexpectedly.

By sticks and stones that flash and wink,   3960
The witches fart, the billies stink.

VOICE. Here comes old Baubo[8] riding now
Alone astride a mother sow.

CHORUS. Give honor then to whom it's due![9]

Frau Baubo forward! Lead the crew!   3965
A proper pig and mother too,
The witches' train will follow you.

VOICE. Which way did you come?

VOICE.   By the Ilsenstone, dearie,
Took a peep into the cliff-owl's eyrie,
Oh, how she stared!

VOICE.   O, hell and blast!   3970
You're riding too fast!

VOICE. She skins you and scores,
Look at these sores!

WITCHES IN CHORUS.

The road is wide, the road is long,[1]
Ah, what an antic, frantic throng!   3975
The pitchfork pokes, the broomstick thrusts,
The infant chokes, the mother busts.[2]

WARLOCKS.[3] FIRST HALF-CHORUS.

Like snails in shells we crawl and poke,
Outrun by all the womenfolk;
For in the Devil's Handicaps   3980
Girls lead us by a thousand steps.

SECOND HALF-CHORUS.

We do not take it much to heart;
Girls have a thousand paces' start,
But as she pants and swings her rump,
Man leaps it in a single jump.   3985

VOICE. [*above*] You there, join up, the Rock Lane crew!

VOICES. [*below*][4] We'd gladly fly aloft with you.
We're washed all clean and scrubbed all sore,
But barren too, for evermore.

BOTH CHORUSES. The wind is mute, the star is fled,   3990
The hazy moon would hide its head.
In rushing flight the magic choir
Spurts forth a myriad sparks of fire.

VOICE. [*from below*] Halt! Halt!

---

8. Originally the name of a lewd nurse in Classical mythology who tries to console Demeter after her daughter Persephone is carried off by Hades. Here it suggests any fantastic female creature. The idea of a witch riding a pig is of uncertain origin.

9. A parody of Romans 13:7, "honor to whom honor is due."

1. A parody of Matthew 7:13–14: "Enter by the narrow gate; for the gate is wide and the way is easy, that leads to destruction, and those who enter by it are many. For the gate is narrow and the way is hard, that leads to life, and those who find it are few."

2. An allusion to the cutting open of a pregnant woman's womb by the force of a witch's broomstick, so that both infant and mother die.

3. The distinction of sexes between witches and warlocks was originally intended to anticipate the sexual orgies to take place at the summit of the Brocken.

4. No adequate explanation for the voices from below has been given. Clearly some satirical allusion is intended, perhaps to the Reformation.

VOICES. [*from above*] Who calls there from the craggy
    fault?   3995
VOICE. [*below*] Wait for me! Wait for me!
  Three hundred years I climb and sweat,
  And haven't reached the summit yet.
  I want my kin and company!
BOTH CHORUSES. The stick, the broom buoy up and float,   4000
             So does the fork, so does the goat;
             Who cannot rise aloft tonight
             Must be forever lost from sight.
HALF-WITCH. [*below*] I'm sadly lagging in the race;
  The others are so far ahead!   4005
  I cannot rest content in bed,
  Nor yet attain the witches' pace.
CHORUS OF THE WITCHES.
             The ointment[5] makes the witches hale,
             A patch of rag will do for sail,
             Each trough a schooner under weigh;   4010
             He'll never fly, who won't today.
BOTH CHORUSES. And as above the peak we flow,
             You others trail along below
             And all the heather overflood
             With your array of hexenhood!   4015
    [*They glide down.[6]*]
MEPHISTOPHELES. It throngs and rustles, thrusts and clatters,
  It swirls and hisses, sucks and chatters,
  It glows and sputters, burns and stinks,
  A sea of hexendom, methinks!
  Hold tight! or we'll be parted in two winks.   4020
  Where are you?
FAUST. [*in the distance*] Here!
MEPHISTOPHELES.   So far adrift already?
  I must assert my birthright. Steady!
  Make room! It's Nick, Squire Nick, sweet mob, give ground!
  Here, doctor, take my hand, and in one bound
  Let us escape the crush and flee.   4025
  This is too wild for even the likes of me.
  Close by there shines a most peculiar glow;
  There's something draws me to that undergrowth.
  Come, come! We'll slip in from below.
FAUST. You Prince of Paradox! Lead on, I am not loath.   4030
  It does appear a queer proceeding, though.
  We go to taste Walpurgis with the elves,
  And promptly start to isolate ourselves.
MEPHISTOPHELES. Look at that flame of varying hue!
  There sits a merry clique for you.   4035

---

5. Witches were said to smear their
broomsticks with the fat of unborn ba-
bies to make them fly (see lines 3976–
77).

6. The swarm of witches settles down on
an open plateau like a flock of birds
landing.

No feeling lonesome at a small affair.
FAUST. I'd rather be up over there!
  I spy a glow and fumes awhirl.
  There flocks the crowd to Evil-kind;[7]
  There many a riddle should unfurl.   4040
MEPHISTOPHELES. And many a one be newly twined.
  You let the great world spin and riot,
  We'll nest contented in our quiet.
  You know, an old tradition runs
  That the great world produces little ones.   4045
  Here bare young witchlets prance and hover,
  There old ones wisely under cover.
  Be sociable, just for my sake;
  It's lots of fun and little ache.
  There, listen, instruments start blaring!   4050
  A hellish screech! But soon one gets past caring.
  Come on, step up, it cannot be refused,
  I'll introduce you, you will be amused,
  And change of company will keep you so.
  What say you, friend? We are not tightly penned.   4055
  Let your eyes rove, you hardly see the end.
  A hundred fires are burning in a row;
  There's dancing, chatter, brewing, drinking, wooing—
  Now name me anything that's more worth doing!
FAUST. Do you intend to gain us recognition   4060
  By showing off as devil or magician?
MEPHISTOPHELES. My custom is to go incognito,
  A state occasion calls for medals, though.
  While not by star and garter decked,
  I find the cloven hoof here held in high respect.   4065
  You see the snail there crawling up?[8] It glides about,
  It can but snoop and slide,
  Yet with no other guide has smelled me out.
  I could not hide myself here if I tried.
  Come now from fire to fire with me as tutor;   4070
  I am the broker here and you the suitor.
  [*to some figures sitting about dying embers*[9]] Well now, old
      gentlemen, why sit apart and fiddle?
  You'd please me better in the very middle,
  Amid the youngsters' swirl and foam;
  One surely is alone enough at home.   4075
A GENERAL. My trust in nations is but feeble!
  One may have served them ever so well;
  Just as on women, so upon the people
  Youth always works the strongest spell.

---

7. Possibly an allusion to Satan, at the summit of the Brocken.
8. The snail may be associated with the group of aged indolents encountered shortly.
9. Much scholarly labor has been expended in attempts to explain the satirical implications of these figures, to no avail.

A CABINET MINISTER. They've strayed so far away from law and
    creed,   4080
  That's why I like the old and pious;
  The time when we were rated highest,
  That was the golden age indeed!
SOCIAL CLIMBER. We none of us have played the dunce,
  And often acted as we oughtn't;   4085
  Now we've attained what was important,
  It's unimportant all at once.
AUTHOR. How many living now amongst us
  Can read a piece that's halfway clever!
  And as for our delightful youngsters,   4090
  They are more impudent than ever.
MEPHISTOPHELES. [*who suddenly appears very old*[1]]
  On this my last ascent of the witching mountain
  I find the masses ripe for the Last Accounting,
  For since my keg is running dregs,
  The world must be on its last legs.   4095
PEDDLING WITCH.[2] Good sirs, do not pass by like that,
  Or you might miss a pretty chance!
  Spare me a more attentive glance,
  My stock is well worth looking at.
  There's nothing here to which an armful   4100
  Of earthly merchandise compares,
  No single thing but has been harmful
  To mortal man and his affairs.
  There is no sword here has not tasted gore,
  No cup from which into a healthy frame   4105
  Some searing venom did not pour,
  No trinket here but that has brought to shame
  Some lovely woman, nor a dagger but designed
  To pierce a trusting ally from behind.
MEPHISTOPHELES. You are behind the times, dear cousin;   4110
  What's done is done, what's past is trite;
  Your stuff is fifteen to the dozen,
  For only novelties excite.
FAUST. This entertainment gives me pause—
  The strangest fair that ever was!   4115
MEPHISTOPHELES. Uphill now, all the surging crew;
  You think you're pushing, but they're pushing you.
FAUST. Who is this?
MEPHISTOPHELES.   Take a good look at her!
  It's Lilith.[3]

1. Mephistopheles, by appearing old, parodies the inactivity of the old men.
2. As at any village fair, the peddler's booth is set up with wares for sale.
3. In response to the two separate creation myths in Genesis (where God creates man and woman, 1:27, and then creates Eve from Adam's rib, 2:18ff.), rabbinical tradition argued that Adam's first wife was Lilith, an evil spirit of the night who seduces men and harms little children. (The Hebrew *lilith*—see Isaiah 34:14—means "night hag.")

FAUST.   Who?
MEPHISTOPHELES.   Adam's first wife. Beware,
 Yield not to the allure of those fair tresses!   4120
 Her sole adornment is her lovely hair;
 Once a young man is captured in that snare,
 He is not soon released from her caresses.
FAUST. Those two there, the old crone and the young thing,
 Already had a merry old fling!   4125
MEPHISTOPHELES. There's none tonight would seek repose.
 Here's a new dance; come on, it's time we chose!
FAUST. [*dancing with the* YOUNG ONE]
  In a fair dream that once I dreamed,
  An apple-tree appeared to me,
  On it two pretty apples gleamed,   4130
  They beckoned me; I climbed the tree.[4]
THE FAIR ONE.
  You've thought such apples[5] very nice
  Since Adam's fall in Paradise.
  I'm happy to report to you,
  My little orchard bears them too.   4135
MEPHISTOPHELES. [*with* THE OLD ONE[6]]
  In a wild dream that once I dreamed
  I saw a cloven tree, it seemed,
  It had a black almighty hole;
  Black as it was, it pleased my soul.
THE OLD ONE. I welcome to my leafy roof   4140
  The baron with the cloven hoof!
  I hope he's brought a piston tall
  To plug the mighty hole withal.
PROCTOPHANTASMIAC.[7] How dare you, you abandoned crew?
 It's long been proved and well propounded   4145
 That ghosts are utterly unfounded!
 And here you even dance as humans do!
THE FAIR ONE. [*dancing*] What is he doing at our spree?
FAUST. [*dancing*] Oh, he goes everywhere, you see.
 What others dance, he must appraise.   4150
 Unless he prattles over every phase,
 There simply wasn't any dancing.
 What most annoys him is when we're advancing,

4. An echo of the Song of Songs 7:8–9, "I say I will climb the palm tree and lay hold of its branches. Oh, may your breasts be like clusters of the vine, and the scent of your breath like apples, and your kisses like the best wine that goes down smoothly, gliding over lips and teeth."

5. The witch applies the metaphor of her breasts as apples to the myth of the fall, when Eve, tempted by the serpent, gave the apple to Adam.

6. Critics have surmised that this may be the Witch from the scene "Witch's Kitchen."

7. What follows (lines 4144–75) is a satirical attack on Friedrich Nicolai (1773–1811), a minor writer and publisher in Berlin who wrote a parody of Goethe's novel *The Sorrows of Young Werther*. As a rationalist of the Enlightenment (see line 4159), he opposed the use of any supernatural elements in literature. Supposedly, however, he himself had been haunted at one time by spirits —specifically a ghost in Tegel, a suburb of Berlin (see line 4161)—and submitted to a cure involving the application of leeches to the posterior. Goethe thus gives him an appropriate name from the Greek *proktos*, "anus."

We could just go in circles, if you will,
As he does in his creaking mill,   4155
And we might win his qualified assent;
The more so if we pay him due acknowledgment.

PROCTOPHANTASMIAC. Still here? This is unheard of, I declare!
  Clear out! We have enlightened! Much they care.
  That devil's brood, they squirm through and finagle;   4160
  We're so advanced, and still it spooks in Tegel.
  How hard I swat at ghosts and sweep away,
  It's never clean; unheard of, I must say!

THE FAIR ONE. Be off and stop annoying us, you hear?

PROCTOPHANTASMIAC. Ghosts, to your faces I declare   4165
  That spirit tyranny I will not bear;
  My intellect can't banish it, I fear.
        [*The dancing continues.*]
  This hasn't been my lucky day, I know it;
  But I don't grudge the trip for it,
  And still have hopes before I quit   4170
  To conquer both the devil and the poet.

MEPHISTOPHELES. He'll squat into a puddle soon, you'll find,
  That's what he does by way of purges,
  And when the leeches feast on his behind,
  He's cured of spirits and spiritual urges.   4175
  [*to* FAUST, *who has left the dancing*] Why did you let that
      pretty damsel go,
  Who sang so sweetly as you romped?

FAUST. Imagine—in mid-song there jumped
  A red mouse from her mouth.[8]

MEPHISTOPHELES.   Oh yes?
  Well, what of that! who cares at such a feast,   4180
  While he is dallying with a shepherdess?
  It wasn't a gray mouse at least.

FAUST. And then I saw—

MEPHISTOPHELES.   What?

FAUST.   Look, Mephisto, yonder,
  Lone and apart, the maiden pale and sweet?
  But haltingly she seems to wander,   4185
  As if advancing with unparted feet.
  There would appear to me, I swear,
  A likeness to dear Gretchen there.

MEPHISTOPHELES. Leave that alone; no good can come of it.
  It is a wraith,[9] a lifeless counterfeit,   4190
  A changeling perilously met.
  She clots a man's blood with her staring threat,

8. Goethe borrowed this incident from one of his sources, which describes how a little red mouse jumps out of the mouth of a sleeping girl.
9. The term in German, *Idol*, from the Greek *eidolon*, means a "spiritless image." How or why this appears to Faust here is uncertain, especially as he can have no knowledge of Gretchen's fate since he left her. In the original draft for the "Walpurgis Night" Goethe intended the final scene to represent Gretchen's execution, in which the head of the wraith would fall off and blood gush forth.

And he may turn into a monolith;
You've heard, of course, of the Medusa myth.[1]

FAUST. Not so—a dead girl's eyes I see   4195
That no dear hand closed as she died.
This is the breast that Gretchen proffered me,
This the enchanting body I enjoyed.

MEPHISTOPHELES. You gullible fool, it's all a magic spell!
Each sees in her the one he loves too well.   4200

FAUST. What torment, yet how sweetly relished!
That gaze—I cannot seek escape.
How strangely is the graceful neck embellished
By a red strand from throat to nape,
A scarlet knife-edge, as it were!   4205

MEPHISTOPHELES. Quite so! I too see it on her.
You're apt to find her walking head in hand;
Perseus cut off her head, you understand.
You're always off upon some fancy!
Come up that little hillock there—   4210
Here's quite a merry Prater fair![2]
Unless I'm fooled by necromancy,
It is indeed a stage I see.
What's playing here?

SERVIBILIS.[3]   You're just in time to see
The last of seven courses on the play-bill;[4]   4215
Here that's the usual evening's repast.
An amateur writes up the fable,
And amateurs make up the cast.
I make a callow exit now, excuse me!
I am the immature who lifts the curtain.   4220

MEPHISTOPHELES. To see you on the Blocksberg will amuse me;
That's one place where you all belong for certain.

WALPURGIS NIGHT'S DREAM†

OR

THE GOLDEN WEDDING OF OBERON AND TITANIA

Intermezzo

STAGEMASTER. Well, tonight we rest a spell,
Mieding's valiant breed;[1]

1. Mephistopheles associates the cut through the neck of the wraith with the myth of the beheading by Perseus (see line 4208) of the Medusa, one of the Gorgons, whose face turned men to stone.
2. A transition to the "Intermezzo." The Prater is a famous amusement park in Vienna, first opened to the public by the Emperor Joseph II in 1766. The anachronism is clearly intentional.
3. It has been argued that this curtain-raiser may represent satirically the Rec-

tor of the school in Weimar, Karl August Böttiger (1760–1835), a fawning courtier who took an active interest in the Weimar Theater.
4. The "Intermezzo" is conceived on the analogy of a Greek satyr play, following a double tragic trilogy as the seventh item.
1. Johann Martin Mieding (died 1782), a Weimar carpenter, was stage-master for the amateur theater of the Court, in which Goethe also participated.

Ancient mountains, moisty dell,   4225
Are all the props we need.

HERALD.   Weddings, to be golden praised,
Should fifty years pass muster;
To me, contention's sieges raised
Is gold of finer luster.   4230

OBERON.   At my side if spirits be,
Show forth these hours, invited;
King and Royal Consort, see,
Troth have freshly plighted,

PUCK.[2]   Enter Puck and turns athwart   4235
And shifts his feet at dancing;
Hundreds follow to cavort
And share his joyous prancing.

ARIEL.[3]   Ariel strikes his lyre pure
To strains of heavenly cadence;   4240
Masks bizarre his song will lure,
But also lures fair maidens.

OBERON.   Where spouses strive for concord fair,
On our example start them;
To foster fondness in a pair   4245
You only need to part them.

TITANIA.   Husband sulking, wife in moods?
Then swiftly up and grip her;
Lead her to southern latitudes,
Him to the northern Dipper.   4250

ORCHESTRA TUTTI. [*fortissimo*]
Jack-a-fly and Tim-a-bug
With kindred and relation,
Grassy cricket, leafy frog
Provide the orchestration!

SOLO.[4]   Here's the bagpipe's tootle-sack,   4255
A soap-bubble its belly;
Hear it leak and squeak and quack
Up through its crooked sally.

SPIRIT AS YET IN GESTATION.[5]
Spider claw and hoptoad paunch
And winglets to the gnome!   4260
No true beastie will you launch,
Albeit a little poem.

---

2. The elf from Shakespeare's *Midsummer Night's Dream*, who here leads the dancing chorus of spirits.
3. A spirit of the air, from Shakespeare's *Tempest*.
4. A soap bubble speaks with the sound of a bagpipe.
5. A grotesque mixture of insects, like a creature from a painting by Bosch or Breughel.

PAIR OF PARTNERS.
Tiny step and springy skip
Through honey dew and fragrance;
Bravely tripped, though scarce a trip 4265
Aloft to airy regions.

CURIOUS TRAVELER.[6]
Is this not mummery for fun?
Should I believe my eyes?
Fair immortal Oberon
Here too tonight? Surprise! 4270

ORTHODOX.[7] Neither tail nor talons, true,
And yet past doubt or cavil:
As with the gods of Greece, here too
We're up against a devil.

NORTHERN ARTIST.[8]
My catch today remains for fair 4275
On sketch and fragment levels,
I'm well in train though to prepare
For my Italian Travels.

PURIST. Alas! an evil day for me:
Lewd speech, and diction clouded; 4280
In all the witch-host here, I see
No more than two are powdered.

YOUNG WITCH. A powdered head and covering frock
Are good for gray old hexen;
So I sit naked on my buck 4285
And show up firm and buxom.

MATRON. We have too much of *savoir-faire*
To bandy words with witches;
But you may rot, for all I care,
As young and tender bitches. 4290

BANDMASTER. Jack-a-fly and Tim-a-bug,
Don't swarm about the naked!
Grassy cricket, leafy frog,
You *can* keep time, I take it?

WEATHERVANE.[9] [*pointing one way*]
The best of company, in truth, 4295
All hopeful brides amongst us!

---

6. An allusion to Nicolai (see lines 4144 ff. and note). In 1783–96 he had published a *Description of a Journey through Germany and Switzerland* in twelve large volumes.
7. Count Friedrich Leopold zu Stolberg (1750–1819), poet of the *Sturm und Drang* and translator of Homer, who came to oppose the poets of Weimar from the standpoint of pious Christianity.

8. Goethe himself. He associates himself with the preoccupation of northern European artists with subjects from the Classical realm. Goethe was planning an Italian journey when he wrote this scene in 1797, though ultimately he did not go.
9. The same figure speaks the following two stanzas, a flatterer who totally changes the direction of his opinion according to the audience he addresses.

And bachelors to a man, forsooth,
Most eligible youngsters!

WEATHERVANE. [*pointing other way*]
And if the ground won't split apart
To swallow lads and ladies,   4300
I'm off to take a flying start
And leap straight into Hades.

XENIEN.[1]
Insect-shaped we flutter up,
Sharp little scissors flitting,
To offer unto Beelzebub,   4305
Our father, worship fitting.

HENNINGS.[2]
Look at them milling here in strength,
Ingenuously joking!
They'll have the crust to claim at length
That they are kindly-spoken.   4310

MUSAGETE.
How I should love to lose myself
Amid this witches' pageant,
I'm better with this kind of elf
Than as the Muses' agent.

CI-DEVANT SPIRIT-OF-THE-TIMES.
Here, grab my coat-tail! Any flop   4315
Thus soars above the masses;
The Blocksberg has a spacious top
Like Germany's Parnassus.

CURIOUS TRAVELER.[3]
What do they call this haughty man,
So poker-stiffly walking?   4320
He snoops and sniffs as hard as he can.
"It's Jesuits he's stalking."

CRANE.[4]
I take my pleasure both in clear
And muddy waters angling;
Thus you may see the pious here   4325
Amongst the devils dangling.

THIS WORLD'S CHILD.[5]
Believe me, to the pious all

---

1. A reference to the collection of satirical epigrams published in 1796 by Goethe and Schiller.
2. August Friedrich Hennings (1746–1826), a minor writer and editor who in 1798–99 published a collection of poems entitled *Musagete* in two volumes (see lines 4311 ff.; the title is an epithet of Apollo, "one who leads the Muses"). He also was editor of a literary journal first entitled *Spirit of the Age*, then (after 1800) *Spirit of the Nineteenth Century* (Goethe acknowledges this change of title with his French term *ci-devant*, "erstwhile").
3. Nicolai, as above (lines 4267 ff.),
whose hatred for Catholics was well known.
4. From a comment to Eckermann on February 17, 1829, it is known that Goethe here alludes to Johann Caspar Lavater (1741–1801), the Swiss physiognomist, with whom Goethe came into contact as a young man.
5. A third allusion to Goethe himself, in accord with his earlier poem "Dinner in Coblentz" (1774), where he speaks of himself as sitting between Lavater and Basedow: "prophet to the right, prophet to the left, the world's child in the middle."

Is grist to prayer mills;
Upon the Blocksberg here they call
Lots of conventicles.   4330

DANCER.   Another chorus coming in?
I hear a distant drumming.
Be easy! It's the unison
Of moorland bittern thrumming.

DANCEMASTER.[6]
How all the dancers lift their feet   4335
And manage hook-or-crook-like!
The hunched turn limber, awkward fleet,
Not caring what they look like.

FIDDLER.   This mob is all at daggers drawn,
At odds like ice and fire;   4340
Just on the tootlebag they fawn
Like beasts on Orpheus' lyre.

DOGMATIC.[7]   I shan't be flustered by critique,
For all their doubts and cavils;
There must be something to Old Nick.   4345
Or how could there be devils?

IDEALIST.[8]   This once by fantasy, my bliss,
I feel too harshly saddled;
Forsooth, if I am all of this,
Today I must be addled.   4350

REALIST.[9]   I find their doings hard to stand,
I never was a squirmer;
For once I have two feet on sand
Instead of *terra firma*.

SUPERNATURALIST.[1]
With these carousers I concur,   4355
And do enjoy the ball so!
For from the devils I infer
Benignant spirits also.

SCEPTIC.[2]   Each trails and trusts his will o'wisp
To lead him to the treasure;   4360
The devil-cavil rhyme is crisp,
For me it's made to measure.

6. This and the stanza following were
written much later than the rest of the
"Dream"—apparently early in 1826, in
response to an English translation of the
scene by John Heavyside.
7. Pre-Kantian dogmatists, specifically in
Christian doctrine.
8. Post-Kantian Idealism, especially the
philosophy of Fichte and Schelling.
9. A general allusion to empiricists who

would base their judgment of reality on
observation.
1. An allusion to belief in a transcendent realm, of which the enthusiast Friedrich Heinrich Jacobi (1743–1819) served
as a conspicuous example.
2. Presumably an allusion to such a philosopher as the Scotsman David Hume
(1711–76).

BANDMASTER.   You frog and cricket make us sound
                       Like amateur auditions;
                       You fly and beetle, I'll be bound,   4365
                       I thought you were musicians!

NIMBLE ONES.[3] They call us sports the *Sans-souci*,
                       Our feet are sore from slogging;
                       We carry on right merrily,
                       Each walking on his noggin.   4370

AWKWARD ONES.[4]
                       We've sponged and toadied all we knew,
                       But now have shot our wadding;
                       Our dancing shoes are worn right through,
                       Barefooted we are plodding.

WILL O' THE WISPS.[5]
                       We came directly from the swamp.   4375
                       Where we originated;
                       But here we shine in serried pomp,
                       As glittering gallants rated.

SHOOTING STAR.[6]
                       Wreathed in fire I plunged from high
                       In sparks of starry glitter;   4380
                       Now prostrate in the grass I lie,
                       Who'll help me to a litter?

MASSIVE ONES.[7] Room! More room here! Let us through!
                       Down tender herbs are trodden.
                       Spirits coming, spirits too   4385
                       Come uncouth and plodding.

PUCK.   One needn't lumber so and sway
                       Like elephant babies, must one!
                       Let loudest thumping come today
                       From Puck himself, robust one!   4390

ARIEL.   Whether Nature bountiful
                       Or spirit gave you pinions,
                       Track me lightly up the hill
                       To the rose dominions!

ORCHESTRA. [*pianissimo*]   4395
                       Cloudy drift and vapor's edge
                       Are lighted from above.
                       Leafy sough and breezy sedge,
                       And all is wafted off.

---

3. Opportunists who merely changed their political leanings after the French Revolution "without a care" (i.e., *sans-souci* in French).
4. Aristocratic emigrés from France after the Revolution, who frequently became parasites at the various courts of Europe.
5. Creatures from the swamp who emerged from nowhere through the Revolution to shine in the public arena. (See the Will-o'-the-Wisp in the preceding scene, lines 3855 ff.)
6. Radical revolutionaries whose political day was over.
7. The "masses" released by the Revolution.

DREARY DAY[1]

A Field

FAUST. MEPHISTOPHELES.

FAUST. In misery! Despairing! Long roaming the earth, a wretched waif, and now imprisoned! Locked up in the dungeon as an evildoer to suffer appalling torture, the lovely luckless creature! To this! To this pass!—Faithless, degraded spirit—and this you concealed from me? Yes, stand there, stand! Roll those demon eyes in your head in speechless spite! Stand there and defy me with your unbearable presence! Imprisoned! In unredeemable ruin! Abandoned to evil spirits and to judging, unfeeling mankind! And through it all you lull me with insipid distractions, hide from me her deepening wretchedness, and let her helplessly perish!

MEPHISTOHELES. She is not the first.[2]

FAUST. Cur! Abominable monster!—Transform him, thou infinite spirit,[3] change the viper back into its dog shape, as it was pleased to lope before me of a night, tumbling at the harmless wanderer's feet and dragging him down by the shoulders as he fell. Return him to his favorite guise, that he may crawl on his belly in the sand before me, and I may spurn him with my foot, the offal!—Not the first!—Piteous grief! Too piteous for human soul to grasp, that more than one being should have sunk to this depth of misery, that the first did not atone enough for the guilt of all the rest, writhing in deathly agony before the eyes of the eternally Forgiving! I am rent to the living core by this single one's suffering; you pass with a carefree grin over the fate of thousands!

MEPHISTOPHELES. There we are, back once more at our wits' end, where your human minds snap. Why make common cause with us if you cannot see it through? You would fly, yet are not proof against vertigo? Did we obtrude ourselves on you, or you on us?

FAUST. Do not flash your voracious tusks at me so! I am sickened!—Glorious lofty Spirit, who didst deign to appear before me, who knowest my heart and my soul, why forge me to this profligate who relishes injury and gloats over perdition?[4]

MEPHISTOPHELES. Are you finished?

FAUST. Save her! Or woe unto you! The most hideous curse upon you for millennia!

1. From the earliest stage of composition on *Faust*, the only scene in the published text which is prose. Faust's rage indicates that he has just learned of Gretchen's fate, though the later text of the "Walpurgis Night" (despite the appearance of the wraith) does not fully clarify how this has happened.

2. Such comment is made elsewhere in the literature of infanticide (as in the play *Infanticide* by Heinrich Leopold Wagner, 1747–79) and actually occurs in the documents pertaining to the trial of Susanna Margaretha Brandt in Frankfurt in 1772, thought to be Goethe's source for the Gretchen tragedy.

3. An invocation of the Earth Spirit from "Night," lines 482 ff.

4. This speech may be the germ of Faust's monologue (written in 1788) in "Forest and Cavern," lines 3240–50.

MEPHISTOPHELES. I cannot loose the vengeman's bonds, nor undo his bolts. "Save her!" Who was it that plunged her to her ruin? I or you?

[FAUST *gazes about him savagely.*]

MEPHISTOPHELES. Are you groping for thunder? It is well that it was not given you wretched mortals! To shatter the innocent reasoner—there's true tyrant fashion when seeking relief from any straits.

FAUST. Take me there! She shall be free!

MEPHISTOPHELES. And the danger you court? Know, there still weighs upon the town blood-guilt from your hand. Over the site of the slain hover avenging spirits in wait for the slayer's return.

FAUST. That, too, from you? Murder and death of a world upon your head, monster! Lead me there, I say, and free her!

MEPHISTOPHELES. I will lead you, and what I can perform, hear it! Do I have all the power on earth and in heaven? The gaoler's senses I will befog, you possess yourself of the keys and lead her out by human hand. I will stand guard! The magic steeds are ready, I will carry you off. Thus far my power.

FAUST. Up and away!

NIGHT[5]

Open Field

FAUST, MEPHISTOPHELES, *charging along on black steeds.*

FAUST. Why do they hover there, by the raven-stone?[6]

MEPHISTOPHELES. Who knows what they are brewing and wreaking.   4400

FAUST. Weaving and wavering, bowing and crouching . . .

MEPHISTOPHELES. A witches' guild.[7]

FAUST. Strewing and conjuring . . .

MEPHISTOPHELES. Away! Away!

DUNGEON†

FAUST, *holding a bunch of keys and a lamp, in front of a small iron door.*

FAUST. I shudder with a long-unwonted spell;   4405
  The woe of all mankind rends me apart.
  Behind this sodden wall here does she dwell,
  And her transgression was a trusting heart!

5. Faust and Mephistopheles, on the magic steeds, ride past the gallows where Gretchen is to be executed the following morning.
6. The block on which Gretchen will be beheaded.
7. Possibly influenced by the Witches in Shakespeare's *Macbeth* or similar figures in the famous ballad "Lenore" by Gottfried August Bürger (1747–94). The purpose of these witches is uncertain, though they may be consecrating the place for death according to some occult rite.

You shrink from being here!
You are afraid of seeing her!   4410
Forward! Your tarrying tardies forth her death.
    [*He seizes the lock. Singing is heard from inside.*[1]]
MARGARETE. My mother, the whore
                Who smothered me,
                My father, the knave
                Who made broth of me!   4415
                Wee sister shy
                The bones laid by
                In a cool dale;
                Of a sudden I was a fair nightingale;
                Fly, pretty bird, fly!   4420
FAUST. [*unlocking the door*] She little knows, her lover at the door
    Can hear the clanking chains, the rustling straw.
        [*He enters.*]
MARGARETE. [*trying to hide on her pallet*] Woe! They are coming.
    Bitter death is here!
FAUST. [*softly*] Hush! Hush! I've come to set you free.
MARGARETE. [*writhing up to him*] If you be human, pity my
    despair!   4425
FAUST. No, hush! You'll have the guards on me.
        [*He seizes the chains to unlock them.*]
MARGARETE. [*on her knees*] Say, who has given you this power,
    Headsman, over me?
    You come already at the midnight hour,
    Oh feel for me and let me be!   4430
    I'm due at dawn—is that too long?
        [*She rises to her feet.*]
    I am so young, oh God, so young
    And am to die!
    And I was pretty too, that was my ruin.
    Far is my friend, who once was nigh;   4435
    Torn lies the wreath, the petals strewn.
    Do not so roughly wrench my arm!
    Be gentle—have I done you any harm?
    Oh, let me not in vain implore—
    Have I so much as looked on you before?   4440
FAUST. Oh pity! I can bear no more.
MARGARETE. Now I am wholly in your might.
    Just let me nurse the child before.
    I hugged it to me all last night;

---

1. Gretchen's song is taken from the fairy tale of the "Juniper Tree," later included in the collection of the brothers Grimm. It is a story of primal horror: a wicked stepmother decapitates her young stepson, then serves him to her husband in a stew. After the father has eaten greedily, the grieving sister gathers the boy's bones and buries them beneath the juniper tree which grows upon the grave of their true mother. A miraculous bird suddenly appears in the tree singing the song here repeated by Gretchen in the original oral version.

They've taken it away to make me cry, 4445
And now they say I made it die,
And I shall never again be glad.
They sing songs about me. People are horrid!
An ancient folk tale ends like that,
Why blame me for it?[2] 4450

FAUST. [*throwing himself down*] See at your feet a lover kneeling,
Your grievous bonds to be unsealing!

MARGARETE. [*throwing herself down beside him*] Yes—let us beg
the saints for intercession!
This threshold beneath,
Under these steps, 4455
Hell's depths seethe,
The Devil, gnashing
In wrath appalling,
Crashing and brawling!

FAUST. [*loudly*] Gretchen! Gretchen! 4460

MARGARETE. [*attentively*] That was my dear one calling!
[*She jumps up. The chains fall off.*[3]]
Where is he? I heard him well, he called me.
I am free! There's nobody shall hold me.
To his arms I shall fly,
At his bosom lie! 4465
He called Gretchen! On the threshold he stood,
Through the clangor and howl of the Devil's brood,
Through the sneers, the infernal infuriate drone,
I knew it, the sweet, the enchanting tone.

FAUST. It is I!

MARGARETE. It's you! Oh, say it again! 4470
[*seizing him*] It's he! It is he! Where is all my pain?
The chains, the dungeon where I languish?
You, come to end my anguish!
I am saved![4]
Already I see the street anew, 4475
Where first you came upon my sight,
And the dear garden bright,
Where I and Marthe were awaiting you.

FAUST. [*straining away*] Come with me, come!

MARGARETE. Oh do not hurry!
I love to tarry where you tarry! [*caressing him*] 4480

FAUST. Hurry!
For if you tarry
We shall have much to rue it for.

MARGARETE. What? You can kiss no more?
My friend, so lately gone amiss, 4485

2. Gretchen confuses the song she has
just sung with the songs peddled by bal-
lad-mongers, who presumably will commemorate her own death in such a way.
3. Apparently a miraculous liberation
from her bonds.
4. Not in the *Urfaust*, this anticipates
the Voice from Above at the end of the
scene (see line 4611).

And has forgotten how to kiss?
Why am I fearful now in your embrace?
When from your speeches, from your face
A wave of very heaven overbroke me,
And you would kiss as if you were to choke me?   4490
Kiss me!
Or I'll kiss you!
    [*She embraces him.*]
Oh no—your lips are cold,
Are clay.
Where is your love abiding,   4495
In hiding?
Who took it away?
    [*She turns away from him.*]

FAUST. Take heart, dear love, come, let us go,
  I will caress you with a thousandfold glow;
  Just follow—that is all I beg of you!   4500

MARGARETE. [*turning toward him*] And it is really you? Is it
  all true?

FAUST. It is! Come on!

MARGARETE.   And you cast off this strap,
  Take me again into your lap.
  How is it that you do not shrink from me?
  Why, do you know, my friend, whom you set free?   4505

FAUST. Come, while the night is deep and stilled.

MARGARETE. My mother I killed,
  My child I drowned.
  Was it not given us both, and bound
  Thee too? Thee! No—I can't believe it yet.   4510
  Give me that hand! No, it's no dream!
  My dearest hand! But it feels wet!
  Oh! Wipe it off! It would seem
  There's blood on it.[5]
  Oh God! Whom did it hit?   4515
  Put up that sword,
  I beg of thee!

FAUST. Let what is past be past—oh Lord,
  You're killing me.

MARGARETE. No, no, you must outlive us!   4520
  Here is what manner of graves to give us,
  I charge you, go to it,
  Tomorrow do it.
  The best place give to my mother,
  Right next her put my brother,   4525
  And me at a distance, pray,
  But not too far away!

5. An allusion to Faust's murder of Valentine. The theme of guilt is derived
from the sleepwalking scene in Shakespeare's *Macbeth*, where Lady Macbeth
tries to wash out the spot of blood.

And the little one at my right breast.
There's no one else will lie by me![6]—
To nestle against your side was rest,   4530
Was purest, sweetest happiness!
But now it seems I lost the feel of you,
As if I had to brace myself, as if you too
Repulsed me, spurning my caress;
Yet it is you, as ever kind and dear.   4535

FAUST. Then if you feel it's I, come out from here!

MARGARETE. Out where?

FAUST.   To freedom.

MARGARETE.   Is the grave out there?
Death ambushed? Then I go with you!
From here to the eternal resting-place,   4540
Else not one pace—
You're leaving now? Oh Heinrich, if I could too!

FAUST. You can! Just want to! See, the door is open.

MARGARETE. It must not be; for me there is no hoping.
What use is fleeing? Still they lie in wait for you.   4545
I dread the beggar's staff and purse,
And a sinner's conscience makes it worse!
It's so wretched to err in far-off lands,
And still at last I'll fall into their hands!

FAUST. I'll stay with you.   4550

MARGARETE. Quick, run![7]
Save your little one.
Quick, follow the trail
Up the river dale,
Cross on the trunk   4555
Into the copse,
Left, where the planking stops
Into the lake.
Snatch it, for God's sake,
It hasn't sunk,   4560
Is kicking still!
Save it, save!

FAUST. Oh love—you rave!
One step—and you can leave at will!

MARGARETE. If only we were past that hill!   4565
There sits my mother upon a stone,
It sets my flesh ashiver,
There sits my mother upon a stone,
Her heavy head aquiver;
She won't beckon or nod, her head is too sore,   4570
She has slept so long, she'll awake no more.
She slept so that we might kiss.

---

6. As an executed infanticide, Gretchen would not be allowed burial in hallowed ground.

7. Gretchen imagines herself with Faust as a fugitive beggar, reenacting the drowning of her infant son.

Those were the days of our bliss!

FAUST. No pleading avails, no talking sense.

I must lift you up and carry you hence.   4575

MARGARETE. Let go! I'll suffer no violence!

Don't seize me with such murderous grasp!

Haven't I done all else you asked?

FAUST. The dawn shines gray! Oh love, my love!

MARGARETE. Day! Yes, day is here, it dawns so gray;   4480

This was to be my wedding-day![8]

Tell no one that Gretchen was yours already.

My poor wreath's shredding!

What's done is done!

We shall be one,   4585

But not at a wedding.

The crowd is thronging, no word, no laugh;

The square is milling,

The streets o'erfilling.

There tolls the bell, they break the staff.[9]   4490

How they pounce on me, bind me!

Already I am on the scaffold laid,

All necks shrink back from the winking blade

That will glint and find me.

Mute lies the world like the grave!   4595

FAUST. This day is my undoing!

MEPHISTOPHELES. [*appearing outside*] Up! Or you risk your ruin!

Womanish mutter! Vain chatter and putter!

My stallions shudder,

The night is ending.[1]   4600

MARGARETE. What rises there, from the pit ascending?

He! He! send him away!

What does he want on the solemn day?

He wants me![2]

FAUST.   You shall be whole!

MARGARETE. Judgment of God! To thee I gave my soul!   4605

MEPHISTOPHELES. [*to* FAUST] Come, come! Or I'll forsake both
her and thee.

MARGARETE. Thine I am, Father! Rescue me!

Ye heavenly host of angels, sally

To be my refuge, about me rally![3]

Heinrich! I shrink from thee!   4610

---

8. The association of execution day and wedding day, with the bell tolling and the townspeople gathering, is thematic to Gretchen's derangement, since Faust presumably never intended to marry her.
9. Traditionally, the "sinner's bell" was tolled as the condemned was led to execution, and a staff was broken over the head of the condemned at the gallows as a symbol of the death penalty.
1. The magic stallions must disappear at daybreak.
2. Sensing that Mephistopheles is the devil, Gretchen imagines that he has come to carry her off to Hell.
3. See Psalm 34:7, "The angel of the Lord encamps around those who fear him, and delivers them."

MEPHISTOPHELES. She is condemned!

VOICE. [*from above*]   Redeemed![4]

MEPHISTOPHELES. [*to* FAUST]   Hither! To me!

[*Disappears with* FAUST.]

VOICE. [*from within, dying away*] Heinrich! Heinrich![5]

4. Not in the *Urfaust*, which contained no hint of Gretchen's salvation.

5. This concluding line of *Part 1* echoes the traditional ending of the Faust legend, where eternal damnation is pronounced against Faust: "Fauste! Accusatus es!" "Fauste! Iudicatus es!" "Fauste! Fauste! In aeternum damnatus es!" In contrast to the assurance of Gretchen's salvation, Mephistopheles may thus seem to drag Faust off to damnation.

The Tragedy's Second Part in Five Acts

Act I

CHARMING LANDSCAPE†

FAUST, *bedded on a flowery mead, weary, restless, seeking sleep. Twilight. A ring of* SPIRITS, *graceful little shapes, floating and weaving.*

ARIEL.[1] [*singing, to the accompaniment of Aeolian harps*[2]]
When the vernal blossom showers
Wafting sink on all the earth,
And the fields their verdant dowers   4615
Shine to all of mortal birth,
Elfin power of fairies dainty
Hies to help where help it can,
Be he wicked, be he saintly,
Pitying the luckless man.   4620
Ye who surround this head with aerial wheeling,
Here prove the noble elfin way of healing,
Soothe now the wearied heart's contention dire,
Withdraw the searing arrows of remorse,
Of horrors suffered cleanse his soul entire.   4625
Four are the vigils of the night's dim course,[3]
With kindly care to plenish them conspire.
First rest his head upon the cooling pillow,
Then bathe him in the dew of Lethe's bourn;[4]
And soon the cramp-enrigored limbs grow willow,   4630
As strengthened he will rest against the morn;
Do fairest duty of the sprite—
Return him to the sacred light.

1. The same spirit of the air from Shakespeare's *Tempest* who concluded the "Walpurgis Night's Dream" (lines 4391 ff.). It may be assumed that he has come directly to this "charming landscape" with his companion spirits from the Intermezzo.
2. See "Dedication," line 28 and note.
3. An allusion to the traditional watches of the night, extending in three-hour periods from six in the evening to six in the morning. The four pauses would occur at 9:00 P.M., midnight, 3:00 A.M. and 6:00 A.M., respectively.
4. Drinking the waters of the river Lethe, according to Classical mythology, caused the mind to forget its earthly existence.

CHORUS. [*in alternating solos, duos, groups, and unison*[5]]
When an aerial mildness vagrant
Green-embowered lowland rings,   4635
Swathing mists and ambience fragrant
Dusk in its descending brings,
Languor dulcet, lisping lowly,
Lulls the heart to child's repose,
On the weary sufferer slowly   4640
These diurnal portals close.

Night has sunk already, darkling,
Ranking star on holy star,
Lambent lantern, tiny sparkling,
Shimmer near and glimmer far;   4645
There in cloudless night aglimmer,
Mirrored here in watery planes,
Sealing blissful rest, the shimmer
Of the moon in splendor reigns.

Rueful hours are fading, ending,   4650
Ache and bliss are washed away;
Bode it now! Already mending,
Trust the newly pledging day.
Vales are greening, hillocks swelling,
Bushes shady rest afford,   4655
And in pliant silver welling,
Crops are swaying harvestward.

Send your gaze to yonder brightness,
Wish on wish at will to reap,
You are cradled but in lightness,   4660
Cast it off, the shell of sleep!
Scruple not to be audacious
As the doubting rabble gasp;
All is open to the gracious
Who perceive and swiftly grasp.   4665
[*A stupendous clangor proclaims the approach of the sun.*]

ARIEL.   Hark the storm of hours rounding,
Clear to spirit ear rebounding,
Knell of day's renewal sounding!
Granite portals groan and clatter,
Wheels of Phoebus roll and spatter,   4670
What great din the dawning brings!
Trumpet-blaring and fanfaring,
Ears bedazing, eyes beglaring,
Fear to hear unheard-of things.
Blossom clusters seek to hide in,   4675

---

5. Goethe's original manuscript for this song contained four separate musical notations, indicating also the appropriate vigil of the night: Sérénade (evening song), Notturno (night song), Mattutino (morning song), and Réveille (call to awaken).

> Deep in sheltered hush abiding,
> Down the crags, beneath the leaf;
> If it strikes you, you are deaf.

FAUST. Revived, life's pulse is throbbing fresh and heady,
Gently to greet the dawn's ethereal wreathing;   4680
This night, too, earth, you have persisted steady
And, newly quickened, at my feet are breathing;
Fresh joy to grant you have already striven.
Already set resolve astir and seething
Toward peaks of being to be ever driven.—   4685
In luminous haze the world would pierce its cover,
The woods resound to myriad notes of living,
Down clefts and vales where drifts of vapor hover,
Cerulean clarity is downward seeping,
And twigs and branches, freshly laved, recover   4690
From fragrant depths of their enchanted sleeping;
Where leaf and petal drip from dewy shower,
Now hue on hue from somber ground are leaping,
And all about me turns to Eden's bower.

Raise up your gaze!—The mountain titans waken,   4695
Swift to proclaim the consecrated hour,
Of deathless lucence they have first partaken,
Before the day to lowlands here inclined it.
But now the alp's green slants have also shaken
The dusk, for gleam and contour newly minded,   4700
And light descends triumphant, stepwise darting;—
He clears the rim!—Alas, already blinded,
I turn aside, my mortal vision smarting.

Thus also, as we yearningly aspire
And find at last fulfillment's portals parting,   4705
Wrung within tender reach our prime desire,
There will erupt from those eternal porches,
Dumbfounding us, exorbitance of fire;
We only meant to kindle up life's torches,
And flame engulfs us, seas of torrid blazes!   4710
Love? Hatred? Which? envelops us and scorches,
Sends pain and joy in vast alternate phases,
Till we gaze back upon our homely planet
And shelter in most young of youthful hazes.

So, sun in back, my eye too weak to scan it,   4715
I rather follow, with entrancement growing,
The cataract that cleaves the jagged granite,
From fall to fall, in thousand leaps, outthrowing
A score of thousand streams in its revolving,
From upflung foam a soaring lacework blowing.   4720
But in what splendor from this storm evolving,

Vaults up the shimmering arc, in variance lasting,
Now purely limned and now in air dissolving,
A cooling fragrance all about it casting.
This mirrors all aspiring human action.   4725
On this your mind for clearer insight fasten:
That life is ours by colorful refraction.

IMPERIAL RESIDENCE[1]†

Throne Room

COUNCIL OF STATE *awaiting the* EMPEROR. *Trumpets.*

[COURT ATTENDANTS *of every sort, splendidly attired, step forward.*]
[*The* EMPEROR *reaches his throne, on his right the* ASTROLOGER.]

EMPEROR. My trusty well-beloved, well met,
  Assembled here from far and near;—
  The Magus is beside me here,   4730
  The Fool, though—he is missing yet.
SQUIRE. Why, hard behind your train of state
  He seemed to drop of his own weight;
  They bore his Lardship off from here,
  If dead or drunken was not clear.[2]   4735
SECOND SQUIRE. At once, with wondrous speed of pace
  Intrudes another in his place,
  In costly garb, but such a fop
  That people stare at him and stop;
  The sentries fling before his face   4740
  Their halberds crossed, his zeal to cool—
  Yet here he is, the daring fool!
MEPHISTOPHELES. [*kneeling near the throne*] What is desired and
      yet rejected?
  What is upbraided, and yet nursed?
  What is unceasingly protected?   4745
  What bitterly denounced and cursed?
  Whom must we shun by common warning?
  Whom are we glad to call by name?
  What would approach your royal awning?
  What is self-banished from the same?   4750
EMPEROR. Save us your riddles for the nonce!
  Conundrums are *de trop* for once;

1. Faust's visit to the court of the Holy Roman Emperor had been a central aspect of the Faust legend from the earliest chapbook of 1587. That Goethe intended initially to follow this tradition is apparent from the "Outline of the Contents for *Part II*," which he dictated for his autobiography in 1816 (see below).
2. Goethe acknowledged (in a conversation with Eckermann, October 1, 1827; see below) that the true jester had been removed by Mephistopheles.

These gentlemen will pose a few.—
I'd gladly hear them solved by you.
My former Fool, I fear, went far and wide;   **4755**
Assume his place and step up to my side.
    [MEPHISTOPHELES *ascends and takes his stand at left.*]
CROWD MUTTERING.[3] Another fool—For new dismay—
Whence did he come—How find his way—
The old one fell—He shot his wad—
There was a keg—Here is a rod—   **4760**
EMPEROR. Well, then, Our trusty ones who love Us,
Be welcome both from near and far,
You meet beneath a favoring star,
For hail and bliss are writ on high above us.
But why, with Carnival so near,   **4765**
The time we banish care and fear,
In bearded masquerade appear,
Serenely bent on pure enjoyment,
Should we consult in toilsome state employment?
Still, since you feel there is no other way,   **4770**
We are convened—each have his say.
CHANCELLOR. The highest Good has like a halo shone
About the Emperor's head, and he alone
May validly accord it from above:
The equity of Law!—What all men love,   **4775**
What all demand, desire, can't do without,
His office must dispense it all about.
But oh! what good is reason to man's mind,
To hands good will, to hearts intention kind,
When Commonwealth's in feverish upheaval,   **4780**
And evil rankly overhatches evil?
Who from this lofty hall could train his sight
Onto the realm, would view a nightmare fright,
Where failing plies misshapen failing,
A lawful lawlessness prevailing,   **4785**
A world of errors in its courses trailing.

This one a flock, that one a wife will seize,
From altars, cross and candle, jewelled host,
Of their possessions many years may boast
Unscathed of body, in untroubled ease.   **4790**
Now plaintiffs crowd the justice-dwelling,
The judge on lofty pillow lolls,
While just outside it, fiercely swelling,
The floodtide of rebellion rolls.
He robs and rapes without repentance   **4795**
Whom base accomplices support,
And Guilty! sounds the lying sentence,
Where innocence is sole resort.

3. Each half line in the following four lines (as in similar instances four times more in this scene—lines 4885–88, 4951–54, 4973–76, 4993–98) is spoken by an individual in the crowd of assembled courtiers.

The world is rent by mutual maiming,
Destroys what should be held in awe;   4800
The sense of right seems past reclaiming
Which solely leads us to the Law!
A man of pure intention bends
To bribes and flattery in time,
A judge who cannot punish ends   4805
By throwing in his lot with crime.
Would that my picture, somber as it was,
Could have been veiled in darker gauze.
    [*Pause.*]
Remedial counsels must be offered:
Privation dealt, privation suffered,   4810
Leave very Majesty bereft.

QUARTERMASTER. What wild unrest, these savage days!
A man is either slain or slays,
To all command remaining deaf.
Within their walls the burgomasters,   4815
Upon his rocky perch the knight,
They have conspired to outlast us
And hold their forces gathered tight.
The mercenary soldier rages,
Impatiently demands his pay,   4820
And if we did not owe him wages,
He would long since have run away.
If one denies what all expected,
One has stirred up a hornet's nest;
The realm they were to have protected   4825
Lies ravaged now and sore distressed.
Forfeit is half the earth's dominion,
They prey and loot without redress,
And though there still are kings, in their opinion
This hardly could concern them less.   4830

TREASURER. Who trusts in allies now or clients?
The subsidies in which we placed reliance
Run dry like water in a spout.
Oh Lord, in your dominions vast
To whom have all the titles passed?
Look where you will, incumbents new stand out,
And each would lord it all unheeding;
All we can do is just look on;
So many rights we have been ceding,
No right remains for us to lean upon.   4840
As for the parties, as they're called,
You cannot trust them nowadays;
You may be scolded or extolled,
Indifferent are abuse and praise.
The Ghibellines and Guelfs at war[4]   4845

4. An allusion to two warring factions in the Empire during the twelfth and thirteenth centuries, totally anachronistic here; presumably indicating any such warring factions.

Have gone in hiding to regroup;
Who helps his neighbor any more?
Each wants to cook his private soup.
The ports of gold are tightly jammed,
Each one has scraped and raked and crammed,   4850
But our exchequer is to let.

MARSHAL. To me, too, fate such ills dispenses:
Each day is to curtail expenses,
Each puts us deeper into debt,
And growing anguish will extort.   4855
The cooks and scullions need not fear;
Of boar and stag, of hare and deer,
Of ducks and geese and Gallic hens,
Allowances in kind, fixed rents,
There's still an inflow of a sort.   4860
But wine at last is running short.
Where cask on cask the vaults would stow us,
Prime vintages of premier growers,
My lords' relentless swillings show us
The final barrel's final drop.   4865
The City Council has to draw its pegs,
We're down to jugs and bowls from kegs,
Beneath the table lies the sop.
I am to settle all accounts,
The Jew will not rebate an ounce,   4870
Liens and attachments will pronounce
Which swallow up the next year's crop.
The swine are short of fattening forage,
We sleep on pillows under mortgage,
At table serve premasticated bread.   4875

EMPEROR. [*after some reflection, to* MEPHISTOPHELES] And you,
      fool, have no tale of woe to add?

MEPHISTOPHELES. Not I. To see the radiance effused
By you and yours! Could confidence be bruised
Where sovereignty brooks no insolence,
Where instant force stands ready for defense,   4880
Where goodwill acts, braced by intelligence,
And bounteous energy, instructed by good sense?
What could toward misadventure be combining,
Or gloom, where galaxies like these are shining?

PEOPLE MUTTERING. There is a rogue—Knows how to cast—   4885
He plays his fish—Both loose and fast—
What's up his sleeve—We know these jokes—
Some plan, what else—Another hoax—

MEPHISTOPHELES. Who in this world has not some lack or need?
One this, one that—here it is cash. Indeed,   4890
There is no gathering it off the pavement;
Yet wisdom taps its most profound encavement
In lodes and masonwork, where gold unstinted
Waits underground, both minted and unminted;

And who can raise it to the light of day?   4895
Man's gifts of Nature and of Mind, I say.
CHANCELLOR. Nature and Mind—un-Christianlike address,
Your atheist burns at the stake for less,
Because such talk is dangerous and wild.
Nature is sin, the Mind is Satan,   4900
Doubt they engender in their mating,
Their epicene misshapen child.
Not for this Empire! Only two professions
Have graced of old His Majesty's possessions
And worthily support his throne: 4905
Divines and knights—they quell upheaval,
And as twin shields against all evil
Call justly church and state their own.
The vulgar spirits of sedition
With aid and comfort, though, are plied;   4910
By whom? The heretic! The black magician!
Corrupting town and countryside.
Their kind it is you would be smuggling
Into this Court with jests and juggling;
A noisome changeling you are suckling,   4915
The wizard and the fool live hide in hide.
MEPHISTOPHELES. I recognize the learned scholar's speech!
What is not there to touch is out of reach,
What is impalpable is wholly missed,
The incomputable does not exist,   4920
What you can't weigh is air upon your scale,
What you don't coin you think does not avail.
EMPEROR. All this will hardly whisk our woes away;
What is your Lenten sermon good for, pray?
I'm sick of the perennial how and when;   4925
We're short of money—well, procure it then.
MEPHISTOPHELES. I can perform as much, more than you say;
It's easy—easy in a difficult way;
The stuff lies there all ready, yet to reach it—
There is the subtle art, and who can teach it?   4930
Just think: on those calamitous occasions
When land and folk were swept by armed invasions,
How this or that man, deep in terror's meshes,
Would rush to hide all that he held most precious.
This was in ancient Roman times the way,   4935
And ever since, till yesterday, today.
These hoards lie buried in the ground, and it—
The soil's the Emperor's, his the benefit.
TREASURER. This, from a fool, is not devoid of wit;
Indeed, thus runs an old Imperial writ.[5]   4940
CHANCELLOR. Gold bait—it smacks of Satan, not Messias;
That scheme sounds neither sound to me nor pious.

5. According to ancient law, any buried treasure lying below the cut of a plow would belong to the Emperor.

MARSHAL. For means to make our style at Court more regal
  I should be glad to be a shade illegal.
QUARTERMASTER. The fool is clever, pledges each his share;   4945
  You pay the soldier—how? he does not care.
MEPHISTOPHELES. Lest you suspect yourselves by me defrauded,
  Here is a man to ask! Astrologer much-lauded,
  Of every orbit knows the house, the hours;
  You tell us then: What say the heavenly powers?[6]   4950
MUTTERING. They're hand in glove—Two rogues as one—
  A royal fool—A charlatan—
  An ancient tune—And played to death—
  The Magus speaks—The Fool lends breath—
ASTROLOGER. [*speaking while* MEPHISTOPHELES *prompts*] The Sun
    himself is gold of pure assay,   4955
  Mercurius the Envoy serves for pay,
  Dame Venus charmed you all with her sweet grace;
  Early and late shows you her lovely face;
  Chaste Luna, all caprices, minces,
  Mars, though he miss you, yet his threat convinces;   4960
  Jupiter shines the brightest even so,
  Saturn is great, though distance dims his glow,
  As metal we do not respect him much,
  In value low, yet heavy to the touch.
  Yes! Sol and Luna in conjunction seen,   4965
  To silver gold, turns all the world serene.
  With this you may engarner all the rest,
  Palace and garden, rosy cheek and breast,
  All this provides the deeply learned man,[7]
  Who may accomplish what no other can.   4970
EMPEROR. I hear twice-echoed his address,
  And yet I hardly doubt it less.
MUTTERING. Oh, let us off—All warmed-up stuff—
  It's number mystic—Alchymistic—
  I heard it oft—False hope it puffed—   4975
  You probe the joke—It's up in smoke—
MEPHISTOPHELES. There they all stand amazed and snivel,
  Trust not the riches to be found,
  The one of mandrake root will drivel,
  The other of the coal-black hound.[8]   4980
  What use is it for one to giggle,
  The other of Black Art to wail,
  When all the time his soles will tickle,

6. The speech by the Astrologer which follows is spoken to promptings by Mephistopheles, indicating that the skepticism expressed by the crowd is well founded. The entire speech, however faithful to traditional astrological lore, is willfully mystifying and whimsical. Sun and moon, "Sol and Luna" (line 4965), representing the metals gold and silver, are said to be in conjunction, signifying happy times when all things may be accomplished.
7. An allusion to Faust.
8. The mandrake root, said to grow in human form beneath a gallows when the sperm of a hanged man fell to the earth, could be pulled out only by a "coal-black" dog according to an elaborate ritual. The root was thought to provide its owner with miraculous powers.

And his accustomed footstep fail?

You all can feel the secret virtue 4985
Of Nature constantly at work,
As rising effluents alert you
To powers that deep within her lurk.[9]
When every limb will twitch and tweak,
Uncanny signs disturb the mind,
There resolutely delve and seek, 4990
There lies the fiddler, lures the find!
MUTTERING. I drag my foot like weight of lead—
I feel the gout—My arm is dead—
My big toe itches— 4995
My back's in stitches—
By all such signs, here should be found
The very richest treasure-ground.
EMPEROR. To work! I fear you are adepter
At pledge than proof; go test your lather 5000
Of lies at once, let us foregather
In those fine halls. Downed sword and scepter,
With these imperial hands I shall,
If you speak truth, dig deep and well,
Or if you lie, send you to Hell. 5005
MEPHISTOPHELES. I'd find the way myself, came worst to worst . . .
Let me impress upon you first
What unclaimed riches many a place would yield.
A peasant ploughing in the field
Will lift a treasure from the furrow's fold, 5010
Or, as he scrapes a nitre-crusted wall,
Recoil, rejoice to see a roll of gold,
Pure gold, into his frugal fingers fall.
What vaultings must await exploding,
What shafts and passageways well worth unloading 5015
Be thrust at by the treasure-boding
New neighbors of the underground!
In long-sealed cellars to the seekers
Plump golden salvers, bowls, and beakers
In rich refulgent rows abound. 5020
Here goblets glow with ruby glare,
And, to employ them then and there,
An ancient vintage waits the taste;
But—as by experts truly told—
Its staves long sunk away in mold, 5025
In keg of tartar now encased.[1]
Such rare intoxicating essence,

9. An allusion to the notion that certain persons are sensitive to the magnetic force of buried metals. As he describes this, to lend support to the plan to uncover such treasures, Mephistopheles casts a spell on the crowd to cause them to have such feelings of sympathetic response.

1. According to popular belief, the tartar which forms as a deposit from old wine on the inside of old casks can be hard enough to contain the wine even after the wooden staves rot away.

As well as jeweled incandescence,
In dread nocturnal darkness hide.
The sage will search it readily enough;   5030
To see in light of day is trivial stuff,
It is in gloom that mysteries abide.

EMPEROR. Those you may keep! I like the noonday's lustre.
If something is of worth, it should pass muster.
Who can tell friend from villain in the night,   5035
When all the cows are black, all catseyes bright?
Those hoards of gold below ground, coin and cup,
Go pull your plough and pry them up.

MEPHISTOPHELES. Seize pick and spade yourself and battle,
Your peasant labor reaps great spoil,   5040
You'll see a flock of golden cattle
Be wrested from the harrowed soil.
Joyful, unstinting, from the treasure trove
Then deck yourself, adorn your lady love;
A rainbow shower of gems will freshly arm   5045
Both majesty and feminine charm.

EMPEROR. Get on, get on! How long shall we be bored?

ASTROLOGER. [MEPHISTOPHELES *prompting him as before*] Such
    urgent craving deign to quell, my Lord,
Let first the motley pageantry unroll;
A scattered purpose will not win the goal.   5050
In calm atonement let us shrive desire,
Seek to deserve the lower through the higher.
Who wants the good should be it first;
Who would sip joy should tame his thirst;
Let him tread ripened grapes who asks for wine;   5055
Who hopes for wonders, tread the path divine.

EMPEROR. So let the time in merriment be passed!
Then we shall welcome the Ash Wednesday Fast.
Meanwhile we celebrate in any case
Gay Carnival at all the wilder pace.   5060
[*Trumpets. Exeunt.*]

MEPHISTOPHELES. How luck and merit blend in men's affairs,
That never dawns upon this foolish lot;
If the philosopher's stone were theirs,
Stone would seek sage and find him not.

SPACIOUS HALL

*With Adjacent Apartments, Decorated and Festively
Adorned for the Carnival*[1]†

1. Goethe's "Carnival Masque" is modeled on festivals of the Italian courts during the Renaissance (familiar to him from such literary sources as Grazzini's book on the Florentine masques of the early sixteenth century under Lorenzo the Magnificent) and on eighteenth-century forms, as Goethe witnessed them during his Italian journey and described them in his essay on the Roman carnival.

HERALD.[2] Place not in Germany this revel,   5065
  With dance of fool and death and devil,
  Expect a feast of joy, not grief.[3]
  Our Lord, in his Italian questing,
  His profit in your pleasure vesting,
  The lofty Alpine bulwark breasting,   5070
  Has won himself a happy fief.
  First to the sacred soles he bent,
  For the Imperial rule to sue,
  And when to fetch the crown he went,
  He carried back the fool's cap too.[4]   5075
  Now we are all reborn to fit;
  Every sophisticated man
  Will snugly wrap his head and ears in it;
  It makes of him some sort of addle-wit,
  He hides therein such wisdom as he can.   5080
  I see the throng already starting,
  With cozy pairing, veering, parting,
  An eager concourse, group on group.
  Surge in, flow out, my busy jollies;
  Why, all the world, not just your troupe,   5085
  With all its hundred thousand follies
  Is but a vast collective dupe.

FLOWER GIRLS.[5] [*singing, to mandolin accompaniment*]
    Finery, to earn your favor,
    We have donned for this night's sport,
    Maids of Florence, come to savor   5090
    Splendors of the German court;

    Chestnut locks we twined with tippets
    Of the gayest floral art;
    Silken flosses, silken snippets,
    Playing their appointed part.   5095

    For we count it gift of reason,
    Altogether worth your praise,
    That our flowers outbloom each season
    In their artificial glaze.[6]

    Colored scraps and slips assorted   5100
    Found in symmetry their due;
    Any bit you're free to snort at,
    But the whole will dazzle you.

---

2. The first part of the masque (to line 5456) is introduced and staged by the Herald, who serves as a master of ceremonies.
3. The Herald alludes by contrast to German carnival practice (the *Fast-nacht*) and perhaps to the medieval "Dance of Death."
4. These lines suggest that the Emperor brought back the Italian masque when he visited Rome for his coronation by the Pope (whose slippers he kissed, line 5072).
5. These are apparently natives of Florence dressed in a traditional costume of the Italian masque.
6. The flowers are artificial, imported in Goethe's day from Italy.

Flower girls appeal, admit it,
Charmingly to eyes and hearts;   5105
For a bond of nature fitted
Female temper for the arts.

HERALD. Show us on your head the precious
   Burden carried in each basket,
   From your hampers what is freshest,   5110
   What each fancies, let him ask it.
   Quick, let lanes in leafy shrouding
   Into garden paths be made us,
   Worthy of our eager crowding
   Are both merchandise and traders.   5115

FLOWER GIRLS. Strike your bargains, gaily playing,
            But tonight no bargain binds!
            By an apt and pithy saying
            May each know the thing he finds.[7]

OLIVE BRANCH BEARING FRUIT. Bursts of bloom I envy none,   5120
   All contrarity I shun—
   Blight on all for which I stand.
   Am I not the country's marrow,
   Warrant sure to plow and harrow,
   Sign of peace to every land?   5125
   Here I hope to—happy duty—
   Grace a head of worth and beauty.

WREATH OF GOLDEN CORN-EARS. Wreaths to charm and to embellish
   Ceres'[8] gifts will make on you:
   What is welfare's foremost relish   5130
   Be to you adornment too.

FANCY WREATH. Hollyhock and mallow aping,
   Wondrous blossom from the moss!
   This is none of Nature's shaping,
   Fashion, though, may breed it thus.   5135

FANCY BOUQUET.
            It would stump botanic masters
            All the way to Theophrastus[9]
            To define me, yet I rather
            Hope to please the one or other,
            One to whom I would consign me   5140
            If into her hairs she'd twine me,
            If she should decide to bear me
            Off and at her bosom wear me.

ROSEBUDS. [*challenge*]
            Let the motley fancies flower
            For the fashion of the hour,   5145
            Wondrously and subtly molded,

---

7. The Flower Girls here introduce figures dressed to represent the kind of
flower which they are selling.
8. Ceres was the Roman goddess of the
grain.
9. Theophrastus of Lesbos (b. 390 B.C.),
a Greek philosopher, student of Aristotle, who wrote several works on plants.

Nature never thus unfolded:
Golden bells on verdant stalks
Peep from out luxurious locks!—
But we—stay concealed, reminders   5150
Of delight for lucky finders.
Summer come, itself proclaiming
Season of the rosebud's flaming,
Who but finds it bliss enchanting?
Charms of pledging, charms of granting   5155
In the realm of Flora[1] strike
Gaze and sense and heart alike.

[*Under the greenery of leafy lanes the* FLOWER GIRLS
daintily arrange their wares.]

GARDENERS. [*singing to the accompaniment of lutes*][2]
Let the blossoms' meretricious
Compliments adorn your tresses,
Fruits attract without caresses,   5160
In the tasting prove delicious.
Fruit in tawny-purple flushes
Buy! Your palate, tongue, and budget,
Not the eye, are fit to judge it—
Peach and plum and cherry luscious.   5165

Fruits for joy and taste to sample
At their ripest and most ample!
For the rose are poems written,
But the apple should be bitten.

Suffer us to build a neighbor   5170
To your youthful floral spray,
Heaping bounty ripe, we labor
To erect a twin display.
Gay with bunting, booth and arbor,
Gaily vine-beribboned bower,   5175
Everything together harbor,
Bud and foliage, fruit and flower.

[*Alternating in song, accompanied by mandolins and lutes,
the two choruses continue to dress and heap their wares up
by stages and to invite customers.*]

[*Enter* MOTHER *and* DAUGHTER.[3]]

MOTHER.   When you were my tiny girl
I primped you in your carriage,
Sweet of face and fine of curl,   5180
Fairest in the parish;
Thought of you—so high—allied

---

1. The Roman goddess of flowers.
2. The Gardeners, accompanied by archaic bass lutes (in contrast to the mandolins which accompanied the Flower Girls), offer ripe fruit for sale in competition with the flowers.

3. In association with the playful juxtaposition of the sale of flowers and sensuous pleasure, this anxious mother uses the opportunity to put her daughter on display, as if she also were for sale.

To the richest man for bride,
Saw my girl in marriage.

Many years have since, alas,   5185
Uselessly been squandered,
Spooners, suitors, used to pass,
Stopped and swiftly wandered.
One to whirling reel you begged,
One your elbow subtly egged   5190
To endearments pondered.

Feasts we would on purpose plan
Every time fell short there,
Games of forfeit and third-man⁴
Didn't what they ought there.   5195
But tonight, love, bait your trap,
Fools are loose, so spread your lap,
One may well be caught there.

[PLAYMATES, *young and beautiful, join the scene; uncon-
strained chattering is heard.* FISHERMEN *and* BIRDCATCHERS,
*equipped with nets, rods, lime-twigs, and other gear, mingle
with the pretty girls. Efforts on both sides to attract, cap-
tivate, evade, and detain occasion most agreeable dialogues.*]

WOODCUTTERS. [*entering, boisterous and uncouth*]⁵
Give room! Untrammeled!
We must be limber,   5200
We fell the timber,
Crunch, crash! We're rugged,
And where we lug it
Someone is pommeled.
If praise is needed,   5205
Weigh this and heed it:
Unless the crude ones
Performed their own,
How would the shrewd ones
Get on alone,   5210
For all they're petted?
You hark to reason!
You'd die a-freezing
Unless we sweated.

PULCINELLI.⁶ [*awkward to the point of farce*]
You are the zanies,   5215
For drudging sent.
We are the brainies
Who never bent;
For our caps,

4. Parlor games familiar in Goethe's time.
5. In contrast to the dance-like pantomime of Flower Girls and Gardeners, the masque now shifts to clumsier groups representing various fringes of human society.
6. Maskers wearing the traditional clown costume of Italian popular comedy, including dunce caps and colorful, baggy suits.

Jackets, and flaps   5220
Are feather-light wraps.
We take our pleasure
As market trippers,
In constant leisure
And floppy slippers,   5225
On saunters bent
Or standing and gaping,
Each other japing;
Upon such calls
Through crowded stalls   5230
With eel-like slipping
We join for skipping,
Wild merriment.
You may commend us
Or reprehend us,   5235
We are content.

PARASITES.[7] [*suggestively fawning*]
You trusty porters
With your good takers,
The charcoal-makers,
Are who support us.   5240
For all that bowing,
Nodding, allowing,
Involute phrases'
Dubious praises,
Blow hot and cold,   5245
As one may hold,
What could it profit?
Take heaven's fire,
Say lightning dire
Were splintered off it—   5250
If wood were missing
Or kindling sawed of it,
Would hearth be hissing
The long and broad of it?
Such broiling and frizzling,   5255
Such boiling and sizzling!
Smack-lips are stirred,
Plate-lickers spurred
By roasts delicious,
By whiff of fishes,   5260
To feats of fable
At patron's table.

TOPER. [*under the influence*][8]
Just so nothing is contrary!

---

7. Stock figures from ancient comedy, possibly representing political opportunists.

8. The costume of the drunkard was traditional to the carnival. He invites all whom he meets to drink along with him.

Ah, I feel so fine and free;
Lusty mood and chanties merry,   5265
All myself procured for me.
So I'm drinking, drink-a-drink!
Click your glasses, clink-a-clink!
Hallo, back there, you come up!
Clink with me and down your cup.   5270

How my missus railed and butted,
Bridling at these motley drapes,
And, however much I strutted,
Scolded me a jackanapes.
But I'm drinking! Drink-a-drink!   5275
Glasses tinkling, clink-a-clink!
Toast you, all you masks-on-sticks!
Let it tinkle as it clicks.

I'm all right here, do not shake me,
For the place is fine for thirst.   5280
If the landlord will not stake me,
Wife or maid will, worst to worst.
Still I'm drinking! Drink-a-drink!
Up, you others! Clink-a-clink!
Everyone, to everyone!   5285
Seems to me the thing's well done.

Let my pleasures overtake me;
If they get a little strong,
Let me lie and do not wake me,
I've been on my feet too long.   5290

CHORUS.   Every brother drink, oh drink!
Toast each other, tink-a-tink!
Firmly sit your bench, each one,
That one down there is all done.

[*The* HERALD *announces various* POETS, *poets of nature,
bards of Court and Chivalry, lyricists as well as rhapsodists.
In the throng of competitors of every sort no one allows the
other to recite. One shuffles by with a few words*][9]

SATIRIST.   As a poet-pamphleteer,   5295
What would be my delight?
If they let me sing and cite
What no one wants to hear.

[*The* POETS *nocturnal and sepulchral beg to be excused
because they are just then engaged in most interesting
conversation with a freshly-formed vampire, which might
possibly give rise to a new mode of literature;*][1] *the* HERALD

---

9. Goethe intended to write verses sati-
rizing various contemporary schools of
poetry but did not complete the scene.
Poets of nature were writers of ballads
and folk songs; bards of Court and
Chivalry were pseudo-medieval poets

who imitated the romances and the
Minnesang.
1. An allusion to supernatural and
Gothic tendencies in later Romantic fiction (such as E. T. A. Hoffmann's *Night
Pieces* of 1817 and Polidori's *Vampire* of
1819).

must admit the force of this, and meanwhile calls upon
Greek mythology, which even in modern guise loses noth-
ing of its character or charm.]
[*The* GRACES.[2]]

AGLAIA. It is grace we bring to living;
Equal grace impart to giving.   5300

HEGEMONE. Equal grace be in receiving,
Graceful is a wish's achieving.

EUPHROSYNE. And in bounds of tranquil living,
Highest grace be in thanksgiving.
[*The* PARCAE.[3]]

ATROPOS. Me, the eldest, they selected   5305
To be spinning here this once;
Much is mused on, much reflected,
As the tender life-thread runs.

Finest flax I sought for sleaving,
Screened you soft and limber strands;
How to smooth it slim and even
Cunning finger understands.

Lest of revelry and dancing
You too lavishly partake,
Mark this tenuous thread's advancing   5315
And beware! For it might break!

CLOTHO. I have latterly been handed,
You must know, the shears of fate;
For our Elder's[4] ways were branded
Unacceptable of late.   5320

Rankly useless strands she nurses
Over-long in air and light,
Hopes of utmost worth she curses,
Snapping, to sepulchral night.

Yet I too have erred already   5325
Scores of times, in youthful way;
To contain myself and steady,
See, my shears are sheathed today.

So I gladly curb my powers,
Look with kindness on this fair;   5330
You, exempt these festive hours,
Revel on with never a care.

2. The Graces were goddesses of social
intercourse in general. The name "Hegemone" ("the one who leads the way")
is substituted for the more traditional
"Thalia." "Aglaia" ("the resplendent
one") and "Euphrosyne" ("the merry
one") are the other two traditional
names.

3. The three Parcae (Fates) were traditionally associated with spinning the
thread of human life (Clotho), measuring its length (Lachesis), and cutting it
at death (Atropos). Their roles are playfully confused for this festival occasion.
4. The Elder is Atropos.

LACHESIS. I, who am alone discerning,
Kept the sorting of the thread,
And my reel, though ever turning,   5335
Never yet has oversped.

Fibers sliding, fibers spooling,
Each upon its track I guide,
Every outflow overruling,   5340
Bend it to a rounded glide.

If I once forgot or slumbered,
I would fear for mankind bane,
Hours are counted, years are numbered,
And the weaver takes the skein.

HERALD. Who now approach, you will not recognize,   5345
However steeped in ancient screeds you be;
You would esteem them welcome company,
To look at them, who so much ill devise.

They are the Furies,[5] no one will believe us,
Are pretty, young in years, well-shapen, kind;   5350
But try to mingle with them, you will find
How serpentinely sore such doves may grieve us.

They're vicious—but today, 'mid all and sundry,
When every fool will advertise his faults,
They too forgo dissembling their assaults,   5355
And own themselves a plague on town and country.
    [*The* FURIES.]

ALECTO. No good to warn you, you will trust us still,
We are a pretty, young, insinuating coven;
If one among you has a loving-doving,
We'll stroke him under chin and ears until—   5360

Till eye to eye with him we may confide:
For this one, that one she is also primping,
Is hollow-headed, pigeon-chested, limping,
And good for nothing, if his promised bride.
His bride will next be molded in our fingers: 5365
Her friend has, not so many weeks ago,
Disparaged her before Miss So-and-so!—
They make it up, but yet a something lingers.

MEGAERA. All these are harmless games! for, once they marry,
The task is mine; I know how to embroil   5370
The fairest happiness in whim and bile;
The hours are variable, men will vary.

None firmly clasps the wished within his arm

---

5. The Furies were traditionally associated with anger (Alecto), envy (Megaera), and vengeance (Tisiphone).
Here they perform social roles as the
cause of, respectively, lovers' quarrels,
infidelity in marriage, and the jilted lover's revenge.

Without for yet more wished inanely lusting,
From highest bliss of which he has the custom;   5375
He flees the sun and goes the frost to warm.

All this I am most expert at pursuing,
By sending Asmodeus,[6] faithful devil,
At proper time to sow out what is evil,
And thus by pairs the human race undoing.   5380
TISIPHONE. Not barbed tongues, but poison, dagger
    Do I sharpen for the traitor,
    Change your love and sooner, later,
    Under vengeance you will stagger.

    What of sweetness may perfuse it   5385
    Must be turned to gall and tartar;
    There's no bargaining, no barter
    Over circumstance—he rues it.

    No one urge me to forgive!
    At the cliffs my cause I monish,   5390
    Echo, listen! answers 'punish!';
    He who changes shall not live.
HERALD. Be pleased to step aside, if you don't mind,
What now approaches is not of your kind.[7]
A cumbrous mountain lumbering up one sees,   5395
Its flanks ornate with colored tapestries;
A snaking trunk, a head with tusks immense,
A mystery—but I reveal its sense.
A lady rides his neck, shaped slimly-nicely,
With slender wand she guides his course precisely.   5400
The other, upright, glorious to see,
Blinds me with luster of high majesty.
Below, two noble ladies shackles carry,
The one of anxious mien, the other merry,
One wishing, one perceiving herself free.   5405
Let each announce who she might be.
FEAR.   Smouldering torches, candles, lanterns
    Glint through this disordered train,
    Oh, amid these lying phantoms
    I am prisoned by this chain.   5410

    Off, you tittering detractors!
    Suspect are your grins to see;
    All my foes and malefactors
    On this night beleaguer me.

6. Asmodeus is an evil spirit from Jewish demonology who causes discord between husband and wife.
7. As the climax of the allegorical sequence the pageant of Victory appears. The elephant presumably represents Power, and the lady leading him is Intelligence. Seated upon his back is Victory on her throne, and on either side walk Fear and Hope, two ladies in chains. Goethe may here have been influenced by accounts of processions in antiquity which used elephants (as in the *Triumph of Caesar* by the Italian painter Andrea Mantegna, 1431–1506).

Ha! a friend has turned to foe   5415
His disguise I know unasked;
That one sought my death, I know,
There he creeps away, unmasked.

Anywhere I'd gladly wander
To the outside world in flight;   5420
But the threat of ruin yonder
Holds me here 'twixt fog and fright.

HOPE.   Dearest sisters, friendly greetings.
Though two nights of festive meetings
Saw you mummed by mask and curtain,   5425
Still I know of you for certain
You will stand unveiled tomorrow.
And if by the torches' blaze
We were ill at ease and drooping,
Surely then, in smiling days,   5430
We shall roam sweet pastures, musing,
As may please us, free of sorrow,
Now alone, now gaily grouping,
Still or active, by our choosing,
Free of care's incessant driving,   5435
Never lacking, ever striving;
Like an ever-welcome guest
We feel certain of our ground:
We are confident the best
Must be somewhere to be found.   5440

INTELLIGENCE.   Two worst foes of man's existence,
Fear and Hope, in chains enslaved,
I retain at prudent distance;
All step back there! you are saved.

See this live colossus, cumbrous,   5445
Turret-laden, in my sway,
How untiringly he lumbers
Step by step his arduous way.

Lastly, though, enthroned on high,
See the goddess with her spacious   5450
Wing-spread, ever poised to fly
For the prize of the audacious.

Rays of gloria proclaim her,
Shining far and wide wherever;
And Victoria we name her,   5455
Patroness of all endeavor.

ZOILO-THERSITES.[8] Bah! Pooh! I enter right on cue

---

8. Mephistopheles, still in his role of court jester, enters as the traditional anti-masque, in the guise of the Classical debunkers: Zoilos, a scathing critic of Homer, and Thersites, the ugly and dissident rogue from the *Iliad* (II).

To scold the worthless lot of you!
But what I choose for target fair
Is Lady Victory up there,   5460
No doubt she thinks her snowy wings
Make her an eagle, of all things,
And that whichever way she stirs
All folk and property are hers;
But when a feat has earned its prize,   5465
It promptly makes my hackles rise.
For high laid low, and low made high,
The crooked straight, the straight awry,
Just that keeps me in health and mirth,
That's how I relish things on earth.   5470
HERALD. Then feel, you wretched mongrel-birth,
The pious mace's master-blow,
There, writhe and curl you ever so!⁹—
But how the dwarfish double stump
So swiftly forms a nauseous clump!—   5475
The clump becomes an egg—o wonder!
And now balloons and bursts asunder.
A double issue, hatched from that,
Falls out, an adder and a bat;
In dust the one is wriggling off,   5480
The other blackly darts aloft,
To reunite their stratagem;
I would not make a third with them.¹
MUTTERING. Quick! there's dancing, bands at play—
No! I wish I were away—   5485
Don't you feel all snarled and clewed
By that godless phantom brood?
Something swooped and touched my hair—
At my foot I was aware—
None of us is injured here—   5490
Still we all are put in fear—
What the monsters counted on
They have done—the fun is gone.
HERALD. Ever since I first accepted
Herald's duty at the pageants,   5495
I have watched the gate and kept it
Closed to any baneful agents
Apt to mar the festive flavor;
And I neither wink nor waver.
Yet I fear that ghostly raiders   5500
Through the windows might invade us,
And from spooks and spells that bait you
I could never liberate you.

---

9. The Herald strikes him with his staff,
as Odysseus struck Thersites in the *Iliad*
(II.265).
1. Mephistopheles, employing his devilish
magic, transforms himself into a gigantic
egg which hatches into an adder and a
bat.

If the dwarf was suspect-seeming,
Yonder, look! a mighty streaming.   5505
Of the figures there, my station
Calls for due interpretation.
But what passes comprehension,
Explanation also passes,
Help you all my good intention!—   5510
See it sweeping through the masses?[2]—
Splendid chariot, with four horses,
All the crowd with ease percourses;
Yet it crosses never parting,
I see no one sideways darting.   5515
Colorful, it glitters yonder—
Errant sparkles gleam and wander,
Magic lantern, one might ponder?—
Storms up with tempestuous snort.
All make way! I shudder!   5520

BOY CHARIOTEER.[3]   Halt!
Steeds of mine, your pinions idle,
Honor the accustomed bridle,
As I curb you, curb your fire,
Rush along when I inspire—
To these rooms let us add luster!   5525
Look about you, how they cluster,
Our admirers, round on round.
Herald, up, as you are bound,
And before afar we flee,
Name us here, describe and show us;
We are allegories, see,
And as such you ought to know us.

HERALD. I could not tell your name by sight;
But to describe you—that I might.

BOY CHARIOTEER. Why don't you try!   5535

HERALD.   One may aver:
For one thing, you are young and fair.
A half-grown boy; the ladies, though, might own
That they would gladly see you fully grown.
You seem to me a ladies' man *in spe*,
A native-born seducer, I should say.   5540

BOY CHARIOTEER. Not bad at all! Go on, let's see—
You earn yourself the riddle's merry key.

HERALD. The eye's black lightning, ringlets dusky,
Cheered by a jewelled band for crown!

2. This new float, prepared by Mephistopheles and Faust, is unexpected and beyond the Herald's ability to interpret. Upon a splendid carriage hitched to dragons (cf. lines 5677 ff.) rides Plutus, the god of wealth (Faust in disguise), pulled by the Boy Charioteer.

3. In a conversation with Eckermann (December 20, 1829; see below) Goethe called this allegorical figure the personification of poetry, an embodiment of the same spirit who appears in Act III as Euphorion, offspring of Faust and Helena.

And what a captivating gown   5545
Flows from your shoulders to the buskin
With purple hem and glittery down!
You could be slanged a girl with ease,
But as you are, for weal or woe,
The girls would eye you even so.   5550
They'd help you learn your ABC's.

BOY CHARIOTEER. And this one, who, a form of splendor,
Enthroned upon the chariot glows?

HERALD. He seems a monarch, rich and tender,
He prospers whom his favor chose!   5555
There's nothing left for his endeavor,
For any hardship spies his gaze,
His pure delight in giving ever
Both bliss and luxury outweighs.

BOY CHARIOTEER. You must not rest content with these—   5560
Supply more details if you please.

HERALD. How can one capture worth and grace?
We saw the healthful, rounded face,
The swelling lips, the cheeks full-blown
That by the splendid turban shone;   5565
The robe's luxurious caress!
And what of his august address?
Renown and reign is what I sense.

BOY CHARIOTEER. Plutus, the god of opulence,[4]
Comes driving up in pomp and state,   5570
His Majesty can hardly wait.

HERALD. Now tell us who, and how, yourself may be?

BOY CHARIOTEER. I am profusion, I am poetry;[5]
The poet who fulfills himself
By squandering his inmost wealth.   5575
I, too, am rich beyond all measure,
Count myself Plutus-like in treasure,
I quicken and adorn his feast,
By lavishing what he has least.

HERALD. This boasting suits you all too well,   5580
Now for a sample of your spell.

BOY CHARIOTEER. I snap my fingers, see! it gleams
About the wheels in sparkles, beams.
A string of pearls goes skimming there;
    [*Keeps snapping his fingers all about.*]
There, golden clasps for neck and ear;   5585
Now precious combs and diadems,
Now, set in rings, the choicest gems;
Sometimes a flick of flame I throw,
To see what it might set aglow.

4. The Greek word *ploutos* means "wealth." There is an ancient connection with the Greek and Roman god of the underworld, Pluto (cf. Plato, *Cratylus,* 403A), "so called because riches arise from the earth."
5. See note to line 5521.

HERALD. Look, grasping, snatching, my fine host!   5590
  The giver comes to grief almost.
  Bright gems, his snapping fingers pour them,
  And right and left, they're snapping for them.
  But now the scheme is twisted meanly:
  What one has grasped, however keenly,   5595
  Affords but wretched ownership,
  The keepsake flutters from his grip,
  Like dream dissolves the pearly band,
  And beetles scamper in his hand,
  When he, poor fellow, throws them out,   5600
  Around his head they buzz about,
  The others, for more solid prize,
  Are left with wanton butterflies.
  The scamp, for rich rewards foretold
  He offers but the gleam of gold!   5605

BOY CHARIOTEER. How to announce the masks, you know, I gather,
  Their inwardness to fathom, though, is rather
  Beyond the herald's courtly sphere;
  Acuter sight is needed here.
  But any acrimony I eschew;   5610
  With speech and question, Sire, I turn to you.
  [*to* PLUTUS] Did you not to my hands entrust
  The chariot's fourfold rushing gust?
  Did I not steer it as you led me?
  Am I not where your finger sped me?   5615
  Did I not fly on pinions eager
  To win the palm for your quadriga?
  For you, as often as I fought
  I came triumphant from the quarrel;
  If now your brow is decked with laurel,   5620
  By this my mind and hand was it not wrought?

PLUTUS. If testimony's due for all to hear it,
  I gladly say: You're spirit of my spirit.
  Your deeds enact my mind alone,
  Your wealth is greater than my own.   5625
  This twig of green, your service to redeem,
  Above all crowns and circlets I esteem;
  Hear all this truthful eulogy:
  My cherished son, I take delight in thee.[6]

BOY CHARIOTEER. The greatest gifts at my command,   5630
  See! I have spread with lavish hand.[7]
  On this or that one's head there flare
  The flamelets that I scattered there,
  From one onto the next it skips,

---

6. A playful paraphrase of the Father's words at the baptism of Christ, Matthew 3:17, "This is my beloved Son, with whom I am well pleased."
7. Possibly an allusion to the spirit at Pentecost, which seized the apostles, appearing as a flame above their heads and causing them to speak in tongues (Acts 2:1–4).

On this one rests, from that one slips,   5635
But seldom glares in upward rush
To glow in sudden transient flush;
On many, unaware of it,
It sadly guts as soon as lit.

FEMALE GOSSIP. The one up on the chariot there,   5640
            He is a charlatan, I swear;
            Hunched up in back, an owlish clown,
            By thirst and hunger shriveled down,
            As no one ever saw him yet;
            He cannot feel a pinch, I bet.[8]   5645

THE STARVELING. Shoo, sickening females, let me go,
You I can never suit, I know.
When yet the wifely virtues shone,
As *Avaritia* I was known;
Domestic rules were sound and stout: 5650
They meant much in, and nothing out!
I scrounged for chest and cabinet;
Now they would make a vice of it.
Since women, though, have not been craving
Of late to learn the art of saving,   5655
And like your true delinquent shopper
Have three desires for every copper,
The hapless husband sorely frets,
Whichever way he looks are debts;
And what her distaff may recover   5660
Goes for the body of her lover;
Or dining better, drinking more
With the philanderers' plaguey corps;
This makes my love of gold more tender:
My name is Greed, and male my gender!   5665

LEADER OF THE WOMEN. Share, dragon, dragon's hoarding honors!
It's all just make-believe and bluff:
He's come to sic our husbands on us,
Who are quite troublesome enough.

WOMEN EN MASSE. That scarecrow! Slap him off his wagon!   5670
            Scare us, that dried-up gallow-log?
            We, shy before his shriveled mug?
            Who minds a wood-and-paper dragon?
            Let's up and at him, kick and slug!

HERALD. To order! Order, by my mace!—   5675
But hardly needed is my calling,
See how the grisly monsters, crawling
Within the quickly-yielded space,
Their double pairs of wings unspread.[9]

---

8. This "starveling" whom they describe is Mephistopheles in yet another disguise, who first calls himself *Avaritia* (line 5649), then Greed (line 5665).

9. These allegorical dragons are attached to the float (see note to line 5510) as guardians of the treasure, presumably controlled by the Boy Charioteer.

The dragons undulate in ire   5680
Their scaly gorges, spewing fire;
The place is clear, the crowd has fled.
  [PLUTUS *descends from the chariot*.]
HERALD. Now he descends, how like a king!
  He makes a sign, the dragons swing
  The heavy coffer down the chariot   5685
  Whereon both gold and Greed were carried,
  And set it down before his feet;
  A marvel, was the way of it.
PLUTUS. [*to* CHARIOTEER] Now you are rid of weights that over-
    whelm,
  Are free and fresh; now briskly to your realm![1]   5690
  Here it is not! Here we are hemmed, surrounded
  By weird contortions, checkered, wild, confounded.
  Where clear your gaze to clear and lovely regions,
  But in yourself your trust and sole allegiance,
  Where only please the beautiful, the good,   5695
  There go create your world—to solitude!
BOY CHARIOTEER. As I will be your cherished envoy, then,
  So I shall love you as my next of kin.
  Where you reside is plenty; where I rest
  All feel themselves most gloriously blessed.   5700
  They often veer in life's perplexity:
  Should they devote themselves to you? to me?
  While idleness rewards your devotees,
  My followers can never rest at ease.
  Nor are my actions furtive or concealed,   5705
  I only have to breathe to stand revealed.
  Farewell! You grudge me not my bliss, I know,
  But your first lisp will fetch me, even so.
    [*Exits, as he came*.]
PLUTUS. Time now to loose the hoard of gems and metal!
  To strike the locks I use the Herald's rod.   5710
  It opens! Watch! In brazen bowl and kettle
  It starts uncoiling, wells with golden blood,
  Upmost the wealth of chain and ring and crown;
  It seethes and would, engulfing, melt it down.
CRIES OF THE CROWD, ALTERNATING.
            Look here! and there! just see it brim,   5715
            It fills the coffer to the rim;
            Great vessels, gold ones, swallowing,
            Great rolls of coinage wallowing.—
            The ducats flip like newly struck,
            My heart goes skipping with such luck—   5720
            To look on all I hankered for!
            There they go rolling on the floor.—

1. This recalls Prospero's farewell speech   (V.i.318 ff.): "Then to the elements/Be
to Ariel in Shakespeare's *Tempest*   free, and fare thou well!"

It's offered you, just don't delay,
You stoop and get up rich that way.—
And we fall to and lightning-swift   5725
Pounce on the chest and make short shrift.

HERALD. Why do you scramble, fools? What for?
This is all mummery, no more;
All that is asked tonight is mirth;
You think they'd give you gold or worth?   5730
Why, in this game to entertain
Tin tokens would be excess gain.
You dolts! a graceful trick, forsooth,
Must promptly count for clumsy truth.
What's truth to you—when all you've pawed   5735
By random grabs was musty fraud?
Mummed Plutus, hero of the masque,
Drive me this rabble off, I ask.

PLUTUS. What could be fitter than your mace?
Lend it to me for a short space.—   5740
I dip it, quick, in seething heat.—
Now, masques! be nimble on your feet.
Bright flash, sparks spurting to and fro!
The end already is aglow.
Whoever has too rashly neared   5745
At once is mercilessly seared—
With this I start upon my round.

TUMULT AND SHOUTS.
Help! it's all up with us! Give ground,
Escape who can escape from here!—
Stand back, make room there, in the rear!   5750
Hot sparks are flying in my face.—
I feel the heavy glowing mace—
We're lost and done for, one and all.—
Give way, you masquers' serried wall!
Fall back, fall back, insane array!   5755
Oh, had I wings, I'd fly away.—

PLUTUS. The circle is already cleared,
And no one, I believe, is seared.
The rabble shrinks,
Scared off, methinks.—   5760
For pledge of order now restored
I draw, invisibly, a cord.

HERALD. You worked a brilliant feat of force,
How much I owe your shrewd resource!

PLUTUS. Be patient yet, my noble friend: 5765
Not all the tumult's at an end.

GREED. At least now anyone who wishes
Can get a pleasant ringside view;
For idle gaping, or forbidden dishes,
You'll find that women always head the queue.   5770

No, I am not yet altogether brittle!
A handsome woman's handsome yet;
And since today it costs me little,
Let me go boldly courting for a bit.
But since in crowded spots as here   5775
Not every word will reach to every ear,
I'll try the trick, and hope I shall not miss it,
By being pantomimically explicit.[2]
Hand, foot, and gesture will not do, I see,
I'll have to reach for some burlesquerie.   5780
Like pliant clay I will work up the gold,
That stuff complies with any shape you mold.

HERALD. What's he about, the antic stick?
A starveling with a parlor trick?
To dough he's kneading all the gold,   5785
It softens for him, fit to mold,
But squeeze and lump it as he will,
Its form remains misshapen still.
He now turns to the women's side,
They all cry out and try to hide,   5790
With bearing mightily disgusted;
The rogue, I see, could not be trusted.
I greatly fear he seeks his glee
By injuring morality.
I must not stand for such offense.   5795
Pass me my staff, to drive him hence.

PLUTUS. It's foolery, let him proceed;
He little knows the menace in the offing,
There soon will not be scope for him to scoff in;
The law is mighty, mightier is need.   5800

TURMOIL AND SONG.
          The savage host stride up in strength,
          Down mountain height and valley's length,
          And irresistible their gait:
          Great Pan is whom they celebrate.
          What no one knows, they've known it long,   5805
          Into the vacant space they throng.[3]

PLUTUS. I know you well and the Great Pan you lead!
Together you have ventured daring deed.
Full well I know what only few can know,

2. True to the devil's traditional sexual role, Mephistopheles molds the magic gold into a gigantic phallus with which he threatens and shocks the ladies present.

3. The appearance of this group of wild men—a traditional costume in Baroque allegorical masques—presumably follows the plan of events which the Herald had been announcing. As indicated (line 5805), only his followers, along with the Herald and Plutus-Faust (Mephistopheles as Greed speaks no lines after 5782 and perhaps has left the stage), know that the figure of Pan is the Emperor himself. The name "Pan" is associated through a false etymology with the Greek neuter adjective *pan*, "all" (cf. line 5873), which is appropriate to the Emperor's status as absolute monarch; but the goat-god Pan, as lord of woods and protector of shepherds, is in fact identified mythologically with excess, wildness, lechery, and debauch.

And open this tight circle, as I owe.   5810
May a propitious fate attend them!
Most wondrous things might come to be;
They know not where their strides may send them,
They are proceeding carelessly.

DISCORDANT SONG.[4]
  You dolled-up show of tinsel fun!   5815
  They come up crude, they come up rough,
  By soaring leap, at flying run,
  Robust their nature is, and tough.

FAUNS.[5] In dancing flocks
 The faunic folk,   5820
 With wreath of oak
 On twisting locks,
An ear, drawn finely to a point,
Onto the curly head is joint,
Snub nose in a blunted face asprawl   5825
With women does you no harm at all.
Where faun for the dance plump hand should proffer,
The fairest would scarcely decline the offer.

SATYR.[6] Here skips the satyr, next in rank,
With foot of goat and skinny shank,   5830
He needs them sinewy and lank,
For chamois-like on mountain heights
He gladly scans the lofty sights.
Refreshed in freedom's aura then,
He jeers at the families of men,   5835
Who deep in lowland reek and stew
So blandly think they are living, too,
Whereas he knows he holds secure
That upper world, untouched and pure.[7]

GNOMES.[8] The little men come tripping there.   5840
They'd rather not go pair and pair;
With lantern bright and smock of moss,
They dance in swarms, and intercross,
Each for its own self laboring so,

4. The followers of Pan (here and above, lines 5801 ff.) usurp the Herald's role as announcer, referring to themselves in the third person as "the savage host" (line 5801) and addressing the assembled crowd as "You dolled-up show of tinsel fun!"
5. Named for Faunus, a nature god often confused with Pan, fauns were minor Roman deities, later represented as sexually active hybrids of goat and youth, with short horns, pointed ears, and (as they say) oak wreaths in their hair.
6. Satyrs, the Greek counterpart of fauns, were usually followers of the god Dionysus and were familiar (by repre-

sensation at least) from the satyr plays of the Greek tragic festivals, where they indulged in ribald and lewd acts as a kind of slapstick comedy.
7. Here Goethe alludes also to the literary mode of satire (lines 5834 ff.), which derives from a Latin tradition (*saturna*) unrelated to the Greek satyrs.
8. "The little men" (the term *gnomes* was invented by Paracelsus in the sixteenth century, synonymous with "pygmies") are hobgoblins or dwarfs of Germanic folklore who live within the earth and guard its treasures. They are represented here as miners, carrying their lanterns and wearing smocks of moss (line 5842).

A teeming mass of ants that glow,   5845
And hurry, scurry to and fro
And back and forth their errands go.

To worthy brownie-folk allied,
As mountain-surgeons certified:
We bleed the lofty mountain chains,   5850
And tap their brimming fountain-veins;
The metals all ahead we throw
With miner's hail: Luck-ho! Luck-ho![9]
And quite sincerely thus we hail:
We wish the kindly people well.   5855

And yet the gold that we unseal
Is what they use to pimp and steal,
Our iron arms the haughty man,
Though wholesale murder be his plan.
Who these commandments[1] takes in vain   5860
Holds all the others in disdain.
All this is not our fault, you see,
So bear with it, for so do we.

GIANTS.[2] The Wild Men named, and so renowned,
The heights of Harz is where they're found,   5865
Like Nature naked in their might,
And all of giant girth and height.
A trunk of fir in each right hand,
About the waist a bushy band
Of leaves and branches rudely twined;   5870
Such bodyguard no pope could find.

NYMPHS IN CHORUS. [*surrounding* GREAT PAN] He too draws near!—
Now recognize
The whole world here
In Great Pan's guise.   5875
Surround, you gayest, his advance,
About him weave in graceful dance,
For, being grave, in kindly way,
He'd have the company be gay.
Beneath the vaulted roof of blue   5880
He stayed intently wakeful too,
But brooklets lisp to him and seep,
Small breezes gently rock him to sleep.
And when he takes his midday ease,
No leaf will stir upon the trees;   5885
But wholesome herbs with fragrant balm

9. The theme of mining precious metals is purposefully associated with Mephistopheles' plan to dig up the buried treasures of the realm. "Luck-ho!" (*Glück auf!*) is the traditional miner's greeting.
1. An allusion to the Biblical ten commandments, specifically the three concerning murder, theft, and adultery (as suggested by lines 5857 ff.).
2. "Wild men" from the Harz mountains, figures from Germanic mythology. Here they also support the coat-of-arms of the eighteenth century kingdom of Prussia and thus seem plausible (though anachronistic) bodyguards for the Emperor as Pan.

Perfume the ether's tranquil calm;
Nor may the nymph stay on her toes
But falls aslumber where she goes.
When of a sudden unawares   5890
His mighty voice resounds and blares,
Like ocean roar and lightning crash,
All wits are scattered in a flash,
Brave armies break and run astray,
And heroes tremble in the fray.³   5895
So praise him to whom praise is due,
Hail him who led us here to you!⁴

DEPUTATION OF GNOMES. [*to* GREAT PAN]⁵
When the heart-lode rich and shining
Threads its streaks from cleft to cleft,
Only to astute divining   5900
Shows its labyrinthine weft,

We, where cryptic tunnels darkle,
Vault our troglodytic lair,
But where day's pure breezes sparkle
You vouchsafe us treasures fair.   5905

Here we now discover bubbling
Wondrous fountain ready-breached,
Promising to yield, untroubling,
What before could scarce be reached.

Its full gain is in your giving.   5910
Take it in safekeeping, Lord:
Benefice for all the living
In your hands is any hoard.

PLUTUS. [*to* HERALD] We must compose ourselves in high as-
   surance,
And let occur what will with stout endurance.   5915
Your pluck is of the highest, after all.
There soon will come to pass most gruesome riot,
Age after age will stubbornly deny it:
Inscribe it truly in your protocol.

HERALD. [*touching the mace still held by* PLUTUS]⁶
The gnomes conduct Great Pan, their Sire,   5920

---

3. An allusion to the terror caused by
the shout of the god Pan, described here
in association with the sublime forces in
nature, lightning and the roar of the sea.
4. An ironic paraphrase of St. Paul's
epistle to the Romans 13:7, "Render
. . . honor to whom honor is due."
5. The ballad which follows is filled with
the technical terminology of mining.
6. The episode which follows was
adapted by Goethe from an incident described in the *Historical Chronicle* of Johann Ludwig Gottfried (1619). At a carnival entertainment for the Court of

King Charles VI of France in 1394 the
King appeared with six of his lords in
the costume of wild men or satyrs. One
of the ladies present seized hold of the
King in his disguise, trying to see who
he was. Another lord took a torch from
a servant to get a better light, and the
costume caught fire. The other costumed
figures rushed in to help quench the fire,
and their costumes were also ignited. As
a result, four of the lords were burned
to death and the King himself emerged
in a state of mental derangement, to
which he had already been prone.

Sedately to the source of fire,
It surges up from depths profound,
Then sinks and settles to the ground,
And dark the gaping mouth is found;
Wells up once more to seethe and sear, 5925
Great Pan observes it in good cheer,
Rejoicing in the wondrous sight,
And pearly foam spurts left and right.
In portents dark like these should he confide?
He stoops and gazes deep inside.— 5930
But now we see his beard fall in!—
Whose could it be, that shaven chin?
His hand conceals it from our view.—
A great mischance might now ensue,
The beard caught fire, back upward flew, 5935
Sets hair and chest and wreath aglow,
Serenity is turned to woe.—
To quench the fire in throngs they came,
But none escape a share of flame,
And as they thrash and as they slap, 5940
New brands are stirred for new mishap;
Entangled in the fiery haze,
The whole masked huddle stands ablaze.

But what report is passed, I hear,
From mouth to mouth, from ear to ear? 5945
O memorably ill-starred night,
That brought on us such grievous plight!
Tomorrow will proclaim it true,
What nobody will wish he knew;
Yet everywhere their outcries go: 5950
"The Emperor" is stricken so.
On fire are—were it but untrue!—
The Emperor and his retinue.
So cursed be they who tempted him,
Enlaced themselves in resinous trim, 5955
Stampeded here, a raucous host,
For universal holocaust.
O youthful spirit, will you ever
Exuberance with judgment season?
O sovereignty, will you never 5960
Compound supremacy with reason?

The glade[7] already stands on fire,
With pointed tongues it flicks still higher,
The cross-beamed ceiling soon it dooms,
A wholesale conflagration looms. 5965
Ah, brimful is our cup of grief,
I know not who can bring relief.
The splendor of Imperial might

7. A reference to the hall (or stage), decorated to resemble a woodland scene.

Will be the ash-heap of one night.
PLUTUS.[8] Fright enough has now been spread,   5970
Now relief be wrought instead!—
Hallowed staff let smite the ground,
Make it quiver and resound!
Spacious ether, it is willed,
Let with fragrant cool be filled.   5975
Waft, you foggy wisps and wander,
Sated vapors, here and yonder,
Damp the twisted whorls of flame;
Trickling, purling, cloudlets curling,
Seeping, steeping, gently drenching,   5980
Dousing every place and quenching,
You, the soothing, smoothing, slightening,
Milden into summer lightning
Rank incendiary game.[9]—
For where spirits seek to harm us,   5985
Magic art shall shield and arm us.

PLEASANCE†

Morning Sun

The EMPEROR, COURTIERS, FAUST, MEPHISTOPHELES, *dressed decently and inconspicuously in current fashion; both kneeling.*

FAUST. You pardon, Sire, the pyromantic sport?
EMPEROR. [*beckoning them to rise*] I would have more amusement of this sort.—
I all at once stood in a fiery sphere,
I almost fancied I was Pluto here.   5990
Of night and coal there yawned a rocky gorge
Aglow with lights. From this or that hot forge
A myriad raging flames whirled ever higher
And flared into a wall, a vault of fire.
Into the loftiest sky-dome it was raised,   5995
Which ever faded as it ever blazed.
Far off through twisted fiery trunks and steeples
I saw the endless moving files of peoples
In serried concourse press to where I stood,
And render homage as they always would.   6000
I recognized a courtier now and then—
Of thousand salamanders seemed my reign!
MEPHISTOPHELES. You rule them, Sire—for every element

8. Perhaps abandoning his mask (as Mephistopheles will later do at the end of Act III), Faust here speaks both as master of ceremonies, having usurped the Herald's staff, and as demonic magician, presumably relying on Mephistopheles' assistance.

9. Faust's incantatory lines describe a process of quenching the fire with water which implies some pre-arranged sprinkling system, unless (as is also likely) both the fire and the water are to be understood as products of Mephistopheles' magic.

Owes Majesty unquestioning assent.
You sampled now the fire's obedient ravage:[1]   6005
Next plunge into the sea at its most savage,
And scarcely do you tread its pearly ground,
When all about you forms a glorious round;
For undulating nile-green swells, upwelling
With coral edges, mold a splendored dwelling   6010
With you for center. Every step you do,
The glassy palaces advance with you,
Alive the very confines of your shelter
With darting swarms, a glistening, cross-laced welter.
The mild new gleam draws portents of the ocean,   6015
They bound and lunge—the walls arrest their motion.
Gold dragons sport, prismatic scales and claws,
There gapes a shark, you laugh into his jaws.
How much your Court may teem with fond dependents,
You've never had such thronging of attendants.   6020
Yet they will not impede the loveliest view:
Inquisitive young nereids press too
Against the crystal carapace's limit.
The youngest fish-like, curious and timid,
The elder wise. Soon Thetis learns of this,   6025
Grants the new Peleus her salute and kiss.—
Forthwith a seat on Mount Olympus fair . . .
EMPEROR. I'll let you off the regions of the air,
One reaches all too soon that lofty berth.
MEPHISTOPHELES. And you, great Sire, already have the Earth.   6030
EMPEROR. What pleasing turn of fate has brought you here,
Straight from Arabian Nights, it would appear?
If you have Shehrazade's rich invention,
I pledge you my most generous attention.[2]
Stand ever ready when the world of day,   6035
As oft it does, seems made of loathly clay.
MARSHAL. [*entering in haste*] Exalted Sire, in all my days to this
I never hoped to tell of higher bliss
Than what, most seasonably gay,
Sends me before your throne today.   6040
Account upon account is squared,
The usurers' talons have been pared,
I'm rid of such infernal care,
That Heaven could not seem more fair.
QUARTERMASTER. [*following in haste*] Paid in advance the soldier's
    due,   6045

1. In what follows Mephistopheles envisions an underwater domain, including
the Nereids, in particular Thetis (line
6025), wife of Peleus and mother of
Achilles, anticipating the role of these
sea nymphs in the "Classical Walpurgis
Night."

2. The anonymous collection of Arabian tales, *The Thousand and One
Nights*, told each night by Scheherazade
to her tyrannical husband, the Emperor
of the Indies, to prevent him from putting her to death, as he had threatened.

The Army's all been pledged anew;
The man-at-arms feels born all over,
Mine Host and wenches are in clover.
EMPEROR. How does your breath come deep and free!
The furrowed face, all wreathed in glee! 6050
How briskly now you cross the hall!
TREASURER. [*joining*] Enquire of these, to whom we owe it all.
FAUST. The full report's the Chancellor's to render.
CHANCELLOR. [*approaching slowly*] Whose waning years are gilded
    with new splendor.
See then and hear ye the momentous screed 6055
Which turned all woe to happiness indeed.
[*He reads.*]
"To All it may Concern upon Our Earth:
This paper is a thousand guilders worth.
There lies, sure warrant of it and full measure,
Beneath Our earth a wealth of buried treasure. 6060
As for this wealth, the means are now in train
To raise it and redeem the scrip again."[3]
EMPEROR. I sense gross fraud here, blasphemous counterfeit!
Who dared to forge the Emperor's name and writ?
Has no one thought to punish such a crime? 6065
TREASURER. Recall—Your own self signed it at the time,
Only last night. You stood in Great Pan's mask,
And with the Chancellor we approached to ask:
"Allow yourself high festive joy and nourish
The common weal with but a pen's brief flourish."[4] 6070
You signed; that night by men of thousand arts
The thing was multipled a thousand parts;
So that like blessing should to all accrue,
We stamped up all the lower series too,
Tens, Thirties, Fifties, Hundreds did we edit, 6075
The good it did folk, you would hardly credit.
Your city, else half molded in stagnation,
Now teems revived in prosperous elation!
Although your name has long been widely blessed,
It's not been spelt with such fond interest. 6080
The alphabet has now been proved redundant:
In this sign everyone finds grace abundant.
EMPEROR. It circulates like gold of true assay?
The Court, the Army take it in full pay?
I scarce believe it, though you say I ought. 6085
MARSHAL. The fugitives could never now be caught;
The stuff was scattered broadside in a wink.
The money-changers' benches groan and clink,

---

3. The use of paper money (called *assignats* in France) developed in Europe during the eighteenth century and resulted in fraud and inflation during the old régime and the French Revolution.

4. The Chancellor and Treasurer must have constituted the Deputation of Gnomes in the "Carnival Masque" (lines 5898–5913).

Each single sheet is honored in their court
In gold and silver, though a trifle short.   6090
To butcher, baker, inn it next flits down;
Just feasting seems to busy half the town,
The other half show off their fine new clothes.
The draper cuts the bolt, the tailor sews,
Here cellars toast the Emperor, barrels plashing,   6095
There waiters jostle, steaming platters clashing.
MEPHISTOPHELES. You roam the terraces alone, it happens,
And meet a beauty decked in costly trappings,
One eye by haughty peacock feathers hidden:
The other winks, by such a voucher bidden;   6100
More swiftly than by turn of speech or wit
The rich rewards of love are lured by it.
One is no longer plagued by purse or package,
A note borne next the heart is easy baggage,
It aptly couples there with love epistles.   6105
In priestly breviaries it chastely nestles,
The soldier, too, for ease of hips and loins
May now discard the ponderous belt of coins.
Your Highness pardon if this stately matter
I seem to slander by such lowly chatter.   6110
FAUST. The plethora of treasure which, congealed,
The depths of Your dominions hold concealed
Lies unexploited. Concept most immense
Is to such wealth a negligible fence,
Imagination in its loftiest flight   6115
Will not encompass it, strain as it might.
Yet spirits gifted with profoundest sense
Place in the boundless . . . boundless confidence.
MEPHISTOPHELES. Such currency, in gold and jewels' place,
Is neat, it bears its value on its face,   6120
One may without much bargaining or barter
Enflame onself with Bacchus', Venus' ardor;
If metal's wanted, there's the banker's pile,
If he falls short, one digs a little while.
Gold dish and jewelry are auctioned off,   6125
The paper, validated soon enough,
Disarms the wag who with his darts would stab it.
They ask for nothing else now, it's a habit.
Henceforth the crown lands guard an ample store
Of specie, gems, and scrip, as not before.   6130
EMPEROR. The Empire owes you signal benefit;
May the reward be of a kind with it.
Receive the Empire's inner soil in fief,
Its treasures' fit custodians-in-chief.
You know the hoards, far-flung and well-protected,   6135
When digging's to be done, you shall direct it.
Unite, chiefs of my surface and sub-surface,

Rejoice to clothe with dignity your office,
As upper now and nether world, elate
In close-bound harmony, collaborate.   6140
TREASURER. There shall not be the faintest breath of trouble:
I cherish a magician for my double.
[*Exit with* FAUST.]
EMPEROR. I'll grant a gift to everyone at Court;
What will they use it for? Let each report.
PAGE. [*receiving*] I'll live as gaily as in paradise.   6145
ANOTHER. [*likewise*] I'm off to buy my love a chain and locket.
CHAMBERLAIN. [*accepting*] From now on I drink wine at twice the
price.
ANOTHER. [*likewise*] My word, the dice are itching in my pocket.
BARON. [*with deliberation*] I'll clear of debt my manor house
and field.
ANOTHER. [*likewise*] I'll lay it by, more interest to yield.   6150
EMPEROR. I hoped for pluck and zest for ventures new;
I should have known you, and what each would do.
For all new bloom of wealth, it's plain to see
That each remains just what he used to be.
FOOL.[5] [*approaching*] You deal out favors—let me have a few. 6155
EMPEROR. So you revived in time to waste these too!
FOOL. Those magic leaves! I cannot grasp them quite.
EMPEROR. No wonder, for you do not use them right.
FOOL. Some more come fluttering down—what should I do?
EMPEROR. They fell your way, so let them fall to you.   6160
[*Exit.*]
FOOL. Five thousand guilders—wondrously collected!
MEPHISTOPHELES. Wineskin on legs! Have you been resurrected?
FOOL. Been often raised, but never to such profit.
MEPHISTOPHELES. You're in a sweat with the excitement of it.
FOOL. Look—does this really work in money's stead?   6165
MEPHISTOPHELES. Enough to keep you drunk and overfed.
FOOL. Can house and land and ox be bought for it?
MEPHISTOPHELES. Why not? Just make your bid and seal a writ.
FOOL. A hunt, a trout-stream, park and lodge?
MEPHISTOPHELES.   Yes, all!
I'd love to see you in your manor-hall!   6170
FOOL. This night I dote on deeds of property!
[*Exit.*]
MEPHISTOPHELES. [*solus*] Not every jester is a fool, you see!

DARK GALLERY†

FAUST. MEPHISTOPHELES.

MEPHISTOPHELES. Why do you draw me down these somber
hallways?

---

5. The true court jester, who had been
removed by Mephistopheles at the outset
of his sojourn at the court (lines 4731
ff.).

Is there not sport enough within,
There in the motley court-throng, always   6175
Good for a swindle and a grin?
FAUST. Don't tell me that, it is a threadbare ruse,
  You've rubbed it thin like worn-out shoes.
  These to's and fro's are just your way
  To keep from being brought to bay.   6180
  But I am pestered, courtiers fret me,
  The Marshall and the Chamberlain beset me;
  The Emperor bids, there must be no delay,
  Helen and Paris he must see straightway;
  Ideals female and male, ideally mated,   6185
  He would inspect distinctly corporated.
  To work! I must not be forsworn or feckless.
MEPHISTOPHELES. The promise was nonsensically reckless;
FAUST. You failed, my friend, to see the hitch
  In all the hoaxes you were using.   6190
  First we arranged to make him rich,
  Now we're expected to amuse him.
MEPHISTOPHELES. You think it's just a sleight-of-hand;
  But here the climbing looms more steeply,
  You stray on deeply alien land,   6195
  Perhaps incur new guilt at random;
  You'd magic Helen up as cheaply
  As now the guilders' paper phantom.
  With witches' switches, troll-spawn, polter-poultice
  I'm always at your service at short notice,   6200
  But devil's trulls, though not as cheap as beans,
  Can hardly stand for Grecian heroines.
FAUST. Again that barrel-organ litany!
  With you one always flounders past reliance;
  A veritable fount of non-compliance,   6205
  For every trick you ask an added fee.
  I know it can be done with but a mutter,
  Two winks, and you can have her on the spot.
MEPHISTOPHELES. I have no commerce with that pagan clutter,
  They have their segregated plot.   6210
  There is a way, though.
FAUST.   Speak, and do not fiddle!
MEPHISTOPHELES. I loathe to touch on more exalted riddle.—
  Goddesses sit enthroned in reverend loneliness,
  Space is as naught about them, time is less;
  The very mention of them is distress.   6215
  They are—the Mothers.
FAUST. [*starting*]   Mothers!
MEPHISTOPHELES.   Are you awed?
FAUST. The Mothers! Why, it strikes a singular chord.
MEPHISTOPHELES. And so it ought. Goddesses undivined
  By mortals, named with shrinking by our kind.

Go delve the downmost for their habitat;   6220
Blame but yourself that it has come to that.

FAUST. Where is the road?

MEPHISTOPHELES.   No road! Into the unacceded,
The inaccessible; toward the never-pleaded,
The never-pleadable. How is your mood?
There are no locks to probe, no bolts to shift;   6225
By desolations harrowed you will drift.
Can you conceive of wastes of solitude?

FAUST. I'd hope you'd spare me verbal witching;
This reeks of the old sorcery kitchen,[1]
Of times long buried and unrued;   6230
Did I not move in worldly company?
Not study, and not lecture, vacancy?—
I spoke, with reason, as I thought, endowed,
And contradiction sounded doubly loud.
I even had to seek from rank affliction   6235
Escape in wilderness and dereliction;
And, not to be quite outcast and alone,
At last enlist myself the devil's own.

MEPHISTOPHELES. And had you even swum the trackless ocean,
Lost in its utter boundlessness,   6240
You still saw wave on wave in constant motion,
Though for your life in terror and distress.
Still there were sights. You would have seen a shift
Of dolphins cleave the emerald calm, the drift
Of clouds, sun, moon and stars revolve in harness;   6245
There you see Nothing—vacant gaping farness,
Mark not your own step as you stride,
Nor point of rest where you abide.

FAUST. You speak your part of mystagogue in chief
That ever played on neophyte's belief,   6250
With just the sign reversed—send me to limbo
As if to make my strength and craft more nimble;
You use me, like the tomcat one remembers,
To scrabble out your chestnut from the embers.[2]
But I am game! Let me explore that scope,   6255
Within your Naught to find the All, I hope.

MEPHISTOPHELES. A compliment before our ways must part:
You are no stranger to the devil's art;
Here, take this key.

FAUST.   This little bit?

MEPHISTOPHELES. First grasp it well and then belittle it.   6260

FAUST. It grows within my hand! It glitters, glows!

MEPHISTOPHELES. Ah—do you sense the virtue it bestows?
This key will scent the true site from the others;

1. The Witch's Kitchen in *Part I*.
2. In a fable of La Fontaine (Book 9, number 17), the cat Raton is persuaded by the monkey Bertrand to pull chestnuts out of the fire for him.

Follow it down—it leads you to the Mothers.

FAUST. [*with a shudder*] The Mothers! Still it strikes a shock
    of fear.   6265
What is this word that I am loath to hear?

MEPHISTOPHELES. Are you in blinkers, rear at a new word?
    Would only hear what you already heard?
    Shy at no further sound, weird as it be,
    Long since no more at odds with oddity.   6270

FAUST. Yet not in torpor would I comfort find;
    Awe is the finest portion of mankind;
    However scarce the world may make this sense—
    In awe one feels profoundly the immense.

MEPHISTOPHELES. Well then, sink down! Or I might call
    it: soar!   6275
    It's all one and the same. Escape the norming
    Of what has formed, to forms' unbounded swarming!
    Delight in what long since has been no more;
    Like cloud-drifts whirl the shades of past existence;
    You wield the key and make them keep their distance.   6280

FAUST. [*enraptured*] Yes! clutching it, I feel my strength
    redoubled,
My stride braced for the goal, my heart untroubled.

MEPHISTOPHELES. A glowing tripod will at last give sign
    That you have reached the deepest, nethermost shrine;[3]
    And by its light you will behold the Mothers;   6285
    Some may be seated, upright, walking others,
    As it may chance. Formation, transformation,
    The eternal mind's eternal recreation,
    Enswathed in likenesses of manifold entity;
    They see you not, for only wraiths they see.   6290
    Then arm your heart, for peril here is great,
    Sight on the tripod and approach it straight
    And touch it with the key!

    [FAUST *strikes an attitude of peremptory command with
    the key.*]

MEPHISTOPHELES. [*inspecting him*] That is the pose to take!
    Then it will trail, true servant, in your wake;
    You calmly rise, on fortune's buoyant air,   6295
    Return with it before they are aware.
    Once you have brought it here, you have retrieved it,
    May summon hero, heroine from night's retreat,
    The very first to have essayed that feat;
    It will be done, and you will have achieved it.   6300
    Its incense fumes, by magical arranging,
    Henceforth to godly figures must be changing.

FAUST. How do I start?

---

3. The tripod, glowing with some burning substance, suggests the traditional ac-
coutrements of the ancient oracles, as at
Delphi, associated with the ecstatic
trance of the priestess.

MEPHISTOPHELES.   Your essence downward prise;
  Sink down by stamping, stamping you will rise.
    [FAUST *stamps and sinks out of sight.*]
MEPHISTOPHELES. Let's hope the key still has the former
    knack!   6305
  I wonder if we'll ever see him back.

BRIGHTLY LIT BALLROOMS

The EMPEROR *and* PRINCES, *the* COURT *in movement.*

CHAMBERLAIN. [*to* MEPHISTOPHELES] You owe us still the spirit
    scene, you know;
  The master is impatient—start the show.
MARSHAL. His Grace was pleased this moment to enquire;
  You! Don't dishonor Majesty's desire.   6310
MEPHISTOPHELES. Why, for this very thing my mate went out,
  He knows quite well what he's about,
  He labors, shut from human eyes,
  In quiet strains with all his heart;
  For who would raise that treasure, beauty's prize,   6315
  Needs wisdom of the Magi, highest art.
MARSHAL. It does not matter by what kind of skill—
  Let all be ready, is the Emperor's will.
BLONDE. [*to* MEPHISTOPHELES] A word, dear Sir! You see an
    unflawed face,
  But in the summertime, it's a disgrace!   6320
  Then in their hundreds reddish spots and brownish
  Make my complexion look so coarse and clownish.
  Some salve!
MEPHISTOPHELES.   A pity! Luscious little thing,
  And spotted like a leopard cub, come spring.
  Take frog-spawn, tongue of hoptoad, cohobated,   6325
  By the full moon's light duly distillated,
  And as the moon wanes, spread it neatly on:
  When May arrives, the freckles will be gone.
BRUNETTE. On favors bent, the fawning crowd advances.
  I beg a remedy! A frozen foot   6330
  Inhibits me at walking and at dances,
  To drop a curtsey even I'm hard put.
MEPHISTOPHELES. If you would let me kick you with my foot . . .
BRUNETTE. Well—I am told that courting couples love it.
MEPHISTOPHELES. My kick, child, has a meaning far above it;   6335
  Hair of the dog, whatever ill you pick.
  Foot for a foot, all parts are cured like that.
  Come close! Here goes! Mind, there's no tit for tat.
BRUNETTE. [*screaming*] Ow! Oh! that hurts! that was a dreadful
    kick,
  Like from a horse.   6340

MEPHISTOPHELES.   But it has done the trick.
  You'll dance now as you please, all light and level,
  Play footie, too, at table as you revel.
LADY. [*pressing forward*] Oh, let me pass! Too painfully I smart,
  The seething rancor sears my inmost heart;
  Till yesterday he sought my eye with glee,   6345
  Now chats with *her* and turns his back on me.
MEPHISTOPHELES. The thing's precarious, to be sure, but hark.
  Steal up to him in close proximity;
  Here, take this coal and make a stealthy mark
  On shoulder, sleeve, or coat, whatever part;   6350
  Remorse will sweetly stab him to the heart.
  But you must promptly swallow down this ember
  And take no water and no wine, remember;
  He'll languish at your door before it's dark.
LADY. It is not poison?   6355
MEPHISTOPHELES. [*indignantly*] What a slur to cast!
  To find its like you'd walk a pretty stretch;
  The stake to which I went this coal to fetch[1]—
  We used to stoke it harder in the past.
PAGE. I am in love—she thinks it puppy stuff.
MEPHISTOPHELES. [*aside*] Where listen first? This thing is
    getting tough.   6360
  [*to the* PAGE] Don't try the very youngest ones just yet;
  Those longer in the tooth are your best bet.[2]
  [*others crowd up*] More yet! They're coming at me hard and
    fast.
  I'll be reduced to telling truth at last.
  The worst resort! The plight is pressing, though.—   6365
  O, Mothers! Mothers! Won't you let Faust go?
  [*looking about*] In the great hall I see the lights' dim blur,
  The entire court is all at once astir.
  I see them move in decorous array
  Through distant gallery, long passageway.   6370
  There—they assemble in the spacious Hall
  Of Chivalry, it hardly holds them all.
  With costly carpeting wide walls ornate,
  The nooks and niches decked with armor plate:
  This surely needs no magic spells or elves;   6375
  Here spirits find their way all by themselves.

HALL OF CHIVALRY†

Dim Illumination

[EMPEROR *and* COURT *have made their entrance.*]

1. Coal from the ashes of a fire used to burn a witch or a heretic, which, according to superstition, possessed rare magical powers.

2. Recalls the final advice offered to the Student about his studies by Mephistopheles in *Part I* (lines 2011 ff.).

HERALD. Announcement of the play, my wonted office,
    The spirits' secretive employment ruins;
    One vainly dares by proper reasoned preface
    To fathom the inexplicable doings.   6380
    All readied are the chairs and settles all;
    The Emperor they seat to face the wall,
    There he may view in peace the warlike rages—
    On tapestry—of our heroic ages.
    Now all are seated, Lord and courtiers' bustle,   6385
    Deep in the background crowded benches jostle;
    And love with love, this somber ghostly hour,
    Most lovingly beside each other cower.
    And so, all being in their proper places,
    We're ready; let the spirits show their paces!   6390
    [*Trumpets.*]
ASTROLOGER. Begin the play, the stage assume its shape,
    The lord commands it, let the firm walls gape!
    Here magic is at hand, all hindrance banish,
    As if rolled up by surf, the carpets vanish,
    The wall splits up, it turns about,   6395
    A deep-spaced theater seems fitted out,
    All lighted for us by a mystic glare,
    And I to the proscenium repair.[1]
MEPHISTOPHELES. [*from the prompter's box*] From here I hope to
    gain the crowd's support,
    For prompting is Old Nick's rhetoric forte.   6400
    [*to the* ASTROLOGER] You know the pulse of stars and their
    direction,
    You should pick up my whispers to perfection.
ASTROLOGER. Here is revealed to view by wondrous might,
    Quite massive, too, an ancient temple site.
    Like unto Atlas holding up the skies,   6405
    In rows aligned, sufficient columns rise;
    For all the mass they bear, they won't fall short,
    Just two would lend an edifice support.
ARCHITECT. So this is Classic! It deserves no prize,
    It's clumsy, over-heavy to my eyes.   6410
    The coarse is counted noble, bulk sublime.
    I like slim pillars, striving up in endless climb;
    The pointed apex elevates the mind;
    That style uplifts us most of all, I find.
ASTROLOGER. Receive with awe the hour by stars conferred;   6415
    Let reason be restrained by magic word;
    Instead, from farthest space let wander free
    Magnificent audacious fantasy.

1. The walls open inward to establish a deeper space on the stage, with an indefinite openness ("mystic glare") subsequently to be filled with the façade of a Doric temple (lines 6403–8). Both the Astrologer and Mephistopheles (concealed from the audience within the prompter's box) are placed on the proscenium at the edge of the stage looking into the set.

Lay eyes upon your bold desire-in-chief,
It is impossible, and hence deserves belief.[2]   6420
    [FAUST *mounts the proscenium from the other side.*]

ASTROLOGER. In priestly garb and wreath, a wondrous man,
  Who now completes what boldly he began.
  From hollow crypt a tripod climbs with him,
  I sense already incense fragrance dim.
  Now he prepares the lofty work to bless,   6425
  Naught henceforth can befall but happiness.

FAUST. [*with magnificent pathos*] You I invoke, great Mothers, you
    whose throne
  Is boundless space, who dwell forever lone
  And yet in company. Encircling you,
  Life's images are floating, live, yet lifeless too,   6430
  What was, in all its gleam and effigy,
  There is astir; eternal it would be.
  You, sovereign powers, assign it to diurnal
  Bright tabernacle and to vault nocturnal.
  The ones, the lovely course of life embraces,   6435
  The others but the bold magician[3] traces;
  He confidently shows, a lavish host,
  To each the wondrous, what he craves the most.

ASTROLOGER. The glowing key has barely touched the rim,
  And foggy vapor makes the spaces dim,   6440
  It steals within, with cloudy billow glides,
  It stretches, clusters, twines to pairs, divides.
  And now—the master stroke of spirits know:
  Their wafting drifts make music as they go.
  Of aerial notes who knows what eerie croon,   6445
  As they proceed, all changes into tune.[4]
  The columns ranked, the very triglyphs ring,[5]
  Now the entire temple seems to sing.
  The mist descends; from out the gauzy space
  A comely youth steps forth with rhythmic pace.   6450
  My office rests—who needs to be apprised?
  By all sweet Paris will be recognized!
    [PARIS *steps forth.*]

LADY. Oh, what a glow of freshly blossomed youth!
SECOND LADY. As fresh and juicy as a peach, in truth!
THIRD LADY. That finely sculptured, sweetly swelling lip!   6455
FOURTH LADY. A cup from which you would be pleased to sip?
FIFTH LADY. He's very handsome, yes, though underbred.
SIXTH LADY. Some more finesse would stand him in good stead.

---

2. Tertullian, a Carthaginian theologian (160?–230?), asserted about Christ's resurrection, in his treatise *On the Body of Christ*, chapter 5, "It is certain, because it is impossible."

3. Goethe's manuscript for this line first read "the bold poet." The word *Dichter* was later crossed out and *Magier* written above it.

4. A reference to the shapes which form out of the cloud from the tripod and subsequently assume the forms of Paris and Helena.

5. A figure in the frieze of a Doric temple consisting of a protruding block with three parallel vertical channels on its face.

KNIGHT. I sense an aura of the shepherd lad,[6]
  No prince in him, no courtliness—too bad.   6460
ANOTHER. Well, yes—half naked he's a likely whelp;
  To see him wearing armor, though, would help.
LADY. Now he sits down, so sinuously sweet.
KNIGHT. You think his lap would make a cozy seat?
OTHERS. How gracefully his head sinks on his arm!   6465
CHAMBERLAIN. The lout! This might pass muster on a farm!
LADY. You men must always carp and be unpleasant.
THE FORMER. To loll and wallow when the Emperor's present!
LADY. It's just a play—he thinks that no one sees.
THE FORMER. The stage itself here owes proprieties.   6470
LADY. Soft slumber now has overcome the fair!
THE FORMER. Soon he will snore! Most natural, I swear!
YOUNG LADY. [*rapturously*] What fragrance mingles with the
      incense fume?
  So fresh— deep in my heart it seems to bloom.
OLDER LADY. It's true! A breath of soul-pervading essence,   6475
  It comes from him!
OLDEST LADY.   The bloom of adolescence,
  Ambrosia,[7] by the youth exuded here
  And wafted outward on the atmosphere.
      [HELENA *steps forth*.]
MEPHISTOPHELES. So this is she! She'd steal no sleep from me.
  She's pretty, yes, but not my cup of tea.   6480
ASTROLOGER. This once for me there's nothing left to do,
  As man of honor I confess it true.
  Beauty made flesh, and had I tongues of fire![8]
  Of beauty they have sung to many a lyre;
  Who glimpses her is reft of every sense,   6485
  Who calls her his—too rich his recompense.
FAUST. Have I yet eyes? Is deep within my breast
  All beauty's fount incontinently lavished?
  Most blessèd gain has brought me my dread quest;
  How was the world inane to me, bleak, ravished!   6490
  What is it now, since my new priesthood's term?
  As never yet, desired, enduring, firm!
  Ah, may I lose life's very breath and germ
  If I am ever rehabituated!—
  The pleasing shape of which I was enamored,   6495
  By magic mirroring beglamored,
  Was to this form a wraith, of froth created!—
  To thee I vow the stirring of all force,
  All passion's sum and source,
  Desire, love, worship, adoration, frenzy!   6500

---

6. Paris had herded sheep for his father, King Priam of Troy, on Mount Ida, where the three goddesses appeared to him with the golden apple of Eris. We may surmise that the event here represented occurs just after Paris has made his judgment in favor of Aphrodite.

7. A traditional food of the gods, bestowing immortality.
8. An allusion to Acts 2:3–4., "And there appeared to them tongues as of fire, distributed and resting on each one of them."

MEPHISTOPHELES. [*from prompter's box*] Don't blow your part,
    man! Will you curb your fancy!
OLDER LADY. Good height, good figure—just the head too small.
YOUNGER LADY. What clumsy ankles, look! They spoil it all.
DIPLOMAT. I have seen princesses with less appeal,
    She seems to me a beauty, head to heel.   6505
COURTIER. She nears the sleeper now with gentle stealth.
LADY. How coarse, beside that purest youth and health!
POET. He shines with her reflected beauty's glow.
LADY. Endymion and Luna! A tableau![9]
THE FORMER. Quite so. It seems the goddess, downward
    sinking,   6510
  Leans over, of his aura to be drinking.
  Ah, enviable!—A kiss!—The crowning touch.
CHAPERONE. Right here in public! This is just too much!
FAUST. Dread favor to the stripling!—
MEPHISTOPHELES.   Hush! Be still!
  Let the poor ghost disport itself at will.   6515
COURTIER. She lightly tiptoes off; he's waking, though.
LADY. She's looking back! I could have told you so.
COURTIER. He marvels! Well, a wonder *did* occur.
LADY. What she can see is no surprise to *her*.
COURTIER. She turns to him with wellbred elegance.   6520
LADY. I see she's planning to become his teacher;
  In such a matter all you males are dense,
  He fancies too he is the first to reach her.
KNIGHT. You let her be! Majestic and refined!
LADY. The strumpet! She's a downright vulgar kind!   6525
PAGE. To be where he is now—I wouldn't mind.
COURTIER. There's few, I think, would find these meshes cruel!
LADY. It's passed through many a hand before, that jewel,
  What's more, the gilt on it is rather worn.
OTHERS. She was no good ten years since she was born.[1]   6530
KNIGHT. Each takes the best in season he can get;
  I think these fair remains would do me yet.
SAVANT. I must say, though I see her from close in,
  I have my doubts that she is genuine.
  The present tends to court exaggeration,   6535
  That's why I rather trust documentation.
  There I do read she was the special joy
  Of every grizzlebearded man in Troy.[2]

---

9. In response to Endymion's surpassing beauty, the goddess of the moon, Luna, fell in love with him. When Jupiter discovered this, he offered Endymion a choice between death and eternal sleep. He chose the latter and continued to be watched over by the moon.

1. Helena was abducted by Theseus when she was ten years old (see lines 7415–26 and 8848 ff.).

2. An allusion to Homer's *Iliad* (III.156 ff.), where the old men of Troy, watching the battle from the walls of the city, observe Helen as she passes them: "Surely there is no blame on Trojans and strong-greaved Achaians if for long time they suffer hardship for a woman like this one. Terrible is the likeness of her face to immortal goddesses."

The situation fits here to a tee:
I am not young, and yet she pleases me. 6540

ASTROLOGER. No longer boy! Bold man of hero race,
He sweeps her helpless into his embrace.
With newly strengthened arm he lifts her up,
What—not abducting her?

FAUST.   Audacious pup!
You dare! Halt, hear me? Let her go at once! 6545

MEPHISTOPHELES. It's your own work, this ghostly mask, you dunce!

ASTROLOGER. One final word! Now things have gone so far,
I call the play *The Rape of Helena.*

FAUST. What rape! Is it for nothing here I stand?
Does this key count for nothing in my hand? 6550
It led through wave and swell and awesome strand
Of desolation back here to firm land.
Here I stand firm, here it's realities,
The mind may battle spirits, based on these,
The greater double realm prepare at ease. 6555
Far as she was, how can she be more near!
She will be doubly mine if rescued here.
Dare! Mothers! Mothers! it is yours to give!
Who knew her once, without her cannot live.

ASTROLOGER. What would you? Faustus! Faust! With violence loud 6560
He seizes her, the shape begins to cloud.
He wields the key, turns it to touch upon
The youth!—Woe to us, woe! All vanished! Gone!
[*Explosion;*[3] FAUST *lies on the ground. The spirits dissolve into mist.*]

MEPHISTOPHELES. [*taking* FAUST *upon his shoulder*] There now!
You take aboard damned fools, don't wonder
At last the very Devil is dragged under. 6565
[*Darkness, tumult.*]

Act II

NARROW, HIGH-VAULTED GOTHIC CHAMBER[†]

Erstwhile Faust's, Unchanged

MEPHISTOPHELES. [*stepping out from behind a curtain. As he lifts it and looks back,* FAUST *is disclosed stretched on an antique bed.*] Lie on here, luckless dreamer, bound

---

3. Two sources have been suggested for the explosion here. First, a poem by Hans Sachs, *Story of the Emperor Maximilian,* where Maximilian attempts to embrace the conjured spirit of his dead wife, who vanishes "amid noise and smoke and loud tumult." Second, a story by Anthony Hamilton (1646–1720), *Faustus, the Enchanter,* where Queen Elizabeth seeks to embrace the shade of the Fair Rosamund, conjured up by Faustus, causing thunderclaps to shake the palace and a thick smoke to fill the gallery. After the tumult has subsided, Faust is found lying on his back.

By gyves of love not soon unpried!
Whom Helena has stupefied,
He will not easily come round.
[*looking about*] As I look up, and here, and there, I find it   6570
All quite intact here and unmodified;
The colored panes, I think, are further blinded,[1]
The spiders' webs have multiplied;
The paper's yellowed, ink dried up, but still
All is in order, stacked and level;[2]   6575
Here even lies the very quill
With which Faust signed himself unto the Devil.
Yes! Here is stuck within the rim
A droplet of the blood I lured from him.[3]
A single item of this sort   6580
Would grace the foremost antiquarian's hoard.
Here, too, on the same hook the same old gowning;[4]
Reminds me of that bit of clowning
When I dispensed instructions to that youth,
Whereon perhaps he browses still. Forsooth!   6585
I swear I feel a little yen,
Old smoke-warm shroud, in your disguise
To swagger as a lecturer again,
In consciousness of being wholly wise;
A trick that scholars seem to know,   6590
The Devil dropped it long ago.
> [*He takes down the fur and shakes it; cicadas, beetles, and farfarellas fly from it.[5]*]

CHORUS OF INSECTS. Well met! We are hailing
> Our patron of yore,
> We're buzzing and sailing,
> Have known you before.   6595
> Each singly, dear Father,
> You planted us once,
> In thousands now rather
> We issue to dance.
> The rogue will not surface,   6600
> He hides himself so,
> The lice in the fur-piece
> Are quicker to show.

MEPHISTOPHELES. How they surprise and cheer me, the young fry!
Just sow, and you will harvest by and by.   6605
I shake once more the venerable vair,

---

1. See Faust's mention of the stained-glass windows in his opening monologue, line 401.
2. See the renewal of the monologue in "Night," lines 656–85.
3. See the pact scene, 1714–41.
4. See the Student scene, when Mephistopheles wore the same robe (lines 1868–2048).

5. These insects may recall Faust's reference to "a universe of moths" in his earlier monologue in "Night," lines 658–59. "Farfarella," a variant of the Italian *farfalletta*, a diminutive of "moth," may derive from Dante's *Inferno* (XXI.123), where "Farfarello" is one of the names assigned to the demons who guard the pit of the barrators.

Still more come fluttering forth now here and there.—
Soar up! About! In myriad nooks aside
Bestir yourselves, my little dears, to hide.
There, where old reticules are found,   6610
Here, in the ancient parchments browned,
Where in the dust old potsherds wallow,
In yonder deathshead's staring hollow.
This den of antiquated evils
Must ever shelter whims and weevils.   6615
    [*He slips into the fur.*]
Once more enfold my shoulders, pray,
I am the Dean again today.
But what's the use adopting just the name,
Let's get some folk who recognize the claim!
    [*He pulls at the bell, which resounds with a piercing
    clangor; whereof the halls tremble and the doors burst open.*]

FAMULUS. [*tottering up the long dark passage*] What a booming!
    What a shaking!   6620
Staircase trembles, wall is quaking;
Through the colored panes ashiver
Summer lightning flashes quiver.
Ceiling cracks, and from its shifting
Plaster clatters, chalk is sifting.   6625
And the door, securely bolted,
Wonder! from its haspings jolted.—
What! Oh dread! A giant hulking
There in Faust's old furpiece skulking!
As he gazes, as he beckons,   6630
I'll be on my knees in seconds.
Shall I linger, shall I flee?
Oh, what will become of me!

MEPHISTOPHELES. [*beckoning*] Come here, my friend!—Your name
    is Nicodemus.[6]

FAMULUS. Most Reverend Sir! That is my name—*Oremus.*[7]   6635

MEPHISTOPHELES. Not that!

FAMULUS.   I'm glad! You know me, it appears.

MEPHISTOPHELES. I do; a student still, though up in years,
An ivied mossback! Even a learned man
Will study on because that's all he can.
And so a middling house of cards one piles,   6640
No genius ever laid the final tiles.
But your professor is no slouch, at all:
The noble Doctor Wagner, known to all!
The arbiter of learned circles now,
Authority to whom they all kowtow,   6645
Wisdom's continual augmentor.

---

6. "Nicodemus" was the name of a
Pharisee who visited Jesus by night
(John 3:1).

7. Latin for "let us pray," indicating a
pious gesture to ward off evil spirits.

Of students, auditors, about this center
A great assembly daily flocks.
Sole luminary of the Faculty,
He like St. Peter wields the key,[8]   6650
The lower and the higher he unlocks.
And as he shines supreme and sparkles,
No fame, no name can hold its own,
Faust's reputation even darkles,
For his researches stand alone.   6655

FAMULUS. Permit, Your Worship, if I say to you,
If you will pardon my gainsaying you,
That what you have surmised is far from true:
For modesty is his allotted part.
The great man's enigmatic disappearance   6660
He never could accept—his reappearance
Is source of hope and solace to his heart.
The Doctor's rooms are in the same repair
As he abandoned them, untouched to date
Their former master they await.   6665
I hardly dare to venture there.
What could it be, this hour's strange star?—
The masonry, methinks, is riven,
Doorposts were shaken, bolts undriven,
Or you had never come this far.   6670

MEPHISTOPHELES. What is the man engaged upon?
Lead me to him, or bring him on.

FAMULUS. Oh, his decree was too severe,
I doubt that I dare ask him here.
For months, to guard the great work from intrusion,   6675
He's lived in most secluded of seclusion.
This frailest of the erudite
Looks like a charcoal-burner quite,
In soot from ear to nose entire,
Eyes red from blowing on the fire,   6680
Each panting moment now he longs;
His tune the ringing of the tongs.

MEPHISTOPHELES. Would he prohibit me admission?
I am the man to further his ambition.

[*Exit* FAMULUS. MEPHISTOPHELES *seats himself with mock
gravity*.]

I barely settle in this chair,   6685
And lo! a guest—no stranger—stirs back there.
But now he holds the freshest Bachelor's brief;
He will be fresh beyond belief.

BACCALAUREUS.[9] [*storming up the passage*]

---

8. In founding his church upon the rock
of Simon Peter, Christ gave him "the
keys of the kingdom of heaven" (Matthew 16:19).

9. The freshman of the *Urfaust* has now
achieved his baccalaureate, the lowest of
the university degrees. In discussing this
scene with Eckermann (December 6,
1829; see below), Goethe insisted that
this figure was intended to parody the
arrogance of students in the early Restoration after the fall of Napoleon, who
belonged to radical fraternities (the so-
called *Burschenschaften*).

Gate and door, I see, are open,
At long last, then, there is hoping   6690
They can't cure the living carcass
Any more in mold and darkness,
Trussing, stunting, till they've killed you,
Dead of life as if of mildew.

Sagging, tilting edifices,   6695
All about to fall to pieces—
We must quit them on the double
Or they'll smother us in rubble.
Though I'm daring like no other,
No wild horses drag me farther.   6700

What, I wonder, will befall me?
This is just where I recall me
Heart in mouth, all in a pother
Years ago and fresh from Mother,
When those greybeards used to awe me,   6705
And their guff was gospel for me.

From these musty tomes they drew it,
Pickled wisdom as they knew it,
Knew it, aye, and knew it worthless,
Made their lives and others' mirthless.   6710
Wait a while!—That far-off cloister
Still contains some dim old oyster!

There he perches—well, I never!
In his old brown fur as ever,
Still the same museum piece,   6715
Huddled in its shaggy fleece.
Wise he seemed before I knew him,
When I hadn't yet seen through him,
Him or any bearded bogey—
Let me have at the old fogey!   6720
Unless that hairless noggin lists with mud
Washed by, old man, by Lethe's turbid flood,
You will acknowledge here a former pupil,
Released from academic drill and scruple.
I find you still just as I left you then;   6725
I, though, am quite a different specimen.
MEPHISTOPHELES. I'm glad you answered to my ringing.
I held you then in high esteem;
The chrysalis, the caterpillar clinging,
Presage the butterfly's resplendent gleam.   6730
You took as much delight as little girls
In your lace collar and your head of curls.
You never wore a queue that I recall?
And now you sport a Swedish poll.
You look so resolute and trim to boot,   6735

Just don't go home quite in the absolute.[1]

BACCALAUREUS. Old man—we took our former stations,
But note the time is not the same,
And spare us your equivocations;
We're smarter now than when we came.   6740
You led this good young fellow by the nose,
It did not take much doing, I suppose,
What no one now would dare to do.

MEPHISTOPHELES. If one tells youngsters what is really true,
But is not up the greenhorns' avenue,   6745
And then, quite painfully, years hence,
They come to know it at their own expense,
They think they cut it all off their own loaf;
Then they opine their master was an oaf.

BACCALAUREUS. A fraud, more like. Where is the teacher who   6750
Would tell us to our faces what is true?
They all know how to brew it strong or mild,
Now grave, now smiling, for the docile child.

MEPHISTOPHELES. A time for learning, true, is set for each;
You, I can see, are quite prepared to teach.   6755
In many a moon, why, in a sun or more,
You must have gained experience galore.

BACCALAUREUS. Experience hogwash! Froth and grit!
In no way equal to the spirit.
What has been always known, admit,   6760
Is worthless and devoid of merit . . .

MEPHISTOPHELES. [*after a pause*] Methought so long ago. I was a
        dunce,
I feel quite stale and silly all at once.

BACCALAUREUS. I am so glad! You may see reason yet;
The first old man of insight I have met!   6765

MEPHISTOPHELES. At hidden hoards of treasure I would nibble,
And horrifying slag I took for it.

BACCALAUREUS. Your balding dome amounts, then, not to quibble,
Just to those hollow ones there, you admit?[2]

MEPHISTOPHELES. [*goodnaturedly*] You know how rude you're be-
        ing, I surmise?   6770

BACCALAUREUS. In German, if one is polite, one lies.[3]

MEPHISTOPHELES. [*who has been inching closer to the proscenium
        in his roller chair, to the stalls*]
Up here I'm running out of light and air,
Might I find refuge with you over there?

BACCALAUREUS. I find conceit untimely in a man
Who wants to count where he no longer can.   6775

---

1. The Baccalaureus, butterfly-like, wears
the latest student fashions, including the
close-cropped hairdo (which replaced the
powdered wigs of the eighteenth century) called "Swedish poll" because it
was thought to have been introduced by
Swedes.
2. An allusion to the skull which was already here in "Night," line 664.
3. A commonplace about the German
language as blunt and rude.

Man's life is in his blood, and where, in truth,
Is blood as lively ever as in youth?
There is fresh blood that briskly circulates
And out of very life new life creates.
All is in motion, all astir with deeds,   6780
The weak succumbs, the vigorous succeeds.
While we won half the world, what were you doing?
Deliberating, contemplating, stewing,
Daydreaming, where each plan another breeds.
I swear, old age is like a frigid fever,   6785
Of aches and shakes and crotchets bred.
One who is thirty years or over
Already is as good as dead.
It would be best if you were put away.
MEPHISTOPHELES. This leaves the Devil nothing much to say.   6790
BACCALAUREUS. He can't exist without my will, I claim.
MEPHISTOPHELES. [*aside*] Old Nick will shortly trip you, all the
        same.
BACCALAUREUS. Ah—this is youth's most noble destiny!
    The world was not, until I made it be;[4]
    I guided up the sun from out the sea;   6795
    The moon began her changing course with me;
    And lo! the day adorned itself to meet me,
    The earth turned green and blossomed forth to greet me.
    I beckoned, and upon that earliest night
    The firmament made all its splendors bright.   6800
    Who, tell me, if not I, freed all you thinkers
    From narrow philistines' confining blinkers?
    But I, true to my spirit's dictates, free,
    In joy pursue the flame that burns in me,
    And pace along, entranced with my own kind,   6805
    The light before me, darkness left behind.
        [*Exit.*]
MEPHISTOPHELES. Godspeed, Original, in all your glory!—
    How stung you'd be to realize:
    Who can think anything, obtuse or wise,
    That ages back was not an ancient story,—   6810
    But there's no threat in even such romantics,
    A few years hence this will have passed;
    Young must, for all its most outlandish antics,
    Still makes some sort of wine at last.
    [*to the younger public in the stalls who fail to applaud*]
    I see my discourse leaves you cold;   6815
    Dear kids, I do not take offense;
    Recall: the Devil, he is old,
    Grow old yourselves, and he'll make sense!

4. See Goethe's conversation with Eckermann on this scene (December 6, 1829),
below.

LABORATORY†

In the Medieval Manner, Extensive Cumbrous Sets of
Apparatus for Fantastic Purposes

WAGNER. [*at the furnace*] There booms the bell,[1] from sooty wall
    Thrills shuddering reverberation.   6820
    No longer can the doubt endure
    Of most momentous expectation.
    There, there the veils of darkness fall;
    In the alembic's inmost member
    A glow is lit like living ember,   6825
    Yes—like a glorious jewel's spark
    It shoots its flashes through the dark!
    A glare of dazzling white is sent!
    This once, let me not lose the battle!—
    Oh God, the door! What is this rattle?   6830
MEPHISTOPHELES. [*entering*] My welcome! It is kindly meant.
WAGNER. [*apprehensively*] Ah, welcome to the hour's good star.
    [*under his breath*] But word and breath from egress firmly bar.
    A glorious work will shortly be displayed.
MEPHISTOPHELES. [*more softly*] What's going on?
WAGNER. [*more softly*]   A man is being made.   6835
MEPHISTOPHELES. A man? And what young pair in passion
    Did you imprison in the flue?
WAGNER. Oh, God forbid! Begetting in the former fashion
    We laugh to scorn beside the new.
    The tender point from which new life would surge,   6840
    The potent grace that from within would urge,
    And taking, giving, was to limn itself,
    Absorb first kindred, then remote for self,
    Has now been ousted from its age-old sway;
    If brutes delight still in the former way,   6845
    Then man with his superior resource
    Must henceforth have a higher, higher source.
    [*turning to the furnace*] It shines! Now one may properly start
        hoping
    That if, 'mid hundreds of ingredients groping,
    By mixing—for on mixture things depend—   6850
    The stuff of humankind we keep composing,
    In a retort enclosing,
    And cohobating well the blend,
    The quiet toil will prosper in the end.
    [*turning to the furnace*] It's coming now! The swirl is clearing
        duly,   6855
    Conviction, too, more truly, truly:
    What we extolled as Nature's deep conundrum,
    We venture now to penetrate by reason,

---

1. Wagner refers to the bell rung by   no scene had intervened.
Mephistopheles (before line 6620) as if

And what she did organically at random,
We crystallize in proper season. 6860

MEPHISTOPHELES. He who has lived has learned a lot,
To him the world can offer nothing new;
Upon my wanderings from spot to spot
I've come across synthetic people too.

WAGNER. [*still continuing to watch the alembic attentively*]
It swells, it gleams, piles up and on, 6865
In just a moment it is done.
A great design appears at first insane;
But chance will soon seem quaint and blind,
And such an exemplary thinking brain
Will soon by thinkers be designed. 6870
[*watching the alembic in rapture*] The glass grows tuneful with
its lovely power,
It's clouding, clearing, nearly done within!
I see in shapely harmony cower
A dainty little mannikin.
What more do we desire, what more the world? 6875
For now the secret is in reach.
Let this vibration but be heard,
And it will turn to voice, to speech.[2]

HOMUNCULUS. [*in the alembic, to* WAGNER] Well, there, Papa!
How now? It was no jest.
Clutch me affectionately to your breast, 6880
But not too roughly, or the glass might shatter.
Such is, you see, a property of matter:
Things natural find all the world scant space,
While things synthetic want a sheltered place.
[*to* MEPHISTOPHELES] What ho, the rogue! Sir Cousin, you here,
too? 6885
You're right on cue, I am obliged to you.
A thoughtful fate has timed it well enough;
Since I exist, I must be ever active,
I feel like getting down to work right off.
Where I need shortcuts, you should be effective. 6890

WAGNER. A word before! I have been much embarrassed,
By old and young with ceaseless problems harassed.
No one has fathomed—naming one at random—
How body and soul form such a jointless tandem,
A timeless-seeming bond, like brother and brother, 6895
And yet make life so wretched for each other.
Secundo—

MEPHISTOPHELES. Stop! I would consult him rather
Why man and wife fall out with one another?
A poser, friend, a quest that never ends.
Here's work to do—just what the imp intends. 6900

HOMUNCULUS. What's there to work on?

2. See Goethe's conversation with Eckermann of December 20, 1829, below.

MEPHISTOPHELES. [*pointing to a side door*] Here your gifts employ!

WAGNER. [*still gazing into the alembic*] My word, you are a captivating boy!
[*The side door opens, revealing* FAUST *stretched on the
couch.*]

HOMUNCULUS. [*astonished*] Momentous!
[*The alembic slips from* WAGNER's *hands, to float over* FAUST
and illuminate him.][3]

               Fair-environed!—Limpid waters
In a dense grove, young nymphs their garments shedding;
Sweet sight! Now sweeter still. Yet 'mid these daughters   6905
One who outglistens all her lustrous setting,
Of hero kin, perchance of godly name.
She dips a foot into that lucidness;
The flawless body's graceful living flame
Is cooled in pliant crystalline caress.   6910
But there, what whirring rush of pinions flashing,
What churns that lambent glass with stir and splashing?
The timid maidens scatter, and at once
The queen remains alone; but calm her glance,
With woman's proud complacency she sees   6915
The splendid swan prince nestling to her knees,
Intrusive-tame. He grows inured, serene . . .
But of a sudden, mist, a vaporous gauze,
Arises and a close-meshed curtain draws
About the most enchanting scene.   6920

MEPHISTOPHELES. How aptly you have improvised it all!
You are as tiny as your tales are tall.
I cannot see a thing.

HOMUNCULUS.   No wonder. From the North,
In foggy centuries spawned forth,
Knighthood-befuddled, cleric-ridden,   6925
How could your eye be free to roam?
In murk alone you feel at home.
[*gazing about him*] Stonework begrimed and moldy-green,
Weird-curlicued, arch-pointed, mean!—
If he awakes, we face a sorer plight,   6930
He'll catch his death upon the sight.
Wood-pools and swans and naked sirens,
Of such was his foreboding dream;
How could he take to these environs!
I hardly stand them, easy as I seem.   6935
Away with him!

MEPHISTOPHELES. I shouldn't be the sorrier.

HOMUNCULUS. Why, into battle bid the warrior,

3. Homunculus offers a description of
the vision which he perceives Faust to
be experiencing in his dream state. What
follows constitutes a word-painting of a
popular theme in the visual arts; it has
been suggested that Goethe had specifically in mind the painting of Leda by
Corregio (1494–1534), in the Kaiser
Friedrich Museum in Berlin.

The maiden summon to the reel,
And you have answered their appeal.
Just now, if I recall aright,[4]   6940
Is classical Walpurgis Night;
Occasion truly heaven-sent—
Transport him to his element.

MEPHISTOPHELES. The like has never come my way.

HOMUNCULUS. How would it come to your attention, pray?   6945
Romantic ghosts alone are known to you,
A genuine ghost must do the Classic too.[5]

MEPHISTOPHELES. Where is it then, the place where we con-
vene?
Antiquish colleagues roil me sight unseen.

HOMUNCULUS. Northwestward, Satan, lies your pleasure-ground, 6950
Southeastward, though, for this time we are bound.
A spacious plain, Peneios flowing through
Enshrubbed and treed, with bights and meadows still,
The lowland spreads from hill to cloven hill,
Above it lies Pharsalus, old and new.[6]   6955

MEPHISTOPHELES. Oh no! Away! let's have no mention
Of slavery and tyrant in contention.
It bores me; they are hardly through,
And then it all begins anew;
And no one realizes they're in thrall   6960
To Asmodeus,[7] who has staged it all.
They fight for "liberties"—to the observant
In actual fact it's servant against servant.

HOMUNCULUS. Leave men's obstreperous nature its free field,
For each of them must fend as best he can   6965
From boyhood up; at length, there is a man.
Our problem is how this one may be healed.
Here try it if you have a remedy,
If you can't manage it, leave it to me.

MEPHISTOPHELES. Well, many a Brocken trick might be
rehearsed,   6970
But pagan bolts would have to open first.
This Grecian tribe was never up to much!

4. As Goethe indicated in the "Second
Sketch for the Announcement of the
Helena" (see below), Homunculus has
instant and complete "recall" of all
events in history, a universal historical
world calendar.
5. See Goethe's conversation with Eckermann on this scene (December 16,
1829), below.
6. Along the traditional geographical-historical axis of cultural orientation in the
West, Homunculus describes the setting
for the coming "Classical Walpurgis
Night." The River Peneios in Thessaly
runs from the slopes of the Pindus
Mountains through the Vale of Tempe,
between Mt. Olympus and Mt. Ossa,
flowing thence into the Aegean Sea on
the northeast coast of Greece. Pharsalus
(Latin form of the name of the Greek
city of Pharsalos) was located on the
river Apidanos in Thessaly. On the
plains outside the city the epochal battle
took place on August 9, 48 B.C., between
Caesar and Pompey which marked the
transition from the ancient to the modern world and the death of mythological
creatures from the former, who assemble
once a year on the anniversary of the
event to commemorate their own demise.
7. See line 5378 and note.

They lure you with free sensuous play and such,
And tempt men to a cheerful kind of sinning;
While ours seems glum and never half as winning.   6975
What now?
HOMUNCULUS.   Why, you're not shy about your itches;
    If I make mention of Thessalian witches,[8]
    Perhaps I do not have to shout.
MEPHISTOPHELES. [*lecherously*] Hmm! They are persons, those
        Thessalian witches
    That I have often asked about.   6980
    With them night after night to hang one's britches
    Would be discomforting, no doubt;
    But just a spot . . .? Why not!
HOMUNCULUS.   Let's have your wrap,
    Fling it about our knightly brother!
    As it has done before, that scrap   6985
    Will do to lift one and the other;
    I light the way.
WAGNER. [*timidly*]   And I?
HOMUNCULUS.   Why, you—
    You'll find at home important things to do.
    There are old parchments there to be inspected,
    Life elements by rule to be collected   6990
    And circumspectly fitted edge to edge.
    The How needs even more thought than the What.
    While I go on a little pilgrimage
    I may discover to your i the dot.
    Thus to the lofty goal you may advance;
    These will be the rewards for having striven:
    Gold, honor, fame, long span of healthy living,
    And scholarship and virtue—too, perchance.
    Farewell!
WAGNER. [*distressed*] Farewell! my heart is sore, alack!
    I fear I may not ever see you back.   7000
MEPHISTOPHELES. Peneius-ho, then! My young friend
    Should not be underestimated.
    [*ad spectatores*] At last we after all depend
    Upon dependents we created.

CLASSICAL WALPURGIS NIGHT[†]

The Pharsalian Fields

Darkness

ERICHTHO. For dread observance of this night, as oft before,   7005

---

8. The Thessalian witches, devotees of the moon who also transform men into beasts, are derived from Lucan, *Pharsalia*, VI; they are mentioned also in Plato, *Gorgias*, 38, and Aristophanes, *Clouds*, 7897. They appear in the "Classical Walpurgis Night" as Lamiae to confront Mephistopheles (lines 7676–7790).

I here proceed, Erichtho,[1] I, the somber one;
Not as repulsive as the poets in their excess
Have rudely slandered me . . . immoderate as they are
In praise or blame . . . Already bleached appears to me
From the gray tide of tents the vale from end to end,   7010
The afterview of that most dire and awestruck night.
How often has it not recurred! And will recur
Eternally . . . Not one but grudges sovereign rule
To others, most to him who seized it by his strength
And strongly reigns.[2] For he who has not learnt to rule   7015
His inner self, is only too intent to rule
His neighbor's will to suit his own imperious mind.
But here a famous precedent was battled out
How might arrays itself against still greater might,
And Freedom's lovely thousand-blossomed wreath is rent,   7020
Stiff laurel coiled about the ruler's brow instead.
Here Pompey dreamt of early glory's flowering day,
There wakeful Caesar harked the balance-tongues of fate!
These will be matched; and who prevailed, the world knows well.

Watch-fires are glowing, lending crimson flames,   7025
The earth exhales again the reek of blood spilt then,
Lured by the wondrous rare effulgence of the night,
The legion of Hellenic legend gather here.
About each fire there waver mootly, or recline
At ease, the fable-woven shapes of ancient days . . .   7030
There rises, not at full, yet gleaming fair,
The moon and sheds a gentle radiance all about;
The mirage of the tents dissolves, the fires burn blue.

But overhead, unlooked for, what a meteor?[3]
It radiates, and lights some sphere corporeal.   7035
I scent the breath of life. It ill befits me, then,
To close with things alive to which I am of harm.[4]
This yields me ill-renown, and nothing gained.
Already it descends. I prudently withdraw!
    [*Departs.*]
    [*The* AERONAUTS *above.*][5]
HOMUNCULUS.   Sail with us another round   7040
                     Over flame and terrors dread;
                     For such ghostly sights abound

---

1. The witch Erichtho is mentioned for her ugliness in both Ovid, *Heroides*, 15.139, and Lucan, *Pharsalia*, 4.507. Pompey had consulted her on the night before the original battle to learn who the victor would be.
2. Here and in the following lines allusion is made to the political struggle between Pompey and Julius Caesar which caused the battle of Pharsalus.
3. What Erichtho takes to be a meteor is in fact Faust and Mephistopheles rid-

ing through the air on the magic cloak, accompanied by Homunculus in his phial, which casts a dazzling light on all of them.
4. Lucan, *Pharsalia*, VI.510 ff., states that Erichtho shunned human company and inhabited the tombs of the dead.
5. The following exchange corresponds to the chant with the Will-o'-the-Wisp in the "Walpurgis Night" of *Part I*, lines 3871–3912.

In the dale and valley-bed.

MEPHISTOPHELES. When, as in the northland's horrors
                 Through some window-arch, I see   7045
                 These most noisome ghosts before us,
                 Either place is home to me.

HOMUNCULUS.   Look! a bony female striding,
                 Vast of step, before us here.

MEPHISTOPHELES. Through the air she saw us gliding,   7050
                 Likely she is struck with fear.

HOMUNCULUS.   Let her stride away! and stand
                 On his feet your knight; at once
                 He'll revive, and not by chance:
                 He seeks life in fable-land.   7055

FAUST. [*touching the soil*] Where is she?

HOMUNCULUS.   Hard to tell; but ask about,
And you can probably find out.
Explore, before the dawn is here,
From one flame hasten on to others:
He who has dared amongst the Mothers   7060
Has precious little left to fear.

MEPHISTOPHELES. I too feel in my element;
But deem it best for our content
That each should range the fires alone,
To seek adventure on his own.   7065
And then, in order to unite us,
You, midget, flash your ringing flare and light us.

HOMUNCULUS. Here's how it flashes, how it rings.
        [*The glass gives off a powerful drone and glare.*]
Now off to fresh unheard-of things!
        [*Exit.*]

FAUST. [*alone*] Where is she!—Do not question now for
                 long ...   7070
For even were it not the soil that bore,
The surf that rose against her at this shore,
It is the air which spoke her native tongue.
Here! By some magic, here, in Grecian land!
I sensed at once the earth whereon I stand;   7075
As, in my sleep, fresh spirit fired my heart,
Awake, I stand here in Antaeus'[6] part.
Though strangest blend of most unlike and same,
I'll earnestly explore this maze of flame.
        [*Departs.*]

ON THE UPPER PENEIOS[1]

MEPHISTOPHELES. [*prying about*] And as I roam about these spots
                 of flame,   7080

6. Antaeus was a giant, offspring of the
earth, with whom Hercules wrestled. He
renewed his strength whenever his feet
touched the ground.

1. This stage direction has been added by
editors to correspond with the later stage
direction "as before" (preceding line
7495).

I do feel quite estranged and disconcerted;
Stark naked all, just here and yonder shirted:
The sphinxes brazen, griffins bare of shame,[2]
So all the crowd that, curly-fleeced or feathered,
From front and rear display themselves untethered.   7085
We too, of course, are heartily indecent,
But this antique lot feels too live and recent;
Quite à la mode these moot points should be mastered
And fashionably-triply overplastered . . .
A nasty lot! Yet a new guest, to meet them,   7090
Must take the trouble decently to greet them . . .
Salute to you, fair ladies, grizzling sages.

GRIFFIN. [*rasping*] Not grizzling! Griffin! No one likes to be
Addressed as grizzled. Words still bear within
Echoing traces of their origin: 7095
Grey, grumbling, gruesome, graveyard, grimly, grunted,
Alike etymologically fronted,
Affront us.[3]

MEPHISTOPHELES. Take this point: while "grizzled" teases,
The "grip" in the proud name of griffin pleases.

GRIFFIN. [*as above, and continuing henceforth*]
Of course! the association is well-tried,   7100
And widely lauded, if at times decried.
One's grip be laid on maidens, gold, or crowns,
On graspers Lady Fortune seldom frowns.

ANTS. [*of the colossal sort*] You speak of gold, we had collected
masses,
Secreted deep in rock and cave crevasses;   7105
The Arimaspians nosed it out and bagged it,
They're giggling there at how far off they've dragged it.[4]

GRIFFINS. Don't worry, we shall force them to confess.

ARIMASPIANS.[5] Not this free night of merriment.
For by the morning it's all spent,   7110
This time we'll bring it off, we guess.

MEPHISTOPHELES. [*who has seated himself among the* SPHINXES]
How I got settled here in moments!
I understand them, one and all.

SPHINX. We emanate our spectral comments,

---

2. The Sphinxes—traditionally represented with the head and upper body of
a woman, the lower body of a lion—appear with naked breasts; the Griffins—
with the head and wings of an eagle and
the body of a lion—are "shameless" in
the greed with which (according to Herodotus, *History*, 4.13) they traditionally
stood guard over buried treasure.
3. The etymological theory of the Griffins, ie., that names originate as imitation of sounds, associates these creatures
with a concern for origins, just as they
presumably embody the etymological
sense of their name (German *Greif*;

Greek *gryps*), as "grip" or "grasp," in
their beaks and claws.
4. According to ancient legend (as in
Herodotus, 4.27, or Pliny, *Natural History*, 11.31), gigantic ants dug up particles of gold from beneath the earth in
order to build their underground homes.
This gold is the treasure which the Griffins guard so greedily.
5. Also mentioned in Herodotus: one-
eyed monsters from Northern Scythia
who were the traditional enemies of the
Griffins, often attempting to steal their
treasure.

And you make them corporeal.[6]   7115
Now, pending more acquaintance, state your name.

MEPHISTOPHELES. By many names they name me—so they claim;
    Are any Britons here? They're always traveling,[7]
    To track down sites of battles, tumbling brooks,
    Long-tumbled ruins, musty classic nooks;   7120
    For them this place would be the very thing.
    They'd bear me out that in a bygone age
    As *Old Iniquity*[8] I held their stage.

SPHINX. Why so?

MEPHISTOPHELES. I do not know myself what for.

SPHINX. So be it. Are you versed in stellar lore?   7125
    About the present hour, what do you say?

MEPHISTOPHELES. [*looking up*] Star shoots on star, a clipped moon
        shines fair ray,
    And I feel good in this congenial spot,
    What with your lion skin to keep me hot,
    To climb about up yonder is no feast,   7130
    Let's have some riddles, or charades at least.

SPHINX. To make a riddle, just enounce yourself.
    Try and resolve your inmost self and action:
    "To good and bad alike in satisfaction,
    To one, a corslet for ascetic lunging,   7135
    The other, vice-companion for mad plunging,
    And either, just for Father Zeus' distraction."[9]

FIRST GRIFFIN. [*rasping*] I'm sick of him!

SECOND GRIFFIN. [*rasping harder*] Who's he to interfere?

BOTH. The ugly fright, who needs him here?

MEPHISTOPHELES. [*brutally*] You think perhaps the guest's claws
        rip, on balance,   7140
    Not quite as well as do your own sharp talons?

SPHINX. [*mildly*] Do stay as long as you've a mind;
    You'll volunteer to leave us, you will find;
    At home your self-importance may be strong,
    Here you feel out of place, unless I'm wrong.   7145

MEPHISTOPHELES. You look quite appetizing, Sphinx, your top at
        least,
    But gruesome farther down, the part that's beast.

SPHINX. You counterfeit find in us sharp reproof,
    In that our claws and paws are sound;
    You, with your shrunken horse's hoof,   7150

6. Here and in what follows the Sphinx performs its traditional role of setting riddles of identity, as in the legend of Oedipus at Thebes.

7. An anachronistic allusion to the reputation of the British as world travelers in the late eighteenth and early nineteenth centuries.

8. The name "Old Iniquity" (so used in English by Goethe) derives from late medieval morality plays. The same name is used by Shakespeare in *Richard III* (III.i.82) and by Ben Jonson in *The Devil Is an Ass* (Prologue, 49).

9. The answer to this riddle by the Sphinx, which Mephistopheles does not bother to acknowledge, is apparently himself.

Are ill at ease amid our round.

[SIRENS *tuning up for song above.*]

MEPHISTOPHELES. Who are those birds who settled, swaying,
That poplar grove in crown and bough?

SPHINX. Beware! Their sing-song has been slaying
The very finest before now.   7155

SIRENS.[1]   Ah, why be habituated
                          To the hideously wondrous!
                          Hark, we're coming in our hundreds,
                          And with notes well-modulated;
                          Thus for Sirens it is fated.   7160

SPHINXES. [*mocking them to the same tune*]
                          Try to make them leave their branches!
                          Deep in foliage to their haunches,
                          They conceal their claws of raptors,
                          They will turn pernicious captors
                          If you listen to their tune.   7165

SIRENS.   Down with hate! Down envy! Rather,
                          Purest pleasures let us gather,
                          Here beneath the heavens strewn!
                          On the earth, upon the ocean,
                          None but the serenest motion   7170
                          To the welcome guest be shown.

MEPHISTOPHELES. Here is the newest and the choicest
Which pours from strings or human voices,
All interbraided part with part.
This sing-song's lost on me, I fear,   7175
It makes a tingling in my ear,
But never filters to the heart.

SPHINX. Speak not of heart! I doubt but whether
To claim a shrunken pouch of leather
Would not be apter on your part.   7180

FAUST. [*approaching close*] How wondrous, just the aspect of
these creatures!
In the repellent, great and valiant features.
They seem to augur me a happy chance;
Where does it take me back, this earnest glance?
[*referring to the* SPHINXES] In front of such did Oedipus stand
once;[2]   7185
[*referring to the* SIRENS] For these, Ulysses writhed in hempen
bonds;[3]

1. According to legend, the Sirens were nymphs transformed to birds (or at least with the wings of birds) who were banished to an island in the sea where they sang sweet songs that enticed passing mariners to their death by shipwreck on the rocks. In Homer's *Odyssey* they are encountered by Odysseus in his wanderings (Book XII, lines 39–54 and 154–200). Here the Sirens have apparently come inland for the "Classical Walpurgis Night" (cf. the "Second Sketch for the Announcement of the *Helena*," below), and they depart precipitously in immediate response to the earthquake later on, apparently swimming downstream in the River Peneios to the Aegean Sea (cf. lines 7503 ff.).
2. See note to line 7115.
3. See note preceding line 7152.

[*referring to the* ANTS] By such as these was highest treasure
    stored;
[*referring to the* GRIFFINS] By these most vigilantly watched the
    hoard.[4]
By a fresh spirit's breath I feel affected,
Grand are the forms, and grandly recollected.   7190

MEPHISTOPHELES. You used to blast it with abuse
  What now you willingly abide;
  No doubt the lover who pursues
  His love takes monsters in his stride.

FAUST. [*to the* SPHINXES] Abide my question, dames of high
    estate: 7195
  Has one of you seen Helena of late?

SPHINXES. She is above our ken, her days are newer,
  The last of us met Hercules,[5] who slew her.
  Through Chiron,[6] though, you might perchance pursue her;
  This night of ghosts, he's always roved and pranced,   7200
  If he responds, you will be much advanced.

SIRENS. Sad your loss if you repel us! . . .
    When Ulysses came sojourning
    With us, did not pass us spurning,
    He had many tales to tell us;[7]   7205
    To all these we pledge to make you
    Privy if you will betake you
    To our ocean realms of jade.

SPHINX. Noble youth, be not betrayed.
  Than bound Ulysses in your turn,   7210
  Be rather by good counsel bound.[8]
  If highborn Chiron can be found,
  What I foretold, you stand to learn.
    [FAUST *withdraws.*]

MEPHISTOPHELES. [*peevishly*] What whistles croaking, flapping
    past,
  That is too quick for eye to seize,   7215
  Each followed by the next so fast?
  They'd wear out any huntsman, these.

SPHINX. Like winter tempest storming fiercely,
  To arrows of Alcides[9] scarcely
  In range—the swift Stymphalides,[1]   7220

---

4. See note to line 7107.
5. The story that Hercules killed the last of the Sphinxes appears to be an invention by Goethe.
6. Chiron the centaur, who appears in the next scene (lines 7330 ff.), was the tutor of many heroes, including Achilles and the twin half-brothers of Helena, Castor and Pollux.
7. The Sirens here distort the truth as Homer tells it. Ulysses was forewarned of the Sirens and had his men fill their ears with wax and himself tied to the mast of his ship in order to guard against the irresistible lure of their song.
8. This syntactic-metaphorical *salto mortale* was copied from the original for the translator's private collection, and is released with reluctance [*Translator*].
9. Another name for Hercules, grandson of Alcaeus.
1. Monstrous birds with iron beaks and claws from the valley of Stymphalus. Hercules killed them as one of his twelve labors.

With web of goose and vulture's bill
Their croaking hail intends no ill.
All they desire is to join in
And prove themselves our next of kin.

MEPHISTOPHELES. [*as if intimidated*] There's more goes hissing in
    between.   7225

SPHINX. These surely need not make you quake,
    They are the heads of the Lernaean Snake,[2]
    Cut from the trunk, but still convinced of being.
    But say, what will you turn to next?
    What gestures, restless or perplexed?   7230
    Where would you go? Begone and further fare! . . .
    I see, the chorus over there
    Has made you swivel-necked. Don't stand on graces,
    Make your way over, greet some charming faces.
    These are the Lamiae,[3] wenches lewdly tender.   7235
    Of swelling lips and scruples slender,
    Just such as suit the Satyr pack;[4]
    With them, a goatfoot has the inner track.

MEPHISTOPHELES. You're staying? So I find you here again?

SPHINX. Yes. Go and mingle with the airy clan.   7240
    We, by our Old Egyptian past affected,[5]
    Are long accustomed to millennial stays.
    And if our site be but respected,
    We tell the lunar and the solar days:[6]
              Crouched before the pyramids—   7245
              Nations pass the judgment bar,
              Inundation, peace and war—
              And we never blink our lids.

ON THE LOWER PENEIOS[1]

PENEIOS *surrounded by waters and* NYMPHS.

PENEIOS.[2] Sough of sedges, stir your whispers,
    Softly breathe, my reedy sisters,   7250
    Waft, you airy willows, wispy
    Poplar feathers, lull with lisping,

2. The Lernaean Hydra had nine heads, one of which was immortal. As one of his labors Hercules was assigned to kill it. Whenever he cut off a head, two new heads grew in its place. Finally he burned them all off and buried the immortal head.
3. Ghosts who thirst for human flesh and blood and who assume different shapes, especially that of young women, in order to attract their victims (See lines 7676 ff. and 6977.)
4. See note to line 5829.
5. The association of the Sphinxes with ancient Egypt enhances their primeval mystery. Correspondingly, they later remain unmoved by the earthquake and the appearance of Seismos (which they describe, lines 7523–49).
6. The great statue of the Sphinx at Gizeh in Egypt was known to have been carefully placed in such a way as to measure time astronomically.
1. See note to line 6955.
2. Peneios, the river, speaks as a person. Parellels for this may be found in Classical literature and art (the Skamander in the *Iliad*, XXI, and the Tiber in the *Aeneid*, VIII).

Mending interrupted dream! . . .
For a fearsome shiver wakes me,
Deep all-moving quiver shakes me,   7255
From the restful rolling stream.

FAUST. [*stepping toward the riverbank*] Surely, if I trust my senses,
Through these laced arboreal fences,
Tangled boskets, from the beaches
Issue notes like human speeches.   7260
Ripples chatter as they rollick,
Breezes titter like . . . a frolic.

NYMPHS. [*to* FAUST]
            'Twere best of all for thee
            Here to be bedding,
            Cool would restore thee,   7265
            Weariness shedding,
            Savor the heart's rest
            That everywhere flees thee;
            Our wafting and purling
            And whispering ease thee.   7270

FAUST. No slumber now! Oh let me ponder
Those peerless apparitions yonder
My eye envisions. To the core
How wondrously I am affected!
Why, do I dream this? Recollect it?   7275
This blissful sight was mine before.
Still waters stealing through the luscious
Array of softly swaying rushes,
They do not splash, scarce seep their path;
From every side, a hundred sources   7280
Unite their flawless crystal courses
To form a limpid shelving bath.
Young female forms, their healthy fitness
Redoubled by the mirror's witness
For the enchanted eye's delight!   7285
Then playful fellowship of bathing,
Emboldened swimming, timid wading,
Gay shouts at last and water fight.
On these my eye should rest contented,
Yet, though a feast be here presented,   7290
On more my striving mind is keen.
Beyond the probing gaze will hover,
Where emerald folds of leafy cover
Must harbor the exalted queen.[3]

Marvels! From the bays emerging,   7295
Swans come drifting down, converging,
Poised at motion's purest peak.

3. Leda is queen of the nymphs and
mother of Helen of Troy. The event described is identical to that seen by Faust
in his dream (lines 6903–20), though differences of style, focus, and emphasis
are important.

Grouped in graceful ease, unhastened,
Haughty, though, and self-complacent
As they cradle crown and beak . . .   7300
One, more boldly than the others[4]
Breasting, bridling, leaves his brothers,
Forging swiftly through their flight;
Bulging plumage proudly swelling,
Wave himself, on wavelets welling,   7305
He invades the sacred site . . .
The rest are cruising here and thither
In calmly gleaming shells of feather,
At times with splendid truculence
The timid maidens' minds deflecting,   7310
So that, their guardianship neglecting,
They think but of their own defense.

NYMPHS. Sisters, come and hold your ear
    To the bankment's verdant scallop:
    For I fancy what I hear   7315
    Is the sound of horse's gallop.
    How I wish to learn who might
    Bear swift tidings here this night.

FAUST. Do I hear the earth resounding
    To a charger's rapid pounding?   7320
        Thither glance!
        Happy chance,
    Is it already lent me?
    O peerless wonder sent me!
A horseman cantering ahead   7325
He seems highminded, spirited,
And of a dazzling white his mount . . .
No doubt! I know him from afar,
The famous son of Philyra![5]—
Halt, Chiron! Halt! I would request account . . .   7330

CHIRON. What is it? What about?

FAUST.   Your paces ease!

CHIRON. I do not rest.

FAUST.   Then take me with you, please!

CHIRON. Mount! I may freely ask then and respond.
    Where are you bound? You stand here by the banks,
    I am prepared to carry you beyond.   7335

FAUST. [*mounting*] Whither you wish. Take my eternal thanks . . .
    The famous man, the noble pedagogue
    Who, to his honor, reared a hero folk,
    The circle of the noble Argonauts,[6]
    And all who have enriched the poet's thoughts.   7340

CHIRON. We'd better let it go at that!

4. Jupiter in the form of a swan.
5 Chiron was the son of Saturn and Philyron (see note to line 7199).

6. A group of fifty heroes organized and led by Jason in his quest for the Golden Fleece. Their ship was called the *Argo*.

As mentor, Pallas even had small credit;[7]
You give instruction—then, off their own bat,
They act as though they'd never had it.

FAUST. The leech to whom no plant is strange,   7345
Who knows the roots to deepest range,
Can heal the sick, the wounded ease and bind,
I here embrace in body as in mind!

CHIRON. For heroes stricken where I was
I knew relief and cure to find!   7350
But in the end bequeathed my cause
To quacks—diviner and divine.

FAUST. You show the truly great man's ways,
Who cannot stomach words of praise;
His modesty will squirm and parry,   7355
Pretending to be ordinary.

CHIRON. You have a sycophantic flair
For flattering prince or commoner.

FAUST. But this you will concede me yet:
The greatest of your era you have met,   7360
To emulate the noblest deeds have striven,
In earnest demigodly wise been living.
Now, of your hero friends, whom have you deemed
The doughtiest, whom have you most esteemed?

CHIRON. Within the Argonauts' high round   7365
Each had a virtue all his own, I found,
And by the strength with which he was endowed
He would excel where others bowed.
The Dioscuri,[8] now, could ever boast
Success where youth and beauty count for most.   7370
Resolve and rapid deed to others' profit—
The Boreads[9] had the pleasant favor of it.
Thoughtful and strong, of ready counsel, clever,
Thus Jason ruled, to women pleasing ever.
Frail Orpheus,[1] musing quietly, withal   7375
Would strike the mightiest lyre among them all.
Sharp-eyed Lynceus[2] was, by night and day
He steered the sacred bark past cliff and spray . . .
Concerted toil on perilous quest I laud:
When one achieves, the others all applaud.   7380

FAUST. Of Hercules shall I be learning?

CHIRON. Alas! Do not excite my yearning . . .
Phoebus[3] I never gazed upon,

---

7. In Homer's *Odyssey*, II and III, Pallas Athena appears to Telemachus in the
guise of Mentor, a family friend, to lead
him on his journey to find his father.
8. Castor and Pollux, twin half-brothers
of Helena, sons of Leda.
9. Zetes and Calais, sons of Boreas (the
North Wind).

1. A legendary poet who accompanied
Jason on the *Argo*.
2. An argonaut renowned for his keen-
ness of sight. The watchman in Act III,
lines 9218 ff., and Act V, lines 11143 ff.,
is given the name "Lynceus," presumably with this figure in mind.
3. Apollo, God of the sun.

Of Ares, Hermes[4] saw no sign,
Then stood before my eyes the one   7385
Whom men would worship as divine.
Born to be king above all others,
In youth most splendorous to view;
Meek servant of his elder brother's
And of the loveliest women too.   7390
No like of his will Earth engender,
Nor Hebe[5] lift to Heaven's throne;
Here must the laboring lyre surrender,
In vain do they torment the stone.

FAUST. Though sculptors vaunted each his token,   7395
So grand he never came to view.
Of fairest hero you have spoken,
Now speak of fairest women too!

CHIRON. Bah! Beauty's often lifeless; not in feature
True loveliness is found expressed.   7400
I keep my praises for the nature
That overbrims with joy and zest.
Beauty but blesses her own face,
But irresistible is grace,
Like Helen's when she rode on me.   7405

FAUST. You carried her?

CHIRON.   I did; this back she used.

FAUST. Am I not quite enough confused
Without such seat entrancing me?

CHIRON. Into my hair she sank her fingers, just
As you do now.

FAUST.   Oh, I am lost,   7410
Lost altogether! Tell of her!
She is my prime, my sole desire!
Whence did you bear her? Oh, and where?

CHIRON. I grant with ease what you enquire.
The Dioscuri had redeemed just then   7415
Their little sister, prey to highwaymen,[6]
But these, unused to being foiled of loot,
Took courage and came storming in pursuit.
The marshes near Eleusis[7] bade to slow
The threesome's rapid flight, and so   7420
The brothers waded through, I splashed and swam across.
Then she dismounted and began caressing
My dripping mane, and, self-possessed, addressing,
Endearingly astute, sweet thanks to me.
So charming—young, an old man's joy—was she!   7425

4. Mars, god of war; Mercury, herald
of Jupiter.
5. The goddess Hebe became the wife of
Hercules after his deification.
6. See notes to lines 6530 and 7369. Chiron's participation in the rescue is the
invention of Goethe.
7. A town in Attica ten miles east of
Athens, site of the Eleusinian mysteries.

FAUST. Aged only ten . . . !

CHIRON.   Philologists,[8] I see,
   Have swathed your mind, like theirs, in pedantry.
   A myth-born female is a thing apart,
   Steps forth as needed by the poet's art,
   Never of age nor over age,   7430
   At ever appetizing stage,
   Abducted young, wooed in senescence yet,
   Unbound by chronometric etiquette.

FAUST. Thus Helen too—no lapse of time shall bind her!
   Did not at Pherae[9] great Achilles find her,   7435
   Beyond all time? What bliss more rare or great:
   Love wrested from the tyranny of fate!
   And could I not by fierce desire contrive
   To will the incomparable back alive,
   Peer of the gods, imperishable treasure,   7440
   August and loveable in equal measure?
   I saw her here and now, as you did there,
   So fair as lovely, as desired, so fair.
   The harshest bonds my mind and soul confine,
   I will not live if she can not be mine.   7445

CHIRON. Dear stranger, as a man you are enthused,
   To spirits, though, your mind appears confused.
   Yet here you are in luck, for it so chances
   That yearly I exchange brief words and glances
   With Manto,[1] who in silent imprecation   7450
   Entreats her father—she's Asclepios' daughter—
   That for his own endangered reputation
   He shed in doctors' minds illumination
   And wean them from the wont of brazen slaughter . . .
   Of Sybils[2] she's to me the most attractive,   7455
   Not all contortions, charitably active;
   She shortly may contrive, I dare assure you,
   With power of roots most thoroughly to cure you.

FAUST. I ask not to be cured, my mind is sound,
   Else it would drag, like others', on the ground.   7460

CHIRON. Spurn not the bounty of the noble fount!
   Here, we have reached it. Quick, dismount!

FAUST. Say, whither have you, of a fearsome night,
   Through gravelled waters borne me to alight?

CHIRON. Here Rome and Greece were locked in stubborn
      fight,[3]   7465

8. The manuscript read "Mythologists" (*Mythologen*).
9. After her death Helena was said to have married Achilles, who was released from death to live with her on the island of Leuce. Goethe substituted Pherae, a town in Thessaly near the home of Achilles.
1. Manto was the daughter of Tiresias; to substantiate her medical skills, Goethe introduces her as the daughter of Asclepios, the Greek god of medicine and healing.
2. Sybils were soothsayers prominent in Roman historic legend and literature.
3. The allusion is to the battle of Pydna (168 B.C.), in which the Romans under Aemilius Paullus defeated Perseus, King of Macedonia.

Olympus left, Peneios on their right,
The greatest empire sinking in the sand;
The king in flight, the burgher in command.
Look up! Majestic, close before you loom
The eternal temple[4] walls in moonlit gloom.   7470

MANTO. [*within, dreaming*]
             With hooves' pounding
             The sacred stair resounding,
             Demigods are nigh.

CHIRON.   Quite so!
             Just open an eye!   7475

MANTO. [*wakening*] Welcome! I see you're not remiss.

CHIRON. As steadfast as your temple edifice!

MANTO. Still roving ever, unabating?

CHIRON. You ever dwell in sheltered stillness pure,
While I delight in circulating.   7480

MANTO. Time circles me, while I endure.
And this one?

CHIRON.   Ill-famed night of late
Has whirled him hither in its spate.
For Helen do his addled senses yearn,   7485
It's Helen he would woo and earn,
And knows not how, or where to turn;
Needs more than most the Aesculapian leech.

MANTO. I hold him dear who craves beyond his reach.
      [CHIRON *is far off by now.*]

MANTO. Rejoice, bold youth, come follow me;
This gloomy shaft leads to Persephone.[5]   7490
Within Olympus' hollow root
She hears in stealth prohibited salute.
Here in his time I smuggled Orpheus through,[6]
Make better use of it; take courage, in with you!
      [*They descend.*]

ON THE UPPER PENEIOS, AS BEFORE[1]

SIRENS. Plunge into Peneios' flood!
        There we should be splashing, ranging,
        Tuneful part-song interchanging,
        For the wretched people's good.
        Far from water nothing thrives!
        If we hastened all our host   7500

4. The Temple of Apollo, presided over by Manto.
5. Persephone, Queen of Hades. (See the "Second Sketch for the Announcement of the *Helena*," below.)
6. See note to line 7375. Faust follows the example of Orpheus, who pleaded before Persephone to bring the dead Eurydice back to life.
1. After Faust departs with Manto, the scene shifts back to the place where Mephistopheles earlier met the mythological beasts.

Down to the Aegean coast,
Every bliss would grace our lives.²
[*Earthquake.*]
Backward rush the waves with foaming,
Down their bed no longer roaming;
Earth is shaken, water staunched,   7505
Smoking banks are upward launched.
We must flee! Come, every one!
Such a portent profits none.
Noble merry guests are fleeing
To the feast of the Aegean,   7510
Where the glinting ripples' welling
Wets the beach with gentle swelling;
There, where Luna doubly glistens,³
Dews us with her sacred essence.
There, a careless animation,   7515
Here, dread jolts of earth's foundation;
Hurry, all who know their good!
Haunted is this neighborhood.

SEISMOS.⁴ [*in the depths, grumbling and rumbling*]
One more shove, but stronger, bolder,
One more heave with mighty shoulder!   7520
Thus we rise through earth and boulder
Up where all must give us way.

SPHINXES. What a mind-revolting tremor,
Noisomely uncanny clamor!
What a swerving, lurching, jolting,   7525
Dizzy back and forward bolting!
What unbearable dismay!
Yet we shall not change our roost,
Not if all of hell were loosed.
Now the ground is vaulting, surges,   7530
Wondrous! He of yore emerges,
Hoary ancient, grizzle-pated,
Delos' Island he created,
At a laboring mother's plea
Drove it up from out the sea.⁵   7535
He, with striving, thrusting, prying,
Tautened arms and back applying,

2. The Sirens here look ahead to the festival at the Aegean Sea and its celebration of the creative power of water.
3. The double glistening of Luna is presumably caused by the reflection on the surface of the sea.
4. The name is Greek for "earthquake" and was used as an attribute of Poseidon, god of the sea (cf. Herodotus, *History*, 7.29). According to legend, Poseidon caused the island Delos to rise up in the midst of the Aegean to provide a suitable birthplace for Apollo and Artemis. Goethe owned a copy of Raphael's painting of the liberation of Paul from prison which showed such a giant breaking free from below the earth.
5. See note preceding line 7519. The mother of Apollo and Artemis, Leto, was being pursued by Hera, angry at the infidelity of her husband Zeus in begetting the twins, and Poseidon created Delos to provide a refuge for her.

Atlas-like[6] in straining toil,
Lifts the ground with sward and soil,
Gravel, pebble, sand, the bed   7540
Of our tranquil riverstead.
So he tears a gash with gloating
Through the valley's quiet coating.
With untiring labor tense,
Caryatid[7] of bulk immense;   7545
Heaves a fearful rocky prison,
From the ground but halfway risen;
But no more must be permitted,
Note it, here are Sphinxes seated.

SEISMOS. This is of my unaided making,   7550
  As should be granted everywhere;
Had I not buffeted and shaken,
How would the world have been so fair?
How could your lofty peaks be drifting
Proud in the pure ethereal blue,   7555
Had I not done the strenuous lifting
For picturesquely ravished view?
When in the sight of highest ancestry,
Of Chaos, Night,[8] I proved myself robust,
And with the Titans for my company   7560
Ossa and Pelion[9] for playballs tossed.
We frolicked on there, youth in seething sap,
Till, wearying, right at the last,
On Mt. Parnassus wantonly we cast
Both of the others like a double cap . . .[1]   7565
Now merry concourse rallies yonder
Apollo and his Muses fair,
For Jove himself, with all his thunder,
I raised aloft his easy-chair.[2]
Now likewise, with stupendous heaving,   7570
I from the deeps thrust up and out
And loudly challenge to new living
Gay dwellers for me hereabout.

SPHINXES. Ancient is, one would surmise,
  What here castled up is found,   7575
Had it not before our eyes
Wrung itself from out the ground.

6. An allusion to the Titan who was thought to support the vault of heaven upon his shoulders.
7. In Classical Greek architecture, the name for a supporting column carved in the form of a woman, derived from the maidens of Caryae (Karyai) in Laconia, who wore a ring upon their heads for carrying baskets.
8. Seismos claims that his parents are Chaos and Night, in Hesiod's *Theogony* the primal powers who created the earth.

9. Pelion and Ossa are mountains in northeastern Greece. The Titans were said to have tried to scale heaven by piling Ossa on Mt. Olympus and Pelion on Ossa.
1. Mt. Parnassus has twin peaks which are not otherwise associated with Pelion and Ossa.
2. Seismos here claims to have built the halls of the Olympians, the "easy-chair" of Jove and the place where Apollo and the Muses sing.

There bush-lined woods are spreading up the side,
While rock on rock surge up with thrust and slide;[3]
A sphinx this cannot incommode   7580
Or trouble in her sanctified abode.

GRIFFINS. Gold in slices, gold in slivers
In the cracks and crannies quivers.
Such a hoard, let no one snatch it;
Up, you emmets, pick and catch it!   7585

CHORUS OF ANTS. As giant then
Labored to lift it,
Scrabble-feet you,
Scurry to sift it!
In and out, nimbly!   7590
In every cleaving
There is a crumblet
Worth the retrieving.
However little,
Be nothing left,   7595
Take pains and scuttle
To every cleft.
Scan every fold,
You teeming flock,
Hurry in the gold,   7600
Let go the rock.

GRIFFINS. Come up! Come up! bring gold in heaps,
We lay our claws on it for keeps;
They serve for bolts of surest kind,
The greatest hoard is well enshrined.   7605

PYGMIES.[4] Truly, we have found our spot here,
Little knowing how or where.
Do not ask us how we got here,
For the fact is, we are there!
To support high spirits, fitting   7610
We consider any land;
Anywhere a rock is splitting,
Promptly there's a dwarf on hand.
Dwarf and dwarvess, quick and steady,
Exemplary couples all,   7615
Hard to say if things already
Worked like this before the Fall.
But we find this of the best,
Thank our star for pleasant setting;
For in East as well as West   7620
Mother Earth enjoys begetting.

3. The newly formed mountain immediately becomes overgrown with plants and
trees, a swift recapitulation of geological
history.
4. According to Greek legend (Homer's
Iliad, III. 6 ff.), the Pygmies who dwelt
on the shore of Oceanus fought an annual war with migrating cranes. These
figures have been made by Goethe to resemble the gnomes (or "dwarfs") of the
carnival in Act I (lines 5840 ff.).

DACTYLS.[5]   If overnights
           She bore little wights,
           She'll bear least ones to boot,
           Who'll find partners to suit.   7625

PYGMY ELDEST.   Hurry, make haste
           To be properly placed!
           To work, and bustle;
           Speed is our muscle!
           While peace is yet,   7630
           Your forge be set,
           Weapon and shield
           The host to yield.
           You emmets all,
           Surge you and sprawl,   7635
           Ore for us haul!
           And Dactyls canny,
           Tiny but many,
           Yours to secure
           Timber, be sure   7640
           To nurse sly flame
           In well-stacked frame
           Coal to procure.

GENERALISSIMO.[6]   With arrow and bow
           A-hunting, ho!   7645
           That tarn is teaming
           With egrets gleaming,
           Countlessly nesting ones,
           Haughtily breasting ones,
           Shoot all together!   7650
           Shoot the whole host;
           That we may boast
           Helmet and feather.

EMMETS AND DACTYLS.
           Who saves our lives!
           We bring the ore,   7655
           They forge but gyves.
           To rise defiant
           Is premature,
           We must be pliant.

THE CRANES OF IBYCUS.[7]
           Cries of murder, deathly anguish!   7660
           Flailing pinions falter, languish!

5. These little creatures, named for the Greek *dactylos* ("fingers"), are used by the Pygmies as slave labor to mine and forge the gold (along with the Ants, or Emmets, below, lines 7634 ff.).
6. This pompous military leader of the Pygmies apparently wants to kill the egrets (or herons) in order to use their feathers for decorating his helmet.

7. The Cranes, traditional enemies of the Pygmies, are here named after Ibycus, an ancient Greek poet, who was killed —according to a ballad by Schiller, from which Goethe derives his title—by robbers and subsequently avenged by a flock of cranes who publicly identified the murderers.

What a wailing, what a moan
Sends aloft its plaintive tone!
Ah, already all are dead,
With their blood the lake is red;   7665
Avarice misshapen, gory,
Rapes the egret's noble glory.
On the helmets, there! it waves
Of those bowleg fat-paunch knaves.
Flight companions of the seaways,   7670
Comrades of our serried relays,
You to vengeance here we call
In a cause akin to all;
No one spare his strength or blood,
Feud eternal to this brood![8]   7675

[*They disperse in the air with hoarse cries.*]

MEPHISTOPHELES. [*on the plain*][9] With northern witches my
control was sounder,
But with these foreign sprites I seem to flounder.
The Blocksberg[1] makes so snug a rendezvous,
Wherever one may be, there's others too.
Frau *Ilse* on her *Stone* maintains her stand,   7680
Upon his *Peak* Herr *Heinrich* is on hand,
The *Snorers* snarl at *Misery*,[2] no doubt,
But all of this will last millennia out.
But here, you take a step, and there's no telling
When earth blows up at you like bladders swelling! . . . 7685
I roam a level valley, all serene,
Abruptly rearing at my back is seen
A mountain—small indeed to earn the name,
To part me from my sphinxes, all the same,
Quite high enough—here many a flame is bounding   7690
All down the vale, the prodigy surrounding . . .
That wanton company of roguish flirts[3]
Still skips and skims before me, tempts and skirts.
Step softly now! Too much inured to snatching,
One takes in dubious dainties for the catching.   7695

LAMIAE.[4] [*drawing* MEPHISTOPHELES *after them*]

8. The call to arms of the Cranes may be modeled on the opening chorus in Aristophanes's *Birds*, where the bird chorus prepares to attack the intruders from Athens.

9. We are here to assume a cinematic shift of scene from the surface of the newly formed mountain down to the plain, where we pick up Mephistopheles in his pursuit of the Lamiae (which began at the end of the scene on the Upper Peneios, line 7248).

1. An allusion to the setting of the "Walpurgis Night."

2. Mephistopheles is here punning on the names of some of the places in the Harz Mountains in the vicinity of the Brocken, where the "Walpurgis Night" of *Part I*

took place (see note preceding line 3835). They were there left in their German forms: *Ilsenstein* ("Stone of Frau Ilse"), *Heinrichshöhe* ("Peak of Herr Heinrich"), *Schnarcher* ("Snorers"), and *Elend* ("Misery") (see line 3880).

3. Mephistopheles refers to the Lamiae, whom he is pursuing.

4. See note to line 7235. In contrast to the primal complacency of the Sphinxes, the Lamiae are constantly moving, constantly changing, constantly deceiving. The Lamiae are also analogous to the witches of the "Walpurgis Night" in *Part I* in their coarse sexual temptation of Mephistopheles.

Faster and faster!
And on and on!
Then lag and chatter
With rapid patter.
It is such fun   7700
So to be easing
The old whoremaster
To heavy penance.
With rigid tendons
He dogs us, humping   7705
Along and stumping,
Dragging his leg;
Wherever we tease him,
Clatters his peg![5]

MEPHISTOPHELES. [*stopping*] Accursed are menfolk! Dupes and rubes   7710
Since Adam's fall, befuddled boobs!
Who ends up wise, though old and hoar?
Were you not fool enough before?
One knows they're rotten to the core, their faces
All paint and rouge, the rest held up by laces.   7715
There's nothing sound there, nothing answers, lives,
Wherever you may touch them, something gives.
You see it, touch it, know it in advance,
And yet, just let the baggage pipe, you dance!

LAMIAE. [*pausing*] He's wondering, hesitating; stay!   7720
Turn back again, don't let him get away.

MEPHISTOPHELES. [*striding ahead*] Don't be a fool! avoid the stitches
That mark the web of doubt and cavil;
If there were not any witches,
Who the deuce would play the devil!   7725

LAMIAE. [*most captivatingly*] Ring this hero round and urge him,
Surely, in his heart emerging,
Love for one of us will burgeon.

MEPHISTOPHELES. Twilight, I confess it freely,
Shows you quite attractive really,   7730
I give credit where it's due.

EMPUSA.[6] [*intruding*] Due to me, no less than you!
Take me in your circle too.

LAMIAE. She's out of place, the pushy one,
She always comes and spoils our fun.   7735

EMPUSA. [*to* MEPHISTOPHELES] Your little cousin greet, I beg,
Empusa with the donkey-leg;
Yours is a horse-foot, I regret,
Sir Cousin—still, a warm well-met!

5. An allusion to the devil's cloven hoof.
6. This horrifying ghost was said to be able to change its shape at will. Usually appearing to travelers, it could be chased away with shouts and curses. Goethe chose to have it appear with the head of an ass in satirical association with Mephistopheles' hoof. The "donkey-leg" (line 7737) was traditional.

MEPHISTOPHELES. Here was I, braced for new sensations, 7740
  And all I find is near relations;
  The world, there's well-thumbed tomes to tell us,
  Is thick with kin, from Harz to Hellas!
EMPUSA. My habit is direct and bold;
  The shapes I choose are manifold, 7745
  But in your honor, I was led
  To don this little ass's head.
MEPHISTOPHELES. I notice that these people's sense
  Of family is most intense;
  But come what may, and all the same, 7750
  The ass I'd just as soon disclaim.
LAMIAE. Let go this nasty fright, she'll scare
  What has a fair and lovely air;
  What fair and lovely was before,
  When she comes up, is so no more! 7755
MEPHISTOPHELES. These dainty slinky cousins here
  Will all bear watching too, I fear;
  The roses on their cheeks may please,
  But warn of metamorphoses.
LAMIAE. There's lots of us, just show some pluck! 7760
  Fall to! and if you are in luck,
  The winning ticket you may snatch.
  Why all this drooling gibberish?
  Is this your wooing, you poor fish?
  You strut about like some prize catch!— 7765
  Now he's amongst us as we ask;
  Give way now, each let down her mask
  And lay her inner nature bare.
MEPHISTOPHELES. I choose the fairest of the fair . . .
  [*embracing her*] A scrawny broomstick! Oh despair! 7770
  [*seizing another*] And this one? . . . What a hideous fright!
LAMIAE. You think it doesn't serve you right?
MEPHISTOPHELES. This charmer I should like to nip . . .
  A lizard slithering from my grip!
  Her braid feels like a snake, all slick, 7775
  I'll grab that lanky one instead . . .
  Now I embrace a thyrsus stick![7]
  And with a pine-cone for a head.
  Where will it end? . . . That chubby one
  May yet provide a bit of fun; 7780
  Here goes—the last one that I woo!
  All lush and mushy, as is sold
  To pashas for its weight in gold . . .
  Oh, phew! the puffball bursts in two!
LAMIAE. Now dart asunder, veer and hover, 7785
  Now lightning lunges blackly cover

7. A staff, tipped with a pine cone and twined with ivy, which was carried by the Maenads, followers of the god Dionysus, at feasts and celebrations in his honor.

The interloping witch's spawn!
From eery random circles drawn
Swoop down on noiseless wings of bat!
He's getting off too easily at that.   7790
MEPHISTOPHELES. [*shaking himself*] Not much new wisdom do I
    carry forth;
Absurdness here, absurdity up north,
Ghosts, here as yonder, problematic,
Poets and public, both pathetic.
It was all mummery, no more,   7795
Phantasmagoria, as before.
At luring masquers I would run,
And what I touched left me aghast . . .
I find to be deceived quite fun—
If only it were made to last.   7800
[*losing his way among the rocks*]⁸ Where am I now? Where
    should I stumble?
This was a path, now it's a jumble.
The way was level, free of trouble,
Now I am up against all rubble.
I clamber up and down in vain,   7805
Where will I find my Sphinx again?
I never dreamt so wild a sight,
Such mountains in a single night!
A pretty lusty witches' trot!
They bring their Blocksberg to the spot.   7810
OREAS.⁹ [*from the living rock*] Up here to me! Old is my height,
Kept its primeval shape and site.
Revere the dizzying rocky brinks,
The Pindus chain's most forward links.¹
Just as unshaken stood my head   7815
When over me Great Pompey fled.²
Whereas the shapes of fancy born
Fade on the cock's crow at the dawn.³
I watch such figments rise up now and then
And of a sudden sink again.   7820
MEPHISTOPHELES. Be honored, venerable head!
By noble oak engarlanded;
Not Luna's very clearest light
Can penetrate your somber night.—
But by those bushes makes its way   7825

8. Mephistopheles has apparently wandered to the limits of the plain and now begins to climb about the rocks and cliffs of the Pindus Mountains (see line 7814).
9. This is the term for a mountain nymph, identified with the spirit of this "living rock" (i.e., a primal rock such as granite).
1. The Pindus is a mountain range running north to south in the west of Thessaly, in northwest Greece.
2. See note to line 6955. According to Plutarch, after his defeat at Pharsalus Pompey fled past Larissa and Tempe (towns in Thessaly) to the sea.
3. An allusion to the mountain Seismos, which has suddenly appeared in the midst of the "Classical Walpurgis Night" and will apparently disappear again with the following dawn.

A light that sheds a modest ray.
How paths do cross in this affair!
Homunculus! I do declare.
Where do you come from, Sparkleface?

HOMUNCULUS. I float like this from place to place,   7830
Keen on the finest manner of becoming;
I cannot wait to smash my glass and flare;
But judging by the morning's slumming,
To venture into this I hardly dare.
In confidence, I'm tracking down a pair   7835
Of sages[4] whom I want to question next;
I listened: Nature! Nature! went the text.
These I should like to fasten on as teachers;
They're bound to know the way of earthly creatures;
I think I see a chance at last to learn   7840
Which is the wisest way for me to turn.

MEPHISTOPHELES. You'd better try by your own lights.
For anywhere that spook holds sway
Philosopher has right of way.
And to ingratiate his art he makes   7845
A dozen new ones in two shakes.
By going wrong alone you come to rights!
If you would be, become by your own lights.

HOMUNCULUS. Good counsel, though, is not a gift to flout.

MEPHISTOPHELES. Away then! We shall see how it turns out.   7850
[*They separate.*]

ANAXAGORAS. [*to* THALES][5] Your stubborn mind will not be moved?
You want still more than this to stand disproved?

THALES. The wave will bend to any wind and tide,
But from the jagged cliff it holds aside.

ANAXAGORAS. That cliff exists by dint of swathes of flame.   7855

THALES. It is in moisture, though, that life became.

HOMUNCULUS. [*between the two*] Admit me to your company,
I too aspire to come to be!

ANAXAGORAS. Have you, oh Thales, in but one night's flood
Raised such a mountain from a mass of mud?   7860

THALES. Never was Nature and her fluid power
Indentured yet to day and night and hour.
She shapes each form to her controlling course
And be the scale immense, eschews all force.

ANAXAGORAS. But not so here! Here fierce Plutonian plasmas,   7865
Explosive rage of vast Aeolic miasmas,[6]

---

4. A reference to Thales and Anaxagoras (see the next note).
5. Anaxagoras (ca. 500–430 B.C.) was an Athenian philosopher who concerned himself above all with the nature of the material world, proposing (among other controversial doctrines) that the heavenly bodies consist of burning masses of stone, instead of spiritual powers or gods. Thales of Miletus (ca. 620–546 B.C.), earliest of the pre-Socratic philoso-phers, was concerned with cosmological-theological speculation, possibly influenced by Aegyptian or Phoenician lore. He taught—according to Aristotle in his *Metaphysics*—that water was the primal element of the material world.
6. The winds and fires of volcanic explosion are described in mythological allusions to Pluto, god of the underworld, and Aeolus, god of the winds.

Broke through the level bottom's ancient crust,
That a new mountain could arise, and must.
THALES. What is the sequel, now that this is past?
    It is in place, and that is good at last.   7870
    This sort of quarrel fritters time away
    And only leads the credulous astray.
ANAXAGORAS. With Myrmidons the mountain teems,
    Who occupy all chinks and seams,
    With pygmies, emmets, gnomes, Tom Thumbs,   7875
    And their minute but active chums.[7]
    [*to* HOMUNCULUS]. You never have set high your sight,
    Lived sparsely like an anchorite;
    If you can take to governing,
    I plan to have you crowned as king.   7880
HOMUNCULUS. What says my Thales?
THALES.   He objects;
    With little men go little acts,
    Among the great a small one grows.
    See there![8] the cranes' black thundercloud,
    It threatens the excited crowd,   7885
    And you with them, if you were king.
    With raking claws and beaks like talons
    They dive upon the pygmy columns,
    Pale doom like lightning flickering.
    An outrage felled the egret ranks,   7890
    Encircling their pacific banks.
    Those very missiles' murderous rain
    Draws cruel blood-revenge in train,
    Brings nearest kin in fury red
    For tainted pygmy-blood to shed.   7895
    Shield, helmet, spear, what use are these?
    What good to dwarves the egret feather?[9]
    How dactyls, emmets cringe together!
    Now breaks the host, now melts, now flees.
ANAXAGORAS. [*after a pause, solemnly*] While hitherto I praised
        those underground,   7900
    In this case my appeal is upward bound . . .
    To Thee on high, unagingly the same,
    Of threefold form and threefold name,
    Out of my people's woe I cry to thee,
    Diana, Luna, Hecate![1]   7905
    Thou inmost-sensing, soul-enlarging,

---

7. Anaxagoras re-introduces a perspective on the figures moving about the mountain of Seismos, both the Ants (Emmets) digging the gold and the Pygmies and Dactyls at war with the Cranes, all observed apparently from a separate vantage point. "Myrmidons" (line 7873) were the warriors who fought under Achilles at Troy, originally created by Zeus out of ants (*myrmēkes*) to repeople plague-stricken Aegina, the island kingdom of Achilles' pious grandsire, Aeacus.

8. Thales describes the action of the battle between the Pygmies and the Cranes.

9. A reference to the helmet feathers extracted from the egrets slaughtered by the Pygmies (see note preceding line 7644).

1. Anaxagoras invokes the moon as a goddess of triple-name.

Thou placid seeming, fiercely charging,
Unclose Thy shadows' fearful maw to sight,
Without a spell reveal the ancient might.
  [*Pause.*]

               Has prayer brought curse?   7910
               Has my cry uncurbed
               Those heights, disturbed
               The order of the universe?

Already ever greater, closer, nears
Her seat of majesty, inscribed in spheres,   7915
Appalling, monstrous to the sight!
A dusky red its darkling light . . .
No! Orb of threatening might, halt your pursuing!
Or we and land and sea are swept to ruin.
So those Thessalian women—could it be?—   7920
Trusting their lawless tuneful sorcery,
Did sing you down, and from you wrested
What is with direst peril vested? . . .
The glowing shield is swathed in dark—
Now rent with lighting flash and spark!   7925
What rushing hiss! what rattling spatter!
Now thunders, monstrous stormwinds scatter!—
Fall at the throne in humble suing!
Forgiveness! For it was my doing.
  [*He prostrates himself on the ground.*]

THALES. The things this man contrived to see and hear!   7930
As to what happened I am less than clear;
In what he witnessed I shared even less.
These hours are out of joint, we must confess,
And Luna rocks her slanted face
Quite cozily in her old place.   7935

HOMUNCULUS. The mound, look, where the pygmies sat,
It's pointed now where it was flat.
I felt a shock of force appalling,
Out of the moon a rock had fallen,
And instantly, without ado,   7940
Both friend and foe it crushed and slew.
Yet praise is due to arts, you know,
By which in one night, one creative throw,
Both from above and from below,
This mountain edifice was wrought.   7945

THALES. Rest easy! It was all in thought.
Let them go hang, the nasty brood!
That you were not their king is good.
Now to the happy sea-feast we repair,
For wondrous guests they hope to honor there.   7950
  [*They depart.*]

MEPHISTOPHELES. [*climbing on the opposite side*] Here I must
      toil up stairs of slanting rocks,
Across unyielding roots of ancient oaks!

Upon my homely Harz, the whiff of resin
Is redolent of pitch, which I find pleasant;
Second to sulphur . . . Here, among these Greeks,   7955
You hardly sense a trace of suchlike reeks;
I feel an itch to nose out, all the same,
With what they stoke hell's agony and flame.
DRYAD.[2] In your own land apply your native wit,
Abroad, you haven't the resource for it.   7960
Toward the homeland you should leave off peering,
The grandeur of these sacred oaks revering.
MEPHISTOPHELES. One thinks of that which one forsook;
The wonted stands for Eden in one's book.
But tell me, what in yonder lair   7965
By murky light is triply huddling?
DRYAD. The Phorcyads![3] To their cavern dare,
Address them, if you can for shudd'ring.
MEPHISTOPHELES. Why not? I gape at what I see within it.
Proud as I am, I must admit   7970
I never saw the like of it,
The hideous mandrake is not in it! . . .[4]
Can the transgressions loathed of yore
At all seem ugly any more
Upon this triple ogre's sight?   7975
I think these monsters would offend us
Where Hell yawns at its most horrendous.
And here they roost in beauty's land of fable
That bears the honorable classic label . . .
They stir, have sensed me now, I'd say,   7980
With whistling twitter, vampire bats at bay.
PHORCYAD. Sisters, pass me the eye, that it make query
Who dares approach our sanctuary so nearly.
MEPHISTOPHELES. Oh most revered! May I solicit leave
To venture near and threefold grace receive?   7985
Unknown indeed, without recommendation
I come, yet by all signs a far relation.
I have laid eyes on gods of ancient awe,
To Ops and Rhea[5] deeply bowed of yore.
The Parcae,[6] yours and Chaos' sisters hoar,   7990
I saw them yesterday—or day before;
But none to match you did I ever see,
And I fall silent now in ecstasy.
PHORCYADS. He seems a spirit of judicious mind.
MEPHISTOPHELES. How comes it that no poet lauds your kind?   7995
Say! What accounts for this, how could it be
You worthiest I never saw in effigy?

---

2. A tree nymph.
3. Three of the daughters of Phorcys, also called "Graiae," were gray-haired, ancient witches who shared one eye and one tooth. They were said to live in a place where neither the sun nor the moon shone.

4. See note to line 4980.
5. Ops, the Roman goddess of sowing and harvest, and Rhea, the wife of Saturn, were often identified with one another.
6. The three Fates (see note preceding line 5305).

Let chisel strain your splendor to describe,
Not Juno, Pallas, Venus[7] and their tribe.
PHORCYADS. In stillest night and solitude confined,   8000
The thought of it has never crossed our mind!
MEPHISTOPHELES. How could it, seeing that the world you shun,
See no one here and are beheld by none.
For that, you would have to inhabit places
Where pomp divides a throne with art's high graces,   8005
Where nimbly every day at double speed
A hero from a marble slab is freed.
Where . . .
PHORCYADS.   Give us peace from the temptation of it!
If we knew better even, would we profit?
Sprung forth from Night, to the nocturnal prone,   8010
Wholly to all, half to ourselves unknown.
MEPHISTOPHELES. In such a case this is no special bother,
One may transmit one's self unto another.
Your threesome finds one eye, one tooth enough,
Then for mythology it could not be too tough   8015
To lodge in two the essence of the three
And leave the likeness of the third to me,
For a brief time.
ONE.   How does it seem to you?
THE OTHERS. Excepting eye and tooth—yes, it would do!
MEPHISTOPHELES. With that you have excluded just the best;   8020
How could the form's full rigor be expressed?
ONE. Just close one eye, 'twill do it even so,
Let forthwith but a single eye-tooth show,
In profile then you will attain the semblance
Of a perfected sisterly resemblance.   8025
MEPHISTOPHELES. Too kind! So be it!
PHORCYADS.   Be it!
MEPHISTOPHELES. [*as* PHORCYAS, *in profile*] There, it's done,
I stand as Chaos's beloved son!
PHORCYADS. We stem from Chaos by undoubted right.
MEPHISTOPHELES. Oh pain! they'll call me an hermaphrodite.
PHORCYADS. In our new triad, what adornment new!
Of eyes as well as teeth, we now have two.[8]
MEPHISTOPHELES. But I must hide from everybody's sight,
To give the devils of the Pit a fright.
          [*Exit.*]

ROCKY INLETS OF THE AEGEAN SEA†

The Moon at Rest at the Zenith[1]

7. Juno, Minerva (Pallas Athena), and
Venus here represent the Olympian goddesses.
8. Mephistopheles, in assuming the guise
of Phorcyas, has lent the Phorcyads one
of his eyes and teeth.

1. The entire festival takes place at a
moment of suspended time, the climax
of the mythical process which unfolds
throughout the "Classical Walpurgis
Night."

SIRENS [*reclining here and there on the cliffs, piping and singing*][2]

> While Thessalian witching women
> Once in spectral lunar dimming   8035
> Impiously drew you down,
> Now gaze calmly from your sweeping
> Vault of night on tremulous leaping,
> Quivering wavelets mildly gleaming,
> And illuminate the teeming
> Forms now rising from the waves.
> Eager for your service know us,
> Grace, oh fairest Luna, show us!

NEREIDS AND TRITONS. [*in the shape of sea prodigies*][3]

> Make a louder, sharper sounding,
> Through the ocean sea resounding,   8045
> Dwellers of the deep call here!
> At the tempest's fearsome riot
> We withdrew to depths of quiet,
> Tuneful singing draws us near.

> See, we take most joyous pleasure   8050
> Donning chains of golden treasure,
> Into precious crown-gems shining
> Clasps and jeweled girdles joining,
> All of it your hoard and prey.
> Barks that bore them, men and master,   8055
> You have sung them to disaster,
> You, the demons of our bay.

SIRENS.

> Well we know, in cool of ocean
> Fish rejoice in gliding motion,
> Veering void of grief or wish;   8060
> But—you swarms in festive moving,
> Now we hope to find you proving
> That you can be more than fish.

NEREIDS AND TRITONS.

> Ere we came, and unreminded,
> We ourselves had long designed it,   8065
> Sisters, brothers, be not late!
> On a voyage, not the longest,
> Gathering witness of the strongest,
> That we top the fish's estate.
> [*They depart.*]

SIRENS.   Off, and vanished straight!   8070
> Toward Samothrace[4]
> With favoring wind they race.

---

2. The Sirens play a central role throughout this scene, providing the musical continuity of the celebration.
3. Presumably mermaids and mermen with fish tails who emerge from the depths in response to the song of the Sirens. The Nereids are daughters of Nereus, one of the two old men of the sea who appear shortly. The Tritons are offspring of Poseidon, god of the sea; they carry conch shells which they blow like trumpets at Poseidon's command to soothe the restless waves.
4. An island in the northeast Aegean Sea famous for its ancient mystery rites and the cult of the so-called great gods.

What sends them speeding, so keen,
To the lofty Cabiri's[5] demesne?†
Gods they, deep wonderment waking,   8075
Themselves ever newly remaking,
And never knowing their own state.

On your heights, we pray,
Gracious Luna, stay;
Let moon-dusk be dense,   8080
Lest day drive us hence.

THALES. [*on the shore, to* HOMUNCULUS] I'd gladly lead you to
    old Nereus[6] too;
His cavern is not far from here, it's true,
His head, though, is as hard as rock,
Cantankerous old vinegar-crock.   8085
Not the entire human race
Can ever please him, sour-face.
He sees the future, though—a lore
Which everyone respects him for,
And pays him honor for its sake;   8090
He's granted many a kindness, too.

HOMUNCULUS. Knock at the door, let's try him, do!
There'll scarce be glass and flame at stake.

NEREUS. Are these men's voices that my ears impart!
What instant wrath they stir deep in my heart!   8095
Those artifacts, to godly likeness prone,
Yet sentenced to be ever but their own.
Gray years I could have savored godlike rest,
But was impelled to benefit their best;
And when at last account of deeds was rendered,   8100
My counsel might as well have not been tendered.

THALES. Yet you, Sea Elder, hold their confidence;
You are the wise one, do not drive us hence!
This flame here, quasi-human though it be,
Puts all its trust in your advice, you see.   8105

NEREUS. Advice! Do men respect it? It is fated
That sapient word congeal in hardened ears.
How grimly have not deeds themselves berated,
And still the tribe in self-will perseveres.
How I gave Paris fatherly advice   8110

5. The generic name for the deities celebrated in the mysteries of Samothrace,
Kabeiroi, non-Greek, possibly Phoenician, in origin. Goethe was attracted to
these obscure deities by contemporary
speculation concerning their significance,
particularly by Friedrich Creuzer, *Symbolism and Mythology of the Ancient
Peoples* (1810–12, Vol. II, pp. 302 ff.),
and by the philosopher Schelling's mono-
graph *On the Gods of Samothrace*
(1815). Both Creuzer and Schelling were
convinced that the Cabiri represent the
earliest, most primitive deities of Greek
mythology, from which all subsequent
Hellenic religion and culture developed.
6. This ancient and prophetic sea god is
provided with uniquely Goethean features as an aged father and sage, "cantankerous" and pessimistic about mankind, who subsequently enjoys and comprehends the moment of epiphany with
a fullness unsurpassed by any of the
other participants (see lines 8134–35,
8150, and 8424).

Lest his quick lust an alien wife entice![7]
There stood he boldly on the Grecian shore,
And I foretold him what I saw in store:
Smoke-stifled air, infused with crimson glow,
Roof-trees ablaze, assault and death below: 8115
Troy's day of doom, in epic rhythms cast,
As dread as well-known to millennia past.
That pup, he counted sport what old men tell,
He took his lust for guide, and Ilion fell—
Titanic corpse, stiff after long ordeal,   8120
To Pindus' eagles a most welcome meal.[8]
Ulysses,[9] too! Why, did I not foretell
The cyclops' savagery, and Circe's spell?
His own delays, his comrades' reckless whim,
Who knows what else! And did that profit him?   8125
Till late enough, and soundly tossed before,
By grace of waves he reached a friendly shore.

THALES. True, such misconduct gives the wise man pain;
The good man, though, will try it once again.
A dram of thanks in pleasure will outweigh   8130
Some hundredweights of thanklessness, I say.
No less a thing than this one is our plea:
This boy would know how best to come to be.

NEREUS. No, chase me not this rarest mood away!
Quite other things await me yet today.[1]   8135
For I have summoned hither all my daughters,
The comely Dorids, Graces of the waters.
Not your earth's soil and not Olympus bears
A lovely being of such graceful airs.
They fling themselves, most captivating motion,   8140
From sea-dragons to Neptune's steeds of ocean,
Most gently wedded to the brine their will,
So that the very spume would raise them still.
In opal flush of Venus' shell-coach gliding,
Now comes the fairest, Galatea,[2] riding,   8145
Who, since the Cyprian's face was turned elsewhere,
Won Paphos' awe and reigns as goddess there.
Thus ever after she has owned, the fairest,
Both temple-town and chariot-throne as heiress.

Be off! In father's hour of joy depart   8150
Harsh words from lips, and hatred from the heart.
Be off to Proteus now! Ask how one can

---

7. Paris supposedly sought the advice of Nereus before he abducted Helena.
8. The fallen city is personified as a corpse which is fed upon by the eagles of the Pindus mountains.
9. The consultation of Nereus by Ulysses concerning his wanderings after the fall of Troy appears to be Goethe's invention.

1. Nereus offers a detailed description of the festival procession which is to come, thus serving as herald or stage manager.
2. Galatea has inherited the place of the Cyprian Venus or Aphrodite, goddess of love, and will ride in the shell which first carried the goddess when she was born from the foam of the sea.

Take shape and vary, of that wonder-man.
    [*Departs toward the sea.*]
THALES. There's nothing gained for us by this foray,
    Proteus, if met, at once dissolves away;   8155
    Even at bay at last, what he propounds
    Is what discountenances and astounds.
    Still, counsel is what you depend upon,
    Let us attempt it then, and wander on!
        [*They depart.*]
SIRENS. [*above, on the cliffs*]
        What from afar comes gliding   8160
        The realm of billows riding?
        As if by Aeol's choosing
        Some snowy sails were cruising,
        So bright they are with radiance,
        Transfigured ocean-maidens.   8165
        Down, let us seek the beaches,
        Already voices reach us.
NEREIDS AND TRITONS. What we bear you, will call
        For rejoicing by all.
        Chelone's[3] huge shell here   8170
        Gleams forth with shape austere:
        They're deities we bring;
        High anthems you must sing.
SIRENS.   Little in height,
        Awsome in might,   8175
        Saviors at sea,[4]
        Revered from gray antiquity.
NEREIDS AND TRITONS. Cabiri here we bear
        To hold a peaceful fair;
        Where they hold sacred honors,   8180
        Neptune will smile upon us.
SIRENS.   We yield you the prize,
        Should vessel capsize,
        Invincible, you
        Will salvage the crew.   8185
NEREIDS AND TRITONS. Three we took off beside us,
        The fourth of them denied us,
        He told us he had the call,
        And thought for one and all.[5]
SIRENS.   One god may be brought   8190
        By another to naught.
        All powers revere ye,
        All injury fear ye.
NEREIDS AND TRITONS. Seven we know them to be.

3. A nymph transformed by Hermes into a sea tortoise. The creatures of the sea carry the Cabiri upon a gigantic tortoise shell.
4. The Cabiri were traditionally regarded as beneficial to sailors, rescuing them from shipwrecks.
5. See note to line 8074. Goethe here follows Schelling's argument on the hierarchy of the Cabiri.

SIRENS.	Where are the other three?	8195
NEREIDS AND TRITONS.	That's asking more than we know,	

Enquire on Olympus, though;
That's where the eighth, too, must be sought
Whom no one yet has given thought!
Aware of us in grace, 8200
But none as yet in place.

Far horizons they beseech,
Peerless, distance-cherishers,
Ever-famished perishers
For the out-of-reach. 8205

SIRENS. It is our way,
Wherever its sway,
In sun or moon, to pray,
It's bound to pay.

NEREIDS AND TRITONS. How matchless our renown, behold, 8210
To usher in this pageant!

SIRENS. The heroes of legend,
Of theirs we grow weary,
Wherever, however extolled,
They carried off the fleece of gold, 8215
You, the Cabiri.[6]
[*repeated in unison*]
They carried off the fleece of gold,
We! ⎱
You! ⎰ the Cabiri.

[NEREIDS *and* TRITONS *pass by*.]

HOMUNCULUS. These freakish shapes, I judge them pots
Of clayware, frail and battered; 8220
Now sages clash with them, and lots
Of hardened heads are shattered.

THALES. That's just what's in demand on earth,
It's rust that gives the coin its worth.

PROTEUS.[7] [*unnoticed*] This warms my fabler's heart, for the more
striking, 8225
The more I find things to my liking.

THALES. Where are you, Proteus?

PROTEUS. [*as if ventriloquizing, now near, now far*] Here! and
here!

THALES. Come, I forgive the tired jest;
But spare a friend vain prattle, I suggest!
I know you're not where you appear. 8230

PROTEUS. [*as if from afar*] Farewell!

6. For their achievement in bringing the Cabiri the Nereids and Tritons are praised as superior to the ancient heroes, even to the Argonauts, who carried off the golden fleece.

7. The old man of the sea is famous for his power of self-transformation even in Homer, where Menelaos describes his confrontation with Proteus in the *Odyssey*, IV. Proteus here represents the power of nature in constant change and variety.

THALES. [*under his breath to Homunculus*] He is quite near. Now
    flash your flare,
  He is as nosy as a bear;
  However shaped, wherever moored,
  By flames of fire he will be lured.
HOMUNCULUS. A flood of light, then, watch me pass;   8235
  Yet modestly, or I might burst the glass.
PROTEUS. [*in the shape of a giant turtle*] What shines so exquisitely
    fair?
THALES. [*covering up* HOMUNCULUS] Good! Look at it more closely
    if you care.
  Just do not grudge the little trouble
  To show yourself on feet humanly double.   8240
  By our indulgence be it, with our will,
  If someone wants to view what we conceal.
PROTEUS. [*nobly shaped*] You still excel in worldly cleverness.
THALES. In changing shapes you take delight no less. [*having re-
    vealed* HOMUNCULUS]
PROTEUS. [*astonished*] A shining little dwarf! Never did see! 8245
THALES. He begs advice, would gladly come to be.
  He has, so I have heard him say,
  Been born but half in some prodigious way.
  Of intellectual traits he has no dearth,
  But sorely lacks the solid clay of earth.   8250
  So far the glass is all that keeps him weighted,
  But he would gladly soon be corporated.
PROTEUS. A genuine spinster's progeny,
  You are before you ought to be!
THALES. [*under his breath*] In other ways, too, things are
    critical.   8255
  I think he is—hermaphroditical.[8]
PROTEUS. The more assuredly then it thrives,
  He'll suit, whichever form arrives.
  No need to ponder this a minute,
  In the broad sea you must begin it!   8260
  There first the tiny way you try,
  The tiniest life contently chewing,
  Thus you grow larger by and by
  And shape yourself for higher doing.
HOMUNCULUS. Here a most gentle ether breezes,   8265
  It smells so fresh, and the aroma pleases!
PROTEUS. That, my dear boy, I understand!
  Out there the cozy aura gets much denser,
  Upon that narrow tongue of strand
  The nimb ineffably intenser;   8270
  A little further we espy
  That floating train from closer by.
  Come there with me!

8. As pure spirit, Homunculus precedes
all sexual division and contains an ambivalent potential to become either male
or female.

THALES. I'm joining you.

HOMUNCULUS. Thrice-odd spiritual retinue!

[TELCHINES *of Rhodes*[9] *on sea-horses and sea-dragons,*[1] *wielding Neptune's trident.*]

CHORUS. 'Tis we who have fashioned Poseidon's great trident, 8275
The billows to soothe in their turmoil most strident.
When clouds are split wide by the Thund'rer's unfolding,
Poseidon replies to the terrible rolling;
What glare from on high may be jaggedly flashed,
There's wave upon wave from below for it splashed; 8280
And what in between may have quakingly wallowed,
Long tossed, by the nethermost depth it is swallowed;
Wherefore he has lent us the scepter today—
And carefree we float now, all festive and gay.

SIRENS. You, to Helios consecrated, 8285
For this feast-day's blessing fated,
Greetings, at this hour which pays
Luna highest awe and praise!

TELCHINES. All-loveliest Queen of yon canopy vaulted!
You hear with enchantment your brother exalted. 8290
To Rhodes,[2] blessed island, kind hearing you lend,
Whence paeans[3] of praise to him ever ascend.
At onset and closure on each of his days
He sends us his fiery radiant gaze.
The mountains, the cities, the shoreline, the bight, 8295
The god finds them pleasing, so lovely and bright.
No fog wafts about us, and should it creep in,
A beam and a breeze, and the island is clean.
His shape finds the god there in hundredfold guise,
As youth, as colossus, yet gentle and wise. 8300
We wrought this, we first ones, who nobly began
To cast godly might in choice likeness of man.

PROTEUS. You let them swagger, let them praise!
The sun-god's sacred living rays
Make sport of works in rigid style. 8305
There they will smelt and mold undaunted,
And once it's cast in bronze, they vaunt it,
Imagining it is worth while.
How does it end, this proud renown?
The godly images stood tall— 8310
A jolt of earth destroyed them all;
Long since they have been melted down.[4]

9. A primitive, diminutive people, representative of a chthonic cult associated with the cabiritic mysteries. They were the first to learn how to work with bronze and iron, and they forged the trident of Poseidon, god of the sea, whom they served also as tutors. As primitive metal workers or smiths, these creatures represent the earliest stage of human craftsmanship and art.
1. The Telchines ride upon fantastic mythological creatures (called Hippocampi) with the bodies of horses and the tails of dolphins.
2. The island where the Telchines lived was sacred to Apollo.
3. A formal ode of celebration dedicated to Apollo.
4. The Colossus of Rhodes is reported to have been destroyed by an earthquake in 223 B.C. and the metal from it melted down and sold.

Terrestrial life, whatever sort,
Is and remains an irksome sport;
To ocean, life is better married;   8315
To timeless floods you shall be carried
By Proteus-Dolphin.
[*He transforms himself.*]
                              Done, you see!
And there most prosperously fare you,
Upon this arching back I bear you
And wed you to the ocean sea.   8320

THALES. Espouse the recommended part,
Begin creation from the start.
For swift enactment gird your will!
You move there by eternal norms,
Through thousand, countless thousand forms,   8325
There's time enough for manship still.[5]
[HOMUNCULUS *mounts* PROTEUS-DOLPHIN.]

PROTEUS. Come with me into moisty distance,
To lead a long and broad existence,
And cruise at will the wide and nether;
But higher orders do not covet,   8330
Once you are human and above it,
You will be done for altogether.

THALES. It all depends, each to his fad;
A fine man of his time is not so bad.

PROTEUS. [*to* THALES] You mean perhaps a type like yours!   8335
That for some little time endures;
Indeed, amid a wan and ghostly cast
I've seen you now for many ages past.

SIRENS. [*on the cliff*]
                    Who about the moon has planted
                    Cloudlets in a ring so bright?   8340
                    Doves they are, by love enchanted,
                    Wings as dazzling-white as light.[6]
                    It is Paphos that released them,
                    Sent her love-enraptured swarm;
                    All perfected is our feast then,   8345
                    Fully clear our joy and calm.

NEREUS. [*approaching* THALES] True, a wanderer might rather
Call this halo "emanation;"
We, the spirits, have another
And the proper explanation.   8350
Doves they are, my daughter's pages,
Which her roving shell escort,

5. Thales describes a process of organic
evolution through stages of metamorphosis with which Goethe as poet and scientist essentially agreed.
6. The doves of Aphrodite from the seat
of her cult at Paphos had originally
served to pull the carriage in which the
goddess rode. Here, since Galatea rides
in the scallop shell which had conveyed
the goddess across the water after her
seabirth, the doves function as the attendants of her train, flying ahead of the
others.

Flight of rare and wondrous sort,
Learnt from immemorial ages.

THALES. No good man would prize it lowly,   8355
    Nor can I but call it best,
    When one nurtures something holy
    In the warm and tranquil nest.

PSYLLI AND MARSI.[7] [*on bulls, calves, and rams of the sea*]
    In Cyprus' rugged cave recesses,
    By Poseidon unburied,   8360
    By Seismos unharried,[8]
    Fanned ever by breezy caresses,
    As of old, and time without end,
    Bliss-aware leisure we spend,
    Cytheria's[9] chariot we tend,   8365
    And lead, at the whisper of night,
    Through the waves' cross-broidered delight,
    To the tribe of the day, out of sight,
    Forward the loveliest maid.
    On our still courses defying   8370
    Both eagle and winged lion,
    Crescent and cross as well;[1]
    However aloft it may reign and dwell,
    Changeably stir and mill,
    Harry each other and kill,   8375
    Crops and towns wreak ill,
    Forth, as ever begun,
    We usher the loveliest lady on.

SIRENS.   Softly gliding, gently pacing,
    Round the chariot, ring on ring,   8380
    File on file now interlacing,
    Serpentine meandering,
    Buxom Nereids, come near,
    Pleasing-wild unto the sight,
    Bring, sweet Dorids, Galatea,   8385
    Her high mother's image quite.[2]
    Grave she seems like godly faces,
    Shares immortals' earnest worth,
    Yet with all the luring graces
    Of the loveliest maid of earth.   8390

7. Obscure, primeval inhabitants of Cyprus, the island of Aphrodite, who here declare that they have tended the shell of the goddess since she first came ashore there. They represent the earliest stage of human culture, cave dwellers like the Cyclops of Homer's *Odyssey*, IX.

8. Just as the sea is momentarily blessed and becalmed for the festival, so also the caves of the Psylli and Marsi are said to be free of the destructive forces of either Poseidon, the sea god, or Seismos, the earthquake.

9. A title of Aphrodite associated with her cult on the island of Cythera.

1. These four heraldic signs—the eagle, the winged lion, the cross, and the crescent moon—are identified with the historical sequence of powers which have held Cyprus: Rome, Venice, the Christian crusaders, and Turkey.

2. The Nereids, who earlier appeared with the Tritons to fetch the Cabiri (lines 8044 ff.), and the Dorids are sisters, named respectively for their father (Nereus) and their mother (the sea nymph Doris).

DORIDS. [*in chorus, as they glide past* NEREUS, *all on dolphins*]
            Luna, light and shade, to render
            Youth's bloom clearer, we desire;
            Cherished bridegrooms now we tender
            Suppliantly to our sire.[3]
     [*to* NEREUS.]
            These are lads we rescued, headed   8395
            For the breakers' grim-toothed face,
            Warmed to light of living, bedded
            Soft on moss and reedy lace,
            Who with fervent kisses tender
            Now their faithful thanks must render;   8400
            Show the charming ones your grace!
NEREUS.   It must pay off in double measure
           To blend, as you do, charity and pleasure.
DORIDS.   Father, if you don't dislike us
            For the joy from ocean wrung,   8405
            Be they clasped, immortal like us,
            To our breast forever young.
NEREUS. Do let the handsome catch enchant you,
         Each mold her own from youth to man;
         I am unable, though, to grant you   8410
         What only the Olympian can.
         The wave, your changeful fellow-rover,
         Grants love continuance no more,
         And once the tender charm is over,
         You set them gently back ashore.   8415
DORIDS.   Sweet youths, we sadly part, it seems,
            Though warmly fond, we vow it;
            Enduring faith was in our dreams,
            The gods will not allow it.   8420
YOUTHS.   Just pour us out such further bliss,
            Brave sailor-lads implore,
            We've never known a life like this,
            And look for nothing more.
     [GALATEA *approaches in her shell chariot.*][4]
NEREUS. It's you, oh my dearest!
GALATEA.   Dear Father, well met!
         What bliss! Oh my dolphins, do tarry just yet![5]   8425
NEREUS. Past it glides, the hurrying throng,
         In plunging circular motion;
         What do they care for fervent heart's devotion!
         Ah—would they only carry me along!
         Yet a single loving gaze   8430
         All the empty year outweighs.

---

3. The Dorids, traditionally fifty in number, ride upon dolphins (similar to Homunculus on Proteus), accompanied by young sailors whom they have rescued from shipwrecks.
4. The iconographic high-point of the festival is here achieved with the epiphany of Galatea.
5. Galatea's call echoes the terms used by Faust in his wager with Mephistopheles (line 1699).

THALES. Hail! Hail again, glad sight!
New burgeons my delight,
With truth and beauty I feel rife . . .
From the water has sprung all life!! 8435
All is sustained by its endeavor!
Vouchsafe us, Ocean, your rule forever.
But for you, rain-clouds sending,
Freshets richly spending,
Streams now here now yonder bending, 8440
Noble rivers ending,
Where would the earth be, where lowland and mountain?
Of life's renewal, you are the fountain.
ECHO. [*chorus of all the circles*] Of life's renewal you are the fount.
NEREUS. They turn and roll in far-off haze, 8445
No longer render gaze for gaze;
In drawn-out curving chain,
To prove their festive vein,
The thronging circles swirl and veer.
Galatea's throne, though, shell-bedecked, 8450
Now and then I do detect.
It gleams like a star
Through the crowd between;
Through teeming masses love's light is seen,
Were it ever so far, 8455
It shines bright and clear,
Ever true and near.
HOMUNCULUS. In this lovely damp,
Whatever lights my lamp
Is sweetly tender. 8460
PROTEUS. In this live damp alone
Has your bright lamp shone
With sound of splendor.[6]
NEREUS. Amid the attendants, what secret untested
Would now be to wondering eyes manifested? 8465
What glares at the shell, by Galatea's feet,
Now mightily glowing, now gracious, now sweet,
As though by the pulses of love it were stirred?
THALES. Homunculus is it, by Proteus ensnared . . .
These symptoms betoken imperious craving, 8470
The clamorous drone of an agonized raving;
He'll crash at her glittering throne and be shattered;
It's flaming, now flashes, already is scattered.[7]
SIRENS. What lights us the billows, what fiery wonder
Sets blazing their clashes and sparkling asunder? 8475
It lightens and wavers and brightens the height:
The bodies, they glow on the courses of night,

6. In these final speeches of Proteus and Homunculus, now far out at sea, the lyrical-musical quality of the festival achieves its highest fulfillment.
7. The final speeches of Nereus and Thales constitute a question and an answer, in which the mythical father-figure, the old man of the sea, must learn the meaning of what is happening from the human philosopher.

And ringed is the whole by the luminous wall;[8]
May Eros[9] then reign who engendered it all!

> Hail the sea, the ocean swelling!   8480
> Wreathed in sacred fiery torrents:
> Hail the fire, the waters welling!
> Hail the singular occurrence!

ALL IN UNISON.[1]

> Hail the gentle airs benignant!
> Hail the deeps with secrets pregnant!   8485
> Solemnly here be ye sung,
> All four elements as one!

Act III†

BEFORE THE PALACE OF MENELAOS AT SPARTA[2]

[*Enter* HELENA *and* CHORUS OF CAPTIVE TROJAN WOMEN.[3]
PANTHALIS,[4] *leader of the chorus.*]

HELENA. Exalted much and much disparaged,[5] Helena,
I leave behind the strand where first we came ashore,
Still in a stupor from the nimble tilt and pitch   8490
Of rolling seas that brought us from the Phrygian[6] plain
Astride high-bristling backs, thanks to Poseidon's[7] grace
And Euros'[8] strength, to inlets of the native land.[9]
King Menelaos is rejoicing down below
In his return amidst the bravest of his host.   8495

8. The Sirens conclude the festival by offering their response to the mystery of Homunculus' self-sacrifice in exalted, hymnic tones. What they perceive and describe is the blending and fusion of opposites—of fire and water, of spirit and substance, of the masculine and feminine—through which life is created in the sea.
9. Not the playful Cupid of later mythology, nor even exclusively the daimon celebrated in Plato's *Symposium*, but a much more ancient, even primal, concept, the original creative force which produces life and light out of chaos. By implication, Homunculus is here the embodiment of Eros, spirit motivated by love (line 8468).
1. Not merely all the participants in the festival but the entire cosmos of ancient Hellas here assumes a single choric voice.
2. The first of the three sections of the *Helena* (lines 8488–9126) consists of an elaborate imitation of the form and structure of Greek tragedy, specifically the drama of Euripides. The meter of the dialogue (with some exceptions in the final scene, for which see note to line 8909), is iambic trimeter, a six-

stress iambic line used in Greek drama, which Goethe—in his initial draft of the *Helena* in 1800—was the first to imitate in German. The stage is also set in imitation of the ancient Greek theater, with the façade of a palace as the backdrop and a main entrance through the central palace doors.
3. A similar chorus of captive Trojan women is used by Euripides in *The Trojan Women* and *Hecuba*.
4. The name derives from Pausanias' description of the painting by Polygnotos (fifth century B.C.) of the fall of Troy, which was to be found in the hall of the Cnidians at Delphi, where Panthalis is one of Helen's attendants.
5. Helena refers to her reputation in literature, the history of her praise and abuse at the hands of poets.
6. Inaccurately used for the region about Troy (Troas).
7. The god of the sea.
8. The east wind.
9. Helena's stupor, caused by the motion of the sea, which the rhythm of the lines seeks to imitate, must also allude to the journey from the underworld which she has just completed (though she does not remember it).

But you, bid welcome to me now, oh lofty house,[1]
Which Tyndareos,[2] my father, back from Pallas' hill,[3]
Erected for himself along the nearby slope
And raised in splendor over any Spartan house,
As I with sister Clytemnestra[4] here grew up,   8500
With Castor, too, and Pollux, playing happy games.[5]
Be greeted, then, the bronzen gate's twin portals you!
It was your hospitably wide-flung openness
By which that time to me, elected out of many,
Shone forth bright Menelaos in a suitor's garb.[6]   8505
Now open them to me once more that I fulfill
In faith a pressing royal charge, as behooves a wife.
Allow me entry! and let all be left behind
That stormed about me hitherto so fatefully.
For since the time I left this threshold free of care   8510
For Cytherea's temple, mindful of sacred troth,
But then a pirate seized me, the Phrygian, on that quest,[7]
Full many things have passed which people far and wide
Are fond of telling, yet which grate on the ear of one
Of whom reports spun out have grown to a fairy-tale.   8515

CHORUS.[8] Do not disdain, oh wondrous Queen,
    The proud possession of the highest good!
    For on you alone was bestowed the greatest bliss,
    The fame of beauty, surpassing all the rest.
    The hero's name rings out before him,   8520
    Lends pride to his gait,
    Yet straight away the most stiffnecked man
    To all-conquering beauty bends his mind.

HELENA. Enough! together with my lord I voyaged here
    And to his city now am sent ahead by him;   8525
    Yet what there may be in his heart I cannot guess.
    Is it as wife I come here? Is it as a queen?
    Is it as victim for the Prince's bitter smart
    And for the Greeks' so long sustained calamities?

1. Helena's address to the palace may be an imitation of similar speeches by the Herald in Aeschylus' *Agamemnon*, lines 518–19, or by Menelaos in Euripides' *Orestes*, lines 356 ff., where both characters are also returning from Troy.
2. King of Sparta and, according to variant genealogical accounts, the father of Helena, Clytemnestra, Castor, and Pollux. According to the alternative myth of Leda and the swan (see lines 6904 ff. and 7277 ff.), Helena's father was the god Zeus.
3. The Acropolis of Athens, sacred to Pallas Athena.
4. Clytemnestra married Agamemnon and Helena married his brother Menelaos.
5. See note to line 7369.
6. Helena alludes to her marriage with Menelaos, who won her hand in competition with many other princely suitors.
7. According to one version of the myth, Paris (the Phrygian "pirate") met Helen at the temple of Aphrodite on the island of Cythera. Paris had awarded the golden apple of Eris, the prize of beauty, to Aphrodite in response to her promise to unite him, as a reward, with the world's most beautiful woman (see note to line 6469). This allusion also recalls the spirit show of Paris and Helena in "Hall of Chivalry" (lines 6421–6565).
8. The three choral insertions to the prologue (lines 8516–23, 8560–67, 8591–8603) are interrelated by metrical responsion to constitute a choral ode, as strophe, antistrophe, and epode respectively. Goethe's imitation of the form of the Greek choral ode in the *Helena* is essentially without precedent in German drama.

A conquest am I—whether captive too, who knows!   8530
For fate and repute did the immortals allot me indeed
Equivocally, of beautiful form the hazardous
Concomitants, who even at this threshold here
Attend my side with presence of portentous gloom.[9]
Still in the hollow ship my lord would look at me   8535
But seldom, nor let fall a single word of cheer.
Like one who harbors ill did he sit facing me.
But presently, as sailing up the bay-shore deep
Of the Eurotas,[1] the leading vessels' beaks were just
Saluting the land, he spoke, as though by a god impelled: 8540
Here shall my warriors disembark, in order due,
I shall review their lines, drawn up along the beach,
But you move onward, keep ascending up the bank,
Endowed with fruit, of sacred Eurotas, on and up,
And guide the steeds onto the moisty meadow's sheen   8545
Until you shall have made your way to the lovely plain
Where Lacedaemon,[2] once a spacious fertile field,
By somber mountains closely neighbored, holds its site.
Then, entering the lofty-towered princely house,
Hold muster for me of the serving-maids whom I   8550
Relinquished there, with the astute old stewardess.[3]
Let her display to you the treasure's rich array,
As by your father handed down, and by myself
In war and peace, by steady increment, amassed.
There you will find it all maintained in order: for,   8555
Such his prerogative, the prince on his return
Finds all within his house in faithful keeping still,
Each thing in its own place, just as he left it there.
For in the serf no power resides to make a change.
CHORUS. Let now feast on the glorious hoard,   8560
          The ever increased, your eyes and heart;
          For the neck-chain's shimmer, the diadem's glow,
          They loll in pride there, vaunting themselves;
          But enter boldly and challenge them,
          They will marshall their strength,   8565
          I rejoice to look on as beauty contends
          Against gold and pearls and the pride of gems.
HELENA. Then there ensued the Master's further imperious word:
    Once you are done surveying all in order due,
    Then take as many tripods as you deem of need,   8570
    And sundry vessels such as one at sacrifice
    Wants close at hand as he performs the sacred rite,

9. The description of Helena's supposed homecoming and her relation to Menelaos derives from Euripides' *Orestes*, where upon his arrival at Argos Menelaos sends Helena ahead to the palace to pour libations on Clytemnestra's grave, and from *The Trojan Women* (lines 860–1059), where Menelaos indicates to Hecuba that he will sacrifice Helena after he returns with her to Sparta.
1. The main river of Laconia, on the banks of which the city of Sparta was located, about twenty miles inland from its mouth.
2. Another name for Sparta.
3. Phorcyas-Mephisto.

The caldrons and the bowls, the shallow salver too,
Set purest water from the holy fountain by
In its tall pitchers, and the well-dried kindling too,   8575
Swift to accept the flame, keep there in readiness,
A well-honed knife should not be lacking, for the last.
All the remainder, though, I leave unto your care.
Thus spoke he, urging my departure; but no thing
That draws life's breath did he in his ordaining
        mark   8580
For slaughter worshipful of the Olympian gods.
This gives me pause, yet I, dismissing undue care,
Commit it all into the hands of gods on high,
Who bring to pass what they may harbor in their thought,
And whether it by human minds be judged benign   8585
Or else of evil, we, the mortals, suffer it.[4]
At times, one sacrificing has raised the heavy axe
In consecration to the earth-bowed victim's neck,
And could not consummate it, being hindered by
The foe's approach, or intervention by a god.   8590
CHORUS. What may come to pass you will not divine;
        Therefore, oh Queen, stride on
        Stout of heart.
        Blessing or ill on man
        Unexpectedly falls;   8595
        Even forewarned we believe it not.
        Did not Troy burn, did we not see
        Death before us, infamous death?
        And are we not here,
        Joined to you, joyful in service,   8600
        Seeing the dazzling sun of the heavens,
        And of earth what is fairest,
        You, whose favor has blessed us?
HELENA. Be that as might be! It behooves me, come what may,
To mount without delay into the royal house,   8605
Which, almost forfeited, long missed, and longed-for much,
Stands once again before my eyes, I know not how.
My feet no longer take me up so pluckily
Those lofty stairs I used to skip up as a child.
        [*Exit.*]
CHORUS. Cast any suffering   8610
        Far away, sisters, you
        Dolefully captive ones;
        Share in our lady's bliss,
        Helena's happiness,
        Who joyously, on feet   8615
        Returning belatedly, to be sure,

4. Helena's puzzlement concerning the lack of an animal to be slaughtered suggests an allusion to the story of Abra- ham and Isaac (Genesis 22:7), where Isaac also asks about the missing victim.

But all the firmer for that,
Nears her paternal hearth.

Honor the holy
Gods who restore us,   8620
Homeward to joy conduct us!
One unbound, after all,
Floats as on pinions
Over the roughest ground, while in vain
The prisoner eats out his heart,   8625
Over the dungeon's pinnacles
Arms spread wide in yearning.

But her an immortal seized
In the distance,
Out of Ilion's dust   8630
Bore her back here
Into the old, the newly adorned
House of her father,
After ineffable
Joys and torments   8635
To be mindful afresh
Of earliest times of youth.

PANTHALIS. [*as leader of the chorus*] Abandon now the joy-
   embowered path of song
And to the portals of the door apply your gaze.
What do I see, oh sisters? Is it not the Queen   8640
Returning, vehement emotion in her steps?
What is it? what, exalted Queen, could you have met
Within the halls of your own house in welcome's stead
To shatter your composure? You conceal it not;
It is abhorrence that I read upon your brow,   8645
A noble indignation struggling with surprise.

HELENA. [*who has left the portals open, in accents of emotion*][5]
Ignoble panic ill becomes the child of Zeus,[6]
The fleeting brush of terror's fingers touch her not;
But the stark horror which, since time's first origin
Uncoiled from hoar Night's womb, of many shapes as yet   8650
Like glowing clouds from out the mountain's fiery maw,
Comes rolling up, will shake a very hero's heart.
Thus awe-inspiringly the Stygian[7] gods have marked
The entrance to my house today that I as soon
Let the oft-trodden, sorely longed-for threshold go   8655
And seek my distance from it, like a guest dismissed.
Yet no! I have withdrawn here to the light, nor shall

---

5. Helena's return from the palace recalls a similar incident in Aeschylus' *Eumenides*, where the Pythian priestess enters the temple at Delphi only to emerge
again immediately in panic at the sight
of the Furies asleep around the altar.

6. Helena alludes to the alternative myth
of her birth, whereas she earlier called
Tyndareos her father (see line 8497).
7. The gods of the underworld, named
for the river Styx.

You drive me farther, powers, whoever you may be.
On consecration will I set my mind, then, cleansed,
Let the hearth's embers greet the lady like the lord.   8660
CHORUS LEADER. Reveal, oh noble Lady, to your serving maids,
Who reverently stand by you, what has occurred.
HELENA. What I have seen, you shall lay eyes upon yourselves,
    Unless it be that ancient Night at once engulfed
    Her form back in her womb's portentous depth.   8665
    But I will put it into words so you may know:
    When mindful of the task at hand, I gravely stepped
    Into the somber mid-space of the royal house,
    The hush of vacant passageways astonished me.
    No sound of purposefully passing traffic met   8670
    The ear, nor swiftly bustling busyness the gaze,
    And not a maid appeared to me, no stewardess,
    Who used to welcome any stranger graciously.
    But when I neared the shelter of the fireplace,
    I saw, by barely smoldering embers' tepid glow,   8675
    A rangy shrouded female sitting on the ground,
    Recalling not a sleeper, more a musing shape.
    In accents of command I summon her to work,
    Supposing her the stewardess installed perchance
    At his departure by my husband's providence;   8680
    But all enfolded she continues motionless;
    At length, upon my threat, she raises her right arm
    As if to banish me away from hearth and hall.
    I turn away from her, incensed, and hasten straight
    Toward the steps that reach the ornate thalamus   8685
    Upon its dais, and close to it, the treasure-room.
    The portent, though, springs up abruptly from the ground,
    Imperiously bars my way, and shows itself
    Of stature gaunt, and hollow, bloody-blear of eye,
    And weird of shape as to confound the eye and mind.   8690
    However, I address the breeze; for quite in vain
    The word will strain creatively to build up shapes.
    Look—there she is! She even ventures forth to light!
    Here we are masters till the King our lord arrives.
    Night's dread abortions are by Phoebus, beauty's friend,   8695
    Thrust off and banished into caverns, or subdued.

[PHORCYAS *appears on the threshold between the doorposts.*]
CHORUS. Much have I lived through, although the tresses
        Youthfully cluster about my temples!
        Many the terrors that I witnessed,
        War's desolation, Ilion's night   8700
        When it fell.[8]

8. The description of the fall of Troy may derive in part from the conclusion of Euripides' *Trojan Women*, where the burning city is described. More likely, however, Goethe is following the longer and more vivid description in Book II of Virgil's *Aeneid*, where Aeneas describes to Dido the fall of the city.

Through the beclouded, dust-swirling tumult of
Warriors raging, I heard the awesome
Hail of the gods, hearkened discord's
Brazen-voiced clangor clash downfield   8705
Toward the wall.[9]

Still they were standing, ah,
Ilion's walls, but the flaming blaze
Coursed already from neighbor to neighbor,
Spreading farther from here to there   8710
By its own tempest's blast
Through the night-shrouded city.

Fleeing, I saw through reek and glow
And the blaze of the flickering flame
Frightful wrath of approaching gods,   8715
Striding portents,
Titan shapes, through dusky
Flame-reddened smoky writhing.[1]

Yet, did I see it or did
Fear-smothered spirit shape   8720
So tangled a skein? This I
Never could tell, but that I stand
Eye to eye with this horror here,
That I can tell for certain;
Could I not grasp it with my hand,   8725
Were it not for the peril of it
Staying my will with panic?

Which might you be, then,
Of Phorcys' daughters?
For to his kindred   8730
I must compare you.
Perchance as one of the gray-born—
Of but one eye and one tooth
Turn by turn partaking—
Graiae are you not come?[2]   8735

Dare you then, monster,
Thus beside beauty
Stand before Phoebus'
Arbiter's gazes?
Fear not to venture forth, however,   8740
For the ugly his sight omits,

9. The association of violent destruction
in battle with the shout of a god is Homeric, as when Ares or Poseidon shout
with the voice of ten thousand men
(*Iliad*, V.859 ff. and XIV.147–48). Eris,
"discord" (whose "clangor" is mentioned here, line 8705), also shouts in
this way (*Iliad*, XI.2–12).
1. The Chorus begins to confuse in its
memory the fall of Troy with the supernatural powers of the underworld.
2. The Chorus correctly associates
Mephistopheles' guise with the Phorcyads, or Graiae (see note to line 7967).

As his holy eye has not
Ever perceived the shadows.

But us mortals, alas, condemns   8745
All too grievous misfortune
To the ineffable anguish of eye
Which what is luckless, forever deplorable,
Stirs in lovers of beauty.

Aye then, listen, you, as you dare
Meet us brazenly, hear a ban,   8750
Hear all menace of scolding speech,
Hear execration from lips of the fortunate
Who are fashioned by gods above.

PHORCYAS. Old is the saying, yet enduring its high truth,
That Modesty and Beauty never hand in hand   8755
Pursue their way along the verdant road of earth.[3]
So deeply rooted dwells in both an ancient hate
That wheresoever it might happen that their paths
Should meet, each on the other turns a hostile back.
Then both again, more vehemently, rush apart,   8760
Modesty sad of heart, but Beauty brazenly,
Till Orcus'[4] hollow night wraps her about at last,
Unless it be old age has chastened her before.
Now you I find, bold hussies, wantonly poured forth
This way from alien parts, enclamored like the hoarse 8765
And raucous-sounding flight of cranes that overhead
In elongated cloud its croaking riot sends
Below, and lures the quiet wayfarer to raise
His gaze aloft; yet they go drifting on their way
While he goes his; just so it will turn out with us.   8770

Who are you, pray, to take upon yourselves to rave
Like Maenads[5] wild, or drunk, about the King's great house?
Yes, who are you, to meet the royal stewardess
With such a howl as does a pack of hounds the moon?
You think it is concealed from me what kith you are,   8775
Young brood, begot of war, reared up in battle-clash?
Man-mad, as readily seducing as seduced,
Who sap the strength of citizen and warrior both.
I watch your throng, and seem to see a locust-swarm
Swoop down and cover up the fields' green crops.   8780
Devourers of the thrift of others! Sneaking thieves
Destroying young prosperity just up from seed,
Cheap booty goods, knocked down at sale, at barter, you!

3. Phorcyas begins with a familiar saying which derives from a Roman idea
(as in Juvenal, *Satire* 10.297, "Rare indeed is the friendly union of beauty of
form and chaste modesty," or Ovid,
Epistles, 16.288, "There is strife between
exalted form and shame."). What follows is an extended double epic simile in
the Homeric or Vergilian manner.
4. The Classical underworld.
5. The Maenads were drunken or ecstatic followers of Dionysos.

HELENA. Who scolds a lady's waiting maids before her face
   Presumptuously encroaches on her household right;   8785
   For it is hers alone to praise the laudable
   And lay reproof upon what is to blame.
   Moreover, I am well content with the services
   They rendered me when Ilion's mighty eminence
   Beleaguered stood, and fell, and prostrate lay; no less   8790
   When we endured the griefs and dire vicissitudes
   Of errant voyage, where each but regards himself.
   Here I expect like service from the lively band.
   Not what the serf be, asks the lord, but how he serves.
   You hold your peace, therefore, and sneer at them no
      more.   8795
   If hitherto you tended well the royal house
   In absence of the mistress, this speaks well of you;
   But now she comes herself, you in your turn withdraw,
   Lest there be punishment in place of earned reward.
PHORCYAS. To raise domestic threats remains a weighty right   8800
   Well-earned by a god-favored ruler's noble spouse
   In view of prudent governance of many years.
   But since, acknowledged now! you occupy anew
   The former place of Queen and Lady of the House,
   Seize hold of the long-slackened reins and govern now,   8805
   Take charge again of treasure and us all to boot.
   Above all else, protect me, elder that I am,
   Against this gaggle who, beside your beauty's swan,
   Are but a swarm of cacklesome, ill-feathered geese.
CHORUS LEADER.[6] How ugly is, seen next to beauty,
   ugliness.   8810
PHORCYAS. How foolish is, seen next to wisdom, foolishness.
   [*From here on, single* CHORETIDS *step out of the* CHORUS *to
   make retorts.*]
CHORETID I. Of father Erebus[7] report, report of mother night.
PHORCYAS. Speak you of Scylla,[8] then, your very kith and kin.
CHORETID II. There's many a monster clambering up your pedigree.
PHORCYAS. To Orcus off with you! there seek your kinfolk out.   8815
CHORETID III. The ones who dwell there are all much too young
   for you.
PHORCYAS. Tiresias[9] the Ancient try your lewdness on.

6. Goethe here employs stychomythia, the form of one-line exchange used in Greek tragedy for scenes of rapid pace and emotional intensity. Six separate lines are assigned to six Choretids (solo speakers). These six presumably constitute one half of the Chorus, grouped with the Chorus Leader on one side of Phorcyas. The other half stands with Helena and catches her when she faints (following line 8881).
7. The lowest level of the underworld. In Hesiod, *Theogony*, lines 123 ff., Erebus and Night are the offspring of Chaos, and together they beget the Day and the Aether.
8. A monster with six heads, serpent-shaped and baying with the bark of dogs (see Homer's *Odyssey*, XII.211–59). Scylla was a daughter of Phorcys and thus a sister of the Phorcyads.
9. The blind prophet of Thebes who appears in Sophocles' *Antigone* and *Oedipus the King* as an old man.

CHORETID IV. Orion's[1] wet-nurse was great-great-grandchild to you.

PHORCYAS. By harpies[2] you were reared on offal, I should judge.

CHORETID V. Say, what do you sustain such well-groomed lean-
ness with? 8820

PHORCYAS. Not with the blood that you are all too avid for.

CHORETID VI. It's carcases you lust for, loathsome corpse yourself.

PHORCYAS. It's vampire teeth that glitter in your shameless jowls.

CHORUS LEADER. Yours I could stop, were I to say just who you
are.

PHORCYAS. Name first yourself, then, and the riddle will be
solved. 8825

HELENA. In sorrow, not in anger, do I intervene
Between you and forbid such rash and fierce exchange!
For nothing more of harm can face the ruling lord
Than loyal servants' secret festering enmity.
No longer does the echo of his orders then 8830
Return to him in swift fulfillment's tuneful chord,
No, then a willful tumult all about him roars,
Who is himself distracted, chiding all in vain.
Nor is this all. In your unconscionable wrath
You conjured up unhallowed pictures' frightful shapes, 8835
Which throng about me so that I myself feel snatched
To Orcus, in defiance of the sights of home.
Is this remembrance? or delusion seizing me?
Was I all that? Or am I now? Or shall I be
The nightmare image of that ravager of towns?[3] 8840
The maidens shudder, but as you, the eldest one,
Stand with composure, speak to me a word of sense.

PHORCYAS. To him who recollects long years of varied bliss,
The highest godly boon at last will seem a dream.
But you, by fortune favored past all bounds and goal, 8845
Saw only those by love enardored line your life,
Those swiftly kindled to all manner of bold deed.
Why, Theseus early snatched you up with quickened lust,
Like Heracles in strength, of glorious manly form.

HELENA. Abducted me, ten-year-old slender doe I was, 8850
And then Aphidnus' castle closed on me in Attica.[4]

---

1. The hunter, son of Poseidon, who was killed by Artemis and then transformed by Zeus into a heavenly constellation.

2. Mythical creatures with the heads and breasts of women and the bodies of birds, who pollute whatever they touch.

3. The confusion of past, present, and future time in these questions is important for the sense of timelessness in the *Helena*, in which the heroine participates (though it confuses her). The phrase "ravager of towns," which imitates the type of epithet used by Homer, probably derives from Euripides' *Trojan Women* (lines 892–93), where Hecuba speaks of Helen to Menelaos as follows: "She looks enchanted, and where she looks homes are set on fire;/she captures cities as she captures the eyes of men."

4. Theseus (here compared with Heracles; see lines 7381 ff.) and his companion Pirithous abducted the ten-year-old Helen from a temple of Artemis where they saw her dancing. Theseus then entrusted her to his friend Aphidnus to keep her in his castle, since Helena was still too young for love. Attica is the region of Greece where Athens, the city which Theseus ruled, is located.

PHORCYAS. But soon set free at Castor's and at Pollux' hands,[5]
You stood, by an array of choicest heroes wooed.

HELENA. But secret favor over all, I freely own,
Patroclus[6] won, who was Pelides' second self.   8855

PHORCYAS. To Menelaos did a father's will betrothe you, though,
Bold rover of the seas, but home-preserver too.

HELENA. He gave his daughter, gave the kingdom's governance.
From wedded concourse then sprang forth Hermione.[7]

PHORCYAS. But when afar he boldly seized the prize of Crete,   8860
Into your loneliness came all too fair a guest.[8]

HELENA. Why do you bring to mind that all-but-widowhood,
And what appalling doom emerged from it to me?

PHORCYAS. To me, a free-born Cretan woman, that same quest
Brought in its train enslavement, long captivity.[9]   8865

HELENA. He forthwith then installed you here as stewardess,
Entrusting much, both keep and treasure boldly seized.

PHORCYAS. Which you relinquished, bound for tower-ringed Ilion
And ever inexhaustible delights of love.

HELENA. Do not recall the joys! for all too bitter grief's   8870
Infinitude was poured me over breast and head.

PHORCYAS. And yet they say that you appeared in double shape,
Observed in Ilion as well as Egypt too.[1]

HELENA. Do not confound a turbid mind's confusion quite.
Why, even now I know not which of these I am.   8875

PHORCYAS. And more they say: from out of the realm of shades
Achilles rose at last and joined you too, enflamed!
Who loved you once against all settled rule of fate.[2]

HELENA. I as a myth allied myself to him as myth.
It was a dream, the words themselves proclaim it so.   8880
I fade away, becoming to myself a myth.[3]

[*Swooning, she sinks into the* SEMI-CHORUS' *arms.*]

CHORUS. Silence, silence![4]

---

5. Helena was freed from Theseus by her twin half-brothers (see lines 7369 and 7415).

6. It is uncertain why Helena mentions Patroclus, who was the close friend of Achilles in Homer's *Iliad*, as the favorite among her suitors (Achilles, son of Peleus, is here styled Pelides).

7. Hermione, daughter of Helena and Menelaos, appears as a character in Euripides' *Andromache* and *Orestes*.

8. Menelaos went to Crete after the death of his maternal grandfather, Creteus, to receive his share of the estate, during which time Paris seduced Helena.

9. Possibly derived from the false stories which Odysseus tells of himself as a fugitive from Crete after his return to Ithaca in Homer's *Odyssey* (XIII.256 ff., XIV. 192 ff., XVII. 415 ff., XIX.165 ff.).

1. An allusion to the later legend, which Euripides used satirically in his *Helen*, that Helena was actually carried off by Hermes to Egypt, while a false figure of her (idol) was taken to Ilion (Troy).

2. The spirits of Achilles and Helen were united on the island of Leuce at the request of Achilles, who there begot Euphorion on her (mentioned earlier, line 7435, where Goethe erroneously refers to the city of Pherae).

3. *Idol* in the German, from the Greek *eidolon*, "a phantom or ghost." Helena recognizes that in her marriage with Achilles she was such an "idol," as also in the legend that she never went to Troy; and that here in this place, as a spirit released from the underworld, she is the same. (See line 4190.)

4. The plea by the Chorus for silence because of Helena's swoon follows the example of Euripides' *Orestes* (lines 140 ff.), where both Electra and the Chorus move on tip-toe so as not to wake the sleeping Orestes.

Ill-gazing, ill-speaking as you are!
Past so hideous one-toothed lips
What would indeed waft forth   8885
From such gruesome horrors' maw!

For the wicked in the guise of benevolence,
Wolfish-fierce under woolly sheep's fleece,
Far more terrible seems to me than the three-
Headed Hell-hound's jaws.[5]   8890
Anxious listeners here we stand:
When? how? where might it break forth,
Of such malice
The deeply lurking monster?

Thus you—for kindly-meant, solace-rich discourse,   8895
Lethe-outpouring, most loving-kind speech—
Stir up instead in all that is bygone
Evilest more than good,
Sombering all at once
Not the present's glow alone,   8900
But the future's
Soft glint of hope as it glimmers forth.

Silence, silence!
That the soul of the Queen,
Poised on the brink of flight,   8905
Might yet hold on, hold fast
To that form of all forms
Ever touched by the light of the sun.

[HELENA *has recovered and resumed her place at center.*]
PHORCYAS.[6] Issue forth from fleeting vapors, sun exalted of this day,
  Which, while shrouded yet, delightful, now in dazzling splen-
      dor reigns.   8910
As the world unfolds, you answer with a lovely gaze yourself.
Let them scold me ugly, still I know true beauty well enough.
HELENA. As I, swaying, quit the void that lay about me in my
      swoon,
I would gladly rest me further, for so weary are my limbs:
It behooves a queen, however, as I think it does all men,   8915
To encounter with composure any dire and sudden turn.
PHORCYAS. Now you face us in your grandeur, in your beauty once
      again,
This your gaze bespeaks commandment; speak then, what is
      your command?
HELENA. Be in readiness to render what your brazen strife withheld;
Quick, prepare a sacrifice as by the King's behest to me.   8920
PHORCYAS. All is ready in the palace, basin, tripod, sharpened
      axe,

5. A reference to Cerberus, the dog
which guards the entrance to Hades.
6. Goethe here—as in several parts of
this episode (lines 8909–29, 8957–61,

8966–70, 9067–70, 9122–26)—employs the
archaic trochaic tetrameter favored by
Euripides at moments of emotional intensity in his later plays.

For the sprinkling, incense-burning; indicate the victim now!
HELENA. This he left undesignated.
PHORCYAS.   Left unsaid? O, grievous word!
HELENA. What distress has overcome you?
PHORCYAS.   It is you he meant, o Queen!
HELENA. I?   8925
PHORCYAS. And these.
CHORUS.   O woe, o pity!
PHORCYAS.   You shall fall beneath the axe.
HELENA. Dreadful! yet divined; ah me!
PHORCYAS.   And ineluctable it seems.
CHORUS. Oh! And we? What will befall us?
PHORCYAS.   She will die a noble death;
   As for you: among the rafters on the rooftree's lofty beam
   Shall you twitch and dangle, thrushes which the fowler strung
      in line.[7]

      [HELENA *and* CHORUS *stand in amazement and terror, form-
      ing an expressive, well-arranged tableau.*]

PHORCYAS. Bewraithed!—As if congealed to effigies you stand,   8930
   Scared to be parting from the day that is not yours.
   The spectral breed of man, wherever, just like you
   Renounce unwillingly the lofty sunshine glow;
   Yet no one begs them off or saves them from the end;
   They're all aware of it, yet only few approve.   8935
   Enough, you are undone! To work then, with a will.

      [*She claps her hands, whereupon at the portals appear
      muffled dwarfish figures,[8] which promptly and deftly carry
      out the orders pronounced.*]

   Come here, you saturnine misbrood, round as a ball!
   Come rolling up, you'll find your fill of mischief here.
   The hand-borne altar, golden-horned, make room for that,
   The axe should lie and glint across the silver rim,   8940
   Fill up the ewers, there will be work in rinsing off
   The hideous polluting stain of blackening blood.
   Spread exquisitely here the rug across the dust,
   So that the victim might kneel down in royal wise,
   And duly swathed, head promptly severed, to be sure,   8945
   Yet all decorum satisfied, be laid to rest.

CHORUS LEADER. The Queen is standing to one side here, wrapped
      in thought,
   Whereas her maidens wilt like meadow-grass mown down;
   But I, the eldest, feel impelled by sacred trust
   To seek a word with you, the Great-great-eldest one.   8950
   You are experienced, wise, not ill-disposed to us,

---

7. Phorcyas-Mephisto describes the death
which will be imposed on the Chorus in
terms borrowed from Homer's *Odyssey*
(XXII.462–73), where the faithless servant girls are put to death after the
slaughter of the suitors.

8. The "dwarfish figures" which here appear at Phorcyas-Mephisto's call are presumably infernal spirits who serve him
in his capacity as stage manager of this
show.

I think, though, brainless lot, we judged and used you ill.

Speak, therefore, of such rescue as there might still be.

PHORCYAS. Soon spoken: it depends upon the Queen alone
    To save herself, and you, as bonus lives, with her.[9]   8955
    Resolve is needed, and of the nimblest sort, what's more.

CHORUS. Oh most reverend of Parcae, wisest of the Sibyls you,[1]
    Keep the golden shears from closing, then proclaim us day and
        life;
    For we sense already lifted, swinging, dangling, most
        uncouthly,
    These sweet limbs, which would much rather first take pleasure
        in the dancing,   8960
    Then repose at lover's breast.

HELENA. Leave these to quaver! What I feel is pain, not fear;
    But should you know reprieve, you shall be thanked for it.
    One shrewd and far-seeing is apt indeed to discern
    Within the hopeless the barely possible. Do speak.   8965

CHORUS. Speak and tell us, tell us quickly: how do we escape the
        gruesome
    Nasty noose which ominously, like the meanest sort of neck-
        lace,
    Twines about the neck? Poor wretches, we can sense it all be-
        forehand,
    To unbreathing point, to choking, if you, Rhea,[2] noble mother
    Of all gods, do not relent.   8970

PHORCYAS. And have you patience, then, in silence to hear out
    The long-drawn-out recital? Many a tale it holds.

CHORUS. Patience sufficient! Listening, we at least live on.[3]

PHORCYAS. He who remains at home, preserving choice estate,
    At pains as much to caulk the tall apartments' walls   8975
    As to secure the roof before the thrust of rain,
    Will surely prosper all the long days of his life;
    But he who frivolously crosses, on flighty soles,
    The hallowed straight-rule of his threshold, lawless of mind,
    He will, returning, find the old place, to be sure,   8980
    But altogether changed, if not destroyed outright.

HELENA. Why treat us to this kind of long-familiar saw?
    You have a tale; touch not on what must give offense.

PHORCYAS. It is historical, by no means a reproach.[4]
    From bay to bay, freebooting, Menelaos rowed,   8985
    Islands and littoral all felt his stabbing raids,
    And he returned with spoils, as now abound in there.

---

9. We perhaps are to assume here that one of the conditions for releasing Helena from the underworld to meet with Faust would be that she must herself request it.

1. Phorcyas is addressed as one of the Parcae, or Fates (see lines 5305 ff.), and as a Sibyl, or prophetess.

2. The wife of Kronos or Saturn and mother of the Olympian gods (see line 7989).

3. Possibly a playful allusion to the tales of Scheherazade in the *Thousand and One Nights*. (See line 6032 and note.)

4. In the German, "historical" (*Geschichtlich*) echoes "stories," "tales" (*Geschichten*), in line 8972.

At Ilion he lingered all of tèn long years;
How long he took for his returning I know not.
What is the state right here, though, of the noble house   8990
Of Tyndareos? What of the kingdom all about?

HELENA. Why, can you be so bodily perfused with blame
That you can move your lips no more but to reprove?

PHORCYAS. Deserted stood so many years the rim of hills
Which to the rear of Sparta northward rises high,   8995
Taygetos[5] left behind—where as a playful brook
Eurotas scampers down and then, by reeds spread out,
Flows broadly through our valley, nourishing your swans.
Back in the glen there, quietly a daring clan
Have settled, thrusting up from out Cimmerian[6] night,   9000
And raised themselves a towering keep, unscalable,
From where they harass land and people as they please.[7]

HELENA. They could contrive this? Quite impossible it seems.

PHORCYAS. They had the time; it has been twenty years, or near.

HELENA. Is there one lord? A numerous brigand host in league?   9005

PHORCYAS. They are not brigands; one, however, is their lord.
I do not scold him, though he did descend on me.
He could have taken all, yet chose to be content
With some—not tribute—voluntary gifts, he said.[8]

HELENA. How are his looks?

PHORCYAS.   Not bad! I like him well.   9010
He is high-spirited, bold-tempered, nobly made,
Judicious, too, like few among the Greeks.
They call his kind barbarians, yet I suspect
Their likes might not be cruel as, besieging Troy,
More than one hero ravened like a cannibal.[9]   9015
I note his breadth of soul, to him I'd trust myself.
And there's his castle, too! you should lay eyes on that!
Far different indeed from clumsy mounds of stone
Such as your fathers helter-skelter jumbled up,
Like Cyclopes, walls Cyclopean, crashing down   9020
Raw stone on stone unhewn;[1] there, on the other hand,
All's perpendicular and level, by the rule.[2]
Look at it from the outside: heavenward it sweeps,

---

5. A mountain range to the west of Sparta in the Peloponnesus.
6. According to Homer's *Odyssey* (XI.14 ff.), the Kimmerians are a people dwelling in a land hidden in fog and cloud where the sun never shines.
7. Presumably an allusion to medieval crusader castles, such as that built in the mid-thirteenth century at Mistra in the Peloponnesus by "Frankish" (i.e., West European) knights of the Fourth Crusade.
8. Such gifts would be owed by feudal law to the liege lord.
9. Presumably an allusion to Achilles' statement to the dying Hector in Homer's *Iliad* (xxii.346 ff.), "I wish only that my spirit and fury would drive me

to hack your meat away and eat it raw for the things that you have done to me."
1. A reference to the rough walls and huge stones of Mycenaean fortresses. In Greek drama these fortresses were described as having been built by the Cyclopes (one-eyed giants, familiar from Homer's *Odyssey*, IX), as in Euripides' *Iphigenie at Aulis*, line 265. Rough-hewn Sparta was traditionally contrasted with the splendor of Troy (see *The Trojan Women*, lines 992 ff.).
2. A feature of the Gothic style of architecture, which Goethe and his contemporaries regarded as characteristically Germanic.

So rigid, truly jointed, mirror-smooth as steel.
To try to scale it—why, the very thought slides off.   9025
Within—the spaciousness of courtyards wide, enclosed
By edifice galore, of every kind and end.
There's columns large and small, vaults, arches, arculets,
Arcades and galleries for looking out and in,
Escutcheons, too.

CHORUS.   What are escutcheons?[3]

PHORCYAS.   You have seen   9030
Ajax display upon his shield a serpent coiled.[4]
The Seven against Thebes all bore depicted shapes,
Each on his shield, replete with rich significance.[5]
Here moon and stars on the nocturnal firmament,
There goddess, champion, ladder, swords and torches, too,   9035
And what aggression grimly threatens goodly towns.
It is such figurements our band of heroes too
Display in gleaming hues from dim ancestral times.
There you see lion, eagle, also beak and claw,
The horns of buffalo, wings, roses, peacock-tail,   9040
As well as bars—gold, sable, argent, azure, gules.
The like is hung in great apartments, row on row,
In state-rooms limitless, as wide as all the world;
There's room for you to dance!

CHORUS.   Say, are there partners, too?

PHORCYAS. The best! A golden-curled, boyishly fresh-skinned
    band,   9045
Fragrant with youth! No one but Paris had this scent,
When he approached too near the Queen.

HELENA.   You quite forget
Your proper part; come now to your concluding word.

PHORCYAS. The final word is yours—an earnest, audible yes!
And forthwith I surround you with that castle.[6]   9050

CHORUS.   Speak,
Oh speak that short word, save yourself and us as well!

HELENA. What! should I stand in fear King Menelaos might
Commit such fierce transgression as to do me harm?

PHORCYAS. Have you forgotten the unheard-of way he maimed
Your Deiphobos, the brother of Paris battle-slain,   9055
Who stubbornly besieged and won your widowed bed
And freely relished it? His nose and ears he lopped
And mutilated more—a horror to behold.[7]

HELENA. The thing he did to him, it was on my account.

---

3. The medieval heraldic arms associated
with tournaments and festivals of the
chivalric courts.
4. In Homer's *Iliad*, Ajax is often described as carrying a great shield with
seven layers of leather.
5. In Aeschylus' *Seven Against Thebes*
(lines 378–650) the Messenger describes
the shield of each of the seven chieftains
who have joined with Polyneices to attack the city of Thebes.

6. Phorcyas-Mephisto here indicates the
conditions which must be met in order
for Faust to meet Helena. His statement
also hints at the theatrical nature of the
transformation of scene which he proposes.
7. Menelaos' mutilation of Deiphobos
(who married Helena after the death of
Paris; see Euripides' *Trojan Women*,
lines 959–60) is described in Virgil's
Aeneid (VI.494–97).

PHORCYAS. On his account he now will do the like to you.   9060
  Beauty is indivisible: who held it whole,
  Destroys it rather, execrating partial hold.
    [Trumpets in the distance; the CHORUS *gives a violent
    start.]*[8]
  As blaring trumpets sharply lay on ear and bowels
  A rending grip, thus jealousy will sink its claws
  Into the bosom of the man who can't forget   9065
  What once he owned, and now has lost, to own no more.

CHORUS. Don't you hear the horns resounding? see the glint of
  weaponry?

PHORCYAS. Welcome to the King and Master, gladly shall I lay
  account.

CHORUS. What of us?

PHORCYAS. You know it well: you bear close witness to her death,
  Minding well your own within there; no, there is no help for
  you.   9070
    [Pause.]

HELENA. I have reflected on the step I next may dare.
  You are a froward demon,[9] this I sense full well,
  And feel misgiving lest you bend benign to ill.
  Yet I will follow you into that castle first;
  The rest is mine to know; whatever more the Queen   9075
  Sequesters deep within her breast in this regard,
  Be inaccessible to all. Crone, lead the way!

CHORUS.[1] Oh how gladly speed we thither
    Hurrying footsteps;
    Death at our backs,   9080
    Before us once more
    A looming stronghold's
    Impregnable bastion.
    May it shelter as well
    As Ilion's citadel did,   9085
    Which succumbed at length
    But to treacherous stratagem.[2]
    *[Fog spreads about, shrouding the background, and the fore-
    ground as well, at will.]*
    What? what is this?
    Sisters, look about!
    Was it not smiling day?   9090
    Mists arise in wavering streaks
    From Eurotas' sacred flood;[3]
    Lost to sight already the lovely
    Reed-engarlanded bank;[4]

8. The sound of trumpets, arranged by Phorcyas-Mephisto, causes the Chorus and Helena to believe that the army of Menelaos is really approaching.
9. Helena appears to sense that Phorcyas is indeed a devil, though she would presumably associate him with the Classical underworld.

1. This ode concludes the Classical section of the *Helena.*
2. An allusion to the Trojan Horse.
3. See note to line 8539.
4. Analogous to the scene at the edge of the Peneios in the "Classical Walpurgis Night" (see lines 7249 ff.).

No more, alas, do I see   9095
The soft on-glide of the swans,
Allies in floating joy,
Free in its pride and grace.

Yet, after all,
I hear their call,   9100
Their far-off husky note!
Death-heralding note, they say;[5]
Ah, would that when all is done,
It may not have augured us too
Ruin in promised rescue's stead;   9105
To us, who are swanlike, long,
Fair, and white of neck; nor, oh,
To her, our swan-begotten.[6]
Woe to us, woe!

All is covered by now;   9110
Shrouded in mist all round.
Are we not losing sight of each other?
What is it? Are we walking?
Or merely floating
Trippingly over the hidden ground?   9115
Can you see? Is it not perchance
Hermes[7] floating ahead? Not his golden staff
Flashing, bidding us back again
To ill-favored, gray-dawning Hades,
Full of impalpable figments,   9120
Overthronged, eternally void?
Yes, it darkens of a sudden, lifting mists unveil not brightness,
Gloomy gray and dun of stonework. Masonry confronts the
    vision,
Rigidly defies its ranging. Are we in a court? a dungeon?
Either case is horrifying! Sisters, oh, we are imprisoned,   9125
Captive if we ever were.[8]

INNER COURTYARD OF A CASTLE

Surrounded by Opulent and Fanciful Medieval Architecture

CHORUS LEADER.[1] Forward and foolish, chips off the block of
    womankind!
Fluff driven by the weather, playthings of the hour,

5. Apparently some kind of music is heard (as a demonic *entr'acte*? as an accompaniment to their song?) which the Chorus associates with the legend of the swan's song at the moment of death.
6. Helena is "swan-begotten," recalling the legend of Leda and the swan (see lines 6904 ff. and 7277 ff.).
7. Traditionally, as Psychopompos, Hermes led the dead spirit into the underworld. Here it may be the shape of

Phorcyas-Mephisto which the Chorus sees. They are quite aware that a descent to Hades would be a return to the place from which they came.
8. In their guise as captured Trojan girls, the Chorus associates the medieval fortress with the palace of Sparta as a prison.
1. A loose trimeter continues until the appearance of Faust (line 9192), who speaks in blank verse.

Of fortune or misfortune, neither have you learnt
To take with calm. Does each not contradict the rest   9130
With passion always, and in turn the others her?
In joy and grief, it's howl or laugh in unison.
Now hush! and listening bide whatever our lady may
Highmindedly resolve here for herself and us.

HELENA. Where are you, Pythonissa?[2] whatsoever called;   9135
Step from beneath these vaultings of the somber keep.
Should you have hastened to announce me to the lord,
This wondrous champion here, for worthy welcome's sake,
Accept my thanks and quickly lead me in to him.
I crave an end to roaming; crave repose alone.   9140

CHORUS LEADER. In vain you gaze about, my Queen, to every side;
The odious form is vanished, has remained perhaps
Back in the fog from out the swathes of which we came,
I know not how, with speed, and yet unpacingly.
Or else she errs astray within this citadel's   9145
Moot labyrinth which fuses muchness into one,[3]
To seek the lord anent a princely high-salute.
But look, up there, already swarming into sight
In galleries, at windows, crossing double doors,
A throng of serving-folk,[4] all bustling back and forth;   9150
This heralds grateful rites of lordly welcoming.

CHORUS.[5] My heart sings! oh, just see, over there
          How decorously, with leisurely tread,
          Pages in flower of youth move down
          The orderly train. How? and on whose behest   9155
          Could there emerge, so early trained to the ranks,
          Of boyish youth such splendorous throng?
          What to admire the most? Is it elegant gait,
          Curly locks, perhaps, that cluster the dazzling brow,
          Cheeks, perhaps, that bear twin flush of the peach,   9160
          And just as downy a fleece?
          I long for a bite, yet I shudder and shrink;
          For in similar instance, the mouth only filled,
          Repulsive to mention! with ashes.[6]
          Here come the fairest   9165

---

2. A medieval Latin form of the title used by the priestess of Apollo at Delphi (after the sacred serpent Pytho, slain there by Apollo). It came to refer to any prophetess or seer and here refers to Phorcyas-Mephisto, who has disappeared from the scene (returning only at line 9419) to make way for Faust.
3. This description of Gothic architecture corresponds to the Romantic view of that style, which Goethe shared.
4. Spirits conjured up by Mephistopheles to assist Faust in the encounter with Helena. They function as supernumeraries in the show, remaining silent throughout.
5. The meter of the following speech

approximates the traditional anapestic march-measure often used in Greek drama for the first entrance of the Chorus. Here the Chorus chants in time to the procession of page boys, describing them as they enter the stage.
6. The idea of cheeks which resemble peaches, enticing the Chorus to take a bite, and the apprehension that they will only bite ashes, presumably derives from the apples of Sodom, described by Milton in *Paradise Lost* (X.564 ff.), when the devils in Hell are transformed into serpents. The Chorus apparently recalls a similar experience from the underworld, here surmising (correctly) that the page boys are only spirits like themselves.

Stepping toward us;
What is it they bear?
Steps to a throne,
Carpet and dais,
Canopy, tent-like   9170
Drapery rich;
Billowing over,
Cloud-garlands forming
Over our Lady's head;
For now she has mounted,   9175
Duly bidden, the sumptuous bolster.[7]
Draw you near,
Stair by stair,
Form a solemn file.
Worthy, oh worthy, threefold worthy   9180
Be such a welcome's answering grace!

[*All that is proclaimed by the* CHORUS *is enacted in due order.*]

[FAUST. PAGES *and* SQUIRES *having descended in a long procession, he appears at the top of the staircase in the knightly court garb of the Middle Ages and descends with slow, dignified steps.*]

CHORUS LEADER. [*inspecting him attentively*] This man—unless
    immortals, as they often do,
Have lent him admirable parts, superb address,
And amiable presence for a transient span
Of tenure only,—must be certain of success   9185
In all he undertakes, be it in clash of arms,
Be it in minor skirmish with the fairest maids.
He is in truth to be preferred to many a man
Whom my own eyes in high esteem have seen.
At grave and measured pace of reverent restraint   9190
I see the prince advancing; turn about, oh Queen!

FAUST. [*approaching, a* BOUND MAN *at his side*][8]
In lieu of ceremonial salute,
In lieu of reverent welcome, as were fitting,
I bring you, harshly chained, a servant, who
Failing his duty, wrested mine from me.   9195
Down on thy knees! and to this royal lady
Confession render of thy heavy guilt.
This is, exalted sovereign, the man
Installed, by virtue of his eye's rare blaze,
Keen look-out on the tower's great height, to scan   9200
The scope of heaven and the breadth of earth,
Whatever here or there might come in view,
Might stir down circling hills into the vale
To this firm keep, be it the swell of herds,

7. The page boys construct an elaborate throne with a canopy above it where Helena is to be seated as queen of this court.

8. With his first speech to Helena Faust introduces blank verse, the form used in Shakespearian and German Classical drama.

Perchance a marching host; we shelter those, 9205
Bid check to these. Today, what dereliction!
As you approach he gives no sign, we fail
Of most distinguished honors plainly due
To such exalted guest. For which outrage
His life is forfeit, and his blood were spilt 9210
Long since by his deserts; but you alone
May punish or may pardon, as you please.

HELENA.[9] Such lofty dignity as you award,
 Of source of justice, ruler, be it but
 By way of trial, as I may surmise— 9215
 So I fulfill the judge's premier charge,
 To grant defendants hearing. Speak you, then.

LYNCEUS, WARDEN OF THE TOWER.[1]
   Keep me kneeling, keep me gazing,
   Whether dying, whether living,
   All my soul is freely given
   Her, by Heaven sent, amazing. 9220

   As the glory of the morning
   In the east I would espy,
   Wondrously, without a warning,
   From the south it dazed my eye. 9225

   So it cast my sight in harness
   That in peak and gorge's stead,
   Mid the earth's and heaven's farness
   On this star alone it fed.

   Like the lynx on treetop perching 9230
   I am dowed with sharpest sight;
   Now I blink as though emerging
   From a murky dream of night.

   Could I tell, my senses drifting,
   Moat and gateway, south from north? 9235
   Vapors shifting, vapors lifting,
   Such a goddess gleaming forth!

   Facing her and lost in gazing,
   I imbibed her balmy light,
   By her fairness, all bedazing, 9240
   This poor wretch was dazzled quite.

   I forgot the warden's duty,
   Quite the horn I hold by oath;
   Forfeit is my life—yet beauty
   Conquers guilt and anger both. 9245

9. Helena replies to Faust in blank verse, indicating her willingness to accommodate her form of speech to his.
1. The lyrical form of Lynceus' defense is totally alien to classical literature, a form of ballad stanza from medieval Germanic love poetry, the so-called *Minnesang*.

HELENA. The evil that I brought on him myself
  I must not punish. Woe! what stern decree
  Pursues me, to be fated everywhere
  So to enthrall men's hearts they will not spare
  Themselves nor aught of worth! Abducting now, 9250
  Seducing, battling, snatching there and thither,
  Heroes and demigods, immortals, aye, and demons
  Have carried me at random here and yon.
  Come once, I stirred the world, redoubled—more,
  Now threefold, fourfold I bring woe on woe. 9255
  Release this worthy one, let him go free;
  No shame befall him whom the gods bewitched.

FAUST. In wonderment, o Queen, I see at once
  Unerring markswoman, and here her prey;
  I see the bow from which the arrow sped 9260
  And this one drooping.[2] Arrow follows arrow,
  Striking myself. All over and athwart
  I sense their wingèd whir in space and keep.
  What am I now? You render all at once
  Rebellious my most faithful, insecure 9265
  My battlements. I come to fear my army
  Obeys already her who wins unarmed.
  What choice have I but to consign myself,
  And all I owned in fancy, unto thee?
  Let me in chosen fealty at your feet 9270
  Acknowledge you as mistress unto whom
  By her mere advent fell estate and throne.

  [LYNCEUS *with a casket, and men carrying more after him.*]

LYNCEUS.[3] You witness, lady, my return!
     One gaze the man of wealth would earn;
     He looks at you and feels at once 9275
     Enriched and beggared by the glance.

     What was I once? what now would claim?
     What to desire? at what to aim?
     Alas, the eye's acutest ray
     Against your throne is dashed to spray. 9280

     From out the teeming East we pressed,
     Wrought swift disaster on the West;
     A sea of peoples broad and vast,
     The first knew nothing of the last.

     The first might fall, the second held, 9285
     The third one's halberd flashed and felled;
     Each one enforced a hundredfold,
     A thousand slain could go untold.

2. A poetic commonplace from medieval love poetry, even more from conventions of Petrarchan (i.e., Renaissance) love poetry.
3. The second song of devotion by Lynceus develops further the thematic and historical implications of the encounter between Helena and Faust, as between the Classical and Germanic cultures.

We thrust ahead, we stormed apace,
As masters entered place on place, 9290
And where one day I harshly vexed,
Another robbed and stole the next.

We looked, no sooner looked than seized;
One snatched a girl his fancy pleased,
The next a steer of stolid gait, 9295
And all the horses shared its fate.

But I was fond of seeking out
The rarest ever seen about,
And if another matched my prize,
It turned to sawdust in my eyes. 9300

On treasure traces I would tread
And send my searching gaze ahead,
For me no pocket was too dark,
Transparent every cask and ark.

And mounds of gold became my own, 9305
More splendid still, much precious stone:
But now the emerald counts alone
If green upon your breast it shone.

Let quiver now twixt ear and lips
The oval drop from ocean deeps; 9310
The ruby, though, is put to flight,
The blooming cheek will bleach it quite.

And so the most prodigious hoard,
Here at your footstool be it stored,
In homage at your feet be laid 9315
The spoils with blood of battles paid.

So many chests I dragged before.
As many I could add, and more,
If but my presence you indulge,
The strongrooms shall with treasure bulge. 9320

For you did scarce ascend the throne,
And to the godly form alone
All wisdom, opulence, and power
Already bow, already cower.

All this I tightly clutched as mine, 9325
Now it is loose and turned to thine,
I thought it valid, worthy, fair,
But now I hold it cheap and bare.

All wilted what I held with pride,
As meadow grasses mowed and dried: 9330
Deign to return with one gay glance
Its former worth to it at once!

FAUST. Forthwith remove the burden boldly seized
　　And unrewarded go, though unreproved.
　　All that the castle harbors in its depth　　　　　　　　9335
　　Is hers already. Proffering her particulars
　　Is useless. Go and posit hoard on hoard
　　In ordered piles. Create the unseen splendor's
　　Exalted likeness! Make the vaultings gleam
　　Like the fresh skies, prepare her paradises　　　　　9340
　　Of simulated life devoid of life.
　　Outrun her progress with the ready bloom
　　Of rug on rug unwound; her tread be met
　　By dainty ground, her gaze by that supreme
　　Lucence which dazzles all but the divine.　　　　　9345
LYNCEUS. Master's bidding needs small wit,
　　　　Servant makes light work of it:
　　　　Does not flesh and treasure all
　　　　Own this sovereign beauty's thrall?
　　　　All the host has long been tame,　　　　　　　　9350
　　　　Broadswords all are dull and lame,
　　　　Sun himself but wan and cold
　　　　By the splendor of her mold,
　　　　By the riches of her face
　　　　All is empty, all is base.　　　　　　　　　　　9355
　　[*Exit.*]
HELENA. [*to* FAUST] I wish to speak with you, but first ascend
　　To join me at my side. The vacant place
　　Calls for the master and ensures my own.
FAUST. Be pleased, exalted Queen, to entertain
　　My faithful kneeling homage first; this hand　　　　9360
　　Which to your side would raise me, let me kiss it.
　　Confirm me as co-regent of your realm
　　Uncognizant of borders, and procure yourself
　　Adorer, server, warder, all in one!
HELENA. Manifold wonders do I see and hear,　　　　9365
　　Amazement strikes me, I have much to ask.
　　Yet I desire instruction why that man's
　　Converse rang strange to me, both strange and pleasing.
　　Each sound seems to accommodate the other,
　　And as one word repairs unto the ear,　　　　　　　9370
　　There comes another to caress the first.[4]
FAUST. Already pleased, then, with our nation's parlance,
　　You will be surely ravished by their song,
　　Which satisfies the ear and sense profoundly.
　　But we had safest practice it at once;　　　　　　　9375
　　Exchange of speech allures it, calls it forth.
HELENA. Tell, then, how can I speak with such fair art?
FAUST. It's easy, it must well up from the heart,

4. Goethe alludes to the historical origin of rhyme in Western poetry.

And when the breast with longing overbuoys,
One looks about and asks—
HELENA.   who shares our joys.   9380
FAUST. Now seeks the mind no forth or back from this,
    Alone the present moment—
HELENA.   is our bliss.
FAUST. Is hoard, high prize, possession, earnest, and
    Whence comes its confirmation?
HELENA.   From my hand.
CHORUS. Who would reprehend our princess   9385
        If she grants the castle's lord
        Kind accommodation?
        For confess, all of us are
        Prisoners, not for the first time
        Since the lamentable downfall   9390
        Of Ilion, and the fearsome
        Labyrinthine voyage of grief.

        Ladies to men's love accustomed
        Are not hesitant choosers,
        Rather expert judges.   9395
        Be it shepherds,[5] gold of ringlet,
        Be it fauns of swarthy bristle,
        As occasion may afford,
        To their limbs' luxuriance
        Equal claim they grant in full.   9400

        Near and nearer they are seated,
        One to the other inclining,
        Shoulder to shoulder, knee to knee,
        Hand in hand they sway
        Over the throne's   9405
        High-upholstered opulence.
        Nor does majesty forbear
        Before the people's eyes
        Private affections'
        Exuberant displaying.   9410
HELENA.[6] I feel so far away and yet so near,
    And all too gladly say: Here am I! Here!
FAUST. Breathless I seem, my tongue is faltering, chained;
    This is a dream, and place and day have waned.
HELENA. I feel of life bereft, and yet so new,   9415
    Warp to your weft, unto the stranger true,
FAUST. Probe not in thought the choicest lot, I ask!
    Were it but short, existence still is task.

5. The theme of pastoral poetry anticipates the final section of the *Helena*.
6. This sequence of couplets constitutes
both the consummation of the love between Faust and Helena and also a moment of fulfillment for Faust which
would appear to satisfy the terms of his
wager with Mephistopheles.

PHORCYAS. [*making a violent entrance*][7]
    Spelling-books of love construing,
    Playfully bemused in wooing,   9420
    Vainly cooing, idly suing,
    But there is no time, I say.
    Blind to distant lightning's flaring,
    Listen to the trumpet blaring,
    Ruin is not far away.   9425
    Menelaos is descending
    On your camp with swarms unending,
    Arm yourselves for bitter fray!
    By victorious throngs encumbered,
    Like Deiphobus dismembered,   9430
    You will rue your courting play.
    Trash will dangle by a halter,
    Then in this one at the altar
    Fresh-honed axe will find its prey.

FAUST. Uncouth disturbance! Insolently it intrudes;   9435
  In hazards even I dislike insensate vehemence.
  No messenger so fair but that ill tidings foul him;
  You, ugliest of all, delight but in ill news.
  But this time you shall not prevail; with empty breath
  You agitate the air. There is no danger here,   9440
  And even danger would appear an idle threat.
    [*Signals, explosions from the towers, trumpets and coronets,
    military music, powerful forces marching through.*][8]

FAUST.[9] No—heroes' muster you shall savor,
    Ringed in assembly here at length:
    For none deserves the ladies' favor
    But who can guard them with most strength.   9445
    [*to the commanders, who separate from the columns and
    approach*]

7. Through a parody of their rhyming, Phorcyas-Mephisto intentionally disrupts the illusion of fulfillment which Helena and Faust have achieved. Thematically this intrusion corresponds to a similar occasion in the affair with Gretchen in the "Garden Pavilion" of *Part 1*, lines 3207 ff.

8. A theatrical illusion suggesting that the forces of the castle are rallying to the defense against the approaching army of Menelaos. Critics have argued an historical allusion here to the invasion of the Peleponnesus by Guillaume de Villehardouin early in the thirteenth century, when the principalities of Morea and Achaia were established on the model of the French feudal order, where Norman, French, and German chieftains received fiefdoms (see lines 9466–73).

9. Three separate historical periods are intentionally blended here: 1) the Dorian invasion of Mycenaean Greece in the era shortly after the Trojan war, when all the centers of the heroic age fell and Greece entered an era of darkness and barbarism; 2) the migrations of the Germanic tribes across Europe from the north and east (lines 9448 ff.), gradually overrunning the ancient world during the early centuries of the Christian era; and 3) the invasion of the Peloponnesus by the armies of the crusades in the thirteenth century. An allusion may also be intended to the intervention of European interests in the Greek war for independence from the Turks in the early 1820s, the war in which Lord Byron died in 1824 (which event is commemorated in connection with the death of Euphorion; see notes preceding lines 9903 and 9907).

Incessant in your silent raging,
Sure warrant of the foeman's doom,
You, blossom of the North unaging,
And you, the Orient's pith and bloom.

In steel encased, aglare with flashes,   9450
The band that shattered realms and states,
They tread the earth, it quakes with crashes
And in their wake reverberates.

At Pylos we secured our landing,
The hoary Nestor is no more,   9455
All petty royal troops disbanding,
The boundless host sweep all before.

And forthwith from the fastness yonder
Thrust Menelaos back to sea;
There let the vagrant lurk and plunder,   9460
Such was his bend and destiny.

As dukes I am to hail you captains,
Thus Lacedaemon's queen ordains;
Bring hills and dales for her acceptance,
And yours shall be the Empire's gains.   9465

Corinthus' bays, Teutonic warrior,
You shall defend with shield and wall!
You, Goth, shall guard by trusty barrier
Achaia with her gorges all.

To Elis set the Frank in motion,   9475
The Saxon be Messene's bane,
The Norman go to sweep the ocean
And found great Argolis again.

Then each will hold domestic charter,
Let might and fury outward rage;   9475
But over all enthroned be Sparta,
The Queen's redoubt from age to age.

While you she sees enjoy securely
Domains untouched by want or blight,
You at her feet will seek as surely   9480
Legitimation, law, and light.

[FAUST *descends; the* PRINCES *form a circle about him to
hear more closely his orders and directions.*]

CHORUS. He who craves for himself the prize of beauty,
        Valiant above all,
        Wisely let him look to weapons;
        Blandishing, he won indeed   9485
        What is highest on earth;
        Yet calmly he owns it not:

Shrewdly stealthy ones unblandish,
Boldly brigands snatch her from him;
Let him take thought to prevent it.   9490

Hence our Prince I praise,
Esteem him high before others,
For so allying himself, brave and astute,
That the stalwart stand obedient,
Biding his every beck.   9495
Loyal, they do his bidding,
Each for his own good as much
As rendering thanks to the ruler,
Winning loftiest fame for either besides.

For who will snatch her now   9500
From the potent possessor?
His she is, and ungrudged to him let her be,
Doubly ungrudged by us, whom alike with her,
With surest wall he encompassed within,
With mightiest host without.   9505

FAUST.† The patrimony here awarded—
To each an opulent domain—
Is grand; let them depart to guard it,
We hold the center for our reign.

And they will vie to shelter, reckless   9510
Of leaping waves on every side,
Un-island, thee, by slender hilly necklace
To Europe's last redoubt of mountains tied.

Before all others by the raptured
Of every tribe accounted blest,   9515
Thou sun-land, for my queen recaptured,
That gazed at her the earliest.

When to Eurotas'[1] reedy whispers
She broke in radiance from the shell,
Her noble mother's, twin-born sister's   9520
Eyesight outstabbing by her spell.

This land, all else for you forsaking,
Presents the finest of its worth;
Than all the globe—yours for the taking—
Prefer, o choose the native earth.   9525

Though on its ridge the jagged peak must suffer
The solar arrow with a frigid glare,
The boulders have a blush of green to offer,
The goat collects a toothsome frugal share.

---

1. The river which flows south from Ar-   by Zeus in the form of a swan.
cadia to Sparta, where Leda was seduced

The torrent tumbles, fed by countless rillets,   9530
Already gorges, rises, alps are green.
On meadows stippled with a hundred hillocks
Sedately spreading woolly flocks are seen.

One at a time, with measured caution striding,
The hornèd beasts approach the sheer ascent,   9535
But, shelter for the whole of them providing,
The rocky wall with scores of caves is rent.
There Pan[2] protects them, nymphs of life inhabit
The dewy shade that bushy cliffsides lend,
And serried trees, for higher regions avid,   9540
Their laced array of branches skyward send.

Hoar forests these! The oaktree looms defiant,
And limb on willful limb enjagging jut;
Rising in purity, the maple pliant
Sports with its load, with syrup juice aglut.   9545

And tepid milk in shady rounds of quiet
Wells up maternally for child and lamb;
Not far is fruit, the lowland's ripened diet,
And honey trickles from the hollowed stem.

Their miens, their gazes are serener,   9550
Bliss is inherited like wealth,
Each is immortal in his own demesne here,
They live contented and in health.

One watches the enchanting child[3] attaining,
Down flawless days, to father's vigor then,   9555
And stands amazed—the question still remaining
If these are gods or mortal men?

So was Apollo shaped to shepherd likeness
That of their fairest, one resembled him;
Where Nature works within her own pure cycle,   9560
All worlds link up without an interim.
        [*sitting next to her*]
Thus things for me, for you, have blithely ended,
Let all the past be put behind and gone;
O feel from the all-highest god descended,
To that first world you appertain alone.   9565

No cramping fortress would be rightful
Abode for you; in wiltless verdure set,
To make our residence delightful,
Arcadia encircles Sparta yet.

2. The goat-god who traditionally dwells as lord within the woods and groves of the pastoral landscape.
3. An allusion to Euphorion, whether or not Faust himself explicitly refers to the as yet unborn offspring of his union with Helena.

For refuge lured to smiling harbors, 9570
You fled to fortune's blithest kiss!
These thrones are changing into arbors,
Arcadian-free shall be our bliss!

[*The scene changes completely.*]

[*Closed arbors leaning against a number of rock caverns.
A shady grove extends up to the steep cliffsides surrounding
all.* FAUST *and* HELENA *are not in evidence. The* CHORUS *lies
bedded here and there, asleep.*][4]

PHORCYAS. Who knows how long the maidens have been
slumbering,
Nor can I tell if what with perfect clarity 9575
My eyes beheld, they even dared perchance to dream.
So I will wake them. Let the youngsters be amazed;
You bearded ones no less, who sit and hide below
To find the key at last to wonders worth belief.
Arise! Arise forthwith and swiftly shake your locks; 9580
Have done with sleep, stop blinking, and attend to me![5]

CHORUS.[6] Speak, say on, and let us hear it, what of marvels has
befallen,
We are eager, and the harder to believe your tale, the better,
For we find it poor amusement to be staring at these boulders.

PHORCYAS. Hardly rubbed your eyes, you children, and already time
is slow? 9885
Listen, then: within these caverns, in these grottos, in these
arbors,
Screen and shelter have been granted, as to lovers in an idyll,
To our liege lord and our lady.

CHORUS. What, within there?

PHORCYAS. Yes—secluded
From the world, but me alone they summoned for discreet
attendance.
Thus distinguished, I stood by, but as befits a trusted
servant, 9590
I took care to find employment some way off, turned here and
thither
Seeking mosses, worts, and tree-bark, privy to their divers virtues;
Thus the two remained alone.

4. Goethe here employs a deep stage which distinguishes between a proscenium and a perspective set with receding areas that represent caves (in one of which Faust, Helena, and Euphorion are later discovered). Such a theatrical structure was first developed in Italy in the late sixteenth century, especially in conjunction with the musical drama imitating Greek tragedy that subsequently emerged as opera. The most famous example of this new theatre was the Teatro Olympico in Vicenza, designed by Andrea Palladio (1518–80), which Goethe visited at the start of his Italian journey in the fall of 1786. The visual style of this pastoral stage set may be modeled also on the landscapes of the French painter Nicolas Poussin (1594–1665).
5. The sleeping Chorus is borrowed from Aeschylus' *Eumenides*, where the Furies are discovered asleep around the altar of Apollo at Delphi, having been put under a spell by the god.
6. Goethe imitates (using again the iambic trimeter) the *parabasis* of ancient Greek Comedy, where the Chorus interrupts the dramatic continuity of the play in order to address the audience directly in sharp, satirical terms.

CHORUS. One might think that these enclosures harbored worlds of
   space within them,
   Wood and meadow, lakes and freshets; truly, fairy yarns you
      spin![7]   9595
PHORCYAS. So they do, you callow children! Those are recesses
      unfathomed,
   Hall on hall, and court on courtyard, these I pensively explored.
   All at once, a peal of laughter echoes through the hollow spaces;
   As I watch, a boy is tumbling from our lady's lap to Master's,
   From the father to the mother, tender frolic, fond caresses,   9600
   Teasing love's inane endearments, playful shouts and gay
      exulting
   Variously strike my ear.[8]†
   Naked genius unfledged, a faun exempt of faunic coarseness,
   He will leap on solid ground, which like a springboard counter-
      vailing
   Flings him upward high and higher, till by second, third rebound-
      ing   9605
   He has touched the lofty vault.

   Anxiously his mother calls him: leap and spring as fancy takes
      thee,
   But forbear to fly, untrammeled flight is not vouchsafed to thee.
   Thus the honest father warns him: in the earth inheres resilience
   Which will buoy thee up, if only thou adhere to it on tiptoe,   9610
   Like the son of earth, Antaeus, it will strengthen thee at once.
   Then he skips upon this rocky mass of cliff, and from its edges
   To another, keeps rebounding as a driven ball will bounce.

   All at once, though, he has vanished in a jagged gorge's crevice,
   Lost, it seems to us, already. Mother moans and father
      comforts,   9615
   I attend with frightened shrugging. Then, what startling reappear-
      ance!
   Were there treasures hidden yonder? Drapings striped as if with
      flowers
   Worthily adorn him now.[9]
   Tassels swinging from his forearms, ribbons fluttering at his bosom,
   In his hand the golden lyre, exactly like a little Phoebus,   9620

7. The sense of a fairy tale expressed
here by the Chorus is crucial for the entire last section of the *Helena*.
8. Euphorion was the name of the
offspring born to Helena and Achilles
from their posthumous marriage on the
blessed island of Leuce (see also lines
7435 and 8876). As we know from a
conversation with Eckermann (December
20, 1829; see below), Goethe intended
Euphorion to personify the spirit of
poesy; such is also indicated by the Chorus when they address him as "poesy
pure" (line 9863). Goethe's conception

of Euphorion as a naked Genius suggests
a variation on the painting by Annibale
Carracci (1560–1609) entitled *The Genius of Fame*, which since 1746 had been
in the Johanneum in Dresden. The painting depicts the naked body of a youth
with wings, soaring upward toward the
heavens.
9. The transformation of Euphorion is
associated by Phorcyas-Mephisto with
the theme of buried treasure, so central
to *Faust*. Euphorion emerges from the
depths like a youthful Phoebus Apollo,
the God of poetry and song.

Quite serenely he approaches the projecting edge; we marvel.
And his parents from enchantment each fall in the other's arms.
For what fulgence at his head, a gleam not easily determined,
Whether glittering gold or blaze of high prepotency of mind.
Thus he is proclaimed already by his boyish look and bearing 9625
Heir apparent to all beauty, sentient members agitated
By imperishable music; and as such you are to hear him,
And as such you will behold him in unique astonishment.

CHORUS.   Is this a marvel to you,
      Offspring of Crete? 9630
      Have you not hearkened then
      To lessons from poets' lips,
      Never have heard of Hellas',
      Nor of Ionia's
      Hoary ancestral hoard 9635
      Of goldly and kingly lays?

      All that can ever befall
      These late days of our own
      Apes but with dolorous sound
      Glories of yore. 9640
      Paler is what you relate
      Than the delightful lies—
      More worthy of faith than is truth—
      Fabled of Maia's son.

      He, of finely wrought strength, 9645
      Whom, as a babe scarce born,
      Gossiping gaggle of nurses,
      Sluggish of wit,
      Swaddled in purest down
      Strapped into exquisite wraps; 9650
      Nimble and strong, though, the scamp
      Smoothly withdrew his lissom
      Supply elastic limbs,
      Leaving behind in his stead
      The sedulous purple encumbrance, 9655
      Calmly, a vacant shell;
      As when a butterfly, rid
      Of worn-out chrysalid armor,
      Thrills the unfolded wings
      And boldly its wayward course 9660
      Tumbles through sun-drenched air.

      So does he, the adroitest,
      Patron spirit to be
      Ever to thieves and rogues,
      And all intent upon vantage. 9665
      This he forthwith enacts
      By most dexterous arts.

Nimbly the Lord of the Sea
He robs of the trident, slily in Ares' sight
Steals from its sheath the sword,   9670
Bow, too, and arrow from Phoebus,
And from Hephaistos his tongs;
All but snatches the lightning of Zeus, his father,
But for awe of its fire;
Albeit Eros he bests   9675
At foot-tripping wrestling game,
And from Cytherea's breast
Trims, as she hugs him, the belt.[1]

[*String music, charming and melodiously pure, resounds from
the cavern.*[2] *All take notice and soon appear deeply moved.
From here on until the noted pause, the action is accompanied throughout by full-toned music.*][3]†

PHORCYAS.   Listen, strings, in sweet collusion!
             Quick, be rid of fable play,   9680
             Ancient deities' confusion
             Put to rest, it had its day.

             Rest, old tales, for none will miss you,
             We demand a higher art:
             From the living heart must issue   9685
             What would work upon the heart.

[*She withdraws toward the cliffs.*]

CHORUS.   Dreaded one, if you are giving
             To these graceful notes your ear,
             We, so lately saved for living,
             Melt away in joyous tears.   9690

             Let the sun withdraw its lustre,
             Once the dawn within unfolds,
             From our hearts we amply muster
             What the whole wide world witholds.

[HELENA, FAUST, *and* EUPHORION, *costumed as described
above.*]

---

1. The most famous theft of the young
Hermes is not mentioned here. On the
day of his birth he stole the cattle of
Apollo, then, to appease the older god,
presented him with the gift of the lyre,
which he had invented from the shell of
a tortoise. From this lyre Apollo fashioned music and because of it subsequently became the god of poetry. Euphorion emerges from the crevice into
which he disappeared carrying a golden
lyre (line 9620), "like a little Phoebus."
2. To sound—at least at first—as if
played by Euphorion on his golden lyre.
3. From this point to the death of Euphorion the drama is transformed into
opera, and the text becomes no more
than a libretto for music which Goethe

hoped would be written but which never
has been. This libretto was influenced in
significant ways by a fragmentary sequel
to Mozart's *Magic Flute* which Goethe
wrote in the late 1790s. Goethe envisioned music for *Euphorion*—as he
stated to Eckermann (February 12, 1829;
see below)—in the manner of Mozart's
Don Giovanni. Yet the style of the
opera is not tragic but burlesque. The
heroic grandeur of Euphorion is transformed into a kind of puppet play which
elicits only a sense of resignation and
irony from Faust and Helena and from
Phorcyas-Mephisto and the Chorus.
Goethe's opera-ballet, like a grandiose
shadow game, finally dissolves into thin
air.

EUPHORION.   Hearken childish songs a-singing,   9695
               Take at once your proper parts;
               As you watch my rhythmic springing,
               Skip parentally your hearts.

HELENA.   Love, to lavish human blessing,
               Links a noble pair-to-be;   9700
               Godly joy to be expressing,
               He creates a peerless Three.

FAUST.   All is then enacted rightly;
               I am yours and you are mine;
               See us interwoven tightly   9705
               As we must by love divine.

CHORUS.   Joy of many ages' reaping
               In their offspring's gentle glow
               On this pair descended heaping.
               Oh, their union moves me so!   9710

EUPHORION.   Now let me leap
               Skyward and higher,
               Now let me skip,
               Buoyant desire
               Takes me already   9715
               Into its grip.

FAUST.   But steady, steady!
               Not danger courting,
               Lest heedless sporting
               Bring fall and ruin,   9720
               Our dearest son
               Be our undoing.

EUPHORION.   I will not linger
               In earthbound clinging,
               Let go my finger,   9725
               My locks let go,
               Let go my garments,
               For they are mine!

HELENA.   Oh, think, believe us,
               Here you belong!   9730
               How you would grieve us,
               How sorely wrong
               The fair and hard-won
               Mine, His, and Thine.

CHORUS.   Soon slips, I fear me,   9735
               The knot benign!

HELENA AND FAUST.
               Bridle, oh, bridle,
               Your parents urge,
               Impulses' idle
               Vehement surge!   9740
               Grace our lonely
               Rustic purlieus.

EUPHORION. For your sakes only
        Patience I use.
    [*tracing a winding path through the* CHORUS *and drawing it
    away to dance*]
        This merry tribe I ring,   9745
        Airy and light.
        Now is the tune I sing,
        My movement right?
HELENA.   Yes, you do well to dance,
        Leading these lovely ones,   9750
        Your arts employ.
FAUST.   Would we were done with this!
        I in this flightiness
        Can take no joy.
    [EUPHORION *and* CHORUS, *dancing and singing, move in
    intricate evolutions.*]
CHORUS.   Ah, as you wave your arms'   9755
        Well-shapen pair,
        Your shining ringlets' charms
        Shake in the air,
        As to the ground you put
        Lightly your tender foot,   9760
        As limb on limb repair
        Gracefully here and there,
        You have achieved your goal,
        Enchanting child;
        Have all our hearts beguiled,   9765
        Won every soul.
    [*Pause.*]
EUPHORION. You be as many
        Does of light tread,
        Be from this cranny
        To new game led;   9770
        I'll do the hunting,
        You make escape.
CHORUS.   You, to disarm us,
        Need not be lithe,
        Nothing would charm us   9775
        Or seem as blithe,
        As to embrace you,
        Beauteous shape!
EUPHORION. Through arbors scurry,
        By boulders hurry,   9780
        What's lightly gathered,
        That I disdain,
        But danger weathered
        I count for gain.
HELENA AND FAUST.
        What self-will! What reckless bounding!   9785

          Hopeless to contain his daring.
          There, like hunting-horns resounding,
          Din through woods and valleys blaring;
          What abandon! Wanton roar!

CHORUS. [*hurrying up one by one*]
          Racing on, he left us lagging,   9790
          Passed us by with scorn uncaring,
          There he now approaches, dragging
          Just the wildest in the score.

EUPHORION. [*carrying up a young girl*]
          Here this sturdy lass I carry,
          For my pleasure and enjoyment,   9795
          Her reluctant breast I press
          In delightful forced caress,
          Her resisting lips I kiss,
          Proving strength and willfulness.

GIRL.   Stop! Within this body, pirate,   9800
          Pluck and strength are not at bay,
          Spirits like your self-will fire it,
          Not so lightly brushed away.
          He who thinks me lost and cringing,
          On his arm too much relies!   9805
          Hold me fast, here I go singeing
          Striplings for a lark—surprise!

[*She kindles and flares up as a flame.*]
          Follow me to regions aerial,
          Follow me to somber burial,
          Catch me, catch the vanished prize.   9810

EUPHORION. [*shaking off the last of the flames*]
          Cliffside's confining press,
          Forest and brush,
          Pall in their narrowness,
          Am I not young and fresh?
          Winds they go soaring,   9815
          Waves, they are roaring,
          These from afar I hear,
          Fain would be near.

[*He leaps ever higher up the cliffs.*]

HELENA, FAUST, AND CHORUS.
          Would you ape the chamois' ways?
          Horrid downfall we are dreading!   9820

EUPHORION. Ever upward am I heading,
          Ever farther must I gaze.
          Now I know where I stand!
          In the isle's heartland,
          Pelops' domain within,   9825
          Mainland and ocean kin.

CHORUS.   Would you not gently
          Dwell amid wood and peak?

Let us contently
Vine arbors seek, 9830
Grape-rows the hillocks bound,
Fig-green and apple-gold;
Fast to the lovely ground,
Lovely one, hold!

EUPHORION. Dream ye of peaceful day? 9835
Let dream who may!
War! does the watchword sound,
Triumph! the hills resound.

CHORUS. He who in peace invites
Scourges of war, 9840
Hope and all dear delights
He must abhor.

EUPHORION. Those whom this country bore,
Dangers behind, before,
Boundless and bold of mood, 9845
Prodigal of their blood:
To her undaunted sons'
Sacred resource,
To the embattled ones
May it add force![4] 9850

CHORUS. Lo, aloft, and climbing higher!
Yet his image never shrinks,
Gleam of armor his attire,
As of bronze and steel it winks.

EUPHORION. No escarpment, no immuring, 9855
Trust oneself is all one can;
Fortress firm for sure enduring
Is the iron breast of man.
Lightly armed, field every human
If unconquered ye would dwell; 9860
Be an amazon each woman,
Every child a sentinel.

CHORUS. Poesy pure, august,
Heavenward rise it must,
Glittering, starry bright, 9865
Ever so far, its light
Ever to reach us still,
Hear it we ever will,
Ever delight.[5]

EUPHORION. No, not as child in arms arriving, 9870
As youth in armor let it be,
In ardent spirit soon contriving

---

4. An obscure passage syntactically. The opening subordinate phrases stand in opposition to the main clause of the last two lines ("resource" and "force"; "the embattled ones" and "undaunted sons"), and the pronoun of the final line presumably refers to the war which Euphorion champions.

5. The only instance in the entire Euphorion sequence where he is explicitly associated wtih the spirit of poesy.

To join the strong and bold and free.
Forth fare!
Now, there,   9875
To fame the open road I see.

HELENA AND FAUST.
                Into living ushered scarcely,
                Scarce to smiling day inured,
                Yet by dizzying stairs perversely
                Into parlous spaces lured?   9880
                Are then we
                Naught to thee,
                Lovely bonds a fantasy?

EUPHORION.   Across the ocean hear it thunder,
                There gorge on gorge reverberate,   9885
                Hear host on host, aclash, asunder,
                Deal thrust on thrust in throes of fate.
                And death's thrall
                Is duty's call,
                Fate decreed it once for all.   9890

HELENA, FAUST, AND CHORUS.
                What appalling, grim insistence!
                Is it death, then, duty wills?

EUPHORION.   Shall I watch at idle distance?
                No! I share their needs and ills.

THE FORMER.   Death is by heady   9895
                Rashness foretold!

EUPHORION.   Still! And already
                Pinions unfold!⁶
                Thither! I must! I must!
                Grant me the flight!   9900

[*He launches himself upon the air; his garments carry him for an instant, his head shines, a trail of light marks his wake.*]

CHORUS.   Icarus! Icarus!⁷
                Piteous plight.

[*A beautiful youth plunges down at the parents' feet; one seems to recognize in the body a familiar figure;⁸† but the corporeal vanishes at once; the aureole rises like a meteor to the sky; robe, cloak, and lyre are left behind.*]

HELENA AND FAUST.
                Must agony overwhelm
                Delight so soon?

---

6. Euphorion's assertion that his wings here unfold for flight is contradicted by the stage direction following, which indicates unambiguously that he is suspended momentarily by his garments only.

7. The son of Daedalus, a craftsman of ancient Crete, who tried to escape with his father on artificial wings which melted when he flew too near the sun.

8. George Gordon, Lord Byron (1788–1824). (See the conversation with Eckermann of July 5, 1827, below.) For Goethe, Byron embodied the modern spirit of poetry which we would now call Romantic.

EUPHORION'S VOICE. [*from the deeps*]   9905
          Mother, in this dim realm
          Let me not dwell alone!
[*Pause.*]
CHORUS. [*dirge*]⁹   Never lonely!—Wheresoever
          Dwelling (we do not mistake you),
          As you quit the day forever,
          None of these our hearts forsake you.   9910
          Tears and dirges gladly sparing,
          Envious, we sing your praise:
          Song and soul were fine and daring
          Both in bright and dreary days.

          Born to easeful earthly station,   9915
          High of lineage, great of gift,
          Soon, alas! his own damnation,
          Youthful blossom roughly reft.
          Worldy insight clearer, harder,
          Tuned to every heartstring's tone,   9920
          Finest women's loving ardor,
          And a music all his own.

          But you rushed most vehemently,
          Heedless, into tangling flaw,
          Fell afoul incontinently   9925
          Of propriety and law;
          Yet at last exalted yearning
          Lent to native courage weight,
          Splendid laurels to be earning
          You were minded—not so Fate.   9930

          Who succeeds? That query dismal
          Muffled Destiny leaves moot,
          When misfortune most abysmal
          Strikes the bloodied people mute.
          Yet afresh new anthems sow them,   9935
          Stand in mourning bowed no more:
          For the soil again will grow them
          As it ever has before.
[*Complete pause. The music ends.*]
HELENA. [*to* FAUST]¹ An ancient truth, alas, is proved once more
      through me:
    That beauty and good fortune are but fleetly joined.   9940
    Severed is now the bond of life like that of love,
    Lamenting both, I grievingly pronounce farewell!
    And one last time I fling myself into your arms.

9. In his conversation with Eckermann of July 5, 1827 (below), Goethe noted that the Chorus here completely abandons its role. Nothing remains of Greek drama or even of the *Helena* as Goethe pays his poetic tribute to the dead Byron. (See note preceding line 8488.)
1. Helena, implicitly acknowledging her break with Faust, speaks once again in iambic trimeter.

Persephoneia, gather in the boy and me.
[*She embraces* FAUST; *her corporeal substance vanishes, robe
and veil are left in his arms.*]

PHORCYAS. [*to* FAUST] Hold fast what of it all remains to you.   9945
Do not release the robe. Already demons
Are plucking at its corners and would like
To snatch it down to Hades. Hold it fast!
It is the goddess, whom you lost, no more,
Yet godly still. Make use of the exalted   9950
Inestimable boon and rise aloft,
It bears you swiftly over all that is base
Across the ether, for as long as you may endure.
We meet again, far, passing far from here.
[HELENA's *garments dissolve into clouds, surround* FAUST,
lift him up, and drift past with him.]

PHORCYAS. [*gathers up* EUPHORION's *robe, cloak, and lyre from the
ground, steps up to the proscenium, raises up the exuviae,
and speaks*]
        Still fortunately these endure!   9955
        The flame is vanished, to be sure,
        Yet leaves the world in no distress.
        Enough remains to consecrate the poet,
        Stir guildsmen's greed, collegial pettiness;
        And, ready talent lacking to bestow it,   9960
        I can at least lend out the dress.
[*She seats herself in the proscenium against a column.*]

PANTHALIS. Make haste now, girls! now that we are well rid of
spells,
The Old-Thessalian crone's chaotic thrall of mind;
Likewise the swirl of much-confounded tinkling notes,
Blurring the ear, more sorely still the inner sense.   9965
Downward to Hades! For you saw the Queen make haste
With measured pace that way. Let forthwith in her prints
The footsteps of her loyal maidens now be set.
We find her at the throne of the Inscrutable.

CHORUS. Queens, to be sure, find their pleasure wherever;   9970
        In Hades, even, they take pride of place,
        Proudly joined to their peers,
        In Persephone's innermost counsels;
        But we, in the background,
        Deep in asphodel meads,   9975
        Companioned to lanky poplars
        And barren willows,
        What pastime have we?
        Whispering, bat-fashion,
        Twitters, unpleasing, eerie.   9980

PANTHALIS. He who has earned no name, nor strives for noble
things
Belongs but to the elements, so get you gone!

I yearn to join my Queen; in merit not alone,
But in our loyalty we live as persons still.
[*Exit.*]

ALL. Restored are we to the light of day,   9985
Persons, indeed, no longer,
That we feel, we know.
But never to Hades will we return.
Ever-live Nature
Lays to us spirits   9990
As we to her, full-valid claim.

A PART OF THE CHORUS.[2]† We within these myriad branches'
    whispery quiver, breezy floating,
Lure and dally, softly tempting, up the rootwork founts of
    living,
To the twigs; and now with foliage, now with blossom all-
    abundant,
We adorn the fluttering ringlets free to prosper in the air. 9995
Falls the fruit, at once forgather lustily both flock and people
For the grasping, for the tasting, briskly striding, keenly pressing,
Bowing one and all about us as before the earliest gods.

ANOTHER PART.[3] To these cliffsides' polished mirror gleaming far
    into the distance,
Undulating, nestling gently and caressingly we cling;   10000
Hearken, listen to each sound, the notes of songbirds, reedy
    fluting,
Be it Pan's dread voice, reply is ever ready to go forth;
Zephyrs breathe, we breathe in answer, roll the thunders, ours go
    rolling
Stunning in reverberation, threefold, tenfold, after it.

A THIRD PART.[4] Sisters! Livelier of spirit, we pursue the brooks' swift
    courses;   10005
For the hillocks in the distance tempt us with their rich adorn-
    ment,
Down and ever down, we water, ever welling and meandering,
Now the meadow, now the pastures, soon the garden round the
    house.
There the cypresses' slim tapers point it out above the landscape,
Rising to the ether over span of shore and watery mirror.   10010

A FOURTH PART.[5] Range you others where you fancy, we encom-
    pass, cling with rustling

2. The first group of the Chorus is transformed into tree nymphs (Dryads) such
as Mephistopheles encountered outside
the cave of the Phorcyads in the "Classical Walpurgis Night" (lines 7959 ff.).
3. The second group becomes mountain
nymphs (Oreads) such as Mephistopheles also encountered in the "Classical
Walpurgis Night" (lines 7811 ff.).
4. The third group becomes water
nymphs (Naiads) such as those which
appeared at several points in the "Classical Walpurgis Night": the Nymphs in
the reeds at the Peneios (lines 7263 ff.);
the Sirens of the Aegean (lines 7156 ff.
and 7495 ff., and throughout the final
section); and perhaps even the Nereids
and Dorids who participated in the festival of Galatea.
5. The fourth group of the Chorus enters
directly into the vines and the grapes,
grows to ripeness, and becomes the spirit
of wine produced from the harvest, identical with the god Bacchus.

To the fully planted hillside where the vine greens on its staff;
There through days and hours the vintner's indefatigable passion
Lets us see the fondest fervor's ever dubious reward.
Now with hoe and now with mattock, now at heaping, pruning,
    binding,   10015
He will pray to all the gods, the sun-god, though, to most avail.
Bacchus stirs himself, the pampered, little for his loyal servant,
Rests in arbors, lolls in caverns, trifling with the youngest faun.
All that ever yet he needed for his daydreams' semi-trances
Ever waits for him in wineskins, kept for him in butts and
    pitchers.   10020
Right and left in coolness hidden for eternities of time.
But when all the gods have readied, Helios above the others,
Airing, moisting, warming, blazing, cornucopias of grape,
Of a sudden life resurges where the vintner worked in quiet,
Bushes swish and brush each other, rustles run from stock
    to stock.   10025
Baskets creaking, buckets rattling, shoulder-hampers groaning off,
All toward the mighty wine-press, for the treaders' sturdy dance;
That is when the sacred bounty of the luscious pure-born berries,
Rudely trampled, foams and splatters, all commingling foully
    squashed.
Smiting now the ear, the cymbals' and the timbrels' brazen
    clangor   10030
Hail the wine-god Dionysus out of mysteries revealed;
Forth he steps with goat-foot satyrs, whirling nymphs of goat-feet
    also,
All between, with strident braying blares Silenus' long-eared
    beast.
Naught is spared! The cloven talons trample down all chaste
    decorum,
Senses all are whirled a-stagger, stunned the ear to deafness
    dread.   10035
Drunken groping for the goblets, glutted sodden heads and
    paunches,
Still at pains is one or other, only to increase the turmoil,
For to garner fresher vintage, older skins are swiftly drained![6]
    [*The curtain falls.*]
    [PHORCYAS, *in the proscenium, rears herself to giant stature,*
    but steps down from the buskins and casts off mask and
    veil, revealing herself as MEPHISTOPHELES, *in order to pro-*
    vide in an epilogue such comment on the play as might be
    necessary.][7]

6. In the closing section of the passage Dionysian revels burst loose in overwhelming force, complete with all the drunken company of the god, the satyrs and nymphs, the fat-bellied Silenos and his ass. A totally new tone enters the choral song, as all order and control is destroyed and drunken chaos ensues.

7. Mephistopheles seems to intend an epilogue, which he would speak as he removes his costume, buskins, mask, and veil, rearing up to gigantic proportion—one recalls the monster that emerged from the poodle in the first study scene of *Part I*.

Act IV

HIGH MOUNTAINS

Sheer, jagged pinnacles. A cloud drifts up, settles against the cliff, sinks down onto a projecting ledge. It divides.[1]

FAUST. [*steps forth*]† The most profound of solitudes beholding
    underfoot,
I circumspectly tread the margin of these peaks,   10040
Dismiss my aerial engine, which on cloudless days
Has spirited me gently over land and sea.
It slowly separates from me without dispersing.
The essence forges eastward in compacted train,
The admiring eye pursues it, in amazement lost.   10045
It parts in floating, undulating, changeably;
Yet would adopt a shape . . . Yes! I am not deceived!
On sun-gilt holstery in wondrous splendor laid,
Of titan size, indeed, a godlike female form,
I see it well! Resembling Juno, Leda, Helena,   10050
In what majestic loveliness it wavers in my sight.
Alas, too soon deformed! Distended, shapelessly amassed,
It hulks at orient like a distant arctic range,
Its glamor mirroring deep sense of fleeting days.[2]

About my breast and brow a shining band of mist   10055
Still hovers, though, exhilarating, tender, cool.[3]
Now lightly, hesitantly, it ascends, higher and higher,
Takes form. Am I received by an enchanting shape,
As of long-lost, most cherished boon of earliest youth?[4]
The inmost heart's primordial treasures rise again,   10060
Aurora's[5] love, winged impetus it means to me,
The swiftly felt, first, scarcely comprehended glance,
That, caught and held, outglittered any gem.
Like beauty of the soul, the lovely image is enhanced
And, undissolving, wafts aloft into the ether,   10065
Drawing away with it the best my soul contains.[6]

    [*A seven-mile boot*[7] *pads onstage; another follows presently:*
    MEPHISTOPHELES *dismounts. The boots hurry on.*]

1. The cloud formed from Helena's garments has carried Faust to high rocky peaks somewhere in the Alps. The setting of this scene should be compared to "Charming Landscape," which begins Part II. Faust's monologue also recalls his comments there, lines 4679–4727.
2. The form of the Ideal Feminine has withdrawn to the eastern horizon, where it hovers over icy summits in the shape of a gigantic woman. Goethe alludes here to the cloud formation called *cumulus* in the study by the English scientist Luke Howard *On Modification of Clouds* (London, 1803), which Goethe read in 1815. (See also Goethe's trilogy of poems "On Howard's Theory of Clouds," published 1820–22.)
3. In contrast to the cumulus, this cloud is a cirrus (also following Howard).
4. A schema to Act IV indicates that the contrast of these two clouds is intended to symbolize for Faust the contrast between Helena and Gretchen.
5. Aurora, goddess of the dawn, signifies Faust's first love, Gretchen.
6. The ascent of this cloud prefigures the final ascent in "Mountain Gorges" (lines 12094–95), where Faust's spirit follows the penitent soul of Gretchen.
7. A fairy-tale device borrowed from the seven-league boots in the story of Tom Thumb by Charles Perrault (1628–1703).

MEPHISTOPHELES. Now that was rapid transport for us![8]
 But tell me, what are you about?
 Debarking in the midst of horrors,
 In grimly yawning rock redoubt?   10070
 Though not this very spot, I know it well,
 For properly this was the pit of hell.[9]
FAUST. Of foolish legends you are never short;
 We're in for yet another weird report.
MEPHISTOPHELES. [*seriously*] When the Almighty—I know well
  wherefore—   10075
 From air did banish us to depths of wrath,[1]
 Where all about us from a glowing core
 Eternal blazes ate their flaming path,
 We found ourselves amid excessive brightness
 Pent up in most uncomfortable tightness.   10080
 The devils all together started coughing,
 Blew out from upper and from nether offing;
 Hell swelled with acid stench and sulfur reek,
 What press of gas there was! It reached a titan peak,
 So that at last the level earthen crust,   10085
 Thick as it was, burst with the rending thrust.
 The cloth has now been given a new tweak,
 What was the base one time, is now the peak.
 On this the proper recipes are grounded
 By which the top and bottom are confounded. 10090
 For we escaped the seething servile pool
 To supereminence of aerial rule.
 It is an open secret closely sealed,
 To gentiles only late to be revealed. [*Ephesians vi.12*][2]
FAUST. To me the mountain mass lies nobly mute, 10095
 The whences and the whys I don't dispute.
 When Nature by and in herself was founded,
 In purity the earthen sphere she rounded,
 In summit and in gorge did pleasure seek,
 And threaded cliff to cliff and peak to peak; 10100
 Then did she fashion sloping hills at peace
 And gently down into the vale release.
 All greens and grows, and to her gay abundance
 Your swirling lunacies are sheer redundance.
MEPHISTOPHELES. Oh yes! . . . that seems as clear as day to
  you,   10105

8. An ironic allusion to Luke 1:39, "Mary rose in these days and went into the hill country with haste."
9. According to popular superstitition, mountains were formed when devils coughed in hell. Recall the theme of volcanic explosion in the "Classical Walpurgis Night."
1. An allusion to the fall of the angels with Lucifer after they rebelled against God, for which see Milton's *Paradise Lost* (Books I and VIII).
2. "For our wrestling is not against flesh and blood, but against the powers, against the world rulers of this darkness, against the spiritual hosts of wickedness in the heavenly places." The Biblical references in the last two acts of Part II were added by Goethe's associate and literary advisor, F. W. Riemer (1774–1845).

But to a witness it is just untrue.
Why, I was there when down below us, scalding
With tumbling streams of flame the chasm swelled;
When Moloch's hammer,[3] cliff to boulder welding,
Whole mountain fragments far abroad propelled.   10110
And still the lands with alien masses stare;
Who can explain the force that hurled them there?
Philosophers have shaped no concept for it,
There lies the stone, they simply must ignore it.
And quite in vain the best of brains were racked.—   10115
Alone the artless common people know
And are not fooled by intellect;
Their wisdom ripened long ago:
A wonder! here the Devil's in respect.
My wanderer, with simple faith for crutch,   10120
To Devil's Rock, to Devil's Bridge[4] will trudge.

FAUST. It's quite a fascinating thing to hear
How devils look upon the natural sphere.

MEPHISTOPHELES. Be Nature as it is! What do I care?
It's *point d'honneur!*—Beelzebub[5] was there.   10125
It is by us great things are made and broken,
Upheaval, chaos, violence! this be your token!—
No more with ambiguities to tease you—
Tell me, did nothing on our surface please you?
You have surveyed immeasurable stretches,   10130
The kingdoms of this world and all their riches; [*Matthew iv*][6]
And yet, insatiable as you are,
You've felt no appetite so far?

FAUST. Yes! One great thing did tempt me, one.
You guess at it!   10135

MEPHISTOPHELES.   That's quickly done.
I'd choose a typical metropolis,
At center, bourgeois stomach's gruesome bliss,
Tight crooked alleys, pointed gables, mullions,
Crabbed market stalls of roots and scallions,
Where bleeding joints on benches lie,   10140
Prey to the browsing carrion-fly;
For there at any time you'll find
Ado and stench of every kind.
Then boulevards and spacious squares
To flaunt aristocratic airs;   10145
And on, past any gate's resistance,
The suburbs sprawl into the distance.

---

3. Moloch, god of the Ammonites (Leviticus 18:2), is the most warlike of the devils in Milton's *Paradise Lost* (I.392 ff., II.43 ff.); in Klopstock's *Messiah* (II.352 ff.) he dwells in the mountains.
4. An allusion to the natural geological formation of this name in the Alps on the road through the St. Gotthard pass
5. See note to line 1334.
6. "Again, the devil took him to a very high mountain, and showed him all the kingdoms of the world and the glory of them."

There I'd rejoice in coaches gliding,
The noisy here-and-thither-sliding,
Eternal forward-backward hustle,   10150
The scattered ant-heap's teeming bustle.
And when I rode, and when I strolled,
By myriads I should be extolled,
Be ever central, ever lead.

FAUST. You offer me not bread but pebbles.   10155
One cheers to see the people breed,
In snug accustomed manner feed,
Grow lettered even, start to read—
And all one does is raising rebels.

MEPHISTOPHELES. Then I would build myself, as grandees
        ought,   10160
A pleasance at a pleasant spot,
Hill, forest, lowland, lea, and grange
To splendid gardens rearrange.[7]
In foils of foliage, velvet meadows,
Perspective pathways, artful shadows,   10165
Cascades through rock with rock combined,
And waterworks of every kind;
Where here will soar the awesome central fountain,
There hiss and piss wee bagatelles past counting.
Snug little cabins then I'd have them build,   10170
With fairest ladies to be filled,
And timeless pleasures to be wooed
In charmingly gregarious solitude.
Ladies, I say; for to me, once for all,
But in the plural women count at all.   10175

FAUST. Tawdry and up-to-date! Sardanapal![8]

MEPHISTOPHELES. What goal then, let me guess, won your alle-
        giance?
A high and bold one, I surmise.
Much closer as you soared to lunar regions,
They must be where your fancy flies?   10180

FAUST. By no means! Still this planet's soil
For noble deeds grants scope abounding.
I sense accomplishments astounding,
Feel strength in me for daring toil.

MEPHISTOPHELES. So now you crave a hero's fame?   10185
This tells from whose high company you came.

FAUST. Sway I would gain, a sovereign's thrall!
Renown is naught, the deed is all.

MEPHISTOPHELES. Yet poets will arise to render
Unto posterity your splendor,   10190

---

7. The following description suggests the formal gardens of Baroque and Rococo estates, as in the park at Versailles during the eighteenth century.
8. The King of Assyria, a legendary re- veller and debaucher, and the titular hero of Byron's play *Sardanapalus* (1821), which had been dedicated to Goethe.

Praise folly, folly to engender.
FAUST. Of all this nothing I concede.
What do you know of human need?
All sting and gall, what can your mind
Know of the longings of mankind?   10195
MEPHISTOPHELES. Have it according to your bent!
Confide to me your crotchets' full extent.
FAUST. On the high sea my eye was lately dwelling,
It surged, in towers self upon self upwelling.
Then it subsided and poured forth its breakers   10200
To storm the mainland's broad and shallow acres.
This galled me—showing how unbridled blood
By passionate impulse in rebellious flood
To wry perversity of temper blights
The liberal mind which cherishes all rights.   10205
I thought it chance, gazed on with sharp intent,
The wave held on, then rolling backward went,
Back from the proudly conquered goal it came;
An hour would lapse, but to repeat the game.
MEPHISTOPHELES. [*ad spectatores*] These are not novel tidings to
    my ears,   10210
I've known of it these hundred thousand years.
FAUST. [*continuing, with passion*] Forward it steals, and in a myriad
    starts,
Sterile itself, sterility imparts;
It swells and grows and rolls, and spans
The noisome vacancy of dismal strands.   10215
There wave on wave imbued with power has heaved,
But to withdraw—and nothing is achieved;
Which drives me near to desperate distress!
Such elemental might unharnessed, purposeless![9]
There dares my spirit soar past all it knew;   10220
Here I would struggle, this I would subdue.

And it is possible!—Surge as it may,
Past every hill it winds its pliant way;
However boisterously it cavorted,
Small height will proudly loom to thwart it,   10225
Small depth profound attraction holds.
Straight in my mind plan upon plan unfolds:
Earn for yourself the choice, delicious boast,
To lock the imperious ocean from the coast,
To shrink the borders of the damp expanse,   10230
And gorge it, far off, on its own advance.
This, step by step, my mind led me to see;
This is my wish, in this dare further me!
    [*Drums and warlike music at the audience's back in the
    distance, from the right.*]

9. Faust's concern with the waste of energy involved in the flux of the tides
echoes the argument of a work which

Goethe read while composing this scene,
Tableau of the Baltic Sea by Catteau-
Calleville (1812).

MEPHISTOPHELES. How easy! Do you hear far drums resound?
FAUST. War once again! The sane detest the sound.   10235
MEPHISTOPHELES. War, peace, what matter. The endeavor
  To feather one's own nest is clever.
  You watch, you crouch, you pounce upon your rabbit:
  The opportunity is there, Faust—grab it!
FAUST. That puzzle-box put back upon the shelf!   10240
  In plain and brief, what's up? Explain yourself.
MEPHISTOPHELES. Upon my tour I could not help observing
  That the poor Emperor's plight is most unnerving;
  You know him—when we entertained him,
  With counterfeit of wealth sustained him,   10245
  He thought the world his for a song.
  You see, he came into his title young;
  He ventured to conclude at random
  It would be easy to combine,
  Desirable, and altogether fine,   10250
  To govern and enjoy in tandem.
FAUST. A grave mistake. Who is to order ought
  In ordering his bliss to find.
  His soul with high design is fraught,
  But what—must be revealed to no man's mind.   10255
  What to his trustiest in whispers is propounded
  Is brought about, and all the world's astounded.
  Thus he remains the one on whom all leans,
  The worthiest—; incontinence demeans.[1]
MEPHISTOPHELES. No fear! he did not stint himself—
        not he!   10260
  Meanwhile the realm broke up in anarchy,
  Where large and small made war the length and breadth,
  Where brother brother put to flight, to death,
  Where castle warred on castle, city on city,
  Burgher on noble, feuding without pity,   10265
  The bishop even with his chapter and flock.
  They would draw arms as soon as look.
  Churches knew blood and death, town gates once crossed,
  Merchant and wanderer were as good as lost.
  And all grew vastly bold, for living meant   10270
  Dog must eat dog—and so, somehow, it went.
FAUST. Went, limped and fell, stood up once more to reel
  And took a clumsy tumble, head over heel.
MEPHISTOPHELES. This state of things no one was to deplore,
  Each one was able, each one meant to score.   10275
  The merest pawn would for a rook show off;
  Until at last the best had had enough.
  The most resourceful rose with one accord

---

1 The final phrase here has been much disputed, on the incorrect assumption that Faust here rejects the principle of enjoyment (*Geniessen*: here, "incontinence") which has motivated his activity from the outset of the drama. The contrast intended is no different from that between government and enjoyment mentioned in line 10251.

And said: He who can give us peace is lord.
The Emperor cannot, will not—let us choose,   10280
Let a new Emperor new life infuse,
Make fresh the world and safe for men
So none will suffer, none abuse;
And peace and justice wed again.[2]
FAUST. Sounds holy.   10285
MEPHISTOPHELES.   Right! Such moves the clergy launches,
They were securing their well-nourished paunches.
The clergy more than others took their side.[3]
Revolt swelled up, revolt was sanctified.
So that our Emperor, whom we gave delight,
Is here drawn up, perhaps for his last fight.   10290
FAUST. I feel for him, he was so good and open.
MEPHISTOPHELES. Come, let's look in; while there is life, there's
        hoping.
Let's free him from this narrow valley!
A thousand rescues brings a single sally.
Who knows how yet the cards may stack?   10295
And back in luck, he'll have his vassals back.
        [*They climb across the foothills and inspect the disposition
        of the troops in the valley. Drums and warlike music re-
        sound from below.*]
MEPHISTOPHELES. I see that the position's well secured;
We add our bit, and triumph is assured.
FAUST. What could our intervention mend?
It's fraud! Vain magic, sleight of hand!   10300
MEPHISTOPHELES. It's stratagem that wins the battle!
You'll keep yourself in higher mettle
If you consider your ambition.
If we preserve the Emperor's throne and land,
You may kneel down here and petition   10305
As fief from him the boundless strand.
FAUST. As many things as you've been through—
Go on and win a battle, too.
MEPHISTOPHELES. No—you shall win it! For this show
You are the Generalissimo.   10310
FAUST. Yes, that would be the proper rank!
Give orders where my knowledge is a blank.
MEPHISTOPHELES. Leave to the General Staff the worry,
And the Field Marshall won't be sorry.
Battle disorder—long I sensed it,   10315
And battle order promptly drew against it,
From primal mountains, primal human force;
Happy the man who garners this resource.

2. An allusion to Psalm 85:10, "Right-
eousness and peace have kissed each
other."
3. The clergy oppose the Emperor because their possessions are threatened by
anarchy. In the outline of *Part II* dictated in 1816 (see below) Goethe indicated that Faust would wage war against
the monks after the death of his and
Helena's son. A remnant of that original
plan may be apparent in the dilemma of
the Emperor as described here.

FAUST. What moves in arms there down the glen?
  Did you stir up the mountain men?   10320
MEPHISTOPHELES. No, no—like Quince I just withdrew
  The quintessence of the whole crew.[4]
  [*Enter* THE THREE MIGHTY MEN (*Samuel ii.* 23.8).][5]
MEPHISTOPHELES. Why, there my lads are coming, see?
  Of much disparate ages, you can tell,
  Of different garb and panoply;   10325
  They ought to serve you pretty well.
  [*ad spectatores*] The kids now fancy the historic
  Knight's armor and the vizor's clatter;
  And as the louts are allegoric,
  You all will like them that much better.[6]   10330
PUGNACIOUS. [*young, lightly armed, colorfully dressed*] Let anyone
    as much as eye me,
  Right in the kisser I will blip 'em,
  And those that chicken out and fly me,
  I catch by their back hair and flip 'em.
RAPACIOUS. [*mature, well armed, richly dressed*] Just picking fights
    is nursery stuff,   10335
  You might as well be bashing boards;
  Just go for pickings fat enough
  And ask the questions afterwards.
TENACIOUS. [*elderly, heavily armed, unclothed*] With that affairs
    are hardly bettered,
  A goodly pile is quickly scattered,   10340
  And life will wash it down the drain.
  Takers are smart, but keepers saner;
  Rely upon the old campaigner,
  You won't be clipped of it again.
  [*They descend as a group.*]

IN THE FOOTHILLS

  Drums and martial music from below. The EMPEROR'S *tent is
being pitched.*

  EMPEROR. COMMANDER-IN-CHIEF. AIDES.[1]

COMMANDER-IN-CHIEF. The concept still appears well-
    grounded   10345

4. An allusion to Peter Quince in Shakespeare's *Midsummer Night's Dream*,
who, as author, director, and manager of
the play performed by the tradesmen of
Athens, was its "quintessence"; stressed
on the first syllable.
5. An allusion to "the three mighty
men" who are named as fighting in the
army of King David: Jashobeam, Elea-
zar, and Shammah. They have apparently been summoned by Mephistopheles from Hell.
6. An allusion to modish chivalric and
Gothic novels and plays popular during

the later Romantic period in Germany.
1. This battle scene, like the funeral
games in Homer's *Iliad* or the war in
Heaven in Milton's *Paradise Lost*, imposes a sense of spectacle and cosmic
show upon the reader. Here, as elsewhere in *Faust*, it is Mephistopheles
(with his three infernal henchmen) who
unleashes the demonic powers in the battle. Much of the dramatic and poetic
technique of this scene reflects the tradition of Baroque drama and, especially,
Shakespearian history plays.

To have withdrawn to this convenient dale
The whole force, tightly massed and bounded;
I firmly trust we shall prevail.

EMPEROR. We now must see how it turns out;
This yielding irks me, though, this all-but-rout.   10350

COMMANDER-IN-CHIEF. Be pleased to look at our right flank, o Sire.
Just such terrain as strategists admire;
Passable hills, yet not unduly so,
Advantageous to us, traps to the foe.
We, half concealed, on wavy ground at large;   10355
The cavalry dare not attempt a charge.

EMPEROR. This leaves but praises for my part;
Here may be tested brawn and heart.

COMMANDER-IN-CHIEF. Here, in the central meadow's flat terrain
You see the phalanx[2] poised in fighting vein.   10360
High in the air the halberds glint and blaze,
Catching the sunbeams through the morning haze.
How ominously heaves the mighty square
With thousands all afire to do and dare!
This should attest their massive force for you;   10365
I look to them to cleave the foe in two.

EMPEROR. This handsome view I never had before.
Worth double of its strength is such a corps.

COMMANDER-IN-CHIEF. Of our left flank I offer no report,
Stout heroes occupy the rocky fort.   10370
The cliffs which now with glittering armor stare
Protect the stronghold's vital thoroughfare.
I see an unsuspecting hostile force
Already founder on a bloody course.

EMPEROR. There they come marching up, my two-faced kin,   10375
Who called me uncle, cousin, brother then,
And robbed, by mounting licence of their own,
Of might the scepter, and of awe the throne,
Laid waste the realm by mutual enmity,
And now in rebel concert fall on me.   10380
The rabble wavers in uncertain spirit,
Then breaks and rushes where the currents steer it.

COMMANDER-IN-CHIEF. Here hastes a good man down the rocky
        slope,
Sent for intelligence; success, I hope!

FIRST SCOUT. Yes, our mission is well ended,   10385
        And it was by ruse and pluck
        That both there and back we wended;
        But we bring but little luck,
        Many swear pure dedication,
        As some loyal bands do still;   10390
        But excuse for hesitation:
        Inner ferment, civil ill.

2. A body of heavily armed infantry   with joined shields and long lances.
formed in close, deep ranks and files

EMPEROR. To save its skin is egoism's all,
  Not debt of love, not duty's, honor's call.
  Do you not judge, when your account is due,   10395
  That neighbor's fire[3] will leap to your house too?
COMMANDER-IN-CHIEF. Down climbs the second in the interim,
  But wearily—he shakes in every limb.
SECOND SCOUT. First we smilingly detected
          Rank disorder's riotous throes;   10400
          Then abruptly, unexpected,
          A new Emperor arose.[4]
          Now in predetermined manner
          Trots the multitude to battle;
          Once unfurled the lying banner,   10405
          All come flocking.—Sheep and cattle!
EMPEROR. A rival Emperor profits me—I feel
  My sovereignty's never been more real.
  The armor, first but as a soldier borne,
  With more exalted purpose now is worn.   10410
  At every feast, as brilliant as it was,
  Danger I missed, for lack of other flaws.
  When you advised to tilt at ring and hole,
  My heart beat high, for jousting throbbed my soul.
  And had you not dissuaded me from war,   10415
  A hero's aureole had graced me long before.
  I felt my spirit sealed with hardihood
  When mirrored in that realm of fire I stood.[5]
  The force blazed out at me with hideous clutch,
  It was but make-believe—but grand as such.   10420
  Of feats and fame I have been dimly dreaming,
  Now I make up the fault of wanton seeming.
    [*The heralds are dispatched to challenge the* RIVAL EM-
    PEROR. *Enter* FAUST *in armor, with half-closed visor.* THE
    THREE MIGHTY MEN,[6] *armed and attired as earlier.*]
FAUST. We join you, and I hope, unblamed; indeed,
  Precaution counts no less without a need.
  You know the mountain folk[7] reflect and pore,   10425
  Versed in the scripts of rock and nature lore.
  The spirits, long estranged from lowland sites,
  Prefer more than before the craggy heights.
  They mutely toil through intricate crevasses
  In rich metallic vapors' noble gases;   10430
  In ceaseless separating, testing, blending

3. See Horace, *Epistles,* I.18.84: "It's
your concern when your neighbor's wall
is ablaze."
4. The appearance of a rival emperor to
challenge the authority of the true Emperor may be borrowed from a corresponding theme in Shakespeare's *Richard
III* and *Richard II,* where in each case
the King is challenged and overthrown
by a rival for the throne because of an
abuse of royal privilege and power.

5. See the Emperor's disguise as Pan in
the Carnival Masque (lines 5987–6002).
6. See note preceding line 10323. The supernatural devices in the battle which
follows were borrowed in part from Sir
Walter Scott's *Letters on Demonology
and Witchcraft* (1831), which Goethe
was reading in December, 1830, and January, 1831.
7. An allusion to creatures of folk superstition such as goblins, gnomes, elves.

Their every urge to new invention bending.
With the fine finger of spiritual passion
Their delicate transparent shapes they fashion;
Then, in the crystal's timeless silence furled,   10435
They see the progress of the upper world.

EMPEROR. I've heard this and believe it true, but how,
My worthy man, can this concern us now?

FAUST. The Sabine sorcerer of Norcia,[8] Sire,
Is your devout and honorable squire.   10440
What hideous doom on him was grimly calling,
The faggots crackled, flames flicked up, appalling;
The well-dried logs, heaped criss-cross all about,
With pitch and sulfur-covered rods eked out:
All hope, from man, God, devil was in vain,   10445
But Highness burst apart the glowing chain.
In Rome it was. Still deeply in your debt,
His heart is ever mindful of you yet.
He quite forgot himself from that hour on,
He asks the star, the depth, for you alone.   10450
He urged as foremost care, and made it ours,
To stand by you. Great are the mountain's powers;
There Nature acts prepotently and free,
Thick-witted clergy scolds it sorcery.

EMPEROR. On days of feasting, when the guests we hail,   10455
The gladly entering gladly to regale,
We gaily see each new one's forward thrust
Compress the dwindling floor-space as it must.
How much more welcome still the honest figure
Who proffers for most present help his vigor   10460
At morning hour of such ambiguous valence
Because fate's scales hang over it in balance.
Yet at this solemn moment here, repeal
The valiant sword-arm from the willing steel,
Honor the hour which many thousands draws   10465
To march in arms for or against my cause.
Man trust but self! Who craves for throne and crown,
Let him in person merit such renown.
Be what arose against me now—the ghost
Which "Emperor" styles itself, duke of the host,   10470
Lord of our lands, our vassals' suzerain—
By My hand thrust among the dead again!

FAUST. However turns the course of nemesis,
You do not well to stake your head like this.

8. This story of the Sabine sorcerer of Norcia (an Italian town infamous for sorcery) is presumably invented by Faust (and Mephistopheles) to deceive the Emperor into accepting their demonic assistance. Reference to this is also made on two later occasions (see lines 10606 and 10988). Supposedly the Emperor, on the occasion of his coronation in Rome, pardoned this sorcerer, who was about to be burned to death. For this reason—so Faust claims—the sorcerer has since been devoted to the Emperor and now has conjured the mountain spirits to come to his aid.

Is not the helm adorned with plume and crest?[9]   10475
It shields the head which crowns our pluck with zest.
What could the limbs effect without the head?
For when it slumbers, all are laid abed,
If it is hurt, it lames the others' lives,
Who rise afresh when swiftly it revives.   10480
With speed employs its solid right the arm,
It lifts the shield to guard the skull from harm,
The sword observes its duty, nothing slow,
It strongly parries and returns the blow;
Part in their luck the sturdy foot is granted,   10485
And on the victim's neck is briskly planted.

EMPEROR. Such is my wrath, the proud head I would treat
But as a new-made footstool for my feet![1]

HERALDS. [*returning*]
          Little honor, scant audition
          We encountered in our questing,   10490
          Of our nobly forceful mission
          They made scorn as feeble jesting:
          "Dust are all your Emperor's glories,
          Valley echo's vacant chime;
          To recall him smacks of stories   10495
          Starting "once upon a time.""

FAUST. Now have their wish those ever firm and true
Who were the best and took their stand with you.
There nears the foe, yours keenly bide your wishes,
Bid them attack, the moment is propitious.   10500

EMPEROR. At this point I relinquish the command.
   [*to the* COMMANDER-IN-CHIEF] Let now your duty, Prince, be in
      your hand.

COMMANDER-IN-CHIEF. Then let the right dress lines and take the
   field!
The enemy's left wing, just now ascending,
Before their final step is done, shall yield   10505
To youthful strength of loyalty defending.

FAUST. Give your permission, then, for this live blade
To step into the ranks of your brigade,
To fuse with them in most pervasive way,
And so allied, his robust sport display.   10510
          [*He points to the right.*]

AUDACIOUS. [*steps forward*] Who shows his face to me won't turn
   his back
But with both jowls on him well-minced with mangling,
Who turns his back will find a grisly slack
Of neck and head and top-knot down it dangling.

9. There is a playful association here of
the Emperor as head of state with the
elaborately adorned helmet he wears in
battle. (See the Pygmy Generalissimus in
the "Classical Walpurgis Night," lines
7644–52.)

1. An allusion to Psalm 110:1, "The
Lord said unto my Lord [i.e., King
David], sit thou at my right hand, until
I make thine enemies thy footstool."

And if yours lay about them then 10515
With swords and maces as I scythe,
Then watch the foe, man over man,
Drown in their own gore where they writhe.
[*Exit.*]

COMMANDER-IN-CHIEF. Now let our center phalanx follow, steady,
Launch shrewd assault with all the strength it can, 10520
A little rightward, where our force already
With fierce attack has discomposed their plan.

FAUST. [*pointing to the middle one*] Accept this fellow, too, beneath your sway;
He's lithe and sweeps all obstacles away.

RAPACIOUS. [*steps forward*] High daring of the imperial side 10525
With thirst for plunder be allied;
And on one goal let all be bent:
The rival Emperor's costly tent.
He shall not long be boasting of his throne,
I make the phalanx' forward edge my own. 10530

GRAB-SWAG. [*sutler-woman, nestling against him*][2] Though I'm not
spliced with him, for sure,
He stays my dearest paramour.
What harvest's ripened for our craws!
Woman's a wild thing when she claws,
In looting knows no law or shame; 10535
In victory on! and anything's fair game.
[[*Exeunt both.*]]

COMMANDER-IN-CHIEF. As was to be foreseen, on our left flank
Their right now falls in strength. Each man, each rank
Will now repulse them as they fiercely mass
To gain the rocky narrows of the pass. 10540

FAUST. [*gesturing to the left*] Then, Sir, note this one too; for the
strong arm
To reinforce itself can do no harm.

TENACIOUS. [*stepping forward*] Now finds the left all care dispelled!
Where I am, what is gained is tightly held;
In this my strength resides of old: 10545
No lightning-bolt can break my hold.
[*Exit.*]

MEPHISTOPHELES [*descending from above*] Now watch how, in the
background, masses
From all the jagged rock crevasses
Pour forth in arms, for space contesting,
The narrow mountain paths congesting, 10550
With helm and harness, sword and spear
They form a bulwark in our rear,
Poised to receive their battle task.

---

2. No explanation is given for the appearance of this sutler-woman (though
Goethe may have borrowed her from the
corresponding figure in Schiller's verse
prologue to the drama *Wallenstein*,
"Wallenstein's Camp").

[under his breath, to those in the know] Whence it all came,
    you must not ask.
Of course, I was not slow to clear   10555
The armories of all their gear;
There they all stood, on foot or mounted,
As if still lords of earth accounted;
What knight, king, emperor was before
Is empty snail-shell now, no more;   10560
Specters caparisoned in many a piece
Lend medieval times a pert new lease.[3]
Whatever little imp hides up each cuff—
For this time it looks genuine enough.
[Aloud] Hear them beforehand seethe in anger,   10565
And, jostling, clash with tinny clangor!
The tattered flags surmounting the formations
Have waited for fresh breezes with impatience,
An ancient tribe stands by here, after all,
Glad to be mingling in a modern brawl.   10570
    [Fearful flourish of trumpets from above, noticeable waver-
    ing in the enemy army.]

FAUST. There glimmers the horizon darkling
But here and there with telltale sparkling,
A radiance ominously ruddy;
The weapons glint, already bloody,
The crags, the woods, the atmosphere,   10575
The whole of heaven interfere.

MEPHISTOPHELES. Our right maintains its firm array;
I see, though, from among them jutting,
Our lithe Audacious, hugely strutting,
Abustle in his private way.   10580

EMPEROR. A single arm I first saw flying,
Now there's a dozen flailing, plying,
This is not done in Nature's way.

FAUST. Have you not heard of vapor bands[4]
Which waft along Sicilian strands?   10585
There, wavering clear, in light of day,
On mists of middle air projected,
By special redolence reflected,
A sight to marvel at appears:
Of cities here and thither shifting,   10590
Of gardens up and downward drifting,
As view on view the ether clears.

EMPEROR. How suspect, though! I see appear
The glittering tip of each tall spear;
I see our line—on their bright lances,   10595

---

3. An anachronistic allusion to the early-nineteenth-century fad, especially among wealthy aristocrats, of collecting medieval armor.

4. *Fata morgana*, familiar to Goethe from such works as Athanasius Kircher's *Great Work of Light and Shade* (1646).

Each one, a flickering flamelet[5] dances.
This has too fey an air, I fear.

FAUST. Your pardon, Sire, these are the last
Of spirit natures of the past,
The Dioscuri's lumen cast,   10600
By whom all mariners swore fast;
Their final strength they muster here.

EMPEROR. But say: to whom are we beholden
For Nature's patently unfolding
For us enigmas without peer?   10605

MEPHISTOPHELES. To whom but him, the lofty master[6]
Who in your destiny takes part?
Your foes' designs of dire disaster
Have exercised him deep at heart.
His gratitude will see you saved,   10610
Let even his own death be braved.

EMPEROR. They were parading me with pomp and shout,
I counted now, and meant to try it out,
So I saw fit, without much thought or care,
To help that whitebeard to some cooler air.   10615
The thwarted clergy took it with long faces,
That caper scarcely raised me in their graces.
Years after, am I to detect
This cheerful action's late effect?

FAUST. You cast your bread upon the waters;   10620
Now heavenward your gaze incline!
Methinks He will despatch a sign,
Attend, its sense will soon be taught us.

EMPEROR. An eagle drifts high in the firmament,
A griffin after him with dire intent.[7]   10625

FAUST. Attend! this augurs well, I say.
The griffin is a beast of fable;
How could he flatter himself able
To match true eagles in the fray?

EMPEROR. As I look on, they interloop   10630
In spacious circles—now, one swoop,
They're flying at each other's craws,
Rake breast and neck with cruel claws.

FAUST. Mark how, bedraggled with his mauling,
The wicked griffin reaps but woe,   10635
And lion-tail adroop, is falling
From sight to high-woods far below.

EMPEROR. May sign be equalled by event!
I mark it with astonishment.

5. Electrical discharge known as St. Elmo's fire, visible at the tips of masts of ships when struck by lightning in storms.
6. The sorcerer of Norcia, referred to below as "white beard" (line 10615). (See note to line 10439).

7. The eagle and the griffin represent, respectively, the Emperor and his rival, in the manner perhaps of heraldic coats of arms. For a similar augury predicting the outcome of battle see Homer, *Iliad*, XII.200–209.

MEPHISTOPHELES. [*toward the right*] Our assault, by much
    repeating,   10640
  Has the enemy retreating,
  And, their fighting spirit failing,
  To the right their lines are trailing,
  Causing turmoil as they enter
  Units of their leftward center.   10645
  Our own phalanx' armored edges
  Draw to right and drive their wedges
  In that gap like lightning flashing.—
  Now, like waves to tempest's lashing,
  Foams the rage of equal forces,   10650
  Fiercely clenched with matched resources;
  When was stratagem more splendid?
  Ours the battle-day here ended!
EMPEROR. [*on the left, to* FAUST] Watch! That side wakes grave
    suspicion,
  Hazardous seems our position.   10655
  No more stones flung down the edges,
  Foes have gained the lower ledges,
  Crests already stand deserted.
  Now!—The foe, in mass concerted,
  Nourishing his uprush steady,   10660
  May have gained the pass already.
  End result of impious striving!
  Vain was all your arts' contriving.
    [*Pause.*]
MEPHISTOPHELES. I see my ravens homing yonder,
  What message might they bear, I wonder?[8]   10665
  I greatly fear our issue fails.
EMPEROR. What are these birds of ill about?
  The struggle for the rock redoubt
  Was where they set their sooty sails.
MEPHISTOPHELES. [*to the ravens*] Sit down, quite close, where I
    can hear.   10670
  He is not lost who has your ear,
  Your counsel, being sound, prevails.
FAUST. [*to the* EMPEROR] You are aware of course of pigeons
  Returning from remotest regions
  To brood and food they cherish most.   10675
  So here, but with a change of lease:
  The pigeon mail may serve in peace,
  But war commands the raven-post.
MEPHISTOPHELES. A heavy bane appears to loom,
  Look there! observe the signs of doom   10680
  About our heroes' rocky rim.
  The nearest heights have been percoursed,
  And should the pass itself be forced,

8. On the mythological source of the ravens see note to line 2491.

Our chance of holding out is slim.
EMPEROR. So I am swindled after all!   10685
  I have been quailing in its thrall
  Since first you snared me in that net.
MEPHISTOPHELES. Take heart! We are not beaten yet.
  Cool wins the final trick, not nervous;
  Just near the end things may seem out of hand;   10690
  I have my trusty scouting service,
  Command that I may take command.
COMMANDER-IN-CHIEF. [*who has joined them meanwhile*]
  Your bond with these and close alliance
  I bore with long and pained compliance,
  No lasting luck can magic earn.   10695
  I cannot turn this fight or mend it,
  As they began it, let them end it,
  And so my baton I return.
EMPEROR. No, keep it for the better hours
  That fortune may yet bless us with.   10700
  That gargoyle makes me shrink and cower,
  He and his cozy raven kith.
  [*to* MEPHISTOPHELES] The baton I cannot award you,
  You do not seem the proper man,
  Command what help your arts afford you,   10705
  And let things take what course they can.
    [*Exit into the tent with the* COMMANDER-IN-CHIEF.]
MEPHISTOPHELES. I hope the bludgeon keeps him fit!
  We others would have little use for it,
  It had a cross of sorts stuck on.
FAUST. What shall we do now?   10710
MEPHISTOPHELES.   It's all done—
  Now, cousins swart, to service fleet,
  Off to Great Mountain Lake, the Undines[9] greet,
  And ask them for the semblance of their flow.
  By arts inscrutable and feminine,
  They split the semblant from the genuine,   10715
  And all would swear that what is not is so.
    [*Pause.*]
FAUST. The devastating way our ravens
  Must have beguiled those water maidens!
  Some rills already run, I see.
  From many a spur of rock all bare and arid   10720
  A scampering full-bodied spring is carried,
  All done for is their victory.
MEPHISTOPHELES. This is the weirdest welcome yet,
  The boldest climbers are upset.
FAUST. Already stream to stream roars strongly coupled,   10725
  From gorges they return once more redoubled,
  One flow now casts an arching swell,

9. Water spirits (see note to line 1274).

At once it flattens to the rocky coaming,
Now this, now that way thundering and foaming,
And hurls itself by steps downhill.   10730
What use their resolute, heroic lunging,
The mighty flood engulfs them in its plunging.
Its fury makes me shudder, too, and stare.
MEPHISTOPHELES. I can see nothing of these watery lies,
The spell bewilders only human eyes,   10735
I am amused by the bizarre affair.
In masses, whole platoons, away they bound,
The fools think they are being drowned,
They pant and snort while walking safe and sound,
And ludicrously paddle on dry ground.   10740
Now there's confusion everywhere.
[*The* RAVENS *have returned.*]
I shall commend you at the Master's[1] throne;
If now you would prove masters of your own,
Then hurry to the glowing smithy
Where sparks by dwarf-folk ever busy   10745
From stone and metal are retrieved.
Demand, with much persuasive chatter,
A fire, to glow, to beam, to spatter,
As in a lofty mind conceived.
True, summer lightning in the distance winking,   10750
Stars plunging down too fast for eyelid's blinking,
May happen any summer's night;
But summer lightning in the tangled briar,
Stars sizzling on wet ground and spitting fire,
That's hardly such a common sight.   10755
So don't you put yourselves to undue strain,
First make request for it, and then ordain.
[*Exeunt the* RAVENS. *Things take the prescribed course.*]
MEPHISTOPHELES. To foes obscurities profound!
And step by step on unknown ground!
On every hand an errant spark,   10760
Quick glare, to plunge in sudden dark.
All this is very fair and right,
Now for some noise to stoke the fright.
FAUST. From musty halls the hollow weaponry
In open air feels newly strong and free;   10765
It's clanged and rattled up there for some time,
A wondrous and deceptive chime.[2]
MEPHISTOPHELES. Quite right! there's no more holding them, it
    looks,
The air resounds with knightly donnybrooks,
As in idyllic times of yore.   10770
Pallettes' and brassarts' steely sheens,

1. This reference to a "Master" is ob-   in Goethe's *Faust*).
scure. Some commentators claim it is   2. See lines 10554–64.
Satan (who is not otherwise mentioned

Embodying Guelfs and Ghibellines,[3]
Renew at once their feuding hoar.
Fixed in hereditary groove,
Irreconcilable they prove,   10775
Now far and wide resounds the roar.
When all is said, it's party hate
Works best in every devil's fête,
Down to the very utmost horrors;
With sounds now hideously Panic,   10780
Now shrill and stridently satanic,
It spreads alarm through vale and forest.
    [*Sounds of warlike tumult in the orchestra, eventually
changing to gay martial airs.*]

THE RIVAL EMPEROR'S TENT

A Throne, Rich Appointments

RAPACIOUS, GRAB-SWAG.

GRAB-SWAG. So we were first to get here, see?
RAPACIOUS. No raven flies as fast as we.
GRAB-SWAG. My, what a hoard is here piled up!   10785
  Where do I start? Where do I stop?
RAPACIOUS. The room is loaded fit to burst!
  I don't know what to reach for first.
GRAB-SWAG. That rug would suit me well, for sure;
  My pad is often sadly poor.   10790
RAPACIOUS. Here hangs a mace of steel with spikes;
  I have long hankered for the likes.
GRAB-SWAG. This scarlet cloak with golden seam,
  Of such I often used to dream.
RAPACIOUS. [*taking the weapon*] With this the job is quickly
    done.   10795
  One strikes him dead and passes on.
  You've piled so much upon your hunch,
  And nothing useful in the bunch.
  Leave all that rubbish in its place
  And take away this little case,   10800
  Or that one; nothing but pure gold,
  For army-pay, their bellies hold.
GRAB-SWAG. This thing is murder just to shift;
  I cannot carry it or lift.
RAPACIOUS. Hunch over, quickly! Bend your rump,   10805
  I'll heave it on your sturdy hump.
GRAB-SWAG. It's fit to break my back in two.
  Oh no! that's done it now for you!
    [*The coffer falls and bursts open.*]

3. See note to line 4845.

RAPACIOUS. There lies the yellow gold in heaps;
    Jump to it, rake it up for keeps!   10810
GRAB-SWAG. [*crouching down*] Quick, fill my apron with the stuff!
    We still can carry off enough.
RAPACIOUS. Enough of that! Don't dawdle so!
    [*She gets up.*]
    That apron has a hole—oh no!
    Wherever you may stand or go,   10815
    Our treasure lavishly you sow.
AIDES. [*of our* EMPEROR] Who let you in this place of homage,
    In the imperial hoard to rummage?
RAPACIOUS. We risked our limbs, and life to boot,
    And claim our honest share of loot.   10820
    Such is the rule in enemy tents,
    We're soldiers, see, at all events.
AIDES. That's not our view of soldierdom,
    Both fighting-men and thieving scum;
    To join our Emperor's company,   10825
    An honest soldier one must be.
RAPACIOUS. That honesty's a windy thing,
    You call it "requisitioning."
    You, one and all, end up in clover,
    The trade salute is "hand it over."   10830
    [*to* GRAB-SWAG] Tote what you can, and on your way!
    We are unwelcome guests today.
    [*Exeunt.*]
FIRST AIDE. Say, why did you not promptly trim
    That fellow's shameless snout for him?
SECOND. Somehow I lost my strength to clout him,   10835
    There was a spooky air about them.
THIRD. Me too, my eyes gave out on me,
    It flickered so I could not see.
FOURTH. There's something up, I don't know what:
    The whole day long it was so hot,   10840
    With such a sultry, dismal pall,
    The one would stand, the other fall,
    You groped about and struck a blow,
    And every lunge would fell a foe,
    Your eyes were hung about with mist,   10845
    Your hearing hummed and buzzed and hissed.
    And so it went, and now we're here,
    And how it came about, we've no idea.
    [*Enter the* EMPEROR *with* FOUR PRINCES. *The* AIDES *withdraw.*][4]

4. In this final scene of Act IV, the last part of *Faust* to be composed, Goethe makes use of the Alexandrine, consisting of a six-stress iambic line in rhymed couplets with a caesura after the third stress. The standard verse form of Baroque and Neo-Classical tragedy in the seventeenth and early eighteenth centuries, derived from French drama, the Alexandrine had become associated with pompous and ceremonial public or political action. This scene complements the initial appearance of the Emperor with his counselors in Act I ("Imperial Residence," lines 4728 ff.).

EMPEROR. Be that as it may be! The enemy is shattered,
The remnants of his rout in level country scattered.   10850
Here stands the vacant throne, and treason's treasure-mound,
Smothered in tapestries, constricts us all around.
We, by our palladins in honoured ease protected,
Imperially await the commonwealth's elected;
Tidings of happiness arrive from every side: 10855
Of cheerful loyalty and Empire pacified.
Though interwoven with our fight there was some juggling,
In essence it was still ourselves who did the struggling.
Strange cases often favor fighting-men just so,
A stone falls from the sky, blood rains upon the foe,   10860
From rocky caverns issue wondrous chords resounding,
Which have the foe's heart quailing, but set our hearts bounding.
The adversary lies, by lasting mockery chafed,
The victor, as he triumphs, lauds the grace vouchsafed.
And all intone, unasked, by their spontaneous choices,   10865
"Now let us praise the Lord," sung by a million voices.[5]
Yet for the highest prize, my pious glance I bid
Turn back into my heart, as else it seldom did.
A young, vivacious prince may have glad days to squander;
The years will teach him, though, the moment's weight to
    ponder.   10870
Hence I ally myself forthwith, without delay,
With you four worthy ones for house, estate, and sway.[6]
[*to the first*] Yours was, o Prince, the host's astutely wrought
    complection,
Then, at decisive point, heroic bold direction;
Be active then in peace as may with peace accord,   10875
I name you Arch-Marshal, bestow on you the sword.
ARCH-MARSHAL. Your trusty host, of late engaged on home dis-
    orders,
When it confirms Your throne and person at the borders,
Be it our privilege 'mid festive revelers massed,
In the ancestral hall to order your repast.   10880
Before you borne, beside you held, its shining splendor
Exalted majesty unceasing escort render.
EMPEROR. [*to the second*] He who with gallantry combines a
    gentle grace,
You! be Arch-Chamberlain; it is no easy place.

---

5. A reference to Luther's German version of the Latin hymn "Te Deum laudamus," ascribed to St. Ambrose.
6. The following lines recapitulate the traditional investiture of the Holy Roman Emperor by the princes responsible for electing him: the Elector of Saxony serves as Chief Marshal, the Elector of Brandenburg as Chief Chamberlain, the Elector Palatine as Chief Steward, and the Elector of Bohemia as Chief Cupbearer. Traditionally, the three spiritual princes—the Archbishops of Mainz, Trier, and Cologne—also participated in the election, though only one Archbishop appears in this scene (the Chancellor of Act I, lines 4847 ff.) These princes correspond to the counselors who appear in Act I (the Chief Marshal would have been the Quartermaster; the Chief Chamberlain the Marshal; the Chief Steward the Treasurer; and the Chief Cupbearer, whose youth is emphasized, perhaps the Herald of the Carnival). Goethe was familiar with this ceremonial procedure from personal experience, having witnessed the coronation of Joseph II in Frankfurt in 1764.

O'er all domestic staff you wield supreme observance, 10885
In whose internal strife I find indifferent servants;
Be henceforth honored your example and held blest
How one may please one's lord, the Court, and all the rest.

ARCH-CHAMBERLAIN. It earns one grace to speed the lord's design
    exalted,
Be helpful to the best, nor even hurt the faulted, 10890
Be calm without deceit, clear without trickery,
If You see through me, Sire, that is enough for me.
May fancy in advance that feast-to-come engender?
At table, mine will be the golden bowl to tender,
Mine to receive Your rings, so at the jubilee 10895
Your hand refresh itself, as Your regard does me.

EMPEROR. I am too grave of mind to ponder gay distraction,
But be it so! It too will further cheerful action.
    [*to the third*] You I appoint Arch-Steward! Thus henceforward
    be
Lord of the hunt, the game preserves and fowlery; 10900
At all times serve the choice of favorite dish I mention
As proffered by the month, prepared with due attention.

ARCH-STEWARD. Most pleasant duty be for me a rigid fast
Till You enjoy the cheer of a select repast.
Your kitchen staff and I shall seek by joint persistence, 10905
To hasten on the season, nearer draw the distance.
You spurn the far and early which the board may boast,
It is the plain and hearty that You look for most.

EMPEROR. [*to the fourth*] Since unavoidably we talk of feast and
    revel,
The goblet-bearer you become, my young daredevil. 10910
Arch-Cupbearer, make sure now that our cellars stock
In lavish quantity fine malmsey, claret, hock.
But use restraint yourself, see that you are not tempted
By moment's chance and mirth to think yourself exempted.

ARCH-CUPBEARER. Why, even youth matures to man's estate, my
    Prince, 10915
Before You are aware, once given confidence.
I too transport myself to that great festive morning,
The Emperor's serving board most fittingly adorning
With gold and silver bowls of state and circumstance,
For You the loveliest cup, though, choosing in advance: 10920
A lucent Venice-shell, wherein contentment huddles,
The wine's aroma gains in strength, but not befuddles.
Upon such wondrous gift one well may lean too hard,
Your Majesty's restraint, though, is superior guard.

EMPEROR. What by unquestionable pledge I made your dower 10925
You heard with confidence upon this solemn hour.
The Emperor's word is great and any gift ensures,
Yet noble writ is needful for investitures,
Needful his hand and seal. For its due formulation
The moment brings the proper man to his right station. 10930

[*Enter the* ARCHBISHOP (ARCH-CHANCELLOR).]

EMPEROR. When to the keystone is entrusted the great arch,
Then it is made secure against the ages' march.
Behold four Princes here! Already We expounded
Whereon the welfare of estate and house is founded.
Now shall what in Our realm at large may live and thrive   10935
Be laid, with weight and force, upon Arch-Princes five.
In lands they shall stand out above all other orders,
Wherefore I here and now extend their feudal borders
Out of the fiefs of those who turned from me of late.
I allocate to you many a fine estate,   10940
As well, the privilege to stretch afar your charter
As chance may offer, through reversion, purchase, barter;
Then, you shall wield untrammeled in your own domain
Whatever territorial rights to lords pertain.
Your verdicts passed as Lords Appellate shall be binding: 10945
There shall no recourse lie from your judicial finding.
Then, tax, rent, levy, impost, yours be without stint,
Royalties from safe-conduct, mining, salt, and mint.
For as my gratitude's most signal demonstration,
I raised you little short of the Imperial station.   10950

ARCHBISHOP. Let me in all our names profoundest thanks intone,
You make our might more firm and fortify your own.

EMPEROR. Still higher trust the five of you I thought on giving.
I live yet for my realm, and while I relish living,
My noble forebears' chain draws thoughtful gaze instead   10955
From active enterprise to what must loom ahead.
I, too, in course of time must part from what I cherished:
Then be the realm's Electors, and, old liege-lord perished,
On sacred altar raise the new one, crown on brow,
And peaceful then may end what was so stormy now.   10960

ARCH-CHANCELLOR. With humble bow, yet pride in depth of soul,
     we princes
Obeisance make to you, earth's premier eminences.
While loyal blood our veins amply percourses still
We are the body which you animate at will.

EMPEROR. Thus, in conclusion, be all hitherto instated   10965
For every age to come, by writ perpetuated.
Your sovereign tenure shall be absolutely free,
Yet indivisible be it by Our decree.
However you increased what by Our will was tendered,
All shall to eldest sons in fullness be surrendered.   10970

ARCH-CHANCELLOR. I cheerfully confide this grant of gravest powers
Forthwith to parchment, for the Empire's weal and ours;
Our busy Chancery shall copy, seal, and date it,
Your sacred signature, o Sire, corroborate it.

EMPEROR. And so I give you leave, that each may go his way   10975
In privacy to ponder this auspicious day.

          [*The* LAY PRINCES *depart. The* ARCHBISHOP *remains and
          speaks with rhetorical fervor.*]

ARCHBISHOP. The Bishop stays behind upon the Chancellor's
 leaving,
 Impelled to seek Your ear by most severe misgiving.
 His fatherly concern relief for you would seek.
EMPEROR. At such a joyful hour, what apprehensions? Speak! 10980
ARCHBISHOP. What bitter grief to me to find, at such an hour,
 Your consecrated head in league with Satan's power.
 Secure indeed upon the throne, as one may hope,
 Yet woefully in scorn of God and Father Pope.
 Apprised of it, his sacred judgment's swift conviction 10985
 Will blight your sinful realm with bolts of interdiction.
 He still has not forgotten how Your word unbound
 That doomed magician[7] on the day that you were crowned.
 To Christendom's great harm, your diadem's effulgence
 Shed on that head accursed the ray of first indulgence. 10990
 Beat, then, Your breast, divert from the ill-gotten bliss
 Forthwith a moderate mite back unto holiness.
 That sweep of hills whereon your tent was then erected,
 Where by pernicious spirit-league you were protected,
 Where avid ear you leant unto the Prince of Lies, 10995
 This consecrate to sacred cause in pious wise;
 With mountain and dense forest to their furthest bounding,
 With sloping alps of green to pastures lush redounding,
 With limpid lakes ateem with fish, with countless rills
 Which, busily meandering, plunge down the hills; 11000
 Then the broad dale itself, with paddocks, meadows, shires;
 You will find mercy if contrition thus aspires.
EMPEROR. By my grave fault I am so grievously dismayed,
 At your discretion let the boundary be laid.
ARCHBISHOP. Firstly! the space by such iniquity polluted 11005
 Be forthwith for Our Lord's high service instituted.
 Its sturdy masonry the mind's eye swiftly builds,[8]
 A shaft of morning sun the choir already gilds,
 The edifice expands and grows, the cross-shape forming,
 The nave looms up and on, the faithful spirits warming, 11010
 There, to the worthy portals cluster the devout,
 As first through hills and dales the call of bells rings out.
 From heavenly spires it rings, as they to Heaven aspire,
 The penitent approach, rebirth their pure desire.
 To that great consecration—may the day come soon!— 11015
 Your presence, Sire, will add the highest grace and boon.
EMPEROR. May such a lofty work be pious mind's profession,
 To praise the Lord our God, and cleanse me of transgression.
 Enough! Some surge of spirit I already feel.
ARCHBISHOP. As Chancellor now I urge due form, to sign and
  seal. 11020

7. The sorcerer of Norcia (see note to line 10439).
8. The Archbishop describes the construction of a Gothic cathedral, which serves as an analogue to Faust's reclamation of land in Act V. Goethe may here allude to the plans of his friend Boisserée to secure support from the Prussian King to complete the Cathedral of Cologne.

EMPEROR. A formal deed of transfer to the Church—design it,
Lay it before me and I shall be pleased to sign it.

ARCHBISHOP. [*has taken his leave, but turns back at the exit*]
Then you devote to the emerging work's intent
All land appurtenances, impost, tithe and rent,
Forever. Worthy maintenance exacts high levy,   11025
And costs of careful governance are no less heavy.
To speed construction even on such desert spot,
Some requisitioned booty-gold you will allot.⁹
Besides all this, it needs, I cannot but remember,
Divers remote supplies as lime and slate and timber.   11030
The people do the hauling, from the pulpit taught,
The Church commends him who fares forth in her support.
[*Exit.*]

EMPEROR. The sin I shouldered is a great and irksome yoke,
I reap sore damage from the odious conjuring-folk.

ARCHBISHOP. [*returning once again, with a most profound obeis-
ance*] Your pardon, Sire! You granted that most ill-famed
man   11035
The Empire's coastline; yet on this shall fall the ban
Unless you grant the Holy Purse, as contrite truant,
There, too, the tithe and rent and bounties thence accruant.¹

EMPEROR. [*peevishly*] The land's not there, it lies beneath the ocean
swell.

ARCHBISHOP. Who has the right and patience, wins his day as
well.   11040
Your word shall be our bond, may lapse of time not flout it!
[*Exit*]

EMPEROR. [*alone*] Why not sign over all the realm while we're
about it!

Act V†

OPEN COUNTRY¹

WAYFARER.² Aye, the same dark linden swaying,
Now matured to aged strength,

---

9. See Rapacious' remark, lines 10828 ff.
1. This is the only reference to the bestowal of land upon Faust, earlier mentioned as a plan by Mephistopheles
(lines 10305–6), which had presumably
been one of the original motives for
writing Act IV.
1. Goethe here adapts a tale from Ovid's
Metamorphoses (VIII.611–724; see his
conversation with Eckermann of June 6,
1831, below). In Ovid the poor aged couple Philemon and Baucis receive Jupiter
and Mercury as guests into their simple
hut, the only human beings who offer
generous hospitality to the gods in disguise. In reward they are saved when

the rest of the land is flooded by the
gods and all other mortals drowned.
Their hut is transformed into a temple,
and the aged couple subsequently serve
the gods in the temple until their simultaneous deaths when they are transformed
into trees, an oak and a linden, which
grow together above the temple and provide it with shade.
2. Ovid's gods in disguise are replaced
by an anonymous traveler, returning to
this place to receive hospitality from the
aged couple after years of absence since
an earlier visit. Thematically he offsets
Faust, who now rules in the palace of
his newly created realm.

Welcome, after years of straying,   11045
They salute me back at length!
Aye—the selfsame humble acres!
To that hut of refuge fair
I repaired when storm-lashed breakers
Cast me on the sand-dunes there.   11050
Who received me when I foundered,
I would bless the honest pair,
Hardly to be still encountered,
Old as even then they were.
Those were folk of pious living!   11055
Should I knock, call out? All hail!
If you know the bliss of giving
As of old, and never fail.

BAUCIS. [*a little granny, very old*] Hush! Keep quiet, dear arrival,
    Let him rest, my frail old man!   11060
    Lengthy slumber grants revival
    For brief vigil's active span.

WAYFARER. Is it you, then, Mother, living
    To receive my second thanks,
    For the life-gift jointly given   11065
    To the youth cast on your banks?
    Are you Baucis who devoutly
    Quickened once this faltering lip?
        [*The* HUSBAND *enters.*]
    You Philemon, who so stoutly
    Snatched my hoard from water's grip?   11070
    Silvery pealing from your arbor,
    From your hearth the nimble flame—
    You in gruesome plight were harbor
    Whence relief and comfort came.

    Let me scan the boundless ocean,   11075
    Kneel upon the sandy crest,
    Pour in prayerful devotion
    What would burst my crowded breast.
        [[*He strides forward upon the dune.*]]
PHILEMON. [*to* BAUCIS] Lay the table for us, hurry,
    In our little garden bright.   11080
    He will start aback and scurry,
    See and not believe his sight.
    [*standing beside the wayfarer*] What so fiercely overbore you,
    Rolling breakers, foam-bespewed,
    See as garden-land before you,   11085
    Glimpse of paradise renewed.
    Older, slower to be aiding
    Ready-handed as of yore,
    I beheld, my powers fading,
    Surf already far offshore.   11090
    Clever masters' daring minions

Drained and walled the ocean bed,
Shrank the sea's entrenched dominions,
To be masters in her stead.
Gaze on hamlets, common, stable,   11095
Luscious meadows, grove and eave,—
But enough—let us to table,
For the sun would take his leave.
See the sails from farthest westing
Safe to anchorage repair!   11100
Well the seabirds know their nesting,
For the harbor now is there.
Outward pressed to distant spaces
See the ocean's azure sheen,
Breadth of densely settled places   11105
Right and left and all between.[3]

[*The three at table in the little garden.*]

BAUCIS. Silent? And, it seems, unable
To relieve your hunger, too?

PHILEMON. He would hear the wondrous fable;
Tell him, as you like to do.   11110

BAUCIS. Well! A wonder, do not doubt it!
Still it makes my reason fret;
Something wrong was all about it
That I cannot fathom yet.

PHILEMON. On the Emperor dare one blame it,   11115
Who conferred on him the shore?
Did a herald not proclaim it,
Trumpets flourishing before?
Here a footing first was grounded,
Not far distant from our bluff,   11120
Tents and huts—but green-surrounded,
Rose a palace soon enough.

BAUCIS. Vainly in the daytime labored
Pick and shovel, clink and strike,
Where at night the elf-lights wavered,   11125
By the dawn there stood a dike.[4]
Human victims bled and fevered,
Anguish on the night-air borne,
Fiery torrents pouring seaward
Scored a channel by the morn.   11130
Godless is he, he would savor
This our grove and cabin here;
Now the newly strutting neighbor
As his subjects we should fear.

3. Philemon surveys the city which has been built at Faust's command on the land reclaimed by pushing back the sea behind dikes located far off, near the horizon.

4. Baucis indicates her awareness that devilish powers have been employed in the dark of night. The technology of such dike and dam projects, recalling the labors of lowland Friesen and the Dutch in the late Middle Ages, also reflects Goethe's interest in similar projects during his own day, such as plans for the harbor in Bremen or the Panama Canal.

PHILEMON. Yet he pledged, you have forgotten, 11135
　Homestead fair on new-won land!
BAUCIS. Do not trust the ocean bottom,
　Steadfast on your hill-brow stand!
PHILEMON. To the chapel let us wander,
　Greet the parting sun once more; 11140
　Ring and kneel in worship yonder,
　Trusting God as heretofore.

PALACE

Spacious Ornamental Gardens; Large, Straight Canal

FAUST *in extreme old age,*[1] *walking about in meditation.*

LYNCEUS, THE KEEPER OF THE WATCHTOWER,[2] [*through a speaking-
　tube*] The sun is down, the last few vessels
　Are briskly coursing harborward.
　A sailing lighter slowly nestles 11145
　Up-channel from the open port.
　The colored streamers flutter gaily,
　The rigid davits stoutly rise;
　With you for patron, blest the sailor,
　And blessing yours for late-won prize. 11150
　　[*The little bell tolls on the dune.*]
FAUST. [*starting violently*] That cursed peal! Malign and ground-
　less,
　Like shot from ambush does it pierce;
　Before my eyes my realm is boundless,
　But at my back annoyance leers,
　Reminding me with envious stabbing: 11155
　My lofty title is impure,
　The linden range, the weathered cabin,
　The frail old church are still secure.
　And should I seek my ease there—crawling
　At alien shades my flesh would rear, 11160
　Thorn in my side, encumbrance galling,
　Oh, were I far away from here!
KEEPER OF THE TOWER. [*as above*] To port the flag-gay bark does
　ride
　On the fresh breeze of eventide!
　How high its nimble course is stacked 11165
　With riches crated, cased, and sacked!
　　[*Splendid bark, richly and colorfully laden with products
　　of exotic regions.*]
　　[*Enter* MEPHISTOPHELES, THE THREE MIGHTY MEN.]

---

1. See Goethe's conversation with Eckermann, June 6, 1831 (below), concerning
Faust's age.
2. Presumably the same figure who served
as watchman of the tower in the middle
section of the *Helena*. (See note to line
7377.)

CHORUS. There, overboard
And we're ashore.
Hail to our Lord.
And Patron here!   11170
[*They disembark, the goods are moved ashore.*]
MEPHISTOPHELES. So we have proved we're worth our pay;
The Patron's praise will make us gay.
With credit we have met our task,
In Master's praise we'll gaily bask.
With just two ships we started then,
With twenty we are back again.
What great things we achieved, behold,   11175
Here by our cargo can be told.
Free ocean makes you scruple-free,
Cobwebs of caution swept to sea.
There only counts the timely grip,
You catch a fish, you catch a ship,   11180
And once of three the masters now,
You hook the fourth one anyhow;
The fifth will be in sorry plight,
You have the force, and might is right.
You tend the what and not the wise,   11185
If I know naval enterprise:
For commerce, war, and piracy,
They form a seamless trinity.

THE THREE MIGHTY MEN.
                  Not thanked or hailed,
                  No hail or thanks,   11190
                  Why, did we sail
                  A stench to banks?
                  His face is wry,
                  His brow is grooved,
                  The regal loot   11195
                  Is not approved.

MEPHISTOPHELES.
                  Do not expect
                  A wage to spare,
                  You know you took
                  Your proper share.   11200

THE MEN.   The part we had
                  Was just for fun,
                  We all demand
                  An equal one.

MEPHISTOPHELES.
                  First sort upstairs   11205
                  In hall on hall
                  The precious goods
                  Assembled all.
                  When he takes in

The stately show,   11210
And reckons up
The loot just so;
I bet it's you
He'll stint the least,
He'll give the squadron   11215
Feast on feast.
The pretty birds[3] arrive tomorrow,
You'll find my service prompt and thorough.
[*The cargo is hauled away.*]
MEPHISTOPHELES. [*to* FAUST] With clouded brow and somber-
        gazed
You hear your lofty fortune raised.   11220
Exalted wisdom now is crowned.
At peace are sea and solid ground;
From harboring shore, to speed at large,
The willing sea received the barge;
Say, "from this palace, from this beach,   11225
The world is wholly in my reach."
All started from this very spot,
Here stood the earliest wooden hut;
A shallow groove was scratched before
Where now they ply the busy oar.   11230
Your noble mind, their toiling hands,
Secured the prize of seas and lands.
From here—
FAUST.   That blasted *here*! you see?
That's just what sorely weighs on me.
To your great cunning I confide it,   11235
I feel my heart is stabbed and maimed,
My mind unable to abide it—
Yet as I say it, I'm ashamed.
That aged couple must surrender,
I want their linden for my throne,   11240
The unowned timber-margin slender
Despoils for me the world I own.
There, for the eye's untrammeled roving,
I wish a scaffold to be woven
From branch to branch, for vistas deep   11245
Of my achievement's fullest sweep,
With all-embracing gaze to scan
The masterpiece of sapient man,
As he ordains with thoughtful mind
New homestead for his teeming kind.   11250

Thus we are stretched on cruellest rack,
In riches sensing what we lack.
The tinkling chime, the linden bloom

3. Sailors' slang for ladies of easy virtue who gather at ports of call.

Close in like sanctuary and tomb.
The will's omnipotent command,   11255
Like surf it breaks upon this sand.
How can I rid myself and breathe!
The bell but tinkles, and I seethe.

MEPHISTOPHELES. Of course! Such chief annoyance must
Turn all one's life to ash and dust.   11260
The finer ear, who would deny it,
Recoils from this repulsive riot.
Does not that noisome ding-dong-dingling
Befoul the sky of evening, mingling
With all events its souring ferment,   11265
From first immersion to interment?
Till life seems but a shadow throng
Parading between ding and dong?

FAUST. That stubbornness, perverse and vain,
So blights the most majestic gain   11270
That to one's agonized disgust
One has to tire of being just.

MEPHISTOPHELES. Why should you scruple here and wince?
Have you not colonized long since?

FAUST. Go, then, and clear them from my sight!—   11275
The handsome little farm you know
That I assigned them long ago.

MEPHISTOPHELES. One hauls them off and makes them settle,
And in a trice they're back in fettle;
For, once sustained the rude offense,   11280
A pretty place is recompense.
    [*He gives a strident whistle.*]
    [*Enter* THE THREE.]

MEPHISTOPHELES. Come! As the Master bade to say,
Tomorrow will be Navy Day.

THE THREE. The old gent's welcome was a slight,
A rousing feast will do us right.   11285
    [*Exeunt.*]

MEPHISTOPHELES. [*ad spectatores*] What passes here is far from
new;
There once was Naboth's vineyard, too. [*Kings i.21*][4]

DEEP NIGHT

LYNCEUS, *the keeper on the watchtower of the palace, singing.*

LYNCEUS.   To seeing born,
                  To scanning called,
                  To the watchtower sworn,   11290

4. King Ahab coveted Naboth's vineyard and tried unsuccessfully to buy it from him. The King's wife, Jezebel, therefore plotted against the life of Naboth, after whose death Ahab seized the vineyards, only to be confronted there by the prophet Elijah, who accused him of the murder.

I relish the world.
Sighting the far,
Espying the near,
Moon-disc and star,
Forest and deer.   11295
In all I behold
Ever-comely design,
As its virtues unfold
I take pleasure in mine.
You fortunate eyes,   11300
All you ever did see,
Whatever its guise,
Was so lovely to me![1]

[*Pause.*]

Not for pleasure, though, my master
Placed me on this lofty stand;   11305
What a hideous disaster
Threatens from the darkened land!
Spattering sparks are winking, glaring
Through the linden's doubled gloom,
Fanned by rushing air, the flaring   11310
Burrows deeper and gains room.
Woe! the inner hut's afire
That was moist and mossy green,
Instant rescue would require,
Yet no help is to be seen.   11315
Ah, the poor old pair that tended
Else so watchfully their fire,
Must their age in smoke be ended,
Snuffed in conflagration dire!
Like a glowing fiery steeple   11320
Redly soars the mossy frame,
Scarcely could the honest people
Flee this raging hell of flame!
Through the boughs, their leafy tracing,
Soaring tongues of fire are racing,   11325
Branches furnish ready fuel,
Flash and tumble down the trees;
Ah, the gift of sight is cruel
Showing horrors such as these!
There, the chapel in their falling   11330
Ponderous boughs have battered down,
Pointed serpent tongues appalling
Now engulf each leafy crown.
To the roots agape and trembling
Melt the trunks in scarlet blaze.—   11335

1. Like the Wayfarer who visits the hut of Baucis and Philemon, Lynceus the Watchman stands in thematic opposition to the figure of Faust in Act V. Readers have always felt that in his affirmation of life here as he surveys the landscape he also speaks for the poet of *Faust*.

[*Long pause; sound of singing.*][2]
   To dead centuries assembling
   What throughout them pleased the gaze.
FAUST. [*on the balcony, facing the dunes*] Up on the keep, what
  crooning whimper?
The tone's outhurried by the fact;
My watchman wails; my inmost temper   11340
Is soured by the impatient act.
But where the linden stand is wizened
To piteous ruin, charred and stark,
A look-out frame will soon have risen
To sweep the world in boundless arc.   11345
Thence I shall view the new plantation
Assigned to shelter the old pair,
Who, mindful of benign salvation,
Will spend life's happy evening there.
MEPHISTOPHELES AND THE THREE. [*below*]
Here we return in full career;   11350
It was not smoothly done, I fear.
We knocked, we rapped, we knocked in vain,
No one would open up; again
We knocked and rattled somewhat more,
And inward fell the brittle door.   11355
We called and threatened more than once,
And still we met with no response.
As at such times it will occur,
They wouldn't hear, so didn't stir.
So we fell to without ado   11360
And nimbly moved them out for you.
The couple did not suffer much,
From fear fell lifeless at our touch.
A lurking stranger who was found
And offered fight, was laid aground.   11365
Live embers, knocked about a bit
In brief but furious struggling, lit
Some straw—and now it blazes free,
A funeral pyre for those three.
FAUST. So you have turned deaf ears to me!   11370
I meant exchange, not robbery.
This thoughtless violent affair,
My curse on it, for you to share!
CHORUS. That ancient truth we will recite:
Give way to force, for might is right;   11375
And would you boldly offer strife,
Then risk your house, estate, and—life.
   [*Exeunt.*]

2. The opening section of Lynceus' monologue was sung, his description of the burning of hut and chapel was spoken, and here he commences again with his song, only to be interrupted by Faust, who objects to the sound.

FAUST. [*on the balcony*] The stars withdraw their gleam and wink,
The fiery blazes dwindle, sink;
Still hither, fanned by vagrant drafts,   11380
A veil of smoke and vapor wafts.
Too rashly bid, too swiftly done!—
What wanders here, of shadows spun?[3]

MIDNIGHT[1]

[*Enter* FOUR GRAY CRONES.][2]

THE FIRST. My name, it is Want.
THE SECOND.   My name, it is Debt.
THE THIRD. My name, it is Care.
THE FOURTH.   My name, it is Need.   11385
THREE TOGETHER. We cannot gain entry, the portals are locked,
  A wealthy man lives here, our entrance is blocked.
WANT. I pass into shadow.
DEBT.   I pass into naught.
NEED. The pampered dismiss me from sight and from thought.
CARE. You sisters, you never may enter therein.   11390
  But Care—she will creep through the keyhole unseen.
    [CARE *disappears*.]
WANT. Away, my gray sisters, we may not abide.
DEBT. I, sister, will join you and cleave to your side.
NEED. And Need follows close on the heel of the other.
THREE TOGETHER. Clouds drifting, enveloping star upon star!   11395
  Back yonder, remote, from afar, from afar
  We see him approach, it is———Death, our brother.
FAUST. [*in the palace*] Four I saw enter, go but three;
  Unfathomable was their speech to me.
  Like "Need" it lingered on the breath,   11400
  Then, like a somber echo—"Death."
  It droned as with a muffled ghostly threat.
  I have not fought my way to freedom yet.
  Could I but clear my path at every turning
  Of spells, all magic utterly unlearning;   11405

3. Faust observes the spirit figures which appear in the following scene as they form themselves out of the smoke and vapor of the burning ruins.

1. A manuscript for this and the two scenes which follow it (lines 11384–11831) is preserved in the handwriting of Goethe's secretary which dates from 1825, at the time when work on *Faust* began again after an interruption of more than two decades. It is argued (on the basis of a comment by Goethe to Boisserée in 1815, preserved in the latter's diary, that the ending of *Faust* had already been written at "the best time," i.e., around 1800) that most of what is contained in this manuscript was copied from earlier drafts which derived from the time of work on *Part I*. A sense of proximity in mode and tone between these scenes and the scenes written around 1800, especially the "great lacuna," will be apparent.

2. The appearance of these four allegorical hags recalls the Witches in Shakespeare's *Macbeth*, who confront Macbeth and Banquo on the Scottish heath. Since Schiller adapted Shakespeare's play for the Weimar Theater in the spring of 1800, the analogy may have more than arbitrary validity. Also relevant is Faust's lament concerning Care in the later section of his monologue in "Night" (lines 644–51).

Were I but Man, with Nature for my frame,
The name of human would be worth the claim.

And such I was, before I fell to searching
The dark, with curses world and self besmirching.[3]
So thick is now the air with spook and elf   11410
That no one knows how to extract himself.
Though smiling day with light of reason gleams,
The night entangles us in webs of dreams;
We gaily turn from meadows lush with sap,
A bird will croak; what does it croak? Mishap.   11415
Enmeshed on every hand by superstition,
Events of omen, portent, premonition . . .
Abashed we stand, alone with but our fear.
The door has creaked—and no one enters here.
[*shaken*] Is someone here?
CARE.   The question calls for Yea.   11420
FAUST. And you—who are you?
CARE.   I am here, I say.
FAUST. Remove yourself!
CARE.   I am where I should be.
FAUST. [*incensed at first, then mollified, to himself*]
    Restrain yourself and speak no conjury.
CARE. If there were no ear to hear me,
    Still the pounding heart would fear me;   11425
    In most manifold array
    I exert relentless sway,
    Haunt the seaways, haunt the canyon,
    Ever timorous companion,
    Ever found and never sought,   11430
    Ever paid both curse and court.
Gray Care—am I unknown to you?
FAUST. I only sped the whole word through,
    Clutched any stray temptation by the hair,
    And what fell short, abandoned there,   11435
    And what eluded me, let pass.
    All that I did was covet and attain,
    And crave afresh, and thus with might and main
    Stormed through my life; first powerful and great,
    But now at pace more prudent, more sedate.   11440
    I know full well the earthly sphere of men—
    The yonder view is blocked to mortal ken;
    A fool who squints beyond with blinking eyes,
    Imagining his like above the skies;
    Let him stand firm and gaze about alert;   11445
    To able man this world is not inert;
    What need for him to roam eternities?
    What he perceives, that he may seize,

3. Recall Faust's curse before his pact with Mephistopheles, lines 1583–1606.

Let him stride on upon this planet's face,
When spirits haunt, let him not change his pace,   11450
Find bliss and torment in his onward stride,
Aye—every moment stay unsatisfied.[4]

CARE. Once I mark him and assail him,
    Nothing earthly will avail him,
    Never-ending gloom descending,   11455
    Sun his rise and fall suspending;
    Unimpaired all outer senses,
    Dark on dark the soul enfences,
    Stays his hand of any treasure
    To possess himself at leisure.   11460
    Weal and woe of like redundance,
    He must famish in abundance,
    Be it gladness, be it sorrow,
    He defers it to the morrow,
    Of the future ever heedful,   11465
    Ever laggard of the needful.

FAUST. Desist! This will not work on me!
  Such caterwauling[5] I despise.
  Begone—your wretched litany
  Might well unnerve a man, however wise.   11470

CARE. Be it going, be it coming,
    All resolve is taken from him,
    Down the highway's level coping
    Staggering he trips and groping,
    Deeply mired and farther erring,   11475
    Senses mocking, vision blurring,
    Burden to himself and others;
    Breath sustains no more than smothers,
    Fails to strangle or revive him,
    Hung between despair and striving.   11480
    Thus a langorous pursuing,
    Hard refraining, nauseous doing,
    Now reprieving, now molesting,
    Hollow sleep and shallow resting,
    Keep him shackled to his station   11485
    And prepare him for damnation.

FAUST. Unholy wraiths! For eons you exerted
  Your hateful sway on humankind just so;
  The most indifferent days you have perverted
  To loathsome coils of involuted woe.   11490
  Not lightly is the demon net uncast,
  Strict spirit-bond, I know, is hard to sever;
  And yet your power, o Care, insidiously vast,
  I shall not recognize it ever.

4. Recall the terms of Faust's wager with Mephistopheles, lines 1699–1706.
5. As indicated by the sustained use of feminine rhymes in the speeches by Care, she addresses Faust in a kind of chant and wailing lament, as if to cast a spell.

CARE. Taste of it forthwith, then, as rife   11495
    With curse I turn away offended!
    Man commonly is blind throughout his life,
    My Faust, be blind then as you end it.
    [*She breathes upon him. Exit.*]

FAUST. [*blinded*] The night, it seems, turns deeper still—but shining,
    The light within continues ever bright,[6]   11500
    I hasten to fulfill my thought's designing;
    The master's word alone imparts his might.
    Up, workmen, man for man, arise anew!
    Let blithely savor what I boldly drew.
    Seize spade and shovel, each take up his tool!   11505
    Fulfill at once what was marked off by rule.
    Attendance prompt to orders wise
    Achieves the most alluring prize;
    To bring to fruit the most exalted plans,
    One mind is ample for a thousand hands.   11510

GREAT OUTER PRECINCT OF THE PALACE

Torches

MEPHISTOPHELES. [*as supervisor, in the lead*]
    Step up, step up! Come on, come on!
    You quivering lemur creatures,[1]
    Patched up from sinew, band, and bone,
    Exiguous demi-natures.

LEMURES. [*in chorus*]
    We are aware and are at hand,   11515
    Here at your service find us,
    Was it a broad expanse of land,
    They said had been assigned us?

    A measuring chain is ready too,
    And stakes to mark the plotting,   11520
    What we were summoned here to do
    We knew but have forgotten.

MEPHISTOPHELES. No call here for artistic grace;
    The dig is measured by the digger;
    Your lankiest lie down upon his face,   11525
    The rest cut out the turf to suit his figure;
    As for our forebears it was done,
    Scoop out an oblong tetragon!

---

6. That blindness brings a deeper, more authentic insight is an ancient literary motif, as in Sophocles' *Oedipus the King* (which Goethe may have had in mind here), where the prophet Tiresias, though blind, sees the truth, and the effect of such true sight on Oedipus is to blind him.

1. *Lemures* (Latin), spirits of the evil dead in classical mythology, depicted like skeletons on a bas-relief excavated in a grave near Cumae in southern Italy, which was known to Goethe. (Not to be confused with "lemurs," a nocturnal lower primate.)

From palace down to narrow stall,
That's the inane conclusion, after all.　　　　　11530

LEMURES. [*digging with teasing gestures*]²
　　　　　　When I was young and lived and loved,
　　　　　　It seemed like honey-sipping,
　　　　　　Where pipers skirled and dancers shoved
　　　　　　My feet went tripping, skipping.

　　　　　　Now age with its insidious crutch　　11535
　　　　　　Hit me and sent me groping;
　　　　　　I tripped the grave-door, just a touch,
　　　　　　What fool had left it open?

FAUST. [*issuing from the palace, groping his way by the door-jambs*]
　How gaily ring the spades, a song of mirth!
　It is my host of toiling slaves,　　　　　　11540
　That renders self-content the earth,
　Ordains a border to the waves,
　The sea with rigid bonds enchains.

MEPHISTOPHELES. [*aside*] For us alone you are at pains
　With all your dikes and moles; a revel　　　11545
　For Neptune, the old water-devil,
　Is all you spread, if you but knew.
　You lose, whatever your reliance—
　The elements are sworn to our alliance,
　In ruin issues all you do.　　　　　　　　11550

FAUST. Ho, overseer!

MEPHISTOPHELES. 　　Here!

FAUST. 　　　　　　From every source
　Find me more hands, recruit with vigor
　Spur them with blandishment and rigor,
　Spare neither pay nor lure nor force!
　I want a tally, daily to be rendered,　　　11555
　How much the trench in hand is gaining room.

MEPHISTOPHELES. [*under his breath*] The question, as I under-
　　stand it,
　Is not of room so much as tomb.

FAUST.³ A chain of marshes lines the hills,

2. The song of the Lemures is adapted
from the Gravediggers' song in Shakespeare's *Hamlet* (V.i):

In youth when I did love, did love,
　Methought it was very sweet,
To contract the time for my behove,
　O, methought there was nothing meet.

But age, with his stealing steps,
　Hath clawed me in his clutch,
And hath shipped me into the land,
　As if I had never been such.

Goethe also was familiar with Shakespeare's source, a poem attributed to
Lord Nicholas Vaux (d. 1523), later included by Bishop Percy in his *Reliques
of Ancient English Poetry* (1765) as a
ballad entitled "The Aged Lover Re-
nounceth Love" (Vol. I. Book II, 2).

3. In the manuscript of 1825 Faust's
final monologue is much abbreviated,
consisting of nine lines in all: "from the
ditch which crawls through swamps/and
finally reaches the sea/I win a place for
many millions/there will I also dwell
among them,/stand upon truly my own
ground and earth./ I may say to the moment:/Oh tarry yet, thou art so fair!/
The trace of my earthly days/will not
disappear for aeons." Scholars have
argued (though by no means unanimously) that the revised and longer version of the speech was added by Goethe
as an afterthought early in 1832, after
the entire *Faust* had otherwise been
completed.

Befouling all the land retrievement;   11560
To drain this stagnant pool of ills
Would be the crowning, last achievement.
I'd open room to live for millions
Not safely, but in free resilience.
Lush fallow then to man and cattle yields   11565
Swift crops and comforts from the maiden fields,
New homesteads near the trusty buttress-face
Walled by a bold and horny-handed race.
A land of Eden sheltered here within,
Let tempest rage outside unto the rim,   11570
And as it laps a breach in greedy riot,
Communal spirit hastens to defy it.
Yes—this I hold to with devout insistence,
Wisdom's last verdict goes to say:
He only earns both freedom and existence   11575
Who must reconquer them each day.
And so, ringed all about by perils, here
Youth, manhood, age will spend their strenuous year.
Such teeming would I see upon this land,
On acres free among free people stand.   11580
I might entreat the fleeting minute:
Oh tarry yet, thou art so fair!
My path on earth, the trace I leave within it
Eons untold cannot impair.
Foretasting such high happiness to come,   11585
I savor now my striving's crown and sum.

[FAUST *sinks backward; the* LEMURES *break his fall and lay him on the ground.*]

MEPHISTOPHELES. No joy could sate him, no delight but cloyed,
For changing shapes he lusted to the last;
The final moment, worthless, stale, and void,
The luckless creature, he would hold it fast.   11590
Here he who fought me off so well—
Time triumphs—stranded lies, a whitened shell.
The clock is muted—
CHORUS.   Mute! Like midnight it is stilled.
The hand is falling,
MEPHISTOPHELES.   Fell—it is fulfilled.[4]
CHORUS. It is all over.
MEPHISTOPHELES.   Over! Stupid name.   11595
Why over?
All over and pure nothing—just the same!
What has this constant doing ever brought
But what is done to rake away to naught?
So it is over! How to read this clause?   11600
All over is as good as never was,
And yet it whirls about as if it were.
The Ever-empty is what I prefer.

4. A parody of Christ's last words on the cross, "It is finished" (John 19:30).

ENTOMBMENT[1]

LEMUR. [*solo*][2] Who was it built this house so ill
                With shovel and with spade?   11605
LEMURES. [*in chorus*]
          For thee, dull guest in hempen twill
          It's far too neatly made.
LEMUR. [*solo*] Why is the hall so ill supplied,
            No board or chairs, how came it?
LEMURES. [*in chorus*]
          It is but briefly occupied;   11610
          So many wait to claim it.
MEPHISTOPHELES. There lies the corpse, and when the soul would flit,
    I'll show it straight the bond with blood cemented;
    Yet tricks galore have lately been invented
    To cheat the devil of his writ.   11615
    On novel routes we're yet unknown,
    The former one offends opinions;
    I used to do it all alone,
    Now I am forced to call on minions.

    All round, we are in sorry plight!   11620
    Tradition, custom, old-established right,
    There's nothing to be trusted as it was.
    With its last breath it used to slip the house,
    I'd lie in wait, and like the nimblest mouse
    Snap! I would hold it fast in clenched-up claws.   11625
    Now it hangs back, is loth to leave the place,
    The body's wretched shack, noisome and brooding;
    The elements by their own feuding,
    They must at last evict it in disgrace.
    And though for days and hours I rack my brain,   11630
    The plaguy questions, when? how? where? remain;
    Why, even old man Death's swift pounce runs out,
    The very whether? long remains in doubt;
    I've often lusted at stiff limbs—in vain,
    It was all sham, they stirred, they moved again.   11635
[*with fantastic gestures of conjuration, fugleman-fashion*[3]]
    Step lively! make your paces double-long,
    Knights of the straight, knights of the crooked horn.
    Chips off Old Nick's block, to the manner born,
    And mind you, bring up Hell's jaws[4] right along.

1. An intentional allusion to the iconography of Christ's entombment in medieval art. It has been argued that Goethe was influenced in particular by fourteenth-century frescos of the Camposanto in Pisa depicting the Triumph of Death, the Last Judgment, and Hell.
2. Again the Lemures' song echoes the Gravediggers' song in *Hamlet* (V.i): "A pickaxe and a spade, a spade,/For and a shrouding sheet;/Oh, a pit of clay for to be made/ For such a guest is meet."
3. A reference to the leader of a file of troops in a marching army who would direct the movements of his group.
4 The traditional Hell-mouth of the medieval stage (see note to line 242).

Hell's jaws are many, many! to be sure,   11640
It swallows them by rank and etiquette;
Yet even on this final guided tour
We'll all become less formal soon, I bet.
     [*The ghastly jaws of Hell open at left.*]
With tusks agape, the arching gullet breathes
A raging cataract of flame eternal,   11645
See, in the smoldering distance fumes and seethes
The citadel of flame in blaze infernal,
Up to the fangs the scarlet floodtide surges,
Some of the damned swim up, on rescue bent,
The vast hyena mauls them and engorges,   11650
And they resume their anguished hot descent.
The corners, too, are worth exploring, brim-full
Of greatest horrors in least space confined!
Try as you like to terrify the sinful,
They count it fraud and figment of the mind.   11655
     [*to the* FAT DEVILS *of the short, straight horns*]
Now, paunchy rascals, with your cheeks all burning!
Who stuffed with hellish sulfur fairly glow;
You clumsy cloddish bullnecks never-turning,
You watch for glint of phosphor here below:
That is the little soul, winged psyche, land her   11660
And pluck the wings, it leaves a sordid worm;
Then with my stamp of lordship I will brand her,
And off with her in whirling fiery storm.

So, to patrol the lower station,
You bellows, is your duty, mark;   11665
If that's her chosen habitation,
The matter's somewhat in the dark.
The navel's where she likes to stay,
Look sharp, she may give you the slip that way.
     [*to the* LEAN DEVILS *of the long, crooked horns*]
You, guardsmen loons, great jackanapes unsteady,   11670
Rake through the air with unremitting tries;
Arms stretched aloft, sharp talons at the ready,
To catch the fluttering flibbet as it flies.
She's ill at ease in her old house, I'd say,
And genius seeks the straight and upward way.   11675
     [*Aureole from above, right.*]
HEAVENLY HOST. Follow, ye envoys,[5]
                Heaven-born convoys,
                On leisured wing coast:
                Sinful ones shriving,
                Dust to enliven;   11680
                Bounteous giving

5. *Angeloi* (Greek), "messengers," i.e., angels, surrounded by the heavenly "glory"
(Aureole).

To all things living
Waft in its striving
The hovering host.

MEPHISTOPHELES. A tuneless jangling, nauseous and
  churlish,   11685
Comes from above with the unwelcome day;
The kind of mincing medley, boyish-girlish,
As unctuous taste may relish, I daresay.
You know how we in heinous hour allotted
Annihilation to the human brood: 11690
The blackest infamy we plotted
Just suits their bland beatitude.

Look at the canting holy-oilers!
Thus they have snatched from us so many a prize,
With our own weapons they would foil us;   11695
They too are devils, only in disguise.
If you want shame eternal, lose today!
On to the graveside, hold it come what may!

CHORUS OF ANGELS. [*strewing roses*][6]
    Roses, you glowing ones,
    Balsam bestowing ones!   11700
    Floating and flickering,
    Stealthily quickening,
    Rose-twiglet-whirling ones,
    Rosebud-unfurling ones,
    Hasten to spread.   11705

    Spring, burst out blooming,
    Emerald, red;
    Send grace perfuming
    The sleeper's bed.

MEPHISTOPHELES. [*to the* DEVILS] Why hunch and flinch? Is this
  my hellish host?   11710
Let them strew on and show your mettle.
Back, every lubber, to his post!
To snow in with their childish catch-a-petal
The red-hot devils, seems to be their boast;
It melts and shrivels at your puff—   11715
Now, blowhards, blow!—Enough, enough!
Before your froust the whole swarm withers off.—
Come, not so wildly! shut your snouts and noses!
There—you have blown too strongly for the roses.
The proper dose you never seem to learn.   11720
They shrivel; more, they darken, curl up, burn!
Now it drifts up in flames, pernicious, clear,

6. The association of roses with heaven was traditional. In a fresco by Luca Signorelli (1441–1523) in the Cathedral of Orvieto angels are depicted strewing roses on the blessed. In the final scene (lines 11942 ff.) we learn that the angels have received the roses from the souls of the penitent, one of whom is Gretchen.

Thrust out against it, close together here!
The spirit drains away, all valor spent!
The devils sense a flattering alien scent.   11725

CHORUS OF ANGELS. Blossoms of blessing,
                    Gay flames caressing,
                    Love they are spreading,
                    Ecstasy shedding,
                    As heart would pray.   11730
                    Message of verity,
                    Ether all clarity.
                    To Heaven's company
                    Everywhere day.

MEPHISTOPHELES. O curse! O shame upon such bumpkins!   11735
Here's devils standing on their pumpkins,
Cartwheel on clumsy cartwheel turned,
They plunge to Hell arse-over-face.
My blessings on the scalding bath you earned!
But as for me, I keep my place.   11740
[*battling the fluttering roses*] Off, will-o'-the-wisps! you too!
    shine ever so much,
You're just some nauseous jelly to the touch.
What are you fluttering still? Will you be off!—
It grips my neck like pitch and sulphur stuff.

CHORUS OF ANGELS. What is not yours to keep,   11745
                    Leave it aside,
                    What mars your inmost deep,
                    You must not bide.
                    Thrusts it with mighty force,
                    Hold to the stronger course.   11750
                    Love leads but loving ones
                    In to the source.

MEPHISTOPHELES. My liver burns, my heart, my head as well,
Some super-devilish element!
More pointed far than flames of hell.—   11755
That's why you so prodigiously lament,
Unhappy lovesick lads, who wander, spurned,
Their craning necks to the belovèd turned.

I too! What draws my head that way for me?[7]
Do we not stand in sworn, inveterate enmity?   11760
The sight was else so bitterly averse.
Did something alien steep me through and through?
Those captivating youths, I quite enjoy the view;
What hinders me from uttering a curse?—   11765
And if I get infatuated,
Who will in future be the dunce?
The lawless rascals that I hated,
They seem so very lovely all at once!—

---

7. As a final ironic twist to the devil's role, Mephistopheles is distracted by sexual desire in response to the naked bodies of the young angels, thus abandoning his opposition to them.

You pretty children, let me quiz you:
Are you not too of Lucifer's own kind?   11770
You look so sweet, why, I would like to kiss you,
You turn up just in time, I find.
Somehow I feel so natural, so trustful,
As if a thousand times I'd watched your ways,
So stealthy-kittenishly lustful;   11775
Fair still, more fairly fair, with every gaze.
O, do approach, o grudge me not a glance!
ANGELS. We're coming—why retreat as we advance?
We are approaching, stay then if you can.
      [*The* ANGELS, *drifting all about, occupy the entire space.*]
MEPHISTOPHELES. [*who is being crowded into the proscenium*]
You who berate us fiends and elves,   11780
You are arch-conjurers yourselves;
For you seduce both maid and man.
Ah, what a damnable affair!
Is this love's essence that appeared?
My body is a single blazing flare,   11785
I hardly notice that my neck is seared.—
You waver to and fro, please try descending,
A bit more worldly-like your sweet limbs bending;
Though gravity, I grant, sits well on you,
I'd like, just once, to catch you smiling, too;   11790
I'd cherish the delight of it always;
I have in mind the way that lovers gaze,
A dimpling near the lips, and it is done.
You, lad, I like the best, so lean and tall,
That curate's mien becomes you not at all,   11795
Give me a little wanton wink, come on!
You need a decent naked fashion, too,
That long enfolding robe is over-prim—
They turn around—now for a backward view!
I could just eat them up, the lot of them.   11800
CHORUS OF ANGELS. On to the Light,
                   Loving flames, stream,
                   May Truth redeem
                   Self-damned from blight,
                   That, gladly weaned   11805
                   From evil and cleaned,
                   In the All-Unity
                   Blessèd they be.
MEPHISTOPHELES. [*coming to his senses*] What ails me!—Job-like,
      boil on boil my skin,
All sores I stand and shake with self-disgust,[8]   11810
And yet triumphant, as I come to trust
In my firm inner self and in my kin;

8. An allusion to the suffering Job, beset by diseases inflicted at Satan's behest, suggesting an ironic connection with the earlier use of Job in "Prologue in Heaven" (see note 7, page 8, and interpretive note, page 310).

I know the noble devil parts are safe,
It's only skin the love-spook knows to chafe;
Extinguished are the vicious flames I fought, 11815
And now I curse you all together, as I ought!

CHORUS OF ANGELS. Sheltered by glows
                    All-holiest, mightiest,
                    Bliss with the righteous,
                    Living, he knows. 11820
                    In unison fair
                    Soar now and quire,
                    In purified air
                    May the spirit respire!

[*They soar up, carrying off* FAUST's *immortal essence.*]

MEPHISTOPHELES. [*looking about him*] How can this be? Where
    are they gone away? 11825
You half-baked tribe, you have made off with it,
To heaven they are spiriting my prey;
That's why they came to buzz about this pit!
I have been robbed of costly, peerless profit,
The lofty soul pledged me by solemn forfeit, 11830
They've spirited it slyly from my writ.

Where do I sue now as complainer?
Who will enforce my well-earned right?
You have been fairly cheated, old campaigner,
You have deserved it, grim enough your plight. 11835
This thing was wretchedly mishandled,
A great expense, for shame! is thrown away,
A vulgar lust, absurd amours have dandled
The seasoned devil of his prey.
If to this childish-fatuous spree 11840
One so experienced could descend,
Then no mean folly it must be
That seized upon him in the end.

MOUNTAIN GORGES[1]†

Forests, Cliffs, Wilderness

HOLY ANCHORITES,[2] *scattered up the mountainsides, dwelling among rock-clefts.*

1. The setting of the final scene is argued to derive from several pictorial sources: 1) a Pisan fresco (see note to line 11604) depicting Anchorites in the Theban wilderness, a surging stream below, a dense forest in the middle, ascending cliffs with caves, with hermits surrounded by lions (see lines 11844–51); 2) a painting allegedly by Titian (1477–1576) of St. Jerome in the wilderness, an engraving of which was owned by Goethe; or 3) a detailed description of Montserrat near Barcelona in Wilhelm von Humboldt's book *The Basques*, which Goethe read in 1800.
2. Hermits of the first centuries of the Christian era who lived in the wilderness and practiced self-mortification in order to attain a mystical union with God.

CHORUS AND ECHO.

Wild-forest swaying near,
Ponderous boulders here,   11845
Tree roots entwine and close,
Tree trunks in serried rows.
Gushing up, wave on wave,
Shelter, the deepest cave.
Lions, they slink around,   11850
Kindly, without a sound,
Honor the hallowed grove,
Refuge of sacred love.

PATER ECSTATICUS.[3] [*floating hither and thither*]

Joy ever searing on,
Love's ever-glowing bond,   11855
Seething with ache the breast,
Foaming of God-lust blest.
Arrows, pierce through me,
Lances, undo me,
Bludgeons, come batter me,   11860
Lightning, come shatter me,
That dross might separate
All and evaporate,
Shine but the lasting star,
Timeless love's core.   11865

PATER PROFUNDUS.[4] [*in a deep region*]

When at my feet, with boulders teeming,
Gorge leans on chasm in ponderous sprawl,
A thousand glittering brooklets streaming
To join the flood-spate's gruesome fall,
When, by its own stout urge directed,   11870
The tree thrusts upward, straight and tall,
'Tis by all-potent love effected,
Which fashions all, and fosters all.

As though ravine and woods were waving,
A clamor thunders all about,   11875
And yet, still gracious in their raving,
The floods go plunging down the spout,
To moist the dale their urgent calling;
The lightning's, as it flared and hissed,
To carry freshness in its falling   11880
To ether charged with noisome mist.

3. The first of four titles assigned to the Anchorite fathers: *Ecstaticus, Profundus, Seraphicus,* and *Marianus.* These titles indicate a hierarchy of ascending degrees of divine knowledge. Historically, the title *Ecstaticus* had been used for St. Anthony, Johann Ruysbroek, and Dionysius the Carthusian; levitation had been attributed to, among others, St. Francis Xavier.

4. Traditionally an epithet applied to St. Bernhard of Clairvaux (1091–1153), who appears in Dante's *Paradiso* (Cantos XXXI ff.), replacing Beatrice as the poet's guide, to lead him toward a mystical vision of God.

Love-envoys, they proclaim what merit
Here works its all-creative will.
O may it also light my spirit;
Now chafes the mind, confounded, chill,   11885
In curbs of torpid senses shrinking,
In sharply tightened chains that smart.
Almighty Lord! O soothe my thinking,
Illumine Thou my needy heart.

PATER SERAPHICUS.[5] [*in a middle region*]
What a wispy dawn-cloud hovers   11890
In the spruces' swaying hair;
Do I fathom what it covers?
A young spirit band is there.

CHORUS OF BLESSED BOYS.[6]
Tell us who we are, dear Father.
Tell us, Father, in what place?   11895
We are happy, all together,
Life to us is such mild grace.

PATER SERAPHICUS.
Boys! born at the midnight sleeping,
Scarce unfolded sense and brain,
For their parents, early weeping,   11900
For the angels, cherished gain.
That a loving heart is present,
Well you sense, so closer glide;
Yet earth's jagged paths a pleasant
Fate vouchsafed you not to stride.   11905
Sink into my eyes, employ them,
Fit at world and earth to peer,
As your own you may enjoy them,
Gaze at these environs here.
[*He assumes them within himself.*]
These are trees, and yonder, boulders,   11910
Waterfalls that downward shoot
And with heaving giant shoulders
Further tilt their dizzying route.

BLESSED BOYS. [*from within*]
Mighty vistas strike our gazes,
But too somber is the spot,   11915
Thrills of fear and awe it raises,
Noble, kind one, hold us not.

PATER SERAPHICUS.
To a higher sphere ascending,
Ever grow in hidden wise,

---

5. Traditionally an epithet ascribed to St. Francis of Assisi (1182–1226), founder of the Franciscan order, who led a life of exemplary simplicity.
6. Unbaptized children who died immediately after being born and are thus without sin, yet also without experience of life. Their relation to Pater Seraphicus may be compared with that of Homunculus to Proteus in the final scene of the "Classical Walpurgis Night."

As, in purity unending, 11920
Godly presence fortifies.
For this is the spirit ration
Found where ether is most free,
Timeless loving's revelation,
Which unfolds to ecstasy. 11925

CHORUS OF BLESSED BOYS. [*circling the highest peaks*]
Hand to hand sealing,
Join a gay roundelay,
Reverent feeling,
Make it resound away;
Holiest teaching 11930
Trust without fear,
Know you will reach him
Whom you revere.

ANGELS. [*floating in the higher atmosphere, bearing* FAUST'S
IMMORTAL ESSENCE]
Pure spirits' peer, from evil coil
He was vouchsafed exemption; 11935
"Whoever strives in ceaseless toil,
Him we may grant redemption."
And when on high, transfigured love
Has added intercession,
The blest will throng to him above 11940
With welcoming compassion.[7]

THE YOUNGER ANGELS.
From the hands of pure contrition,
Holy love, those roses showered
Help us to prevail, empowered
To fulfill the lofty mission, 11945
Of this soul-prize to delude them.
Devils scattered as we strewed them,
Fiends inured to hellish anguish
With love's torment learnt to languish;
Petals stung the spawn of evil, 11950
Why, the very Master-Devil
We have pierced with stabbing pain.
Triumph! it was not in vain.

THE MORE PERFECTED ANGELS.
Earth remnants molest us,
To bear them is toil, 11955
Were they asbestos,
They still would soil.
When spirit strength has surged
And the elements to communion
With itself has merged, 11960

7. Concerning this important speech as the key to Faust's salvation, see Goethe's conversation with Eckermann, June 6, 1831, below. (Lines 11936–37 were enclosed in quotation marks in Goethe's manuscript and in all subsequent editions.)

No angel can sever the union
Of two fused in one,
Of twin natures blended,
Eternal love alone
Has strength to end it.[8]   11965

THE YOUNGER ANGELS.

Swathing the lofty cliff,
I divine, stirring near,
Wafting like mist adrift,
Spirit life here.
Now thins the fleece of cloud,   11970
I see a lively crowd
Of blessed boys,
Rid of the weight of earth,
In a circle curled,
They relish the joys   11975
Of fresh spring, rebirth
In the glad upper world.
For a beginning,
Rising bliss winning,
Let him join these!   11980

THE BLESSED BOYS.

Gladly we gather in
Him in the pupal stage;
Glad by the same to win
Angelic gage.
Loosen the flaking film   11985
Left yet to bind him,
Life in the sacred realm
Has grown and fined him.

DOCTOR MARIANUS. [*in the highest, purest cell*][9]

Here is the prospect free,
Spirit uplifting.   11990
Womanly shapes I see
Heavenward drifting.
Star-garlands burgeon,
High at their center
Heaven's crowned Virgin,   11995
Known by her splendor.
                    [*rapt*][1]
Sovereign Mistress of the World,

8. Recall Faust's comments on the two souls within his breast (lines 1112 ff.).
9. As a sublime counter-figure to Doctor Faustus in his study at the outset of the drama, this mystical devotee of the Virgin represents the highest level of spiritual perfection attainable within the human sphere. Thematically he may be compared with Nereus in his devotion to Galatea in the final scene of the "Classi-cal Walpurgis Night." Through Doctor Marianus the theme of the Eternal Feminine is re-introduced to *Faust* in its highest traditional form.
1. The following prayer of rapture addressed to the *Mater Gloriosa* echoes the prayer to the Virgin Mary by St. Bernhard in Dante's *Paradiso*, XXXIII.1–39, which apparently served Goethe as a model for the latter part of this scene.

On the azure awning
Of the Heavens fresh-unfurled,
Let Thy grace be dawning.   12000
What the breast of man doth move,
Tender, earnest feeling,
Deign to sense it and approve
Sacred love's revealing.

As invincible we stood   12005
When Thou badest the pious,
Of a sudden melts our mood
As Thou pacifiest.
Virgin Thou immaculate,
Rich in grace maternal,   12010
Chosen for divine estate,
Crowned our Queen Eternal.

About Her swathing
Cloud wisps tremble,
Expiant maidens'   12015
Airy assembly,
Humbly Her knees in
Penance seeking
Pardon bespeaking.

Nor to Thee the Lord denied it,   12020
Pure Thyself and peerless,
That the easily misguided
Should approach Thee fearless.

In their carnal weakness nursed,
Hard is their salvation;   12025
Who unaided ever burst
Shackles of temptation?
How the foot so swiftly slips
Down the glassy reaches!
Who resists bold eyes and lips   12030
And endearing speeches?

[MATER GLORIOSA[2] *floating on high*.]
CHORUS OF PENITENT WOMEN.

Thou who art soaring
In realms undying,
Hear our imploring,
Thou past all vying,   12035
Rich mercies pouring!

2. The Virgin Mary appears in Glory, accompanied by female attendants, a counterpart to the statue of her as the *Mater Dolorosa* to whom Gretchen prayed in *Part I* (see note 1, page 88, above). Suggested iconographic sources for this vision are paintings of the ascension of Mary, for instance by Titian, in Venice.

MAGNA PECCATRIX. [*Luke vii.* 36][3]
>By the love that at the feet
>Of Thy son and Savior lying,
>Poured them tears for unguent meet,
>Scorn of Pharisees defying;   12040
>By the vessel whence so amply
>Fragrance overpoured the rims,
>By the ringlets that so gently
>Served to dry the sacred limbs—

MULIER SAMARITANA. [*John iv*][4]
>By the wellspring whither erstwhile   12045
>Herds of Abraham were driven,
>By the pail whence to the thirsting
>Savior's lips cool drink was given,
>By the pure and plenteous fountain
>Thence forever outward streaming,   12050
>Ever sparkling and abounding
>Flows for all the world's redeeming—

MARIA AEGYPTIACA. [*Acta Sanctorum*][5]
>By the shrine where what was mortal
>Of the Lord was laid in mourning,
>By the arm that from its portal   12055
>Spurned me back with voice of warning;
>By my forty years' repentance
>Humbly served in desert land,
>By the blissful parting sentence
>I inscribed upon the sand—   12060

THE THREE TOGETHER.
>Thou who those of great transgression
>From Thy presence dost not banish,
>And their treasures of contrition
>Through the eons still replenish,
>Grant this soul, we join in praying,   12065
>Who but once misstepped, unwitting,

3. First of the attendants of the *Mater Gloriosa*, this is the sinful woman who bathed the feet of Christ with her tears when he was eating in the house of Simon the Pharisee, then kissed them and wiped them dry with her hair. Christ then said, "Her sins, which are many, are forgiven, for she loved much" (Luke 7:47).

4. When Christ was traveling through Samaria, he requested of a Samaritan woman that she give him water from the well of Jacob to drink, and she responded to his words by affirming him to be the Messiah.

5. The story of Mary of Egypt is taken from the *Acts of the Saints*, a collection of legends about the saints and martyrs prepared from the seventeenth to the nineteenth centuries. Mary of Egypt had led a life of sin for seventeen years when she felt an invisible hand preventing her from entering the temple in Jerusalem on a festival day. She repented her sins, prayed to the Virgin, and was suddenly transported into the temple. She then went out into the desert beyond the Jordan in response to a voice and lived a life of penance for forty-eight years. She finally died there and was buried in the sand in response to a request which she wrote upon the sand. Mary of Egypt accompanies the "great sinner" of Luke 7 and the Samaritan woman of John 4 because—like Gretchen, whose penitent spirit is shortly to appear—all three were guilty of carnal sin and all three were forgiven when they demonstrated selfless love.

> Unaware that she was straying,
> Such forgiveness as is fitting!

UNA POENITENTIUM, ELSE CALLED GRETCHEN. [*nestling*]

> Incline
> Thou past comparing,   12070
> Thou radiance bearing,
> Thy grace upon my happiness.
> The early-cherished,
> No longer blemished,
> Returns to bliss.[6]   12075

BLESSED BOYS. [*circling closer*]

> He already outgrows us
> In bodily might;
> True care that he owes us
> Will richly requite.
> We early were riven   12080
> From earthly creatures,
> He, wise in living,
> Will fitly teach us.

THE ONE PENITENT, ELSE CALLED GRETCHEN.

> 'Mid spirit choirs fresh life commencing,
> The novice scarce regains his wit,   12085
> The heavenly host but dimly sensing,
> Already he has merged with it.
> Behold! how all terrestrial cumbrance,
> A worn-out guise, cast off at length,
> In first ethereal adumbrance   12090
> He issues forth in youthful strength.
> Vouchsafe me through new morn to lead him,
> Too bright as yet for him to see.[7]

MATER GLORIOSA.

> Come, soar to higher spheres, precede him,
> He will divine and follow thee.   12095

DOCTOR MARIANUS. [*prostrate in adoration*]

> Gaze to meet the saving gaze,[8]
> Contrite all and tender,
> For a blissful fate your ways
> Thankfully surrender.

6. An adaptation of Gretchen's earlier prayer of despair to the *Mater Dolorosa* (see lines 3587 ff.). Not only does Goethe perfectly adapt the prayer to an opposite purpose, but he also has the soul of Gretchen imitate the intercession of Beatrice on behalf of Dante in the *Divine Comedy*. The hierarchy of the *Mater Gloriosa*, her three women, and Gretchen as penitent exactly corresponds to the hierarchy described by Virgil at the outset of the *Inferno* (II.43–126) of the Virgin, St. Lucy, and Beatrice. A corresponding train of saints about the Virgin is then envisioned by Dante in the *Paradiso*, XXXII.

7. The theme of a blinding brightness recalls the theme of the Earth Spirit (line 485 ff.) and the rising sun in "Charming Landscape," lines 4702–3. A corresponding theme of developing vision of a purer light is also central to Dante's progress in the company of Beatrice in the *Paradiso*.

8. The German of this line, *Blicket auf zum Retterblick*, recalls the theme of the "moment" to which Faust aspired: *Augenblick*. It is ironic and important that such affirmation should be spoken by an ecstatic devotee of the Virgin who is "prostrate in adoration."

May each noble mind be seen 12100
Eager for Thy service;
Holy Virgin, Mother, Queen,
Goddess, pour Thy mercies!

CHORUS MYSTICUS.[9]

All in transition
Is but reflection; 12105
What is deficient
Here becomes action;
Human discernment
Here is passed by;
Woman Eternal 12110
Draw us on high.

9. In Goethe's manuscript this Chorus was first called *chorus in excelsis* ("on high"). As with the cosmic choral voice that ends the festival of the "Classical Walpurgis Night" by affirming the triumph of Eros, here a universal voice of the mystical union with the Virgin as highest form of the Eternal Feminine affirms a corresponding sense of fulfillment. The terms of the final chorus, furthermore, without lessening the complexity of the tragedy in any way, also affirm the manner in which the drama as a whole achieves a corresponding affirmation and fulfillment: as "reflection" (*Gleichnis*), as "action" (*Ereignis*), as "deed" (*getan*, which recalls the *Tat* of Faust's translation for *logos*, line 1237). (See also the essay by Hans Eichner, below.)

Interpretive Notes

The task of providing adequate commentary on a literary work so complex and varied as Goethe's *Faust* is inexhaustible, even if a point is reached fairly quickly where too much already seems to have been said. Commentary can easily become an intrusion on the prerogatives of judgment and response which all readers have the right to control and enjoy on their own. At the same time, the history of *Faust* commentaries, which is complex and varied (with examples of futility and failure to document every possible kind of comment), shows that information is not adequate in itself, even though a great deal of information—some of it quite arcane and esoteric—is needed for even a first reading. For this reason I have prepared the following supplementary notes to the drama, intended to serve an entirely different function from that of the footnotes which gloss and explain references and allusions as they occur within the play. These interpretive notes are not intended to overlap or compete with the function of the documents and critical essays in this book. Rather, they are all addressed to particular questions and problems in understanding Goethe's drama, usually in connection with individual scenes. Two criteria above all have been taken into consideration here: the inordinate complexity of literary allusion and imitation in *Faust*, and the thematic and structural interaction among the various scenes.

"Dedication" (lines 1–32). Composed on June 24, 1797 (according to Goethe's diary entry), two days after the poet wrote to Schiller of his plans to recommence work on the uncompleted drama. Apart from intermittent efforts in Italy in 1788 and shortly thereafter to prepare the play for publication as a fragment in his collected works in 1790, over two decades had passed since Goethe had written the various drafts which we know as the *Urfaust* from the transcript prepared by Luise von Göchhausen shortly after Goethe arrived in Weimar in 1775. The dedicatory poem of 1797 thus describes the poet's reponse to these earlier manuscripts as he prepares to pick up where he had left off. The characters of the drama haunt him like spirits half-realized from his past, and this calls to mind the days of his youth and the departed friends who were close to him when he was first writing the play. This sense of distance from the world of Faust—even the world partially created in the earlier manuscripts—combined with feelings of nostalgia and regret is crucial for understanding the point of view of the completed drama (at least in *Part I*).

Critics have noted that Goethe returned to Faust from writing ballads during the spring of 1797 for Schiller's *Musenalmanach* and that the spirit-world of his ballads is closely akin to the attitude and mood which Goethe associates with *Faust* in the "Dedication." The form of the "Dedication," derived from the *ottava rima* of Italian romances and earlier used by Goethe for his incompleted epic *Die Geheimnisse* (which begins with the longer poem also entitled "Dedication"), was associated by him with reflective and melancholy moods and a certain formality of emotional expression. The importance of Schiller for the renewal of Goethe's efforts on *Faust*, which may be traced through his persistent inquiries in their almost daily correspondence, should be kept in mind. Schiller shared the fascination of other early readers of Goethe's work (which they knew from the published *Fragment* of 1790), such as Wilhelm von Humboldt, Schelling, and Friedrich Schlegel, in regard especiallly to the philosophical implications of the tragedy.

"Prelude in the Theater" (lines 33–242). Composed presumably in the period 1798 to 1800 (perhaps soon after the renovation of the Weimar Theater in the summer and fall of 1798), the "Prelude" offers a general view of the theater from the separate perspectives of the theater manager, the dramatic poet, and the actor. All three perspectives were familiar to Goethe, of course, though he should not be identified

with any of the three speakers in the "Prelude," least of all the poet. He offers instead a playfully ironic picture of the theater of his time, juxtaposing its several concerns in such a way that broader, ultimately universal implications are defined which pertain not only to *Faust* but to all drama in any theater. Sources for the "Prelude" are less important than the sense of theater it establishes for the drama of *Faust*, a sense which is both pragmatic—as demonstrated by the arguments of the Director and the Comedian concerning the necessity of a popular success for both profit and applause —and also theoretical—as indicated by the ironic application to the Poet of attitudes toward art and poetry which were familiar to Goethe from the aesthetics of the time (as, for instance, in the essays of Schiller, whose views Goethe largely shared). Some critics have questioned the relevance of the "Prelude" for *Faust*. There can be no question, however, that Goethe meant it to be read as a prelude to the drama, presumably the whole drama (even though *Part II* was not written until much later). Despite its playful and satirical tone, the "Prelude" remains a valuable document for theater history and for the theory of drama in relation to theatrical production. The burden of its argument should also discourage any preoccupation with the philosophy of *Faust* at the expense of its theatricality.

"*Prologue in Heaven*" (*lines 243–353*). Composed presumably in late 1799 or 1800, the "Prologue" achieves an important transformation of the traditional Faust legend. Faust's pact with Mephistopheles not only proceeds from Faust's own decision to work with magic but also from a wager contracted independently between Mephistopheles and the Lord. Neither the use of black magic nor the question of damnation, but rather the nature or condition of man himself, thus becomes the central concern of Goethe's drama. And it is the Lord, not Mephistopheles, who first singles out Faust as the best representative of mankind. Goethe here uses the example of the prologue to *Job* (1:6–12), thus establishing for his Faust the traditional philosophical and existential, as well as theological, implications of Satan's testing of Job. In a comment to Eckermann later in his life (January 18, 1825) Goethe expressed satisfaction concerning this association of Faust and Job. The "Prologue" may also derive certain qualities—particularly with regard to the characterization of the Lord in relation to the heavenly host—from that other attempt to "justify the ways of God to man," Milton's *Paradise Lost* (especially the scene in heaven in Book III). The role of Goethe's Mephistopheles is, of course, diametrically opposed to the role of Milton's Satan, as indicated by the fact that Christ is the interlocutor of God in Milton's scene, whereas Mephistopheles (like Satan in *Job*) has that role in Goethe's "Prologue."

Important for the "Prologue" also, in anticipation of Faust's ultimate salvation in Goethe's drama (another change in the legend to which Goethe here commits himself), is the subordination of Mephistopheles' role to the will of the Lord. The devil in the "Prologue" becomes a somewhat playful and congenial emissary of Heaven, whose complaints about the state of the world and the condition of man (lines 271–92) are mollified by the ironic tone of his entire exchange with the Lord. Goethe thus establishes for his play a transcendental perspective of tolerance, which the reader is invited to share. On the authority of the "Prologue," furthermore, we learn to take Mephistopheles' subsequent self-definition as true, when in his first conversation with Faust he calls himself a "part of that force which would/Do ever evil, and does ever good" (lines 1335–36 and note), though he does not there acknowledge the Lord as the ultimate source of good.

Critics have pointed out a purposeful theatrical-allegorical transformation in the "Prologue" of the realm of Heaven—which should *not* be understood in terms of Christian theology or any other religious doctrine—into a feudal court, very much in accord with ceremonies of state as represented in traditions of Renaissance and Baroque drama (for example, in Shakespeare's history plays). The Lord is presented as a monarch surrounded by his subjects, the hosts of Heaven (see stage direction preceding line 243). The Archangels represent vassals who celebrate the cosmos as the Lord's domain. Mephistopheles' role thus corresponds to that of the court jester, resembling the role of the Comedian in the "Prelude" and also anticipating his disguise in the court of the Emperor in Act I of *Part II*. (Indeed, the entire setting of the court in *Part II* may be read—and presumably was so intended by Goethe—as a parody of the right rule represented by the heavenly court of the "Prologue.") Also important is the balance of transcendental perspectives between the "Prologue" and the final scenes of *Part II* ("Entombment" and "Mountain Gorges," which constitute a kind of epilogue).

Hymn of the Archangels (*lines 243–70*). This hymn may be read as a celebration of the cosmos addressed to the Lord by his chief vassals in direct response to what they perceive from their heavenly vantage point. But the poetic implications of the hymn extend beyond celebration to demonstration through an implicit identity of speaker, statement, and object. Here—as also, in an even more complex manner, in the scene "Charming Landscape," which begins *Part II* (composed a quarter of a century after the "Prologue")—Goethe achieves a mode of poetry which seeks to imitate the life process itself, using imagery of sight and sound to equate the action of the cosmos with its own statement. (Also comparable is the speech from the *Urfaust* in which the Earth Spirit describes its activity, lines 501–9.) The three Archangels presumably derive from their important counterparts in *Paradise Lost* (since Biblical references to them are obscure). All three celebrate cyclical processes from different perspectives: Raphael the circular path of the sun; Gabriel the cycles of night and day and the changing tides of the earth; Michael the motion of storms with their lightning and thunder, as well as the gentler activity of good weather. In their refrain (which restates the final lines of Raphael's stanza) all three affirm the glory of the Lord, himself incomprehensible, as manifested in the permanent life of his creation. The Archangels employ a lyric stanza with regular four-stress iambic lines, alternating rhymes, and feminine-masculine endings. The exalted tone and measured cadence of this opening hymn stands in purposeful contrast to the more familiar, colloquial speech of Mephistopheles which follows it.

"Night" (lines 345–807). Readers of this opening scene to Goethe's drama should keep two important considerations in mind: 1) two separate and quite disparate stages of composition are joined together here, not without considerable effort on the part of the author's synthesizing powers; and 2) the scene as a whole, modeled—at least by the apparent intention of the final stage of composition—on the subgenre of monodrama, which was popular in the eighteenth century and was well known to Goethe (especially from French sources), provides a survey of the entire Faustian dilemma, and indeed of the entire drama of *Faust*, within its own peculiar scope. With regard to the stages of composition, it should be noted that the opening section—the monologue in the study, the contemplation of the Sign of the Macrocosm and the conjuring of the Earth Spirit, and the conversation with the famulus Wagner (lines 354–605)—belongs to the earliest stages of Goethe's work on the drama and coincides (with minor revisions) with the text of the *Urfaust*, which dates from the mid-1770s. In the renewal of the monologue after Wagner leaves an apparent recapitulation of the preceding events occurs, a review by Faust of the confrontation with the Earth Spirit in particular. This transition section of the scene indicates a process of recreation and transformation around 1800 by Goethe as he worked himself back into the mood of the earlier fragment and, simultaneously, carried its perspective forward into his later, more mature view of Faust's dilemma. The medium of this more universal, indeed archetypal, tragedy of man is fully established when the suicide motif is introduced (lines 686 ff.) with the subsequent existential crisis of despair and renewal on the model of Christ's death and resurrection at Easter. There is no indication in the text of the *Urfaust*, which is far more satirical and archaic in tone, that Goethe intended Faust to be associated in any way with Christ, or even that the scene is set in the night before Easter morning. Concerning the structure of the scene as a whole, it should be noted how Goethe exploits his boldest departure from the traditional legend of Faust. Having abandoned the devil entirely in the opening sequence, introducing the Earth Spirit as an apparent substitute, Goethe went on to associate the use of magic and incantation generally with the ritualistic and psychological response of both Faust and the Chorus in the cathedral to the mystery of Christ's resurrection, which is associated both with the renewal of life in nature (as the following scene, "Outside the City Gate," demonstrates) and with the renewal of spiritual energy in the mind of the protagonist through the creative recollection of childhood faith and joy. We thus observe a twofold transformation of the traditional magus in this scene: first, in accord with the boundless striving of the Romantic (or pre-Romantic) will, whereby Faust attempts to challenge the spiritual power of the world; and second, by analogy with Christian myth, whereby Faust's state of mind is transformed and renewed. The opening scene of the drama thus demonstrates how Goethe initially made the Faust of the popular legend into a prototypical Romantic hero and, at the later stage of composition, modified the stance of this hero in such a way that his ultimate salvation is prefigured.

Later Addition to "Night" (lines 607–807). The inner psychological motivation of Faust's second monologue is crucial to the drama, yet difficult to follow. In less than a hundred lines after Wagner leaves, Faust works himself into a suicidal despair, purely through reflection upon the incidents which have preceded. The interruption of Faust's mood by Wagner after the encounter with the Earth Spirit—which must have been primarily satirical in its initial intention—became an interruption of nearly a quarter century for Goethe (see note to "Dedication" above). The effort of recollection for Faust, thinking back to the encounter with the Earth Spirit, brings him face to face with futility, not only because Faust is merely human and incapable of confronting the Spirit as an equal, but more because *as human* he is subject to time and the conditions of life, as represented by his situation in the study. These conditions are referred to, in what approaches a mythical personification, as "gray Care" (line 644), who subsequently appears as the Hag in Act V (lines 11384–510) to blind Faust just before he dies. It has been argued persuasively by critics that this creature at the end of the drama should be regarded as a counter-figure to the Earth Spirit at the beginning. Faust's dilemma, which assumes in this scene an existential despair, is that he stands suspended between these opposing forces, juxtaposing the two in his mind in irreconcilable conflict. Interpreted in this way, the second monologue becomes central to more than Goethe's *Faust*; it is an authoritative expression of what has come to be called Romantic despair. Goethe is here concerned with the fundamental tragic dilemma of the human condition.

Easter Chorus (lines 737–807). Faust responds to the Easter music as to a heavenly visitation. Though he denies all Christian faith himself (lines 765 ff.), as Goethe likewise would have done, he nonetheless acknowledges the validity of the Easter ritual as a miracle of rebirth for the faithful. Such faith, he admits in recalling his own childhood, was once shared by him as well. More important is the function of this visitation within the larger structure of the scene. In contrast to the appearance of the Earth Spirit, which was conjured by Faust through a magical sign, the Easter Chorus comes over him unexpectedly and by surprise, a gift of grace at the moment when he is about to drink the poison. The balance and contrast of these two spiritual visitations is central to Faust's experience both in this opening scene and in the drama as a whole. The Easter resurrection clearly prefigures Faust's ultimate salvation at the end, confirming the earlier prophecy of the Lord in the "Prologue in Heaven" (lines 308–9 and 328–29). And both these visitations constitute a radical departure by Goethe from the traditional Faust legend, which commences with the conjuring of Mephistopheles.

"Outside the City Gate" (lines 808–1177). This scene follows immediately the conclusion of "Night" (and was presumably written more or less in sequence with it, early in 1801), showing the general activity of town and country on the Easter morning introduced by the choruses in the cathedral at the end of the preceding scene. Goethe here establishes a panoramic mode of dramatic action, something like a genre painting, involving an informal procession of figures across the stage who represent typical citizens of the town. Until the appearance of Faust and Wagner (line 901) there is nothing in the scene which directly pertains to the drama. A somewhat playful and satirical tone pervades the entire procession, as if the various activities and preoccupations of human society were being exposed as a source of humor. Such satirical display of mankind, often quite unrelated to Faust himself, occurs frequently later on (e.g., the "Walpurgis Night"), especially in the various allegorical and symbolic scenes of *Part II*. In this scene the poet's most serious concern is found in the effects of Easter, specifically the return of spring to the land, upon all people, young and old, rich and poor, as also later on upon Faust and Wagner. The setting and the structure of the scene also demonstrate the effects of renewal as an emergence, an opening outward. The citizens of the town proceed out of the narrow city gate and into the countryside as if they were being released from the imprisonment of winter and society. Initially, the perspective of the scene is fixed at a convenient vantage point near the gate; later on, after Faust's opening speech (lines 902–40), the setting moves with Faust and Wagner almost cinematically as they make their way, first, to the village with its rustic fesival, then to the top of a hill, where they watch the sun go down, and finally back to the city gate, accompanied by the black poodle, returning at evening to the protection and enclosure of house and (for Faust) study. The scene thus assumes a cyclical structure, moving with Faust as he makes his journey from morning to evening out from the city to the limits of human habitation and activity in nature and then back again to the gate of the city. Within this structure of journey and return, which may stand symbolically for human life in its activity and involvement in the open world of nature, the focal points are found in Faust's speeches: at the outset of his walk (lines 903–40) and at its outer limit (lines 1064–99). Less central, though thematically related to the journey as a whole, is Faust's comment concerning the two separate and opposing forces in the human mind ("Two souls, alas, are dwelling in my breast," line 1112), which motivate, respectively, the going out and the return. Also significant is the balancing of Faust's invocation of the spirits of the air (lines 1118–25), followed by the appearance of the black poodle, which later proves to be Mephistopheles in disguise. Faust does not conjure this devil to appear (he comes, after all, by independent agreement with the Lord in the "Prologue in Heaven"), but the symbolic structure of the scene motivates his entrance into the drama all the same.

Faust's Sunset Speech (lines 1064–99). What follows is another of Faust's great set speeches, in effect a monologue, which may also be regarded as a crucial poetic text for European Romanticism. His mood, as in the opening scene, is a mixture of frustration at his own condition as human being and his desire for infinite satisfaction. Watching the sun as it sets over the horizon, Faust projects this desire upon its departure through an image of spiritual flight. By imagining himself moving in the company of the sun, which increasingly assumes the guise of divinity, Faust also comes to identify himself with this god. He imagines himself moving above the earth, surveying the whole of it from his transcendent vantage point. He conceives of himself as the mythical center of a cosmic activity (lines 1085 ff.), poised between heaven and earth, day and night. As the sun departs and evening begins to come on, Faust returns to consciousness of himself and his position on the hill, acknowledging that his "fancy" (line 1089) was no more than that. His concluding lines affirm through generalization the validity for all men of his transcendental longings and imaginings, that preeminently Faustian feeling of infinite desire, associated in the concluding couplets with the flights of birds in the sky: the lark in its jubilation, the eagle in its heights, and the crane in its migrations.

The Doctrine of Two Souls (lines 1110–17). Faust's comments concerning the two opposite impulses of the human mind have been the subject of much discussion by

Faust scholars. It would be an error to seek any coherent philosophical doctrine in them (as some have done), even though when he wrote the passage Goethe may have had in mind corresponding philosophical doctrines of polar impulses, such as Fichte's theory of the reciprocity of impulses which constitutes all knowledge and even consciousness itself (in his *Wissenschaftslehre* of 1794) and Schiller's dichotomy between what he calls "material impulse" (*Stofftrieb*) and "formal impulse" (*Formtrieb*) in the letters *On Aesthetic Education* of 1795 (which was itself influenced by Fichte). Goethe establishes his duality in *Faust* as a dramatic theme which recurs again and again in various guises throughout the work. One need think only of Mephistopheles' description of human desires to the Lord (lines 304–5) or of the polarity between the Sign of the Macrocosm and the Earth Spirit in Faust's earlier attempt to achieve satisfaction of his desires through magic (lines 429–513). Similarly, in the present scene and the one which follows, Faust's desire to follow the path of the sun is offset by his contentment when he returns again to his study and begins to read his Bible. Within the configuration of characters in the play, however, it should be noted that Wagner, in apparent contrast to Faust—as he himself here emphasizes—is only aware of the second of the two opposing forces, never having felt any longing for infinite vision. Mephistopheles, who is about to enter the drama and will not again depart until after Faust's death, appears to ignore this duality and even to offer Faust the possibility (at least in terms of their wager in the second study scene) of overcoming this contradiction in himself by allowing Mephistopheles to guide him through the domain of human experience. In what ways this attempt succeeds or fails remains one of the central issues in the interpretation of Goethe's drama.

The First Study Scene (lines 1178–1529). When Goethe finally set himself to write the scenes in which Mephistopheles first appears and the pact with Faust is concluded (probably in 1800, perhaps shortly before the preceding scene, "Outside the City Gates," or else early in 1801), he was obliged to make his peace with the popular legend. No single aspect of the Faust tradition, not even the damnation of Faust (which Goethe ultimately transformed to salvation), imposed such unyielding and archaic demands on the author as the initial terms of Faust's meeting with Mephistopheles. Here also Goethe had to establish the nature and the function of the devil for his *Faust* in a manner which would be suitable to the rest of the drama, both what had already been written (i.e., the Gretchen tragedy) and what was yet to come. What Goethe determined to do with these scenes, therefore, was the juxtaposition of two radically contrary motives, which elicit unavoidably quite opposite responses from the reader, leaving an impression of profound ambivalence. On the one hand, almost by force and with a strong dose of poetic irony, Goethe transports us back into the remote context of the popular legend, as if he were imitating the style and tone of the sixteenth-century chapbook or some sub-literary late medieval ballad. On the other hand, both Mephistopheles and the terms of his pact with Faust are accommodated and transformed to accord with Goethe's own intentions for the drama. For these separate motives Goethe also provided quite separate poetic effects. The archaic material of Mephistopheles' appearance and the signing of the pact, much of it derived from the chapbook version of the Faust story by Pfitzer, assume a playful, almost satirical tone, as if the magic and supernaturalism did not take itself quite seriously. There is thus a sense of hocus-pocus to these scenes, a sense of spectacular magic show, as if we were again attending the folk play or puppet show of *Faust*, as Goethe knew it from his childhood. In this Goethe also accommodates himself to the expectations which had been raised by the published *Fragment* of 1790, where basic questions concerning the role of Mephistopheles and the nature of his pact with Faust were left wide open. But Goethe himself had little sympathy with magic and the supernatural in terms of the popular legend. His playful, ironic style, willfully archaic and simplistic, makes this all too apparent. Far more serious and far more difficult is the integration of this traditional material to the drama of Faust as Goethe conceived it, as his various friends and critics responded to it (Schiller and the philosophers at Jena above all), and as the other scenes composed since work had recommenced in 1797 were developing it for the poet. Goethe was required to accommodate himself to the universal and even philosophical concerns of his drama, its implications for him as he saw them around 1800, at the same time that he paid his ironic lip-service to the popular legend. Above all in those sections of the two study scenes which are new to Goethe—Faust's initial mood and his translation from the Bible, some aspects of Mephistopheles's self-definition, the spirit song which is conjured to lull Faust to sleep, Faust's curse against human existence, and especially the wager which emerges from the traditional pact—these aspects of the scene indicate the direction in which Goethe was leading the popular legend, and these above all demand careful attention from the reader.

Faust's Translation of the Bible (lines 1210–37). Faust introduces the theme of Christian revelation as a valid analogue to his own intellectual concern. From Goethe's point of view this would not necessarily indicate the perspective of religion. Historically, Faust was a contemporary of Martin Luther, whose translation of the Bible into German (New Testament, 1524) included the familiar version of the opening verse of John which Faust begins with: "In the beginning was the Word" (*Im Anfang war das Wort*). Here Faust is, in effect, sharing in Luther's labor of translation, though he immediately transforms the text to accord with his own philosophy of life. Within the dramatic situation, the translation of scripture provides an ironic parallel to the appearance of Mephistopheles: both the devil in his guise as poodle and the text of the Gospel as Word of God provide instances of the incarnation of spirit, for which Christ himself is the essential model. Mephistopheles apparently recognizes this as competition and grows increasingly violent in his barking.

Faust's sequence of terms for the Greek *logos* reflects the intellectual background to Romantic thought which Goethe himself participated in during the latter half of the eighteenth century. The rejection of "Word" for "Sense" corresponds to the rejection of traditional rhetorical views of language as mere form or artifice in favor of the sense, the meaning, the feeling which language represents. An analogue to this is provided by Faust himself in the scene from the Gretchen tragedy (composed before 1775), "Marthe's Garden," where Faust discusses religion and refuses to accept any name for God, asserting instead that "Feeling is all!" (line 3456). The alternative choice of term, "Force" (*Kraft*), would correspond to the basic view of life in the era of the German *Sturm und Drang* during the 1770s, which Goethe himself established in large measure through such works as *The Sorrows of Young Werther* and *Götz von Berlichingen*. The final choice of term, "Deed" (*Tat*), is clearly the most Faustian, the most valid for Goethe's drama as a whole, corresponding to the famous couplet in Faust's last monologue in Part II: "He only earns both freedom and existence/Who must reconquer them each day." (lines 11575–76) (See also the Lord's statement about the need for mankind to be active even if the devil must drive men to it, lines 340 ff.) *Logos* as Deed would also correspond to the philosophy of Idealism, as in Fichte's *Wissenschaftslehre* (1794), which argues that experience, consciousness, and even life itself begin when the self posits itself through action (*Tathandlung*). Thus, whether Faust himself is aware of any such implications, Goethe has here transformed the Biblical Word from the context of Luther and the historical Faust to the context of Romantic Idealism, the context in which Goethe was writing and the context to which his *Faust* was addressed.

The Song of the Spirits (lines 1447–1505). The entertainment promised by Mephistopheles provides, of course, his means of escape. The spirits he conjures (presumably the same as were heard earlier in the corridor, lines 1259 ff.) will offer a magical vision which affects all the senses (sound, line 1439; sight, line 1440; smell, line 1442; taste, line 1443; touch, line 1444). The devil's irresistible art lulls Faust to sleep. The spirit song which follows, apart from being one of Goethe's most brilliant lyric poems, establishes a mode of verse with crucial thematic implications for the entire Faust drama, especially *Part II*. The magic of Mephistopheles manifests itself to the senses as demonic art; the expression of this art in the drama, perforce, is verbal, poetic, dependent on Goethe's own art; and the medium of expression is the voice of spirits, representing presumably the voice of nature itself (assuming that these, as others later on, are spirits of nature). The fact that they deceive Faust and hypnotize him is perhaps itself a part of this theme. At the outset of *Part II* the song of the elves will transform and renew Faust (lines 4634 ff.); the spirit show of Helena and Paris will inspire his love for her (lines 6427 ff.); and much of the "Classical Walpurgis Night" and the Helena act may be regarded as the supreme examples of such poetic-mythical phantasmagoria. Further instances of spirit song as the voice of nature would be the song of the Archangels in the "Prologue in Heaven" (lines 243 ff.) and the song of metamorphosis by the Chorus in Act III of *Part II* (lines 9992 ff.), where the singers actually become spirits of nature. With regard to the present song, it should be considered how the mind of the reader, sharing in the response of Faust the listener, moves through a poetic-visionary process, like a mental journey, which creates its own reality as it goes along. Initially a sense of transcendence is affirmed, as if the walls of Faust's study opened up to reveal the whole of nature and the cosmos (lines 1447–56). Within this open domain a sense of spiritual beauty (*Geistige Schöne*, line 1458; here: "graces uplifting") is asserted to overwhelm the participant, soliciting a response—eminently Faustian—of "lovelorn yearning" (*Sehnende Neigung*, line 1461), which leads to a flight across lands, moving swiftly to a kind of garden enclosure or "arbor" (lines 1466, 1470), where lovers exchange vows (lines 1467 ff.). From this retreat of love, apparently through association with the arbor as a grape vine, a Dionysian revel is conjured in which the wine flows forth from the pressed grapes in broad streams, permeating the landscape itself, like rivers flowing to the sea (lines 1471–83). The poem—or whatever spirit participates in what the song says—then moves as a bird in flight, following the sun outwards across the sea to blissful islands, where singing choirs are heard and dancers are seen on meadows (lines 1484–96). From here activity extends in every direction, climbing mountains, swimming lakes, hovering in the air, ascending finally as a blissful celebration (*Seliger Huld*, line 1505; here: "blessed requital") of life itself and of the distant loving stars (lines 1497–1505). (Such visionary experience should also be compared to earlier instances for Faust, e.g., lines 386–97, 1068–99.)

The Pact Scene (lines 1530–2072). As late as April, 1801, as indicated in a letter to Schiller, Goethe intended to write an additional scene, the "Disputation," which would have been placed between the two study scenes. Ultimately he abandoned the plan, leaving only a sketch for its structure and a draft for the opening lines (See

Paralipomena Nos. 11 and 12 to *Faust I, W. A.,* I.14.290 ff.). This academic debate, so far as can be construed from the fragments, would have occurred in a large auditorium with students and faculty in attendance. Mephistopheles, in his guise as wandering scholar, was to challenge Faust in the debate concerning the respective value of experience and intuition or imaginative vision, Mephistopheles defending the former and Faust—despite his central preoccupation with the experience of life—the latter. With reference to a philosophical concern for self-knowledge ("Γνῶϑι σεαυτον in schönen Sinne," Paral. 11) and something called a creative mirror ("schaffender Spiegel," *ibid.*), Faust was to celebrate the inner life of the mind, perhaps sustaining the mood which resulted from the first Study scene, especially the vision of the spirit song. Mephistopheles was to speak as a man of the world, offering information about various natural phenomena (derived apparently from Goethe's own preoccupation at that time with the natural philosophy of Schelling and others). Apparently Mephistopheles was to win a resounding triumph in the debate, with the effect of thrusting Faust's mood once again into profound despair. When composing the second study scene Goethe still intended to write the "Disputation," and the radical reversal of roles and attitudes between Faust and Mephistopheles which has occurred from the first scene to the second in the text as it stands—totally without explanation or apparent cause—can only be understood with reference to the abandoned scene. Some sense of participation in the academic life of Faust's university is still indicated by Mephistopheles at lines 1712–13, where he speaks of the "doctoral feast" to take place that evening. The effect of this change in mood and relationship for the second Study scene is that Faust assumes the stance of negator and denier, even uttering a categorical curse against life itself, and Mephistopheles, who now appears in the dress of a Spanish cavalier—like a figure from the Don Juan legend, ready to lead Faust into the world according to the pact he proposes—must play a conciliatory role, cajoling and encouraging Faust to take up life with him on the devil's terms.

Faust's Curse (lines 1587–1606). The curse which follows is directed against every basic aspect of human existence. The initial metaphor defines the mind, or soul (*Seele,* line 1587), as bound within the body as a "cave of grief," to which the received data of sense impression are "lures and blandishments." First, Faust curses what is termed "smug delusion" (line 1591), apparently the intuition of higher things through the phenomena of the natural world, which Mephistopheles in the "Prologue in Heaven" called "of Heaven's light a glitter" (line 284). Then, Faust curses the world of phenomena itself, as it is perceived by the senses (lines 1593–94). The "lying dreams" which next receive the curse (lines 1595–96) include not only the visions of sleep—mentioned just above in Faust's lament (lines 1562 ff.)—but also the illusions and ideals of mankind regarding immortality. Next, in quick survey Faust includes in his curse those aspects of life which were earlier referred to as Care (lines 644 ff.): property, family, and labor (lines 1597–98), also wealth and the particular deceptive pleasures it provides (lines 1599 ff.). The curse against wine and love (lines 1603–4) calls to mind the vision which the spirit song provided Faust in the preceding scene (lines 1463–83). Faust thus rejects the vision which had such power over him so recently and which will constitute a central preoccupation of much of his subsequent activity through the drama. Finally, rejecting the primal Christian virtues of faith, hope and patience (*spes, fides, patientia*), Faust imposes his curse on those positive and redemptive qualities of mind which he demonstrated at the outset of the first Study scene, after he returned from his Easter walk and when he turned to the Bible. For Mephistopheles this curse upon everything which might have value for Faust's existence indicates that Faust is ready for a pact with the devil.

Faust's Wager (lines 1699–1706). The concept of the "moment" is most important for the drama of *Faust* as a whole. Nor does Goethe allow the reader to lose sight of it, especially in the climactic scenes of *Part II* (see, for example, lines 8424–25, 9411 ff., 11585–86). Faust has in mind not a sense of satisfaction as the completion and negation of striving (see by contrast line 1691), but rather a kind of fulfillment where the temporal and experiential process of such striving would be gathered together within such a moment so that time itself would be transcended. Ultimately this concept is aesthetic, corresponding to idealist theories of beauty in art (as the term "fair"—*schön* in the German, line 1700—indicates). For this reason *Part II* offers a more authoritative demonstration of such a moment and the impossibility of establishing it as a permanent reality in the world. At the same time, with regard to the ultimate role of Gretchen in Faust's salvation and the redeeming power of her love for him, it may be argued that the nearest instance of the fulfillment in the moment which Faust envisions is found in the ultimate self-sacrifice of love. Gretchen demonstrates this in an intuitive manner; Homunculus at the end of the "Classical Walpurgis Night" demonstrates it as a conscious principle of organic life itself. At this point in the drama such possibilities cannot be anticipated, above all since Mephistopheles has no comprehension of this and does not himself participate at all in the instances mentioned. The reader must clarify for himself the meaning of the "moment" for *Faust* as a whole through a critical reading of the drama in its entirety.

Mephistopheles' Monologue (lines 1851–67). This monologue by Mephistopheles, addressed to Faust in his absence while wearing the academic robes of Faust, is crucial for determining the relationship between the two—at least from Mephistopheles' point of view and at this stage in the composition of *Faust*. The speech is also important because it was regarded so seriously by the early philosophical critics of the *Fragment*. Both Schelling (in the brief discussion of *Faust* from his *Philosophy of Art*) and Hegel (in the section on "Desire and Necessity" in *The Phenomenology of Mind*, 1807) quote from this speech. Faust will fall victim to Mephistopheles, so he believes, because he has abandoned "intelligence and science"—following Mephistopheles' bidding (lines 1835–41) and is now subject to the deceptions and illusions of the "liar-in-chief" (literally, "spirit of lies," *Lügengeist*). The description of Faust's infinite stiving (lines 1856–59) essentially corresponds with Faust's nature as we have seen it thus far. Mephistopheles' motive for dragging him through the domain of sensual experience, as expressed in lines 1860–1865, is directly contrary to the terms of their wager in the text of 1800 (lines 1692–1706). Using a figurative allusion to Tantalus, who was tortured in Hell by food and drink close at hand which he could see and smell but never enjoy, Mephistopheles reverses the torture and imagines Faust—"sticking, writhing, flagging"—yearning in vain for relief. Such relief is precisely the opposite of the goal which Faust establishes for their wager. Mephistopheles will win only if he enables Faust to achieve the beautiful moment of fulfillment. As this statement stands within the larger context of the second study scene, Mephistopheles can only be regarded as misunderstanding the wager. The most likely explanation, however, is that Mephistopheles here speaks from a perspective far closer to the traditional pact from the Faust legend, the perspective of the *Fragment* of 1790, which was still a long way from the final stage of composition of *Part I*.

Mephistopheles on the "Iota" (line 2000). The phrase "no jot or tittle" (*kein Jota* in the German) alludes to Matthew 5:18, "For verily I say unto you, Till heaven and earth pass, one jot or one tittle shall in no wise pass from the law, till all be fulfilled" (King James Version). The response by Mephistopheles to the student's claim that every word must stand for a concept is an ironic defense of the autonomy of words as words. Mention of the "jot" (*iota*, the Greek letter *i*) probably recalls—ironically in the mouth of the devil!—the conflict between the Arians and the Athanasians at the Council of Nicaea (325 A.D.) concerning the relation of Father and Son in the Trinity. The issue turned on the distinction between two Greek words, identical except for the iota: *homoousios*, "of the same nature" (argued by the Athanasians), and *homoiousios*, "of similar nature" (argued by the Arians). The Athanasians prevailed and the resulting creed, generally adopted by both the Greek and Roman churches, dropped the iota, thus asserting the identity of Father and Son. This goes directly contrary to Mephistopheles' claim, suggesting that from the ironic perspective of the author, whose views on language would have supported Faust's concern to go beyond word to deed, the student is right here about words and concepts. The irony is heightened, of course, by the fact that the student is not able to defend himself, does not know who Mephistopheles is, and probably does not understand what he is saying anyway.

"Auerbach's Tavern in Leipzig" (lines 2073–2336). The visit to Auerbach's Tavern, a well-known tavern in the city of Leipzig frequented by students of the university, offers relatively little problem for interpretation. The significance of the visit for Faust is found primarily in his disdain of such drinking and debauch. He speaks only two short lines in the entire scene (lines 2183 and 2296), spending the rest of the visit apart as a detached, ultimately a bored, observer. Mephistopheles' justification for the visit (lines 2158 ff.), in a speech added to the version for publication in the *Fragment* of 1790, seems indifferent and unpersuasive, as if it were an afterthought by Goethe. The corresponding speech in the *Urfaust* is: "Now watch how they carry on here! If you enjoy it, I can provide this kind of society every night." Neither the carousal nor the hocus-pocus functions in any serious way for Goethe's drama. The effectiveness of the scene on the stage, which more than a century of theater productions can attest to, derives from the satirical and slapstick elements, in particular from the songs, somewhat less from the magic tricks played on the drinkers by Mephistopheles.

Particularly important here is the manner in which Goethe concedes something to the authority of the popular Faust legend. In this regard "Auerbach's Tavern" provides an appropriate geographical focus, the only place in *Faust, Part I* which is specifically located in reference to actuality. This locale also joins together the widely separate eras of the historical Faustus and the author Goethe through the medium of popular art and legend. According to the chapbooks, Faust visited Auerbach's Tavern when he was in Leipzig in 1526; Goethe then frequented the same place in the 1760s, as long as his friend Behrisch, who apparently was an enthusiastic participant in such drinking, lived at the inn there. Two rather primitive frescos were painted on the walls of the tavern about a century after the supposed visit of the historical Faustus (i.e., ca. 1625) and both were still there in Goethe's day: one showed Faust at a table with a group of students drinking and playing music; the other depicted Faust riding out the door on a wine cask, to the amazement of his drinking partners (lines 2229 ff.). Goethe intentionally incorporated both these incidents into his scene, thus using the place in accord with the artistic representations of the popular tradition associated with it. Yet several important changes are also introduced. Mephistopheles does not figure in the paintings or in the tradition; Faust himself is both the drinker and the magician. In the *Urfaust* Goethe acknowledges this by having Faust himself perform the tricks of magic at the end of the scene (tricks which also derive from the popular legend); in the revised version published in 1790 it is Mephistopheles who performs both Faustian roles, playing the tricks of the wine and the noses as well as singing the song of the flea (which he already sang in the first version). The continuity of tradition is thus preserved, but a radical transformation in the nature and role of Faust himself is implicitly acknowledged. The devil has to be his substitute in performing magic tricks--something which also holds true later in *Part II* in the Court of the Emperor, where Mephistopheles assumes the guise of court jester (see Act I).

"Witch's Kitchen" (lines 2337–2604). Goethe must have recognized from the earliest stages of work on his *Faust* a radical discrepancy in the roles his character plays in the two sections of the drama that ultimately became *Part I.* The entire sequence of scenes—including those written much later, around 1800—from the first monologue through "Auerbach's Tavern" emphasize the intellectual and existential disillusionment of an aging academic, a scholar who is fed up with learning and science, requiring a quality of sterile frustration in a figure generally assumed (see lines 2055 ff., as also "Witch's Kitchen," lines 2341–42) to be about fifty years old. The encounter with Gretchen, however, which fills the latter half of *Part I*, demands that Faust play the role of seducer and libertine, a kind of Don Juan who must be physically attractive to a very young girl. Magical rejuvenation through the devil's powers —a device not otherwise contained in the popular Faust legend at all—must have been planned by Goethe even at the stage of writing the *Urfaust.* The only dramatic function of the scene is thus the drinking of the magical brew by Faust, prepared by the Witch and her simian assistants in the bubbling pot, presumably at the command of Mephistopheles (who here serves as the traditional devil of medieval superstition, even to the point where the Witch calls him Satan, line 2504).

When Goethe came to compose this scene, however, the demands it placed upon him were totally alien to his poetic inclinations. He wrote it during the early spring of 1788, under pressure of a publisher's deadline for his collected works, to be included in Volume 7 as part of *Faust, ein Fragment.* Goethe was in Rome, nearing the end of his Italian journey, steeped in Classical art and culture to a degree unequalled in his subsequent career. He wrote the scene, according to his remarks to Eckermann over forty years later (April 10, 1829), in the gardens of the Villa Borghese, where the atmosphere of primitive, Nordic witchcraft demanded by the scene must have seemed the true antipode of the eternal city and the Italian spring. Such a radical contradiction of mood is appropriately demonstrated in Faust's own state of mind, perhaps as a reflection of Goethe's situation while writing the scene: he is appalled and disgusted by the Witch, her kitchen and companions, and her brew, to the point (lines 2337–46) where he almost refuses to submit to Mephistopheles' youth cure. Here also, perhaps in accord with Mephistopheles' own tactics of such rejuvenation, Faust confronts the magic mirror with its image of a woman, presumably displayed as Classical beauty in the style of paintings of the nude Venus by such Italians as Giorgione or Titian (the former was known to Goethe from the gallery in Dresden; the latter—which Goethe later often praised—is in the Uffizi Gallery, Florence). In a paradox, which must have been intentional, Goethe's Faust is thus rejuvenated in spirit through the unexpected contemplation of the ideal of Classical beauty, which solicits an appropriate erotic response in him, before he is rejuvenated magically in body by drinking the witch's brew.

A further difficulty which this scene has caused to many generations of critics pertains to the magical and incantatory verses of the Witch and her Marmosets (especially lines 1394–2428, 2450–60, 2540–52). Efforts have been made again and again to extract some secret symbol system from these hocus-pocus jingles with their accompanying objects—the glass sphere (line 2402), the sieve (line 2416), the scepter-duster (line 2427) and crown (line 2450), and the Witch's rite of bell, book, and candle, complete with magic circle. By a consensus of modern readers this is all mere nonsense, with no further authority than popular superstition. The language begins at the level of parody, derived from children's jingles, and degenerates to random number games (in the Witch's arithmetic chant, das *Hexen-Einmaleins,* line 2552). Much of the language serves no greater function than its sound suggests, as in the well-known verses of incantation by the witches in *Macbeth,* IV.i: "Double, double, toil and trouble;/Fire burn, and cauldron bubble." Indeed, the cauldron scene in Shakespeare's play was probably very much in Goethe's mind when he wrote "Witch's Kitchen," providing him with his most vivid dramatic source (in addition to popular pictorial examples of such witches which he may have known). Goethe is also concerned here with the theme of bestiality, perhaps in an intentional contrast with "Auerbach's Tavern," especially through the use of the Marmosets and their language. Just as the drinkers at the tavern became more and more bestial in their debauching, so here the animals who behave like human beings—particularly in their ability to speak—demonstrate a perversion of pretense. This is apparent especially in the lines of the animals about their use of language and the question of whether what they say has any meaning: "We rhyme and pun it;/We hark and view;/ . . . /If haply point/Is joined to point/With luck it's meaning!" (lines 2454–55 and 2458 ff.).

They acknowledge that their use of language, and especially the form of verse and rhyme, is purely bestial and has meaning only by chance, not by intention. In this regard the Marmosets bear out the earlier assertion by Mephistopheles to the Student (lines 1994 ff.) that words need not be accompanied by concepts to which they correspond. Here we have an extreme instance—which perhaps goes beyond the limits which even Mephistopheles envisioned—where words are used purely for the sound, totally devoid of sense. From such a perspective, then, the magical rite which is imposed on Faust by the Witch at the end of the scene assumes dubious implications. With its use of music, book, torches, and brew it is clearly a parody of a religious act, in particular of the Christian mass—suggesting that in the perspective of Part I the witch's brew should set off both the poison which Faust was prevented from drinking by the Easter Chorus and the Eucharist itself, which that chorus presumably celebrated to commemorate the resurrection. Goethe seems to be working against himself on purpose. The magic potion which rejuvenates Faust, according to a folk belief with which the poet was not much in sympathy, is placed in association with other symbolic, spiritual acts in the drama which have far greater significance and authority than this event. Apart from the vision of the feminine in the magic mirror, which establishes the central theme of woman as the embodiment of ideal beauty and the erotic as a legitimate aspect of Faust's essential striving, this scene may be taken as an arbitrary theatrical device, providing a pervasive sense of comic self-parody.

"Highway" (after "Witch's Kitchen"). In the text of the *Urfaust,* copied from Goethe's manuscripts by Luise von Göchhausen, a short scene occurs between "Auerbach's Tavern" and the opening of the Gretchen sequence ("Witch's Kitchen," of course, had not yet been written). This scene, which Goethe later cut from the text of the *Fragment,* is the only portion of the original Faust preserved in a manuscript in Goethe's handwriting. The scene deserves consideration, especially insofar as it offsets and balances the later short scene from the *Urfaust,* which Goethe did include in *Part I,* "Night. Open Field" (lines 4399–4404). The text is as follows:

HIGHWAY

A wayside cross, on the hill at right an old castle, in the distance a little peasant hut.

FAUST. What's this, Mephisto, are you pressed?
　　Why drop your eyes before the shrine?
MEPHISTOPHELES. I don't deny that I am prejudiced,
　　But I detest it—just a quirk of mine.

The Gretchen Tragedy (lines 2605–3834). The sequence of scenes concerned with Faust's seduction of Gretchen, composed as part of the *Urfaust* probably in early 1775, constitutes the latter half of *Part I.* This sequence has always fascinated readers of *Faust.* The impact of the so-called Gretchen tragedy on the popular imagination, as measured by subsequent imitations (such as the operas of Berlioz, Boito, or Gounod), has established Faust's role as libertine alongside the tradition of his pact with the devil in equal importance. Here, more even than in the encounter with the Earth Spirit, the author of the *Urfaust* departed radically from any sources in the popular legend. All attempts to locate an analogue to Gretchen in the Faust chapbooks have been futile. In two important ways Goethe introduced a perspective to his drama which was entirely removed from the antiquarian and hocus-pocus qualities of the traditional Faust and which addressed central concerns of later eighteenth-century thought and sensibility. First, the theme of seduction, predominant in domestic, middle-class drama and a preoccupation of the age—from Casanova's *Memoirs* to Beaumarchais's *Marriage of Figaro,* from Laclos's *Liaisons dangereuses* to Mozart's *Don Giovanni*—was united with the essential dynamic power of will in Faust, his striving for infinite knowledge and experience. The philosopher Kierkegaard recognized this when he chose the Gretchen episode alongside *Don Giovanni* as his central examples for the aesthetics of the erotic in *Either/Or* (1843). Second, a dimension of social realism was introduced to *Faust* which carried profound legal and moral implications for Goethe's own time. The theme of infanticide, often involving the seduction of innocent girls who subsequently fell victim to the intolerance of eighteenth-century middle-class society, usually leading to their execution, while the seducer escaped without penalty, attracted many writers, especially among the German *Sturm und Drang,* who all sought to denounce a barbarous injustice. It has been persuasively argued that Goethe himself may have conceived the Gretchen-tragedy in direct response to the execution for infanticide in Frankfurt on January 14, 1772, of Susanna Margarethe Brandt ("Gretchen" is a diminutive for the name "Margarete," which name she is also called in several of Goethe's scenes). Such external evidence also lends support to the impression any reader will receive from the Gretchen tragedy that she, not Faust, is the central figure of the sequence, that it is her tragedy, and that he functions above all as the instrument of her destruction, however authentic his erotic motives may be.

Within the larger context of the drama, however, especially in the later published versions (the *Fragment* of 1790 contained the entire sequence through Gretchen's collapse at the end of the cathedral scene; the conclusion, with a revision of the dungeon scene from its initial prose to verse, was added in *Part I*), the Gretchen tragedy came to assume a significance for Faust and his ultimate salvation which went far beyond the themes of libertinism and infanticide. Gretchen, in her authentic love for Faust, emerges as the most powerful embodiment of the Feminine, that principle which defines the highest object of Faustian desire and ultimately serves—through a recollection of Beatrice's intercession on behalf of Dante in the *Divine Comedy*—as the instrument of Faust's salvation. The essential triangular relationship of the figures in this sequence—seemingly a parody of an eighteenth-century literary cliché: Faust as the agent of erotic desire, Gretchen as the appropriate object of seduction, and Mephistopheles as the instrument of fulfillment or the "go-between"—establishes an archetypal or mythical pattern which is central to the entire drama. In one sense this constitutes the transformation of a traditional demonic seduction (later used, for instance, by Thomas Mann in his novel *Doctor Faustus*, and hinted at by Goethe later in the "Walpurgis Night," when Faust dances with the youthful, naked witch), where sexual enticement through a seemingly beautiful girl, who subsequently proves to be a monster in disguise, serves the devil as the means of trapping the wayward sinner (see in this regard lines 3324–25 in the scene "Forest and Cave"). At a deeper level, however, this pattern establishes a dramatic reenactment of the fall of man, though also with a crucial difference. Contrary to the Biblical account and in opposition to Milton's dramatization of it in *Paradise Lost*, Eve becomes the innocent victim of Adam's erotic desire, not the mediator of Satan in eating the forbidden fruit. Yet Mephistopheles is true to his traditional role as the tempter, however complicated by literary traditions as a pandar or conniving servant (recall Sganarelle and Leporello in the *Don Juan* legend), and his presence legitimizes the mythical analogue to the fall, which might otherwise seem far-fetched. Goethe later acknowledged such implications retrospectively, at the end of the scene "Dungeon" when the voice from above announces that Gretchen is saved (line 4611), and in the reappearance of Gretchen as the "shining band of mist" (line 10055), which Faust observes ascending heavenwards at the outset of Act IV, and lastly as the Penitent Spirit (*Una Poenitentium*, lines 12069–75) in the final scene of the drama, where she intercedes with a prayer to the *Mater Gloriosa* on behalf of Faust's salvation, echoing Gretchen's earlier prayer to the Madonna in "By the City Wall" (lines 3587 ff.).

Most important for the dramatic technique of the Gretchen episode is the influence of Shakespeare, apparent throughout, both in the scenic technique and in the psychology of character. Here Goethe writes as the representative dramatist of the *Sturm und Drang*, an era which was steeped in Shakespeare and which in this instance achieved an imitation of the master which is worthy of him. Apart from various specific borrowings throughout the sequence of scenes (mentioned in the footnotes), Goethe also adapts to his purpose the radically anti-Classical (or anti-Neo-Classical) technique of brief lyric and emotional scenes, which was felt at that time to be eminently Shakespearian. Far more important is the dialectical contrast of dramatic moments which Goethe achieves through this sequence, establishing a complex and varied mood for the Gretchen tragedy which accompanies and itself elicits the appropriate response to its advance from innocence to surrender and to despair and, finally, to madness and destruction. Also Shakespearian, however eighteenth-century in its guise, is the psychology of the heroine, who clearly blends various positive attributes of Shakespeare's heroines with great force and attraction, from Juliet and Ophelia to Desdemona and Imogen, with less apparent analogues to numerous others (such as Lady Anne in *Richard III* or Isabella in *Measure for Measure*). What Goethe establishes above all through an intensive, lyrical focus on his heroine is a direct revelation of her emotional state of mind, externalized often with great dramatic power in scenes which otherwise would seem to be no more than brief songs or monologues (as in "Gretchen's Chamber" with the song at the spinning wheel or in "By the City Wall" with the prayer to the Virgin). Through this mode of drama from within the entire sequence assumes an intensity and an authority of mood which ultimately, in the dungeon scene, goes beyond the limits even of Shakespeare and perhaps to the limits of what is tolerable for any theater audience.

"Forest and Cave" (lines 3217–3373). The concluding section of this scene (lines 3342–69) was already contained in the *Urfaust* as the latter part of a scene immediately following "Cathedral," which began with what became the opening of the Valentine scene (lines 3620–59). The scene "Forest and Cave" as it now stands was composed in Rome early in 1788, as indicated in part by the use of blank verse for Faust's monologue, introduced to German drama (e.g., in Goethe's *Iphigenie* and *Tasso*) at that time from the Shakespearian model. In the *Fragment* of 1790 the scene was located later in the Gretchen sequence, just following "At the Well." This scene constitutes the center of the Gretchen tragedy, its focal point and high point within the thematic concerns of the Faust drama as a whole. Indicative of this is the extent to which the reflective self-analysis by the character Faust in his monologue reestablishes an awareness of his essential condition, his Faustian nature, totally removed from the specific context of his involvement with Gretchen. Goethe clearly intends that the monologue connect thematically the separate sequence of scenes in the Gretchen episode with the situation of Faust in the opening monologue (hence his

direct address here to the Earth Spirit). Such thematic connections were subsequently strengthened when the scenes for the "great lacuna" were composed around 1800. Much of what is stated there, especially in the *logos* scene, when Faust returns to his study after the Easter Walk (lines 1178 ff.), and in the pact scene, especially just following the wager with Mephistopheles (lines 1742–1867, part of which was already contained in the *Fragment*), bears directly on what Faust here asserts in "Forest and Cave."

Critics have been bothered by the question of whether the Earth Spirit is indeed responsible in any way for what Faust has achieved and received. One cannot forget that the Spirit turned its countenance toward Faust in the fire only to overwhelm and reject him. One hypothesis has held that Goethe intended at this stage of composition (the "Prologue in Heaven" had not yet been conceived) to make the Earth Spirit responsible for the appearance of Mephistopheles, as Faust here assumes (and also in lines 3243 ff.). Within the perspective of *Part I*, however, it makes more sense to argue that Faust is merely in error (once again), since he can have no knowledge of the "Prologue in Heaven" anyway or even of how Mephistopheles actually was motivated to appear to him in the guise of the poodle. Such ironic discrepancy between the perspective of Faust the character and the drama *Faust* as a whole is coming to be recognized as an essential aspect of Goethe's work.

Faust's Credo (lines 3431–58). This speech is often referred to as Faust's credo. Goethe again employs a free rhythmic verse form which also quickly abandons rhyme. In this way, recalling the manner of the Earth Spirit in his self-presentation (lines 501–9), the language imitates and to a degree becomes identical with the emotions which it expresses. This is all the more striking because the speech is directly concerned with the problematic status of language in naming what is ineffable. Goethe here addresses the central thematic concern in *Faust* with the relation between word as sign and that which it signifies, specifically the relation between rhetoric and spirit, as represented in the *Urfaust* in the conversations between Faust and Wagner (lines 530–57) and between Mephistopheles and the Student, especially where theology is discussed (lines 1983–2000). The theme is represented at a later stage of composition above all in the *logos* scene (lines 1224–37). Despite the emphasis placed throughout on a personal experience of the divine, an emotional intuition of the God within, the concluding lines—where the famous tag "feeling is all" occurs—consciously call to mind a venerable tradition of theological debate concerning the validity of names for God. It may also be inherent in the ironic technique of such a verbal performance concerning the artifice of words that Faust is equally caught up in his own rhetoric, which constitutes after all yet another strategy of seduction.

The Valentine Scene (lines 3620–3775). The opening section of this scene (lines 3620–59, excluding 3646–49) is contained in the *Urfaust*, located immediately following (rather than before) the scene "Cathedral." It was omitted entirely from the *Fragment* of 1790. The expanded version of *Part I* was presumably composed around 1800, though completed only at the end of March, 1806, shortly before the manuscript was sent to the publisher. The final manuscript of the entire scene is preserved in Goethe's own hand. In addition to the death of Gretchen's brother Valentine and his public denunciation of her before he dies, this scene provides the motive for Faust's flight from the city to avoid arrest for the killing (lines 3712 ff.). Goethe has Mephistopheles mention explicitly (lines 3660 ff.) that it is the evening two nights before the Walpurgis Night, thus anticipating his visit there with Faust (which he presumably intends even before Valentine is killed). This scene brings Faust in his role of libertine, seducer, and lover of Gretchen into close proximity with the Don Juan legend. Whether or not Goethe had Mozart's opera *Don Giovanni* (1787) in mind when he composed the final version of this scene, consideration may be made, on the one hand, of the nighttime duel in the opening scene between Don Giovanni and the Commendatore, father of Donna Anna, whom Don Giovanni has just attempted to seduce, and, on the other, the Canzonetta which Don Giovanni, disguised as Leporello, sings beneath the balcony of Donna Elvira in Act II, accompanying himself on a guitar, as he attempts to seduce Donna Elvira's servant girl. It is interesting to note that the role of Don Juan in both its aspects is assumed more by Mephistopheles than by Faust, first when he sings the song beneath Gretchen's window (lines 3682–97), then when he manipulates the sword that kills Valentine (lines 3704–11).

"Walpurgis Night" (lines 3835–4222). No other scene in Goethe's *Faust* places such difficult demands on the reader for understanding its place and significance in the drama. The essential meaning which Goethe wished to convey resides in the "Walpurgis Night" revels themselves, quite apart from any necessary association with Faust and his pact with Mephistopheles. Indeed, apart from a few obscure eighteenth-century sources (such as the poem "Walpurgisnight" of 1756 by the poet Johann Friedrich Löwen, 1729–71, which Goethe knew), there was no evidence in the Faust tradition for associating him with the legends of the May Day witches' Sabbath. At the time when Goethe returned to work on his *Faust* in 1797, however, this scene above all attracted his attention, and it may have been the first section which he attempted, though without initial success, to add to the drama. Goethe associated *Faust* with the murky spirit world of Nordic, Germanic legend, as represented also by several of the ballads which he had been composing for Schiller's *Musenalmanach*. The

"Walpurgis Night" therefore provides a logical extension of the hocus-pocus and murky superstition established in "Witch's Kitchen" (where the later scene is also mentioned; see lines 2589–90, also 2113–14). By temper and mood the poet in the 1790s strongly preferred Classical art, which he has assimilated in Italy, in opposition to the dark, supernatural world of Nordic witches and demons.

A clear distinction can be made between the initial purpose of the "Walpurgis Night," as derived from Goethe's various literary sources and outlined in his first drafts for the scene, and the ultimate function of the final text in the Faust drama as we have it. This distinction is important for understanding both the "Walpurgis Night" and Goethe's evolving view of the drama during the years when *Part I* was being prepared for publication (1797–1806). The sources used have been traced by scholars from several books borrowed from the Ducal library in Weimar at the time when work on the scene was in progress, especially 1799–1801. For the most part these consist of obscure and pseudo-scientific compendia of medieval folklore from the seventeenth century. These accounts offer a fantastic picture of medieval witches' sabbaths, colored by a mixture of popular superstition and moralistic outrage. The annual revels involved a procession of witches which ascended in the darkness to the summit of the Brocken, where orgiastic revels were held in celebration of Satan, including blatant sexual intercourse and the act of obeisance to Satan by kissing the anus of a goat (traditionally associated with the cult of Satan). That Goethe initially planned to follow the accounts of such satanic debauchery—even to the inclusion of Satan himself, who figures nowhere else in *Faust!*—is apparent from the manuscript draft of the earliest stage of composition on the scene, dating from about 1798–99.

What led Goethe to change his mind about the "Walpurgis Night" and to curtail so drastically the scene he had planned for *Part I*? Critics have tended to read Goethe's *Faust*, especially *Part I*, largely from the perspective of the central character and the problem of his pact with Mephistopheles. The drama has been regarded, in other words, essentially as a tragedy of character, even if that character assumes a representative stance for mankind in general. Recent discussions, however, especially those which have taken *Part II* adequately into account, have come to recognize that Goethe's interest in *Faust* ultimately extended far beyond any immediate concern with character. That this is so in the Carnival of Act I, in the "Classical Walpurgis Night," and in the *Helena* act of *Part II* need hardly be defended. It may also be true of *Part I*, at least tentatively in those scenes which expand the scope of the drama beyond the specifically human realm into a potentially cosmic domain, e.g., the "Prologue in Heaven" and the "Walpurgis Night," especially the "Dream" (see notes on these scenes). Goethe's view of the witches' Sabbath on the Brocken gradually shifted away from the orgiastic revels at the summit, as these were conceived in response to the popular tradition, toward a kind of festival on May Day night which has much more positive and serious implications for the drama of *Faust* as a whole. For this view of the rites of May—just as pagan in origin as the cult of Satan and perhaps originally identical with it—Goethe's chief source for the "Walpurgis Night's Dream" eminently served his purpose: the fairy-folk of Shakespeare's *Midsummer Night's Dream*. (This shift of emphasis is discussed further in the note to the "Dream" which follows.)

"Walpurgis Night's Dream" (lines 4223–4398). Critics have been embarrassed by the apparent lack of direct relevance to the Faust story demonstrated by this "Intermezzo." Even its function as an intermezzo, or *entr'acte*, is unclear, due primarily to Goethe's decision not to conclude the "Walpurgis Night," as first planned, with a climactic scene after the "Dream" at the summit of the Blocksberg in the presence of Satan. The entire dream sequence had been intended to serve as a true interlude both in the Walpurgis Night generally and in the activities of Faust and Mephistopheles as they ascend the mountain. Instead, as the text now stands, the Intermezzo brings the "Walpurgis Night" to a close, thus assuming perforce the role of a surrogate climax, in place of the scene with Satan. It consists of a sequence of single speeches, apparently presented as a kind of pageant before Oberon and Titania, the King and Queen of the fairies (borrowed from Shakespeare's *Midsummer Night's Dream*, which Goethe knew in the original and which had just been translated into German by August Wilhelm Schlegel; with some influence perhaps from several late-eighteenth-century operatic versions of Shakespeare's story, which are of minor importance). The speakers in the interlude include a number of figures who represent as objects of satire in schematic, allegorical fashion various modes and schools of thought and writing in Goethe's own day. Some of these figures are so obscure that even Goethe's own audience would not have recognized them. What, then, does such a piece have to do with *Faust*?

Above all one must consider how the source from Shakespeare has been adapted here and how the "Dream" itself is incorporated into the "Walpurgis Night." A group of amateurs (*dilettantes* in the original, lines 4217–18) perform a story which one of them has written. The amateurs are meant to resemble the group of tradesmen in *A Midsummer Night's Dream*, including Peter Quince and Bottom, who in the final scene present their dramatic version of Pyramus and Thisbe before Duke Theseus and his bride Hippolyta. Goethe thus imposes on the "Intermezzo" an intentional irony of ineptitude, borrowed from his source, though he does not indulge in the same kind of Shakespearian slapstick. By focusing instead on the themes of poetry and letters, then of philosophy and politics, Goethe exposes, through the inadequacy of what is said, characteristic failings of human culture and society, specifically in later eighteenth-century Germany. For whom and for what motive, however, is this exposé presented? In Shakespeare's play the patrons and audience of the mechanicals' entertainment are the rulers of the city and their court, human beings who are celebrating a threefold marriage. The spirits of the wood, who figure so centrally in the play, have nothing to do with this slapstick performance and remain in their natural domain until the epilogue, when Puck, along with Oberon and Titania with their fairy train, enter the palace to bring blessings of fertility to the marriages being consummated. In Goethe's "Intermezzo" the fairy King and Queen are themselves the recipients of such an entertainment, presented to them as part of the celebrations for their golden wedding anniversary. At the same time, however, these fairies (apparently) are themselves a play within a play on the fairy stage as the "Walpurgis Night's Dream." The "Dream" thus consists of a play within a play, or—to be more precise with reference to readers of Goethe's *Faust*—it involves a play within a play within a play. At the outer level is the witches' Sabbath of the "Walpurgis Night"; at the center is the satirical exposé of human folly and failure; and in between is the golden wedding festival of Oberon and Titania.

The "Intermezzo" also shares another aspect of Shakespeare's play. The spirits of *A Midsummer Night's Dream* enjoy a privileged status as natural powers, which may be playful—as demonstrated by Puck, or Robin Goodfellow (who also appears in Goethe's "Dream," essentially in the same role)—but which may also be dangerous to the human community—especially when there is dissension or conflict among them, as there is in the play between Oberon and Titania. Critics have also perceived an exalted tradition behind these fairy monarchs, and we may assume that Goethe was at least intuitively aware of this tradition. Oberon is a variant of the Lord of the May Day rites, a powerful demonic force which was often identified—especially in the context of Christian polemics against such pagan survivals—with Satan himself. As such Oberon would also be the Lord of the "Walpurgis Night." Titania, on the other hand, is a kind of nature goddess, the embodiment of that power of growth and fertility associated with the green world of woods and fields and with the summer as a season of warmth and recreation. In Shakespeare's play strife between these two powers threatens to divide and even destroy the natural world. Their reunion is crucial to the successful conclusion of the comic plot. Goethe presents the "Walpurgis Night's Dream" as an ironic commemoration of the resolution of that strife at the end of *A Midsummer Night's Dream*, but he purposefully confuses the resolution with the human marriages celebrated in Shakespeare's comedy. The golden wedding anniversary of Oberon and Titania marks the resolution, so they themselves imply (lines 4243–50), of fifty years of domestic squabbling in the realm of natural spirits which they rule. The present festival achieves a universal harmony and peace, a sense of fulfillment and bliss which is clearly at odds with both the amateur quality of the theatrical show and the sense of excess and debauch in the witches' Sabbath on the Brocken. Indicative of this resolution in the realm of natural spirits is the appearance of Ariel alongside Puck, a spirit of the air—derived by Goethe from Shakespeare's *Tempest* and subsequently employed in the opening scene of *Faust, Part II*—who seems to embody that ministry of harmonious interaction which the fairy festival is meant to signify. In this regard the "Intermezzo" has nothing in common with either the human world of Faust or the demonic domain of Mephistopheles; yet it reflects ironically on both, if only through contrast.

Completely by surprise Goethe thus affirms an ultimate positive and creative order to the natural world in the midst of apparent categorical denials of such order, both in the setting of the Gretchen story and in the setting of the "Walpurgis Night." Yet the poet must also have had in mind that the May Day rite from Shakespeare, where all strife between Oberon and Titania is resolved, is essentially the same seasonal festival as the Walpurgis Night itself (the night of April 30 to May 1) and that the essential meaning of this festival is regeneration, renewal of life and spirit, indeed salvation, in the sense that the voice from above will affirm it for Gretchen at the end of *Part I* (line 4611), and the elfin chorus directed by Ariel will provide it for Faust at the outset of *Part II*. A corresponding contrast between failure and creativity may also be perceived within the text of the "Walpurgis Night's Dream." The festival of golden harmony among the spirits transforms, at least in part, and offsets the satirical bungling of the amateur performers and the objects of their satire, through a reflection—albeit at a distance and with a sense of contrast—of the authentic art and poetry which is appropriate to the realm of the spirit. This is associated with nature and in particular with Classical myth and culture. Ariel especially brings the powers of heavenly spirits into the "Dream" and later leads everyone to the palace of Oberon on the hill of roses (lines 4393–94).

Finally, all distinctions in the "Dream" between internal and external perspective, between actors and audience may dissolve into the confusion of our own sense of it from reading the sequence of speeches. This confusion is due in large measure to the uniformity and willful inadequacy of the form itself, as a sequence of stanzas in doggerel ballad style. Goethe has imposed on his piece the illusion of a linear progression of cumbersome and isolated utterances, as if it were a ceremonial procession not quite under control or a narrative structure consisting of unrelated units. In contrast to the form, however, the entire complex establishes multiple layers of ironic self-reflection which constantly shift and undercut all sense of dramatic illusion. What Goethe here achieves is a play within a play within a play which is totally devoid of coherent plot and which purposefully juxtaposes various voices at different levels of perspective. It may even be argued that the language of the "Dream" itself is intentionally perverse. Not only are the sparate statements inadequate as expressions of the meaning, but the nature of the "Dream" resists any correlation between statement and meaning, except in terms of the irony of theatrical performance. And we also are caught up in that irony, since we, like Faust, witness that performance and come to recognize that the object of satire is our world of human society. The entire "Dream" thus functions as a sequence of self-reflecting mirrors which may finally project only the image of the spectator back upon himself. Perhaps this is a characteristic of spirit shows and dreams anyway. We emerge with a sense of radical ambivalence, where the separate realms of spirit and human kind are intentionally confused, as also are distinctions between good and evil, nature and the demonic, poetry and dilettantisms. Only through such ironic confusion can the "Dream" finally serve as an adequate substitute for the climax of the "Walpurgis Night" which Goethe had planned to write. The "Dream" provides an ironic alternative to the scene of Satan on the Brocken; but it also provides equally—if only in miniature—an ironic analogue to the *Faust*-drama itself, with regard to both the general condition of Faust's relation to Mephistopheles and the particular situation at this point in the drama concerning Faust's love for Gretchen, which now approaches catastrophe and tragic collapse.

"Dungeon" (lines 4405–4612). In the *Urfaust* this scene is in prose. The omission of it (along with the two preceding) from the *Fragment* may indicate that Goethe already planned at that time to recast it in verse. The changes consist of minor additions and subtle rhythmic shifts in the language which in no way diminish the dramatic power of this remarkable scene and which greatly enhance the emotional control in a complex interaction of opposing moods between Faust and Gretchen that achieves an approximation to musical form. The setting of the scene, which includes a precise visual sense of stage representation, establishes a sense of frame between the outer corridor with the door into Gretchen's cell and the narrow, confining cell itself. The dark enclosed space, which Faust must enter with the keys and lamp secured by Mephistopheles, offsets corresponding scenes earlier in the Gretchen episode, though with opposite implications; the garden pavilion in which the lovers exchange vows of love and the bedroom of Gretchen which Faust entered with Mephistopheles. A thematic parallel with Faust's own Gothic study provides an ironic counterpart as a prison. Gretchen's state of mind, a derangement which indicates withdrawal into herself, complements the enclosure of the cell. Goethe used Shakespearian models here for the madness of the girl, in particular that of Ophelia in *Hamlet*, and also—as an analogue for the tragic encounter between Faust and Gretchen, despite differences in attitude and mood—Desdemona in her bedroom awaiting the arrival of her husband in the final scene of *Othello*. In the radical discontinuity of emotion and apprehension, however, where Faust pleads in increasing desperation for Gretchen to leave with him and she distorts his purpose according to her private vision, no parallel could be found short of the scene on the heath in *King Lear* between the mad King and the blind Gloucester (IV.vi).

"Charming Landscape" (lines 4613–4727). The short scene which begins *Part II* provides a programmatic demonstration of the poetic and symbolic scope that the subsequent five acts will achieve. Here Goethe expresses again, in the twofold perspective of Ariel with his elfin chorus and Faust in his monologue, the central insight of the drama as a whole concerning human life and its relation to the processes of nature. "Charming Landscape" thus assumes a degree of poetic autonomy which frees it from all obligations to dramatic continuity. Efforts by critics to explain how Faust came to this mountain meadow, where he has left Mephistopheles and why, and especially how this sleep and reawakening can be justified in the light of Gretchen's death and Faust's apparent moral guilt—all efforts to deal with these questions are inappropriate, especially since the scene itself takes no cognizance of them. Nor is there any direct relation of this scene to the action which follows in the court of the Emperor; it stands apart and above the drama proper and reflects upon the entirety of it. The most important continuities for this scene extend to other programmatic moments of *Faust*, in particular the scene "Night," in *Part I*, which demonstrates a corresponding mental transformation in Faust at a different level of symbolic intensity. Also important for comparison are the other monologues of Faust, as in the sunset speech of "Outside the City Gate," the scene of "Forest and Cavern," or the opening speech of Act IV. What unites these other moments in the drama with this scene, and indeed unites the drama of *Faust* as a whole, is the fundamental attempt to comprehend human existence in its constantly varying temporal dimension and its constant dependence on the shifting forces of mind and will which motivate all action and thought, with reference to some ultimate and absolute power of spirit or divinity,

either within nature and accessible to human experience or above and beyond the natural world, transcending all knowledge and understanding.

By imitating alien poetic forms Goethe also accommodates here—as so often—the entire scope of the European tradition to his own drama. The spirit Ariel from Shakespeare's *Tempest*, who appeared earlier, is re-introduced. Here Goethe allows the airy spirit of Shakespeare's last play to come into his element, as anticipated in the stanza spoken by Ariel at the end of the "Intermezzo" (lines 4391 ff.). Particularly striking is the similarity of form and tone in the lyrics of Ariel in *The Tempest* and in "Charming Landscape." The dominant meter of Ariel's songs is trochaic, usually in a four-stress line with alternating rhyme or rhyming couplets. The famous song to Prince Ferdinand about his supposedly drowned father, "Full fathom five thy father lies . . ." (I.ii.397 ff.), is a single stanza of eight lines corresponding precisely to the form of both Ariel's opening song (lines 4613 ff.) and the night song of the elfin chorus which follows (lines 4634–65). Poetic effects in Shakespeare, especially phonetic patterns of internal rhyme, alliteration and repetition of consonants, to achieve an almost magical sense of chant or charm, are also imitated. Ariel in Shakespeare is the voice of air, the element to which he is freed by Prospero at the end of the play. In Goethe he speaks with the same voice, indeed represents the spiritual elements of nature so completely that in "Charming Landscape" Ariel affirms the ultimate triumph of his liberation: nature herself sings these songs in a poetic language which perfectly fuses sense and sound.

Goethe's second source is equally pervasive in its implications for the scene. Faust's monologue is written in *terza rima*, the meter of Dante's *Divine Comedy*, a complex form of interlocking rhyme in a continuous sequence of iambic pentameter, which Goethe here imitated for the first time. The persistent, forward motion of Dante's poetic meter (as Goethe stated in a letter to Chancellor Müller) demands a "broad and rich subject matter as the basis for it." *The Divine Comedy* in its massive architectonic structure employs *terza rima* to trace the journey of the visionary mind through the entire range of the cosmos—as asserted by the Stage Director of Goethe's "Prelude in the Theater": "From Heaven through the World to Hell" (line 242). Dante's journey in his poem is more or less continuous from the *Inferno* through the *Purgatorio* to the *Paradiso*. Faust's monologue imitates in miniature the progress of Dante's vision, as indicated by the advance of Faust's mind from the moment of awakening—Dante's poem also begins with an awakening—into the direct presence of divinity, represented by the rising sun. Particularly important as a contrast to Dante is the decisive interruption of continuous flow in the *terza rima*, a categorical breakdown of continuity, which Goethe introduced at two points in the monologue to emphasize the failure of Faust's effort to achieve a direct vision of the absolute. This is indicated by the dashes which occur in mid-line at line 4695: "Raise up your gaze!—" and at line 4702: "He clears the rim!—" Despite the limited scope of Faust's monologue in *terza rima*, the implications of this pattern of reversal and withdrawal —which goes directly against the basic function of the meter in Dante's poem—reflect the meaning of Goethe's *Faust* as a whole.

Faust's monologue begins at the moment of awakening consciousness. The arrival of dawn solicits reciprocal response in the mind of Faust, which manifests itself in renewed desire, indeed in (Faustian) striving toward the highest mode of existence (*Zum höchsten Dasein immerfort zu streben*, line 4685). The speech is divided into four separate verse paragraphs, which indicate four distinct stages of response in Faust. The first is an unfolding, an opening outwards of his desire, which advances into the morning and seeks to permeate the whole of animated nature, regarded as a garden, a "paradise" (line 4694), in which Faust lives and acts. The second indicates the heroic, ultimately tragic thrust of Faust's mind toward confrontation with divinity as it emerges in the light of the sun. Instantaneous blindness at the overwhelming brightness of the sun forces a reversal, which categorically transforms the basic stance of Faust's mind. His retreat manifests itself in reflective discourse: he thinks over what has happened and formulates his thoughts in a language which assumes an intentional generality. At the end of the second paragraph (line 4703) he spoke in an emphatic first-person singular, the first occurrence of the first person as pronominal subject in the monologue. In the third paragraph he shifts to first-person plural, as if he were speaking for all mankind, passing a judgment which assumes the authority not only of personal experience, but also of universal law. When he confronts the sun Faust retreats, not to escape exposure, like the spirits, but to achieve reflective thought, which—as Goethe knew from the entire history of German Idealist speculation—is the necessary condition of all knowledge and understanding. In this way also Faust exemplifies that quality of nobility in the mind which was mentioned at the conclusion of the elfin song, a nobility which "understands" (*versteht*, line 4665) and then "swiftly grasps." The final section of the monologue then introduces one of Goethe's most archetypal images of human experience. The life of man is symbolized in the waterfall as it plummets downwards, crashing from rock cliff to rock cliff. The force of the flowing water corresponds to that will or drive which constitutes Faustian striving. The clash of water and rock throws up a spray or mist of fine water drops into the air above the falls. This hovers and is suspended in a constant motion, imperceptible to the eye as either rise or fall, life's "most youthful veil" (*jugendlichst-*

em Schleier, line 4714; here translated as "most young of youthful hazes"), in which Faust's own life takes shelter. This mist catches the light of the sun as it shines through the air, each tiny droplet of water serving as a crystal through which the light is refracted, forming all together for the perceiving eye a rainbow in its varied color. The image of the rainbow provides a symbol for that aspect of human creativity which may be called art and poetry in the most general sense. This remains accessible to Faust after he has turned away from the light of the divine, providing a comprehensive and sufficient mirroring or "reflection" of human striving: *Der spiegelt ab das menschliche Bestreben* ("This mirrors all aspiring human action," line 4725). That striving which constitutes Faust's essential nature is thus sublimated into a reflection upon itself, indeed a representation of itself—as a work of art, a poem, a drama—in and through which the authentic light of the divine, which is beyond the limits of human vision in direct confrontation, is refracted into the many-hued spectrum of the rainbow. In this sense the final line of Faust's monologue indicates the highest possible achievement of human art and culture as Goethe understood it. That quality or aspect of life which is accessible to man—the same force which beat again in Faust's pulse at the outset of the monologue (lines 4679–80)—is its multi-colored refraction.

"Imperial Residence" (lines 4728–5064). In Goethe's outline of *Part II* from 1816 attention is given to details of situation and motivation, even to historical reference. Faust's visit was to take place at the Imperial Parliament at Augsburg; the Emperor was Maximilian I (reigned 1493 to 1519), who was indeed on the throne during the historical Faust's lifetime; and their meeting was to occur, as in the chapbooks, because the Emperor had heard of Faust's magical powers and wished to meet him—or, at least, according to the outline, so Mephistopheles reports to Faust. The plan for the visit, furthermore, was to have been prepared as part of the opening scene in *Part II,* when Mephistopheles joins Faust in "Charming Landscape" after his monologue in response to the rising sun. The initial encounter with the Emperor, finally, was to have occurred without the presence of Mephistopheles—again, following the outline—so that an exchange would take place reflecting Faust's own abilities to respond to the Emperor's questions. Mephistopheles, according to the outline, would only intervene after Faust had become flustered and confused. This interview was to conclude with the Emperor's request to witness a show of apparitions and spirits, among them presumably Helena. If this outline had been all that Goethe completed of *Part II,* how little we would know of the thematic significance which the entire encounter with the Imperial court later assumed. A reader of the outline may well be tempted to ask whether Goethe himself, even as late as 1816, had any idea what would ultimately emerge for the drama.

Particularly troubling for the reader of *Part II* must be the laconic dismissal of all particulars concerning the actual situation. No longer may we locate the Imperial Residence geographically or even identify the Emperor by name historically. Beyond this, however, the transition from the opening scene to the court has been dropped. Mephistopheles does not appear with Faust at all in the opening scene (as he had earlier done following the monologue in "Forest and Cave," lines 3251 ff., and as he later does also in the opening scene of Act IV, lines 10067 ff.), and—far more drastic a change—Faust himself is completely absent and goes unmentioned in the scene "Throne Room." We are suddenly transported into the presence of the Emperor (who has only this generic title throughout) as he commences a session with his counselors on affairs of state. Mephistopheles then arrives in the guise of court jester, identified by name in his speeches to the reader of the drama and presumably recognizable to the audience in the theater. No explanation apart from passing surmise (lines 4731–42) is offered for the substitution, though the true jester later appears at the end of the scene "Pleasance" (lines 6155 ff.), and the Emperor assigns the jester's place to his devilish substitute at his left side with no questions asked. Faust himself does not appear until the middle of the Carnival Masque, which follows directly after this scene, and his allegorical guise as Plutus, God of Wealth, is unprepared for and totally unexpected even by the Herald (see lines 5494 ff. and note). From the present scene, apart from Mephistopheles's swift intervention in the fiscal affairs of the realm, which occurs in response to a direct request from the Emperor (lines 4876 ff.), we have no indication of what the world of the Emperor might have to do with the thematic concerns of Goethe's *Faust.*

The answer to such questions is provided only by a reading of *Part II* as a whole, especially from the juxtaposition of the last two acts with the opening scenes. Goethe introduces an elaborate thematic exploration of public issues, including questions of both political philosophy and economic reform, which extends throughout the rest of *Faust,* despite numerous symbolic transformations and apparent theatrical and mythological digressions which occur along the way. Within this dimension of the drama the Emperor functions as a separate figure in the action, an analogue in his behavior to Faust himself. At the outset he is immature and irresponsible, newly returned from his coronation in Rome (see lines 5068 ff. and 10439 ff.) and eager to introduce the customs of the Roman carnival to his German court (see lines 5065 ff.). He proves to be inept as a ruler, failing to organize the finances of his realm and failing to assert adequate leadership over his vassals and counselors. The intervention of Mephistopheles thus imposes an infernal solution to the Emperor's ineptitude, for which, beyond all comprehension by the Emperor himself, a devilish price is exacted. Both the financial reform proposed by Mephistopheles and the military assistance he later provides in the war are fraudulent. The paper money introduced to cover the debts of the Empire, despite the elaborate pretense by Mephistopheles to sustain it with the wealth of buried treasure, has no value and provides only temporary relief, followed by drastic inflation and utimately a collapse of credit, concluding (in Act IV) in anarchy, rebellion, and open warfare (see lines 10234–95). Nor would the Emperor stand a chance of victory in that war did not Faust impose the forces of Mephistopheles and his three infernal companions (see lines 10323 ff.) to rout the Rival Emperor and his armies through the use of elemental magic, the semblance of universal fire and water (see the scene "In the Foothills," lines 10345–10782 and notes). The effect of such compromise with the devil, amounting to a kind of unwritten pact with the powers of evil, is then apparent in the final scene of Act IV, where the Emperor attempts to reward his chieftains (including Faust, who subsequently receives the tidal lands for use in his reclamation project in Act V) only to fall under the oppressive moral and material demands of the Church, which through the Archbishop exacts a heavy penance for the Emperor's dubious involvement with the powers of darkness (see lines 10931–11042). Our last view of the Emperor with reference to his Empire at the conclusion of the war (line 11042) suggests that he emerges from his involvement with Faust and Mephistopheles both sadder and wiser, no longer free to rule as he would but at last truly aware of what the responsibility of imperial rule requires of him.

The most important literary model for the entire role of the Emperor is found in the history plays of Shakespeare. In this we observe once again the free departure from the popular legend of Faust (a departure also beyond anything hinted at in the outline of 1816) in order to establish a universal basis for the thematics of the drama. Essential parallels of structure and theme may be detected in the second history cycle by Shakespeare, the sequence of four related plays, *Richard II; Henry IV, Parts I* and *II;* and *Henry V.* Shakespeare there provides a comprehensive survey of historical revolution in the rule of the English kings at the end of the Middle Ages, through a cycle of usurpation, violent civil disorder, and restoration. A grand panorama is portrayed through the reigns of three kings: Richard II, who is deposed by his rival Bolingbroke and later murdered; Henry IV, who must labor under the burden of guilt for his usurpation throughout his reign; and Henry V, the glorious Hal, who reestablishes the glory of the English throne through his miraculous victories in France and his marriage with Katherine, Princess of France. Goethe by contrast collapses the sweep of history into an individual, personal focus upon the young Emperor. Goethe's Emperor displays a number of attributes in common with Prince Hal of the two *Henry IV*s, especially the apparently frivolous pleasure received from feasting and entertainments; yet he clearly fails to develop either a realistic sense of the world or a clear understanding of his own obligations as monarch in the manner of Shakespeare's Hal. Attributes of both Richard II and Henry IV may also be perceived in this monarch, which suggests that all three figures from Shakespeare are here united into one. Richard II abused the privileges of his inherited throne by frivolous and irresponsible behavior, in a manner which closely corresponds to the fraudulent fiscal reform in *Faust*. Open rebellion is also the result of such irresponsibility in both instances. One may even detect in the Rival Emperor of Act Four (who remains curiously out of sight in Goethe's drama) a corresponding figure to Henry Bolingbroke in *Richard II*, who opposes the legitimate King and successfully seizes the throne. In Goethe's *Faust*, due only to the intervention of Mephistopheles, the rebellion is unsuccessful; the emperor retains his rule. At the end, however, alongside any other Shakespearian parallels, we observe a monarch who is compromised and plagued by guilt for his wrongdoings, in a manner that may derive from the melancholy and remorse of Henry IV, the monarch who spends his time devoted to uneasy penance and prayer and whose most famous speech concludes with a line that could well apply to Goethe's Emperor in the situation he faces for the remainder of his reign: "Uneasy lies the head that wears a crown" (*Henry IV, Part II*, III.i). Such echoes of Shakespeare in the characterization of the Emperor remain no more than that, touched upon briefly, in passing, as part of this incidental sub-plot to the drama of *Faust*.

Carnival Masque (lines 5067–5986). The masquerade (as it is called in line 4767), the celebration of the traditional pre-Lenten Carnival by the Emperor's court, extends through nine hundred lines of Act I and could be regarded as a radical digression from the central plot of *Faust*. The most important function of this scene is to establish the peculiar allegorical and symbolical mode of dramatic action, which Goethe later elaborates into the mythical sequence of the "Classical Walpurgis Night" and the Helena act. Important thematic continuity may also be observed between the "Walpurgis Night's Dream" and the Carnival Masque, especially with regard to the use of theater as a medium which blends social satire and a celebration of nature as the true basis of art. In the Carnival this sense of play is focused upon the life of the Emperor's court, particularly upon the economic problems of the Emperor's reign in relation to the frivolous and self-indulgent pleasures which the

Masque itself represents. To this is added, as an unexpected intrusion on the part of Mephistopheles and Faust, a display of the fascination and the danger of gold, demonstrated by the response of the members of the court to the magical treasure chest which is carried on stage by Faust (in his guise as Plutus, god of wealth) and the Boy Charioteer. The crowd of participants is caught up in the attraction of the treasure, further manipulated by Mephistopheles in his guise as Greed, who effects a twofold transformation of the magical gold, first into flames, which threaten to burn the greedy crowd, then into a gigantic phallus, which is used to frighten and threaten the ladies. Finally, with the arrival of the Emperor and his train, disguised as the great god Pan with a wild troupe of fawns, satyrs, gnomes, giants, and nymphs, the thematics of natural force and demonic treasure are united in an explosive, even more dangerous climax. The Emperor has clearly accommodated his role in the Masque to the plan for digging up buried treasure from the ground, which had been proposed by Mephistopheles in the preceding scene. His costume and his companions indicate a confusion of political power and natural domain, whereby the guardians and miners of the hoard serve as subjects of the Emperor. The intrusion of Mephistopheles and Faust, however, with the imposition of a treasure which is the creation not of nature but of infernal magic, administered by the forces of Plutus and "poetry" (the Boy Charioteer), upsets the Emperor's plans of exploitation, tempts him and his train to share in the greed for this gold, and causes the entire Masque (whether or not by intention) to go up in flames, which threaten to burn their victims to death. The involvement of both the Emperor and Faust in the demonic power of the devil's magical gold constitutes a central concern of Goethe's drama. It speaks to the ethical and political aspects of the social world which is represented in *Part II* and also to the more existential and erotic aspects of Faust's encounters with the Feminine, looking back to the Gretchen tragedy of *Part I* and ahead to the Helena sequence of *Part II*, which is about to commence.

"Pleasance" and Paper Money (lines 5988–6172). This scene divides into two sections, both by its content and from the history of its composition. The opening speeches (through line 6036) were written in immediate sequence with the Carnival Masque, probably in the last weeks of 1827 or early in 1828, and included with the text of all of Act I up to this point which Goethe sent in mid-February to be published in Volume 12 of the final edition of his *Collected Works*. The remainder of the scene, which constitutes the so-called paper-money scene, was written somewhat later, perhaps near the end of 1829, when the remaining parts of Act I were completed. The shift of focus from the Emperor's concern for entertainment to the news of the impact of paper currency is thematic to the entire sequence in the Emperor's court. His preoccupation with amusement, appointing Faust to be his "Scheherazade," the source of daily magic shows, constitutes a drastic neglect of duty in the face of financial crisis in his realm. Mephistopheles, however, turns this neglect to his own purpose by manipulating this crisis through a devilish entertainment of his own devising. Indeed, the introduction of the new paper currency proves to have occurred already in the midst of the Carnival Masque, though no one, least of all the Emperor himself, was fully aware at the time what was happening. Goethe would seem to invite by this a reconsideration of the thematic material pertaining to wealth, treasure, and exchange which permeates the entire Masque, in particular with regard to the first meeting of Faust as Plutus and the Emperor as Pan. As Goethe indicated to Eckermann in discussing this scene (December 7, 1829; see below), Mephistopheles had arranged that the Emperor sign a paper in the midst of the Masque which authorized the paper to serve as money. He subsequently caused the paper to be reproduced a thousandfold and circulated throughout the realm. The Emperor suspects fraud so long as he doubts the signature. The assurance of his Treasurer puts him at ease, however, so that the larger question of legitimacy for the paper money never arises. It is not only that the buried treasure without limit that is to cover the paper bills has not been (and will not be) secured, but also that the multiplication of these bills by Mephistopheles perpetrates a potentially unending extension of the supposed resources of the treasury. Does he thus become a counterfeiter, as well as introducing surreptitiously (assuming the sixteenth-century setting) the invention of printing?

Particularly important for the drama is the characteristic quality of this Mephistophelian tactic. The text of the bill with the Emperor's signature may be regarded as duplication in kind, if not in specific intent, of the pact which Faust once signed with the same devil. More than this, the technique of reproduction suggests the same disrespect for the relation of word to sense, of text to substance, of medium to essence, which Mephistopheles displayed in his initial appearances in *Part I*. The lack of an authentic gold base for the paper is no different from the lack of an authentic sense for the words in which this devil deals. Nor is the Emperor's damnation likely to be less complete than Faust's, were it not for the ironic turn of the drama ultimately against Mephistopheles' purpose. In this, also, we may contrast the manner in which the emperor manages his court with that of the Lord over his cosmic realm in the "Prologue in Heaven." The transcendent source of salvation, like the transcendent source of love, ultimately legitimizes the fraudulent medium imposed by Mephistopheles upon his all too willing human agents. A thematic parallel is also suggested between the paper money and the theatrical medium within which the spirit of Helena

328 · *Interpretive Notes (lines 6173–6305)*

subsequently is embodied. The difference, of course, resides in the authenticity of
Faust's spiritual journey to secure her and bring her back into the medium of his
own experience. For that, of course, as Mephistopheles himself acknowledges, the
powers of the Mothers offer special privilege.

"Dark Gallery" (lines 6173–6305). With casual abruptness, as a direct result of the
Emperor's new office for Faust as the master of his revels (see lines 6035–36), the
theme of Helena from the traditional Faust legend is introduced as the subject of an
occasional entertainment. Faust clearly regards the proposal at first as no more than
this, as his initial speech to Mephistopheles makes clear. But the latter describes the
task with unexpected seriousness, contrasting the world of Nordic witchcraft, familiar
from the "Witch's Kitchen" and "Walpurgis Night" in *Part I*, with the more awesome realm of mythical archetypes in which the spirit of a Classical Helena would
reside. Faust still associates this new mode of hocus-pocus with the rituals of the
"Witch's Kitchen" (see lines 6229–30), forgetting that the vision of the Feminine had
also appeared to him there in the magic mirror. Yet even the *sound* of the Mothers
indicates the emergence of something radically new to Goethe's drama. Faust's emotional response further supports this, particularly as indicated by the use of stage
directions for his state of mind at three separate moments in the scene ("starting,"
line 6173; "with a shudder," line 6265; "enraptured," line 6281), a device used only
rarely by Goethe in this drama. Critics and scholars have also been struck with a
ponderous awe in response to the name, which has led to an enormous body of erudite speculation concerning the doctrine implied and its possible sources. What has
often gone unnoticed is the characteristic ironic tone of the entire scene, an instance
of Mephistopheles once again as manipulator and trickster. This seems particularly
apparent in his instructions to Faust, not only concerning the need that he strike the
magical key against the tripod in the midst of the silent Mothers, who are strangely
declared to be unable to see anything but spirits (see line 6290–93), but also in
Faust's heroic posing in rehearsal of his quest. The final couplet of the scene, furthermore, spoken *ad spectatores* by Mephistopheles after Faust has disappeared, indicates
that no very reliable clarification of mystical doctrine is likely to be forthcoming from
this instructor.

In a conversation with Eckermann (January 10, 1830; see below), responding to an
inquiry concerning the origin of the Mothers, Goethe referred to Plutarch as his
source for the name but claimed the rest as free invention. He also quoted a line
from the scene, "Why, it strikes a singular chord" (line 6217), suggesting that the
playful air of mystery—at the ironic expense of Eckermann's serious concern—may
have been precisely the effect he intended for the scene. The source in Plutarch has
been identified as the *Life of Marcellus*, chapter 20, or (less likely) the treatise *On
the Decline of Oracles*, chapter 22. The former concerns the cult of mother goddesses
in Engyon, of ancient Cretan origin, discussed in relation to a certain Nikias, a refu-
gee of the Carthaginian dominance at Engyon and a friend of the Romans in the
time of Marcellus (late third century B.C.). Plutarch emphasizes the service of Marcellus as civilizer of Rome, one of the first to bring Greek art and learning to the
Italian city (as Faust subsequently brings the forms of Helen and Paris to the
Emperor's court). These mother goddesses were identical (according to the world history of Diodorus Siculus, also known to Goethe) with the Corybantes of Crete, associated with the Great Mother, Rhea or Cybele or Demeter. There is a significant
mythological connection here with materials used by Goethe in the concluding festival
of the "Classical Walpurgis Night," in particular the rites of the Cabiri (see note to
line 8074), as also with the myth of the rape of Demeter's daughter Persephone by
Hades and her subsequent establishment as queen of the underworld. It was Goethe's
intention that Faust later participate in the "Classical Walpurgis Night" in order to
visit the underworld and plead through Manto with Persephone for the release of
Helena. All this material suggests, as any perceptive reader of *Faust* will note, that the
initial descent to the Mothers in Act I, despite its appropriate ironic and mystifying
quality, prefigures the more authentic search for Helena that occurs subsequently in
the "Classical Walpurgis Night." Apart from this, all else in "Dark Gallery" should be
considered in the dramatic context of Faust's involvement with the Emperor. Goethe
may also have intended a pun on the name "Mothers," which in German (*Mütter*)
has almost the identical sound as the word "myth" (*Mythe*).

It should also be noted that Goethe makes playful use throughout this scene of
terms appropriate to initiation into a mystery rite. Mephistopheles speaks of steeper
steps into a more deeply alien realm (lines 6194–95), which might recall the procession into a sacred precinct or the temple of the mysteries. His initial speech on the
Mothers indicates what he calls a reluctance to reveal, or "uncover" (*entdecken*), a
more exalted mystery or secret (*Geheimnis*, line 6212). Above all, the phrases
describing the path into the Mother's realm, despite the willful obscurity of abstractions, suggest the vocabulary of mystery: "Into the unacceded,/The inaccessible;
toward the never-pleaded,/The never-pleadable." (lines 6222 ff.) Even the emphasis
on emptiness, solitude and wilderness (lines 6227, 6236) contribute to this sense of
participation in a separate and alien realm of experience. Faust acknowledges these
implications when he addresses Mephistopheles, not without irony, as "mystagogue in
chief" (line 6249), associating himself with the "neophyte." Such implications are

further strengthened by the use of symbolic objects traditionally associated with such mystery rites: the key (line 6259), which would unlock the secret and, in association especially with the theme of treasure, the gate, door, or entrance to the hidden, buried source of the treasure; and the tripod (lines 6283 ff.), glowing with a substance associated with the theme of fire and of aromatic fragrance. All this evidence has invited scholarly speculation, especially with reference to Jungian archetypes, concerning the precise nature of this mystery rite. A reader of *Faust* should bear in mind, however, that our evidence in this scene is limited to what Mephistopheles can tell us, a highly questionable source of information, whose role as mystagogue is equally dubious. Similarly, Faust as neophyte, who at this point has no awareness at all of what to expect, can hardly be looked to for guidance. Nor does the setting of the scene within the Gothic halls of the Emperor's palace provide anything but an ironic opposition to the ancient and mysterious source referred to as the Mothers. Only further developments within the drama itself can provide any valid clarification of what all this mystery portends. One should also bear in mind that the entire Helena act had already been completed when this scene was written, as had also the detailed outline of the "Classical Walpurgis Night" contained in the "Second Sketch for the Announcement of the *Helena*" (see below).

"Hall of Chivalry" and "The Rape of Helena" (lines 6377–6565). This scene, which concludes unexpectedly Faust's stay at the Emperor's court and also concludes the first stage in his developing desire for Helena, constitutes a superb climax to the theme of the theater in Goethe's *Faust*, demonstrating in eminently theatrical terms how the experience of theater relates to visionary experience, both dreams and myth, on the one hand, and, with consummate irony, to the difficult, ultimately indifferent relation between society and art, on the other. Composed quite late in the era of work on *Part II*, probably near the end of 1829 (see the conversation with Eckermann for December 30, below), the scene presupposes the Helena act (completed three years before) and thus consciously prefigures all that is there achieved. It also anticipates the great labor still to be faced by the poet during the first half of 1830, the "Classical Walpurgis Night," and provides the only valid mode of transition into that fantastic mythical realm for Faust, namely the medium of dream vision, which begins in response to this spirit show, proceeds in his unconscious state at the laboratory of Wagner through the dream of Leda, as described by Homunculus (lines 6904–20), and achieves fulfillment in the vision of Leda at the shores of the Peneios after he arrives in Greece and recovers consciousness (lines 7271–95). The sense of theater established in "Hall of Chivalry," furthermore, relates directly to earlier instances of this mode of representation in *Faust*, above all to the sense of cosmic theater or *threatrum mundi* in "Prelude in the Theater" and, even more, in "Prologue in Heaven," also to the more earthly sense of spirit show, with both negative and positive implications, respectively, in the "Walpurgis Night's Dream," the amateur theatrical representation of the golden wedding anniversary of Oberon and Titania, and the more sublime musical performance of Ariel and the elfin chorus in "Charming Landscape," which constituted an ideal transformation of theatrical show into natural event. Closer at hand, finally, and thematically sequential to the social satire of the spirit show for all who participate in "Hall of Chivalry" is the Carnival Masque which first introduced Faust to the Emperor's court, both as a master of revels and as a participant in the Masque. All these implications come together in this scene, as the poet meant they should, to establish the legitimate centrality of the show for *Faust* as a whole.

Also important for understanding Goethe's theatrical technique in this scene is the crucial use he made—hitherto unacknowledged by commentators—of Shakespearian models. On the one hand, with regard to the ironic, ultimately disruptive impact of the theater on society, the "mouse-trap" in *Hamlet*, the play within the play staged by the Players at Hamlet's instructions before King Claudius and the court (III.ii), must have served as the nearest instance of the effect which Goethe wished to achieve. Other possible examples for such play within play could be found, both from Baroque theater in general, with its fascination with illusion and spectacular effects, and from Romantic comedy in particular, such as the plays by Ludwig Tieck written in the late 1790s. Nowhere, however, is the manipulation of audience response in direct relation to a dumb show so crucial to a sense of the true meaning of theatrical performance as in *Hamlet*. This, above all, is the impact of this show, *The Rape of Helena*, as the Astrologer entitles it (line 6548), yet with a crucial ironic difference. In *Hamlet*, in addition to the various sardonic responses elicited by the show in members of the audience, Hamlet included, the entire performance is directed to Claudius as a trap to force into the open his sense of guilt for the murder of Hamlet's father. The play functions as a strategy of exposure: "the play's the thing [says Hamlet]/Wherein I'll catch the conscience of the King" (II.ii.604–5). In *Faust* the impact of the performance turns against its instigator and Faust himself falls victim to the power of illusion. This shift of effect seems central to Goethe's drama, especially as the thematics of vision pertain to the developing quest for ideal Beauty embodied in the Feminine. Faust's surrender to theatrical illusion, which also recalls Don Quixote's famous encounter with Master Peter the puppet player in Cervantes' novel (II.26), is in itself a profoundly Faustian gesture, recalling explicitly his response to the vision of the Feminine in the "Witch's Kitchen" of Part I (lines 2429 ff.), which even then sent him into raptures.

There is yet another source in Shakespeare, however, which deserves mention. Prospero in *The Tempest* provides a theatrical entertainment for his daughter Miranda and her lover Ferdinand, to commemorate and solemnize their betrothal through the offices of spirits, the goddesses Iris, Juno, and Ceres, who appear in the entertainment to celebrate the lovers with music. The parallel to Faust's spirit show of Helena and Paris, especially considering the use of Prospero's magic which alone makes it possible, is striking. But Goethe goes even further in adapting his source to the purpose of *Faust.* Toward the end of the spirit masque in *The Tempest*, Prospero suddenly remembers that intruders are approaching his cave, breaks the theatrical illusion of his own show, and dissipates the spirits with a single quick command. The consternation of the lovers at the sudden conclusion of the pageant results in the famous speech on the *theatrum mundi*, "Our revels now are ended" (IV.i.148 ff.). Goethe imposes precisely the same sense of insubstantiality upon Faust's spirit show but also, as in the use of *Hamlet*, turns the Shakespearian source against his hero. Faust, in contrast to Prospero, loses his sense of reflective distance to the show he has created and surrenders himself to the illusion with an act of violence, trying to seize the spirit of Helena away from the spirit of Paris. Mephistopheles intrudes with a reminder worthy of such a demonic Prospero: "It's your own work, this ghostly mask, you dunce!" (line 6546) The effect, however, is a violent explosion, causing the spirits of the show to dissolve into air—precisely as it occurred in *The Tempest*—but Faust is left unconscious; indeed, his conscious mind has submitted entirely, as we subsequently learn, to the internal dream-vision which constituted the spirit show in the first place. Only by pursuing this vision beyond the realm of social reality into the mythical domain of the "Classical Walpurgis Night," leading finally to his confrontation with Persephone in the underworld, can Faust recover himself again and incidentally achieve this meeting with Helena on equal ground.

What is the content of the spirit show itself? The Astrologer, who may at best speak the sardonic opinions of Mephistopheles, calls it "The Rape of Helena" (line 6548). Yet, from all descriptions of what happens, one might hardly describe it as rape. Indeed, Paris is said to fall asleep (line 6471). Helena then approaches him, awakens him with a kiss (lines 6511–12)—an ironic reversal of the kiss from the fairy tale "Sleeping Beauty"—and then erotically entices the youth, who is amazed at the sight of her, to the point where he embraces her and prepares to carry her off with him. At this point the intrusion by Faust occurs. The scene has clearly depicted the myth of Paris's reward, when on Mount Ida as a shepherd he was approached by the three goddesses Hera, Athena, and Aphrodite and asked to give the golden apple of Eris to the most beautiful of them. Aphrodite, who received the apple, promised Paris the most beautiful of mortal women, Helena. According to the more realistic versions of the myth, as contained for instance in Homer or Aeschylus, Paris actually appeared as a guest at the court of Menelaos in Sparta, where he then seduced and made off with Helena, thus ultimately causing the fall of Troy. In Goethe's version, more fairy-tale-like, as befits a dream vision, Helena apparently appears to the sleeping youth from nowhere, indeed as if in a dream, which he, like Faust, is dreaming, of ideal beauty, that beauty of erotic desire which Aphrodite herself represents. No wonder that Faust feels compelled to intervene, though he does not recognize—as Mephistopheles tries to remind him (line 6546)—that the entire encounter is the projection of his own mind, his own dream. Such implications indicate how skillfully Goethe has here used the spirit show to prefigure the actual encounter between Faust and Helena which is to take place in Act III, indeed to prefigure also the erotic climax of the "Classical Walpurgis Night," where Homunculus sacrifices himself to the nymph Galatea, incarnation of the goddess Aphrodite at the festival, uniting the elements of fire and water, in an act which symbolizes the origin of all life in primal Eros.

"Narrow-Vaulted Gothic Chamber" (lines 6566–6818). The opening scene of Act II, completed early in December 1829 (see the conversation with Eckermann of December 6, below), serves an important thematic and structural function which has not always been recognized. Not only does Goethe here recapitulate exactly the situation of "Charming Landscape," where Faust lies asleep in an Alpine field after the catastrophic encounter with Gretchen—as later in Act IV the same situation will recur in the rocky peaks of the higher Alps after Faust's true encounter with Helena (in contrast to the spirit show just preceding). This scene also recreates the original academic situation with which the drama of Faust began in the Gothic study of the scholar. Faust, though unconscious and carried by Mephistopheles, returns to his study. For the poet of *Faust* this return marked more than a closure to the structure of the drama; more than half a century had passed since the opening monologue in "Night" had been written, more than a quarter century since the scenes in the study for the "great lacuna" were written to complete Part I. Not only had Goethe himself grown from youth to mature poet and beyond, to become the sage of Weimar, but Europe itself, the cultural and social basis of Faust's dilemma as man of learning, had been radically transformed through the French Revolution and the Napoleonic era into the nineteenth century. These historical changes are reflected in Goethe's scene;

even more, they provide thematic transformations of perspective which reflect on the internal development of *Faust* itself. It is essential that the reader bear the earlier study scenes in mind in order to understand this development.

Focal points for Goethe's recapitulation are the intrusions to the study by Wagner (lines 518–601) and by the Student (lines 1868–2050), represented now by the new Famulus and by the Baccalaureus, the same student who first came as freshman and now has achieved his degree. Here also, as elsewhere (for instance, in the original Student scene), Mephistopheles takes the place of Faust in the study, again putting on the academic robes (lines 6586 ff.), which have gathered dust and insects. Both intruders, who come in response to the bell which Mephistopheles rings (lines 6619, 6667, 6728), assume that nothing has changed in the study, despite changes in the world. For the Famulus this is indicated by the preservation of all Faust's scholarly materials as he left them; for the Baccalaureus the assumption manifests itself in blatant arrogance, measuring its own sense of growth against what seems to be a static world of dead learning. Elsewhere in the laboratory, as the following scene demonstrates, Wagner has assumed the place of the absent Faust, though totally lacking in Faustian qualities (as befits the pedant turned professor). What makes the irony of the scene so powerful, especially for Mephistopheles in dealing with these figures, none of whom presumably has any idea who he is, is the fact that Faust himself lies unconscious, concealed behind a curtain (which Mephistopheles raises as he enters, to reveal Faust for the benefit of the audience). We share with him a knowledge of what has happened to Faust, so that the perspective of the scene is turned against the assumptions of all those who inhabit this academic world.

Epochal significance may also be ascribed to the act of ringing the bell by Mephistopheles (following line 6619), which shakes the entire structure of the Gothic hall with its sound and causes all the doors to fly open, doors hitherto locked and sealed as if to symbolize the imprisonment from which Faust first suffered. All three of the figures encountered in this and the following scene appear to recognize the importance of this sound (lines 6667, 6728, 6819–20). Wagner associates the sound of the bell with the critical moment of his chemical experiment, in which—like Mary Shelley's Frankenstein—he seeks to create a human being. The emergence of Homunculus in the next scene, which succeeds (we surmise) only because of the infernal assistance provided at the last moment by Mephistopheles, is only the external sign of what this epoch signifies for the drama. The true liberation of the medieval, Germanic Faustian mind from the imprisonment of the self in its own knowledge is about to occur through the mythical-poetic journey to Greece, the participation in the "Classical Walpurgis Night," and the creation of the "Phantasmagoria" of the Helena act, in which Faust will be married to ideal Classical Beauty and produce Euphorion, the self-consuming spirit of poetry. Liberation of the reflective self through the Feminine by the aid of Mephistopheles: this had been the central theme of the Gretchen tragedy, as it had been prefigured also in the rejuvenation of Faust in the "Witch's Kitchen," when he envisioned the image of the Feminine in the magical mirror. The ringing of the bell should thus be considered in the context of the Faust drama as the primal liberation of the Faustian self at a higher level than anything yet achieved, a liberation which will ironically restore Faust to consciousness within the realm of ancient poetry and myth, enabling him eventually to make his way back to his native Germany with the new purpose that motivates his action in the final acts of the drama.

"Laboratory" and Homunculus (lines 6819–7004). All the paraphernalia of the alchemist's laboratory, otherwise associated in the popular legend with Faust himself, are here gathered visibly by Goethe into a climactic parody of all scientific experiment, for which Wagner, the pedant turned professor, serves as the appropriate practitioner. The conventional concerns of alchemy for such things as the philosopher's stone and the creation of gold out of base metals are here united in the idea of the *homunculus*, the "little chemical man" in the test tube (as Goethe first referred to him in the "Second Sketch for the Announcement of the *Helena*"; see below). The setting of the scene recalls earlier descriptions by Faust of the apparatus of his alchemical and medical experiments (see lines 668 ff., 1034–49), which had yielded, characteristically, either poison (lines 686 ff.) or death (lines 1050–55). Thematic associations with the Witch's Kitchen are also apparent, especially due to the entrance of Mephistopheles, who may be surmised to serve as a kind of infernal catalyst for Wagner's experiment (as Goethe indicated to Eckermann on December 16, 1829; see below). Nor does Goethe abandon the central thematic contrast between medieval and Classical modes, related both to the contrast between Mephistopheles and Homunculus (lines 6923 ff.) and to the opposition of settings in the drama: the dark and oppressive enclosure of the Gothic study and laboratory versus the open, mythical realm of the "Classical Walpurgis Night" (in particular the festival at the Aegean Sea), to which Homunculus will shortly lead Mephistopheles and Faust. It is the same opposition which was already established in the "Witch's Kitchen" when Faust observed the vision of the Feminine in the mirror, a vision of Classical beauty, in total contrast to the medieval hocus-pocus of that scene.

Much scholarly discussion has been devoted to the figure of Homunculus, especially with regard to possible sources. Generally it is now recognized that Goethe was here developing the symbolic implications of his drama—in a manner resembling the originality of the Earth Spirit in the *Urfaust*—for which no sources provide adequate anticipation. It is also important to note that no trace of this figure occurs in the outline of *Part II* which Goethe dictated in 1816 (see below) and that the discussion of Wagner's creation in the "Second Sketch for the Announcement of the *Helena*" of 1826 (see below) does not use the traditional Latin term *homunculus* (literally, "little man"). A large body of obscure material has been gathered in relation to the idea of such an alchemical creation of life, for which the treatise by Paracelsus (1493–1541) *On the Generation of Natural Things* is representative. It was thought that the proper blending in a glass container of male sperm and organic material in an extreme state of putrefaction could, under the right conditions of time and warmth, create a living being. Such a source—and similar cabalistic works like the chapter on *homunculi* in Praetorius' *Anthropodemus Plutonicus*—would have been consulted by Goethe, for instance, in 1768, when he was studying the occult, or in 1798–99, when he was working on the "Walpurgis Night" for *Part I*. Also of interest as a possible source, particularly important for the role of Homunculus in the "Classical Walpurgis Night," are the scientific theories on the origin of life by contemporaries of Goethe, especially by Lorenz Oken concerning the sea as the primal uterus, in which the original seed of mankind came to be. Two attributes of Homunculus are, however, unique to Goethe, as they are also central to *Faust* in relation to the predominant characteristics of the protagonist. First, the creation in the test tube is totally without material substance, pure spirit or mind, which explains the apparent superiority and independence of Homunculus over even Mephistopheles. As Goethe mentioned in the "Second Sketch" of 1826, Wagner's little chemical man contains within himself a universal historical world calendar, which provides him with knowledge of the "Classical Walpurgis Night," something even Mephistopheles has never heard of. Second, according to a natural impulse which is eminently Faustian, pure spirit strives from the moment of its appearance and without cessation to achieve substantiality, to become material, that is, to be alive within the world of nature. In this regard, Homunculus' search for existence is analogous to Faust's search for Helena, as the structure of the "Classical Walpurgis Night" makes apparent.

Especially important for the action of the drama is the coincidence of moments in the laboratory scene, "moments" (lines 6832, 6866, 6886) in the sense of the original wager between Faust and Mephistopheles (lines 1699 ff.). Without any indication of adequate causes for such coincidence, the state of visionary unconsciousness in Faust as a result of the explosion at the end of the spirit show in "Hall of Chivalry" is joined with the creation of Homunculus by Wagner in the laboratory. The only apparent mediating agent between these two events, as so often in *Faust*, is Mephistopheles. Not only had he provided the means (i.e., the magical key) for Faust's journey to the Mothers in order to conjure up the spirits of Helena and Paris, he also brought Faust back to the study after the explosion and there rang the bell, which in its tremendous liberating force is regarded even by Wagner (lines 6819 ff.) as a signal that the great moment is at hand. Mephistopheles also knows full well what Wagner is about and is instrumental somehow in bringing the experiment at last, after apparent frequent failures (line 6829), to successful completion. Further thematic indication of this coincidence is provided by Faust's dream of Leda and the Swan, as Homunculus (who is the only one who can witness it) interprets to Mephistopheles and Wagner (lines 6904–20). No reader should miss the fact that Homunculus is created in close juxtaposition with a dream by Faust of the conception of Helena, the embodiment of the ideal beauty which he seeks. Similarly, as if to prove this thematic significance, the "Classical Walpurgis Night" concludes in an ecstatic moment of fusion and erotic self-procreation. Homunculus dissipates himself into the sea—the primal act of natural generation—and the Helena act begins immediately thereafter. Contrary even to Goethe's own plans for the underworld scene, in which Faust pleads with Persephone through the help of Manto, the act begins with the appearance of Helena herself, newly emerged from the spirit realm and carried over the water of the sea like newborn Aphrodite on her shell.

"Classical Walpurgis Night" (lines 7005–8487). The "Classical Walpurgis Night" constitutes the most complex and difficult poetic sequence in the whole of *Faust*. It was conceived apparently at the time when the Helena act was composed, during the mid-1820s, according to the plan for it contained in Goethe's "Second Sketch for the Announcement of the *Helena*" (see below). No mention of anything corresponding to the "Classical Walpurgis Night" is found in the "Outline of the Contents for *Part II*" of 1816 (see below). It was written almost entirely during the first half of 1830, not much more than a year before Goethe completed the drama. The sequence is conceived as a distant analogue to the more medieval-Germanic witches' Sabbath of the "Walpurgis Night" in *Part I*; but it also introduces the unique poetic realm of the Helena act, providing a bridge from Faust's world in Germany to the Classical world of Greece, from the socio-political realm of the Emperor's court (where the masquerade and the spirit show of Act I have already anticipated the later transformation) to the mythical-poetic realm beyond the limits of geographical space and historical time. In certain ways the "Classical Walpurgis Night" is also designed as the preliminary path of Faust's search for the spirit of Helena in the underworld, recapitulating in

more articulate poetic form his earlier journey to the Mothers. Faust's search also shares in a rich tradition of visionary journeys into the realm of spirits and the dead (the most conspicuous examples are found, of course, in Book Six of Virgil's *Aeneid* and in Dante's *Divine Comedy*). No precedent exists, however, for the mode of action and representation which Goethe chose to employ, introducing a great deal of obscure mythological material in order to present primal, indeed archetypal, experience, which ultimately (in the festival at the shores of the Aegean Sea) goes beyond the limits of individual human existence to offer a celebration of life itself in the broadest, most universal terms. This concluding festival, where Homunculus becomes the central figure, both Faust and Mephistopheles having disappeared from the stage, also provides a purposeful analogue at the cosmic, elemental level for that more individual mythical action which occurs simultaneously in the underworld, as Faust, guided by Manto, pleads with Persephone, queen of the dead, to secure the release of Helena. When Goethe composed the festival at the end of the "Classical Walpurgis Night," he apparently decided that the symbolic and thematic implications of this cosmic celebration of Eros would make the scene of Faust's visit to the underworld superfluous.

Festival at the Aegean Sea (lines 8034–8487). In Goethe's "Second Sketch for the Announcement of the *Helena*" (1826) no mention is made of this climactic festival which concludes the "Classical Walpurgis Night." The idea for what must be the boldest and most obscure poetic sequence in the entire *Faust* drama seems to have occurred to the poet when he had actually begun work on the "Classical Walpurgis Night" early in 1830. Ultimately this scene came to replace the plan to represent Faust's visit to the underworld and his appeal to Persephone for the release of Helena, though Goethe apparently decided on this only after Act II was finished. The festival at the Aegean constitutes the fulfillment of the search by Homunculus for substantiality, achieved through his ultimate fusion with the sea by following the nymph Galatea as she rides on the shell of Aphrodite. This act of sacrifice and renewal was intended to provide both an analogy and a contrast to the subsequent union of Faust and Helena: an analogy insofar as the erotic desire of Homunculus resembles the striving of the Faustian will for ideal beauty; a contrast insofar as the complete transformation of Homunculus provides an instance of fulfillment within the realm of nature which is denied to Faust and to mankind generally. What Goethe came finally to recognize, however, almost as if his mythical drama had taken its author by surprise, was that this festival celebration of erotic fusion provides an adequate and an appropriate alternative to Faust's visit to the dead. The ultimate result of Homunculus's self-sacrifice in response to Galatea far out at sea is the emergence of Helena, the embodiment of ideal beauty, at the outset of Act III, newly arrived (as she believes) at the shores of her native Sparta and still dizzy with the motion of the sea. Her journey from the underworld into life is identical with the journey from the sea to the land, from the domain of the festival of natural creation to the stage of Faust's all too human tragic drama. This connection is both subtle and crucial.

The festival at the Aegean also provides an intentional contrast to the geological events which occur inland earlier in the "Classical Walpurgis Night." The volcanic eruption that brought the giant of the earthquake, Seismos, above ground led to further violence, warfare, and exploitation, and finally destruction from the explosion of the descending meteor. Goethe there indicated his negative opinion of the volcanic theory about creation through violence, whether that creation is defined in geological or in political and social terms. The poet, like Homunculus, clearly prefers the wisdom of Thales to that of Anaxagoras. The events of the festival celebrate the more evolutionary processes of creation which occur within the medium of water. Here, in an important anticipation of later Darwinian theories of evolution, Goethe demonstrates the origin of life in the sea and affirms, through statements made by the elderly sages who witness the festival—Thales, Proteus, and Nereus—that out of this original act of creation will emerge ultimately the higher forms of life, culminating in man.

The Cabiri (lines 8070–8218). In his treatise *On the Gods of Samothrace* (1815), Schelling described the Cabiri as a chain of ascending forces from the primal depths of the earth or the sea upwards to the heavens. The first of them, Axieros, identified with Demeter or Ceres, the Great Mother, consists entirely of desire for growth or creation. The second, Axiokersa, is identified with Persephone or Proserpina, daughter of the first, who then became queen of the underworld when she was carried off by Hades. The third, Axiokersos, is the Egyptian Osiris or the Greek Dionysos, here thought to function as the consort of the daughter in place of Hades. The fourth of the gods, called Kadmilos, is Hermes, messenger or guide, who leads the other gods up from the underworld to the realm of Heaven. The interaction of these deities and their linear ascent is understood by Schelling in terms of a growth or creation of consciousness, proceeding from primal urge through erotic union toward complete consciousness, the latter stage being represented as a heavenly recapitulation of the deities, who thus come to number seven, and even eight, in all. Goethe makes fun of the uncertain number of the Cabiri but intends also, I believe, a very serious association of these gods both with the visitation to the underworld by Faust and with the union of Homunculus and Galatea in the festival. The motive of ascending creation and self-consciousness is common to all three, and in some highly elusive way the entire festival is an authentic celebration of a cabiritic mystery rite, even though the participants derive from separate sources. The entire event, furthermore, is ultimately Faustian in its essential striving toward self-fulfillment and constitutes the appropriate primal prerequisite for the marriage of Faust and Helena in Act III. The significance of the Cabiri, despite the pervasive satirical tone, is as far-reaching as the Faust drama itself.

The Helena Act (lines 8488–10038). The conjuring of Helen of Troy by Mephistopheles to serve as a concubine for Faust was a traditional part of the Faust legend, which Goethe emphasized to have been part of the earliest plan for his drama. The first part of the Helena (as Goethe referred to Act III) was drafted in 1800, corresponding roughly to lines 8488–8802. Concerning Goethe's difficulties in composing the episode at that time, see the exchange of letters with Schiller of September 1800 (see below). In the surviving manuscript of this draft the title is Helena in the Middle Ages. A Satyr Play. The prose sketch of Part II dictated by Goethe in 1816 (see below) indicates the general function of the episode for the drama as envisioned at that time. The final text of Act III (written in 1825–26) was published independently in Goethe's final collected works in 1827 with the title Helena, Classical-Romantic Phantasmagoria, an Interlude to Faust. The draft of Goethe's announcement for this publication is reprinted below. Unusual demands are made on the reader by the Helena, and the work has baffled many critics. It should be noted that, as an Interlude following the "Classical Walpurgis Night," this act assumes the same structural position in Part II as the "Walpurgis Night's Dream" in Part I, which follows the "Walpurgis Night" and is subtitled "Intermezzo." It is also important to bear in mind that Faust descended into the underworld with Manto during the "Classical Walpurgis Night" (after line 7494), where he was to plead before Persephone, queen of the dead, for the release of Helena. Goethe planned to compose this scene in the underworld as a prelude to Act III and subsequently abandoned the plan only after the "Classical Walpurgis Night" was completed in 1830. The reader must assume at the outset of the Helena that Faust has been granted his request. Mephistopheles appears in Act III only in the guise of Phorcyas, which he assumed in the "Classical Walpurgis Night" (see lines 7951–8033). It becomes apparent, especially from the final stage direction to Act III (after line 10038), that Phorcyas-Mephisto functions as a kind of demonic stage manager for the entire Interlude. Though he does not himself bring Helena to Faust, he is responsible for everything which happens after she arrives, especially for the setting and the transformations of scene: from the palace of Menelaos at Sparta, to the inner courtyard of a castle, to the pastoral grove in Arcadia. We are also to imagine (presumably) that all the characters who appear in the act are spirits: the Chorus accompanies Helena from Hades and the attendants of Faust's castle (as also the dwarfs who appear after line 8937) are provided by Mephistopheles. (Possibly an exception to this is Lynceus.) The entire sequence of the Helena thus assumes the status of a theatrical show, a phantasmagoria of the poetic imagination, which not only serves to deceive Helena into the illusion that she is really alive (as it does initially) but establishes also the only possible medium—a literary, poetic, artistic, and theatrical medium—within which it is possible for Faust to be united with Helena. The complexity and the power of Goethe's Helena derive from the thematic implications it assumes for the broader context of Faust as a whole. Helena embodies the ideal of Classical beauty just as Faust represents the Germanic or Romantic spirit of infinite striving, and the offspring of their union, Euphorion, who was described by Goethe as the spirit of poetry, may be called the Byronic spirit of "modern" poetry. The historical scope and structure of the Helena, as Goethe emphasized (see his letter to Boisserée of October 22, 1826, below), extends across three thousand years of the Western cultural tradition, from the fall of Troy, at the time when the supposed historical Helen lived, to the battle of Missolonghi in 1824, when Byron was killed (see note to lines 9907–35). The Helena must thus be understood as a mythical-poetic recapitulation or recreation of that cultural history, a theatrical event in symbolic terms: the marriage of Faust and Helena to produce the self-consuming spirit of modern poetry as the synthesis of the ancient and the medieval, the union of Classicism and Romanticism.

Also important and difficult to follow through the Helena is the developing thematic self-awareness of this phantasmagoria as a mythical reality. The advance of dramatic action is more than a recapitulation of cultural history; a corresponding development of reflective understanding accompanies this action as a perspective or implied response imposed upon characters and audience alike. At the outset, for instance, Helena assumes that she really exists, as if she were arriving home from Troy to Sparta in historical truth. Only gradually, above all through the dialogue exchanged with Phorcyas-Mephisto, does she become aware that she is only a spirit from the underworld, an ideal (however powerful her role as ideal), an Idol (line 8879; here translated as "myth"). Faust experiences less difficulty in accommodating himself to Helena in the central section of the act; yet it is clear from the example of courtly devotion set for him toward his lady and queen by Lynceus (in his two songs, lines 9218–45 and 9273–9332) that Faust, too, must learn the language of love in terms appropriate to the role imposed on him by literary tradition. He thus courts Helena and wins her by teaching her to rhyme (lines 9372–84). Euphorion alone seems incapable of understanding himself in terms of the literary-cultural tradition through which he has come into being; though such lack of reflectivity seems appropriate to the idyllic and operatic medium of his performance, as it also indicates the cause of his tragic fall. The offspring of this poetic union between Classical beauty and Romantic love destroys itself because it cannot comprehend and understand what it is. Equally important for the success of the *Helena* is the implied response imposed upon the audience by this performance. This is indicated, for instance, by the role of Phorcyas-Mephisto as stage manager or master of ceremonies. His presence in the *Helena* provides a constant reminder—or it should do so—that the entire sequence is no more than a poetic or theatrical event, a phantasmagoria upon a stage constructed and directed by the devil and populated with spirits. Our task as audience is to maintain a conscious awareness that this vast panoramic spectacle is no more than that. We submit to the illusions of this theater only at the peril of our understanding. What it means for us as it unfolds and advances is essentially the same, so Goethe implies, as the meaning of our cultural tradition itself, insofar as it is accessible to us through the experience of art. Such experience above all is what the *Helena* is intended to convey, and our response will determine the success of our understanding in regard to what happens to Faust. The result for him, as always, in this greatest instance of striving for the moment of ideal fulfillment, is error and failure. The meaning of all this for us, who only observe it as audience, need not constitute perhaps a corresponding error and failure. That question is left open, however, by the silence of Mephistopheles at the end (after line 10038), when he removes his mask and costume as if "to provide in an epilogue such comment on the play as might be necessary."

"Before the Palace of Menelaos at Sparta" (lines 8488–9126). Goethe's imitation of Greek tragedy in the first section of the *Helena* commands respect as a *tour de force* of poetic form. Totally alien conventions and structures of drama are achieved with sufficient authority to deceive even the spirit heroine and her Chorus into believing, at least for a time, that they have truly returned to ancient Sparta. The basic structure of the sequence corresponds closely to conventions of Euripidean drama familiar to Goethe from the original sources. A number of purposeful variations are also imposed on this structure, however, which provide an eminently Goethean (or is it Mephistophelean?) sense of artifice, to the point where even the characters on the stage recognize that they are participants in an elaborate deception. The basic principle which Goethe follows is an alternation between units of dialogue in spoken verse (iambic trimeter) and formal lyrical odes sung by the Chorus. The long opening speech by Helena (lines 8488–8609) corresponds closely to conventions of the *Prologos* in Euripides, in which the main character presents herself and establishes a sense of the dramatic situation. Helena's speech is indeed very long and rhetorically elaborate, including the formal celebration of the house to which she returns (lines 8502 ff.) and a direct quotation of the speech of instructions which Menelaos supposedly spoke to her (lines 8541–59 and 8568–78). Goethe interrupts her prologue several times, presumably to avoid monotony, by having the Chorus speak separate stanzas in metrical responsion (lines 8516–23 correspond to lines 8560–67 as strophe and antistrophe, lines 8591–8603 are a variation on that unit as epode). It is contrary to the conventions of Attic drama, of course, for the Chorus to enter the theater with the actor who speaks the prologue. The Chorus does not notice this, but presumably Goethe intends to indicate that they have arrived here with Helena, as spirits released from the underworld, in a manner which is alien to the conventions of their role. What follows is a sequence of three formal odes (lines 8610–37; 8697–8753; 8882–8908) interspersed with three episodes, as follows: Panthalis, the Chorus leader, with Helena when she returns in haste from the palace to report on her meeting inside with Phorcyas; Phorcyas and Helena in a formal Agon (or dramatic conflict), in which one half the Chorus also participates as separate Choretids in Stychomythia; all the characters, finally, in an elaborate exchange, which leads to a breakdown in the form of the drama itself. Everything in this sequence pertains to the confrontation of the Grecian spirits with the devil in his disguise, involving both an elaborate exposé of their insubstantiality (which causes Helena to collapse in a faint, line 8881) and a complex manipulation of emotion by Phorcyas, which gradually persuades the Chorus and even Helena to submit to his power (lines 9071 ff.). All three of the choral odes are concerned with the identity of the Chorus in relation to their situation in the drama, both as regards their journey from the underworld (which they confuse in the second ode with the burning of Troy) and the threat of evil which they sense in Phorcyas. The formal Agon of the second episode involves both a sequence of mythological invective between the Chorus and Phorcyas (where Mephistopheles is clearly in his element) and a formal review of the traditional legends of Helena in a double Stychomythia between Phorcyas and the heroine (lines 8848–81), resulting in her final recognition that she is only a "myth." In the final, extended episode Phorcyas, who himself introduces the archaic verse form of trochaic tetrameter (lines 8909–29), which is associated with heightened emotion, purposefully imposes a panic upon both Helena and the Chorus when he insists that they are to be the victims of the supposed sacrifice planned by Menelaos. He calls out a gang of lesser devils disguised as muffled dwarfs (see stage direction after line 8936), and he stages

sound effects of trumpets in the distance, leading the Chorus to believe that the army of Menelaos is approaching (stage direction after line 9062). Along with all this Phorcyas-Mephisto also begins the elaborate transformation of the Classical medium into the medieval German world through the lengthy description he provides of the castle of Faust and his attendants (lines 8984–9049). Clearly both the Chorus and Helena are intrigued by more than the prospect of rescue; the exotic picture painted by Mephistopheles of Gothic splendor with more than a hint of erotic attraction, both in Faust as lord of the house (lines 9006 ff.) and in his youthful attendants, who offer new dances to the Chorus (lines 9044 ff.), gradually captivates even Helena. Two dramatic devices in particular are introduced by Goethe to this final episode which are totally alien to the technique of Greek tragedy: first, the Chorus, speaking apparently in unison, interrupts the dialogue several times out of sheer emotional intensity (see lines 8925 and 8927, 8973, 9029, 9044, and 9050–51; these lines are quite distinct from the units of trochaic tetrameter assigned to the Chorus: 8957–61, 8966–70, 9122–26, also with Phorcyas: 9063–70); second, the moment of crisis and reversal upon which the entire sequence hinges, the moment of decision for Helena is indicated by a stage direction of one word: "Pause" (after line 9070). The dynamics of development and dramatic interaction in Goethe's Greek tragedy are thus anything but Greek in origin, reflecting strategies and devices eminently suited to Mephistopheles in his role as attendant and surreptitious manager-director of the entire show. It should also be noted, finally, that the spectacular set change which seems to involve a dislocation in space from Sparta to the medieval fortress northwards in the Peloponnesus is in fact an elaborate theatrical deception caused by the mists and smoke which Phorcyas-Mephisto conjures forth (see stage direction after line 9087, followed by a detailed descriptive response of the Chorus, lines 9088–9126). And when the smoke clears to reveal the courtyard of the Gothic fortress, Phorcyas-Mephisto has disappeared, surrendering the stage to Faust.

"*Inner Courtyard of a Castle*" (lines 9127–9573). The central section of the *Helena* constitutes Goethe's poetic tribute to the Germanic Middle Ages. Faust appears to Helena within the walls of a Gothic fortress dressed in the ceremonial attire of a medieval knight, not as the historical Faustus of the sixteenth century, but as the representative of what Goethe, along with other historians of literature at that time, called the Romantic age, the era of Christian knighthood and Gothic art, the era of courtly love, *Minnesang* (the medieval German love lyric), and chivalric romances. In thus associating the hero of his drama with the cultural milieu of the Middle Ages, Goethe implicitly acknowledged the affinity of his *Faust* to the enthusiasm for Germanic antiquities which had emerged during the era of the Napoleonic wars, particularly among such Romantic critics as the brothers Schlegel, in the form of a militant patriotic nationalism. The history of Goethe's reluctant and rather skeptical response to this movement is complex and often ambivalent. At the instigation of his friend Boisserée, for instance, he had been persuaded to lend his name in support of the proposal to complete construction of the famous Cologne Cathedral, and he became a genuine admirer of the collection of medieval German and Flemish paintings which Boisserée had assembled in the Rhineland. At the same time, however, he maintained his commitment to the norms of Classical art, even though he tempered his earlier defense of these norms (particular in the program for the visual arts which he developed around 1800 with a group of friends at Weimar, which became known as "the Weimar friends of art") with an implicit historical relativism, which acknowledged the validity of the style and technique of Christian medieval art as appropriate for the culture of that era. Goethe resisted, however, often in open opposition to the temper of his time, all aspects of cultural nationalism. The central section of his *Helena* provides eloquent demonstration of this cosmopolitan relativism, whereby the era of German medieval art is located in a developmental sequence between Classical antiquity and the modern period. Faust may represent this middle age, by virtue of the popular legend of the sixteenth-century conjurer and the reputation which Goethe's own *Faust, Part I*, had quickly achieved among the Romantic nationalists in Germany as the greatest German poem, but the meeting of Faust with Helena, where Classical beauty is wooed and won by the medieval Romantic spirit, results in a radical transformation of both parents in their impetuous and ultimately tragic offspring, Euphorion, the spirit of modern poetry.

Particularly interesting are the various forms of imitation and allusion which Goethe provides in his theatrical recreation of medieval art and poetry. The courtyard of the castle clearly suggests aspects of Gothic architecture, especially as described to the Chorus and Helena by Phorcyas-Mephisto (lines 9017–30), decorated with colorful heraldic emblems, shields and banners. The procession of youths which accompanies Faust when he first enters (described by the Chorus, lines 9148–81) provides a sense of high ceremony, which Faust's appearance and behavior also sustains. The elaborate throne with its carpets and canopy, constructed on the stage by the pages and squires, also establishes an appropriate setting for Helena as the judge and ruler (line 9214), lady and queen, of this court of love. Indeed, it is only with Helena's arrival that the civilizing and transforming power of chivalric love is established in this court, in accord with the highest ethical ideals of medieval poetry and art. Such transformation is apparent both in the songs of celebration which are offered to her by the watchman Lynceus (lines 9218–45 and 9273–9332) and in the mercy which Helena displays in response to his praise, freeing him of all fault despite Faust's initial condemnation for failing to announce her arrival (lines 9192–9212). The songs of Lynceus, it has been claimed, imitate the style and form of the so-called *Minnesang*, especially the poems of Heinrich von Morungen (died 1222) which had been included in Ludwig Tieck's anthology of *Love Songs from the Swabian Epoch* (1803). Helena's beauty is compared by the watchman to the light of the rising sun, which surprised him in approaching from the south and blinded him (recalling a corresponding effect of the rising sun on Faust himself in "Charming Landscape" at the beginning of *Part II*). In the second song by Lynceus, which surveys the triumphant military conquests of the Germanic tribes, Helena is offered the booty of war as tribute to her beauty and her power as the lady of this court. The chest of treasure (which must derive from Mephistopheles, as did the earlier chests with which Gretchen was tempted in *Part I*) contains jewels which enhance the natural beauty of Helena: emeralds (line 9307), pearls (line 9310), and rubies (line 9311), associated with her breasts, her ears and lips, and her cheeks. Through such poetic service to the lady the military attributes of Faust's Germanic fortress—"wisdom, opulence, and power" (line 9323)—are made subservient to Classical beauty. Property is denied, concern for the self is denied, in the complete submission of "I" and "mine" to "thou" and "thine" (lines 9325 ff.).

The high point of Goethe's thematic application of medieval poetics to the meeting between Faust and Helena occurs through the introduction of rhyme (lines 9372–84). She is attracted by the pleasant sound of Lynceus's songs, the accommodation of one word to another, like a caress in the ear of the hearer. Faust then asserts that rhyme is also accompanied by a correspondence of sense, where separate elements of language and meaning are brought into harmonious interaction. This model of Romantic medieval poetry defines the nature of the love which Faust offers Helena, and by learning to rhyme in exchange with him, she also learns to love him. Indeed, the sequence of couplets following a brief choral ode (lines 9411–18) achieves the consummation of their love as a poetic climax. Rhyming is doubled in each couplet, as the lovers seek to express the full meaning of their union. For Helena, the spirit from the underworld, a sense of reality is achieved within the present moment; whereas for Faust language fails, and time and space dissolve into a dream. In their second couplets, respectively, each of the lovers expresses an appropriate sense of paradox: Helena, the Classical beauty in the Romantic domain, feels "bereft" of life and yet renewed, and Faust, seeming to fulfill the conditions of his wager with Mephistopheles, asserts a complete satisfaction with the present moment (*Augenblick* in the German). It is thus a supreme irony that Mephistopheles immediately intervenes, appearing for the first time in Faust's Gothic fortress, to disrupt the poetic union of the lovers through an intentional parody of their rhyming. This interruption indicates how fragile and insubstantial this moment of synthesis actually is, constituting for Faust no more than a vision, a dream, a poetic fiction within the phantasmagoric medium of a theatrical show.

Faust's Survey of Pastoral (lines 9506–9573). Goethe here indicates the significance of the final transformation of scene in the *Helena*. Faust's speech provides a complex résumé of the European pastoral tradition, looking especially to Virgil's use of Arcadia as idealized landscape in his *Eclogues*. Arcadia is spoken of both as the "last redoubt" (line 9513) of Europe, connected by a "branch" of mountains across the isthmus to mainland Greece, an "un-island," and also as the center of the Peloponnesus itself, the middle which will be surrounded, like the fortress of warriors mentioned by the Chorus (line 9505), by the protection of Faust's Germanic chieftains, sheltering the pastoral retreat within. To this is added the emphasis of association with Helena's own birthplace; Sparta and Arcadia are confused by the connecting link of the Eurotas (line 9518), the river which flows south from Arcadia to Sparta, where Leda was confronted by Zeus in his guise as swan—which recalls both the earlier visions of the encounter by Faust (see lines 6904–20 and 7277–94). Faust thus asserts that the landscape of their retreat is also the place of Helena's birth, the origin of her primal and ideal beauty, where she broke out of her egg (line 9519)—a mythical analogue to the emergence of Aphrodite from the sea—to the wonderment of the nymphs of Eurotas' reeds (see lines 7263–70) and her mother and sister, Leda and Clytemnestra. In effect Faust is proposing that he retreat with Helena into the center and the origin of her own native place, where she shall truly reign as a spirit of place (*genius loci*), reaffirming the authenticity of her ideal beauty within the primal, pastoral, ideal landscape. The intricacy and precision of this accommodation of a European poetic tradition to the particular thematic situation of Goethe's drama is astonishing and entirely unique.

The central section of the poem (lines 9526–61), almost formulaic in quality, provides a measured survey of the various aspects of landscape which became almost clichés within the post-Virgilian pastoral tradition. What should be noted here above all is the exercise in abstraction which Goethe has employed, removing these various elements of landscape from their context in the dialogue and action of Virgil's *Eclogues*, where landscape is always part of the background, never depicted as significant in itself alone, since the pastoral mode depends always on a sophisticated sense of situation, involving human relationships between the various idealized shepherd figures. It seems an eminently Romantic shift of emphasis, which Goethe certainly introduced by intention, to represent the landscape itself as the embodiment of the ideal, quite without explicit reference to the human habitation it provides. The landscape is also populated with its appropriate nature spirits—Pan, the goat-god who traditionally dwells as lord within the woods and groves of the pastoral landscape, and his nymphs (lines 9538 ff.), who are presumably no different from those mentioned in connection with the Eurotas (and who will later be joined by the Chorus, when they are all transformed into natural spirits at the very end of the Helena act; see lines 9992 ff.). Also striking, and without parallel in Classical pastoral, is the stanza describing the tall trees, the "hoar forests," of oak and maple (lines 9542 ff.). Emphasis is placed especially on the vertical thrust of their growth, as an urge to reach "higher regions" and an interlacing of their branches as they arch toward the sky. The distinction between oak and maple also seems to assume symbolic implications with reference to this vertical desire: the one "looms defiant," while the other "rises in purity," glutted with its sweet sap. One is tempted to interpret this peculiar element of Goethe's pastoral with reference to Faustian desire, perhaps in specific association with the Gothic forms of his native German tradition, especially in the use of the columns and arches which so strikingly imitate the rising trunks and branches of a forest, striving to reach the divine—a view of Gothic architecture which Goethe had come to share with his friend Boisserée. The final focus of importance in this central section of the poem is the child, an element of the pastoral which may derive from Virgil's famous fourth *Eclogue*, where the expectation of the child's birth brings also the promise that the golden age will be re-established. "The enchanting child" (line 9554) can only be Euphorion, whether or not Faust himself here intends to allude to the as yet unborn offspring of his union with Helena. In accord with the semblance of immortality within the Arcadian realm (lines 9550 ff. and 9556–57), he will seem to be divine, in fact resembling Apollo (lines 9558–59), god of music and poetry, as Apollo had also once joined the shepherds (an allusion to his year's service to King Admetus as shepherd), an indication of the perfect coherence and totality of the pastoral realm. The central part of the poem thus concludes by affirming an ideal of unity which would unite mortal and divine in the expected offspring of this marriage. That such union also has significance for a concept of poetry is suggested by the office of Apollo himself.

A problematic aspect of this poetic recital by Faust is the nature of his authority and the validity of what he says. Goethe makes no concessions to dramatic plausibility, since Faust himself can have no direct experience of what he describes. Yet he speaks with the confidence that the pastoral tradition in poetry itself provides. This confidence also extends to a sense of setting which the poem establishes for the drama, whereby the ideal of harmony and communion which Faust associates with Arcadia in terms of his love for Helena becomes perfectly fused with the reality of place. In a sense the language of the poem itself creates the place, as perhaps has always been true of pastoral poetry. It represents a landscape of the mind, projected upon an imagined remoteness—Sicily for Theocritus, Arcadia for Virgil—which is primal, even original: the Golden World before time began, as Hesiod (*Works and Days,* 109) and Ovid (*Metamorphoses,* I.89) call it and Goethe here alludes to it (line 9565); yet this is also timeless, even out of time, in an eternal spring, where past and future have no meaning. In this sense Helena, as a spirit returned from the underworld and as the embodiment of the ideal of beauty, belongs to Arcadia as the appropriate landscape for that spirit and that ideal. Goethe also alludes to the myth of Helena's marriage with Achilles after death, when they were located—in a manner analogous to Faust and Helena here—upon "blessed ground" (*auf sel'gem Grund,* line 9570; here "smiling harbors"), where their offspring Euphorion was born.

Arcadia, the ideal pastoral landscape, which constitutes the setting for the conclusion of the Helena act, is created by and through Faust's poetic depiction of it. The mechanical change of scene, which appears to happen instantaneously and automatically at the end of the poem (see the stage direction before line 9574), is merely a visual acknowledgment within the theater of what has already been achieved in poetry for the loving pair. Faust also knows that this is so, in a manner quite appropriate to the self-conscious, self-reflective aspect of the pastoral tradition, and he expresses this awareness emphatically in a manner which the reader should not ignore. The last stanza also applies this sense of poetic fulfillment to Helena in terms of her journey from Hades, fully in accord with the myth of her marriage upon the blessed isle: "tempted to dwell upon blessed ground, you fled into the happiest destiny!" And at the very end, commanding the change of scene and the establishment of its appropriate condition, with the authority of Adam giving names to paradise, Faust asserts his absolute expectation that "our bliss" shall be "Arcadian-free" (line 9573).

Phorcyas' Fairytale about Euphorion (lines 9596–9628). Euphorion was the name of the offspring born to Helena and Achilles from their posthumous marriage on the blessed island of Leuce (see also lines 7435 and 8876). He was born with wings. His name derived from the fertility of the land. Jupiter fell in love with him, and since he could not possess him he destroyed him with a thunderbolt on the island of Melos, as Euphorion was fleeing from him. As we know from a conversation with

Eckermann (December 20, 1829; see below), Goethe intended Euphorion to personify the spirit of poetry; such is also indicated by the Chorus when they address him as "poesy pure" (*Heilige Poesie*, line 9863). Phorcyas' tale, however, chiefly owing to its ironic tone, resists such allegorical reduction. What emerges instead, somewhat in the manner of a fairy tale, is a sense of who Euphorion is from what he does. He is born with "a peal of laughter" (line 9598) and immediately tumbles and springs about, as if full-blown, in spontaneous and exuberant manner: "tender frolic, fond caresses, teasing love's inane endearments, playful shouts and gay exulting" (lines 9600–9601). Phorcyas-Mephisto calls him a naked genius without wings (though he suddenly claims to have wings just before his final, fatal leap; see lines 9897–98), a faun without any bestial qualities. His jumps and leaps indicate both a boundless desire, which manifests itself in upward motion, and a power derived from the earth, which Faust associates with the mythological figure of Antaeus (line 9611), the son of earth whose strength never diminished so long as he kept in touch with his parent. Both Helena and Faust, who are quoted by Phorcyas-Mephisto (lines 9607–11), emphasize the peril as well as the strength of this quality. We may surmise that, unlike pure spirits, Euphorion may not achieve free flight—so Helena warns him—but like creatures of nature (which grow out of the earth) he enjoys resilience and strength—so Faust assures him. In this regard the child would appear to exhibit a mixture of attributes derived from his respective parents, who contrast so radically with each other. Goethe's conception of Euphorion as a naked genius without wings suggests an intentional variation on an iconographical source. It seems likely that he may have had in mind a painting by Annibale Carracci (1560–1609)—one of the Italian Baroque painters whom Goethe often mentioned, alongside Raphael, as a master of the medium—entitled *The Genius of Fame* (*Der Genius des Ruhms*, originally, *L'onore*), which since 1746 has been in the Johanneum in Dresden, in the same hall as Raphael's *Sistine Madonna*. The painting depicts the naked body of a youth with wings, soaring upwards toward the heavens. Likelihood of such influence is increased by the climactic assertion of Euphorion just before his abortive attempt to fly that the path to fame (*Ruhm*) is opening before him (line 9876).

The Euphorion Opera (lines 9679–9938). The meaning of this operatic sequence depends in large measure upon the implicit musical form, which can be surmised at best from a careful analysis of the structure as potential song. Without some effort to reconstruct the music which the text demands, the entire sequence will appear superficial and banal. In order to appreciate what Goethe here attempted to achieve, some sense of his expectations for the Euphorion drama as opera must be provided. It is necessary to differentiate the formal units of statement which would have manifested themselves in discrete set pieces both as music and as ballet. This can be done only through careful attention to meter, since everything else in the language, including the substance of what is said and the voice which says it, is made to depend on this implicit musical form. The following meters can be distinguished: 1) trochaic, usually in a ballad stanza (as in the opening section), where it serves as a kind of neutral norm, presumably representing song without dance; 2) dactylic, usually in short two-stressed lines, which suggest a three-four waltz tempo for both music and dance; 3) a short iambic line, which begins with three neutral syllables followed by a strong-stressed feminine ending (x x x x́ x), indicating a kind of folk-dance measure, perhaps the traditional *Ländler*; 4) a slow, four-stressed line with first- and second-stressed syllables juxtaposed (x́ x́ x x x́ x x́), which suggests a stately, martial tempo for heroic, military, ceremonial music; 5) some use of iambic four-stressed lines just before the fall of Euphorion, which suggests a kind of lyrical interlude before the dramatic climax; and 6) a double stanza in trochaic meter—eight lines, four-stressed, alternating rhyme—for the choral dirge at the very end. Everything in this operatic sequence is made subordinate to the actions of Euphorion as the central heroic figure. Both Helena and Faust, along with the Chorus, are reduced to roles in response, observing, reacting, and following the lead of Euphorion. The role of Euphorion is essentially divided into two parts, the first predominantly erotic—proceeding from a solo of pure self-expression through an exchange with the Chorus to an aggressive chase sequence involving motifs of seduction, rape, violence, and destruction—and the second predominantly militant—where the triumphant heroic stance of the martial meter is offset by the tragic leap and fall at the end.

All this may be regarded as an elaborate allegory for the workings of the spirit of poetry; yet Goethe seems to have more than that in mind thematically, especially insofar as there may be an ironic, even a parodistic relationship implied between Euphorion and his father. His flamboyant operatic and balletic tragedy is a kind of *Faust* drama in miniature, involving the same fundamental forces of will and impulse, of Faustian striving, and the same inevitable error and failure, in accord with the universal principle of human action expressed by the Lord in the "Prologue in Heaven" (line 317). The progression of concern from love to war, including acts of violence in both instances, also would seem to reflect Faust's own progress from his love affairs with Gretchen and (now) Helena toward his involvement in the affairs of the empire, leading in Act V to his attempt to establish a new society liberated by Mephistophelian technology. Faust's failure in each instance is no less categorical, even if less flamboyant and spectacular then Euphorion's fall. We certainly are meant to recognize this parallel, just as Faust himself appears to (as indicated by his conspicuous silence). There is hardly a line in the entire opera where Faust may be considered to speak or sing his own mind, and he is completely silent from Euphorion's death (his last words are with Helena and the Chorus, then with Helena, lines 9891–92, 9895–96, 9903–4) until his monologue at the outset of Act IV (lines 10039 ff.).

Byron and Euphorion (stage direction following line 9902). The figure we are meant to recognize in the body of Euphorion is, of course, George Gordon, Lord Byron. Goethe himself made the identification unambiguously in his conversation with Eckermann of July 5, 1827 (see below). What does the association here imply? The authenticity of Byron's genius was beyond question for Goethe; the younger Englishman represented, indeed embodied, the spirit of poetry which he identified with the modern, post-revolutionary era, the period which we would now call Romantic. Goethe said of him (to Eckermann, July 5, 1827): "He was the greatest talent of the century, . . . neither ancient nor romantic but like the present day itself." Euphorion represents precisely the same spirit, especially within the structure of the Helena act as it surveys the entire tradition of Western literature. The death of Euphorion-Byron is the fall of modernism, if not indeed the final collapse of the European poetic tradition. And this fall is inherent in the spirit which is destroyed, as Goethe often emphasized about Byron. His genius was magnificent but destructive, directly in opposition to the moral order of the society in which he lived and even in conflict with the spirit of his age. A magnificent description of the daemonic force which Goethe associated with Byron and intended to demonstrate in Euphorion is provided in the final pages of Goethe's autobiography, *Poetry and Truth*, Book IV, Chapter 20 (written probably in 1831 and published only after the poet's death), which has often been quoted and deserves consideration here:

> . . . the daemonic element appears in its most terrifying aspect when it manifests itself predominantly in a human being. During the course of my life I have been able to observe several such men, sometimes closely, sometimes from afar. They are not always the most admirable persons, not necessarily the most intelligent nor the most gifted, and rarely are they remarkable for their goodness of heart; but an extraordinary force goes out from them, and they have an incredible power over all creatures, yes, even over the elements; and who can say how far such an effect may not extend? All the moral forces banded together are powerless against them; in vain do the more enlightened among mankind strive to render them suspect either as deceivers or as deceived; they attract the masses, and they can only be vanquished by the universe itself with which they are in conflict. It is from observations of this nature that the strange and terrifying saying probably arose: *Nemo contra deum nisi deus ipse* ("No one contrary to God, unless God himself").

Metamorphosis of the Chorus (lines 9992–10038). The concluding choral song, where each of the four sections is taken by a separate group, departs from all sources and models, both Classical and modern. Goethe establishes once again in *Faust* a mode of poetic discourse which is unique and yet perfectly suited to what he wishes to convey. The meter ostensibly is trochaic tetrameter, which offsets and balances the lengthy account by Phorcyas-Mephisto of Euphorion's birth at the outset of the Arcadian sequence. Here, as in the earlier speech, however, Goethe adapts and transforms the Classical verse to fit the kind of experience he wishes to convey. These lines are saturated with bewildering activity. Active verbs in every conceivable grammatical form, especially as participial adjectives and substantives, fill almost every foot of each line in a seemingly endless rolling rhythm that rarely subsides at the end of the line. The effect is to dissolve all sense of separate verses into the illusion of continuous, uninterrupted movement. The closest analogue to this sequence would be the spirit song of the first study scene in *Part I* (lines 1447–1505). Few parallels can be found anywhere in literature to the emotional, near hypnotic effect of this choral sequence, where the ear itself can participate in the natural metamorphoses which are described. The dramatic intention of the poem, of course, is to conclude and resolve the visionary, mythical sequence of *Faust* that began with the "Classical Walpurgis Night" and has come to fill fully one fourth of the entire drama. The manner of resolution, totally without the participation of the central characters, finds an exact parallel in the withdrawal of the spirits at the end of the earlier phantasmagoric interlude, when the amateur theatricals of the "Walpurgis Night's Dream" blended into the rising dawn as Ariel led the troupe of spirits off to the hill of roses. Similarly, in the scene "Charming Landscape" at the outset of *Part II*—a scene which was composed very soon after the Helena act was finished—the elfin chorus which sang the night song of renewal to Faust also retreats at the command of Ariel in response to the emerging day. That retreat of spirits into the protection of the natural realm provides a thematic clarification of the effect intended here. Spirits from the underworld who have assumed the guise of a Greek chorus willingly abandon themselves to a process of ecstatic dissolution in which they blend into and become identical with the various activities of nature. Their voices in song begin to speak in the sounds of nature, thus providing yet a further instance of that mode of poetic language in *Faust* where the processes of nature are expressed directly in words. An implicit irony is also included here in that the seeming loss of personality by the Chorus also achieves a degree of fusion between spirit and substance which offsets Faust's own failure to do the same with Helena in some kind of permanent form. Where his own phantasmagoria concluded by dissipating into mists and silence, the Chorus merge with nature so perfectly that the spirit of antiquity is renewed and fulfilled within the everyday realm of natural activity. The highest and ultimately impossible goal of human striving is thus juxtaposed with a triumphant alternative which is as familiar as the here and now of nature. Goethe also indicates the extent to which such irony is intended by having each part of the Chorus interpret the natural process in which they lose themselves in terms of Classical myth. The radical dichotomy which earlier seemed apparent between the Chorus' response to the account of Euphorion's birth, where they interposed the ancient myth of Hermes (lines 9629–78), and the cult of feeling introduced by Phorcyas-Mephisto in response to the musical form of the Euphorion opera (lines 9679–94), is thus resolved here in the perfect blending of myth and nature and the representation of both in the language of the final choral ode.

Cloud Symbolism in Faust's Monologue on the Alpine Summit (lines 10039–66). Once again the transition to a new section of the action in *Faust* is achieved through a monologue, following the pattern established from the earliest stage of composition in "Night" and subsequently developed in such scenes as "Forest and Cave" and "Charming Landscape." Here Goethe provides a crucial thematic juxtaposition of the two most important manifestations of the Feminine for Faust, represented by the cloud formations which he observes after being deposited on the high rocky summit of the Alps. This juxtaposition is known from a sketch for Act IV (*Paralipomena* 179) to signify the contrast between Helena and Gretchen, even though the latter name is not mentioned in the text. This momentary vision of the Feminine also constitutes its departure from Faust for the final two acts of the drama, as it abandons the hero to the affairs of the world, the war of the Emperor and the colonizing of the tidal shores. There the sinister dominance of Mephistopheles, who has played so subordinate a role throughout the "Classical Walpurgis Night" and the *Helena*, quickly becomes apparent. But Goethe also intended the fleeting glimpse of a symbolic manifestation of Gretchen to anticipate the final scene of the drama, "Mountain Gorges," where her spirit appears as a Penitent in company with the Mater Dolorosa to plead for Faust's salvation. (It bears consideration that the final scene had apparently been written in December, 1830, some months before the monologue for Act IV was composed.)

Goethe's use of cloud symbolism is quite precise, based on years of scientific study. In purposeful correlation with the manifestation of mist and rainbow thrown up by the waterfall in "Charming Landscape," these cloud formations constitute a suspension of the element of water, the creative element of life as shown in the final scene of the "Classical Walpurgis Night," in the quite separate elements of air and ether, where the visual manifestation of its form embodies that quality of beauty, attributed as always to the Feminine, which signifies the highest norm of art and inspires the highest mode of Faustian desire. To understand the implications of this symbolism one should consult Goethe's essay "On Cloud Formations" from his journal *On Science,* where he openly acknowledges his use of terminology from the English meterologist Luke Howard, a terminology still in use today. Howard's essay "On the Modifications of Clouds" (1803) had been brought to Goethe's attention and greatly interested him in his efforts to understand different cloud formations. Goethe distinguishes essentially three kinds of clouds according to their relative height in the atmosphere, as well as by their characteristic shapes: 1) *stratus* are those mists and fogs which gather over swamps and moist fields and which often hover about the lower slopes of mountains, usually extending horizontally above the surface of the earth; 2) *cumulus* are the massive and often splendid shapes which are best seen at the horizon and extend in rows over great distance, as for instance—so Goethe mentions—in India, where they move northwards from the southern peninsula to the mountains; and 3) *cirrus* are the varied strips, wisps, and flecks which form in the highest atmosphere and extend across the sky in elaborate patterns. In Faust's monologue the cloud which carried him from Greece, formed from Helena's garments, moves eastward toward the horizon as a cumulus, where it hovers in gigantic parody of the shape of the feminine: "resembling Juno, Leda, Helena" (line 10050). This form is then changed to resemble a range of icy mountains, suggesting that cloud formation which Goethe proposed to call (departing from Howard) *paries,* or the wall, where the horizon appears to be closed off by clouds which extend without interruption vertically from earth to sky. The Classical ideal of beauty has thus departed from Faust toward the east and even presents him with a sense of distant barrier. By contrast to this, the brighter wisp of cirrus, which brings recollection of Gretchen again to Faust, ascends upward to the highest atmosphere, where it retains its shape, inspiring once more a longing for ascent which now prefigures the ultimate ascension of Faust at the end of the drama. This image of the Feminine signifies "beauty of the soul" (line 10064) and inspires, far more than had been the case with Helena, the noblest qualities of Faust, his most auhentic love for the Feminine, for which finally he is saved.

Act V (lines 11043–11843. Goethe indicated in the prose summary of *Part II* which he dictated in 1816 that the ending of *Faust* had already been written and that the action he was summarizing would finally establish a connection with that ending as already achieved (see below). In a conversation with his friend Boisserée in the preceding year he indicated the same satisfaction with what had already been accomplished as conclusion for the drama, a product of what he termed "the best time," i.e., the years around 1800, when *Part I* of *Faust* was completed in close association with such friends as Schiller and the philosophers at Jena. Similar confidence in the earlier material is expressed also at various points in the later conversations with Eckermann, where Goethe addresses his labors at closing the gap, which was finally achieved in the first half of 1831 when Act IV was composed. Scholars have now provided further documentation on the composition of Act V, demonstrating that one of the crucial manuscripts (the so-called H²), containing a fair copy for the three scenes "Midnight," "Great Outer Precinct of the Palace," and "Entombment" (lines 11384–11831), was prepared in 1825–26, when Goethe first began work again on *Part II*, as a final text from draft material for these scenes, now lost to us, which had probably been written a quarter century earlier. This means that the core of Act V, including the meeting of Faust with Care and his death, reflects the perspective of composition for the drama at the time when the "great lacuna" of the *Urfaust* was filled. The significance of this for the reader of *Faust* cannot be overemphasized, even though the continuity of the ending with the rest of *Part II* is achieved with complete authority, especially through the Philemon and Baucis episode in the opening scenes, "Open Country," "Palace," and "Deep Night" (lines 11043–11383), which was composed in April and May, 1831. At the same time it must be emphasized that the final scene, "Mountain Gorges" (lines 11844–12111), constitutes a separate epilogue to the drama, balanced as frame intentionally with the "Prologue in Heaven," and it raises problems of interpretation quite separate from Act V itself (see note to that scene, below). The reader of Act V must suspend the cosmic perspective of *Part II*, though without any sense of contradiction, in order to reestablish the perspective of *Part I*, in particular the pact scene, as the appropriate dramatic continuum for the end of Faust's life. The drama returns quite appropriately to focus upon the dilemma of its hero, recollecting the use which Goethe had made of the traditional Faust legend in establishing the tragedy of man in *Part I*, while simultaneously providing a more universal awareness of contrary alternatives to the Faustian mode of existence, at least in the opening scenes of the final act.

The figure of Care has always caused difficulty for readers of *Part II*, especially because her appearance is so unexpected, despite the very precise dramatic and ethical motivation offered in the murder of Philemon and Baucis. The Four Gray Crones of "Midnight" materialize out of the smoke from the burning wreckage of the cottage and chapel, as indicated by Faust's speech at the end of "Deep Night" (lines 11378–83). Yet the Crones themselves are totally alien to the mood and the manner of even the most supernatural qualities of *Part II*. They are refugees from popular superstition, the spirit world of ghosts and demons, witches and wraiths, as represented in *Part I* by such scenes as "Witch's Kitchen" and "Walpurgis Night." A close parallel with the Witches in Shakespeare's *Macbeth*, hags of the blasted heath, may be supported by the fact that Schiller adapted the play for production at the Weimar Theater in 1800, at a time which may reasonably be argued to coincide with the initial composition of Goethe's scene. This quality is heightened ironically by Faust's opening speech in the scene (lines 11398–11419), where a categorical abhorrence for the supernatural is expressed, which he regards as all-pervasive and oppressive around him, even in the atmosphere of the night and the air of his own chamber. Such an attitude provides a significant contrast to the accommodation of the demonic which was achieved with such effort in the two study scenes of *Part I*. Some critics have even perceived an element of remorse in Faust at this point, approaching a sense of regret for his entire career with Mephistopheles. Yet the role of Care herself must be defined within a frame of reference quite separate from the pact with the devil, especially since we have no reason to believe that Mephistopheles himself is at all responsible for the appearance of Care or is even aware of her presence. In this regard the comments made by Faust in the latter part of the opening scene of the drama may be of some assistance (lines 634–651). The general implications of Care as an alien counter-force to the power of the spirit in its dynamic, creative activity may indicate an irresolvable dilemma for the human condition, which is represented in the drama by Faust himself. The confrontation with the Crone, resulting in blindness, indicates a failure of purpose for Faust as the creator of his own new world. The basis of this failure is defined in ethical terms, since Care approaches as a direct consequence of the arrogant selfishness which causes the death of Philemon and Baucis. Yet the significance of such failure also goes beyond the limits of good and evil, implicating the hero of Goethe's drama in what may truly be regarded as a tragic fall. Nor does this failure diminish in the light of his subsequent salvation, which proceeds from a totally independent act of grace, instigated by the agents of heaven, in particular by the spirit of Gretchen as a penitent. Care may indeed be regarded as contrast-figure to the Feminine in the drama, a kind of negative ground to the projected goal of Faustian striving. Accordingly, the fall of Faust before Care provides a perfect analogue to the fall of Gretchen herself in *Part I*, and the sense of tragedy in both instances is complete and uncompromising. The figure of Care also resembles, more than any other figure in *Faust*, the Evil Spirit which overwhelms Gretchen in the cathedral scene. Yet both spirits also provide what must be perceived as a destructive power analogous to Mephistopheles himself.

The dramatic perspective of Act V is expanded intentionally by Goethe beyond the subjective limits of Faust's own fall. It is important to see the statements of such figures as the Wayfarer in "Open Country" and Lynceus in "Palace" and "Deep Night" as offering viable alternatives for human existence in contradistinction to Faust. The same may be said also for the couple Baucis and Philemon, who have endured to old age in a rustic simplicity and natural piety; yet they prove incapable of accommodating themselves to the new society being created by the infernal technology of Faust's industrial revolution, thus offering no sense of an alternative to the hero. They are merely his victims. The Wayfarer and the Watchman are no more effective in surviving or resisting Faust's economic and social policy, but we feel nonetheless that they stand apart from his ethos with some authority. The Wayfarer had earlier landed on these shores as a shipwreck, tended at that time by Baucis and Philemon, who offered him their hospitality in a manner which recalls the myth of their service to Jupiter and Mercury. We also sense in the final lines spoken by this figure (lines 11075–79), as he approaches the place where the shore used to be, that he has gathered a fullness of experience, a traveler's sense of the "boundless ocean," which sustains his stance of "prayerful devotion" in the face of nature and life itself. In contrast to the man of travels, who has traversed the open spaces of the world, Lynceus with his all-perceiving eyes, surveys these spaces from a fixed center in the tower, gathering to himself the same sense of life's fullness and providing also an affirmation of all nature. The song of Lynceus at the outset of "Deep Night" (lines 11288–11302) has long been regarded as one of Goethe's finest lyrics, as well as one of the last he wrote. The stance established in the song, ironically, resembles that which Faust himself had expressed in his monologue at the outset of *Part II*, in response to the rising sun in "Charming Landscape." But the character himself has gone contrary to such a stance, which may also reflect the distance of twenty-five years in the history of the composition of *Faust* between the action of Faust's fall and the authoritative instances of affirmation which Goethe provides at the end of his drama.

A corresponding contrast of values and attitudes may also be perceived between Faust's situation in Act V, a situation which demands consideration in relation to the wager with Mephistopheles and the question of victory or defeat in the hands of the devil, and the setting of salvation in "Mountain Gorges," where the spirit of Faust enjoys the beneficence of a grace which is totally alien to the world of his new society and completely separate from any causal connection to his fall and death. Readers who look to the events of Act V for any hint whatsoever concerning the cause of Faust's salvation will be disappointed. The very best that can be argued—as has often been done—is that the final speech of Faust, his monologue at the edge of his grave (lines 11559–86), offers a projected ideal of society, a kind of utopian prefiguration, which represents the highest impulse of the Faustian spirit. But critics have often neglected the absolute ironic contrast between Faust's vision and the agents of perverse and inhuman power which now control his city. Mephistopheles has summoned forth the Lemures, who sing grotesque ditties as they dig Faust's grave. Nor is there any reason to doubt that they shall inherit the entire realm which Faust leaves behind. Faust's spirit is saved by the intervention of a transcendent power of redemption, identified with the response of the Feminine to authentic love; but the worldly city built by Mephistopheles and his henchmen at the instigation of Faust, which is surely meant to represent the city in which mankind shall have to live in future time —and all readers of *Faust* must also locate themselves there—is abandoned to the control of demonic and inhumn powers. This sense of loss to the world as a whole, which is not diminished in any way whatsoever by Faust's subsequent salvation in the epilogue, is a central aspect of that tragic fall which Act V represents. No reader of Goethe's *Faust* should take lightly the implications of its generic subtitle: *A Tragedy*.

Characteristically, however, Goethe prevents any single response from dominating the final act of *Faust*. The mood of Faust's final scene, poised between utopian vision and collapse into the hands of the Lemures, is replaced immediately by infernal slapstick. The popular tradition of devil as comic relief, and particularly as the butt of a cosmic joke, is allowed to take possession of Mephistopheles, regardless of the complexity and versatility which he has achieved in the course of the drama. "Entombment" provides a parody of a medieval morality, as the traditional Hell-mouth opens on the stage, belching forth grotesque devils, who provide Mephistopheles with troops to oppose the host of angels which suddenly descends without warning to claim the soul of Faust. The pitched battle which concludes the scene brings ignominious defeat for Mephistopheles, as he allows himself to be aroused sexually by the sight of the heavenly cherubs, apparently conceived by Goethe on the model of the *putti* and *amoretti* of Renaissance paintings. Many questions remain unanswered within the scene itself. Mephistopheles appeals to some sense of justice, like Shakespeare's Shylock when he is hooted out of court, receiving no satisfaction from a system which, from the very outset in "Prologue in Heaven," had little sympathy for the devil's point of view. And the salvation of Faust is here at best a spontaneous effect of his death, for which the angels offer no word of explanation. Nor do they feel any need to explain the heavenly grace which they represent, assuming that they have any conscious awareness that they do so. All such explanation, not through rational argument but through the dramatic representation of transcendence itself as an ultimate mystery, is provided in the scene "Mountain Gorges," which concludes the drama as a whole.

Mountain Gorges, Forest, Cliffs, Wilderness (lines 11844–12111). Two problems have caused difficulty for readers concerning the final scene of *Faust*, both closely related to each other: first, the question of Faust's salvation and its cause within the context of the drama as a whole; second, the apparent Christian vision of the scene, which many have viewed as a surrender by the poet to some kind of theological doctrine, even if the entire scene remains only a symbol for a mystical experience of transcendence. A thematic continuity for this scene with the drama may nonetheless be established, especially if the close proximity of composition is kept in mind between "Mountain Gorges" and the festive conclusion of the "Classical Walpurgis Night." Goethe appears to have completed both scenes during December, 1830. Both scenes offer a celebration of the highest manifestations of the feminine principle, and both demonstrate a mode of activity in response to this principle by the spirit—masculine desire or Faustian striving—which is uniquely free of the limitations of the human condition, as also of the control of the demonic. Mephistopheles is completely absent from both the festival and the ascension. In the former instance the response of Homunculus to Galatea concludes in a climactic act of self-surrender and primal procreation which constitutes a cosmic celebration of Eros. In "Mountain Gorges" the spirit of Faust, who is silent throughout and apparently passive as a recipient of grace, enjoys a similar privilege, culminating in a response to the penitent spirit of Gretchen which leads him upwards into higher regions pursuing the train of the Glorious Mother. The symbolic implications of such a union between the Faustian spirit and the Eternal Feminine establish an ideal norm against which everything else in *Faust* may be measured.

Yet the attainment of such a union clearly lies beyond the limits of human life itself, as demonstrated by the entire career of Faust and all the error and suffering it causes. No interpretation of Goethe's drama should consider the final scene as some kind of reward or fulfillment for Faustian striving in its own terms. Death has been the prerequisite of his salvation and the cause of his grace lies beyond anything that Faust himself has achieved, except for remaining true to himself in his constant striving. In this regard the speech of the Angels, which Goethe himself considered to be the key to Faust's salvation (see his conversation with Eckermann of June 6, 1831, below), should be taken seriously: they are able to rescue a spirit that has been ceaseless in its active striving, but only if love from above intervenes on behalf of that spirit (lines 11934–41). The Angels have been sent to rescue Faust by the *Mater Gloriosa*, presumably in response to the intercession of Gretchen. A splendid irony for the conclusion of Goethe's drama, considering the earlier consequences of Gretchen's love for Faust and the subsequent perambulations of his career in *Part II*. Nor should this intercession be interpreted in any way as a moral act of forgiveness, which would make a travesty of Gretchen's tragic death. Salvation here occurs within the realm of pure spirit as a strictly gratuitous act by the Eternal Feminine.

The Christian iconography of this ascension assumes no more authority as doctrine than had the feudal court of the Lord in "Prologue in Heaven" or the entire apparatus of mythology in the "Classical Walpurgis Night." The literary tradition which Goethe here accommodates to his finale, however, is more important. It seems unquestionable to me that Dante's mystical ascent in the final cantos of the *Paradiso* provided the model for Faust's salvation, especially in the central role of the Virgin with her train as the focal point for the poet's power of vision, a power developed through his love for Beatrice. She is his companion in the ascent through the heavens toward the Virgin, with whom she finds her appropriate place—like Gretchen by the *Mater Gloriosa*—among the devotees of the Madonna. Also apparent as an analogue to Dante is the use Goethe makes of the Holy Anchorites, who do homage to the Mother in a complex hierarchy of devotion and celebration. These figures recall the various saints and mystics in the final third of Dante's poem. The role of Doctor Marianus is crucial in this regard. The highest of the devotees of the Virgin, in his cell at the mountain summit he serves as an extreme counter-figure to Doctor Faust in his study at the outset of the drama. Doctor Marianus also resembles the figure of Nereus, father of Galatea, in the "Classical Walpurgis Night," in that both demonstrate an extreme of selfless devotion to the Feminine, which includes a complete sublimation of personal desire. We last observe Doctor Marianus just before the concluding Chorus Mysticus as he prostrates himself in adoration before the Madonna, expressing thanks for her continuing grace. The hero of *Faust*, apotheosized beyond death in a silence of response, is offset by this mystical devotee, who celebrates the object of his devotions in prayer and hymns. The perspective of the entire "Mountain Gorges" from the opening Chorus and Echo to the final Chorus Mysticus is firmly located with the father figures: Pater Ecstaticus, Pater Seraphicus, Pater Profundus, and Doctor Marianus. We may surmise that this perspective is also shared by the poet of the scene, thus indicating a differentiation between character and implied author which is crucial for our understanding of the drama. Not only does the spirit of Faust ascend in its silence beyond the limits of our vision, located below within the landscape of the Holy Anchorites; but the sense of symbol (*Gleichnis*) attributed by the closing chorus to the drama as a whole suggests that the medium of its language provides at best the *form* of devotions or celebrations for that which must remain "inaccessible" (*unzulänglich*) and "indescribable" (*unbeschreiblich*). The irony of such differentiation in perspective is not relaxed, even in the final lines of the play, for the plurality indicated in the pronoun of response to the Eternal Feminine—which must include the reader of *Faust* along with its poet—still recognizes implicitly the unavoidable separation of place and contrast of activity between ourselves and the dead hero of the drama.

Cyrus Hamlin

The Composition of *Faust*

The following table provides a schematic overview of the entire work in terms of its formal structure. At the simplest level this structure may be defined according to the titles of individual scenes (most of them given by the poet), here listed with the appropriate line numbers. Beyond this, the table provides a summary of the metrical forms that appear in the various scenes (sometimes in astonishing complexity even within single scenes), and also the dates of composition scene by scene, insofar as these can be definitely or approximately fixed.

METRICAL FORM

The range and variety of verse forms in *Faust* is more complex than in any other work of literature. Goethe undertook to imitate and adapt forms from the entire tradition of Western poetry. The variety of verse forms is especially great in *Part II*, which contains several scenes depending sometimes on a sense of earlier poetic structures, sometimes on quasi-musical effects; examples are the Carnival Masque in Act I, the "Classical Walpurgis Night" in Act II, the entire Helena act, and the closing scene of the tragedy. But the flexibility and the dramatic effectiveness of much of *Faust* depends on the use of what is often called the "*Faust* verse" (sometimes referred to in Germany as "madrigal verse"). In German poetic drama it had become customary by the end of the eighteenth century to use Shakespearian blank verse (unrhymed iambic pentameter). Goethe had begun work on *Faust*, however, using an adaptation of the traditional and popular poetic form from sixteenth-century German literature (the era of the historical Faustus) called *Knittelvers*. This is a very free poetic line, often iambic with four stresses, but often varying the number of stressed syllables and the pattern of unstressed syllables, and using a varying rhyme scheme with both masculine and feminine endings. For Goethe this verse form had from the start a quaint, archaic, somewhat rough-hewn quality, like the style of old woodcuts. As his work on *Faust* proceeded, however, especially in the Gretchen tragedy and, later, in the section written around 1800 for *Part I*, Goethe developed this archaic and crude verse form into a highly sophisticated and subtle instrument of stylistic and poetic variation.

DATES OF COMPOSITION

Goethe worked on *Faust* for more than sixty years from its conception around 1770, when he was a young man in his twenties, to its completion in 1831, a year before his death. The documentary evidence for reconstructing his labors is enormous, including Goethe's own comments in his diaries and correspondence, and the many manuscripts of *Faust* which have been preserved (especially of *Part II*). Any outline of the dates of composition scene by scene must acknowledge that individual scenes may have a complex evolution, extending over many years (consider the scenes "Midnight," "Great Outer Precinct of the Palace," and "Entombment" in Act V), so that the final text results from a process of development which is no longer visible in the text; and also that dates of composition for individual scenes, and even for sections of individual scenes and single lines, can often be given by approximation only, even where the evidence from documents is fairly precise. Reconstructing the process of composition remains a highly artificial and abstract venture; even if we know from a particular manuscript that Goethe worked on a particular scene on a particular day, this does not necessarily tell us anything about how the scene was written or why.

In general, the history of composition for *Faust* falls into six periods, each of which ended when Goethe set the project aside for several years or decided to publish some newly completed part of it.

a. The *Urfaust*, or "original *Faust*" (ca. 1772–75). We know very little about when Goethe first began writing *Faust*, though there is evidence to suggest that the earliest scenes (which in the text of the *Urfaust* as we have it may already have been the result of considerable revision; and who can tell how many scenes were thrown away or completely lost?) were probably written in the last three years before Goethe moved to Weimar late in 1775. It is generally acknowledged that the composition of the Gretchen tragedy was a more or less coherent creative endeavor, perhaps done fairly quickly, and perhaps one of the later parts of the *Urfaust* to be written. (Our text of the *Urfaust* derives from a transcription by Luise von Göchhausen, a lady of the court at Weimar; it was prepared from Goethe's manuscript, soon after he settled in Weimar, and rediscovered in 1887.)

b. *Faust. A Fragment* (1788–90). In March and April, 1788, when Goethe was in Rome, he undertook to prepare *Faust* for publication in an edition of his *Collected Works*. The scenes "Witch's Kitchen" and "Forest and Cave" were composed at that time in the form in which we know them. Further work occurred after Goethe returned to Weimar in late 1789, involving the recasting into verse of prose scenes from the original (e.g., "Auerbach's Tavern").

c. *The Tragedy, Part I* (1787–1806). Work on *Faust, Part I,* began again in June, 1797, in response to repeated urging from Schiller (see pp. 406–12, below). At that time (June 24) Goethe wrote the "Dedication," organized the materials in his manuscript, and outlined his plans for work to be done. By the end of 1797 the "Walpurgis Night's Dream" was complete (though not originally intended for *Faust* at all), and a draft for most of the Walpurgis Night as we have it was written in the following year or so, along with a numbered sequence and sketch of scenes for the play. The scene "Dungeon" appears to have been recast from prose to verse in April and May, 1798. The "Prelude in the Theater" was probably composed in conjunction with Goethe's work on the renovation of the Weimar Theater in the summer and fall of 1798. The "Prologue in Heaven" was presumably written soon after Goethe's study of Milton's *Paradise Lost* in the summer of 1799. Sustained work on the "great lacuna" (lines 606–1769), a crucial part of the drama which Goethe had put off writing for twenty-five years, appears to have occurred during 1800–1801, along with further work on the "Walpurgis Night." Nothing further was done on *Part I* until early 1806, when Goethe prepared his final manuscript for publication in Volume 8 of the new edition of his *Collected Works*.

d. *Helena. Classical-Romantic Phantasmagoria. Interlude to "Faust"* (1825–26). Goethe began work again on *Faust* in March 1825 by turning to the first draft of the *Helena* (lines 8488–8802), which had been written in September, 1800. He continued composing Act III until early June, 1826. After minor revisions, it was sent to the publisher that autumn to be included in Volume 4 of the final edition of the *Collected Works* (*Ausgabe letzter Hand*).

e. In February and March, 1825, Goethe revised earlier drafts of three scenes for Act V ("Midnight," "Great Outer Precinct of the Palace," and "Entombment"), which had been written in 1800–1801. A manuscript fair copy of these scenes was prepared by Goethe's scribe in March and April, 1826.

Act I of *Part II* (lines 4613–6036) was published separately in Volume 12 of the final edition of the *Collected Works*, which appeared in 1828. The scenes in the Emperor's court (Imperial Residence) were composed in sequence during the latter half of 1826 and most of 1827. The opening scene of *Part II*, "Charming Landscape," was composed in two sections: Faust's monologue in *terza rima* (lines 4679–4727) in the spring of 1826; Ariel's song and the elfin chorus (4613–78) in the summer of 1827.

f. The concluding scenes of Act I ("Pleasance," "Dark Gallery," "Brightly Lit Ballrooms," and "Hall of Chivalry") and the opening scenes of Act II ("Narrow, High-Vaulted Gothic Chamber" and "Laboratory") were composed during the latter part of 1829. The "Classical Walpurgis Night" was begun during the first half of 1830 and completed in December of that year, at the same time that the final scene of Act V, "Mountain Gorges," was written. Act IV and the opening scenes of Act V ("Open Country," "Palace," and "Deep Night") were written during the first half of 1831. Goethe sealed up the completed manuscript of *Part II* in July, 1831, for publication after his death. It appeared in 1832 as the first volume of his *Posthumous Works*.

Analytical Table

Scene (with Line Numbers)	Metrical Form	Date of Composition[1]
Dedication (1–32)	*ottava rima*	June 24, 1797 (C)
Prelude in the Theater (33–242)	*Faust* verse	late 1798 (C)
Prologue in Heaven (243–353)	*Faust* verse, with hymn in four-stress iambics, eight-line stanzas	late 1799 (C)
THE TRAGEDY'S FIRST PART		
Night (354–807)		
a) 354–605, excluding 598–601	*Knittelvers* and *Faust* verse, with free rhythm	ca. 1772–73 (A)
b) 598–601 and 606–807	*Faust* verse, with choral hymn in two-stress dactylics	probably 1799–1800 (C)
Outside the City Gate (808–1177)	*Faust* verse, with songs	1800–1801 (C)
Study (I) (1178–1529)	*Faust* verse, with eight-line stanzas, four-stress iambics, free verse (Spirits), short line incantations, and song in two-stress short line	1800–1801 (C)
Study (II) (1530–2072)		
a) 1530–1769	*Faust* verse, with spirit-chorus in free verse	1800–1801 (C)
b) 1770–1867 and 2051–72	*Faust* verse	1788–89 (B)
c) 1868–2050	*Faust* verse	before 1775 (A); revised 1789 (B)

1. First publication (including the copy by Luise von Göchhausen) is indicated following date of composition by a letter in parenthesis, as follows: (A) *Urfaust*; (B) *Fragment*; (C) *Part I*; (D) *Helena*; (E) *Act I, Part II*; (F) *Part II*.

Analytical Table

Scene (with Line Numbers)	Metrical Form	Date of Composition[1]
Auerbach's Tavern in Leipzig (2073–2336)	*Faust* verse, with songs and chants	before late 1775 in prose (A); revised as verse 1789 (B)
Witch's Kitchen (2337–2604)	*Faust* verse, with chants and spells	March–April, 1788 (B)
[Gretchen tragedy] (2605–3834)	*Faust* verse (with exceptions as noted)	1774–75 (A); revised 1789 (B)
Street (2605–77)	(with ballad)	
Evening (2678–2804)		
On a Walk (2805–64)		
The Neighbor's House (2865–3024)		
Street (3025–72)		
Garden (3073–3204)		
A Garden Pavilion (3205–16)		
Forest and Cave (3217–3373)	(with monologue in blank verse)	
a) 3217–3341		1788–89 (B; after "At the Well")
b) 3342–69		before late 1775 (A; part of Valentine scene, after "Cathedral")
Gretchen's Chamber (3374–3413)	four-line stanzas in two-stress loose iambics	
Marthe's Garden (3414–3543)	(with "credo" in short-line free verse)	
At the Well (3544–85)		
By the City Wall (3586–3619)	prayer, with varying line and stanza	

350

Analytical Table

Scene (with Line Numbers)	Metrical Form	Date of Composition[1]
Night ("Valentine scene") (3620–3775)		1775(A) (see "Forest and Cave")
a) 3620–45 and 3650–59		
b) 3646–49 and 3660–3995	(with song)	March, 1806 (C)
Cathedral (3776–3834)	free verse, with choral hymn in Latin	1775(A)
Walpurgis Night (3835–4222)	*Faust* verse, with songs and chants	1798–99 and 1800–1801; completed early 1806 (C)
Walpurgis Night's Dream or the Golden Wedding of Oberon and Titania. Intermezzo (4223–4398)	trochaic ballad stanza	1797; revised December (C)
4335–42		added 1826 for *Collected Works*
Dreary Day. Field	prose	perhaps 1772–73 (A)
Night. Open Field (4399–4404)	free verse	before late 1775 (A)
Dungeon (4405–4612)	*Faust* verse, with song and irregular short lines	before late 1775 in prose (A); revised as verse April–May, 1798 (C)
THE TRAGEDY'S PART TWO IN FIVE ACTS		
Act One (4613–6565)		
Charming Landscape (4613–4727)		
a) 4613–78	song (four-stress trochaics in eight-line stanzas), with *Faust* verse	summer, 1827
b) 4678–4727	terza rima	spring, 1826

1. First publication (including the copy by Luise von Göchhausen) is indicated following date of composition by a letter in parenthesis, as follows: (A) *Urfaust*; (B) *Fragment*; (C) *Part I*; (D) *Helena*; (E) *Act I, Part II* (to line 6036); (F) *Part II*.

Analytical Table

Scene (with Line Numbers)	Metrical Form	Date of Composition[1]
Imperial Residence[2] (4728–6565)		
Throne Room (4728–5064) Spacious Hall ("Carnival Masque," 5065–5986)	*Faust* verse	summer, 1827 (E) autumn and winter, 1827 (E)
a) Procession with Herald (5065–5456)	*Faust* verse (Herald); varying four-stress trochaics and iambics, often in four-line stanzas	
b) Allegory of Plutus (5457–5800)	*Faust* verse (with brief sequence of four-stress trochaics)	
c) Pan and his train (5801–5986)	*Faust* verse; two-stress iambics; four-stress trochaics in four-line stanzas; four-stress trochaics	
Pleasance (5988–6172)	*Faust* verse	early 1826 (E)
a) 5988–6036		late 1829 (F)
b) 6037–6172		late 1829 (F)
Dark Gallery (6173–6306)	*Faust* verse	late 1829 (F)
Brightly Lit Ballrooms (6307–76)	*Faust* verse	late 1829 (F)
Hall of Chivalry (6377–6565)	*Faust* verse	
Act Two (6566–8487)		
[Faust's Study] (6566–7004)		
Narrow, High-Vaulted Gothic Chamber (6566–6818)	*Faust* verse, with chorus and four-stress trochaic six-line stanzas	late 1829 (F)
Laboratory (6819–7004)	*Faust* verse	late 1829 (F)

2. The first act of Part II may be properly said to commence after "Charming Landscape," which serves as a symbolic prelude to the entire second part of *Faust*. The stage direction for the opening scene in the Emperor's court, "Imperial Residence," applies to the entire first act.

Analytical Table

Scene (with Line Numbers)	Metrical Form	Date of Composition[1]
Classical Walpurgis Night (7005–8487)		January to June, 1830; completed December, 1830 (F)
Pharsalian Fields (7005–79)	iambic trimeter; four-stress trochaics	
On the Upper Peneios (7080–7248)	Faust verse; four-stress trochaics	
On the Lower Peneios (7249–7494)	Faust verse, with four-stress trochaics, dactylic chant, and free rhythm	
On the Upper Peneios, as before (7495–8033)	four-stress trochaics; Faust verse; songs; free rhythm	
Rocky Inlets of the Aegean Sea (8034–8487)	dialogue in Faust verse, with alternating episodes in four-stress trochaics, irregular three-stress line, anapestic choral verse, iambic and dactylic systems, with variants of all these.	
Act Three (8488–10038)		March, 1825 to June, 1826; final revisions to early 1827 (D)
[Helena. Classical-Romantic Phantasmagoria. Interlude to Faust] (8488–10038)		
Before the Palace of Menelaos in Sparta (8488–9126)	imitation Greek tragedy: dialogue in iambic trimeter, with choral odes in responding stanzas and occasional trochaic tetrameter	

1. First publication is indicated following date of composition by a letter in parenthesis, as follows: (A) *Urfaust;* (B) *Fragment;* (C) *Part I;* (D) *Helena;* (E) *Act I, Part II* (to line 6036); (F) *Part II.*

Analytical Table

Scene (with Line Numbers)	Metric Form	Date of Composition[1]
Inner Courtyard of a Fortress (9127–9573)	gradual shift from iambic trimeter to blank verse, with interludes of choral odes and songs in ballad stanza, concluding with pastoral lyric in iambic stanzas	
Arcadia (9574–10038) Parabasis [Prelude] (9574–9673) Euphorion opera (9674–9938)	trochaic tetrameter; choral ode sequence of musical forms: prelude in trochaic stanzas; dance sequence with solos, choruses, and ensemble in a variety of short lines, leading to a climax in ceremonial measure (six-syllable line with varying stress pattern), followed by couplets and choral dirge	
[Postlude] (9939–10038)	sequence of speeches in iambic trimeter, blank verse, and *Faust* verse, with free verse and trochaic tetrameter	
Act Four (10039–11042) High Mountains (10039–10344) In the Foothills (10345–10782) The Rival Emperor's Tent (10783–11042)	iambic trimeter; *Faust* verse *Faust verse*, with four-stress trochaics *Faust verse*; Alexandrines	Early February to late July, 1831 (F)
Act Five (11043–11142) Open Country (11043–11142) Palace (11143–11287)	four-stress trochaics *Faust* verse, with iambic short lines	April–May, 1831 (F) April–May, 1831 (F)

Analytical Table

Scene (with Line Numbers)	Metrical Form	Date of Composition[1]
Deep Night (11288–11383)	song in anapestic short lines; four-stress trochaics; *Faust* verse	April–May, 1831 (F)
Midnight (11384–11510)	four-stress anapestic chant; alternating *Faust* verse and four-stress trochaics	draft ca. 1800–1801; fair copy February–March, 1825 (F)
Great Outer Precinct of the Palace (11511–11603)	song; *Faust* verse	draft ca. 1800–1801; fair copy February–March, 1825 (F)
Entombment (11604–11843)	song; *Faust* verse, alternating with two-stress irregular dactylics	draft ca. 1800–1801; fair copy February–March, 1825 (F)
Mountain Gorges (11844–12111)	profusion of varying lyric and choral forms (dactylic and iambic systems with varying lengths of line)	December, 1830 (F)

1. First publication is indicated following date of composition by a letter in parenthesis, as follows: (A) *Urfaust*; (B) *Fragment*; (C) *Part I*; (D) *Helena*; (E) *Act I, Part II* (to line 6036); (F) *Part II*.

WALTER ARNDT

Translating *Faust*

Faust is a work of poetry, i.e., one in which cognitive import and formal-aesthetic impact depend on one another and are intimately blended. Without the latter, the former loses not just its verbal bloom but some of its nature: Faust tends to become a petulant or bombastic fantast, Gretchen a prattling petit-bourgeoise, Mephisto a cheaply cynical ward-heeler of Hell, not unlike Ivan Karamazov's seedy visitor, to whom he stood godfather. The impact of the roving, dazzling, enigmatic world drama, and within it the import, is brought to bear upon the reader through a great wealth and variety of scanned and rhymed forms, and in that vigorous, idiosyncratic, often slapdash hand which makes, one fancies, any six consecutive lines of Goethe unmistakable. To me it is axiomatic, therefore, that *Faust* must be brought into English with as near as possible the same formal opulence and the same signature.

There are reported to be in existence, in Goethe collections or in the book trade, close to fifty English versions of *Part I* and about a dozen of *Part II*. Most of them, if not failures from the start, have been rendered inadequate by time. The task of a new translator is to be, on one hand, more Goethean than the many versions which abandon the original for some verbal vehicle more congenial to the translator than to the poet, ostensibly smarter, racier, more "English"; and for a line with enough bumps and potholes in it to keep the passenger on his toes and feeling Modern. This is easy. But it is also his task to produce a translation which improves on more form-respecting versions by attaining a higher fidelity over both long and short run; following the metrics with less shirking of the musically indispensable feminine rhymes; maintaining a fresher diction, but with the original's quota of necessary archaisms; and reaching a higher poetic level without smoothing or prettifying the original. This is more difficult, but not beyond reach. Let me discuss some of the given data of this task.

It is beginning to dawn on critics again that rhyme, in both original and translated poetry, is far from being a childish paste-on ornament, a gratuitous upping of the cost of expression, onerous, supererogatory, and, at best, slightly unfair to the plain, honest "meaning" around it. Yet my mole-like researches over the weary years compel me to report that 68.7 out of every 100 reviewers of translations from and into rhymed verse still sooner or later lift a sorrowing forefinger to say that "the rhyme tyrannizes the meaning." The rhyme, one should say to the forefinger, is an inseparable quality of the seamless whole which makes up the poetic artifact; it is part of the "meaning," and the "meaning" is part of it. There is, of course, poor or obtrusive or inappropriate rhyming, as there is poor scansion and skewed wording. But it does not in itself "tyrannize" anything, it debases the artifact as a whole, as would clumsy invention, insensitive diction, mistranslation. It is "bad" as a natural metallic ingredient is bad which gives an alloy a look or ring poorer than another might have done, had it been in its place in the untraceable process of geological formation.

Rhymes, even between closely cognate dialects like English and German, can of course never consist of phonetically and semantically near-identical cognates as between original and translation. Couples like *Land/Band* and *land/band* may seem useful, but cannot be poetically, i.e., associatively, identical for either rhyme member, let alone between the couples. Therefore rhymes have to sway, i.e., newly co-determine, the total impact in the new medium —even the best and most elegant of them—but no more than did the good and bad ones of the original.

The linguistically innocent critic of translations in verse seldom realizes that formal elements, especially rhyme, "tyrannize," (i.e., co-determine) the original poems as much as the translated ones. They do, of course, and properly so; for it implies no reproach to either poet or translator to recognize that assonance, sonority, rhythm, rhyme, on one hand, and syntax, grammar, phonology, semasiology of the linguistic code, on the other, are all hierarchical degrees and ranges of restriction. They are weights, arms, and torques of the artistic balance between freedom and necessity of expression. And the translator has, not by one optional or idiosyncratic theory of translation, but by the nature of verbal art, exactly the same ranges of freedom and barriers of constraint in his target language as the poet had in his, if his mastery of it is comparable. The poet follows now rhyme, now reason, now metric, now musical lures along no set course; resisting, manipulating, yielding to, and merging their subtle simultaneous pulls, the many vectors which combine in the resultant, the poem or passage. This is exctly what the translator does. He, it is true, labors under the piquant additional restraint of having so to combine his fresh and different vectors that the micro- and macrocosmic resultants closely resemble those of the original. But the handicap is not so much that he has to rhyme. This music is so intimately part of the poetic statement he has before him (which functionally is to him what nascent image and half-formed intent was to the original poet before he made it) that a rhymeless rendering would not occur to him and he would not recognize it as equivalent if it did. It is rather that, more often than not, the cognitively most nearly equivalent choice and grouping of words is not poetically equivalent, and judicious departure from the original is actually closer approach to it. And further, it is that fidelity enjoins him to try to match the weak and flat spots of the original as well as the high points. Hence the sardonic paradox that the translator as a rule will fail out of necessity to match

some of the chief glories of the original, and fail out of fidelity to
remedy any of its weaknesses; with obvious effect on the overall
level of achievement. No wonder that to the naked eye there are
many good poets, but almost no good verse translators in the most
exacting sense of the term.

Joseph Brodsky is perhaps the first foreign poet of rank who came
to this country with sufficient English to sense and savor Gogol-
esque quackery naturalized. He instantly diagnosed our infectious
new hobby of Verse Prospecting with Native Bearer: "translation" of
foreign poetry by American poets destitute of foreign language,
often even more totally lost to prosody than to modesty, whose
working originals consist essentially of the pickings of complaisant
native minds. More in sorrow than in anger, for some of the Pros-
pectors had been generous hosts to him here, Brodsky spoke of this
in 1974[1] in connection with a recent rash of Mandelshtam "translations":

> Translation is a search for an equivalent, not for a substitute.
> Mandelstăm is a formal poet in the highest sense of the word.
> For him a poem began with a sound, with a "sonorous molded
> shape of form," as he himself called it. Logically, a translator
> should begin his work with a search for at least a metrical equiva-
> lent to the original form. Some translated poems indicate that
> the translators are aware of this. But the tension involved is too
> high, it excessively shackles individuality; calls for the use of an
> "instrument of poetry in our own time" are too strident—and the
> translators rush to find substitutes. This happens primarily
> because these translators are themselves poets and their own indi-
> viduality is dearest of all to them. Their conception of individual-
> ity precludes the possibility of sacrifice, which from my point of
> view is the primary feature of mature individuality, and also the
> primary requirement of any (even technical) translation.

Genuine translation, to Brodsky, is sacrifice and service, which
smacks of unfreedom. But there is no "if" to the translator's freedom having to do with the "wealth" of the base language vis-à-vis
the supposed "poverty" of the target language. Aside from possible
structural conveniences or shortcomings of a language, such as the
abundance or paucity of feminine rhymes, I believe this notion to
be another fallacy. As between languages long in cultured use, any
poverty complained of is a quality of the translator, not of the
target language. There are other big ifs, of course, not having to do
with linguistic-poetic balance of freedom and necessity, which do
affect the outcome. An obvious one concerns the linguistic and cultural at-home-ness of the translator in the base language. Another
turns on his stamina, horsemanship, and self-effacement in riding,
under severe handicaps, a set obstacle course after the champion
who chose it, who usually cannot be consulted, and in point of his-

1. *New York Review of Books*, February 7, 1974, p. 14.

torical and linguistic time may be long round the bend. There are other ifs, recently touched upon in my introduction to *Pushkin Threefold*.[2]

Among some practitioners, critics, and editors of what professional austerity long decreed be called verse, not poetry, rhymed poetry is only now beginning to regain its honest name and standing. It is likely to be an uphill struggle. For some thirty years those who could do it but had tired of it, and a host of epigones who could not do it and were relieved that one could now set up shop without it and be actually in the swim because of the disability, have pronounced rhymed verse dead, as dead as "the novel." Some of the respectful reviewers of Barker Fairley's recent prose paraphrase of *Faust* (there were others who, very properly, strewed ashes in their hair and keened) are instructive in their old-fashioned reflexes—especially the one in the *Times Literary Supplement*.[3] "A new verse *Faust* would be a feeble anachronism" (as feeble perhaps as Pasternak's brilliant renderings of Shakespeare, fit only to be broken down into stumbling prose?). "The dramatic poem and the drama in verse have now ceased to be forms which working poets use," he adds, with fine irrelevance to translation; unless he has a notion that such forms now have no live public even in the original. The fact is that Shakespeare, the French Alexandrine dramatists, and Goethe have an inexhaustible public; and it does not consist of aesthetic has-beens and arrested sentimentalists who consider it *de rigueur* to take the kids to meet the culture uncles of their own youth, as they were taken in their time. It consists largely of people who go because these verse dramas are somehow capable of making their hair stand on end with the grandeur and magic of the language alone, even if not always with pity and terror; a thing which Fairley's denatured *Faust*, along with nine out of ten plays of the *vagues* and vogues, is hopelessly incapable of. Therefore, though there may be no major poet at the moment writing verse drama, one is tempted to wonder whether one who could not if the spirit moved him should be called a major poet. Might Lowell, for one, be capable of actually translating instead of "imitating" the great Russian poets he likes to link his name to? Perhaps; but while imitation is an ego trip, translation is service and sacrifice, offering only the rewards of craftsmanship exercised and enthusiasm transmitted. It is perfectly obvious why Richard Wilbur wanted to, and had to, cast his new English renditions of Molière meticulously in metric forms like the original—a feat of art and craft several magnitudes above that of a prose rendering in difficulty, but infinitely worth it, infinitely finer in effect. To an artist who has it at his command, and to the reader or listener who knows the original, it was

2. *Pushkin Threefold: Narrative, Lyric, Polemic, and Ribald Verse. The Originals with Linear and Metric Translations* (New York, E. P. Dutton, 1972, pp. xxv–xlix.
3. P. 1625, December 31, 1971.

clearly the sole solution which could do elementary justice to the stringent demands of the model. As for negative examples—which could be more extreme (perhaps second to, perhaps next to, Nabo-kov's *Onegin*) than Fairley's *Faust?* What could be a more sadden-ing act, on the part of a revered Goethe scholar, than this methodi-cal wrecking operation, performed by the ponderous steel ball of a paradoxical "prose accuracy," upon the whole splendidly intricate body of Goethe's metric architecture? What could be plainer than the fact that in the transference, the bringing home of a work of poetry from another language, fidelity and prose are mutually exclu-sive goals? Only the sort of musty, once-modish prejudice aired in *TLS* offers some clue to why many translators and reviewers seem unable to grasp that simple truth.

It is more important in translating *Faust* than, possibly, other narrative and dramatic poetry to follow the poet's changes of meter and level of diction very strictly. Besides all else it is, this poem is a sovereign *Glasperlenspiel*, by the *magister ludi* of German literature, with almost all the forms and modes of German poetry, native and imported, used up to his time. Tampering with this half serious, half delicately parodical suite of fugues by dismantling some or all in favor of a translator's necessarily more frugal "poetic idiom," or on the plea, overt or implicit, that certain meters are somehow un-English or have "no standing in English metric tradition," smacks of either élitist misapprehension or virtue made of discreditable necessity. To most potential new readers of *Faust* in English out-side of Britain no meter whatever has any particular "standing." If they read modern verse, they have been conditioned to associate poetry with "free form" or no form. Confronted with the panoply of meters and rhyme schemes, from loosest to strictest, from dime-ter to hexameter, in *Faust*, such a reader is offered an instructive, intriguing, and—one cannot but assume—enjoyable introduction to the broad musical and rhythmic possibilities of poetry—much as was the English reader before any of the successive poetics of our litera-ture had developed any tradition. As for the more adept reader, why should it be presumed that he would want a German poem de-germanized wherever—and there are not so many instances—its met-ric forms differ startlingly from the English and Classical ones he knows best?

A case may indeed be made for what might be called imitation of forms instead of exact naturalization by translation; i.e., replacing each mode used or sampled by Goethe, save the ones shared by both languages, by an English one having "standing" in the particular genre and context where it occurs in *Faust*. It would be no mean task to undertake this and in every case successfully recreate within a different meter the content-shape conveyed by Goethe, preserving the proper scope and specific gravity of a poetic statement often bound to a line unit. Ignoring this, though, the idea palpitates bracingly; it seems now subtle, now self-evident. Yet on closer inspection it looks more like a blossom of the desk blotter, more real to the amateur reviewer than to the translator. What if the original is *sui generis*? What if, as part of its *raison d'être* or its point or its special signature, it plays with more metric forms than the target language has any possible "traditional" equivalents for? What if it has adopted (the contrary case) a single one, but one so rigorous, subtle and novel that it becomes a major element in its total impact and must be imitated, lest half the total work be lost *a priori*? Such happened to be the situation in three of the major tasks of translation I have undertaken: in Pushkin's *Eugene Onegin*, in his *Ruslan and Liud- mila*, and in *Faust*. The hunt-the-meter notion also proved inapplic- able, for different reasons, to the unique verse cartoons of Wilhelm Busch, and of course to Rilke. The gravitational field of a native Eng- lish "form" for Faust being quite predictably nonexistent, one had better yield to the powerful magnet of the original form and pro- duce a "base-oriented" rather than a "target-oriented" translation. One will then rely on that form's own power in English to stimu- late a tradition—just as the original poet really had to do, to some degree, among his own public. By now there can be few German readers who come across more than two or three familiar meters in Faust; and I doubt that it matters.

To illustrate that for the poet the form determines the content in the short run almost as much as vice versa, one need only look at one example out of many which occur typically in the neighbor- hood of now famous "taglines." In *Part I*, lines 241–42, Goethe was obviously tempted by the rhetorical promise of *Vom Himmel durch die Welt zur Hölle* ("from Heaven through the world to Hell") as a coda line to the Prelude. There being to *Hölle* only about a dozen rhymes, of which all but *Welle, Stelle, Falle, Schelle, Schwelle, Schnelle* (in their nominal and verbal functions) are bur- lesque or alien to this context, he filled the end of 241 in with *Schnelle* ("speed"), compensated the unmotivated haste with *bedächtiger* ("deliberate"), and chose the kindred *wandelt* ("amble," more or less) for the verb of motion called for by the coda line. *Mit bedächtiger Schnelle*, not a particularly pithy or per- tinent phrase here or in the Supreme Court order, is therefore not sacred verbiage to the translator to the same degree as the coda line is, just as it was not to the poet. Goethe could have put, say, *an des Schöpfers Stelle* ("in the creator's place") or *an des Dichters Stelle*, ("in the poet's place") or *Und treibet auf des Geistes Welle* ("and drifts on the surge of the spirit"), or any of a number of reasonably apt phrases, each, one dares submit, as likely and acceptable fillers as the one he settled on. A good many of the rhyme-paired lines in any poet show one "wanted" and one "co-opted" rhyme word in this way, and this is not "tyranny" but value placed on a formal fea- ture; and the less the second "shows" as "co-opted" to the hearer's critical-aesthetic sense, the more skillful or inspired has the co-option proved. For that matter, a whole passage may take shape under its aegis. This is probably true over long passages in *Faust*, which is a way of saying that it is a poem of astonishingly sustained density and brilliance; and that is where the translator is most severely up against it, and finds himself tunneling through and chipping at a half-dozen flawed near-solutions and perhaps never getting close enough. Other lines and passages, though, do constitute relative troughs in the level of tension, felicity, and point. This is part, then, of what I had in mind when denying the tyranny of rhyme on the translator: it is impossibly restrictive only if he takes, or is exhorted to take, the precise diction in the (relatively speaking) filler passages more seriously and literally than did the poet. The judgment as to what is essence and what is, in this sense, accretion tends to be instantly settled by a spontaneous aesthetic reaction.

A more puzzling case, possibly in some sense a counter-example to the couple cited above, also occurs in the Prelude, in lines 140–41: *Ist es der Einklang nicht, der aus dem Busen dringt* [chosen rhyme word, presumably]/*Und in sein Herz die Welt zurücke schlingt* [co-opted word, presumably]. Now here, with the many verb stems in *-ing-* or *-ink-* and their composites, there are some thirty rhyme words at hand, few very remote or special; yet Goethe settles on *schlingt* with the odd and ambiguous phrase preceding it. "Is it not the accord ["concord," "chord," "harmony"] which emanates from the bosom and snares ["ties," "winds," even "swallows"] the world back into his heart"—what does this mean? Would one co-opt *schlingt* from among so many choices unless one positively "meant" it? And if so, did it suggest itself as part or as origin of so obscure and equivocal a phrase? Is it actually the "chosen" word? Yet can a chord or harmony either "swallow" or "snare," "sling" or "wind" anything "back"? But this sentence, and not a few others, are minor textual puzzles rather than clear instances of lopsided rhyming. They are the scholiast's meat, and the queasy translator may cull from the maze of competitive *Arznei-gärten* of *Faust* scholarship what healing herbs he can.

It follows from the preceding that sometimes, where the poetic statement or image is not particularly lapidary or cogent, and diction somewhat unbuttoned or random, the translator may sacrifice maximum fidelity for the sake of good rhyme and happy phrasing, not always easily come by elsewhere. In the converse case, the opposite sacrifice has to be faced, barring the rare *trouvaille*. Since German, like Russian, with its trailing syllables and wealth of endings is vastly richer in offhand unforced rhymes—especially, of course, feminine ones—than English, impure rhymes, half-rhymes, and, rarely, little more than assonances have been resorted to in some impasses. The demanding octave form, as in the Dedication and the Prelude, poses this purely linguistic quandary in a rather extreme degree; not to mention the *terza rima* . . .

Faust, as German children have often complained, is unduly padded with quotations.[4] This has meant that often, in the circumstances described above, a better line or passage of translation was sacrificed, without full conviction, to a more pedestrian one closer to the original. This is a principle I deprecate over the long run, thinking more highly of the translation as a verbal organism living in the target language than of the claims of maximum fidelity in detail. This is essentially a teleological question: do you want to know pretty exactly what Goethe says in *Faust*, where exactly he places what verbal counters, or do you want pretty exactly the same sum of aesthetic experience which German readers derive from *Faust*? The difference is the one referred to by those forbidding terms "base-oriented" and "target-oriented" translation. In any case, if by and large both claims cannot be met concurrently, there is some inadequacy in the translator's equipment.

A final longish word is perhaps in order here on *imitatio mali*: aspects of fidelity which amount to close imitation of flaws and artful instigation of yawns. I have striven almost everywhere for a precise or very close reproduction of Goethe's metrics, his lines, his diction in the line, and its occasional special effects. This cultural and musical fidelity is far from runaway literalness à la Nabokov, which out of worship of the text and antiquarian self-indulgence maims lexicon and syntax of the target language. It must be driven only as far beyond the limit of aesthetic response or approval as the original may drive the translator and other readers. But this far it should be driven. In other words, where at times Goethe's chosen meters, modes of diction, or lexical ventures add up to effects tedious or offensive to the reader of the original, I submit that these passages must "come out" just as feeble or overripe or convoluted or ludicrous as they went in. It is silly to decide, for example, that one won't use Alexandrines in an English *Faust* because they just never work properly (remember Pope's quip[5]) but will substitute iambic pentameters, if it turns out that Alexandrines stick in German gullets in just the same way. In doing so one would be improving on the original and would then have to urge the Germans to do the same with their version.

The long "antiquish" passages of *Part II*, Act III, are thought by many—more native Germans perhaps than foreign devotees—to be among the more uninspired and unnatural stretches of verse in

---

4. Lest this remark seem obscure: German schoolchildren reading *Faust* often do not realize that they have penetrated to the source of half the popular saws and tags in educated language, and grumble that half the text *besteht aus Zitaten*. British children, we know, tend to take exception to Shakespeare on the same grounds.

5. "A needless Alexandrine ends the song,
That like a wounded snake drags its slow length along."

Faust. They are, while not the origin, certainly the most prominent examples after the eighteenth century of a specious "Grecian" diction in German. The watershed of taste lies perhaps between those who have and those who have not been subjected at some impressionable age to J. H. Voss's born-archaic German translations of Homer. Here, it is felt with rising discomfort, the noble simplicity obviously sought by Goethe is slowly dissipated down those arrays of stately, mannered, overlong lines with all the predicates in the wrong places. Nor is aid forthcoming from any credible integration of those lofty-falutin' figures and groups into the drama at this point, through unpredictable action or deft individuation of characters, however statuesque and myth-encrusted they may be. Thus there is little that could wrap flesh about this wafting of exiguous asphodel whiffs, this gesturing and posturing of a thrice-diluted and ill-transplanted myth. The situation of course is a poser: Helena, for instance, has to evoke credibly the Helen of Homer and the legends; not too much more, not too much less, because her dramatic existence is in her reincarnation in the longing mind of the Homer-conditioned Faust and his nobly Hellenomaniac author. Her actions, in order to establish her, must be circumscribed also (initially and to a degree) by the fable of the legend. But if she is to effect anything credible in the drama, she should come alive as well. She should bowl the reader over with her charm and waywardness, her youth and passion, and make it amply clear why she is in such demand, why even her shade is "enough, and better than a feast." In order to be Helen, she must surely still intoxicate; and to rely for this entirely on the ghostly wine of Homer over three millennia demonstrably does not work. She is actually given all the scope she could need by her translation into Faust's *Burg*; but she remains, there too, an entity composed of memories and surface gestures, which do not encompass and testify to her substance, but constitute it, like the bed-sheet of the conventional ghost. She strides, faints, is seated, reclines, reminisces, mysteriously extrudes Euphorion, and drifts off; alas, none too soon and to no one's regret—hardly even Faust's.

The Classical and Classicist meters employed are all archaic to the modern German reader. They are difficult to get used to and to read naturally, in ascending degree from the eight-foot trochaics of Phorcyas to the clubfoot chaotics (as they must appear) of the Chorus. The mood of mutinous incredulity produced in the German reader by these metrics, while certainly not an end in itself, must be faithfully induced also in the English-speaking reader. This naturally goes against the grain of the protective translator and the one who has not enough native "feel" for the German to dare think anything bad. It should be easiest with the more markedly pseudo-archaic, quasi-expressionist contortions of lexicon, morphology, and syntax, deliberately contrived by Goethe for the Chorus of Helen's

Trojan maids, in imitation of what he had been taught were similar traits of the archaic choric diction of antique tragedy. The baroque jewel beginning line 8895 is perhaps an extreme example. Readers who can only look this up in my translation and perhaps other translations are earnestly assured that the original text is perhaps a shade more unfit for voluntary consumption—and was so in the 1830s too. But here is the point: smoothing these passages out into less mind-boggling and unsayable constructs, while perfectly possible, would be perfectly silly. Others than Goethe may have been more authentic, more successful, certainly more "readable" in their imitations of Attic choric diction in German. But Goethe did it in this characteristic way, which he himself, one feels sure, did not think of as "good German verse" but as a passable verbal evocation of that primitive, solemn, forbidding thing, the voice of the fifth-century Greek chorus. He was translating, as it were, from an authentic Greek fragment that no one else knew about; and his understanding of this voice and its cadences as he blended it into his wispy third-remove Helena tale is a small part, but a part, of the work's authenticity. In short, all this material must in English remain as "bad" as his—as gnarled or as second-hand "poetic" or whatever.

It will be readily seen that there is a small dilemma of *amour-propre* here. Most of the Chorus text and much else *ought* to sound "translated" in the English version, because it does in the German. This is unfortunate for the translator's prestige, but can't be helped. One mild example of the mix is 8508–8515: the fulsome but lucid wording of 8508–9, the quite charming and lifelike jumping of syntactic gears at the start of 8512, the obvious attempt to stretch the material in the same line to fill it ("a pirate, the Phrygian" for "a [or 'the'] Phrygian pirate"), which is rewarded by a small felicity, namely the rapid one-two suggestion of, first, an obscure kidnapping, then the "world-famous" affair with the dazzling prince in the Phrygian cap. Lastly, 8508–9 shows one of the frequent Goethean cliff-hanger adverbs that seem to cry for surgical tape to hold them in the line or scissors to snip them off. The following version is a very close facsimile of the original, with its three oddities that are as un-English as they are un-German in the original:

> Let me go in! and let it all be left behind
> That stormed about me unto this time, fatefully.

The first oddity is the "stormed about me," somewhat queerer in English than in German. The second is the archaism "unto," tried here to give some account of the German *hieher*, already archaic or regional in Goethe's time, but of course not meant to be odd by Goethe. (Do we in translation smooth out items that take the reader of the original—contemporary and/or present—aback, if the author did not mean them to do that?) The third oddity is the stuck-on adverb at the end. My inclination, it must be clear now, is to leave this just as it is, if possible. But practice often shows that proper attention to such desirable oddities, as to any other feature, raises metric difficulties not worth incurring, or might have to be bought at the cost of other fidelities. So here, in the version adopted, I cancelled the ungrammatical "it" and the double "let" of the first line, and got rid of the "unto this time" (as a phrase, a spurious archaism anyway). I paid for these tiny *rapprochements* by the tiny forgery of not showing Goethe's dangling adverb, but pulling it in with a rhetorical "so" that fits the tone of the passage:

> Allow me entry! and let all be left behind
> That stormed about me hitherto so fatefully.

Translation appears to rival matrimony in the myriad minute sacrifices, compromises, betrayals, and felicities which go into its fabric.

Non-linguists possibly do not realize clearly that many (not all) of the worries, i.e., opportunities for fidelity, in *Faust* exist only by virtue of the close kinship between the two Germanic languages we are dealing with here. *Faust* in Turkish would throw up some of the same, but many more much starker and more disheartening problems of equivalence, running not along but across the grains of linguistic structure and cultural heritage. This should make the reader bless his barbaric Saxon heritage which still readily permits the naturalization of a complex masterpiece after a millenium of English deviation from common Germanic.

It should be noted that the language used in the translation is that of a British-educated writer. There are probably some Americanisms, but far more numerous Briticisms. A few of the word stresses, despite my efforts to find common denominators where possible, may deviate from U.S. practice and interfere with the scansion at first. An example would be *altérnate* for the adjective 'every other,' a word apparently lost from U.S. parlance. In triphthongal words like *flower* and *fire* I have generally followed traditional British prosody in scanning them as monosyllables, although the Shakespearean dissyllabic scansion is perfectly tenable, these being phonometrically one-and-a-half morae long in America. Line-by-line numerical correspondence between the original and the translation has been maintained to the exclusion of added or omitted lines and with few major transpositions within a passage. It will be apparent also that an effort has been made, not uniformly successful, to preserve Goethe's prosody, down to the number of feet in every line, in all the seven or more classes of meters he uses, from two to eight feet in length.

At various stages of my pleasant working holiday with *Faust* I have been corrected, instructed, cheered, and spurred on by Henry Hatfield, Harold Jantz, Edson Chick, George Salamon, Frank Ryder, Stuart Atkins, and not least, by my ever equable friend and indefatigable fellow-editor, Cyrus Hamlin, whose ever-deepening insight into *Faust* and salutary rigor proved of inestimable value. They are responsible for many of the virtues and none of the short-comings of this "carrying across," and I am deeply grateful to them; as I am to Alice Weymouth and Aniela Plummer for woman-fully reducing ever more rough and insalubrious drafts to fair copy. My dear wife and children, some of whom shared in my several *dies Fausti* and were subjected to occasional readings, did me the honor of laughing hard at numerous lines, including many of humorous intent.

Warm appreciation is also expressed to the humanists, scientists, and poets of Dartmouth College, who through their Humanities Faculty Development Fund and Committee on Research supported this work over both the academic quarters employed in adding *Part II* to the translation.

CYRUS HAMLIN

Reading *Faust*

The great monuments of literature and art provide the legitimacy and authenticity for what we call human culture. Not only do these works provide us with the ideas and the experiences which direct the lives we live: they do that, of course, and the best moments of any lifetime are bound to be prefigured, if not actually conditioned and at times even caused, by the models of humanity which are accessible to us in their most perfect form in literature and art. But it also holds true that humanity itself is the creation of poetry in the broadest sense of that which is made and established by the imagination of mankind. The true subject of our greatest works, held up to us as if in a magic mirror to transform the image which we project onto them, is the ideal of our own humanity. Why else should we read Goethe's *Faust*, which may be regarded as one of the supreme monuments of all time, a work of such scope and com-plexity that any reader will find its riches inexhaustible? No one is likely to question the legitimacy and authenticity of that reputation, handed down to us almost without interruption through more than a century and a half, which has established *Faust* on a level of cul-tural importance equal to the Homeric epics, Dante's *Divine Comedy*, or Cervantes' *Don Quixote*. Yet we may be in some doubt, even if the text of *Faust* is familiar from close study in the original German, as to just how such a sense of humanity may be achieved here for the general reader. Teachers of undergraduate courses in literature, where *Faust* is appropriately included among the essential texts for study in translation, may share this doubt with a sense of perplexity. Few other masterworks of our cultural tradition seem to resist communication so stubbornly and in so many ways as this monstrous German tragedy about the learned doctor who entered into a contract with the devil. Why are there such difficulties, and what may be done to surmount them?

Two separate considerations are responsible above all for our sense of distance from *Faust*, as for travelers confronted by a remote and very high mountain. The way is uncertain both because we depend on those who have prepared it for us and because the accessibility of the summit itself is in doubt. One of our difficulties as readers of *Faust* derives from the effects of scholarship and criticism, which imposes at the very least a burden of expectation; the other difficulty is inherent in the work itself, which seems to defy all familiar assumptions about coherence of structure and unity of meaning. On the one hand, *Faust* suffers from the history of its own reception, which began with a triumph of possibilities and advanced quickly toward an orthodoxy of public culture, where Goethe's drama has provided a measure for the uses and abuses of literary judgment through each succeeding generation. On the other hand, the drama invites a constant revision of response because the unique history of its own composition so clearly involved the same kind of activity, reflecting the progress of a supremely productive poetic mind through more than sixty years of creative work. It would be a serious error, I believe, for any reader of *Faust*—including those who approach it for the first time and have no direct access to the original German—to ignore the effects of these histories, the history of reception and the history of composition, for the meaning the drama may have for him.

I

It has become a commonplace of criticism to argue that each generation must reinterpret the masterworks of literature anew. Our Shakespeare is not the Shakespeare of our fathers or our grandfathers; and the history of the use and abuse by critics of Homer, Virgil, Dante, Milton, and others has been the subject of large and learned treatises. My point about *Faust* may be less familiar, namely that the history of a work's "reception" also has an unavoidable effect upon the work itself. Even if we know nothing about the views of earlier scholars and critics, our reading will be affected by what they have done. It has been suggested that the great books move through time like ships upon the sea, accumulating the effects of scholarship like barnacles and seaweed. Though the structure remains unimpaired, the appearance changes. *Faust* cannot be for us precisely what it was for Goethe and for his contemporaries. Simply to recognize that this is so, through a general sense of distance and of change, can help a reader to approach the drama more effectively.

Three separate aspects of *Faust* criticism, which have all contributed to its public reputation in important ways, should be mentioned: philosophical interpretations, antiquarian research into the Faust legend, and the association of *Faust* with Germany.

Among the documents assembled in this volume are comments on *Faust* by the leading philosophical critics of Goethe's own time: Friedrich Schlegel, Schelling, and, above all, Hegel. The paraphrase of *Faust* contained in the *Phenomenology of Mind* (1807) is unfamiliar to most Goethe scholars and is unlikely to elicit much sympathy from the modern reader for the obscurities of its conceptual abstractions. Yet the attitude of Hegel toward *Faust* is representative of the single most important response to Goethe's work during the first half of the nineteenth century. *Faust* quickly achieved the reputation of being a philosophical poem, and its central concern was identified with the dilemma of human experience itself, as understood by Fichte and the Idealists, on beyond Hegel to Schopenhauer, Kierkegaard, and the earlier Existentialist thinkers. Faust became synonymous with the self-conscious mind, whether this was understood in terms of Romanticism, German philosophy, or the entire history of Western thought. Goethe himself attempted to minimize the philosophical implications of his work, as indicated by his comments to Eckermann on May 6, 1827 (see below); but *Faust* itself has sustained the legitimacy of such a response and has come to be regarded, willy-nilly, as a philosophical poem. To ignore this or to pretend that it did not or should not have happened would be folly.

The literature of antiquarian research concerning the history of the Faust legend has become so enormous that no one, not even the most dedicated Faust scholar, can any longer survey the entire material. Faust lore and the studies of Faust lore fill whole libraries. Here again we may take for granted the effects of scholarship. No one would question the almost archetypal or mythical significance for Western thought of the obscure sixteenth-century necromancer. Faust enjoys a status comparable to Prometheus within our cultural tradition, and this status explains in part the position of Goethe's *Faust* in the canon of our literature. What is difficult to bear in mind is the degree to which Goethe's drama is itself responsible for the entire literature on the Faust legend. Before Goethe began work on his play during the so-called *Sturm und Drang* of the 1770s, little attention had been paid to the Faust legend apart from popular, sub-literary forms of the theater, such as the puppet shows. The chapbooks on Faust, which had been elaborated and expanded into tedious moral tracts during the seventeenth century, had for the general reading public all but disappeared from memory by Goethe's time. Even Marlowe's great drama had been neglected for generations, as indicated by the fact that Goethe only became

familiar with the play years after *Part I* of his *Faust* had been published. But our knowledge of the earlier history of the Faust legend
is the result of several generations of dedicated scholarship, above
all by the Positivist critics in Germany during the latter half of the
nineteenth century. Their discoveries about the legend have added a
further dimension of awareness to Goethe's *Faust* which at first it
contained only by implication. Clearly we were expected by the
poet to recognize that an obscure and ancient tale was being
reworked in the drama. But Goethe would have been astonished,
and no doubt amused, at the vast learning which has been applied
to the exploration of that obscure background. At one extreme such
antiquarian approaches treat *Faust* as if it were a historical document, an attempt by Goethe to recreate the life and times of the sixteenth-century necromancer. My own conviction, which is reflected
in the selection of materials included in this volume, is that we
must never forget that *Faust* is the masterpiece of a poet writing
during the Romantic era and that we need not actually know any
more about the legend than Goethe did in order to understand his
drama. The burden of scholarship, in this instance, can distort and
mislead the unwary reader.

The two selections on *Faust* by Mme. de Staël and Heine which
conclude the section of criticism by Goethe's contemporaries point
to a third important aspect of the baggage of scholarship which the
drama has been made to bear. Both writers were addressing primarily the reading public of France with the purpose of interpreting
the peculiarities of Germany, its literature and culture. Both also
regard *Faust* as a representative German poem. Heine even allows
himself the remark that "the German people is itself that learned
Doctor Faustus," a remark which has often been reechoed since in
various situations and with various implications. The fortunes of
Goethe's *Faust* have accompanied in large measure the fortunes of
the German nation. And with the rise of nationalism throughout
the nineteenth century, leading to the catastrophes of the world
wars in the twentieth, *Faust* has also lost all innocence as a strictly
poetic work, due to the political and ideological associations which
have frequently been associated with it. A learned study in German
by Hans Schwerte of what he calls the Faustian aspect of German
culture and thought (*Faust und das Faustische*) proves conclusively
that the excessive, often militant claims which have been made for
the German state and the German "soul" have included an explicit
identification with the absolutist demands put by Faust to the
devil. Thomas Mann's novel *Doktor Faustus*, composed during the
final years of the Nazi era, before the ultimate collapse of Germany
at the end of World War II, pursues the problematic identification
of the Faust legend with both the German genius and the German
nation in what must be regarded as an authoritative poetic achievement, fully as comprehensive in its way as Goethe's drama. It is no

longer possible to read *Faust* without responding in some way to the effects of subsequent German history. The association of the two, and at times their identification, has been made too often and too vehemently to be ignored. Especially during the early decades of this century, due to the influence of "intellectual history" (*Geistesgeschichte*) as a critical method and Spengler's *Decline of the West* as an ideology, the radical application of the legend to the nation left a permanent mark upon the reputation of the drama. One indication of this has been a marked decline in the number of studies which have been published on *Faust* in Germany since 1945. An apparent embarrassment, if not at times a positive aversion, may be felt among German readers toward their greatest poem because of its unavoidable association with their recent political past.

II

A full quarter of a century has now intervened since the catastrophe of 1945, and new directions of criticism have established viable contexts for the renewed study of Goethe's masterpiece. Almost without exception the selections included under the heading of "Modern Criticism" have been written since the war, some of them in the last two or three years. To a degree, of course, criteria of expediency and suitability determined the selection of essays. Some general suggestions may nonetheless be offered about the implications of this material for the continuing study of *Faust*. It may even be possible to outline the directions which criticism should pursue during the years to come. Readers of *Faust* in an English translation may feel handicapped, as must always be the case, because the text of the original is beyond access. Yet there is also an advantage to the perspective of distance which a reader in English brings to *Faust*, a greater range of response, a freedom, and an openness which should enable Goethe's work to communicate its meaning more directly and more forcefully and in ways which may be related more easily to our own lives than is the case for many German readers.

Among the possible guidelines which may be offered for beginning readers of Faust, three concerns deserve emphasis here, because they are all essential to any valid interpretation of the work and also because they can sometimes work against each other if they are not all kept in mind. They may be termed the philosophical, the dramatic and the formal. A few comments with reference to the drama itself may assist further study of what they imply.

By philosophical concern I do not mean that *Faust* should be regarded as strictly a philosophical work nor that it should serve the purposes of philosophical speculation. Yet the Idealist critics were correct in asserting that the problem of Faust which Goethe is exploring in his drama indeed constitutes a profound dilemma of the self as it struggles to live in the world and to achieve understanding of itself in relation to the world. These were the concerns of Goethe as a poet and a thinker, as they were also the particular concerns of Idealist philosophy from Kant to Hegel and are also, indeed, central concerns for literature and philosophy throughout the Western tradition. Goethe knew this, perhaps only intuitively at first, when he drafted the opening monologue of Faust and his confrontation, first, with the sign of the Macrocosm and, second, with the Earth Spirit. Later on, especially during the final stages of composition of *Part I*, Goethe may be considered to have adapted theoretical issues which were being discussed at the court of Weimar and the University of Jena during the last decade of the eighteenth century, issues which were familiar to him and which he often discussed, for instance, in his correspondence with Schiller. It is especially in the "great lacuna," the section in *Part I* from the end of the scene with Wagner (line 605) to the conclusion of the pact scene (line 1770), which was composed around the turn of the century, that the full philosophical implications of Faust's dilemma are articulated. Nor do these implications diminish in the composition of *Part II* much later in Goethe's life, long after the heyday of Idealism had passed (which is indicated by the parody of Idealism in the scene with the Baccalaureus early in Act II). The sequence of monologues by Faust provides one forceful and convenient focus for the sequential development of the essential problem of the drama: the monologue in "Forest and Cave" of *Part I* (composed when Goethe was in Rome in 1788); the speech in *terza rima* in the scene "Charming Landscape" at the outset of *Part II*; the monologue in the "High Mountains" at the beginning of Act IV; and Faust's final soliloquy just before his death in the "Great Outer Precinct of the Palace" in Act V. Finally, however, it should be emphasized that the true measure of Goethe's achievement with regard to the philosophical problem of Faust can be provided only by the drama in its entirety. The meaning of Faust's career is much nore complex than the sum of his own reflective comments.

The dramatic concern of *Faust* presents itself to us, initially at least, through the interaction of the characters, especially the central figures of Faust and Mephistopheles, Gretchen, and Helena, the Emperor and (to a lesser degree) Wagner. There is a coherent plot to the drama of Faust's career, however open and seemingly inconsequential in the advance of incidents, and the entire work does finally invite consideration—however difficult in actual practice—as a theatrical presentation. It is important, of course, that readers avoid the bias of inappropriate traditions and maintain an awareness of the shifting, expanding application of conventions from the drama and the theater. As a drama *Faust* may be regarded as truly unique, *sui generis*, within both the context of Goethe's work and the German drama of his time (the drama of Lessing, Schiller, and the later Romantics), and also within the broader contexts of European literature, even though so many separate traditions from Shakespeare to Greek tragedy, from medieval pageantry to the Baroque masque, from opera to mythological phantasmagoria, are introduced at intervals, especially during *Part II*. In some ways *Faust* might be regarded as a *summum* of European drama; yet, equally, it remains without exact precedent and parallel. A reader must learn the rules of the work, so to speak, as it proceeds. And above all the conventions and assumptions which seem adequate to one scene or sequence must not be expected to apply to what follows. The problems for interpretation are enormous, but so is the excitement and the challenge. Goethe maintains the control of a master playwright throughout, and no single literary, thematic, or intellectual problem is not resolved in fundamentally dramatic terms. Every reader must come to grips with *Faust* as drama.

The formal concern of Faust, finally, is the most complex and the most misunderstood aspect of this great work. Careful study has been made by scholars and critics of the various literary forms and styles which Goethe employs in his drama. Studies have also been made of the various sources, models, and norms which Goethe imitated, to the point where no single section of *Faust* remains without some apparent relationship to the history of literary forms and styles, and few traditions of literary composition from the ancient world to Goethe's own era are not represented somewhere in the course of the work. It has been remarked that *Faust* is a kind of anthology of Goethe's entire career, and also of German literature throughout its great Romantic era, with numerous echoes as well from earlier periods. But it may also be argued, and has been occasionally, that the work subsumes within itself the entire tradition of Western literature from its origins through Goethe's own time. This is, of course, a considerable factor for the formal complexity of the work. But there is more.

The various poetic forms which Goethe employs in *Faust* also function thematically and symbolically in various ways, to a greater or lesser degree, throughout the drama. As an example of this one might mention the remarkable sequence of figures of youth in *Part II* who are all associated in one way or another with poetry, creativity, the power of Eros: Ariel in "Charming Landscape"; the Boy Charioteer in the Carnival Masque of Act I; Homunculus in Act II; Euphorion in the Helena act; and Lynceus the Watchman in Acts III and V. It has been increasingly recognized in recent decades that the ultimate structural coherence of *Faust* could never be defined adequately in strictly dramatic terms; nor could the concerns of Faust the character himself explain the full complexity of the work (especially in those later portions where Faust is not even present!). Some principle of thematic interaction must be applied to the work as a whole, whereby the various figures, motifs, forms, and styles may be seen to interact within a myriad of interlinking patterns to constitute a vast fabric, which ultimately comprehends much of what Goethe had to say about human life, about the world, about time and history, about the ultimate values and the ultimate powers which govern everything in our experience. *Faust* is an encyclopedic work in the same degree that the Homeric epics or Dante's *Divine Comedy* are encyclopedic. But the nature of its totality, the formal structure with which that totality is achieved, is far more complex and elusive—so it seems to me—than any other comparable work in Western literature. One might look to Joyce's *Ulysses* for a similar range of styles and diversity of incidents joined together in a thematic or symbolic way; but Joyce, writing within the form of prose fiction (however diversified that was for him!), did not attempt anything like the imitation of varied poetic and literary forms, as distinct from the variety of style and satire in the novel, which Goethe, especially in *Part II*, achieved with a virtuosity and an eloquence which seems to have astonished even the poet himself. It is difficult to offer advice to students who are struggling to comprehend this aspect of Faust; and it is here, of course, where the study of a translation becomes a most severe handicap (though the present translation is remarkably successful in recreating the precise form of the original). Whoever would hope to grasp the ultimate complexity of this work, so it appears, must be prepared to devote years of effort to the endeavor. Yet it may be encouraging to observe one's own progress with each rereading; and the testimony of devoted readers suggests that the pleasures and rewards of continued effort make it all well worth while.

III

That second consideration for assessing the difficulty of reading *Faust* which was mentioned at the outset, the complexity of its history of composition, is always surveyed in the introductions to editions and has occupied considerable time and effort of scholarship. Especially during the latter part of the nineteenth century, after the Goethe Archives were opened at Weimar, detailed evidence was gathered from all available documents concerning the different stages of Goethe's work on the drama. The general outline has long since become public knowledge: the so-called *Urfaust* was written in the years just preceding Goethe's move to Weimar in 1775; the remaining sections of *Part I* (apart from a few scenes written in Italy) were added during the era of Goethe's association with Schiller from 1797 to about 1801, at which time some fragments of *Part II* (the beginning of the *Helena* and much of Act V) were also drafted; and the bulk of *Part II*, beginning with the Helena act

(Act III), was written from 1825 to the end of Goethe's life. All this is well known and does not in itself explain why the history of composition ought to affect our reading of *Faust*. My point here has to do with the consequences of this history for reading the drama itself.

The most important decision made by Goethe in the long, complex process of preparing *Faust* for publication was to abide by all the earlier stages which had already been made public and not to attempt any further changes. This meant that the text of the *Fragment* of 1790 had to be incorporated into the text of *Part I* published in 1808; similarly the text of *Part I* was binding for the much later text of *Part II*, just as the text of the *Helena* published in 1827 was binding for the sections of *Part II* composed later (including the "Classical Walpurgis Night," composed in the first half of 1830, which was initially intended to lead up to Act III—as outlined in the prose "Announcement" of 1826—but which ultimately achieved an independent status in its own right). Much debate has occurred since the 1830s concerning the unity of *Faust* as a whole. Critics have been divided at different eras to different degrees into "unitarians" and "fragmentarians." And the problem remains, even if the debate has subsided: how is it possible to comprehend the work in its entirety, quite apart from the distinction of *Parts I* and *II*, while taking into account nonetheless the inordinately complex history of its composition? I would suggest that a reader must maintain an openness and even a plurality of perspectives as he reads. *Faust* should not be regarded as an assemblage of sections, a kind of patchwork, which merely juxtaposes the separate stages of its composition like the chapters in a continuing autobiography. The various parts are truly incorporated, integrated, embodied (one searches for an adequate metaphor to describe what is ultimately inexplicable) into a comprehensive and a living whole. This totality does not, however, correspond to any familiar notion of artistic unity, least of all to the commonplace Romantic view of an organic unity for art. There is a diversity, a multiplicity, within the unity of *Faust* which allows the entire intellectual, spiritual process of development —a process which extended over a sixty year period, in close relation to the intellectual and poetic growth of Goethe himself—to be preserved in a continuum that accepts diversity and difference, indeed exploits it, for the greater enhancement of the whole. How can this be understood by a reader of *Faust* as he reads?

Each new level of composition establishes its own perspective on the whole of *Faust*. Ignoring particular details which would complicate the picture, I would argue that there are fundamentally three perspectives that are essential to an understanding: 1) the perspective of the young Goethe, the perspective of the *Urfaust*, which is embodied (though somewhat revised) within the text of the *Fragment* of 1790; 2) the perspective of the Classical Goethe, of the mature poet of about fifty years writing at the height of his powers, the perspective of the later additions to *Part I*, composed around 1800 and published (for the most part) in 1808; and 3) the perspective of the sage of Weimar, the master of letters and the spokesman for "World Literature" (*Weltliteratur*), the perspective of *Part II* (for the most part), which was composed between 1825 and 1831. The distinction between these three will be apparent to any reader. Nor will it be questioned that each of these perspectives (in its chronological turn) expands the perspective of the work as a whole. At the first stage the perspective is spontaneous, vigorous, even impetuous; the use of the Faust legend is largely satirical (the attack of an impatient student on his academic mentors), largely antiquarian (the imposition of an alien tone upon a situation and a problem close at hand: this may be felt especially in the Gretchen tragedy, which is a masterpiece of *Sturm-und-Drang* drama, using a plot that belongs to the eighteenth century). The Classical stage of composition establishes a perspective which sees Faust as representative of mankind and deals with a universal dilemma, relating the pact with Mephistopheles to philosophical concepts, ideas about the mind and the world and the nature of human experience. The final stage of composition then broadens the perspective of the drama beyond all particular, individual concerns to explore and celebrate the workings of the cosmos itself in mythical-symbolic terms, transforming Faust and Mephistopheles into mere participants in the events (along with so many others: the Emperor and his Court; the allegorical figures of the Masque; Homunculus and all the fantastic creatures of the "Classical Walpurgis Night": especially the old men, Peneios, Chiron, Anaxagoras and Thales, Nereus and Proteus, but also the youths and maidens, Galatea and her sisters, and the choric celebrants at the Aegean Sea; then the mythical personages of the Helena act, especially Helena and Euphorion, Mephistopheles as Phorcyas and the Chorus of Trojan girls; the three henchmen of Mephistopheles in Acts IV and V, the Counter-Emperor and the forces at war, Baucis and Philemon and the Traveler, Care and her three sisters, the devils and the angels of the burial scene, the father figures of "Mountain Gorges": Pater Ecstaticus, Pater Profundus, and Pater Seraphicus, and the devotee of the Virgin, Doctor Marianus; and also the Mater Gloriosa with her three attendants: Magna Peccatrix, Mulier Samaritana, and Maria Aegyptica, along with the penitent spirit who had formally been Gretchen). The list of figures is bewildering and itself serves to suggest that the drama of *Faust* has become the drama of life itself. Added to this (as hinted in the discussion of form above) is the very sophisticated, yet purposeful assimilation into *Part II* of the entire range of literary forms and traditions which constituted for Goethe what he called World Literature, transcending the poet's own subjective perspective and transcending also the particular perspective of his era, the age of

Romanticism, and of his nation, the perspective of German literature.

All this suggests just how complex the act of understanding this
work must be. And all three perspectives which I have described
here also interact upon each other in a creative and a reciprocal
manner, so that the perceptive mind will always maintain at least
an awareness of all three despite the specific dominance of any one
of them in a particular section of the drama. I would suggest that
the three perspectives should be regarded as concentric circles surrounding a center (the unspoken and perhaps unknown source for
the meaning of the work as a whole); and in the process of reading
Faust we move between and through these separate circles of
perspective in a complex process of interaction that enables us to
focus on each particular at the same time that we maintain an
awareness of the whole. And of course we are assisted in this by the
appropriate, even natural sequence of growth which occurs from the
first perspective to the second, then from the second to the third.
Our working sense of the totality of *Faust* expands as we read:
beginning (after the three opening scenes) with the immediacy of
the original monologue and night scene, then expanding to the
perspective of the Classical stage, only to shift back again for "Auerbach's Tavern" and much of the Gretchen tragedy (though individual scenes require that we keep the second circle of perspective also
in mind); finally moving to the third circle in *Part II*, which
advances by stages into the medium of myth and symbol, attaining
the limits of poetry and art and even life itself (especially at the
end of the "Classical Walpurgis Night" and throughout the Helena
act), only to narrow its focus once again in Acts IV and V in such
a way that we are required to reintroduce the concerns of the earlier, Classical perspective in the section dealing with the blinding
and the death of Faust; and, finally, where the spirit of Gretchen
appears in the last scene (having been anticipated already in Faust's
monologue at the outset of Act IV), the perspective of the *Urfaust*
is established again to affirm the ultimate validity of its immediate
and personal concern (through Gretchen's abiding love for Faust)
within the vast, universal design of salvation which is celebrated at
the very end.

IV

A few words should be said concerning the present edition of
Faust in English translation and its relation to the interests of the
general student of literature. There can be no question that the
three basic perspectives of *Faust* described above have demonstrated
again and again across the years that each is suited to a different
kind of audience. Ths earliest perspective, that of the *Urfaust*, has
the broadest appeal and has been, indeed, almost entirely responsi-

ble for the singular popularity of Goethe's work—or better: of this part of Goethe's work—in every generation. This dimension of *Faust* is also closest to the popular legend, regardless of the sophistication with which Goethe, even at the earliest stages of composition, adapted that legend to his purpose. And it may also be argued that this aspect of the drama has itself become a kind of folk legend, familiar even to those who have never read Goethe. In part this is due to the adaptations of other writers, notably in the operatic versions of the nineteenth century by Berlioz, by Boito, and especially by Gounod; yet also in part it derives from the broad reputation of the work among the general public. The Speck Collection at Yale contains, for instance, the most varied nineteenth century illustrations to *Faust*, including pictures on metal breadboxes and on matchbook covers. Nor should the particular and genuine pleasures of this dimension of *Faust* be ignored by even the most sophisticated reader: pleasures related to the dilemma of learning (where most of us probably identify more with Wagner and the Student than with Faust) and pleasures related to the problematics of love and seduction and to the almost universal sentimental appeal of Gretchen, both in her innocence and in her ultimate suffering. The element of magic and incantation also plays its appropriate role here, though Goethe never took it seriously as such, and neither should we: it is also part of the fun. The scene "Auerbach's Tavern" is paradigmatic of this popular aspect. These qualities of *Faust*, qualities of the first circle of perspective, should be appreciated and enjoyed. Nor is there any other English version, so far as I know, which surpasses the present translation in recreating the various tones and flavors, sometimes coarse, sometimes sentimental, sometimes parodistic, sometimes bittersweet, sometimes slapstick, which Goethe achieved in his language here. Readers of the present edition should have no trouble perceiving this aspect of *Faust* in the translation and in enjoying it for its own sake. The main emphasis of this edition, however, and the level of audience to which it is primarily addressed lie elsewhere.

The perspective of *Faust* which Goethe established above all during the later, so-called Classical, period of composition does not address so broad a public, nor does it yield its particular pleasures so easily. Yet the reputation of Goethe's drama as a masterpiece of literature depends to a large extent upon the problematic, both philosophical and dramatic, which is achieved at this level of the work. The intellectual profundity and the human value of this second circle of perspective are inexhaustible and deserve careful study. The rich implications of language and situation in such scenes as the "Prologue in Heaven" or the latter half of "Night," the Easter walk "Outside the City Gates" and the two study scenes (the latter with the pact of Mephistopheles), are unsurpassed in European drama for the clarification they provide concerning the nature of man and the tragic dilemma of the human condition. Goethe's *Faust* here bears comparison with the best work of Sophocles and Shakespeare, which provided (at least indirectly) the norm for that kind of drama against which Goethe would have expected his work to be measured. At this level, I believe, the present edition—both the translation and the selection of criticism—provides more precise and comprehensive guidance to the general student, who presumably has no direct access to the original German, than any other *Faust* heretofore available in English. It is this aspect of *Faust* which has seemed to both the translator and the editor to be best suited to study by the general student of literature, and it is within this perspective that Goethe's work will best stand comparison with the rest of the canon of European masterpieces.

Of course, there is much more which *Faust* offers, a plenitude of riches throughout *Part II* of the drama, that invites the imagination to explore the limits of poetry, culture, society in both its ethical and political values, the workings of nature, and the mysteries of the spirit. Nothing of importance for any serious student of our cultural heritage is excluded from Goethe's cosmic drama; and everything in the drama, however obscure in its symbolism or its mode of allusion, establishes a highly articulate and sophisticated connection and link to the continuities of our world and our history. Goethe's *Faust* may be regarded as a supreme instance of faith in man's humanity and the accumulated wisdom of all human experience, however varied and contradictory. *Faust* is both accumulative and conservative in the most precise sense: the sweep of its action and language gathers in the entirety of our tradition, remakes it into the vision and the idiom of its own performance. A reader of the drama who responds adequately to that performance, will emerge at the end with a conviction, not that this is the truth about the human condition, but that here we perceive a sense of the limit to which the mind can proceed toward grasping that truth and representing it in the domain of art and poetry. Like all great myths of the self, *Faust* constitutes a drama of discovery, moving through the totality of its lifetime with limited means and with compromising commitments, accompanied by the devil and ultimately failing (as the Lord predicted) to achieve fulfillment or satisfaction, perhaps failing even to secure the validity of its own convictions. It is also the journey of the reader through the poem. What Goethe offers us is an image of our own search for understanding, which can go to the limits of the mind, which will nonetheless and unavoidably fail to secure and affirm the meaning of that limit, but which may receive in the midst of its final failure that gift of grace which poetry can and does provide from a source beyond itself and beyond our understanding.

Backgrounds and Sources

The History of the Damnable Life and Deserved Death of Doctor John Faustus (1592) †

* * *

How Doctor Faustus began to practice in his devilish art, and how he conjured the devil, making him to appear and meet him on the morrow at his own house. Chap. 2.

You have heard before, that all Faustus' mind was set to study the arts of necromancy and conjuration, the which exercise he followed day and night: and taking to him the wings of an eagle, thought to fly over the whole world, and to know the secrets of heaven and earth; for his speculation was so wonderful, being expert in using his *vocabula*, figures, characters, conjurations, and other ceremonial actions, that in all the haste he put in practice to bring the devil before him. And taking his way to a thick wood near to Wittenberg, called in the German tongue *Spisser Waldt*: that is in English the Spisser's Wood (as Faustus would oftentimes boast of it among his crew being in his jollity,) he came into the same wood towards evening into a crossway, where he made with a wand a circle in the dust, and within that many more circles and characters: and thus he passed away the time, until it was nine or ten of the clock in the night, then began Doctor Faustus to call for Mephostophiles the spirit, and to charge him in the name of Beelzebub to appear there personally without any long stay: then presently the devil began so great a rumor in the wood, as if heaven and earth would have come together with wind, the trees bowing their tops to the ground, then fell the devil to blare as if the whole wood had been full of lions, and suddenly about the circle ran the devil as if a thousand wagons had been running together on paved stones. After this at the four corners of the wood it thundered horribly, with such lightnings as if the whole world, to his seeming, had been on fire. Faustus all this while half amazed at the devil's so long tarrying, and doubting whether he were best to abide any more such horrible conjurings, thought to leave his circle and depart; whereupon the devil made him such music of all sorts, as if the nymphs themselves had been in place: whereat Faustus was revived and stood stoutly in his circle aspecting his purpose, and began again to conjure the spirit Mephostophiles in the name of the prince of devils to appear in his likeness: whereat suddenly over his head

---

† The single literary source for the entire Faust legend is the original German chapbook *The History of Dr. Johann Faustus*, published in Frankfurt 1587 by Johann Spiess. Many later adaptations and expansions of this text were made during the seventeenth and early eighteenth centuries, including the earliest and anonymous translation into English published in 1592 (from which the present excerpt is taken), which served as the basis for Christopher Marlowe's play *The Tragical History of Doctor Faustus* (1588). Very few copies of the original chapbook survive, and it is certain that Goethe had access only to the later versions of Faust's life.

hung hovering in the air a mighty dragon: then calls Faustus again after his devilish manner, at which there was a monstrous cry in the wood, as if hell had been open, and all the tormented souls crying to God for mercy; presently not three fathoms above his head fell a flame in manner of a lightning, and changed itself into a globe: yet Faustus feared it not, but did persuade himself that the devil should give him his request before he would leave: Oftentimes after to his companions he would boast, that he had the stoutest head (under the cope of heaven) at commandment: whereat they answered, they knew none stouter than the pope or emperor: but Doctor Faustus said, the head that is my servant is above all on earth, and repeated certain words out of Saint Paul to the Ephesians to make his argument good: The prince of this world is upon earth and under heaven. Well, let us come again to his conjuration where we left him at his fiery globe: Faustus, vexed at the spirits so long tarrying, used his charms with full purpose not to depart before he had his intent, and crying on Mephostophiles the spirit; suddenly the globe opened and sprang up in height of a man: so burning a time, in the end it converted to the shape of a fiery man. This pleasant beast ran about the circle a great while, and lastly appeared in manner of a gray friar, asking Faustus what was his request. Faustus commanded that the next morning at twelve of the clock he should appear to him at his house; but the devil would in no wise grant. Faustus began again to conjure him in the name of Beelzebub, that he should fulfill his request: whereupon the spirit agreed, and so they departed each one his way.

The conference of Doctor Faustus with the spirit Mephostophiles the morning following at his own house. Chap. 3.

Doctor Faustus having commanded the spirit to be with him, at his hour appointed he came and appeared in his chamber, demanding of Faustus what his desire was: then began Doctor Faustus anew with him to conjure him that he should be obedient unto him, and to answer him certain articles, and to fulfill them in all points.

1. That the spirit should serve him and be obedient unto him in all things that he asked of him from that hour until the hour of his death.

2. Further, anything that he desired of him he should bring it to him.

3. Also, that in all Faustus his demands or interrogations, the spirit should tell him nothing but that which is true.

Hereupon the spirit answered and laid his case forth, that he had no such power of himself, until he had first given his prince (that was ruler over him) to understand thereof, and to know if he could obtain so much of his lord: therefore speak further that I may do thy whole desire to my prince: for it is not in my power to fulfill without his leave. Show me the cause why (said Faustus). The spirit answered: Faustus, thou shalt understand, that with us it is even as well a kingdom, as with you on earth: yea, we have our rulers and servants, as I myself am one, and we name our whole number the legion of devils at his commandment, that we call the *Oriental* through his pride and high mind, yet he hath nothwithstanding a legion of devils at his commandment, that we call the Oriental princes; for his power is great and infinite. Also there is a host in *Meridie*, in *Septentrio*, in *Occidente*:[1] and for that Lucifer hath his kingdom under heaven, we must change and give ourselves unto men to serve them at their pleasure. It is also certain, we have never as yet opened unto any man the truth of our dwelling, neither of our ruling, neither what our power is, neither have we given any man any gift, or learned him any thing, except he promise to be ours.

Doctor Faustus upon this arose where he sat, and said, I will have my request, and yet I will not be damned. The spirit answered, Then shalt thou want thy desire, and yet art thou mine notwithstanding: if any man would detain thee it is vain, for thine infidelity hath confounded thee.

Hereupon spoke Faustus: Get thee hence from me, and take Saint Valentine's farewell and Crisam with thee, yet I conjure thee that thou be here at evening, and bethink thyself on that I have asked thee, and ask thy prince's counsel therein. Mephostophiles the spirit, thus answered, vanished away, leaving Faustus in his study, where he sat pondering with himself how he might obtain his request of the devil without loss of his soul: yet fully he was resolved in himself, rather than to want his pleasure, to do whatsoever the spirit and his lord should condition upon.

The second time of the spirits appearing to Faustus in his house, and of their parley. Chap. 4.

Faustus continuing in his devilish cogitations, never moving out of the place where the spirit left him (such was his fervent love to the devil) the night approaching, this swift flying spirit appeared to Faustus, offering himself with all submission to his service, with full authority from his prince to do whatsoever he would request, if so be Faustus would promise to be his: this answer I bring thee, and an answer must thou make by me again, yet will I hear what is thy desire, because thou hast sworn me to be here at this time. Doctor Faustus gave him this answer, though faintly (for his soul's sake), that his request was none other but to become a devil, or at the least a limb of him, and that the spirit should agree unto these articles as follows.

1. That he might be a spirit in shape and quality.

1. The four points of the compass: east, south, north, and west.

2. That Mephostophiles should be his servant, and at his commandment.

3. That Mephostophiles should bring him anything, and do for him whatsoever.

4. That all times he should be in his house, invisible to all men, except only to himself, and at his commandment to show himself.

5. Lastly, that *Mephostophiles* should at all times appear at his command, in what form or shape soever he would.

Upon these points the spirit answered Doctor Faustus, that all this should be granted him and fulfilled, and more if he would agree unto him upon certain articles as follows.

First, that Doctor Faustus should give himself to his lord Lucifer, body and soul.

Secondly, for confirmation of the same, he should make him a writing, written with his own blood.

Thirdly, that he would be an enemy to all Christian people.

Fourthly, that he would deny his Christian belief.

Fifthly, that he let not any man change his opinion, if so be any man should go about to dissuade, or withdraw him from it.

Further, the spirit promised Faustus to give him certain years to live in health and pleasure, and when such years were expired, that then Faustus should be fetched away, and if he should hold these articles and conditions, that then he should have all whatsoever his heart would wish or desire; and that Faustus should quickly perceive himself to be a spirit in all manner of actions whatsoever. Hereupon Doctor Faustus his mind was so inflamed, that he forgot his soul, and promised Mephostophiles to hold all things as he had mentioned them: he thought the devil was not so black as they used to paint him, nor hell so hot as the people say, &c.

The third parley between Doctor Faustus and Mephostophiles about a conclusion. Chap. 5.

After Doctor Faustus had made his promise to the devil, in the morning betimes he called the spirit before him and commanded him that he should always come to him like a friar, after the order of Saint Francis, with a bell in his hand like Saint Anthony, and to ring it once or twice before he appeared, that he might know of his certain coming: then Faustus demanded the spirit, what was his name? The spirit answered, my name is as thou sayest, Mephostophiles, and I am a prince, but servant to Lucifer: and all the circuit from *Septentrio* to the *Meridian*, I rule under him. Even at these words was this wicked wretch Faustus inflamed, to hear himself to have gotten so great a potentate to be his servant, forgot the Lord his maker, and Christ his redeemer, became an enemy unto all mankind, yea, worse than the giants whom the poets fain to climb the hills to make war with the gods: not unlike that enemy of God and his Christ, that for his pride was cast into hell: so likewise Faustus forgot that the high climbers catch the greatest falls, and that the sweetest meat requires the sourest sauce.

After a while, Faustus promised Mephostophiles to write and make his obligation, with full assurance of the articles in the chapter before rehearsed. A pitiful case (Christian reader) for certainly this letter or obligation was found in his house after his most lamentable end, with all the rest of his damnable practices used in his whole life. Therefore I wish all Christians to take an example by this wicked Faustus, and to be comforted in Christ, contenting themselves with that vocation whereunto it hath pleased God to call them, and not to esteem the vain delights of this life, as did this unhappy Faustus, in giving his soul to the devil: and to confirm it the more assuredly, he took a small penknife, and pricked a vein in his left hand, and for certainty thereupon, were seen on his hand these words written, as if they had been written with blood, *ó homo fuge*: whereat the spirit vanished, but Faustus continued in his damnable mind, and made his writing as followeth.

How Doctor Faustus set his blood in a saucer on warm ashes, and wrote as follows. Chap. 6.

I Johannes Faustus, Doctor, do openly acknowledge with mine own hand, to the greater force and strengthening of this letter, that since I began to study and speculate the course and order of the elements, I have not found through the gift that is given me from above, any such learning and wisdom, that can bring me to my desires: and for that I find, that men are unable to instruct me any farther in the matter, now have I, Doctor John Faustus, unto the hellish prince of Orient and his messenger Mephostophiles, given both body and soul, upon such condition, that they shall learn me, and fulfill my desire in all things, as they have promised and vowed unto me, with due obedience unto me, according unto the articles mentioned between us.

Further, I covenant and grant with them by these presents, that at the end of 24 years next ensuing the date of this present letter, they being expired, and I in the meantime, during the said years be served of them at my will, they accomplishing my desires to the full in all points as we are agreed, that then I give them full power to do with me at their pleasure, to rule, to send, fetch, or carry me or mine, be it either body, soul, flesh, blood, or goods, into their habitation, be it wheresoever: and hereupon, I defy God and his Christ, all the host of heaven, and all living creatures that bear the shape of God, yea all that lives; and again I say it, and it shall be so. And to the more strengthening of this writing, I have written it with mine own hand and blood, being in perfect memory, and hereupon I subscribe to it with my name and title, calling all the infernal, middle, and supreme powers to witness of this my letter and subscription.

John Faustus, approved in the elements
and the spiritual doctor

Dr. Johannes Faustus. Puppet Play,
Now First Done into English (1893) †

Act I

SCENE I

FAUST *in his study, seated at a table laden with folios.*

FAUST. I've now arrived at such a pitch of learning,
    That to a laughing stock for men I'm turning;
    All books I've searched, from preface to conclusion
    And still, the philosophic stone,[1] to my confusion,
    I fail to find. My learning is in vain,
    My labor brings but hunger, want and pain!
    No decent coat is left upon my back.
    Of all things but of debt, I suffer, pinch and lack.
    Those sleepless nights, who will repay to me,
    That vainly I devoted to theology?
    Away, then, law and medicine's idle fancy,
    Henceforth I'll put my trust in necromancy,
    And, entering into compact with the devil,
    Learn nature's secret from the powers of evil!
    But e'er I reach this consummation tragic,
    I must become an adept in the art of magic.
VOICE TO THE LEFT. Woulds't thou wise and happy be,
    Choose magic; leave theology.
VOICE TO THE RIGHT. Faustus! Heed not magic's tempting voice,
    But make theology thy choice.
FAUST. Voices around me on each side I hear,
    To which shall I listen, to which give an ear?
    I will question them both, then give judgment aright;
    So, tell me thy name, oh thou voice on my right!
VOICE TO THE RIGHT. The spirit that guards thee.
FAUST.   So each one may say.
    Now, there on my left hand, who art thou, I pray?
VOICE TO THE LEFT. I am sent by Inferno's great monarch to
    bless

---

† The tradition of puppet plays dealing with the legend of Faustus, which extended well into the nineteenth century in German popular theater at a sub-literary level, influenced Goethe's early view of the Faust legend as much as the prose histories. These plays, performed by itinerant players without written scripts, were known to Goethe from direct experience in Frankfurt during his childhood. The extract included here is taken (for convenience) from an English translation of a late-nineteenth-century published version of these German puppet plays.
1. The fabled stone of the alchemists, which would turn base metals to gold.

Thee with gifts of perfection and pure happiness.

FAUST. And were't thou the devil's own kinsman, yet still
Thou art welcome, if only thou work me my will.
So accepting the left and refusing the right,
I shall reach the perfection of earthly delight.

VOICE TO LEFT. Ha, ha!

VOICE TO RIGHT. Thy poor soul!

FAUST.   It mislikes me to hear
How the bad spirit laughs, while the good drops a tear.

                *   *   *

Act II

SCENE I

FAUST *alone. Afterwards* SPIRITS.

FAUST. Strange! The students have disappeared, and are nowhere to be found. All the same, I have their book, and being alone, can herewith begin the study of Magic.

    [*Opens book and reads.*]

Ah! That is how it is done; nothing could be simpler, and yet I have puzzled over it for years!

    [*Looses his girdle, lays it on the ground in a circle, enters circle.*]

Now I will summon the spirits.

    [*Waves his wand, murmuring unintelligible words* * * *]
                                            *   *   *

    [FAUST *summons and interrogates seven spirits, none of whom satisfies him.*][2]

FAUST. * * * Ultimus! Declare thy name.

SPIRIT VIII. Mephistopheles!

FAUST. How swift art thou?

MEPHISTOPHELES. As human thought.

FAUST. Done with you! As human thought! What more could I desire than to behold shaped in fulfilment my rising thought? Why God Almighty can no more. *Eritis sicut deus!*[3] Will you serve me?

MEPHISTOPHELES. If Pluto but permit.

FAUST. And who may Pluto be?

MEPHISTOPHELES. My master.

FAUST. Go! ask your lord to let you serve me eight-and-forty years, hereafter, I will be your bondsman; but come again in human form. I like not apes, and standing in this circle wearies me. Tell your master, too, that I demand to taste of every earthly joy, and to possess fair presence and great fame; true answer, likewise, I must have to every question.

MEPHISTOPHELES. In a moment I am here again.

    [*Disappears, returning in human form, clothed in scarlet garments, covered by a long black cloak, and having a horn on his forehead.* FAUST *steps out of circle.*]

---

2. Editor's interpolation.   3. See *Faust*, line 2048 and note.

MEPHISTOPHELES. Your demands are granted by my lord; but four-and-twenty years are the longest term of service for which I may engage.

FAUST. Four-and-twenty years! Sure that means many a happy day and night. Good! I accept!

MEPHISTOPHELES. If so, give me a little bond—for life and death.

FAUST. If you must have it then, in black and white, fetch ink, for that in my horn has long been dry.

MEPHISTOPHELES. Not black but red on white. Your signature alone is needed; the bond itself is ready written out, *optima forma*,[4] fair and clear; your signature in blood completes it. See! here's a needle, prick your finger with it.

FAUST. Produce the bond, ere signing, I would read.

MEPHISTOPHELES. Mercurius, appear!

[*A raven appears with the bond in its bill.*]

FAUST. [*takes and reads*] I, Johannes, Dr. Faustus, Professor, make the following agreement with Mephistopheles:

   I. To abjure God and the Christian faith.

  II. After four-and-twenty years, reckoning 365 days to the year, to become his bondsman.

 III. During these four-and-twenty years, neither to wash, nor to shave, nor comb my hair, nor to cut my nails.

 IV. To foreswear marriage.

FAUST. Strange! These two last and least conditions seem the hardest. Now—but why pick and choose? I'll take them as they stand, one with another.

MEPHISTOPHELES. Then sign; here is a pen.

[*Gives crow-quill from his hat.*]

FAUST. Freely my blood shall flow upon this day
When to thy Lord my soul I sign away.
Behold the ruddy stream, which seems to brand
In scarlet letters, flaming on my hand.
Great *H* and *F* that all too plainly say
From the impending doom *"Homo fuge!"*[5]
Yet! *F* might stand for Faust and *H* for Honor great,
But whether fickle Chance it be or fixèd Fate,
I may no longer stand in doubt and hesitate.
The deed is signed, is sealed, repentance were too late
Yet I would clasp the parchment, but that o'er me creep
Strange languors of a faint and death-like sleep.

[FAUST *falls asleep in his chair.* * * *]

G. E. LESSING

Letter on Literature XVII (1759) †

"No one," say the authors of the *Bibliothek*, "will deny that the

---

4. "In the best form" (Latin).
5. "Man, flee!" (Latin).
† Translated by Dolores Signori (with

assistance from Walter Arndt and Cyrus Hamlin).

German stage has Professor Gottsched to thank for a great part of its initial improvement."[1]

I am this no one; I flatly deny it. One could well wish that Herr Gottsched had never meddled with the theater. His fancied improvements either affect negligible details or are actual impairments.

When Frau Neuber flourished,[2] and many felt called upon to do meritorious service to her and the stage, our dramatic poesy was indeed in a most wretched state. There were no recognized rules; there was no concern for models. Our heroic and political dramas were full of nonsense, bombast, filth, and low wit. Our comedies relied entirely on disguises and tricks of magic; their wittiest jokes were fist fights. One did not exactly need a subtle and profound mind to appreciate this fault. Nor was Herr Gottsched the first to appreciate it; he was merely the first to credit himself with sufficient power to remedy it. And how did he set about this? He understood a little French and began to translate; he encouraged anyone who could rhyme and understand *Oui, Monsieur* to translate also; he put together his play *Cato*, as a Swiss critic has remarked, with paste and scissors;[3] he put together *Darius*, the *Oysters*, *Elise* and the *Goat on Trial*, *Aurelius* and the *Little Wit*, *Banise* and the *Hypochondriac* without paste and scissors; he placed a curse upon improvising; he had the Harlequin ceremoniously driven out of the theater, which was itself the greatest harlequin joke ever played;[4] in short, he did not desire so much to reform our old theater as to create an entirely new one. And what sort of a new one? A Frenchified one; without considering whether such a Frenchified theater was suitable to a German mode of thought.

From our earlier dramatic literature, which he banished, he could sufficiently have observed that we share the taste of the English more than that of the French; that in our tragedies we want to see and think more than the timid French tragedy offers; that the great, the terrifying, the melancholic have a better effect on us than the pretty, the delicate, the lovelorn; that an excess of simplicity wears

1. The *Letters Concerning Contemporary Literature*, of which this is the seventeenth, were published in Berlin from 1759 on by Gotthold Ephraim Lessing (1729–1781) in collaboration with Moses Mendelssohn and Friedrich Nicolai. This letter begins with an allusion to the *Library of Belles Lettres and the Liberal Arts* (Vol. III, 1), published in Leipzig. Johann Christoph Gottsched (1700–1766), a professor at Leipzig, was the leading theorist in Germany at that time as well as a practicing playwright. His dogmatic preference for all forms of French Neo-Classical literature over more popular German traditions (such as the Harlequin figure in comedy) had achieved almost absolute authority in the German theater at the time when Lessing was writing.

2. Friederike Karoline Neuber, "die Neuberin" (1697–1760), was an actress as well as the leader of a troupe of players engaged by Gottsched to perform plays which he either wrote or adapted.

3. The following plays are from a collection, *German Theater after the Rules of the Ancient Greeks and Romans* (1740–50), assembled by Gottsched.

4. The Harlequin (or "Hans Wurst") derived from the Italian *commedia dell'arte* figure of popular comedy, especially in South Germany and Austria during the seventeenth and earlier eighteenth centuries. Gottsched had viciously attacked this form of improvised theater in favor of the more refined Neo-classical conventions of comedy as derived from France.

us out more than an excess of complexity; and so on. He ought therefore, to have followed this track, and it would have led him directly to the English theater.—Do not, on any account, say that he tried to make use of this also, citing his *Cato* as proof. For precisely the fact that he regards Addison's *Cato* as the best English tragedy[5] shows clearly that he here saw only with the eyes of the French, and that he was not then familiar with Shakespeare, Johnson, Beaumont and Fletcher, among others, with whom out of pride he later refused to get acquainted.

If Shakespeare's masterpieces had been translated for our Germans with a few modest changes, I am certain that it would have had a better effect than being indoctrinated with Corneille and Racine.[6] For one thing, our people would have relished the former far more than the latter; for another, those plays would have roused quite different minds among us than can be claimed for these. A genius can be inspired only by a genius, and most easily by one who seems to owe everything only to nature and who does not scare you away with the tedious accomplishments of art.

Judging also by the standards of Classical drama, Shakespeare is a far greater tragic poet than Corneille, although the latter knew the Classics very well and the former hardly at all. Corneille approaches them in matters of mechanical contrivance, Shakespeare in matters of substance. The Englishman almost always attains the goal of tragedy, however singular and peculiar to himself are the paths he chooses; the Frenchman almost never attains that goal, although he follows the beaten track of the Classics. Apart from Sophocles' *Oedipus* no play can have more power over our passions than *Othello*, *King Lear*, *Hamlet*, to name but these. Has Corneille a single tragedy which has moved you even half so much as Voltaire's *Zaïre*?[7] And Voltaire's *Zaïre*—how far beneath *Othello, the Moor of Venice*, of which it is a feeble copy, and from which the whole character of Orosman is derived?

With little effort I could prove to you in detail that our old plays really had much about them that was English. To mention only the best known of these: *Doctor Faust* has a great many scenes which only a Shakespearean genius could have conceived. And how infatuated Germany was, and still is to some extent, with its *Doctor Faust!* One of my friends preserves an old draft of this tragedy and he has communicated to me a scene from it which certainly contains much that is great.[8] Are you eager to read it? Here it is!— Faust demands the swiftest spirit of Hell for his service. He per-

5. Joseph Addison (1672–1719); his tragedy *Cato* was staged for the first time in 1713.
6. Pierre Corneille (1606–84) and Jean Racine (1639–99). The tragedies of these playwrights, along with the prefaces of the former in particular, had established the norms of Neo-classical tragedy.
7. François-Marie Arouet (Voltaire)

(1694–1778), author of the tragedy *Zaïre* (1732).
8. Lessing here pretends that the following scene is borrowed from the work of a friend. In fact it is part of his own *Faust*, which he is supposed to have completed. The play was never published, and the manuscript was subsequently lost.

forms his incantations; seven of them appear; and now begins the third scene of the second act.

Faust and the Seven Spirits

FAUST. You? You are the swiftest spirits of hell?

ALL THE SPIRITS. We are.

FAUST. Are all seven of you equally swift?

ALL THE SPIRITS. No.

FAUST. And which of you is the swiftest?

ALL THE SPIRITS. I am!

FAUST. A miracle! only six liars among seven devils—I must get to know you better.

FIRST SPIRIT. That you will! Some day!

FAUST. Some day! What do you mean by that? Do devils preach atonement too?

FIRST SPIRIT. Yes indeed, to the stubborn.—But do not delay us.

FAUST. What is your name? And how fast are you?

FIRST SPIRIT. You could have a sample sooner than an answer.

FAUST. Very good. Look here; what am I doing?

FIRST SPIRIT. You are moving your finger quickly through the flame of the light.—

FAUST. And not burning myself. Go, do likewise; pass seven times just as quickly through the flames of Hell and do not burn yourself.—Are you silent? Do you stay?—So devils boast also? Yes, indeed; no sin so small that you are willing to do without it. Second spirit, what are you called?

SECOND SPIRIT. Chil; which in your dull language is, "shaft of the plague."

FAUST. And how swift are you?

SECOND SPIRIT. Do you think that I beat my name in vain?— Swift as shafts of the plague.

FAUST. Then go and serve a doctor! For me you are far too slow. —You, third spirit, what is your name?

THIRD SPIRIT. I am called Dilla, for I am carried by the wings of the wind.

FAUST. And you, fourth spirit?—

FOURTH SPIRIT. My name is Jutta, for I move on the beams of light.

FAUST. O you, whose swiftness can be expressed in finite figures, you miserable ones—

FIFTH SPIRIT. Do not honor them with your annoyance. They are only Satan's messengers in the material world. We are his messengers in the world of the spirits; you will find us swifter.

FAUST. And how swift are you?

FIFTH SPIRIT. As swift as the thoughts of man.

FAUST. That is something!—But the thoughts of man are not always swift. Not when truth and virtue summon them. How sluggish they are then!—You can be swift if you want to be so, but who will guarantee me that you want to be swift at all times? No, I shall trust you as little as I ought to have trusted myself. Alas!—[*To the sixth spirit*] Tell me, how swift are you?

SIXTH SPIRIT. As fast as the vengeance of the avenger.

FAUST. Of the avenger? Which avenger?

SIXTH SPIRIT. Of the mighty one, the frightful one, who reserved the right of revenge for himself alone because revenge amused him.—

FAUST. Devil! You blaspheme, for I see that you tremble.—Swift, you say, as the vengeance of the—I nearly named him! No, let him not be named among us! His revenge would be swift? Swift?—And I am still living? And I am still sinning?—

SIXTH SPIRIT. To let you go on sinning is revenge already!

FAUST. And that a devil should have to teach me this!—Though not until today! No, his revenge is not swift, and if you are not quicker than his revenge, you might as well go.—[*To the seventh spirit*]—How fast are you?

SEVENTH SPIRIT. Mortal incapable of being pleased, if I too am not swift enough for you—

FAUST. Then say, how fast?

SEVENTH SPIRIT. No more and no less than the transition from good to bad.—

FAUST. Ha! You are my devil! As quick as the transition from good to bad!—Yes, that is swift; nothing is swifter than that!—Away from here, you snails of Orcus! Away!—As the transition from good to bad! I have experienced how swift that is! I have experienced that! *and so on.*—

What do you say to this scene? You wish for a German play that has nothing but such scenes? So do I!

The Author on the Drama

Various documents, both public and private, have been preserved from many stages in Goethe's work on *Faust*, which offer valuable indications of his own purpose and attitude concerning his work. The following selection, many of which are here translated into English for the first time, provides a chronological survey of Goethe's views.

Faust Plan of 1800†

Ideal striving to achieve an influence upon and a feeling
     for the whole of Nature.
The appearance of the Spirit as Ge-
     nius of the World and of Action.

Conflict between Form and the Formless.
Preference for formless content
Over empty form.
Content provides form
Form is never without content.
Such contradictions, instead of uniting them,
     make them more disparate.
Bright, clear scientific striving Wagner
Dull, warm ———— ———— Student
~~Life's Deeds Essence~~

                       viewed from without
Enjoyment of Life by the person   Part I   in a stupor
                                 Passion
     directed outwards and Enjoyment with Consciousness.
Enjoyment of Deeds second   ————   Beauty.
     from within.
Enjoyment of Creation   Epilogue in Chaos on the way
                           to Hell.

Outline of the Contents for *Part II* (1816) ‡

At the beginning of the second part Faust is discovered sleeping. He is surrounded by choruses of spirits who conjure up for him in visible symbols and charming songs the joys of honor, fame, power

---

† The precise date of the writing of this plan (translated by C. Hamlin) is not known, but it clearly reflects Goethe's general view of the drama at the time when he returned to the composition of *Part I* (ca. 1797–1800). For a detailed discussion of its importance, see Wolfgang Binder's essay, below. Mention of the division of the drama into two parts indicates that the plan must have been written after that decision was made

(probably in 1800).
‡ The following text was dictated by Goethe in December, 1816, for inclusion in the fourth volume of his autobiography *Poetry and Truth*. After discussing the early stages of composition for *Faust*, he intended to outline the unwritten *Part II*, since he did not believe at that time that he would ever complete the drama. Goethe was subsequently per-

and sovereignty. In flattering words and melodies they disguise what are actually derisive propositions. He awakens feeling strengthened, all previous dependence upon sensuality and passion cast off, his mind, purified and fresh, striving towards the highest.

Mephistopheles appears to him and gives him an amusing and stimulating description of the Imperial Parliament at Augsburg, which has been summoned by the Emperor Maximilian; he pretends that it is all taking place down on the square beneath the window, where Faust, however, can see nothing. Finally, Mephistopheles claims to see the Emperor speaking with a prince at a window of the town hall and assures Faust that the Emperor is asking about him, his whereabouts, and whether by any chance he could be brought to the court. Faust lets himself be persuaded, and his magic cloak makes the journey swifter. In Augsburg they land before an empty hall, and Mephistopheles goes out to spy. Faust meanwhile lapses into his earlier abstruse speculations and his demands upon himself, and, when the former returns, Faust sets the remarkable condition that Mephistopheles not enter the assembly hall but remain at the door; further, that in the Emperor's presence no kind of magic or deception shall occur. Mephistopheles consents. The scene shifts to a large hall where the Emperor, just finished with a banquet, goes to a window with a prince and acknowledges that he desires Faust's cloak in order to hunt in the Tyrol and be back again for tomorrow's session. Faust is announced and graciously received. The Emperor's questions all concern earthly dilemmas and how magic could solve them. Faust's replies suggest higher demands and higher means. The Emperor does not understand him, the courtier even less. The conversation becomes confused, falters, and Faust, bewildered, looks round for Mephistopheles, who immediately steps behind him and answers in his name. Now the conversation becomes animated, several people move closer, and everyone is pleased with the extraordinary guest. The Emperor demands to see apparitions, and they are promised. Faust leaves to make preparations. At that moment Mephistopheles assumes Faust's guise to entertain women and young ladies and eventually is considered to be quite invaluable, since by lightly touching a wart on the hand or somewhat more smartly kicking a corn with his disguised hoof he effects a cure; and a blond young lady even allows him to dab her face with his lean and pointed fingers, since her pocket-mirror immediately gives her the comforting assurance that

---

suaded by Eckermann to delete the outline from the published version of his autobiography, in hopes that the drama would indeed be finished eventually. The text of the outline was only published in 1888 in the critical apparatus to the Weimar edition of *Faust, Part II* (Paralipomenon 63). Of particular inter-est to observe here is how straightforward Goethe's view of *Part II* still was in 1816. What he describes is not essentially different in its dramatic mode (like an echo from medieval Romance) from *Part I*. (The translation is by Dolores Signori and Cyrus Hamlin.)

one freckle after another is disappearing. Evening approaches, a magical theater builds itself. The figure of Helena appears. Observations by the ladies about this beauty of beauties enliven the otherwise awesome scene. Paris enters and is subjected by the men to the same treatment which Helena received from the women. Faust, in disguise, agrees with both sides and this leads to a very amusing scene.

They cannot reach an agreement concerning the choice of the third apparition, and the summoned spirits become restless; several important ones appear together. Strange relationships develop, until at last the theater and the phantoms disappear simultaneously. The real Faust, illuminated by three lamps, lies unconscious in the background. Mephistopheles takes to his heels, something of the duality involved is suspected, no one feels at ease about the matter.

When Mephistopheles encounters Faust again, he finds the latter consumed by an intense passion. He has fallen in love with Helena and now demands that the conjurer procure and deliver her into his arms. Difficulties are perceived. Helena belongs to Orcus, and, though she can be conjured forth by magic, she cannot be held fast. Faust will not give up, and Mephistopheles undertakes the task. Infinite longing by Faust for highest beauty once it has been glimpsed. An old castle, whose lord is off to wars in Palestine, but whose steward is a magician, serves as dwelling for the new Paris. Helena appears; corporeality is restored to her by a magic ring. She believes she has just come from Troy and is arriving in Sparta. She finds everything bleak, desires company, especially masculine, which throughout her life she was never able to do without. Faust enters and, as a German knight, appears wondrous strange at the side of the heroic figure from antiquity. She finds him loathsome, but because he knows how to flatter, she gradually submits to him, and he becomes the successor of so many heroes and demi-gods. A son results from this union, who, as soon as he comes into the world, dances, sings, and cleaves the air with a fencer's thrusts. Now, one must understand that the castle is surrounded by a magical boundary, within which alone these half-realities can come to be. The ever-growing boy is a source of much joy to his mother. He is allowed everything but to cross a certain brook. One holiday, however, he hears music from beyond and sees the countryfolk and soldiers dancing. He crosses the boundary, mingles with them and gets into a quarrel, injures many but at last is killed by a sacred sword. The magician-steward saves the corpse. The mother is inconsolable; and as Helena wrings her hands in despair, she brushes off the ring and falls into Faust's arms, who, however, embraces only her empty garment. Mother and son have disappeared. Mephistopheles, who up to this point has witnessed everything in the guise of an old housekeeper, tries to comfort his friend and infuse a desire for property into him. The lord of the castle has been killed in Palestine, monks want to seize his lands, and their benedictions destroy the magic circle. Mephistopheles advises physical force and provides Faust with three henchmen named Raufebold, Habebald, Haltefest. Faust now believes himself sufficiently equipped and dismisses Mephistopheles and the steward, wages war with the monks, avenges the death of his son, and wins extensive lands. Meanwhile he grows old, and how things go from there will be demonstrated when we eventually assemble the fragments, or rather the discontinuously produced passages already composed for this second part, thereby salvaging some things which will be of interest to readers.

Second Sketch for the Announcement of the *Helena* (1826) †

HELENA. CLASSICAL-ROMANTIC PHANTASMAGORIA. INTERLUDE TO *Faust*

The character of Faust, at the exalted level to which our new version has raised him out of the old rough-hewn folktale, represents a man who, feeling impatient and uncomfortable within the general limits of earthly life, regards the possession of highest knowledge and the enjoyment of richest goods as inadequate to satisfy his longing in the very least, a mind which, turning in every direction, always returns in a more unhappy state.

Such a disposition is so similar to the modern one that a number of clever heads have felt impelled to attempt to solve the problem. The way in which I have come to terms with it has won approval; excellent minds have thought about it and commented on my text, which I have acknowledged with gratitude.[1] I was astonished, however, that those who undertook to continue and complete my fragment did not arrive at the obvious thought, that in composing a second part one must necessarily transcend completely the melancholy sphere of the drama thus far [i.e., *Part I*] and lead such a man into higher regions through more dignified circumstances.

How I had begun to do this for my part lay at hand for me in private, leading me occasionally to attempt at least part of the

---

† In 1826 Goethe decided to publish the newly completed text of the third act of *Faust, Part II*, as an independent unit within his final collected works (*Ausgabe letzter Hand*). The act thus appeared under the independent title given here. In order to clarify the context of this strange piece within the still unpublished and largely unwritten second part of his drama, Goethe drafted several descriptive prose summaries during the latter months of the same year. The text, here translated for the first time into English by Cyrus Hamlin and Dolores Signori, is the longest of these, though only the first six paragraphs were actually published

(in the journal *Ueber Kunst und Alterthum*, which Goethe edited).
1. Among the comments on *Faust* by Goethe's contemporaries included in this edition, which Goethe may here have had in mind, would certainly be the correspondence with Schiller, the review by A. W. Schlegel, and perhaps the more perceptive discussions by Friedrich Schlegel and by Schelling (assuming that they were known to Goethe). Other published comments by younger friends and admirers of *Faust*, which are now of historical interest only, must also have been in Goethe's mind.

sequel, but I carefully concealed my secret from one and all, always in the hope of advancing the work toward a desired conclusion. But now I must no longer hold back and, with the publication of my collected endeavors, keep no more secrets from my readers; indeed I feel obliged to offer gradually all my efforts—even in fragmentary form.

Therefore I have decided to communicate at once, in the very next printer's lot, the above minor drama, complete in itself, which is to be fitted into the Second Part of *Faust*.[2]

But in order to bridge somewhat the large gulf between the well-known pathetic conclusion of *Part I* and the entrance of a Grecian heroine, for the moment I offer for kind acceptance first a summary of what occurs in between and hope it will suffice for the present.[3]

It is related in the old legend, we must know, and the puppet play of *Faust* does not fail to show this scene, that Faust in his peremptory arrogance demands from Mephistopheles possession of the beautiful Helen of Greece, and that after initial resistance Mephistopheles complies. We felt it our duty not to omit such a significant motif from our version. What follows, we hope, will clarify for the moment how we have tried to meet this need and what approach seemed suitable to us.

At a great banquet at the German Emperor's court Faust and Mephistopheles are requested to conjure up apparitions. Unwilling, yet under pressure, they call forth the desired idols of Helena and Paris.[4] Paris appears, the women's rapture knows no bounds; the men try to cool this enthusiasm with specific critical comments, but in vain. Helena appears, the men are beside themselves; the women observe her attentively and manage to point out mockingly that her heroic feet are too large and her ivory-colored complexion is probably painted on, but especially they contrive, through obloquy all too well founded in her actual history, to throw a dubious light on her magnificent person. Carried away by this sublime and beautiful figure, Faust is emboldened to push Paris away as he leans to her embrace; a thunderbolt strikes him down, the apparitions disappear, and the festival ends in turmoil.

Faust comes to his senses again out of a long catatonic sleep, during which his dreams have been visibly and circumstantially

2. The *Helena* was actually published in Volume IV of Goethe's collected works in the year 1827. At that time none of the "Classical Walpurgis Night," which is here described in such detail, had yet been composed.

3. It should be remembered that Goethe was here dictating a draft for a prose summary which was not in fact published during his lifetime. Much of the obscurity in the paragraphs which follow

derives (as Goethe himself must have sensed) from the nature of the mythical drama itself, which could only be clarified in poetic terms through the actual process of composition. This subsequently occurred four years later during 1830.

4. Goethe here outlines the scenes which were finally included at the end of Act I in *Part II*.

enacted before the eyes of the audience.[5] He appears in an exalted mood and, completely absorbed by his supreme vision, insists vehemently that Mephistopheles enable him to possess Helena. Not wishing to admit that he has no say in the Classical Hades, indeed that he is not even welcome there, Mephistopheles resorts to his former, well-proven method of making his master jump about in all directions. This leads us to quite a variety of things which deserve attention. Finally, to assuage the growing impatience of Faust, he advises him to visit, merely in passing on the way to their destination, the recently appointed Professor and Doctor Wagner, whom they find in his laboratory, greatly rejoicing at the creation of a little chemical man.[6]

Suddenly this creature bursts out of his glowing glass container and steps forth as a nimble, well-formed little dwarf. The formula for his creation is hinted at in a mystic way. He offers a demonstration of his abilities; in particular, it turns out that he embodies a universal historical world calendar—that is, he can tell at any moment at those times when sun, moon, earth, and planets have been in the same position what has occurred among men since the creation of Adam. As a sample of this he announces on the spot that the present night coincides precisely with that hour when the Battle of Pharsalia was prepared for, and which both Caesar and Pompey passed sleeplessly. On this point he gets into an argument with Mephistopheles, who, on the basis of Benedictine reckoning, will not believe that that great epochal event occurred at this hour, but claims that it took place several days later. The point is made that the devil should not use monks as his authority. Since he stubbornly insists upon this right, however, their dispute is in danger of lapsing into an interminable chronological controversy, when the little chemical man offers further proof of his profound historical-mythical skill by drawing attention to the fact that this was also the moment when the festival of the Classical Walpurgis Night began, which had been held in Thessaly ever since the beginning of the mythical world and, in accord with the complete coherence of world history as determined by its epochs, was the actual cause of that disastrous event.[7] All four decide to travel there [i.e., to Pharsalia]. Despite their haste, Wagner does not forget to take along a clean phial, to collect here and there, if he can, the neces-

5. In the final version of the drama Faust reawakens only when he touches the ground of Greece (at the beginning of the "Classical Walpurgis Night"). His dream of the conception of Helen when Leda was ravished by Zeus in the guise of a swan is described by Homunculus in Wagner's laboratory (lines 6904–20).
6. Goethe does not yet speak here of Homunculus, though he offers a vivid sense of Wagner's fantastic chemical ex-

periment (how close to Mary Shelley's *Frankenstein*!).
7. Much of the information concerning the Battle of Pharsalia was derived from the Latin poet Lucan, who wrote an epic on the event. The whole idea of the "Classical Walpurgis Night," however, is Goethe's own idea, one of the most incredible poetic conceptions in the history of literature.

sary elements for making a little chemical woman. He puts the glass container into his left breast-pocket, the little chemical man into his right one; and thus they entrust themselves to Mephistopheles' magic cloak.[8] A boundless swarming profusion of geographical-historical remarks from the mouth of the little man in the pocket, concerning the regions they drift over, allows them no chance to compose themselves, what with the arrow-like speed of their flight, until finally they reach the plain of Thessaly by the light of a clear though waning moon. Here on the heath they first encounter Erichto [sic], who is eagerly inhaling the inextirpable reek of decay which clings to these fields. Erichtonius joins her, and their kinship, which was unknown to antiquity, is proved etymologically. Unfortunately she must often carry him on her arm, since he is not good at walking, and indeed, when this infant prodigy evinces a strange passion for the little chemical man, must take the latter on her other arm, a situation by no means calculated to restrain Mephistopheles from making malicious comments.[9]

Faust has entered into a conversation with a crouching Sphinx, in which the most abstruse questions are foiled *ad infinitum* by equally puzzling answers. In a similar pose close by, a watchful Griffin, one of the guardians of gold, interjects without producing any enlightenment. A colossal Ant, another hoarder of gold, joins them and makes the conversation even more confusing.

But now that reason in conflict with itself must despair, trust in the senses is to be undermined too. Empusa appears, wearing a donkey's head in honor of the present festival. By constantly changing her form she stimulates the other, well-defined figures, not, to be sure, to metamorphosis, but to continual impatience.[1]

Now there appear Sphinxes, Griffins, and Ants, in numbers multiplied past counting, developing as it were out of themselves.[2] Back and forth, what is more, swarms and runs the entire plethora of monsters from antiquity, Chimeras, Tragelaphs, Crickets, and, in their midst, many-headed serpents in vast number. Harpies flutter and sway in vague circles like bats; the dragon Python itself appears in multiple form, and the Stymphalian vultures, sharp-beaked, with webbed feet, whip past one by one, swift as arrows. But suddenly, with tuneful song, a flock of Sirens hovers over them all like a cloud. They plunge into the Peneus [sic!] to bathe amid splashing

---

8. In the final drama the trip to Greece is also made on Mephistopheles' magic cloak. Goethe subsequently decided, presumably for practical reasons of dramatic execution, not to have Wagner go along. The whole motif of a little chemical woman was subsequently dropped, to be replaced by the festival of Galatea and Homunculus' spiritual fusion with the sea.
9. Erichtho speaks the Prologue to the final "Classical Walpurgis Night." The role of Erichtonius was abandoned in the final drama.
1. Empusa with the donkey's head appears quite late in the text of the "Classical Walpurgis Night" (lines 7732–55).
2. This scene of general confusion was subsequently included in abbreviated form near the beginning of the "Classical Walpurgis Night" (lines 7214–48). The various creatures are explained in the footnotes to that passage.

and piping, then they perch on trees in the glade next to the river and sing their loveliest songs.[3] First comes an apology by the Nereids and Tritons, who, in spite of the sea's proximity, are prevented by their physique from participating in this festival. Then they urgently invite the entire party to enjoy themselves, one and all, in the various waters and gulfs, and also on the islands and coasts, of the area; part of the crowd accepts this enticing invitation and plunges seaward.

Our travelers, more or less accustomed to such spirit pranks, hardly take notice of all that is buzzing around them. The little chemical man, crawling along on the earth, gleans from the humus a great many phosphorescent atoms, some radiating a blue, others a purple fire. He conscientiously consigns them to Wagner's phial, though he doubts the possibility of creating a little chemical woman from them. But when Wagner shakes them hard in order to observe them more closely, followers of Pompey and Caesar appear ranked in cohorts in a boisterous effort to reclaim these components of their individuality needed for legitimate resurrection. They almost succeed in possessing themselves of these despiritualized bits of matter; but the four winds, whose courses this night are in continual collision, take the present owner into their protection, and the spirits must resign themselves to being told by all that the components of their Roman grandeur have long ago been scattered to the four winds, absorbed and transformed by a million phases of evolution.[4]

This does not reduce the tumult but appeases it for a moment in that attention is turned to the center of the vast plain.[5] There the earth quakes, then swells up to form a mountain chain, north to Scotusa and south to the Peneus, which even threatens to block the river. The head and shoulders of Enceladus come writhing forth; he has made a point of working his way here beneath land and sea in celebration of this important hour. Flickering flames leap out of various chasms; and the natural philosophers, Thales and Anaxagoras,[6] who would not miss this occasion for anything, start a violent quarrel concerning this event, the one attributing it all to water and moisture, the other viewing everything in terms of molten, melting masses; each declaims his solo over the roar of the general chorus; both quote from Homer and each cites the past and present as proof. Thales in vain offers as evidence spring floods and deluges,

3. In the final drama the Sirens play an even greater role than Goethe here envisions for them, due to the addition of the festival at the Aegean, for which they constitute a kind of chorus.
4. All the events here described with reference to Wagner's intended role in the "Classical Walpurgis Night" were subsequently omitted.
5. The volcanic explosion which produces the mountain Seismos (instead of

Enceladus) occurs on the upper Peneios in the "Classical Walpurgis Night" (lines 7495–7675).
6. The argument between the two pre-Socratic philosophers, Thales (who is popularly believed to have derived all life from water) and Anaxagoras (who supposed that fire was the origin of life), occurs in the presence of Homunculus in the final drama (lines 7851–7950).

speaking with pompous, didactic complacency; Anaxagoras, as fiery as the element which possesses him, speaks a more impassioned language and prophesies a rain of stones, which, to be sure, at the next moment falls down from the moon. The crowd extols him as a demi-god, and his opponent is forced to retreat to the seashore.

As yet the peaks and gorges of the mountain are not firm or fixed when, swarming out of gaping crevices on all sides, armies of Pygmies occupy the upper arm and shoulders of the still-crouching giant, and use these as a dance floor and playground; meanwhile armies of croaking Cranes beyond number circle the summit of the giant's head and his hair as if it were an impenetrable forest, and announce an entertaining battle before the general festival concludes.[7]

All this and more is to be imagined, if it can be, as taking place simultaneously. Mephistopheles meanwhile has made the acquaintance of Enyo [one of the Phorcyads], whose grandiose ugliness comes close to unnerving him and startling him into making impolite and insulting remarks.[8] But he pulls himself together and, in consideration of her exalted ancestors and her considerable influence, he tries to win her favor. He comes to an understanding with her and forms an alliance, of which the public terms do not promise much, but the secret ones are all the more remarkable and fraught with consequences. As for Faust, he has approached Chiron, the centaur, who as a neighboring mountain-dweller is making his usual rounds.[9] A serious pedagogical conversation with this prototypical private tutor is, if not interrupted, at least disturbed by a circle of Lamiae, who intrude incessantly between Faust and Chiron; they are charming creatures of every kind, fair, dark, large, small, delicate or strong of limb; each speaks or sings, strides about or dances, hurries past or gesticulates, so that, if Faust had not absorbed the highest image of beauty within himself, he would necessarily be seduced.[1] But Chiron himself, ancient and imperturbable, wishes to clarify for his thoughtful new acquaintance the principles by which he educated his distinguished heroes, whereupon the Argonauts and finally Achilles are described.[2] But when the pedagogue considers the outcome of his efforts, little that is gratifying emerges; for the heroes live and act as if they had never been educated.

When Chiron now hears of Faust's desire and intention, he

7. The battle between the Pygmies and the Cranes occurs soon after the appearance of Seismos in the "Classical Walpurgis Night" (lines 7606–75), though its repercussions are also described in the scene with the philosophers.
8. In the final drama Mephistopheles visits all three of the Phorcyads, none of whom is actually named (lines 7951–8033).
9. The meeting between Faust and Chiron at the banks of the Peneios was placed fairly early in the final text (lines

7319–7488). The encounter with the river nymphs which immediately precedes this meeting in the drama was apparently not yet conceived.
1. The temptation by the Lamiae occurs in the "Classical Walpurgis Night" quite independent of Faust, and Mephistopheles, quite appropriately, is their dupe (lines 7676–7800).
2. The pedagogical speeches by Chiron occur in lines 7365–7462, though the emphasis finally falls much more upon Faust's fascination with Helen.

rejoices to meet again at long last a man who demands the impossible, since he always used to approve the same in his pupils. At the same time he offers assistance and direction to the modern hero, carries him back and forth on his broad back across all the fords and gravel-banks of the Peneus, passes Larissa on the right, and shows his rider here and there the places where Perseus, the unfortunate King of Macedonia, stopped for a few minutes to catch his breath during his most terrifying flight.[3] Thus they make their way downstream to the foot of Olympus; here they encounter a long procession of sibyls,[4] many more than twelve in number. Chiron describes the first who pass as old acquaintances and then commends his charge to the judicious, kindly daughter of Tiresias, Manto.[5]

The latter informs him that the entrance to Orcus is about to open, since the hour is approaching when formerly the mountain had to split open to allow so many great souls to descend. This indeed happens, and, the horoscope of the moment being favorable, they all climb down together in silence.[6] Suddenly Manto covers her charge with her veil and pushes him away from the path against the rock wall, so that he is afraid of being smothered to death. Soon, when he is released, she explains this precaution: the Gorgon's head which for centuries has been growing ever larger, was advancing up the chasm towards them;[7] Proserpina likes to keep it away from the level of the festival because the assembled ghosts and monsters, losing all composure at the sight of the head, would scatter immediately. Manto herself, highly endowed being though she is, dare not gaze at it; had Faust glimpsed it, he would have been destroyed immediately, so that nothing of either his body or his spirit would ever again have been found in the universe. They finally arrive at the vast court of Proserpina, crowded with many shapes; here there is opportunity for an infinitude of incidents, until Faust, when he is presented, is favorably received as a second Orpheus,[8] though his request is considered to be somewhat strange. The speech of Manto as his representative must be impressive; she first invokes the power of precedent and recounts in detail the favor

3. Such a geographical survey, including any allusion to Perseus, was subsequently omitted from the final drama.
4. See the footnote to *Faust*, line 7455.
5. The scene with Manto, brief and yet astonishingly effective, occurs in lines 7465–94.
6. The entire sequence of the descent to Hades as here envisioned was subsequently abandoned, apparently only at the very last stage of composition in 1830. It may perhaps be argued that the scene at the Aegean Sea which concludes the "Classical Walpurgis Night" was seen to be an adequate symbolic substitute for Faust's visit to the underworld.
7. According to ancient myth, the head of Gorgo (some sources speak of three

Gorgons) would turn anyone to stone who looked at it. Goethe appears to have had some specific allegorical intention for introducing this figure here. He subsequently abandoned the plan when he composed the final text.
8. Orpheus, the mythical singer, descended into Hades to request the return to life of his dead wife Eurydice. This was granted by Persephone (or Proserpina) on the condition that he not turn back to look at her until they had returned to the upper world. Orpheus turned at the last minute before they emerged and Eurydice was lost to him. The parallel between Faust and Orpheus is mentioned by Manto in line 7493.

received by Protesilaus, Alcestis, and Euridice.[9] Did not Helena herself once before receive permission to return to life in order to ally herself to Achilles, whom she had earlier loved?[1] Of the further course and current of her speech we may divulge nothing here, least of all the peroration which causes the Queen, moved to tears, to give her consent, and refer the petitioners to the three judges, in whose memory of bronze all is engraved which seems to disappear in Lethe's stream as it flows past their feet.

It now turns out that previously Helena had been allowed to return to life on condition that she restrict herself to the island of Leucas. Now she may return under the same conditions to the land of Sparta, to appear there, as if truly alive, in a house modeled on that of Menelaus. There it would be up to the new suitor how far he might influence her volatile spirit and impressionable mind, and win her favor.[2]

At this point, the announced Interlude of *Helena* begins, which is adequately related to the main course of the drama yet, for reasons which will become apparent, is offered separately for the time being.

This brief sketch should, of course, have been executed and embellished with all the advantages of the poetic and rhetorical arts and then presented to the public; as it stands, however, it may serve for the moment to clarify the events which need to be fully known and carefully considered as antecedents to the announced *Helena*, the Classical-Romantic Phantasmagoric Interlude to *Faust*.

From Goethe's Correspondence with Schiller, 1794–1801[†]

Schiller to Goethe

JENA, NOVEMBER 29, 1794

No less great is my desire to read those parts of your *Faust* which are as yet unpublished; for I can honestly say that what I have read

9. All three of those here named were released from Hades under certain conditions for the sake of those in life who loved them: 1) Protesilaus, first of the Greeks killed at Troy, was allowed to return to his wife, Laodamia, for three hours; 2) Alcestis, wife of Admetus (see Euripides' play), was brought back from death by Hercules; 3) Euridice was the wife of Orpheus (see the previous note).
1. This obscure legend of Helena's return to life to marry Achilles is mentioned in *Faust*; see lines 7435 ff. and note.
2. Goethe here indicates a condition for Helena's existence for Faust in Act III which is only indirectly apparent in the final text. The reason why she is ultimately lost to Faust at the end of the act is not adequately explained by this.
† Goethe's close friendship with Fried-

rich Schiller (1759–1805) from 1794 until the latter's death was important for the development of thought and work for both writers. The almost daily exchange of letters between Jena, where Schiller lived until 1800 when he moved to Weimar, and the nearby Duchy of Weimar, where Goethe had resided since 1775, allows us to follow this development of ideas in detail. The excerpts included here reveal the extent to which Schiller took an active role in persuading the older poet to return to *Faust* during the years from 1797 to 1801, leading to the eventual publication of *Part I* soon after Schiller's death. The letters are reprinted from *Correspondence Between Schiller and Goethe from 1794 to 1805*, translated by L. Dora Schmitz (London: George Bell and Sons, 1890).

of it is to me like the torso of an Hercules.[1] There reigns in those scenes the power and the fulness of genius which unmistakably reveals the first master, and I should like as far as possible to follow the great and bold spirit that breathes in them.

Goethe to Schiller

WEIMAR, DECEMBER 2, 1794

Of *Faust* I cannot as yet let you have anything. I cannot make up my mind to untie the packet in which it is imprisoned. I could not copy without working it out, and I have no courage for that. If anything could induce me to do this at some future time it would certainly be your interest in it.

Goethe to Schiller

WEIMAR, JUNE 22, 1797

As it is extremely necessary that in my present restless state I should set myself something to do, I have determined to take up my *Faust* and, if not to finish it, at all events to bring it a good deal further, by breaking up what has been printed and arranging it in large masses with what is already finished or invented, and of thus further preparing the development of the play, which is in reality as yet only an idea.[2] I have merely taken up this idea and its representation again, and have pretty well made up my mind about it. I only wish, however, that you would be so good as to think the matter over on one of your sleepless nights, and to tell me the demands which you would require of the whole, and in this manner to narrate and to interpret to me my own dreams like a true prophet.

As the different parts of this poem—in what relates to mood—might be treated differently, provided only that they be kept subordinate to the spirit and tone of the whole, and as, moreover, the whole work is subjective, I can work at it at odd moments, and am therefore at present able to do something to it.

Schiller to Goethe

JENA, JUNE 23, 1797

Your resolution to set to work at your *Faust* was indeed a surprise to me, especially just now, when you are thinking of a trip to Italy. But I have at once and for all given up the idea of measuring you

1. Schiller refers to the *Fragment* of 1790, included by Goethe in his collected works (see August Wilhelm Schlegel's review, below), which Schiller must have read in its published form.
2. From Goethe's diary we know that the poem "Dedication," which speaks of the experience of returning to *Faust* after decades of neglect, was composed on June 24, 1797, two days after this letter was written.

by the usual standard of logic, and am therefore convinced before-hand that your genius will see you well through the task.

The request you make that I should tell you of my requirements and *desideria,* is not so easily fulfilled; but as far as I can I will try to discover your thread, and if that cannot be managed, will do so as if I had accidentally found the fragments of *Faust* and had myself to work them out. This much only I will here remark, that *Faust*—the piece itself I mean—in spite of all its poetic individuality, cannot quite ward off the demand for a symbolical treatment, as probably is the case with your own idea. The duality of human nature and the unsuccessful endeavour to unite in man the godlike and the physical, is never lost sight of; and as the story runs and must run into what is fantastic and formless, people will not consent to remain by the subject, but will be led from it to ideas. In short, the demands on *Faust* are both philosophical and poetical, and you may turn in whichever direction you please, the nature of the subject will force you to treat it philosophically, and the imagination will have to accommodate itself to serve a rational idea.

But I can scarcely be telling you anything new by saying this, for you have already, in a great measure, begun to satisfy this demand in what you have already, accomplished.

Goethe to Schiller

WEIMAR, JUNE 24, 1797

Thank you for your first words on my reawakening *Faust.* We shall probably not differ in our views of this work, and yet quite a different kind of courage comes over one when one sees one's thoughts and projects characterised by another; and your sympathy is fruitful in more than one sense.

I shall now first of all endeavour to finish the large masses that are already invented and half wrought out, put them into some connection with what has been printed, and go on in this way till the circle is exhausted.

Schiller to Goethe

JENA, JUNE 26, 1797

Your *Faust* I have now again read through, and I feel actually giddy from the *dénouement.*[3] This, however, is very natural, for the matter is based upon some special conception, and so long as this is not grasped, a subject much less rich than the present one would put reason into a state of dilemma. What I am anxious about in

3. Schiller presumably is referring to the conclusion of the drama (i.e., the traditional damnation of Faust), which had not yet been written at the time. Whether he had any notion that Goethe would ultimately have his hero saved, or whether Goethe himself so intended at that time, is uncertain.

regard to it is that, in accordance with its character, *Faust* appears to require a totality of material if, at the end, the idea is to appear completely carried out; and I know of no poetic framework for holding together a mass that springs up to such a height. However, you will know what you have to do.

For instance, it was, as I think, appropriate that *Faust* should be led into active life, and whatever sphere you may select from this mass, it nevertheless seems to me that his nature will demand too great an amount of circumstantiality and breadth.

As regards the treatment, I find the greatest difficulty to be that of proceeding happily between what is jest and earnest. Reason and common sense seem to me in this subject to be struggling as if for life and death. In the present fragmentary state of *Faust* this is felt very much, but expectation is led to look to the fully-developed whole. The devil gains his point in face of common sense by his realism and *Faust* his in the face of the heart. At times, however, they seem to exchange their parts, and the devil takes reason under his protection against *Faust*.

One difficulty I also find in the fact that the devil annuls his existence, which is idealistic, by his character which is realistic. Reason alone can believe in him, and it is only common sense that can allow and comprehend his existence as he is.

I am in fact very anxious to see how the popular tale will link itself to the philosophical portion of the whole.

Goethe to Schiller

WEIMAR, JUNE 27, 1797

Your remarks about *Faust* gave me great pleasure, naturally they coincide very well with my own projects and plans, only that I shall make this barbarous composition accommodate itself more to my wishes, and I propose rather to touch upon than to fufil the highest demands. In this manner, reason and common sense will probably beat each other about like two boxers, and afterwards sit down amicably together. I will take care that the parts are pleasing and entertaining, and that they offer subjects for thought; in the poem itself, which will ever remain a fragment, I may apply our new theory of the epic poem.[4]

Goethe to Schiller

WEIMAR, MAY 5, 1798

My *Faust* I have brought a good bit further. The old and very confused manuscript still on hand has been copied, and the parts

---

4. This alludes to the short essay "On Epic and Dramatic Poetry," which had been written jointly by Goethe and Schiller through their correspondence during 1797 and which Goethe subsequently published in his journal *Ueber Kunst und Alterthum* in 1827.

arranged in separate boxes and numbered according to a detailed scheme; hence I shall now be able to make use of every moment when I feel in the humour for it, work out the various parts, and sooner or later have them put together.

A very curious thing struck me while doing this: some tragic scenes I had written in prose, and owing to their naturalness and power, as compared with the rest, are quite unbearable.

Schiller to Goethe

JENA, MAY 8, 1798

I congratulate you upon your progress with *Faust*. As soon as you definitely know what has still to be done to the subject, it may be said to be all but finished, for to me the most difficult part about it seems to be its *limitlessness*. A remark you made lately that on account of some of your tragic scenes having been written in prose, they proved powerfully affecting, confirms an earlier experience of yours in the case of Marianne in your *Meister*,[5] in which case likewise pure realism violently affects a pathetic situation and produces a seriousness which is not poetical: for according to my idea, it belongs to the nature of poetry that it should ever unite within itself seriousness and play.

Schiller to Goethe

WEIMAR, SEPTEMBER 13, 1800

I congratulate you upon the advance you have made in your *Faust*. But be sure not to allow yourself to be disturbed by the thought that it would be a pity to barbarise beautiful figures and situations, should such be met with. A similar case might often present itself to you in the second part of *Faust*, and I should be glad, once and for all, to silence your poetic conscience on this point. The barbarous element in the treatment which is imposed upon you by the spirit of the whole, cannot destroy its higher character or do away with what is beautiful in it; it can only modify it and prepare it for some other faculty of soul.[6] Just that which is higher and more elevated in the motives, gives a peculiar charm to the work, and Helena here stands as a symbol of all the beautiful forms which will stray into it. It is a very great merit to proceed consciously from

5. The character of Marianne in Goethe's novel *Wilhelm Meister's Apprenticeship* is the hero's first love, who bears his child and subsequently dies rejected because of a misunderstanding.
6. Schiller refers to the medieval milieu of *Faust* as "barbaric" in accord with the normative Classical aesthetics which he shared with Goethe during the latter 1790s. There is no question that Goethe agreed with him at that time, feeling generally estranged from the legend of Faust.

what is pure to what is impure, in place of soaring up from what is impure to what is pure, as is the case with us other barbarians.[7]

Goethe to Schiller

JENA, SEPTEMBER 16, 1800

The consolation you give me in your letter that the union of what is pure with what is adventurous cannot give rise to a poetic monstrosity altogether objectionable, I have already found confirmed by experience, inasmuch as this amalgamation gives rise to strange results in which I myself take some interest.

Schiller to Goethe

WEIMAR, SEPTEMBER 23, 1800

The recital, the other day, made a great and significant impression upon me; one feels the noble, sublime spirit of ancient tragedy come wafting towards one from the monologue, and its effect is the right one, for it excites what is deepest, in a calm and yet powerful manner.[8] If you were not to bring back anything poetical from Jena but this and what you have already settled in your own mind about the further course of this tragic part, your stay in Jena would have met with its reward. If you succeed with this synthesis of what is noble and barbarous, as I have no doubt will be the case, you will have found the key to the remaining portion of the whole, and it will then not be difficult for you—as it were—analytically to determine and dispute the meaning and spirit of the other portions from this point; for the summit, as you yourself call it, must be seen from, and look towards all the various points of the whole.

Goethe to Schiller

OBER-ROSSLA, APRIL 6, 1801

Faust also has meanwhile had something done to it. I hope that soon the only thing wanting in the great gap will be the disputation,[9] that, it is true, will have to be looked upon as a distinct piece·

7. As Goethe wrote to Schiller on September 12 (the letter is not included here), he had begun to work on the Helena episode for *Faust*. Several hundred lines written at that time for the opening of Act III in *Part II* survive in manuscript. Goethe emphasizes that the heroine attracts his attention because of her ideal Classical beauty but that he finds no way of reconciling this to the medieval ("barbarous") setting of *Faust*. He did not find the way until twenty-five years later.

8. Schiller visited Goethe on September 21, when the latter was in Jena, and Goethe read to him Helena's monologue from the draft for that sequence of *Faust*.

9. Here Goethe refers to the uncompleted lacuna in the drama between the opening scene (after Wagner leaves) and the end of the pact scene (before the student comes in), lines 605–1770, as the "great gap," which he managed to fill only at the time of this letter. The "disputation," a scene subsequently abandoned, was to have occurred between the two study scenes (see the interpretive note to the pact scene, p. 314, above, and Emil Staiger's discussion, below.)

of work, and one which will not be accomplished at a moment's notice.

From Goethe's Letters and His Conversations with Eckermann†

Conversation, Monday, January 10, 1825
[*Goethe responds to an English visitor who reports that he has been reading* Faust, *Part I, and finds it hard going.*]

"Really," said * * * [Goethe], "I would not have advised you to undertake *Faust*. It is mad stuff, and goes quite beyond all ordinary feeling. But since you have done it of your own accord, without asking my advice, you will see how you will get through. Faust is so strange an individual, that only few can sympathize with his internal condition. Then the character of Mephistopheles is, on account of his irony, and also because he is a living result of an extensive acquaintance with the world, also very difficult. But you will see what lights open upon you. * * *"

Conversation, Tuesday, January 18, 1825
[*Goethe discusses the creative use of poetic sources by poets.*]

"The world," said Goethe, "remains always the same; situations are repeated; one people lives, loves, and feels like another; why should not one poet write like another? The situations of life are alike, why then should those of poems be unlike?"

* * *

"Lord Byron, * * * " said I, "is no wiser, when he takes *Faust* to pieces, and thinks you found one thing here, the other there."

"The greater part of those fine things cited by Lord Byron," said Goethe, "I have never even read; much less did I think of them when I was writing *Faust*. But Lord Byron is only great as a poet; as soon as he reflects, he is a child. He knows not how to help himself against stupid attacks of the same kind made upon him by his own countrymen. He ought to have expressed himself more strongly

---

† Johann Peter Eckermann (1792–1854) was a close associate of Goethe during the last years of his life, being in almost daily contact. He served as co-editor of the unpublished literary remains (including *Faust, Part II*) and he also collected and published his *Conversations with Goethe* in 1836–48 (here taken from the translation by John Oxenford, 1850). Regarding himself as an intimate biographer (somewhat on the model of Boswell for Samuel Johnson), Eckermann offers very detailed, often word-for-word accounts of his meetings with the elder poet. Whether or not he is strictly accurate in what is reported, the work remains an invaluable source of information, especially with regard to the thought and opinions of Goethe on every conceivable subject, including *Faust*. To a large extent (if we may trust what Eckermann says), it was he who first persuaded Goethe to think seriously during the early 1820s of trying to complete the second part of his drama.

The letters to Boisserée and Zelter and the letter of March 17, 1832, to Wilhelm von Humboldt are taken from Goethe, *Selected Letters*, translated by M. von Herzfeld and C. Melvil Sym, 1957. Reprinted by permission of the Edinburgh University Press.

against them. 'What is there is mine,' he should have said; 'and whether I got it from a book or from life, is of no consequence; the only point is whether I have made a right use of it.' Walter Scott used a scene from my *Egmont*, and he had a right to do so; and because he did it well, he deserves praise. He has also copied the character of my Mignon in one of his romances; but whether with equal judgment, is another question. Lord Byron's transformed Devil[1] is a continuation of Mephistopheles, and quite right too. If, from the whim of originality, he had departed from the model, he would certainly have fared worse. Thus, my Mephistopheles sings a song from Shakespeare [see lines 3682–97], and why should he not? Why should I give myself the trouble of inventing one of my own, when this said just what was wanted? Also, if the prologue to my *Faust* is something like the beginning of Job, that is again quite right, and I am rather to be praised than censured."

To Sulpiz Boisserée,[2] October 22, 1826
[*On the* Helena]

Helena is one of my oldest conceptions, as old as that of *Faust* itself, and though I have changed its form again and again, the idea has always been the same. I showed Schiller as much of it as I had done at the beginning of the century; our correspondence tells how he kept encouraging me to go on with it. I did so; but nothing but the fullness of time could round off this work that now covers a good three thousand years from the Sack of Troy to the destruction of Missolonghi. The whole thing is a kind of phantasmagoria, of course, but with real unity of place and action.

That is enough about it. Is it not perhaps worse than if I had said nothing? Whatever value is to be put on the work, I have never written anything like it, so it can count as the very latest.

Conversation, Monday evening, January 15, 1827
[*Goethe comments on the difficulties of composition with regard to the as yet unwritten Classical Walpurgis Night.*]

I turned the conversation to the second part of *Faust*; especially the "Classical Walpurgis Night," which existed as yet only as a sketch, and which Goethe had told me he meant to print in that

1. A reference to Byron's play *The Deformed Transformed* (1824).
2. Sulpiz Boisserée (1783–1853), enthusiast for medieval art and architecture, first met Goethe in 1811, when he solicited support from the older poet for a project to publish engravings of the uncompleted cathedral of Cologne. Goethe visited Boisserée in the Rhineland in 1814 and 1815 in order to study his collection of medieval German and Flemish painting. The younger collector and art historian became a devoted correspondent until Goethe's death, and he followed the progress on *Faust, Part II*, a work of particular interest to medieval enthusiasts, with eager expectation.

form.[3] I had ventured to advise him not to do so; for if it were once printed it would be always left in this unfinished state. Goethe must have thought that over in the meantime, for he now told me that he had resolved not to print the sketch.

* * *

"Why," he replied, "one goes on, and must go on; but it is difficult."

" 'Tis well," said I, "that your outline is so complete."

"The outline is indeed complete," said Goethe; "but the most difficult part is yet to be done; and, in the execution of parts, everything depends too much on luck. The 'Classical Walpurgis Night' must be written in rhyme, and yet the whole must have an antique character. It is not easy to find a suitable sort of verse;—and then the dialogue!"

"Is not that also in the plan?" said I.

"The *what* is there," replied Goethe, "but not the *how*. Then, only think what is to be said on that mad night! Faust's speech to Proserpine, when he would move her to give him Helena—what a speech should that be, when Proserpine herself is moved to tears! All this is not easy to do, and depends much on good luck; nay, almost entirely on the mood and strength at the moment."

Conversation, Thursday evening, January 25, 1827
[*Goethe comments on the* Helena *as he prepares to send off the manuscript for independent publication.*]

A sealed packet lay upon the table. Goethe laid his hand upon it. "This," said he, "is *Helena*, which is going to Cotta to be printed."

I felt the importance of the moment. For, as it is with a newly-built vessel on its first going to sea, whose destiny is hid from us, so is it with the intellectual creation of a great master, going forth into the world.

"I have till now," said Goethe, "been always finding little things to add or to touch up; but I must finish, and I am glad it is going to the post, so that I can turn to something else. Let it meet its fate. My comfort is, the general culture of Germany stands at an incredibly high point; so I need not fear such a production will long remain misunderstood and without effect."

"There is a whole antiquity in it," said I.

"Yes," said Goethe, "the philologists will find work."

"I have no fear," said I, "about the antique part; for there we have the most minute detail, the most thorough development of individuals, and each personage says just what he should. But the

3. Here Eckermann refers to the prose summary of the "Classical Walpurgis Night," which is contained in the "Second Sketch for the Announcement of the *Helena*," above. According to what Eckermann says here, it was he who persuaded Goethe not to publish the sketch in hopes that the work itself would ultimately be written.

modern romantic part is very difficult, for half the history of the world lies behind it; the material is so rich that it can only be lightly indicated, and heavy demands are made upon the reader."

"Yet," said Goethe, "it all appeals to the senses, and on the stage would satisfy the eye: more I did not intend. Let the crowd of spectators take pleasure in the spectacle; the higher import will not escape the initiated—as with the *Magic Flute* and other things."[4]

"It will produce a most unusual effect on the stage," said I, "that a piece should begin as a tragedy and end as an opera. But something is required to represent the grandeur of these persons, and to speak the sublime language and verse."

"The first part," said Goethe, "requires the first tragic artists; and the operatic part must be sustained by the first vocalists, male and female. That of Helena ought to be played, not by one, but by two great female artists; for we seldom find that a fine vocalist has sufficient talent as a tragic actress."

"The whole," said I, "will furnish an occasion for great splendour of scenery and costume. I look forward to its representation. If we could only get a good composer."

"It should be one," said Goethe, "who, like Meyerbeer, has lived long in Italy, so that he combines his German nature with the Italian style and manner.[5] However, that will be found somehow or other; I only rejoice that I am rid of it. Of the notion that the chorus does not descend into the lower world, but rather disperses itself among the elements on the cheerful surface of the earth, I am not a little proud."

"It is a new sort of immortality," said I.

Conversation, Sunday, May 6, 1827
[*Goethe responds to the inquiries of a German reader concerning the central "idea" of* Faust.]

"The Germans are, certainly, strange people. By their deep thoughts and ideas, which they seek in everything and fix upon everything, they make life much more burdensome than is necessary. Only have the courage to give yourself up to your impressions: allow yourself to be delighted, moved, elevated; nay, instructed and inspired for something great: but do not imagine all is vanity, if it is not abstract thought and idea.

"They come and ask what idea I meant to embody in my *Faust*;

4. Goethe regarded Mozart's *Magic Flute* (1791) as the norm for the opera of fancy which he imitated in the text of his *Helena*, especially the last third of the act, in which he explicitly insists upon a musical-operatic accompaniment. Goethe's interest in Mozart's opera was sufficient to persuade him to write a sequel, for which he would have hoped a corresponding musical genius might have been found as composer.

5. Giacomo Meyerbeer (1791–1864), whose work in grand opera achieved international acclaim during the second decade of the nineteenth century, apparently seemed the most suitable alternative to the dead Mozart as a possible composer for the operatic sections of *Faust, Part II.*

as if I knew myself, and could inform them. "From heaven, through the world, to hell," would indeed be something;[6] but this is no idea, only a course of action. And further: that the devil loses the wager, and that a man continually struggling from difficult errors towards something better, should be redeemed, is an effective —and, to many, a good enlightening—thought; but it is no idea at the foundation of the whole, and of every individual scene. It would have been a fine thing indeed if I had strung so rich, varied, and highly diversified a life as I have brought to view in *Faust* upon the slender string of one pervading idea.

"It was, in short," continued Goethe, "not in my line, as a poet, to strive to embody anything *abstract*. I received in my mind impressions, and those of a sensuous, animated, charming, varied, hundredfold kind—just as a lively imagination presented them; and I had, as a poet, nothing more to do than to round off and elaborate artistically such views and impressions, and by means of a lively representation so to bring them forward that others might receive the same impression in hearing or reading my representation of them.

"If I still wished, as a poet, to represent any idea, I would do it in short poems, where a decided unity could prevail, and where a complete survey would be easy; * * * I am rather of the opinion, that the more incommensurable, and the more incomprehensible to the understanding, a poetic production is, so much the better it is."

To Karl Friedrich Zelter,[7] May 24, 1827

[On the beginning of Act IV]

And now let me tell you in confidence that helpful good spirits have led me back to *Faust* just where descending from the cloud [that brought him from ancient Greece] he meets his evil genius once more. Don't tell anyone about this; but I should like you to know that I think I shall go forward boldly from this point and fill in the gap between it and the ending that has been ready for a long time.

To Christian Gottfried Nees von Esenbeck,[8] May 25, 1827

[On the Helena]

Patiently and secretly I am making progress [*with Faust*], as will be apparent to you from the three thousand years of *Helena*. For sixty years now I have been tracking it down, in order to force at

---

6. Goethe quotes from *Faust, Part I*, line 242.
7. Carl Friedrich Zelter (1758–1832), composer and musician in Berlin, was one of Goethe's most intimate correspondents during the period from 1796

until the poet's death.
8. Christian Gottfried Nees von Esenbeck (1776–1858), a physician and botanist, corresponded with Goethe especially on matters of natural science during the last two decades or so of Goethe's life.

least something from it. * * * There are various things in it which I value because they have been on my mind for so many long years, for they derive from a time which will never come again and require only a bit of ingenious editing: complete plans, drafted schematically, with certain details already worked out. And it takes only a pure and inspired decisiveness on my part, hence the work has a validity as a kind of whole and will surely please many readers. Thus with an all-out effort last year I finally brought my *Helena* to harmonious life. How many times this piece had been shaped and reshaped over the vast reach of years. Now finally it will abide in a fixed form within its moment of time.

Conversation, Thursday, July 5, 1827
[*Goethe comments on the* Helena.]

Goethe spoke further of *Helena*, now it had again become a subject of discourse. "I at first intended a very different close," said he. "I modified it in various ways, and once very well, but I will not tell you how. Then this conclusion with Lord Byron and Missolonghi was suggested to me by the events of the day, and I gave up all the rest.[9] You have observed the character of the chorus is quite destroyed by the mourning song: until this time it has never belied its girlish nature; but here of a sudden it becomes nobly reflecting, and says things such as it has never thought or could think."

* * *

"I wonder," said Goethe, laughing, "what the German critics will say? Will they have freedom and boldness enough to get over this? Understanding will be attempted in the manner of the French; they will not consider that the imagination has its own laws, to which the understanding cannot and should not penetrate.

"If imagination did not originate things that must ever be problems to the understanding, there would be but little for the imagination to do. It is this which separates poetry from prose—in which understanding always is, and always should be, at home."

To Karl Jakob Ludwig Iken,[1] September 23, 1827
[*On the* Helena]

Let me first express my pleasure that you communicate your interest in my *Helena*. Considering the high level of culture among the best minds of our homeland, I indeed expected such a favorable response; yet the fulfillment of such hopes and desires is always most enjoyable and necessary. I had this in mind when I at last

9. An allusion to the final chorus of the Arcadian sequence in the *Helena*, lines 9907–38, where the death of Euphorion is lamented in terms that include an allusion to the death of Lord Byron at the Battle of Missolonghi in Greece in 1824.

1. Karl Jakob Ludwig Iken (1789–1841), scholar and editor of a newspaper in Bremen, interested particularly in matters relating to Greece, corresponded occasionally with Goethe during the 1820s.

completed this work, so long intended and prepared for, and even as I worked I balanced the cost in time and energy and in strict perseverance against such a profit. I never doubted that those readers for whom I was really writing would quickly grasp the main point of this composition. It is high time that the vehement opposition of Classicists and Romantics be resolved. The essential thing is that we develop our minds; from what point we do so would be insignificant, were it not for the danger of being misled by false models. We are grateful to richer and purer insights into Greek and Roman literature for liberating us from monastic barbarism during the fifteenth and sixteenth centuries. From such a lofty vantage point can we not learn to appreciate everything in its true physical and aesthetic worth, both what is ancient and what is modern?

In hopes of such a sympathetic response I let myself go completely while composing my *Helena,* without worrying at all about its public or even any individual reader, convinced that whoever could grasp and comprehend the whole would gradually assimilate the details with affectionate patience. On one hand, nothing will remain a secret to the philologist, who will indeed take pleasure in the recreation of the antiquity which he already knows; on the other hand, a sensitive reader will penetrate what is playfully concealed here and there; *"Eleusis servat, quod ostendat revisentibus."*[2] And in this instance I would be delighted if the mysterious provides the occasion for friends to return to it again and again.

With regard to other obscure passages in both my earlier and my recent poems I offer the following for consideration: Since many of our experiences cannot be expressed plainly and directly, I long ago chose the following means for revealing my secret meaning to attentive readers, by using images which are set against each other and which simultaneously mirror themselves in each other. Since everything which I have expressed is based upon my experience of life, may I perhaps suggest and hope that my readers will want to experience my poems again and will do so. And certainly each of my readers will discover for himself that from time to time something new appears pleasurably in particular aspects of things which are already familiar to him in general, something which truly pertains to us, since it indicates mental development and thereby leads us on to fresh growth. But this happens to us with everything that presents or contains something of substance.

Conversation, Monday, October 1, 1827
[*Goethe discusses the scene "Imperial Residence. Throne Room."*]

* * * Went to Goethe, who read to me the second scene of his new *Faust.*

2. "Eleusis keeps what it only shows to those who revisit it" (Seneca, *Natural Questions,* VII.31.6).

"In the emperor," said he, "I have endeavoured to represent a prince who has all the necessary qualities for losing his land, and at last succeeds in so doing. He does not concern himself about the welfare of his kingdom and his subjects; he only thinks of himself and how he can amuse himself with something new. The land is without law and justice; the judge is on the side of the criminals; atrocious crimes are committed with impunity. The army is without pay, without discipline, and roams about plundering to help itself as it can. The state treasury is empty, and without hope of replenishment. In the emperor's own household, there is scarcity in both kitchen and cellar. The marshal, who cannot devise means to get on from day to day, is already in the hands of the Jews; to whom everything is pawned, so that bread already eaten comes to the emperor's table.

"The counsellor of state wishes to remonstrate with his Majesty upon all these evils, and advises as to their remedy; but the gracious sovereign is very unwilling to lend his sublime ear to anything so disagreeable. Here now is the true element for Mephisto, who quickly supplants the former fool, and is at once at the side of the emperor as fool and counsellor."

Goethe read the scene and the interspersed murmuring of the crowd excellently, and I had a very pleasant evening.

Conversation, Thursday, February 12, 1829
[*Concerning the music which Goethe envisioned for* Faust]

"Yet I do not give up hope," said I, "of seeing suitable music composed for *Faust*."

"Quite impossible!" said Goethe. "The awful and repulsive passages that must occasionally occur are not in the style of the time. The music should be like that of *Don Juan*. Mozart should have composed for *Faust*.[3] Meyerbeer would pehaps be capable; but he would not touch anything of the kind; he is too much engaged with the Italian theatres."

Conversation, Sunday, December 6, 1829
[*Concerning the length of time between planning and composing* Faust]

To-day after dinner, Goethe read me the first scene of the second act of *Faust*. The effect was great. We are once more transported into Faust's study, where Mephistopheles finds all as he had left it.

3. A reference to Mozart's opera *Don Giovanni*. It is significant that Goethe does not mention Beethoven as an appropriate composer for *Faust*, though Goethe had met Beethoven in the early years of the century. Beethoven, of course, had died by this time, and *Faust* would not find its appropriate operatic setting until Berlioz composed the *Damnation of Faust* from the French translation by Gérard de Nerval (consisting mainly of *Part I*) in the mid-1830s.

He takes from the hook Faust's old study-gown, and a thousand moths and insects flutter out from it. By the directions of Mephistopheles as to where these are to settle down, the locality is brought very clearly before our eyes. He puts on the gown, intending to play the master once more, while Faust lies behind a curtain in a state of paralysis. He pulls the bell, which gives such an awful tone among the old solitary convent-halls that the doors spring open and the walls tremble. The servant rushes in, and finds in Faust's seat Mephistopheles, whom he does not recognize but for whom he has respect. In answer to inquiries he gives news of Wagner, who has now become a celebrated man, and is hoping for the return of his master—he is, we hear, at this moment very busy in his laboratory, trying to make a Homunculus. The servant retires, and the Bachelor enters—the same whom we knew some years before as a shy young student when Mephistopheles (in Faust's gown) made game of him. He is now a man, and so full of conceit that even Mephistopheles can do nothing with him, but moves his chair farther and farther and at last addresses the pit.

Goethe read the scene to the end. I was pleased with his youthful productive strength, and with the closeness of the whole. "As the conception," said Goethe, "is so old—for I have had it in my mind for fifty years—the materials have accumulated to such a degree that the difficulty is to separate and reject. The invention of the second part is really as old as I say; but it may be an advantage that I have not written it down till now when my knowledge of the world is so much clearer. I am like one who in his youth has a great deal of small silver and copper money; which in the course of his life he constantly changes for the better, so that at last the property of his youth stands before him in pieces of pure gold."

We spoke about the character of the Bachelor. "Is he not meant," said I, "to represent a certain class of ideal philosophers?"

"No," said Goethe, "the arrogance peculiar to youth, of which we had such striking examples after our war for freedom, is personified in him. Indeed, everyone believes in his youth that the world really began with him, and that all merely exists for his sake.

"Thus, in the East, there was a man who every morning collected his people about him, and would not go to work till he had commanded the sun to rise. But he was wise enough not to command till the sun of its own accord was on the point of appearing."

Conversation, Wednesday, December 16, 1829
[Goethe comments on Homunculus' relation to Mephistopheles.]

To-day, after dinner, Goethe read me the second scene of the second act of *Faust*, where Mephistopheles visits Wagner, who is on the point of making a human being by chemical means. The work succeeds; the Homunculus appears in the phial, as a shining being, and is at once active. He repels Wagner's questions upon incomprehensible subjects; reasoning is not his business; he wishes to *act*, and begins with our hero, Faust, who, in his paralysed condition, needs a higher aid. As a being to whom the present is perfectly clear and transparent, the Homunculus sees into the soul of the sleeping Faust; who, enraptured by a lovely dream, beholds Leda visited by swans, while she is bathing in a pleasant spot. The Homunculus, by describing this dream, brings a most charming picture before our eyes. Mephistopheles sees nothing of it, and the Homunculus taunts him with his northern nature.

"Generally," said Goethe, "you will perceive that Mephistopheles appears to disadvantage beside the Homunculus,[4] who is like him in clearness of intellect, and so much superior in his tendency to the beautiful and to a useful activity. He styles him cousin; for such spiritual beings as this Homunculus, not saddened and limited by a thorough assumption of humanity, were classed with the dæmons, and thus there is a sort of relationship between the two."

"Certainly," said I, "Mephistopheles here appears a subordinate; yet I cannot help thinking he has had a secret influence on the production of the Homunculus. We have known him in this way before; and, indeed, in the *Helena* he always appears as secretly working. Thus he again elevates himself with regard to the whole, and in his lofy repose he can well afford to put up with a little in particulars."

"Your feeling of the position is very correct," said Goethe; "indeed, I have doubted whether I ought not to put some verses into the mouth of Mephistopheles when he goes to Wagner and when the Homunculus is still in a state of formation, so that his co-operation may be expressed."

"It would do no harm," said I. "Yet this is intimated by the words with which Mephistopheles closes the scene:

> At last we after all depend
> Upon dependents we created. [lines 7003–4]

"True," said Goethe, "that would be almost enough for the attentive; but I will think about some additional verses."

"But those concluding words are very great, and will not easily be penetrated to their full extent."

"I think," said Goethe, "I have given them a bone to pick. A father who has six sons is a lost man, let him do what he may. Kings and ministers, too, who have raised many persons to high places, may have something to think about from their own experience."

Faust's dream about Leda again came into my head, and I regarded this as a most important feature.

4. Goethe presumably here alludes only to the scene in Wagner's laboratory, which he was working on at the time.

"It is wonderful to me," said I, "how the several parts of such a work bear upon, perfect, and sustain one another! By this dream of Leda, *Helena* gains its proper foundation. There we have a constant allusion to swans and the child of a swan; but here we have the act itself, and when we come afterwards to *Helena*, with the sensible impression of such a situation, how much more clear and perfect does all appear!"

Goethe said I was right.

"You will see," said he, "that in these earlier acts the chords of the classic and romantic are constantly struck; so that, as on a rising ground, where both forms of poetry are brought out and in some sort balance one another, we may ascend to *Helena*.

"The French," continued Goethe, "now begin to think aright on these matters. Classic and romantic, say they, are equally good: the only point is to use these forms with judgment, and to be capable of excellence—you can be absurd in both, and then one is as worthless as the other. This, I think, is rational enough, and may content us for a while."

Conversation, Sunday, December 20, 1829
[*Goethe comments on Euphorion and the Boy Charioteer (from the Carnival in Act I).*]

Meanwhile, *Faust* came once more into my head, and I talked of the way to render the Homunculus clear on the stage. "If we do not see the little man himself," said I, "we must see the light in the bottle, and his important words must be uttered in a way that would surpass the capacity of a child."

"Wagner," said Goethe, "must not let the bottle go out of his hands, and the voice must sound as if it came from the bottle. It would be a part for a ventriloquist such as I have heard. A man of that kind would solve the difficulty."

We then talked of the Grand Carnival, and the possibility of representing it upon the stage. "It would be a little more than the market-place at Naples," said I.

"It would require a very large theatre," said Goethe, "and is hardly to be imagined."

"I hope to see it some day," was my answer. "I look forward especially to the elephant, led by Prudence, and surmounted by Victory, with Hope and Fear in chains on each side. This is an allegory that could not easily be surpassed."

"The elephant would not be the first on the stage," said Goethe. "At Paris there is one, which forms an entire character. He belongs to a popular party, and takes the crown from one king and places it on another, which must indeed have an imposing effect. Then, when he is called at the end of the piece, he appears quite alone, makes his bow, and retires. So you see we might reckon on an elephant for our carnival. But the whole scene is much too large, and requires an uncommon kind of manager."

"Still, it is so brilliant and effective that a stage will scarcely allow it to escape. Then how it builds itself up, and becomes more and more striking! First, there are the beautiful gardeners, male and female; who decorate the stage, and at the same time form a mass, so that the various objects as they increase in importance are never without spectators and a background. Then, after the elephants, there is the team of dragons, coming from the background, through the air, and soaring overhead. Then the appearance of the great Pan; and how at last all seems afire, until put out by the wet clouds that roll to the spot. With all this carried out as you have conceived, the public will, in its amazement, confess that it has not senses and intellect enough to appreciate such spectacular riches."

"Pray, no more about the public," said Goethe; "I wish to hear nothing about it. The chief point is, that the piece is written; the world may now do with it as it pleases and use it as far as it can."

We then talked of the Boy Charioteer.[5]

"That Faust is concealed under the mask of Plutus, and Mephistopheles under that of Avarice, you will have already perceived. But who is the Boy Charioteer?"

I hesitated, and could not answer.

"It is Euphorion," said Goethe.

"But how can he appear in the carnival here, when he is not born till the third act?"

"Euphorion," replied Goethe, "is not a human, but an allegorical being. In him is personified poetry; which is bound to neither time, place, nor person. The same spirit who afterwards chooses to be Euphorion appears here as the Boy Charioteer, and is so far like a spectre that he can be present everywhere and at all times."

Conversation, Wednesday, December 30, 1829
[*Goethe discusses the paper-money scene and the spirit show of Paris and Helena in Act I.*]

To-day, after dinner, Goethe read me the next scene.

"Now they have got money at the imperial court," said he, "they want to be amused. The Emperor wishes to see Paris and Helen; and through magical art they are to appear in person. However, since Mephistopheles has nothing to do with Greek antiquity, and has no power over such personages, this task is assigned to Faust, who succeeds in it perfectly. The scene showing the means Faust must adopt to render the apparition possible is not complete yet,

5. The Boy Charioteer is a central allegorical character in the Carnival Masque of Act I. Euphorion, of course, is the offspring of Faust and Helena in Act III, which was composed first (and may thus justify the inverse sequence in Goethe's thinking here) but comes later in *Part II* of *Faust*.

but I will read it to you next time. The actual appearance of Paris and Helen you shall hear to-day."

Conversation, Sunday, January 3, 1830
[*General remarks on* Faust]

* * * [Goethe] had taken up the latest French translation of his *Faust*, by Gérard; which he turned over, and seemed occasionally to read.

"Some singular thoughts pass through my head," said he. "This book is now read in a language over which Voltaire ruled fifty years ago. You cannot understand my thoughts upon this subject, and have no idea of the influence Voltaire and his great contemporaries had in my youth, and how they governed the whole civilized world. My biography does not clearly show the influence of these men in my youth, and what pains it cost me to defend myself against them and to maintain my own ground in a true relation to nature."

* * *

He praised Gérard's translation as very successful, although mostly in prose.

"I do not like," he said, "to read my *Faust* any more in German; but in this French translation all seems again fresh, new, and spirited. *Faust* is, however, quite incommensurable, and all attempts to bring it nearer to the understanding are vain. Also, the first part is the product of a rather dark state in the individual. However, this very darkness has a charm for men's minds; and they work upon it till they are tired, as upon all insoluble problems."

Conversation, Sunday, January 10, 1830
[*Goethe discusses the Mothers scene in Act I ("Dark Gallery").*]

This afternoon, Goethe afforded me great pleasure by reading the scene in which Faust visits the Mothers.

The novelty and unexpectedness of the subject, and Goethe's manner of reading the scene, struck me so forcibly that I felt myself wholly transported into the situation of Faust when he shudders at the communication from Mephistopheles.

Although I had heard and felt the whole, yet so much remained an enigma to me that I asked Goethe for some explanation. But he, as usual, wrapped himself up in mystery, as he looked on me with wide-open eyes and repeated the words:

The Mothers! Why, it strikes a singular chord. [line 6217]

"I can reveal to you no more," said he, "except that I found in Plutarch that in ancient Greece mention was made of the Mothers as divinities. This is all that I owe to others, the rest is my own invention. Take the manuscript home with you, study it carefully, and see what you can make of it."

Conversation, Sunday January 24, 1830
[*Goethe comments on the "Classical Walpurgis Night."*]

We then talked about the "Classical Walpurgis Night," the beginning of which Goethe had lately read me.

"The mythological figures that crowd upon me," said he, "are innumerable; but I restrain myself, and select those that produce the proper pictorial effect. Faust has now met Chiron, and I hope I shall be successful with the scene.[6] If I work hard I shall have done the 'Walpurgis Night' in a couple of months. Nothing more shall take me off *Faust*; for it will be odd enough if I live to finish it, and yet it is possible. The fifth act is as good as done, and the fourth will almost write itself."

Conversation, Sunday, February 13, 1831
[*Concerning the final stage of composition*]

* * * Goethe * * * told me he was going on with the fourth act of *Faust*, and had satisfied himself with the beginning.

"I had," said he, "long since the *what*, as you know, but was not quite satisfied about the *how*; hence it is the more pleasant that good thoughts have come to me.

"I will now go on inventing, to supply the whole gap, from the *Helena* to the fifth act, which is finished, and will write down a detailed plan, that I may work with comfort and security on those parts that first attract me.

"This act acquires quite a peculiar character, so that, like an independent little world, it does not touch the rest, and is only connected with the whole by a slight reference to what precedes and follows."

"It will then," said I, "be perfectly in character with the rest; for, in fact, 'Auerbach's Cellar,' 'Witch's Kitchen,' the Blocksberg, the Imperial Diet, the masquerade, the paper money, the laboratory, the 'Classical Walpurgis Night,' the *Helena* are all of them little independent worlds, which, each being complete in itself, do indeed work upon each other, yet come but little in contact. The great point with the poet is to express a manifold world, and he uses the story of a celebrated hero merely as a sort of thread on which he may string what he pleases. * * *"

"You are perfectly right," said Goethe; "and the only matter of

6. An allusion to Faust's meeting with the centaur Chiron in the "Classical Wal-purgis Night" (lines 7331–7488).

importance is, that the single masses should be clear and significant, while the whole always remains incommensurable—and even on that account, like an unsolved problem, constantly lures mankind to study it again and again."

I asked about *Faust*, and what progress he had made with it.

"That," said Goethe, "will not again let me loose. I daily think and invent more and more of it. I have now had the whole manuscript of the second part stitched together, that it may lie a palpable mass before me. The place of the yet-lacking fourth act I have filled with white paper; and undoubtedly what is finished will allure and urge me to complete what has yet to be done. There is more than people think in these matters of sense, and we must aid the spiritual by all manner of devices."

He sent for the stitched *Faust*, and I was surprised to see how much he had written; for a good folio volume was before me.

"And all," said I, "has been done in the six years that I have been here; and yet, amid so many other occupations, you could have devoted but little time to it. We see how much a work grows, even if we add something only now and then!"

"That is a conviction that strengthens with age," said Goethe; "while youth believes all must be done in a single day. If fortune favour, and I continue in good health, I hope in the next spring months to get a great way on with the fourth act. It was, as you know, invented long since; but the other parts have, in course of execution, grown so much, that I can now use only the outline of my first invention, and must fill out this introduced portion so as to make it of a piece with the rest."

"A far richer world is displayed," said I, "in this second part than in the first."

"I should think so," said Goethe. "The first part is almost entirely subjective; it proceeded entirely from a perplexed impassioned individual, and his semi-darkness is probably highly pleasing to mankind. But in the second part there is scarcely anything of the subjective; here is seen a higher, broader, clearer, more passionless world, and he who has not looked about him and had some experience will not know what to make of it."

"There will be found exercise for thought," said I; "some learning may also be needful. I am glad that I have read Schelling's little book on the Cabiri, and that I now know the drift of that famous passage in the 'Walpurgis Night.' "[7]

"I have always found," said Goethe laughing, "that it is well to know something."

7. See footnote to line 8074.

"The old 'Walpurgis Night,' " said Goethe, "is monarchical, since the devil is there respected throughout as a decided chief. But the 'Classical Walpurgis Night' is thoroughly republican; since all stand on a plain near one another, so that each is as prominent as his associates, and nobody is subordinate or troubled about the rest."

"Moreover," said I, "in the Classical assembly all are sharply-outlined individualities; while, on the German Blocksberg, each individuality is lost in the general witch-mass."

"Therefore," said Goethe, "Mephistopheles knows what is meant when the Homunculus speaks to him of *Thessalian* witches.[8] A connoisseur of antiquity will have something suggested by these words, while to the unlearned it remains a mere name."

"Antiquity," said I, "must be very living to you, else you could not make all these figures step so freshly into life, and treat them with such freedom as you do."

"Without a lifelong occupation with plastic art," said Goethe, "it would not have been possible to me. The difficulty was in observing due moderation amid such plenty, and avoiding all figures that did not perfectly fit into my plan. I made, for instance, no use of the Minotaur, the Harpies, and certain other monsters."

"But what you have exhibited in that night," said I, "is so grouped, and fits so well together, that it can be easily recalled by the imagination and made into a picture. The painters will certainly not allow such good subjects to escape them; and I especially hope to see Mephistopheles among the Phorcyades, when he tries the famous mask in profile."

"There are a few pleasantries there," said Goethe, "which will more or less occupy the world. Suppose the French are the first to perceive *Helena*, and to see what can be done with it for the stage. They will spoil the piece as it is; but they will make a wise use of it for their own purpose, and that is all we can expect or desire. To Phorcyas they will certainly add a chorus of monsters, as is indeed already indicated in one passage."

"It would be a great matter," said I, "if a clever poet of the romantic school treated the piece as an opera throughout, and Rossini collected all his great talent for a grand composition, to produce an effect with the *Helena*. It affords opportunities for magnificent scenes, surprising transformations, brilliant costumes, and charming ballets, which are not easily to be found elsewhere; not to mention that this abundance of sensible material rests on the foundation of an ingenious fable that could scarcely be excelled."

"We will wait for what the gods bring us," said Goethe; "such things are not to be hurried. The great matter is for people to enter

8. See line 6977.

into it, and for managers, poets, and composers to see their advantage in it."

Goethe showed me to-day the beginning of the fifth act of *Faust*, hitherto wanting. I read to the place where the cottage of Philemon and Baucis is burned, and Faust, standing by night on the balcony of his palace, smells the smoke, which is borne to him by a light breeze.

"These names, Philemon and Baucis," said I, "transport me to the Phrygian coast, reminding me of the famous couple of antiquity. But our scene belongs to modern days, and a Christian landscape."

"My Philemon and Baucis," said Goethe, "have nothing to do with that renowned ancient couple or the tradition connected with them. I gave this couple the names merely to elevate the characters. The persons and relations are similar, and hence the use of the names has a good effect."

We then spoke of Faust, whom the hereditary portion of his character—discontent—has not left even in his old age, and who, amid all the treasures of the world, and in a new dominion of his own making, is annoyed by a couple of lindens, a cottage, and a bell, which are not his. He is therein not unlike Ahab, King of Israel, who fancied he possessed nothing, unless he could also make the vineyard of Naboth his own.

"Faust," said Goethe, "when he appears in the fifth act, should, according to my design, be exactly a hundred years old, and I rather think it would be well expressly to say so in some passage."

We then spoke of the conclusion, and Goethe directed my attention to the passage:

> Pure spirits' peer, from evil coil
> He was vouchsafed exemption;
> "Whoever strives in ceaseless toil
> Him we may grant redemption."
> And when on high, transfigured love
> Has added intercession,
> The blest will throng to him above
> With welcoming compassion. [lines 11934–41]

"In these lines," said he, "is contained the key to Faust's salvation. In Faust himself there is an activity that becomes constantly higher and purer to the end, and from above there is eternal love coming to his aid. This harmonizes perfectly with our religious views; according to which we can obtain heavenly bliss, not through our own strength alone, but with the assistance of divine grace.

To Heinrich Meyer,[9] July 20, 1831
[*On* Faust, Part II]

It is always surprising to me how egoism, which is isolated from everything, revolutionary in part and secluded in part, permeates all kinds of lively activities. Let me only acknowledge that I have withdrawn my own into the innermost aspect of my work and have been organizing the second part of my *Faust*, which I began serious work on again four years ago, filling in the important gaps and joining the existing material together from the perspective of the conclusion and from the beginning toward the conclusion. I hope I have succeeded in eliminating all discontinuity between the earlier and the later material.

For a long time I knew what I wanted, indeed even how I wanted it, and I carried it around within me for many years like a fairy tale, only composing particular passages which attracted my attention from time to time. But this second part was not to be, and could not be, as fragmentary as the first. Common sense plays a greater role in it, as will have been apparent from that part of it which has already been printed. It finally required, to be sure, really strong resolution to work it into a whole, so that it would stand up to the scrutiny of an educated mind. For that reason I firmly resolved that it must be completed before my birthday. And so it will be. The whole thing now lies before me and I have only incidentals to correct. Then I will seal it up, and then, whatever happens, it will increase the specific substance of those volumes of my work still to appear. Though it still contains problems enough, since —like world history and human history—each problem solved creates a new one to be solved, it is certain to provide pleasure for those who can respond to a gesture, a hint or a delicate intimation. Such a reader will even find more in it than I could give. And thus a great stone has been pushed over the mountaintop and rolled down the other side. But immediately there are others lying behind me which also need to be dealt with, in order that what is written may be fulfilled: "Such labor has God given to man."

To Wilhelm von Humboldt,[1] December 1, 1831
[*On* Faust *generally*]

Concerning my *Faust* there is much to say and there is little to say. In a happy moment the following passage came to mind:

9. Johann Heinrich Meyer (1760–1832), art historian and active member of the so-called friends of art in Weimar (*Weimarer Kunstfreunde*), who strongly supported Goethe's classical taste in art during the period following the poet's Italian journey in 1786–88, remained a close friend, collaborator, and correspondent of the poet until Goethe's death.
1. Wilhelm von Humboldt (1767–1835), statesman, historian, linguist, and general man of letters, became a close associate of both Goethe and Schiller during the mid-1790s, especially on matters pertaining to literature and aesthetics. His later correspondence with Goethe constitutes one of the most important documents for German nineteenth-century as well as for Goethe's later thought.

> Call yourselves poets by vocation?
> Then order up your poetry. [lines 220–21]

And by means of a mysterious psychological tranformation, which perhaps deserves to be studied, I believe that I have elevated my mind to a kind of productivity which brought all this forth in a full state of consciousness and which pleases me still, even though perhaps I could never swim again in such a river, a productivity which Aristotle and other prosaic minds would ascribe to a kind of madness. The difficulty in achieving this consisted in the fact that the second part of *Faust*, the published sections of which have perhaps attracted your attention, has been thought through for fifty years in all its aims and motifs and has been worked through in fragments —according to my pleasure with one or another incident—, though the whole of it remained full of gaps.

Now common sense will make greater demands of the second part than the first and for this reason it was necessary to work more in anticipation of the needs of an intelligent reader, even though there is enough left over by way of transitions to be supplied for him. It was necessary to fill in certain gaps both for historical and aesthetic continuity; and I kept this up until finally it seemed advisable to cry out: "Close the irrigation canal, the fields have had enough."

And then I had to find the courage to seal up my bound copy of the play, which contains a mixture of printed and unprinted material, so that I would not be tempted to add still further here and there; whereby indeed I regret not being able to share this with my most valued friends—something a poet does so gladly.

To Wilhelm von Humboldt,[2] March 17, 1832
[Last words on Faust]

After a long involuntary pause I am beginning like this, and yet simply impromptu. The Ancients said that the animals are taught through their organs; let me add to this, so are men, but they have the advantage of teaching their organs in return.

Every action, and so every talent, needs some inborn faculty which acts naturally, and unconsciously carries with it the necessary aptitude, and which, therefore, continues to act in such a way that though its law is implicit in it, its course in the end may be aimless and purposeless.

The earlier man becomes aware that there exists some craft, some art that can help him towards a controlled heightening of his natural abilities, the happier he is; whatever he may receive from without does not harm his innate individuality. The best genius is that

---

2. This is the last letter which Goethe wrote. Final changes in the manuscript of *Faust* had been made (according to Goethe's diary notations) during January, 1832. He became ill on March 16 and died on March 22.

which absorbs everything within itself, knows how to appropriate everything, without this in the least impairing its fundamental dispositions, called its character, but rather enhancing and furthering them throughout as much as possible.

Here begin the manifold relations between the conscious and the unconscious. Take for instance a talented musician, composing an important score; consciousness and unconsciousness will be like warp and weft, a simile I am fond of using.

Through practice, teaching, reflection, success, failure, furtherance and resistance, and again and again reflection, man's organs unconsciously and in a free activity link what he acquires with his innate gifts, so that a unity results which leaves the world amazed.

These general remarks may serve as a rapid answer to your question, and as an explanation to the note I return herewith.

For more than sixty years the conception of *Faust* has lain here before my mind with the clearness of youth, though the sequence with less fulness. I have let the idea go quietly along with me through life and have only worked out the scenes that interested me most from time to time. So in the second part gaps remained, waiting for this kind of interest before they could be joined to the rest. It was difficult to do through conscious effort and strength of personality something that really should have been the spontaneous work of active nature. But it surely would not be right if this were not possible after my long life of thought and action, and I am not afraid of people being able to pick out the new from the old, the later from the earlier work. We can leave that to future readers.

It would naturally be an infinite joy to me if during my lifetime, too, I could dedicate these serious jests to my valued friends everywhere. I have always been grateful for their interest and should like to hear their response. But the present age is so senseless and confused that I know I should only be poorly rewarded for my many years of sincere effort at erecting this strange building. It would be driven like a wrack on the shore and lie there, getting gradually covered by the sands of time. The world is ruled to-day by bewildering wrong counsel, urging bewildered wrong action. My most important task is to go on developing as much as possible whatever is and remains in me, distilling my own particular abilities again and again. You, my friend, are doing the same up there in your castle.

Tell me about your work, too; as you know, Riemer is still busy on the same sort of studies as we are, and our evening conversations often touch on these subjects. Forgive this long delayed letter. In spite of my retirement, there is seldom a time when I am in the mood to remind myself of those mysteries of life.

Contemporary Reactions

AUGUST WILHELM SCHLEGEL

[Review of the *Fragment* of 1790]†

"Faust, a Fragment." The meaning of this dramatic poem lies
too deep, is too far-reaching, and, since the piece is only a fragment,
too little developed not to run the risk that a large proportion of
readers will overlook it and dwell instead upon lesser works. Faust,
as Goethe has heightened and expanded the folk legend for his
purposes, is a man for whose understanding science and for
whose stormy heart ethically moderate enjoyment are too confining; whose feelings carry within themselves the mark of inborn nobility and genuine love of nature; and whose actions are
uncertain, aimless, and corruptible; a man who, at one moment,
pushes himself beyond the limits of mortality in order to establish
alliances with higher spirits and, at the next, surrenders himself to
the devil for unrestrained sensual gratification; noble enough not to
be infected by the insensitive mockery of the demon who serves
him in the satisfaction of his desires, and not strong enough to
master the passions which make such a guide necessary to him.
Equally removed from comfortable, inactive repose and from the
joy of successful activity, Faust has squandered his life in endless
research. At last he tears himself free, rejects all science as the dead
skeleton of nature, and hurries to embrace living nature herself.
Bold enthusiasm carries him upwards into the world of spirits. New
youth is given him. A girl who lives alone in modest seclusion and
childish contentment attracts him and falls victim to his passion.
He destroys her domestic peace: this good, weak creature perishes
from love and remorse. All this is presented overpoweringly and, in
Goethe's manner, tossed off with a degree of carelessness and yet
with the utmost truth. But the poet takes us no further. In certain
respects, to be sure, Faust's fate has long since been decided: his
path, once he has taken it, leads unavoidably to ruin. But will this
apply only to his external condition or will it also affect the inner
man? Will he remain true to himself and, even in the final instance,
still deserve human compassion because he falls as a human being
with great abilities? Or will the depraved spirit to whom he has surrendered himself bring him to the point where he becomes himself
the creator of evil, himself a devil?—This question still remains
unanswered.

Just as the design of this play is unique (for it cannot in any way
be compared with any of Goethe's own works, nor with those of

---

† August Wilhelm Schlegel (1767–1845),
who subsequently emerged as the leading
practical critic of European Romanticism, here offers an immediate response
to the first public appearance of
Goethe's drama, the *Fragment* of 1790.

(From *Göttingische Anzeige von gelehr-
ten Sachen* [1790], Stück 154; in *Collected Works*, ed. Böcking [Leipzig,
1846], X, 16 ff. Translated by Dolores
Signori and Cyrus Hamlin.)

any other dramatic poet), so also is its treatment. No single tone, or style, or general norm holds sway, to which the particular ideas must adapt and arrange themselves. The poet has set only one law for himself: to follow the freest ranging of his mind. Hence the sudden transitions from popular simplicity to philosophical profundity, from mysterious, magical oracles to expressions of general common sense, from the sublime to the burlesque. In the versification, too, one finds just as diverse an alternation: here the meter of Hans Sachs,[1] there rhymed lines of all measures and lengths; here and there also irregular lyrical rhythms. In many places one misses that polish of versification which is the work of mechanical diligence; nowhere is there a lack of energy or expression. Here too a superior mind reveals itself, which can afford to ignore discretion and yet never miss its mark.

FRIEDRICH SCHLEGEL

[On *Hamlet* and *Faust* as Philosophical Tragedies][†]

* * * True philosphical poetry interests not only the understanding but also the intellect. Poetry which is "characteristic" develops and advances naturally to philosophical tragedy which is the complete antithesis of aesthetic tragedy. The latter is the consummation of beautiful poetry, consisting of purely lyrical elements whose ultimate effect is the highest harmony. The former is the highest artistic form of didactic poetry, consisting of purely characteristic elements, whose ultimate effect is the highest disharmony. Its catastrophe is tragic, but not its entire substance: for the prevailing purity of the tragic element (an essential condition of aesthetic tragedy) would impair the truth of characteristic and philosophical art.

This is not the place to develop in detail the as yet completely unknown theory of philosophical tragedy. Yet let me illustrate the concept of this poetic form as I conceive it with a single example, which is a very interesting phenomenon in itself and, in addition, one of the most important documents for the "characteristic" quality of modern poetry and which for content and perfect coherence is so far the most admirable of its kind.—*Hamlet* is often misunder-

---

1. See note 5, p. 451, below.
† Friedrich Schlegel (1772–1829; younger brother of August Wilhelm), in his essay "On the Study of Greek Poesy" (1795), from which the passage here included is taken (*Prosaische Jugendschriften*, ed. Jacob Minor [Vienna 1906], Vol. I, pp. 106–8, 114; here translated by Cyrus Hamlin), first elaborated the basic polarity between Classical and Romantic poetry, which subsequently achieved European notoriety. Within this polarity Schlegel argued for a fundamental distinction between aesthetic tragedy, exemplified by the drama of Sophocles, and philosophical tragedy, here discussed with specific reference to Shakespeare's *Hamlet* as norm. Mention of *Faust*, which remains no more than that here, indicates how Goethe's play came to replace Shakespeare as the model for Romantic philosophical tragedy.

stood when it is praised for particular passages. A rather inconsistent tolerance, if the whole is really so disjointed, so senseless as is often silently assumed! In reality the coherence of Shakespeare's dramas is so simple and lucid that it should be comprehended in its own right by open and unbiased minds. The basis of this coherence, however, often lies so deeply hidden—the invisible ties, the connections are so delicate—that even the most ingenious critical analysis will fail if it lacks tact, if false expectations or false principles are applied. In *Hamlet* all the individual parts develop necessarily from a common center and relate back to it again. Nothing is extraneous, superfluous, or accidental in this masterpiece of artistic wisdom. The center of the whole is found in the character of the hero. Because of his unique situation all the power of his noble nature is concentrated in his reason, and his power to act is completely destroyed. His spirit is divided, as if torn apart in opposite directions on the rack; it collapses and perishes from an excess of idle reason, which oppresses him more painfully than do all those with whom he comes into contact. There exists perhaps no more perfect representation of irresolvable discord, which is the true subject of philosophical tragedy, than such an utter disparity between the reflective and the active power as in the character of Hamlet. The total effect of this tragedy is one of maximum despair. All the impressions it makes, which individually seem large and important, become trivial and disappear in the face of what here appears as the final, unique result of all being and thought: the eternal, colossal dissonance which infinitely separates mankind and fate.

In the entire realm of modern poetry this drama is one of the most important documents for the aesthetic historian. In it the mind of its creator is most visible; what appears sporadically throughout the other works of the poet is here perfectly united. Shakespeare among all artists is the one who most completely and most strikingly embodies the spirit of modern poetry. He unites the most charming blossoms of romantic fantasy and the gigantic dimension of the Gothic heroic age with the subtlest strains of modern social life and the most profound and extensive poetic philosophy. With regard to these last two (i.e., social life and philosophy), it might appear at times that he had anticipated the developments of our own age. Who has surpassed him in the inexhaustible supply of what is interesting? in intensity of all passions? in the inimitable truth of the "characteristic"? in unique originality? He spans to the fullest extent the particular aesthetic advantages of every kind of modern writer, highest excellence and, with regard to the singularity of the moderns, even the eccentric peculiarities and errors which they carry with them. Without exaggeration he may be called the peak of modern poetry. How rich he is in individual beauties of every kind! How often he so nearly achieves the highest which can be attained! * * *

The character of the aesthetic development of our age and our nation betrays itself in a remarkable and magnificent phenomenon. Goethe's poetry is the dawn of genuine art and pure beauty.—The sensual power which sustains our age and our people was only the smallest of the advantages with which he first appeared as a young man. The philosophical content, the "characteristic" truth of his later works can be compared with the inexhaustible wealth of Shakespeare. Indeed, if *Faust* were to be completed, it would probably far surpass *Hamlet*, the English poet's masterpiece, with which it seems to share a common purpose. What in *Hamlet* is only fate, event— weakness, is in *Faust* disposition, action—strength. Hamlet's mood and his inclination are the result of his external situation; Faust's corresponding inclination is his natural character.* * *

FRIEDRICH SCHELLING

[On *Faust* as Tragicomedy]†

In moving from tragedy to comedy [in this discussion of contemporary drama] it is without doubt most appropriate to mention the greatest German poem, Goethe's *Faust*. But it is difficult to offer a sufficiently convincing judgment concerning the spirit of the whole based on what we possess of it thus far. So my claim that this poem is by intention far more Aristophanic than tragic may seem striking, in face of the usual view.

Therefore I shall content myself with offering a very general view of this poem, so far as I think I understand it.

Not only is there a sense of fate in the plot; here the "In-Itself" of the universe and of nature confronts as an insurmountable necessity the knowledge of the individual as an individual. The subject as subject cannot enjoy the infinite as infinite, which is nonetheless a necessary inclination of the subject. Here, therefore, is an eternal contradiction. At the same time, the power of fate, which here

† The lecture course by Friedrich W. Schelling (1775–1854) on the "philosophy of art" (reprinted from the *Collected Works* [1859], Vol. I, v, pp. 731 ff.; translated by Cyrus Hamlin), was delivered a number of times over a period of years from 1799 to 1804. Schelling's discussion of Goethe's *Faust* is brief and very general, based entirely on the published text of the *Fragment* of 1790, though even on the basis of this incomplete text Schelling asserts that *Faust* is the greatest German poem and the prototype of philosophical tragedy. Also important is Schelling's emphasis on the unique blending of the tragic and the comic in *Faust*, by which he means the imposition of Mephistophelean irony (which is very close to what came to be called Romantic irony) upon a tragic conflict of existential proportions. Schelling addresses himself to the new philosophical theory of tragedy by shifting his attention away from "plot" (the traditional focus of Aristotelian theory) to the interaction of opposing forces: the individual or subject (that is, Faust himself) and necessity or fate, here called "the 'In-Itself' of the universe and of nature." Schelling is also the first critic of Goethe's drama to intuit the eventual salvation of the hero, and he is the first reader of the drama to identify Faust with the human condition, associating the popular legend with a basic tendency in what he refers to as the "German temper."

stands in opposition to and in conflict with the subject, is more ideal, as also holds no less true for the plot. A suspended harmony could here be established in two directions, and the conflict could seek a twofold solution. The point of departure is the insatiable thirst to behold and, as subject, to enjoy the inner essence of things; and its initial direction is to satisfy ecstatically this insatiable desire beyond the aims and limits of reason, as expressed in this passage from *Faust*:

> Go, spurn intelligence and science,
> Man's lodestar and supreme reliance,
> Be furthered by the liar-in-chief
> In works of fraud and make-believe,
> And I shall have you dead to rights. [lines 1851–54]

The other way out for the mind's unsatisfied striving is that of plunging into the world, to experience earth's sorrow and happiness. In this direction as well the result is decisive; here, too, it is eternally impossible for the finite to participate in the infinite; which is expressed in these words:

> Fate has endowed him with a forward-driving
> Impetuousness that reaches past all sights,
> And which, precipitately striving,
> Would overleap the earth's delights.
> Through dissipation I will drag him,
> Through shallow insignificance,
> I'll have him sticking, writhing, flagging,
> And for his parched incontinence
> Have food and drink suspended at lip level;
> In vain will he be yearning for relief. [lines 1856–65]

In Goethe's *Faust* both these tendencies are represented or, rather, immediately united, so that the one proceeds directly from the other.

For dramatic reasons greater weight had to be placed on the second tendency, the encounter of such a mind with the world. So far as we can tell from the *Fragment*, we clearly recognize that *Faust* is intended to advance in this direction to the heights of tragedy.

Yet the cheerful quality of the whole, even in the first draft, the truth of its misguided striving, the authenticity of a demand for the highest life, already allows us to expect that the conflict will be resolved at a higher level and that Faust will attain fulfillment by being raised up to higher spheres.

In this regard, strange as it may seem, this poem has a significance which is truly comparable to Dante, though it is more of a comedy and divine more in a poetic sense than Dante's *Divine Comedy*.

The wild life into which Faust throws himself becomes by a necessary consequence a Hell for him. His initial purification from the pangs of knowledge and false imagination, in accord with the playful intention of the work as a whole, will have to consist in an initiation into the basic principles of devilry, as the appropriate basis for an enlightened perspective on the world—just as his fulfillment will consist in rising above himself, by which he may perceive and learn to enjoy what is essential.

Even so little concerning the nature of this poem, which in part must be intuited more than known, shows how completely original it is in every aspect, a work comparable only to itself and completely self-contained. The kind of fate [it demonstrates] is unique and would deserve to be called a new discovery, were it not to an extent already present in the German temper and thus represented in its essential form in the mythological person of Faust.

Through this singular conflict, which begins in knowledge, the poem has assumed an epistemological aspect, so that if any poem may be called philosophical, then Goethe's *Faust* above all deserves this distinction. A magnificent spirit, which here unites the power of this exceptional poet with the profundity of a philosopher, has opened in this poem an eternally fresh source of knowledge, which would itself suffice to renew science (*Wissenschaft*) in our time and to infuse into it the freshness of a new life. Whoever seeks to penetrate the true sanctuary of nature, let him be nourished by these tones from a higher world and let him drink in its power in early youth, a power which emanates from this poem, as if in dense rays of light, and which thus moves the inner heart of the world.

GEORG WILHELM FRIEDRICH HEGEL

[Paraphrase of *Faust,* from *The Phenomenology of Mind*]†

In so far as [self-consciousness] has risen from out of the substance of ethical life and the quiescent state of thought, and attained its conscious independence, it has left behind the law of

---

† Hegel (1770–1831), *Phenomenology of Mind* (1807), from the section "Desire and Necessity," translated by Sir James Black Baillie. Readers of this most difficult and abstruse philosophical work have long acknowledged Hegel's argument to include here an intentional allusion to Goethe's *Faust*, if only because of the four lines quoted in modified form from the *Fragment* of 1790. What Hegel provides in fact is a kind of paraphrase through abstraction, whereby the situation of Faust, as represented dramatically by Goethe in the *Fragment*, is translated into the conceptual dynamics of the developing Spirit which constitutes the argument of Hegel's *Phenomenology*. This provides at best an abstract analogue for Goethe's drama which cannot in any sense serve as a commentary on it. The importance of this passage for assessing the impact of Goethe's *Faust*, even in the very limited scope of the first published *Fragment*, on the development of Idealist philosophy justifies its inclusion here, even though the language is bound to remain obscure to any reader unfamiliar with the vocabulary of the *Phenomenology of Spirit*.

custom and of substantial existence, the kinds of knowledge acquired through observation, and the sphere of theory; these lie behind it as a gray shadow that is just vanishing. For this latter is rather a knowledge of something, the independent existence (*Für-sichseyn*) and actuality of which are other than those of self-consciousness. It is not the seemingly divine spirit of universality in knowledge and action, wherein (all individual) feeling and enjoyment are stilled, that has passed into and fills this new level of self-consciousness; but the spirit of the earth, a spirit which holds that being alone as true reality which is the reality of individual consciousness.

> It repudiates sense and science
> The highest gifts possessed by men—
> It has gone over to the devil,
> And must be o'erthrown.[1]

It plunges thus into life, and carries to its completion the pure individuality in which it appears. It does not so much make its own happiness as take it directly and enjoy it. The grey shades of science, laws and principles, which alone stand between it and its own reality, vanish like a lifeless mist that cannot contend against the living certainty of its reality. It takes to itself life much as a ripe fruit is plucked, which comes to meet the hand that takes it.

MADAME DE STAËL

"Faustus"†

Among the pieces written for the performance of puppets, there is one entitled "Dr. Faustus, or Fatal Science," which has always had great success in Germany. Lessing took up this subject before Goethe. This wondrous history is a tradition very generally known. Several English authors have written the life of this same Dr. Faustus, and some of them have even attributed to him the art of printing—his profound knowledge did not preserve him from being weary of life, and in order to escape from it, he tried to enter into a com-

1. Hegel cites the first two and the last two lines of Mephistopheles' soliloquy, without indicating the omission of the middle section. He also transforms intentionally the rhetorical-dramatic form of the original, where Mephistopheles addresses the absent Faust in the imperative. Even more significant is the inversion of the next to last line in the speech. Where Mephistopheles asserts that Faust would "needs come to grief if he *had not* surrendered himself to the devil, Hegel states that self-consciousness will come to grief precisely *because* it *has* surrendered itself to the devil.
† The book by Mme. de Staël (1766–1817) *On Germany*—the excerpt given here is from the original English edition, published by John Murray (London, 1814), Vol. II, pp. 181–85—became the single most important source for the dissemination of German Romantic ideas throughout Europe. Mme. de Staël's comments indicate the kind of impact which Goethe's *Faust, Part I* had on the sensibility of the reading public in the later Romantic era.

pact with the devil, who concludes the whole by carrying him off. From these slender materials Goethe has furnished the astonishing work, of which I will now try to give some idea.

Certainly, we must not expect to find in it either taste, or measure, or the art that selects and terminates; but if the imagination could figure to itself an intellectual chaos, such as the material chaos has often been painted, the "Faustus" of Goethe should have been composed at that epoch. It cannot be exceeded in boldness of conception, and the recollection of this production is always attended with a sensation of giddiness. The Devil is the hero of the piece; the author has not conceived him like a hideous phantom, such as he is usually represented to children; he has made him, if we may so express ourselves, the evil Being *par excellence*, before whom all others * * * are only novices, scarcely worthy to be the servants of Mephistopheles (this is the name of the dæmon who has made himself the friend of Faustus). Goethe wished to display in this character, at once real and fanciful, the bitterest pleasantry that contempt can inspire, and at the same time an audacious gaiety that amuses. There is an infernal irony in the discourses of Mephistopheles, which extends itself to the whole creation, and criticizes the universe like a bad book of which the Devil has made himself the censor.

Mephistopheles makes sport with genius itself, as with the most ridiculous of all absurdities, when it leads men to take a serious interest in any thing, that exists in the world, and above all when it gives them confidence in their own individual strength. It is singular that, supreme wickedness and divine wisdom coincide in this respect; that they equally recognize the vanity and weakness of all earthly things: but the one proclaims this truth only to disgust men with what is good, the other only to elevate them above what is evil.

If the play of "Faustus" contained only a lively and philosophical pleasantry, an analogous spirit may be found in many of Voltaire's writings; but we perceive in this piece an imagination of a very different nature. It is not only that it displays to us the moral world, such as it is, annihilated, but that Hell itself is substituted in the room of it. There is a potency of sorcery, a poetry belonging to the principle of evil, a delirium of wickedness, a distraction of thought, which make us shudder, laugh, and cry, in a breath. It seems as if the government of the world were, for a moment, entrusted to the hands of the Dæmon. You tremble because he is pitiless, you laugh because he humbles the satisfaction of self-love, you weep, because human nature, thus contemplated from the depths of hell, inspires a painful compassion.

Milton has drawn his Satan larger than man; Michael Angelo and Dante have given him the hideous figure of the brute combined with the human shape. The Mephistopheles of Goethe is a civilized Devil. He handles with dexterity that ridicule, so trifling in appearance, which is nevertheless often found to consist with a profundity of malice; he treats all sensibility as silliness or affectation; his figure is ugly, low, and crooked; he is awkward without timidity, disdainful without pride; he affects something of tenderness with the women, because it is only in their company that he needs to deceive, in order to seduce; and what he understands by seduction, is to minister to the passions of others; for he cannot even imitate love. This is the only dissimulation that is impossible to him.

The character of Mephistopheles supposes an inexhaustible knowledge of social life, of nature, and of the marvellous. This play of "Faustus," is the night-mare of the imagination, but it is a night-mare that redoubles its strength. It discovers the diabolical revelation of incredulity,—of that incredulity which attaches itself to everything that can ever exist of good in this world; and perhaps this might be a dangerous revelation, if the circumstances produced by the perfidious intentions of Mephistopheles did not inspire a horror of his arrogant language, and make known the wickedness which it covers.

In the character of Faustus, all the weaknesses of humanity are concentrated: desire of knowledge, and fatigue of labour; wish of success and satiety of pleasure. It presents a perfect model of the changeful and versatile being whose sentiments are yet more ephemeral than the short existence of which he complains. Faustus has more ambition than strength; and this inward agitation produces his revolt against nature, and makes him have recourse to all manner of sorceries, in order to escape from the hard but necessary conditions imposed upon mortality. * * *

HEINRICH HEINE

[Faust] †

I would not be a German if at the mention of *Faust* I were not to express some interpretive thoughts on it. For everyone from the greatest thinker to the most insignificant literary scorekeeper, from the philosopher down to the doctor of philosophy whets his wits on this book. For that matter, it is really as spacious as the Bible and, like it, embraces heaven and earth, together with man and his exegesis. Here again, the subject matter is the main reason for the popularity of *Faust*; however, that he searched out his material in folk

† From *The Romantic School* by the poet Heinrich Heine (1797–1856). Translated by Dolores Signori, with the assistance of Walter Arndt; from *Heine's Collected Works*, ed. H. Kaufmann (Berlin: Aufbau Verlag, 1961), Vol. V, pp. 55 ff. This work was published in France in 1833 as a reply to the views of Madame de Staël (see the previous selection). Heine is concerned with the public reputation of the Faust legend beyond the confines of Germany, especially with reference to the sub-literary, popular mode in which this legend had been transmitted.

legends is proof of Goethe's unconscious profundity, his genius, which always contrived to grasp what was closest at hand and appropriate. I can assume the content of *Faust* to be familiar; for the book has recently become famous even in France. However I do not know whether the old folk legend itself is known *here*, whether in this country, too, at annual fairs a grey book, poorly printed on blotting paper and decorated with rough woodcuts, is sold, in which you may read in great detail how the arch-magician Johannes Faustus, a learned doctor who had studied all sciences, in the end threw away his books and formed an alliance with the devil, whereby he was able to enjoy all sensual pleasures on earth, but in exchange had to give his soul over to infernal perdition. Whenever the people of the Middle Ages saw great intellectual potency anywhere they ascribed it to a dæmonic pact; Albert Magnus, Raimund Lullus, Theophrastus Paracelsus, Agrippa von Nettesheim, even Roger Bacon[1] in England were considered sorcerers, necromancers, exorcists. But legend and song report far stranger things of Doctor Faustus, who demanded not only knowledge of all things but also the most tangible of pleasures from the devil; and this, significantly enough, is the Faust who invented the printing-press and lived at the time when sermons began to be preached against strict Church authority, and independent research started; hence with Faust ends the medieval religious era, and there begins the modern, critical era of science. It is indeed very significant that at precisely the time when by public belief Faust lived, the Reformation began, and that he himself is supposed to have founded the art which secures for knowledge a victory over faith, namely the printing press; an art, however, which also robbed us of the Catholic peace of mind and plunged us into doubt and revolutions—or, as someone else would put it, finally delivered us into the power of the devil. But no, knowledge, the understanding of things through the intellect, science gives us at last the pleasures of which religious faith, Catholic Christianity, has cheated us for so long; we apprehend that men are called not only to a heavenly but also to an earthly equality; the political brotherhood preached to us by philosophy is more beneficial to us than the purely spiritual brotherhood which Christianity has procured for us; and knowledge becomes word, and the word becomes deed, and we can attain the Kingdom of God during our life on this earth; if on top of it we may still partake of that heavenly bliss after death which Christianity so specifically promises us, we shall be all the better pleased.

1. Albertus Magnus (1200–1280), German scholastic philosopher, whose interest in natural science led him to study combinations of metals; Raimund Lullus (1235–1316), Catalan mystic and poet who used his great learning to propagate the Christian faith throughout the Mohammedan world; Theophrastus Paracelsus (1493–1541), Swiss physician and alchemist (see also the note to *Faust*, line 6835); Agrippa von Nettesheim (1486–1535), German physician and philosopher, who wrote a defense of magic, *De occulta philosophia*; Roger Bacon (ca. 1214–92), English scholastic philosopher, who had a keen interest in natural science and in controlled experiments.

The German people in its profundity long ago intuitively surmised this: for the German people is itself that learned Doctor
Faustus, that spiritualist who finally through his intellect has
grasped the inadequacy of the intellect and demands material pleasures and restores to the flesh its rights; yet, still caught up in the
symbolism of Catholic poetry where God is considered the representative of the spirit and the devil representative of the flesh, they
characterized that reinstatement of the flesh as a fall from God, as
an alliance with the devil.

It will still be some time, though, before what was prophesied
with such profound meaning in that poem materializes among the
German people, before it understands, by the intellect itself, the
usurpations of the intellect, and vindicates the rights of the flesh.
That, then, will be the revolution, the great daughter of the Reformation.

Modern Criticism

Faust as a Whole

HERMANN WEIGAND

Goethe's *Faust:* An Introduction for Students and Teachers of General Literature†

I

The history of Doctor Faustus, the celebrated magician who sold his soul to the devil in return for a stipulated term of personal services, the revelation of occult mysteries, and diversified entertainment, was a thrilling horror story with an edifying moral. First published in 1587, it was sold like other "chapbooks" at country fairs year after year, undergoing a variety of versions. Without any pretension to literary form, it catered to the undiscriminating taste of a growing middle class reading public in an age of printing, discovery, and religious controversy. It was immediately snapped up by Christopher Marlowe and turned into a play for the Elizabethan stage. Before long the theme supplied one of the lasting attractions with which troupes of travelling puppet players diverted their audiences. In the third quarter of the eighteenth century, young Goethe made the acquaintance of both the chapbook and the puppet show. Child of an age that experienced the world in terms very different from those of the age of the Reformation, Goethe sensed that the theme of Doctor Faustus harbored unlimited possibilities for expressing the altered and expanded aspirations of the human soul. In the early 1770's he began to toss off the first scenes of a projected *Faust* play. When in the fall of 1775 he came to the little duchy of Weimar, where he was destined to spend the rest of his mature life, he brought with him a substantial number of worked-out scenes which luckily have come down to us in an unauthorized copy discovered more than fifty years after Goethe's death.

The theme had implications beyond what Goethe had first imagined. He worked at it intermittently, but despairing of rounding it out, he published an unfinished version in 1790, *Faust, ein Fragment.* Under the prodding of Schiller, during the next decade, he set to work afresh and finally published *Faust, Part One* in 1808, carrying

† From *The German Quarterly,* Vol. 37 (1964), pp. 467–86, and Vol. 38 (1965), pp. 1–13. Reprinted by permission of *The German Quarterly.*

the work to the death of Gretchen, the Gretchen action constituting the most poignant episode in the *Faust* drama, but an episode
only. Long before this, he had gotten to work on a second part,
enormously differing from the first in style, setting, and perspective.
Portions of *Part Two* were published during Goethe's lifetime. But
when he finally put the concluding touch to his manuscript, in the
year before his death, he sealed it up for posterity. The complete
Faust drama was given to the world in 1832, some sixty years after
Goethe had first set to work on it. *Faust* has become the legacy of a
lifetime. It embodies the most mature distillate of the wisdom of
Germany's greatest poet.

The age of the Reformation saw the career of Faust as an object
lesson and a warning. To the age of Goethe it was natural, on the
other hand, to look upon the doctor-magician as a blurred and distorted prototype of man's ideal aspirations. This is the premise that
explains Goethe's abiding attraction to the theme. Faust appealed
to Goethe as a symbol of man's emancipation from authority.
Regardless of whether Faust's path would eventually lead him to
perdition or to salvation, his courage in daring to trespass upon the
realm of the forbidden makes him a heroic figure charged with positive value. This is the age of the Enlightenment, and obedience is
not one of its watchwords. The Judaeo-Christian pattern of thought
continues to persist as the general framework of the philosopher's
speculations and the poet's imaginings, but for the free spirits of the
age it has lost the sanction of any ironclad dogmatism. A century
earlier, Milton still founded his great poem of *Paradise Lost* on the
theme of "man's first disobedience." This involved the axiomatic
acknowledgment of divine arbitrary authority. The eighteenth century, on the other hand, was set to challenge all arbitrary authority,
in the spiritual as well as the secular sphere. Mere power as such
could compel submission but not induce reverence. Thus what had
been branded as sin could take on the aspect of a higher glory. The
criterion of moral value must now be sought in the essential nature
of reason. Thus Schiller, lecturing to his students on the fall of man
with the biblical story as his text, is ready to concede that the fall pre-
cipitated a catastrophe. But he takes pains to point out that the fall
was also an absolutely necessary first step in the higher development
of mankind. With the fall, the mind of man embarks on the realization of its limitless potentialities. Without it, he would forever
have remained a child of Nature, innocent but ignorant, unable to
develop the faculties of distinguishing between good and evil. And
let us recall in this context the famous emancipatory gesture of
Goethe's older contemporary, Lessing: If God were to stand before
me, holding in his closed right hand the absolute truth, and in his
left hand the unceasing search for truth but with the proviso of
being doomed to stray from it for ever and ever,—if, thus standing
before me he asked me to choose, I would humbly say: Father,

the absolute truth is for you alone, give me what your left hand holds. Autonomy as the premise of human dignity was never more pointedly formulated.

Autonomy involves pride, and pride, we remember, was the cardinal sin of the fallen angels. Their rebellion sprang from "superbia." But even Milton could not refrain from endowing Satan, archfiend and seducer of man, with qualities of strength, steadfastness, and endurance that lent him more than a tinge of the heroic. Faust also exhibits a pride that the Church would have branded as sinful, though it is by no means nihilistic in its aim. All in all, the situation conspires to make us approach the personality of Faust with a highly favorable prejudice.

Let us go afield a moment longer before entering the portals of Goethe's poem.

The spirit of Faust stops at nothing in its quest for self-realization. An exponent of this spirit, Faust, the individual, assumes symbolic significance as the extreme exemplar of the deepest drives of western civilization. Self-realization, properly considered, is a program without inner or outer limits. It is the spirit of total experiment probing the recesses of the individual soul, the relation of the individual to society, the relation of man to his terrestrial environment, the relation of man to the universe. The hazard of self-destruction in the pursuit of this quest is a risk to be faced. In a supreme moment of his career Faust exclaims: "Being is duty, fleet as it may be" [line 9418]. Total self-realization is imperative, even if it were only for a moment. * * *

Without question, Goethe projected in the personality of Faust a sublimely noble aspiration of the human spirit. This does not mean, of course, that Goethe glorified Faust uncritically. That he was not blind to his dark and sinister side no thoughtful reader of the play can overlook. Even before his association with the Evil One, Faust is labeled a "superman" in a deeply ironical context. And with a deliberate eye to restoring a balance, he again employs the word "Übermensch" in one of those very personal stanzas which he set at the head of his collected poems, in "Dedication," 1784.[1]

In this poem Goethe uses the device of allegory to report on a vision during an early morning walk. When the mists that contested the power of the rising sun have vanished, the poet is dazzled by an apparition hovering in their place. He recognizes the female form as the Goddess of Truth and hails her with passionate joy. She has been his intimate since his childhood days, whereas his companions preferred to stray in pursuit of error. After this outburst the Goddess indulgently smiles upon him and replies: "Thou seest how wise, how necessary it was to reveal only a small part of my

---

1. See note preceding line 6 of *Faust*. The poem referred to is not the "Dedication" to *Faust*.

essence to you [she lumps him with his companions.] Scarcely having overcome the crudest error, scarcely having mastered thy first childish wilfulness, thou deemest thyself straightway a superman who can afford to ignore the ordinary duties. Art thou really so different from the others? Get to know thyself. Live in peace with the world."

This poem, acknowledging Goethe's identification with Faust's immoderate aspirations, at the same time reduces his own stature to modest proportions and avows his dedication to a life of cooperation and service.

After these preliminaries are we ready to enter the portals of Goethe's dramatic poem? Almost, but not quite. Like a stately edifice, the *Faust* drama has a gate, a portico, and an elevated platform which we must traverse before passing into the interior.

The gate takes the form of a poem in which the poet, at an advanced stage of his life, invokes anew the airy shapes that haunted the young man's imagination and now press in upon him demanding that he endow them with substance. While the poem is cast in a melancholy mood, the portico, entitled "Prelude in the Theater," treats us to a spirited improvisation in which the director, the poet, and the clown discuss the impending production from a variety of angles, mixing business sense, seriousness, and fun along with satirical shafts aimed at the expectant public. We pass right on to the elevated platform, the "Prologue in Heaven." Here we pause, to note the scene, the songs of glory, and the ensuing dialogue with the utmost care, for this is our initiation, in the heavenly regions, into the action that will take place on earth. The Prologue at once characterizes the *Faust* poem as epic drama, for as in the epics of the ancients, * * * the terrestrial action has its counterpart in the councils of the supernatural powers.

The "Prologue" is a brilliant stage scene revealing the heavenly powers in the best anthropomorphic tradition—the Lord, flanked by three archangels, with the lesser hosts in the background. The paeans of praise deserve the student's closest attention in their blending of the old and the new astronomy (the sun and the lesser planets revolving around a motionless earth, and the earth in rotation), their Pythagorean reference to the music of the spheres,[2] their simple mythology (the setting of the sun at journey's end), their literary synesthesia (the rendering of light in terms of sound), their references to the forces of the tides and meteorology, and finally their climactic allusion to the still, small voice of the prophet Elijah's vision (I Kings 19:12).[3] The setting is solemn and dignified,

2. An allusion to the Ptolemaic astronomical system (the old astronomy), in which the earth is located at the center of concentric spheres that define the motion of the sun, moon, and planets.
3. ". . . and after the earthquake a fire,

but the Lord was not in the fire; and after the fire a still small voice. And when Elijah heard it, he wrapped his face in his mantle and went out and stood at the entrance of the cave."

but the ensuing dialogue is at once shot through with satire and humor.

We see the Lord of the universe engaged in an inspection tour that has brought him to the vicinity of the earth. Closely following the analogy of the Book of Job, Satan-Mephisto, the rogue, to the Lord the least distasteful of all the spirits of negation, comes to pay his respects to the Lord with guarded mock reverence for the Almighty, with jibes at the "retinue" and a parodistic echo of their strains of praise, and he launches into a tirade of criticism leveled at man, the diminutive god of creation, and at the Creator for having endowed him with the ambiguous gift of reason. When the Lord interrupts with a reference to Faust, the most exalted exemplar of the breed, Mephisto gives full rein to his satirical vein, characterizing Faust as mad and proposing a wager to the Lord that, granted permission to ply him with his arts of seduction, he will succeed in deviating this soul to his own ends. The Lord, with great tolerance and unperturbed confidence in the sound kernel of Faust's soul, grants the desired permission for the duration of Faust's sojourn on earth, implying that there is more to come. The Lord's generalization about "a worthy soul" with obvious application to Faust, his "servant," shows that his contempt of the "good" transcends the standards that associate the term with divinely and socially sanctioned norms of moral behavior. His unfathomable tolerance of the self-assertive spark differentiates him radically from the biblical Jehovah whose wrath doomed disobedient man to perdition.

Inasmuch as the Lord of the "Prologue" must be taken as the source of infinite goodness, power, foreknowledge, and wisdom, there can be no doubt as to the ultimate discomfiture of Mephisto. That Faust will be saved in the end is programmatically certain. It may be puzzling in terms of this view that Goethe entitled his poetic drama a tragedy. Would not the outcome have equally justified the title of comedy in the sense used by Dante?[4] But the solemnity of the action, in analogy to Greek drama, may have been decisive in warranting this label. This, however, is a question that the reader of the whole drama may be left to ponder.

The first four scenes of the human drama, a unified sequence spanning two nights and two days, show how the impatient, frustrated idealist is induced to form with the "spirit which perpetually denies" [line 1338] an association that is destined to cast its shadow over the rest of his earthly life. The first scene develops Faust's situation and his personality in a dazzling variety of facets. It unfolds chiefly by way of a very extended dramatic monologue, interrupted by dialogue passages that allow no monotony to de-

4. Dante's *Divine Comedy* describes a visionary journey which begins in Hell and ends in Paradise. It is generally assumed that Dante used the term "comedy" in his title because his poem moves in a progression from damnation to salvation. A comedy would thus be a drama with a happy ending.

velop—the apparition of the Earth Spirit, the dialogue with his assistant Wagner, and the pealing of the bells and the chorus of Easter voices at the climactic moment. On stage the dramatic monologue usually suffers drastic cuts. Its extreme length and subtlety overtax the capacities of both the average theater audience and all but the greatest actors. But for the reader who yields to its spell every line carries its own emotional charge born of Faust's situation and the visible and tangible associations that stream down from the clutter of the high, musty study. With two exceptions: (1) The opening paragraph is a deliberately archaic piece of exposition, evoking the age of the Reformation and the verse form of its most popular poet, Hans Sachs, by its prosy diction and the mechanical rhythm of its four-beat couplets.[5] (2) Later on we come across one more passage where Faust, in the trough of the emotions that toss him, reflects in general terms on the theme of anxiety as the most corroding affliction of the human race. This does not seem to relate to his immediate state of mind, but we are forewarned of what is coming when Care, in the guise of a spectral sister, confronts Faust on the last night of his life as his most sinister assailant. But apart from these two passages all the rest of Faust's monologue has the compelling power of spontaneous improvisation. This effect is achieved by a most felicitous blending of form with content that has been the despair of all translators. The lyrical pitch of the diction, vocabulary, and sentence structure varies from mood to mood. The lines are not of a set length but swell from four- to five- and six-beat waves to return at will to lesser undulations. The rhyme scheme operates with equal freedom, now joining lines in couplets, now looping two pairs, now circling an inner by an outer pair, now binding triple lines or triple pairs together, employing a free alternation of one syllable rhymes with those of two. These few remarks on form must suffice. They apply in large measure to the whole of Part One of the drama. In Part Two the problems of form are far too complex even to be touched upon here.

The middle-aged scholar, who recapitulates his career in the opening lines, is a man wearied and exhausted to the breaking point. He has mastered all the substance and all the techniques of the total medieval university curriculum. The intangible abstractions of logic, metaphysics, and theology have left him disillusioned. He is equally fed up with the procedures and yields of the practical professions, law and medicine. The satirical colloquium to which Mephisto treats the eager Freshman in a later scene merely transposes all of Faust's feelings on these matters into a humorous key. Faust is in deadly earnest. Words have assumed a hollow ring. Words are a device to conceal fundamental ignorance. Words provide no tool for a breakthrough from the world of appearance to the world of

5. Hans Sachs (1494–1576), German poet and leading *Meistersinger* of the Nurem-
berg school, renowned for his use of the *Knittelvers*, or doggerel rhyme.

essence. In scene after scene Faust harps on this central fact. This is his frustration. He conceives of the world in terms of a pantheistic reinterpretation of Scripture. Creation (God, Nature) is a divine, eternally emerging process. He affirms it with all his soul. Is he not cast in the Creator's own image, part of His essence? Is it not his birthright, then, to participate consciously in the sublime dynamic process? Is he not higher than the angels—mere ministrants they? This is the repeated starting point of his broodings after his rejection by the Earth Spirit. Meanwhile, in the opening passage, he gives only a passing glance to the thought that riches and honors, attending the pursuit of worldly success, have passed him by. In his frustration he has taken recourse to magic as a possible shortcut to the spiritual revelation he longs for with every fiber of his being, Impatience dictates this bold and forbidden course, a fever pitch of frenzied affirmation. At this stage the spirit of negation is utterly foreign to him ("a worthy soul" [line 328], the Lord termed him). Faust is a rebel only as regards the barriers of sense that keep him from communing directly with the divine spirit. Philosophically speaking, he storms against being hemmed in by space, time, and causality. * * *

Yet even while overreaching himself, Faust tempers his folly with some discretion. Contemplating the magic symbols drawn by the renowned master's own hand, he turns from the figure suggesting the workings of the universal spirit as too vast for his comprehension. He hails the Earth Spirit, the lesser deity that dwells in the earth like the soul of man in the body, as the more fitting object for his empathy. His ardor is rewarded by a manifestation. Recoiling in terror from the insupportable light, he hears himself gently reassured and chided with mild irony. Then, with a superhuman burst of courage Faust rises to the challenge of the unique moment to proffer himself to the apparition's embrace, only to find himself put in his place by a terse, definitive rejection. But before Faust has time to come to terms with his humiliation his assistant's knock at the door dispels the mood.

Faust dislikes and despises Wagner's fawning airs and his careerist aspirations. That he reveals no trace of these personal feelings either in the midnight discourse or on the next day's afternoon walk, bears testimony to his generosity and humanity. Faust is no cynic. He does not vent his pessimism in taunts and sarcasms leveled at his fellow man. He strives to educate by example and precept. Throughout the dialogue, the issue is sharply drawn between sincerity and scheming, simplicity and pretension, dedication and self-seeking, between earnest self-examination and easy complacency.

After Wagner has left, Faust's mind returns to the vision, to assess its impact. His ego has suffered an annihilating deflation. His buoyant feeling of participating in the creative pulse, on a par with the gods, has been cruelly exposed as brash presumption. Sharp

despair yields to the softer hurt of self-pity, inducing a mood of quieter, almost impersonal meditation on the theme of anxiety. But his
brooding soon reactivates the sting of his having been called a
worm. He indulges in self-laceration as he develops the parallel
between the worm groveling in the dust and his own life. Now the
paraphernalia of his cluttered study meet his eye to mock his existence. Item after item—the stacked books and rolls, the grinning
skull, the obsolete and useless machinery on which his misguided
father pinned his faith—stare him in the face as so much dust. But
when he spies the vial that harbors the potent poison that he has
decocted, his mind veers to a different tack. In a twinkling he has
rebounded from his despair to salute suicide as the most thrilling of
all adventures. His imagination straightway paints the exploit in the
most glowing poetic colors. All his manly self-esteem is revived at
the thought of setting his course to the Unknown, of facing a
Beyond that childish imaginings have invested with unspeakable horrors, of facing what might prove to be total annihilation, not in a
frenzied access of blind impulse, but open-eyed, calm, serene. In a
state of tempered euphoria Faust takes from the shelf the precious
chalice, removes its case, and, reminiscing on its festive function in
the days of his youth, he pours the poison and raises the cup to his
lips. The Easter bells and chorus stay his hand. Though they cannot
rekindle his faith in the miracle of the resurrection, memories of the
fervent piety of his childhood crowd in upon him. His mood is
softened, and the momentum for taking the irretrievable step is lost.

The scene of the Easter walk reinforces some important aspects
of Faust's personality that were only lightly touched on in the initial scene. Faust's deep love of Nature, already glimpsed in his invocation of the moon, finds full expression in the rapturous lyric passage with which he greets the spring landscape and its festive human
throng. He mingles with the simple folk and receives the tribute of
their love and respect with unaffected modesty. Their praise of his
dedication and success during the plague he counters with the
admonition to give credit where it is due, to the Helper above. To
infect them with irreverent skepticism is the last thing he desires.
But most important, the allusion to the plague has touched in
Faust's soul a complex of confused and bitter grief. He confesses
the young man's importunate piety, the ascetic zeal with which he
tried to bend the will of Heaven to his desire. Evidently, Faust is of
the stuff that great saints are made of. Then he speaks with guarded
criticism of his father as having been deluded into the blind alley of
alchemy: dispensing his nefarious concoctions in good faith, he and
his colleagues perpetrated wholesale murder surpassing the ravages
of the plague. The honest intent may exonerate his father, but it
cannot efface a deep sense of guilt on Faust's own part. And the
extreme emotional outburst about "the brazen killers" [line 1055]
helps us to see two enigmatical lines of scene 1 in perspective. The

lines, "what you received but as your fathers' heir, make it your own to gain possession of it" [lines 682–83] had seemed to interrupt the expression of a desire to be rid of all that had been handed down to him, with a puzzling *non sequitur*. Those lines make sense as the quoting by Faust of a familiar adage. But in his mouth the adage has the ring of bitter irony as the repudiation of his traditional heritage. The end of the scene introduces the poodle in the guise of which Mephisto is to make his debut.

Returned to the study that on the previous night had twice seen the superman poised on the brink of annihilation, Faust is about to make the acquaintance of his satanic companion. Scene 3, a theatrical show-piece, unfolds in three stages—the problem of scriptural translation, the exorcism, and Faust's dialogue with the traveling scholar. This scene shows Faust at his best. Having bathed in the fresh air of the woodland hills, he is cleansed and tranquil, at peace with himself, and aglow with the love of God and his fellow men. In this mood he yields to the impulse to translate a New Testament passage from the Greek. No believer in the dogma of the Church, but in search of revelation everywhere, he finds its purest spring in the New Testament. Characteristically, he turns to the opening chapter of the Gospel According to Saint John which, in contrast to the three "synoptic" gospels, exhibits a blend of Hellenistic mysticism with the Jewish ideas of the promised Messiah. The very first verse stymies Faust's efforts: "In the beginning was the word." The word, the "logos," a term of the most elusive connotations, is not fit to be rendered by the prosy German equivalent, "das Wort," an empty husk against which he had railed bitterly. He casts about for a term that might more adequately spread its aura over the page. In this effort he appears as the double of Martin Luther, who set his aim to render the spirit of the gospel rather than the letter. Faust's concentration is disturbed by the antics of the restless poodle.

When repeated attempts to quiet the animal fail, Faust senses that there is something wrong, and the transformation of the dog into a monster presently confirms his suspicion. Not for a moment at a loss to meet the challenge of what he assumes to be an elementary spirit, he recalls the magic formulas that are applicable in such a case. He proceeds to smoke out the spirit with a systematic series of exorcisms. Readers who wish to inform themselves on the nature, appearance, and habits of the elementary spirits as well as on their commerce with mankind, will find their curiosity satisfied by a highly ingenious "scientific" tract on the subject (available in English translation) by the renowned Swiss physician, naturalist, and philosopher Paracelsus,[6] a contemporary of our Doctor Faustus.
* * *

When his sundry exorcisms all fail to work, Faust changes his diagnosis: since this is not a neutral elementary spirit, it must be a

6. See note to line 6835 of *Faust*.

demon out of hell. This calls for more potent incantations. Work-ing himself up to a fever pitch of excitement, Faust cudgels the recal-citrant monster with spells that circumscribe the mystery of the eter-nal only-begotten and his passion. These, and the threat of the irre-sistible Trinitarian thunderbolt, take effect: in place of the shape-less monster there stands the harmless figure of a travelling scholar.

Do we find this confusing? This man, who had dismissed hell as a figment of morbid fantasy, this man, who had expressed his disbe-lief in the glad Easter tidings—this same Faust has now worked a miracle with magic spells that derive their potency from the assump-tion of the Christian mysteries as valid realities! That is paradoxical. We note this only in passing; for Faust is not the man to solve the riddle of the Beyond. His mind dwells in a kind of limbo swarming with mutually contradictory images and concepts. For the moment he is completely occupied with his visitor.

What strikes us throughout the ensuing dialogue is Faust's com-posure, his superior control in the presence of the infernal emissary. The first interchange establishes Faust as master of the situation. Assuming a condescending tone, he displays active curiosity with-out a trace of nervousness: he listens to the riddling answers, the boasts, and tantrums of his visitor with grave concern and mild amusement. To the spirit of negation he opposes his deep, positive reverence for the eternal mysteries of Nature's creative workings. The professor even lectures the devil on the folly of his impotent negativism and admonishes him to mend his ways.

To his surprise Faust discovers that the devil has allowed himself to be caught in a trap. The handling of this all but incredible situa-tion (against the background of the folk image of the devil as an essentially stupid fellow, easily tricked) shows a most ingenious interplay of chance and design: the poodle, evidently bent on no more than a bit of preliminary reconnoitering, has been forced to show his hand prematurely. Faust's self-confidence is heightened by the discovery that he has the visitor in his power. When his prod-ding questions bring out the fact that demons who invade the human realm are governed by strict rules of behavior, it is Faust who takes the initiative in broaching the idea of a pact, and it is Mephisto, caught off guard, who has to resort to a delaying action. Eventually Mephisto, apparently resigned to the situation, puts his captor to sleep by a ruse and makes his escape. Faust awakens in a state of redoubled frustration.

The next scene brings the great showdown, Faust's wager and pact with Mephisto. The time, the morning after; and Faust in a morning-after mood, a colossal hangover after the series of emotional shock waves that had battered him continuously for two nights and a day—the ups and downs of the blinding apparition called forth by his incantation; the great rebound of the suicidal venture, frustrated by the Easter bells; the lyrical exaltation of the Easter walk, brusquely turned into deepest despondency by memories of his part in the plague; the recovery of his buoyancy by the spectacle of the sunset; the serene atmosphere of high peace that prompted his turning to the gospel; the terrific excitement of the exorcism; the sense of mastery in his dialogue with the spirit of negation; the glimpse of a new approach to the cosmic mysteries; and finally, the sense of let-down and utter humiliation on awakening from his trance. All this has left him at a dead center of total exhaustion.

On this morning the tables are turned. The initiative has passed to Mephisto. Even before the smart cavalier enters the study, Faust's irritability is established as he is made to repeat the invitation to enter three times. He is in a devastated mood. There is no fight left in him. He is querulous, petulant, whining. His emotional tone is slack, unstrung. His harping on the theme of renunciation, his complaints about the staleness of his days and the terrors that haunt his nights mark him as the victim of an anxiety neurosis in the making. His attempts to wax lyrical in his laments appear forced, reminding us of the distorted tones of a worn-out record. Each of Mephisto's amused taunts and jibes makes him wince. Before long he flies into an uncontrollable rage that finds expression in a tirade of curses so all-inclusive as to leave no value intact. His foremost curse is leveled against the pride of his pretension to superman status. Next he reviles the sentimental softness that kept him from following through with his intended suicide. He then curses all the lure of the world of sense with its challenge and its invitations to pleasure. The climax is reached in the curse that he hurls against the highest boon of love, meaning, without question, not the love of the sexes, but the core of the Gospel message: "For God so loved the world. . . ." In the wake of this blasphemy he curses the other cardinal Christian virtues, faith and hope, topping off his tirade with a curse against patience, the virtue most alien to his impulsive temperament. With these curses Faust, so positive heretofore in his reverent affirmation of the creative process as divine, has yielded to the spirit of negation. His curses are an echo of the tempter's nihilism. They mark a turning point. Henceforth the infection of radical evil festers in Faust's blood.

Naturally, this violent swing of the pendulum provides for its own correction. In the remainder of this inexhaustibly rich scene Faust soon regains his balance. When Mephisto approaches him with a concrete proposal for their permanent association, with the forfeiture of Faust's soul in the Beyond as the price, Faust counters with a wager that shows him an alert and shrewd bargainer. The substance of the wager on which he conditions the pact is that Mephisto will never succeed in extinguishing the restless urge that makes Faust forever reach beyond the illusory satisfaction of the moment; that Mephisto will never succeed in lulling him into a sense of ease and contentment.

In the text of the play the crucial lines of the wager read as follows:

> *If the swift moment I entreat:*
> *Tarry a while! you are so fair!*
> Then forge the shackles to my feet,
> Then I will gladly perish there!
> Then let them toll the passing-bell,
> Then of your servitude be free,
> The clock may stop, its *hands fall still,*
> And time be over then for me! [lines 1699–1706]

Two lines that formulate the condition, are followed by seven swift, short sentences that draw the conclusion. The four times repeated *then* reverberates like the measured strokes of a gong. The words I have set in italics are destined to recur verbatim at the moment of Faust's death. Mephisto underlines the significance of the pronouncement with the reminder to Faust: "Reflect upon it— *we* shall not forget it" [line 1707]. There is superb irony in the fact that, when Faust has breathed his last, Mephisto misquotes a crucial word and has to stand corrected by his minions, who have remembered the exact wording.

After Faust has reluctantly gone through with the "farce" of signing the contract with a drop of his blood, he expatiates in a series of swiftly changing moods on the meaning of the momentous step he has taken. Dejection and elation spell each other off. The immediate vista is a mad, pointless whirl of dissipation. A moment later his energies rebound with the resolve, now that all prospects of an intellectual breakthrough have gone sour, to encompass in his individual person the totality of *experience* open to mankind, the whole gamut of the emotional life of the race, all its joys and pains, with ultimate annihilation as the end. Mephisto finds amusement in pointing out to him that he still persists in his aim to unite incompatibles, and once more Faust wallows in the trough of dejection. The impasse is broken by Mephisto's arrangements for the two of them to set out at once on a life of adventure in the world, leaving the musty study behind. As Faust goes to gather up some necessaries for the trip on the magic cloak, Mephisto regales the eager Freshman with his satirical wisdom.

Now follow the scenes of Auerbach's cellar in Leipzig that night, and the visit next day to the witch's kitchen to accomplish Faust's physical rejuvenation. They need not detain us long. The roisterous atmosphere of the wine cellar, where Mephisto befuddles the drunken students with his magic tricks, may bring to mind the grosser aspects of Shakespeare's Falstaff scenes. It is entertaining in its triple perspective of the students' coarse antics, Mephisto's delight in leading them by the nose, and Faust's bored impassivity throughout.

In the witch's kitchen the situation is similar: Mephisto has a wonderful time enjoying first the grave nonsense of the animals that watch the boiling cauldron in the absence of their mistress, then in relishing the hysterical fury of the witch making her way down the chimney, and her consternation in recognizing the intruder as her master. Faust shows not the slightest interest in all the nonsense and obscenity. Only one thing catches Faust's attention, a magic mirror. It dazzles him with the elusive shifting image of the most beautiful woman the world has ever seen, Helen of Troy. He reluctantly leaves it to submit to the ritual hocus-pocus of the potion that is to rekindle in his veins the sexual fire of adolescence.

The stage is now set for the Gretchen tragedy, the absorbing theme of the last third of Part One. In the over-all drama of *Faust* the Gretchen action is only an episode, but it is developed with a spontaneity, a richness of delineation as regards the personality of Gretchen and her milieu, a depth of feeling, and a poignancy of tragic ruin that no sensitive reader is proof against. Thanks to Mephisto, who engineers the seduction, many of the scenes sparkle with infinite vivacity and humor. As a matter of fact, Mephisto's initiative and resourcefulness make him more and more the star performer, eclipsing the hero, whose unresolved tensions, unfolding in new situations but without major surprises, reduce him, dramatically speaking, to a more passive role. (This tendency, in fact, prevails throughout the greater portion of Part Two. Only at relatively brief intervals of special intensity does Faust come to the fore and take the lead. And it is only in the final act that Faust fully regains the undisputed summit as the dramatic protagonist.)

The Gretchen action develops swiftly. In the space of a few days Faust, fluctuating between carnal desire and adoration, has won the love and unquestioning trust of the artless girl. From now on we lose track of the passage of time. It is idle to ask how many days Faust spends alone, in the tranquil retreat of Forest and Cavern, enveloped by Gretchen's hallowed aura, welling over with grateful prayers to the Earth Spirit, to whom Faust attributes the new turn of his life, feeling a sense of brotherly intimacy with the birds and beasts of the wilderness, exploring the treasures of his own breast, and imagining himself in the company of the noblest spirits of bygone ages. It is idle to measure the degree of Gretchen's perturbation over her lover's disappearance by the calendar.

Mephisto brings Faust out of the clouds back to the work in hand. When the lovers meet again, Faust is put on the defensive by Gretchen's insistent questions about his religious beliefs, showing her concern for his salvation, and by her undisguised aversion for his companion. Gretchen's plain speaking is one of her most endearing qualities. In the matter-of-factness of her approach she is prosy and unimaginative, quite unlike the sentimental "romantic" heroines commonly met with in fiction. Faust is prompted to express his undogmatic pantheistic faith in exquisitely lyrical language, and Gretchen is half reassured. He is less successful in his embarrassed defense of Mephisto. The meeting ends with Gretchen's agreeing to doctor her mother's bedtime drink.

When the curtain rises again, events have taken their inevitable course. At the well Gretchen becomes reflectively aware of the harsh condemnation her own social class metes out to any girl caught straying from the straight and narrow path, and the double standard that prevails regarding the man's part in the affair. Before the icon of the Virgin she bares her prostrated soul. The next thing, her brother, stung by the wagging of loose tongues, ambushes the strangers serenading the sister whose beauty and virtue he had idolized. He is killed, and his dying words strike the poor girl's heart with fiendish cruelty. The killers have fled, the idyll is over.

Scattered hints, which no reader notices, show that all has taken place in one short month. Mephisto, accompanying Faust on his fatal tryst, alludes to the great adventure in store for them two nights later, the witches' sabbath on the eve of Saint Walpurga.[7] The calendar date of this is fixed as the night ushering in the first of May. That night, as they trudge up the mountain, the Brocken, at the approach of midnight, Mephisto utters a couple of remarkably beautiful lines about the rising moon:

> How drearily the moon-disk's ragged cinder
> Swims up with its belated reddish glow. [lines 3851–52]

The gibbous moon, rising late in the evening four or five nights after the full, places full moon about April 25. This is the second spring full moon. It fixes the date of the first spring full moon as around March 25. Inasmuch as Easter falls on the first Sunday after the first spring full moon, Easter must have been celebrated somewhere between March 26 and 31. We know that the time that elapsed between Faust's frustrated attempt at suicide and his rejuvenation in the witch's kitchen amounted to no more than four days. (On the eve of Easter, his vision and suicide attempt; on Easter day, the afternoon walk followed by the exorcism of the poodle in the study; on Easter Monday, the wager and pact with Mephisto, followed by the visit to Auerbach's wine cellar; on the next day, their visit to the witch's kitchen.) This places Faust's accosting of Gretchen somewhere between March 29 and April 3. From that point on to the night of Valentin's murder, April 28, the time stages of the developing love idyll are left vague.

Before we return to Faust we get one more glimpse of Gretchen in an early stage of her long martyrdom. From the scene in the cathedral we learn that her plight has infinitely worsened since her brother's death. Not only that the first stirrings of pregnancy fill her with

7. See note following line 3834 of *Faust*.

forebodings, she bears a crushing burden of guilt on her mother's account, who faces a long period of purgatory, having died in her sleep (like Hamlet's father)[8] without the ministrations of the Church. There can be no doubt about the circumstances: a precautionary overdose of the sleeping potion must have proved fatal to her mother—this on the very night of Valentin's murder. Had it occurred earlier, the fact would have had to be brought out in the play, and Gretchen's overwrought conscience would have made a later tryst unthinkable. When are we to suppose the scene in the cathedral to take place? As we know, the night of Walpurgis follows hard on the heels of Valentin's murder, only two days intervening. Perhaps the idea that we see Gretchen attending a requiem service for her mother and brother cannot be ruled out, but Gretchen's awareness of her pregnancy makes the assumption of a later date more likely. If so, Goethe did wisely in sacrificing the chronological sequence to the continuity of mood of the Gretchen action. The nine months of anguish that undermine her sanity are shrouded in obscurity. We see her for the last time in chains in a prison cell. Her mind is unhinged. She has done away with her baby. The executioner's sword awaits her at the dawn of day.

After the cathedral scene, a violent shift of mood and locale takes us to the witches' rendezvous on the Brocken with Faust and Mephisto as spectators and participants in the tumultuous annual convocation. This is a virtuoso performance of poetic genius. The language is strained to evoke a bewildering medley of eerie sound, light, and movement in the surge of the demonic elemental forces. Faust and Mephisto, their way lighted by a will-o'-the-wisp, are caught in the tugging updraft and the crush of the flying hosts and detached individuals, all straining to reach the summit for the celebration of the black mass. The modern theater, and particularly the film, finds a challenge in translating this feast of the imagination into a spectacle for the senses, but in accomplishing this it inevitably reduces the suggestive magic of the poetic word to a mere shadow.

In the carnival of obscene animal energy we never get to see the climactic performance on the summit, presided over by "Herr Urian." Mephisto's caprice shunts Faust away from the upward surging throng into the quieter byways of a camping area. At this sideshow we meet a group of motley characters, oldsters, has-beens, who got bogged down in their flight because the vital spark failed them. These impotents expatiate nostalgically on the good old days when they called the tune, and Mephisto gleefully apes them. From general satire, directed against types, the focus disconcertingly shifts to personal satire: Goethe lampoons a literary enemy, Friedrich Nico-

8. An ironic allusion to the fact that   was murdered while sleeping.
Hamlet's father, like Gretchen's mother,

lai, the old warhorse of the German Enlightenment.[9] The many topical allusions were relished by contemporaries in the know but are pointless without a detailed commentary today.

And what of Faust? He had felt the stiff climb among the knobby crags as a zestful challenge. To his inner eye the mountainside had unveiled itself as a living matrix of treasure in the making. Eagerly looking forward to the main spectacle, he had been drawn off to a sideshow. He had danced with a young witch but lost appetite when a red mouse slipped out of her mouth. Then he had spied the wraith of a girl, and Mephisto's warning to avert his eyes from the "Gorgon" had only served to rivet his gaze on the wide-open dead eyes and the gliding gait of the apparition. More and more it had taken on the semblance of Gretchen, and a red line, no wider than the back of a knife, circling her throat, had loomed as a portent of her fate. There we leave Faust, to turn to the anticlimactic conclusion of the "Walpurgisnacht" scene, with some final jibes against half-baked plays and amateurish performances.

Very abruptly the end of the Gretchen tragedy is now enacted. The discontinuity is extreme, as regards both the time and the form. The gap of nine months in Faust's life since his flight after Valentin's murder is a blank. Somehow Mephisto's magic must have succeeded in blocking Faust's memories of Gretchen and in stifling the voice of his conscience regarding her fate until the last night of her life. Then, learning what has happened to her and what awaits her, Faust breaks into violent recriminations against the satanic seducer, only to have his own guilt spelled out to him with pitiless matter-of-factness. The medium of this scene is prose—the rhetorical, exclamatory and at the same time long-winded prose of the Storm and Stress movement of the 1770s. Goethe left the scene "Dreary Day. Field." intact as a relic of his earliest work on the subject of *Faust*. The reference in the scene to the dog who amused himself during Faust's nightly strolls with playing practical jokes on harmless wanderers must belong to a phase of the composition before Goethe had hit upon the happy expedient of the exorcism scene as the means of introducing Mephisto to Faust.

Part One of *Faust* ends with the scene of the attempted rescue, an overwhelming finale. The personality of the wretched girl in the prison cell is completely shattered, but every fractured piece suggests the one-time perfection now irretrievably destroyed. In the wandering of her unhinged mind she bears a striking resemblance to Shakespeare's *Ophelia*,[1] but with this difference: Ophelia, innocent victim of cruel fate, evokes a mood of pure pathos, while Gretchen, involved despite herself in fearful guilt, is a truly tragic victim. Physical dread and a desire to atone rend her bosom. Instinctively she senses the sinister aura of her one-time lover and shrinks from his touch. In a final flash of lucidity she throws herself upon the

9. See note to line 4144 of *Faust*.   1. See note to lines 4423 ff. of *Faust*.

merciful judgment of God, and a voice from the Beyond proclaims her salvation.

The Gretchen episode was the final stage of Faust's career in the world of man outside the confining walls of the study. For Faust, the pure love of Gretchen will be forever imbedded in his memory as the deepest spiritual blessing vouchsafed to him by a kindly Providence, and as the ineradicable reminder of his darkest hour. When he finally departs from the earthly stage the intercession of Gretchen will weight the scales in the achievement of his redemption.

II

Part Two strikes the reader rather as a new beginning than the continuation of the *Faust* drama. The method, the perspective, the focus, the form in all its aspects, are radically new. Psychological drama, though not abandoned, is subordinated to symbolical drama. The Faust of Part Two is more a representative of mankind in its strivings and errings than an individual. The action is divided into five acts of such length as to preclude presentation on the stage in a single evening. The development is epic rather than dramatic. Instead of a forward movement focused upon the outcome of Faust's association with the forces of Evil, the scenes are crowded with pageantry and spectacles in many of which Faust's presence is unobserved or he is off-stage altogether. The versification is subtle and experimental in the extreme. The poetic style and vocabulary are full of innovations that it took German poetry generations to assimilate. The time of Part Two ranges over half a century. Yet of this total span only a minimal portion is accounted for by the action presented. In the present sketch the most fleeting glance at all but the final act must suffice. Only then, on the final day of Faust's life, does the dramatic action resume its forward thrust.

The first scene of act I shows us Faust asleep at the approach of sunrise in a smiling spring landscape. Ariel and his elfin host guard Faust's slumber. Their song helps to banish the images of horror and anguish from his memory. After this symbolical opening Faust awakens. In a grave and measured monologue in *terza rima*[2] verse he communes with Mother Earth. As he drinks in the morning atmosphere, the dew, the myriad sounds of stirring life, the play of lights and colors, we participate through his lines in a process of recuperation amounting to a total rebirth. His reaction to the sunrise translates itself, in his reflective consciousness, into a grandiose symbol of the new approach to life on which he sets his course: blinded by the dazzling light, he turns his back upon the sun, and his gaze is caught by the iridescent play of a rainbow above the waterfall—a spectacle of enduring form despite the renewal from

---

2. A verse form consisting of a series of triplets having ten-syllable or eleven-syllable lines, of which the middle line of one triplet rhymes with the first and third lines of the following triplet. See also note to lines 4679–4727 of *Faust*.

moment to moment of the vapor particles constituting its substance. The barren quest of the absolute is renounced in favor of the more profitable pursuit of exploring the infinite variety of the world of phenomena. This symbol of the rainbow recalls Plato's famous parable of the shadows of semblances thrown on the wall of a cave, as man's closest approach to cognition of reality, but it is zestfully affirmative rather than pessimistic. It is, of course, Goethe's own credo, and in a moment such as this the image of Faust completely blends with that of his author. Insofar as this insight is Faust's, it is one of those momentary flashes of heightened realization that illuminate the landscape of the mind for a fleeting moment, only to be pushed into the background by the preoccupations of daily life. (Strangely enough, there are moments in Part Two when even the voice of Mephisto loses its negativism and becomes indistinguishable from that of Goethe, as in the definitely good-natured send-off given the Baccalaureus, who storms ahead on the very quest of the absolute renounced by Faust, and with the imagery of light and darkness employed in reverse.) This is only to point out that the champions of strict consistency are hard put to it in their interpretation of *Faust Two.*

The scene now changes to the Imperial Court. There is a pleasure-loving young emperor, whose realm is fast drifting into a state of chaos. A satirical tone prevails in the presentation of the many woes that beset the government most inconveniently at a time when all thoughts are normally bent on pleasure. Into this pre-Lenten carnival atmosphere Mephisto and Faust make their entry. For them as for us readers, the bourgeois world has been left behind for good. Mephisto at once gains the emperor's favor in the mask of a court fool, who turns out to be more ingenious than all the grave ministers of the realm. His advice solves the most pressing problem of the moment—that of the exchequer. On the flimsiest security, indeed a phantom security, he gets the treasury to issue an unlimited supply of paper money. Henceforth nothing is allowed to interfere with the carnival mood. We are treated to a most elaborate mummery, itself an evening's entertainment, consisting for the most part of well-rehearsed gay and allegorical pantomime and song, but interspersed with features of dazzling pageantry that only the master magician could have improvised. The emperor himself participates as a masquer along with Faust and Mephisto. At the climactic moment His Majesty threatens to come to grief. Magic flames from a spring of liquid gold spurt and envelop the palace. But the ensuing panic is quelled at once by its promoter and the emperor expresses himself the next morning as jolly well pleased by the show. But, his appetite whetted by the quality of the entertainment, he asks Faust to conjure up Paris and Helen from the underworld as a spectacle for his court, and Faust, trusting in his companion's infinite resoucefulness, promises that it shall be done.

Dramatically speaking, the lavish pageantry of the night before is an elaborate device to trigger the main business of acts I-III. This is nothing less than to reenact one of the major episodes of the sixteenth century *Faust Book* and achieve so staggeringly impossible a wishdream as the physical union of Faust with the all-time paragon of beauty, the fabulous Helen of Troy. Goethe seized upon this theme to symbolize the passionate dedication to the quest of beauty as one of the supreme drives of mankind. At the midpoint of his earthly career, Faust, dynamo of insatiable energy, is kindled with the passion to achieve in the here and now of the world of sense a union with the phantom of absolute beauty that resides in the shadowy world of Hades or in the realm of Platonic ideas. By a singular grace of the Powers his dream is vouchsafed fulfillment for one brief moment. The realization of the absolute takes tangible shape in the offspring of their union, the radiant boy Euphorion. He is the incarnation of the poetic spirit. But sired by absolutes, he, in his turn, is bent on the impossible. Bounding aloft from the cliff to try his wings, he plunges to his death, another Icarus, and Helen slips from Faust's embrace to rejoin her child in the Underworld.

Three long acts develop the story. In act I, Faust, coached by Mephisto in a scene of wondrous awe, penetrates into the realm of the "Mothers" and brings back the famous couple. As they are subjected to admiration and criticism by the court, uncontrollable jealousy and passion for her possession make Faust touch the phantom Helen. He is knocked unconscious by an explosion and carried off by Mephisto to be deposited in his old study.

In act II there is first a superbly humorous interlude: disguised in Faust's old mantle, Mephisto has a spirited colloquy with the erstwhile Freshman, now a sophisticated philosopher sporting a bachelor's degree. This scene reactivates our time sense. It places the action of acts I and II, along with the "timeless" moment of act III, at a point several years beyond the close of Part One. Together with act IV, all the second part except for the last act may be supposed to transpire in a single season.

We next follow Mephisto into an adjoining laboratory where Wagner, Faust's former assistant, now a professor with an enormous reputation, has been laboring for months on end to produce an artificial man, a homunculus, by the art of alchemy. Thanks to Mephisto's presence the miracle comes off: a sprightly mannikin in a test tube slips from Wagner's grasp to hover, weightless, in the atmosphere and greet daddy Wagner and cousin Mephisto with merry chatter. Hearing of Faust's plight, the little creature slips through the doorway to gaze on the unconscious form, and his supernatural intuition spells out the sleeper's vision—the divine swan embracing Leda to sire Helen. He knows that if Faust were to awaken in the study the shock would kill him. But the resourcefulness of our mannikin is equal to the emergency. It so happens, he says, that this very night is the classical counterpart of the witches' sabbath. All the creatures of classical myth are now gathering for their annual rendezvous in northeastern Greece. Let Mephisto carry Faust on his magic cloak, and he himself will lead the way. Straightway they are off, leaving Wagner to attend to his laboratory. By this ingenious device Faust is transported to Greece. As soon as he sets foot on the sacred soil he awakens. His first words are: Where is she? He is possessed of only one thought, to find her. The three now strike out on separate paths to explore the inexhaustible world of wonders. Following each of them in turn, the reader is put through a most thoroughgoing refresher course in classical mythology. As for Faust, he learns from the sphinxes that the celebrated centaur Chiron is abroad and most likely to be of help in locating Helen. Luckily Faust encounters Chiron and, astride the restlessly trotting monster's back, he ventures to report his quest. The genial centaur, infinitely amused at this mortal man's harebrained whim, nevertheless takes him to the priestess Manto, who guards the approach to the Underworld at the foot of Mount Olympus. She hears Faust's plea sympathetically and promises to lead him down to the great goddess Persephone, who alone can grant it.

In this way it comes about that in act III Helen has actually been released from the Underworld to live again for a timeless moment. After long preliminaries of anxious suspense in which Mephisto, having donned the shape of a monstrous mythical hag, plays a sinister but helpful part, Helen and her retinue of maidens, just returned from Troy, find refuge from the bloody designs of Menelaos in a medieval castle built by Faust on Greek soil. Faust is pictured as the overlord of a victorious host of northern warriors that has established itself on the Peloponnesus. Faust's and Helen's exchange of greetings turns into a duet of mutual homage. Helen's union with Faust symbolizes a fusion of the genius of the Germanic north with that of Greek antiquity. The whole act—a phantasmagoria Goethe called it—is a *tour de force* of the poetic imagination without a parallel in Goethe's work. As anticipated above, the mirage of perfection is shattered by the death of their offspring, Euphorion.

If acts I–III were focused upon the experience of beauty—the aesthetic sphere—as a momentous enrichment of Faust's (and mankind's) expanding development, act IV introduces a new theme to engage man's restless imagination. It is the challenge of the physical environment, the will to understand and control the forces of Nature. It is man's will to power in the face of the inert or hostile elements.

The great turn had been prepared for, when Helen vanished. Faust is borne aloft by the garments Helen has left behind. Soaring with the clouds over mountain and sea, Faust's gaze is arrested by the spectacle of the tides, their ceaseless ebb and flow. It impresses him as a symbol of enormous power wasting itself in futile repetition. There dawns upon him the idea of a task, a project: to curb the sea, to reclaim a vast expanse of shore line by a network of dikes. This is a challenge to appeal to his own indomitable energies that have been idly wasting themselves. This is a job for Mephisto and his minions to execute.

Most of act IV is taken up with the machinery for acquiring the rights to the shore line as a sovereign fief from the Emperor, whom Faust had served. This cannot concern us here. But the Faust we meet again in act V has devoted, we must suppose, half a lifetime to this constantly expanding project. Faust has now become a great lord. His eye roams over a limitless expanse of newly created land, flourishing with human habitations, gardens, and woodland. He has built a palace with a high observation tower, and his fleets gather in a distant harbor from which a canal extends to the palace. To judge by Faust's and Mephisto's words, Faust's realm encompasses the world. We cannot suppress an uneasy feeling that this is more than a slip of rhetorical exaggeration: Has Mephisto's new obsequiousness of manner deluded Faust into a state of megalomania? Treasure is being brought from all parts of the earth, and the work goes on ceaselessly. But there is one feature to mar Faust's pride of absolute rule: on a high dune, landward from the palace, there dwells a very ancient couple with rights antedating his. Their thatched hut and tiny chapel shaded by a clump of hoary linden trees is a thorn in his flesh. They have refused his offer to sell on advantageous terms. Day after day the tinkle of the chapel bell exasperates him. Does it awaken uneasy echoes of the church bells that made him set down the poisoned chalice on that first Easter morning? Be that as it may, the tiny knoll sets limits to his craving for absolute sway. He chafes and upbraids his imagination for finding the knoll denied him pricelessly desirable. To Mephisto, returned from an overseas expedition, he confesses his sense of torment and his sense of humiliation in admitting to it, and he acknowledges that the couple are in their legal rights. But it all boils down to his prodding Mephisto to talk him into an act of benevolent violence. The order for their dispossession results in unforeseen catastrophe: the old couple die of fright as the door is battered down. A guest, who puts up a fight, is murdered, in the scuffle the hut catches fire, and Faust must hear his watchman on the tower report the fire that reduces the hut and the chapel to ashes and leaves charred hollow trunks where the lindens had stood. Faust is seized with remorse. Once again his impatience has got the better of him. Was not impatience his cardinal sin? On the day of the wager and pact, when in his bitterness he had uttered his all-encompassing curse, had he not saved up the curse on Patience as the final line of his tirade? But he persuades himself to take the calamity lightly; in place of the destroyed lindens he will erect a lookout tower and from there he will see the neat cottage which his generosity had assigned to the dispossessed couple. And when Mephisto and his three mighty henchmen return to report on their mission, Faust reacts in the manner typical of overlords: he puts the blame for the violence on them and dismisses them with his curse.

Of course, Faust had not intended the consequences of his rash command, but he might have anticipated them if his sense of frustration had not blinded him, and in any case he had committed a deliberate violation of human rights. Such unscrupulousness as to means is typical of persons who are accustomed to the exercise of great power. The bloody deed leaves a stain on Faust's great achievement. To dismiss it as a trifle in view of the immense benefits accruing to mankind from Faust's titanic project would be idle because these benefits were incidental to the exercise of his energy. Faust was no philanthropist. He envisioned the task as a great means to express himself. There was no altruistic motive, for better or worse, to color the project of that great egoist. But, first appearances to the contrary, Faust did not dismiss his responsibility lightly. His brief soliloquy, dwelling on his inveterate impetuosity, shows that his conscience is deeply troubled. And now as he is about to be assailed from another quarter, we see him give evidence of an ethical resilience that more than reconciles us to his faults. "Too rashly bid, too swiftly done" [line 11382]. Faust's repentance is sincere, but he does not waste his energies in morbid brooding over an act that cannot be undone.

Now comes the visitation of the four weird sisters, spectral apparitions that personify Want, Distress, Debt or Guilt ("Schuld" stands for both), and Care. The first three find their entry to the palace barred. They have no power to molest a rich man. Not even "Schuld" in the sense of guilt; for objective wrongdoing must have an acute sense of wrongdoing as its subjective counterpart, to be troublesome. Care, however, can slip through the keyhole, where other potential disturbances of tranquillity are barred. As the three depart, they hail the approach of Brother Death in the background. Faust has been troubled by the spectral images and their low spoken words which he has half divined rather than understood. But he clearly caught the last word uttered, Death, and knows it is a portent of the fact that his life has run its course. Frail as he is, at the outermost edge of the human life span, his mind, forever active and restless, finds the thought of death repugnant. "I have not fought my way to freedom yet" [line 11403], he protests. His ruminations revolve about the fatal misstep of his youth, his involvement with magic, the dread curse, the vilification of the world and himself, the curse that culminated in the blast against Patience, as he enlisted the services of the Evil One. If he could only undo it, he meditates, and the pathos of the fateful decision is fully upon him. Now (like the sorcerer's apprentice) he finds himself irremediably entangled in a web of apparitions and portents, a prey to forces he cannot control. At this moment his soliloquy becomes a dialogue with the spectral sister of whose entry he has become aware. He tries to dismiss her with an imperious command, but she refuses to budge. He reacts violently, but, about to have recourse to the magic powers with which he has saddled himself, he checks himself with the soft spoken admonition: "Restrain yourself and speak no conjury" [line 11422].

This line, spoken under his breath, is the significant turning point in Faust's personal drama. Though ever so late, with death at his door, for once he has not yielded to that impatience which was the fatal flaw of his personality. He has taken a first step to reverse the pattern of his responses to life. This is decisive. This is a metaphysical act in terms of Schiller's dictum: "'The first step upward, ideally considered, is equivalent to traversing the whole road to the goal."

Now the weird sister announces her identity, and in three long passages of a whining, monotonous, staccato rhythm that suggest the wheedling persistence of a mosquito buzzing about the ear, she assaults the fortress of his will, hoping to reduce him to a bundle of nerves, prey to an anxiety neurosis. Three times he stands up to her assault maintaining the integrity of his personality in passages that rank among the finest in the play. His control never slips. He gives a thumbnail sketch of the course of his life, pronouncing an agnostic credo as to the Beyond, lashing out against the crooning tormentor, writhing under the pain of her relentless hypnotizing drone, but the integrity of his will is proof against her assaults. Let us not imagine for a moment that this is simply a rhetorical confrontation. The danger to Faust is very real. We turn back to the very first night of the *Faust* drama, where Faust, during one of his fluctuations between ecstasy and despair over his having been vouchsafed the vision of the Earth Spirit, lapsed into reflections about the power of "Sorge," Care, to torment man with apprehensions of ills that never come to pass. That, to be sure, was the one passage among all those memorable first night monologues which seemed least prompted by his desperate personal situation, approaching, rather, in the ring of its tone a mood of general reflection on human life. But two days later, at the time of Mephisto's second call that led to the wager and pact, Faust had exhibited a facet of his temperament that differed from anything we had observed heretofore. Whereas, on the preceding evening, he had replied to the riddling and the tantrums of Mephisto, the travelling scholar, with composure, superior raillery, and the active curiosity of a man in full command of that startlingly novel situation, this time he is completely out of sorts, he is petulant, querulous, whining, unnerved, pouring out lamentations about the emptiness of his days and the haunting, affrighting dreams of his nights and bridling at Mephisto's jibes. The Faust of that mood, when at last provoked into uttering the all-embracing curse, showed all the symptoms of an anxiety neurosis. This lassitude, the show of a personality quite unstrung, was very different in kind from the bold superhuman gesture with which he had hailed the Earth Spirit, the dark, tense despair of his brooding after having been rejected, and of the euphoric serenity with which he had grasped the poisoned chalice. We see then that the danger of his succumbing to a neurosis that would have left him at loose ends was very real. It is in these terms that we must evaluate Faust's triumph over the specter of Care on the last night of his life.

Care is routed. Unable to enter the inner fortress of Faust's personality, she departs from the palace, but in doing so she exhibits her demonic power: she breathes upon him and casts a spell, making Faust go blind. "Man commonly is blind throughout his life," she comments; "My Faust, be blind then as you end it" [lines 11497-98].

As a rule, commentators have tried to read a deep symbolism into the spell that reduces Faust to blindness, such as: Having been a man of clear-eyed determination all his life, he falls a prey to delusion in the end; he loses his faculty to appraise mankind realistically and surrenders to a utopian optimism. I think the whole attempt to read a symbolical meaning into Faust's blindness is a mistake. Rather, a mythical interpretation is in order. All is then both simple and humanly moving. Faust has matched his energies against an assailant from the non-human, infernal regions. Astonishingly enough, he has come off the victor. But is it customary, we ask, for a mortal to emerge from so unequal a contest unscathed? No, indeed, this would run counter to all tradition. He bears the mark of it on him for the rest of his life. The first analogical example that comes to mind is the biblical story of Jacob wrestling with the angel. Jacob triumphs, but his halting walk ever after serves as a reminder that the angel had touched his hip.[3] Like everything biblical, the story of Jacob was so familiar to Goethe that he may have counted on the awareness of the analogy to come to mind automatically. We find something similar, in fact, in the story of the Fall where it is predicted that the seed of woman shall bruise the head of the serpent but suffer its sting in his heel. * * * In the case of Faust a peculiar pathos attaches to his being stricken with blindness as a compensatory penalty of his victory over the Demon: it happens to him at night, in the last hour of his life, and in the small span of time left him he possibly never registers any awareness of what has happened to him. The night closing in about him simply acts as a stimulus to heighten his fervor for pushing the task to which his life is dedicated.

We summarize: On this last night of his life, Faust has again

---

3. "And Jacob was left alone; and a man wrestled with him until the breaking of day. When the man saw that he did not prevail against Jacob, he touched the hollow of his thigh; and Jacob's thigh was put out of joint as he wrestled with him" (Genesis 32:24).

been carried away by an excess of impatience to the perpetration of a highhanded act of injustice that resulted in destruction and murder. He has subsequently repented of this abuse of his power. Then, when assailed by the spectral demon of Care, he had, in the nick of time, remembered to check his impatience. The hypnotic crooning had prompted him to pass his life in review and, in full acknowledgment of early decisions irretrievably made, he had deeply repented of his cardinal sin of impatience that led to his all embracing curse and his involvement with the powers of darkness. In this he had successfully countered the Demon's assault, but the victory that left his personality whole has left its mark on his body. The curtain now rises on the scene of Faust's death.

Faust's is a natural death, we emphasize, a death long overdue: Faust has already felt the summons himself, and Mephisto, aware of the impending end, has set his minions to work digging a grave. Faust, afire with his task, aware that his physical energies are ebbing, urges the expansion of his work force. The clanking of the spades lifting the sods for his grave fires him to another vision of his successful taming of the sea. Mephisto's sarcastic comment on the upshot of the project, unheard by Faust, is ambiguous. Is he right in his gleeful prophecy that the elements, in league with the demons, will ultimately take over and reduce the whole expenditure of man's energies to nothing—either because magic was enlisted to engineer the project, or because in the long run no work of man can stand up against the inexorable superior power of the elements? Or is he again, as the spirit that forever negates, indulging that wish for annihilation that expressed itself in a tantrum during his first dialogue with Faust? It does not matter. These malicious glosses of Mephisto are confined to the material level. They have no bearing on the spiritual values of the undaunted dying visionary.

During the few moments of life left him Faust continues to grow. A moment ago we saw him reject—in principle—his lifetime association with magic and the infernal powers as a mistaken approach. Now a breakthrough of another kind occurs. Whereas the earlier one concerned his relation to Nature and the mystery of the universe, this one concerns his relation to mankind. Faust's social sense had not been developed. Social relations have played a small part in his experience. Except for Gretchen, whom he both worshiped and abandoned, he has never been close to any human being. He has never had a friend or felt the need of one—a strange lack indeed for a man who had programmatically set out to encompass the whole range of human experience in his person. In the Emperor's court he remained aloof from the dignitaries. Since the great idea of confining the sea dawned upon him, he has treated men only as means to his ends. His will had been supreme. They had only supplied the hands to carry out his plan. "To bring to fruit the most exalted plans, *one* mind is ample for a thousand hands" [lines

11509–10]. He had been a great benefactor for mankind, but all the benefactions accrued as an incidental to his sense of self-realization. It is in this regard that Faust's final utterance achieves a new breakthrough: for the first time he no longer thinks of man in terms of rule and obedience. He has a vision of a self-contained human society of free men, animated by the balanced operation of the two basic principles of competition and cooperation—competition as the drive directed against the nonhuman element, cooperation in the effective exercise of that drive in a society actuated by a common zeal. This is an idyllic vision, to be sure, an extreme simplification. The forces operating in human society will never range themselves to conform to so neat a design of polarity—certainly not in a democracy as we know it, and even though Goethe's eye dwelt with fascination on the new order taking shape in America. To a new direction, rather than to a goal achieved, Faust sets his sights. This is for him, at the last moment of his life, the embodiment of wisdom, the spirit that gives the stamp of value to collective human activity. Having outlined this creed in a phrasing which echoes the central formulation of the wager scene, though translated from statement to contingent hypothesis, Faust falls dead.

In breathing his last, Faust has uttered the key phrase of the wager that conditioned his pact with Mephisto. In the thousands of lines intervening, that situation has never been alluded to. Does its recurrence now stir an echo in Mephisto's ear? If so, he betrays no sign of it, as he shakes his head bemused by the unaccountable taste of this mortal. He admits, moreover, in plain words: Me he withstood so valiantly, now Time masters him at last. Then after further multiple echoes of the pact's phrasing, he concludes: "Es ist vollbracht," it is accomplished. The German "vollbracht" is a parodistic echo of Christ's last word on the Cross. Does the word here signify a burst of exultation or a sigh of relief? Be that as it may, the spectral grave-diggers cut in with a correction: "It is all over" [line 11595]. Let time be past, over, done for me, were the words with which Faust concluded the rhetorically ringing lines of his wager. This correction touches off a tantrum of nihilistic rage in Mephisto in which he rings the changes on that senseless word "over."

Having recovered himself, he stakes his confidence on Faust's signature. He orders the hellish host that has gathered to keep a sharp lookout for the precious soul and snatch it at the moment it leaves the body. There follows a scene of magnificently farcical humor. Hosts of angels are circling above the grave; they sing and scatter roses that, falling on the devils, pain them with more than hellish fire. They take flight. Worse still, Mephisto's lascivious appetite is beguiled by the pleasing forms of the boy angels, and, his attention distracted, the soul is snatched and borne aloft.

The postlude that ends the drama with magnificent recourse to Catholic imagery lets us glimpse various levels of Purgatory—Purgatory, not as a place of torment, but as the unending process of purgation and purification on the part of individual souls and groups dedicated to the deepening contemplation of the divine mysteries. We hear the fervent chants of various fathers of the Church, bearing exalted names. We hear the voices of the very young, who come into mortal life only to leave it again at once. We hear a chorus of penitent women adoring the Blessed Virgin, and in their number there is one that bears the features of Gretchen. Her voice thrills with gratitude to the divine Mother for having heard her intercession for her wayward lover. All of this scene is designed to be executed after the manner of a richly orchestrated oratorio.

Faust's salvation is a highly unorthodox affair. Let the Lord make a defense of his tolerance to the theologians. Arrogantly erect to the last, no humble penitent sinner suing for mercy, Faust is nevertheless rated a sound and perfectible substance by the divine arbiter. On his credit side is his ceaseless striving to expand his personality, despite his constant lapse into error. Perhaps the realization of the part played by Gretchen in his redemption will temper his nature with a little of that sweet humility which is both a gift of divine grace and a visible sign of its bestowal.

Backgrounds to *Faust*

HANS MAYER

Faust, Enlightenment, *Sturm und Drang*†

In a letter of Brecht,[1] as yet unpublished, it is stated: "Despite the legitimate wish for positive models one must not reject the creative stature of great figures like that of *Faustus*, whose effect can be positive in the social sense. Literature shows that tragedy can fulfill some functions of comedy, I mean a certain social purification." Again his well-known propensity for paradox! Classical German aesthetic theory, in which tragedy was ranked as the highest art form, would presumably have conceded that comedy could master, at a pinch and in an auxiliary capacity, the task of tragedy, which, in the alleged meaning of Aristotle, is to bring about purification of the passions. Brecht, as a playwright striving for a non-Aristotelian dramatic theory, speaks of the task of social purification. The highest art to him appears to be comedy. In an auxiliary capacity, to be sure, tragedy can perhaps be entrusted with the same function.

In regard to a figure such as Faustus, there are two more points worthy of note; the first is that Brecht considers the Faust figure still of topical relevance. The letter was written to postulate the enduring quality of the problem of Faust, in spite of Goethe. Moreover, like almost all his predecessors in the history of versions of Faust, Brecht sees Faust as a figure of tragedy.

Perhaps the author of the *Life of Galileo*, who served as advisor to Hanns Eisler[2] in his effort to write an opera libretto entitled *Johann Faustus*, was unaware that his demand for a continuous testing of contemporary drama against the Faust theme (which was of course secretly directed against Goethe), had already been raised during Goethe's life as a thesis of Romantic poetics. The first German imitation of Christopher Marlowe's *Tragical History of*

† From *Zur Deutschen Klassik und Romantik* (Pfullingen: Neske Verlag, 1963), pp. 7–29. Reprinted by permission of Verlag Günther Neske. Translated by Dolores Signori and Cyrus Hamlin. This essay offers a survey of the important though often obscure historical situation (the Enlightenment and the *Sturm und Drang* of the 1760s and 1770s) in which the young Goethe first conceived his *Faust*. A polarity of alternatives between reason and order versus the emotions
and spontaneity characterizes the conflicting attitudes which are associated with these two movements.

1. Bertolt Brecht (1898–1956), poet, dramatist, and theorist of Marxism in the theater. Brecht is usually regarded as an outspoken critic of the literary tradition who had little interest in norms of tragedy and themes such as Faust.

2. Hans Eisler (1898–1962), Marxist composer and librettist for Brecht, student of Arnold Schönberg.

Doctor Faustus appeared in Berlin in 1818. Wilhelm Müller had translated it; the translation had been suggested by Ludwig Achim von Arnim.[3] Arnim's foreword, written in Berlin and given the date November 19, 1817, is notable. His observations on the history and function of the problem of Faust turn out to be highly topical. The Romantic poet and critic protests against the assertion that enough had been done with Faust, that German literature "had been stricken with Fausts."[4] Arnim retorts: "We ought to say, on the contrary, that not enough Fausts have as yet been written, and it is only to be regretted that each Faust, without wishing to absorb the others, does not express only its variation on the theme of perdition sensed and dreaded; in this way each one in its peculiar manner would touch upon the general issue." Here, in a double sense, a "recantation" of the Goethean Faust is being carried out. In one sense, Goethe's version is valued merely as a transitional stage which ought not to stop the onward march of Faust poets. More than this, Arnim willfully interprets Goethe's basic design in terms of the pre-Goethean Faust tradition, as determined chiefly by the 1587 chapbook. As Friedrich Schlegel, at the beginnings of the Romantic school, had already remarked concerning Goethe's novel Wilhelm Meister, praising and scathing the work at the same time, the readers of the novel "cannot help feeling disappointed at the end, since nothing emerges from all these educational efforts but modest amiability," likewise Arnim, almost twenty years later, undertakes a re-interpretation of Goethe's Faust tragedy that is both praising and scathing. He understands the first part of the tragedy, the only part known at the time, as a warning in accord with Christian religion against all arrogance of knowledge. "The further the greed for learning spreads, the higher the arrogance grows of individuals who think they have accomplished something and thus idolize themselves, the more learning demands self-denial, the more the indulgence in learning spreads, the more deeply will be felt the serious truth of Goethe's Faust." To the Romantic the Faust figure again becomes the incarnation of pernicious hubris; there seems to be no longer any question that Faust, in the new versions constantly in demand, will ever be able to end otherwise than in the traditional journey to Hell.

Here is an initial turning point in the history of Faust versions after Goethe. Whether one thinks of Grabbe's Don Juan and Faust, of the Faustian-mythical Merlin drama of Karl Immermann, or of Lenau's lyrical Faust scenes,[5] the finale always, when compared with Goethe's tragedy, has the effect of a retraction, of a

3. The first German translation of Marlowe's Doctor Faustus, by Wilhelm Müller (1794–1827), appeared in 1818 with a foreword by the poet Achim von Arnim (1781–1831).
4. A German pun: mit Fäusten geschlagen is either "beaten with fists" or "stricken with Fausts."

5. Christian Dietrich Grabbe (1801–36) published his tragedy Don Juan and Faust in 1829. Karl Immermann (1796–1840) published his drama Merlin. A Myth in 1832. Nikolaus Lenau (1802–50) published his poem Faust, more an imitation of Byron than of Goethe, in 1835.

renewed acquiescence in the tradition of moralistic treaties against sacrilegious arrogance and eternal perdition. In German literary history, Goethe's Faust interpretation has proven equally magnificent and precarious, equally bold and without consequence. Only the literary stragglers felt it to be exemplary. The potent artist, on the other hand, whether he be an Achim von Arnim or a Brecht or a Thomas Mann, demanded re-investigation of the case, a new hearing, as it were, about the Goethean judgment, each time before a new court of appeals.

The singularity of Goethe's ideological and structural design— singularity in poetic power as well as in intellectual stance—already proves itself in this turn from the classical to the romantic conception of Faust. This singularity becomes even more distinct when one attempts to trace the path that led historically to Goethe's intellectual position. Here, too, Arnim rather clearly recognized the reasons for the recurrent fascination which the Faust theme has been able to exert. Arnim well knew the dull emotions of the dull masses of men, their fear of demons, and their mystical terrors. He saw the Faust genealogy as follows:

> The older age was simpler, it knew only magic, and whoever let go of the mysterious blessings of religion in the sacraments risked being ruined through the mysterious curse of sensuality; and precisely because these sacraments were entrusted to a consecrated order of priests, either exclusively or for purposes of dispensation, the degree of danger in these sacraments doubled. Consecrated in mystery, they stood high above the human race; their fall was therefore all the more terrible. Combined with a command of the sciences, among which natural history especially was associated with witchcraft, this was the reason why so many monks, even bishops, acquired the reputation of being in league with the devil.

Here, if one leaves aside Arnim's all too obviously tract-like demands upon state and religion, lies a very faithful starting point in interpreting the origins of the Faust theme. In general, the Faust commentaries tend to begin with the historical figure of the arch-magician, supposedly originating in Knittlingen, and then turn to the Frankfurt edition of the chapbook of 1587. Arnim points back to the Middle Ages, to the situation before the Reformation. The Catholic priest, as magician, is placed in a double conflict on the one hand between sensuality and the priestly sacrament, and on the other between the judgment which he must secretly pass on himself and his prestige among the people, in the lay world. This tradition of a Catholic origin remained artistically alive and fruitful for some time to come. One of its most famous artistic realizations appeared in 1602, fifteen years after the chapbook of Doctor Faustus. It was the "Comico-Tragœdia" *Cenodoxus*, composed by the Jesuit Jakob Bidermann, a history of the famous doctor of Paris who was torn between inner arrogance and a hybrid agnosticism, but who never-

theless was considered by the world to be an exemplary man. Cenodoxus, that is *kenè dóxa*, empty opinion, vanity, objective conflict
between inner being and social appearance. This tradition too is
taken up by Goethe and endowed with a moving spirituality. The
conversation with Wagner during the Easter walk testifies to this.

> Now people's cheers to me ring jeering fun.
> Could you but read within my soul the story
> How little father and son
> Were truly worthy of such glory! [lines 1030–33]

The Reformation meant a decisive transformation. The Lutheran
minister has a different status vis-à-vis the congregation and society
from that of the Catholic bearer of the sacrament. He ceases to be
a magical figure. Achim von Arnim sees the process as follows:

> With the Reformation, which took the mystery from the
> priesthood and gave it entirely to science, there also disappears
> the element, inherent in theological study, which the people find
> suspicious, and this suspicion falls entirely upon scientific activity,
> especially upon the study of chemistry, which henceforth is sup-
> posed to have led many adepts, as if to a higher light, into the
> power of the devil. Finally there arose among educated people an
> anguish over the separation of the sciences from the active world,
> grief about the narrow boundaries of their certainty.

There begins the secularization of the Faust figure. The chapbook
of 1587 is unmistakably Lutheran in its outlook. The later treatment too, of 1599 by Widman, of 1674 by Pfitzer, or of 1725 by
the "Person of Christian Purpose" are cautionary literature according to the Protestant persuasion, directed against secularized learning and attitudes of godless scholarship. It is highly peculiar in this
connection that traces of the original medieval-Catholic view of
Faust often shine through. In the Frankfurt Faust book of 1587 the
Faust figure shows marked Catholic characteristics. * * *

The spirited play by Shakespeare's contemporary, Christopher
Marlowe, is profoundly antithetical in its attitude. Atheistic features
are unmistakable and surely helped to provoke the Queen's decree,
and also perhaps to shorten abruptly Marlowe's life.[6] With respect
to many features, all later dramatizations of the Faust theme show
Marlowe's influence. To be sure, Goethe did not become
acquainted with the original through Wilhelm Müller's translation
until 1818, whereupon he immediately admired it. However, the
stamp of Marlowe had penetrated the plays of the English traveling
actors, and then the puppet shows, and thus indirectly exerted the
effect of a traditional form even upon Goethe. Already in Marlowe
the prologue and epilogue are present, and the *Tragical History*
begins with Faust's great monologue concerning *vanitas* in the
affairs of all university faculties. Quotations from Aristotle, Galenus,
the *corpus iuris*, the Vulgate are meant to underline this. Already in

---

6. Marlowe died in 1593 in a duel, possibly in a quarrel related to his atheism.

Marlowe, Faust's meditation is interrupted by the appearance of his famulus Wagner. For the rest, Doctor Faustus is shown to be a genuine product of Elizabethan drama, with blank verse for the discussions between Faust and Mephistopheles and prose for the conversations between the students and Wagner and in the scenes of clowning and slapstick, as in Shakespeare. Reflective comments and boisterous fun, spoofs on papistry and trivial magic tricks. Mephistopheles is a lachrymose spirit of warning, but also a fallen angel. For him, Hell is wherever he is. The ambivalence of the Faust figure includes genuine atheism, but also remorse and the attempt to turn back. There is ambivalence, too, in Marlowe's position: the anti-Catholic current which requires Doctor Faustus to appear, as in the chapbook, as a figure of warning, is unmistakable, but just as unmistakable is the lascivious terror, the secret pleasure derived from the actions and sins of Doctor Faustus. No doubt: in quite a different sense from that of the German chapbook, the Faust drama of Christopher Marlowe effects a "social purification" in Brecht's sense.

A direct path leads from Marlowe to Goethe. Of course, this should not be taken as direct transmission, nor even much in accord with the historical study of motifs, although much could be cited here that led from the chapbook to Marlowe, from there to the puppet show, from there to Goethe, encompassing not only the overall design of the tragedy but also details such as the grapes in Auerbach's cellar and the spirits' ire against exorcisms and conjurers. More important is Marlowe's intellectual position in its bearing on the story's secularization, the subversive turning away from Faust as a figure of warning, i.e., a slow but irreversible functional reworking of the character of Faust. Whereas the *first* change of direction had begun with the Reformation, a second was in the making in the process of the European Enlightenment, which culminated in Goethe's Faust figure; which in its turn, however, as Arnim's remarks already foreshadowed, was destined to be supplanted by a new reworking in the course of German literary development. * * *

Calderón's concept in *El mágico prodigioso* (first staged in 1637)[7] is the extreme counter-position to those attempts at secularization which had already become evident in Marlowe. The European Enlightenment in this regard continued the intellectual work of the Renaissance, but also carried to completion the tendency toward secularization which from the very first was implicit in the Reformation. "Lessing continued the work of Luther," Heine wrote in his survey of the history of religion and philosophy in Germany, and he tried hard to demonstrate in detail the parallel effects of Lessing and Luther. Lessing, too, worked on a Faust tragedy; according to his custom he did not take the easy way out, and here,

7. *The Wonder-Working Magician* by Calderón de la Barca (1600–1681), a play about Cyprianus of Antioch, which is set in late antiquity and ends with a Christian martyrdom.

too, to cite the well-known statement from the *Hamburg Drama-turgy*, he could properly boast of his diligence. He spreads his nets, as far as one can see, from the *Gesta Romanorum* across anecdotes from Pauli's *Schimpf und Ernst*, which may have served as a model for his prologue with its assembly of devils, up to the drama *Lucifer* by the Silesian Jesuit Franz Noël.[8] In addition, of course, there were readings in books of black magic and in the abundant literature on witches and exorcism, which Lessing had been able to find in the library at Breslau during the second phase of his work on *Faust*.

The few preserved fragments and communications from Lessing's circle of family and friends make it possible today at least to discern the working method and basic motifs in this Faust drama of the Enlightenment. An "Enlightened" Faust drama: there seems here an immediate contradiction in terms. In the middle of the eighteenth century, a new drama with the entire inventory of the puppet show, with the kind of horrific and coarse action familiar to countless Germans of that time from the various folk plays about Dr. Johann Faust and Christoph Wagner, his famulus? One must not forget that the familiar success of the old dramatizations, which went back directly to the chapbook and which, of course, still used the Hanswurst[9] figure and brought him on stage, not only the puppet stage but also the legitimate stage, continued until far into the age of Goethe. In August, 1833, one such was played in Munich in Schweiger's Popular Theater in the suburb of Au; other versions, at almost the same time, were given in Hamburg at St. Pauli and at Offenbach am Main by a traveling troupe. In the forties, Faust, Wagner, and Hanswurst appeared in the traveling theaters of Ostfriesland, and as late as the fifteenth of July, 1889, the theater director Dressler had the (so-called) authentic Doctor Faustus performed in the summer theater at Plagwitz near Leipzig, and had considerable success with it, running to a series of repeat performances.

The same elements, however, which contributed to the indestructibility of the popular drama (devil conjuring and the demonic pact, good spirits, evil spirits, voices from on high, hocus-pocus complete with a trip to Hell) made the material an abomination to the educated public of the progressive eighteenth century. Faust and bourgeois Enlightenment—the two were evidently incompatible. What good was dramatic material which simply reveled in improbabilities, in what to intelligent thinking was absurd? Moreover, the thirst for and urge toward knowledge were considered the indestructible property of man. An excess of rational curiosity, as Faust evinces it, could lead to unpleasantness in life, to be sure, but could never be viewed as culpable, nor, therefore, serve as the basis of a tragedy. A

8. *Gesta Romanorum*: an anthology of popular tales in Latin collected in England at the turn of the fourteenth century and used as a historical source by Chaucer and Shakespeare. *Schimpf und Ernst*: a collection of amusing anecdotes written by Johannes Pauli (1450–54—after 1520) appeared in 1522. Franciscus Noël's (1652–1725) drama *Lucifer* was published in 1717.

9. The German "Punch" of the puppet stage.

tragic element in the striving for knowledge—that too seemed to be an intrinsic contradiction to the Enlightenment view of life. At most it offered material for a comedy of character. * * *

One can imagine the horror of his enlightened friends when in 1755 it became known that Lessing was working on a Faust drama. Moses Mendelssohn's letter of November 19, 1755, to Lessing can be considered a representative sample of the attitude of German Enlightenment literature towards the Faust material:

> Where do you stand, dearest Lessing, with your middle-class tragedy? I don't like to call it by that name, for I doubt that you will leave it the name of Faust. A single exclamation: "O Faustus! Faustus!" could make the entire pit start to laugh. Another counselor, you will say, who has no business giving advice! All right, then! Just go ahead and let it stand. I want to have the pleasure then of laughing myself with the Leipzig parterre, and seeing you flare up with each laugh. For one certainly has to laugh, provided your theory of laughter is correct.

In these first years of work on Faust, Lessing seems to have aspired to a lofty tragedy in the English manner, leaning strongly on the chapbook. Part of this was probably Faust's scene with the spirits, which he attached to the famous *Letter on Literature* of February 16, 1759, containing the Gottsched polemic.[1] A new phase of work on Faust began in 1760 in Breslau; allegedly at that time twelve pages of the Faust drama were already finished. A completely new draft, supposedly "without any devilry," then originated in Hamburg, where Lessing thought of having the Faust drama performed in the theater on the Gänsemarkt. But the draft was not then brought to completion. What was available of Lessing's Faust fragments was finally lost with that box which in 1775 was to be sent from Leipzig to the book-dealer Gabler at Braunschweig and from there to Wolfenbüttel, but which never arrived. At that time Lessing was himself traveling from Dresden to Vienna and Italy. The fragment included with the seventeenth *Letter on Literature* was preserved, as well as a handwritten fragment of the so-called Berlin scenario, which outlined the action and train of thought for the prologue and the first four scenes of the first act. Everything else is lost. One has to fall back upon the testimony—to be sure, quite ample—of those who had read Lessing's manuscript. The reports of Karl Lessing, Johann Jakob Engel, and Captain von Blankenburg,[2] at any rate, convey an idea of what Lessing proposed to do. On the most important points, the statements of the witnesses coincide.

According to this information Lessing had been one of the first writers to decide not to end the play with Faust's ruin and damnation. By Engel's report, the certainty of this outcome was already communicated by a heavenly voice to the infernal assembly in the scene which was to open the drama. The angel of providence pro-

1. See Lessing's seventeenth *Letter on Literature*, above.
2. Testimonies are preserved by several

people describing aspects of the play which they had seen in manuscript.

claimed from on high the words: "You are not to triumph!" The commentator recalls. "The angel buries this Faust in a deep sleep and creates in his place a phantom with which the devils make sport until, at the moment when they try to get it completely under their control, it disappears. Everything that occurs with this phantom is a vision for the real, sleeping Faust: he awakens after the devils have departed in shame and rage, and thanks Providence for the warning which she had chosen to give him through such an instructive dream.—He is now firmer than ever in truth and virtue." Quite similar is Blankenburg's report: "Enough, the infernal legions believe they have completed their work; in the fifth act, they begin to sing songs of triumph, when an apparition from on high interrupts them in the most unexpected, and yet most natural and most soothing way: 'Do not triumph,' the angel calls out to them, 'you have not scored a victory over humanity and science; the godhead did not give man the most noble of desires in order to make him eternally unhappy; what you saw and now believe you possess is nothing but a phantom.' " * * *

Here is what we have, then—phantom, dream, salvation. Nevertheless, the play is clearly a tragedy. This is all that survives. A magnificent poetical sketch has been lost. But how does it fit into the categories of Enlightenment thought? Of course, even the general outlook of the Enlightenment did not necessarily exclude disapproval of the Faustian attitude. * * * It is not worldly direction of thought, averted from God, which generates the tragic situation. The drive for apperception carries within itself the seed of tragic conflict. The exaggerated development of a striving that is in itself worthy and healthy seems to Lessing capable of a tragic end, but the fact that he goes on to indicate the possibility of this tragic dénouement, only to retract it again and by means of the parable of the phantom make it into a cautionary play with a moralistic purge, is highly characteristic of his entire dramatic theory and technique. It touches upon the roots of his philosophy of life. Everything is connected with Aristotle—not merely with the Poetics but also with Aristotelian ethics. Aristotle consistently held ethical values to lie in the mean between extremes, which are to be avoided. Valor meant the mean between the extremes of cowardice and rashness. Lessing is wholly a follower of Aristotle when, in the famous seventy-fourth section of the Hamburg Dramaturgy, he concludes with Aristotle that the hero of a tragedy "may be neither an entirely virtuous man nor a complete villain." This thesis is first played off against Corneille, who, Lessing claims, brought not only martyrs onto the stage, and at that "as the most perfect and irreproachable persons," but also the "most loathsome monsters." Then, however, in the seventy-eighth section of the Hamburg Dramaturgy, Lessing applies the notion of the mesotes, Aristotle's concept of the mean, even to the effect of the tragedy on the spectator: "Similarly tragic pity must, with regard to fear, check what is too much and what is too little:

just as, conversely, tragic fear must do regarding compassion." * * *

To come back to Lessing's *Faust*, the fundamental attitude of which becomes discernible only when one confronts it with the basic positions of Lessing, the dramatist as well as the dramatic producer, we find this Faust located right "in the middle" between th irreproachable learned man and the wildly conjuring companion of the devil. The striving for cognition itself—irreproachable in its direction—entailed in the Faust figure the tendency to excess. Given this, there existed the danger of a sudden turn toward the culpable. For Lessing, departure from the mean, from temperate moderation of thought and feeling, can establish positive guilt and create tragic conflicts. He never really departed from this conception. * * *

Lessing's *Faust* stands in a tradition of the mean and of balance. Violation of the mean, of an equilibrium of thought and feeling, creates danger, signifies the path to the tragic. Catharsis is to bring the spectator to reach the "virtuous accomplishment" of equable thought and feeling. This means, however, that with Lessing the drama still (or again) definitely possesses the function of a moral institution. In his book *Lessing and Aristotle*,[3] Max Kommerell recognized that "Lessing will strive less for the catastrophe than for balance, where the outcome of the drama is concerned." There can be no question, though, of a "universal view" by Lessing which "unites within itself a plurality of perspectives," as Kommerell maintains in this context. Behind this seeming plurality there is the profound unity of a mediating artist striving for conciliation, a fact which is closely connected with Lessing's social purpose within the German bourgeoisie—with his strength as well as with his limitation. The way in which Lessing has his Faust become guilty, but yet fundamentally not guilty at all, the way in which he sets up the traditional triumph of hell and thwarts it at the same time through the idea of the dream and the phantom, reveals this more daring struggle by a man of the Enlightenment with the Faust theme, despite its survival only in fragments, to be vintage Lessing.

There is a remarkable document—again involving the Faust material—which brings out sharply the antithesis between Lessing's species of bourgeois Enlightenment and the new bourgeois phase of *Sturm und Drang*. In 1776, i.e. directly after the presumed origin of the *Urfaust*, that exponent of the *Sturm und Drang* Friedrich Müller (the "Painter") had published a fragmentary "Situation from Faust's Life"[4] which, almost predictably, he addressed "to Shakespeare's spirit." When Lessing came to Mannheim a year later (1777) he encountered Müller, who showed him the fragment: "Lessing supposed, when he saw my 'Situation from Faust's Life' during his stay in Mannheim, that I would stop at this scene and

3. **Max** Kommerell, *Lessing und Aristoteles. Untersuchung über die Theorie der Tragödie* (Frankfurt, 1940), p. 32.

4. Friedrich Müller (1749–1825) published this short dramatic fragment in 1776.

lead Faust back through remorse and repentence to his salvation, paraphrasing the parable of the prodigal son; then, after expressing such an expectation, he added that it would be hard to conceive how Faust would want to proceed on such a path." Müller then *developed* a further plan for his Faust which, still fragmentary, appeared in 1778 as *Faust's Life Dramatized*. According to Müller's report, Lessing must have assented to the plan:

> "Very fine," he said at the end and in doing so patted me on the shoulder, "you have seized the bucket properly by the handle, the only way in which one could have dressed up this rich yet terribly droll business and transferred it comfortably from its age to ours. I am pleased," he continued, "that you treat the subject popularly, more ironically than seriously; today, when the devils have already lost so much of their credit, whoever wanted to interpret this material for a realistic presentation, in order to induce, like Dante in his *Divine Comedy* or Klopstock in the *Messiade*, serious conviction and belief, would always risk failure and miss his goal."

On this occasion too, incidentally, he told the painter Müller that he himself had sketched a Faust project twice but then dropped it.

There is an apparent agreement here between the man of the Enlightenment and the exponent of *Sturm and Drang*, but only an apparent one. Their agreement extended only to the common rejection of any devil's hocus-pocus on the stage and to the striving for life-like characters. For the rest, Müller's Faust conception was, however fragmentary the form it presents to us, the genuine work of an exponent of the *Sturm und Drang*. The extensive dedication of 1778 to "my dear, cherished Otto Baron von Gemmingen" reveals clearly what the painter Müller had actually striven for with his Faust: "Faust had always been one of my favorite childhood heroes, because I took him immediately to be a splendid fellow; a fellow who had felt all his strength, felt the curb strapped on him by fortune and fate which he wanted to break, and who is looking for ways and means—who had enough spirit to overcome anything that came in his way and hindered him—who has enough warmth in his breast to embrace fondly a devil who approaches him openly and confidentially." And then: "There are moments in life—who doesn't experience this feeling, who hasn't experienced it a thousand times—when the heart overleaps itself, when the finest, the best of fellows, despite justice and laws, reaches absolutely above himself in his desires. I went at my Faust from this angle."

Here, then, Faust helps himself, a wild fellow, an original genius in the pure tradition of the German *Sturm und Drang*. It is strange, actually, that Lessing did not see or did not want to see this during the conversation in Mannheim. His own Enlightenment Faust had been designed as a tragedy of departure from the mean, and the Faust figure, like the theatergoer, had been led back to spiritual balance. With Müller the element of self-help is seen and expressed quite affirmatively. The tragedy is an external conflict between a figure of power and his inhibiting surroundings. What Lessing had condemned, Müller exalts. Where in Lessing an extreme objectification of the Faust figure took place, Müller identifies the poet with the poem, creator with creature. Müller's Faust amounts to a fictional version of Müller the Painter. The antithesis between the Faust conception of the Enlightenment and that of the exponent of the *Sturm und Drang* appears in the substance as well as in the purpose of these two works.

Since our only concern is to work out the common locus of the exponents of *Sturm und Drang* in the treatment of the Faust theme, it cannot and need not be proved by what means (which remain those of an exponent of *Sturm und Drang*) the Faust figure in the *Urfaust* was to demonstrate the theme of the self-helper. Suffice it to remark here that Goethe's Faust, even in his earliest form, was to be far more than a self-helper in an anarchic time, hence more than a new Gottfried von Berlichingen,[5] and that in Goethe the complex dilemma of learning was presented for the first time (and in a manner which later proved very significant) as an implicit dilemma of the artist. All examination of the *Urfaust* has to start from the premise that it was not a preliminary stage to the later completed tragedy which took shape, but an independent tragedy which shows many similarities with the later completed version but which had to stand on its own and answer for itself, and which failed, miscarried, and thus had to remain a fragment.

* * *

With the beginning of the French Revolution an age came to an end. The first turning-point in the history of the Faust conflict as an ever newly arising social conflict had occurred at the beginning of the sixteenth century. A second one came to pass with the end of the early phase of bourgeois emancipation. We have tried to show why German Enlightenment, and even German *Sturm und Drang*, failed here. What Goethe later achieved was the result of new insights and new experiences of a social and historical kind. There is however success as well as failure in this unfathomably sublime work. The completed Faust is a work of loneliness which shows failure and success in closest proximity, a work no longer carried by the social current, as in its beginnings, but almost outside historical time, most certainly contrary to its own epoch. Achim von Arnim maintained that "the sciences of our age have been guilty of a colossal arrogance through their ingenious development; but this arrogance has created the *Faust* of Goethe in the poet's comprehensive vision." It was, indeed, this dictum of Arnim's which shows colossal arrogance and monstrous misjudgment; however, it also shows why Goethe's contemporaries and descendants had no intention of stopping with his *Faust*.

5. Götz von Berlichingen (1480–1562), German knight and adventurer who rebelled against the emperor in the era of the historical Faustus. His life was the subject of Goethe's play of 1772 by the same name.

Faust and Mephistopheles

EUDO C. MASON

The Erdgeist and Mephisto†

Goethe conceived of his Faust as too noble-minded ever, for the sake of power, fame, wealth, happiness, pleasure or any other acquisition, even knowledge, deliberately and with open eyes to seek communion with or ally himself to the forces of evil as such. He might indeed be, or imagine himself to be, "beyond good and evil," but that alone would fundamentally distinguish him from the Faust of tradition, whose entire character and destiny depend upon there being no possibility for him of transcending good and evil, even in the imagination. Yet Goethe's Faust, though most of the time too titanic and spiritually emancipated to see in the conception of "evil" a reality to be taken seriously, looking down with contempt on those who still "fear Hell and the Devil," and though, so far as evil ever does seem to him a reality, he is too noble-minded ever deliberately to choose it, was somehow to be brought into the traditional Faust situation of being allied with the spirit of evil. He had recognizably still to be Faust. The radical transformation of the sources involved by this loftier conception of the hero's character cost Goethe considerable labor and thought, and created problems for him, some of which he found it extremely difficult to solve.

* * *

One of the chief consequences of Goethe's ennoblement of Faust's character was that his Faust could never, like his traditional prototype, conjure up the devil, that some adequate substitute had to be found for that central, decisive motif of the old legend. This meant in turn that Goethe could not utilize the idea of magic upon which that legend reposed, but had to find some adequate substitute for that too. These are problems which Goethe had already faced and at least in part solved, when he wrote the opening monologue.

What Faust aims at in resorting to magic is to enter into communion with the world of spirits for the sake of the hidden knowl-

† From *Goethe's Faust: Its Genesis and Purport*, by Eudo C. Mason, pp. 119–65. Copyright © 1967 by the University of California Press. Originally published by the University of California Press; reprinted by permission of The Regents of the University of California.

edge they can impart to him. This runs as a *leitmotif* through all the sections of the opening monologue, linking them together and conferring upon them the unity so often denied by the critics. It occurs already in the first thirty-two lines.

> So I resorted to Magic's art,
> To see if by *spirit* mouth and might
> Many a secret may come to light. [lines 377–79]

In the second section this motif is taken up again when Faust longs to hover by moonshine around mountain caves "with spirits." In the third section Faust expresses the hope that from contemplation of Nostradamus' mysterious book in the open countryside his soul may expand, "How spirit with its like communes" [line 425], and then he becomes aware that there is no need for him to quit his study to experience this, for

> You *spirits*, You who float nearby,
> Give me an answer, if you hear! [lines 428–29]

The contemplation of the Sign of the Makrokosmus leads Faust to exclaim in the words of some unidentifiable and probably only putative "sage": "The *world of spirits* is not barred" [line 442]. The Erdgeist scornfully asks the overawed Faust what has become of his breast that "with joyous tremble/Swelled up to soar, *us spirits* to resemble" [lines 492–93]. The same conception is expressed also in "Dreary Day. A Field"—and this is one of the close links between that scene and the opening monologue—when Mephisto jeeringly asks Faust, "Why make common cause with us. . . . Did we obtrude ourselves on you, or you on us?" The Erdgeist takes its leave of Faust at the end of the monologue with the mysterious, much discussed words: "Close to the spirit you comprehend,/Not me!" [lines 512–13].

The conception of magic as communication "with Spirits" is, of course, traditional, and Goethe found plenty of precedents for it in his sources. * * * But though Goethe adheres verbally to the tradition of magic in general and of the Faust legend in particular with his use of the word "spirit" (*Geist/Geister*), he has inconspicuously modified its meaning. The sources all of them quite clearly indicate that the spirits involved are *evil* spirits, in fact devils, and that Faust is all along fully aware of this. * * *

* * * [But] the "spirits" envisaged, apostrophized, and invoked by Goethe's Faust take on a fundamentally different character from those of the chapbooks and puppet-plays. The possibility that any of them might be evil spirits is not touched upon: it simply does not interest Faust and is apparently not meant to interest us either. The one spirit that actually does appear, without in the full magical sense of the word being formally and deliberately conjured up, the Erdgeist, is something distinctly different from what is traditionally

understood by an "evil spirit," still more by "the Devil." The only point where evil spirits are referred to by name in the *Urfaust* is in connection not with Faust and his magical undertakings, but with Gretchen and her conscience: she has, as Faust says in "Dreary Day. A Field," been "abandoned to evil spirits," and we see one of these evil spirits tormenting her in the scene "Cathedral." Faust's assumption in the opening monologue appears to be simply that there is an invisible world of spirits which, just because it is spiritual, must be superior to the merely natural and human world, and that it is a noble and courageous enterprise to communicate with that spiritual world, an enterprise indeed that raises one to the level of a "superman" or even of a "god." These are typical eighteenth-century sentiments, which Goethe himself may be supposed in considerable measure to have shared.

Many commentators find a solution of this problem in the conception of "white" magic, which, as opposed to "black" magic, confined itself to the conjuring up of beneficent, or at least neutral and harmless, spirits and was therefore widely regarded as more or less lawful. * * * But Goethe nowhere explicitly or even implicitly makes use of this distinction between white and black magic, and little reflexion is needed to see why he did not and could not do so. The idea of white magic as such is alien not only to the tradition but also to the essence of the Faust legend. Somehow, even if he does not deliberately practise black magic, Faust has got to find himself allied to the devil, if he is to be Faust at all. One could think of the situation in such a way that Faust, while only intending to practise white magic, finds out too late that he has after all, without knowing it, been practising black magic instead or as well. Such a formula comes near to what Goethe was evidently getting at, but there are still elements in it which are not warranted by the actual text. There is no indication that Faust is conscious of or worried by the distinction between white and black magic, nor would it be in keeping with his turbulent, high-vaulting soul, which "stand[s] not in fear of hell or devil" [line 369], to pick his steps in such a way. What he asks is not whether a spirit is good or evil, but whether it can "hear" him and will "answer" him, whether he can "grasp" it, whether—twice he uses this significant word—he feels it to be "near" to him. In other words he seeks amongst the spirits the one most congenial to himself, to his own needs and aspirations, leaving the issue of good and evil on one side as irrelevant. In excluding the idea of a specifically black magic Goethe has necessarily excluded that of a specifically white magic too. The Erdgeist, whom we should pretty certainly have to assign to the sphere of white magic, and Mephisto, whom we should quite certainly have to assign to the sphere of black magic, belong together to the one undivided but heterogeneous world of spirits and are, so to speak, colleagues—this emerges clearly enough from the way in which Mephisto, taking up the Erdgeist's taunt at Faust for having aspired to "soar, us spirits to resemble," asks Faust: "Why make common cause with *us?*" Goethe's *Faust* depends upon the distinction between white and black magic being disregarded. In this sense and in this connexion the work and the hero can both be said to be beyond good and evil, or at least to aspire to that emancipated condition.

There are many critics, however, who assume that the Erdgeist was only an afterthought of Goethe's and that originally Faust was represented as conjuring up the "Prince of Hell", Lucifer, instead; and there are many more who assume that Goethe planned but failed to write a subsequent scene, in which Faust would have invoked the Devil as such and that, in response to this invocation, either Lucifer or Mephisto would have appeared. The postulate underlying both these theories is that Goethe to begin with had no thoughts of radically altering the purport of the traditional Faust legend and that he therefore originally based his drama unambiguously on black magic. This is, as will be seen, an unnecessary and misleading postulate, for which there is no really valid evidence. One of the most significant features of Goethe's drama is that *his* Faust never conjures up the Devil as such and does not appear as the sort of man who could well be thought of as doing so. The most convincing explanation of the invocation of the Erdgeist and of the "great lacuna" which follows upon it and which was only filled with such difficulty and delay, is that Goethe was from the outset bent upon finding some fundamentally different basis upon which to bring his Faust into the required alliance with Mephisto from that of the old tradition with its unambiguous black magic and diabolism. If he had not all along had this intention, which was eventually fulfilled with much ingenuity after 1797, it is not easy to see why there ever should have been any great gap or any invocation of the Erdgeist. The treatment of the theme on traditional lines could have presented no problems; if nothing more than that had been involved, Goethe would surely have tackled it at once, unhesitatingly and with verve. But there is not the least trace of his having ever done so or intended to do so; on the contrary, the evidence of the *Urfaust*, and particularly of "Dreary Day. A Field," which so many wrongly or rightly regard as the earliest scene to have been written, all shows Goethe departing on these essential points from his sources.

Apart from all other considerations, there are purely formal and technical reasons why Goethe is unlikely ever to have contemplated following up the invocation of the Erdgeist with another invocation scene in which Faust would have conjured up the Devil. Such a scene could hardly have been so devised or executed that it would not have seemed an anti-climax or a repetition detracting from the effectiveness of what had gone before. It would have been well nigh impossible and hardly desirable to adapt the conjuration motif to the Devil so impressively as to outshine the opening scene with the Erdgeist; it would also have been very difficult—and hardly worth attempting—to vary the conjuration motif so radically and extensively in applying it to the Devil that the resulting new scene could have constituted either a fitting dialectical counterpart to the Erdgeist scene, as the Classical Walpurgis Night does, for example, to the Nordic Walpurgis Night or a production so different in character as no longer to challenge comparison with it. It will be found that Goethe never repeats a once successfully treated major motif within one and the same work, unless the second treatment of it can thus either transcend the first, supplement it dialectically at the same level of achievement, or differentiate itself from it fundamentally in tone, interest, and attendant circumstances. None of these possibilities would have been open to him in writing such a second invocation scene for *Faust* as many critics suppose him to have planned. The opening monologue had exhausted the invocation motif. It was a situation in which Faust could only be presented once. What we have in Faust's invocation of the Erdgeist is not something supplementary to a projected invocation of the Devil, but Goethe's substitute for the traditional invocation of the Devil. In any case Faust's own declaration in "Dreary Day. A Field" that he has been "chained" to Mephisto by the "glorious, lofty Spirit," however it is interpreted, precludes the possibility of his having conjured Mephisto up of his own accord.

What has been said here of the unlikelihood of Goethe's ever having planned a second invocation scene in which Faust would have conjured up Mephisto, applies still more strongly to the theory occasionally maintained that he intended Faust to invoke the Erdgeist once more. If, however, the "glorious, lofty Spirit" referred to in "Dreary Day. A Field" and in the "Forest and Cave" scene of 1788 is the Erdgeist—and there is no justification for assuming that it could be anything else—then it must have been part of Goethe's early plan that the Spirit should, without needing to be invoked once more, manifest itself again in some way and play a further part, probably a central part, in the action of the drama. In particular it is to be assumed that Goethe intended to introduce some scene or passage that would have thrown more light on Faust's statement that Mephisto had been "chained" or "given" to him as a companion by the Erdgeist, and possibly also on his feeling that the Spirit "knows his heart and soul." That seems to have been a decisive factor in the earliest conception of the Faust drama which we can reasonably suppose Goethe to have had and which he still thought of carrying out as late as 1788. Eventually, however, in 1797, he hit upon what seemed to him a better way of bringing Faust and Mephisto together, and abandoned the earlier conception, without thinking it necessary to eliminate the existing traces of it or to tidy up the loose ends, as he quite easily could have done, if he had in this case attached as much importance to strict consistency as his critics do. It is possible, however, to recognise fairly clearly what the essentials of that earlier, never executed conception must have been, without resorting to any of the intricate, unverifiable hypotheses regularly indulged in on these questions. Everything depends here upon how Goethe arrived at the idea of his Erdgeist and what he meant by it. Our point of departure should be that Goethe evidently conceived of the Erdgeist in such a way that it was in keeping with its nature to link Faust and Mephisto together in companionship, and of Faust and Mephisto in such a way that it was in keeping with their natures thus to be linked together by the Erdgeist. Those many critics who maintain that it is incompatible with the natures of all or any of the three to stand in this relationship to one another would do well to ask themselves whether they may not have formed *a priori* a mistaken notion of the Erdgeist and perhaps also of Faust and Mephisto. It is intrinsically more likely that they should have done this than that one of the most striking pieces of information given to us by Goethe twice, at an interval of some fifteen years, about the three figures in question, should be spurious.

It is at this point that the nature of Goethe's occult and pansophical studies of 1769 and the first months of 1770 is of major importance for the interpretation of *Faust*. For the idea of "magic" represented by the mysterious book of Nostradamus with its "sacred tokens" and by the unnamed sage, who is quoted as having declared that the world of Spirits is not "barred," is indubitably derived from those studies. The question is only in what way and in what degree it is derived from them, and that is a question on which there is much difference of opinion. The widely, though by no means universally, accepted view is that everything essential in the entire invocation scene is taken from the youthful Goethe's occult reading and can only be properly understood in the light of it. * * * [But] the spirit in which the youthful Goethe indulged in occult reading and alchemistic experiments was fundamentally different from that in which Faust is represented as devoting himself to magic and practicing it. * * * The point of them was that they seemed to provide some way of escape from the purely rationalistic, mechanical, and soulless conception of the universe inculcated by modern science, and thereby to make enthusiastic Christian belief still possible. Only within the framework of eighteenth-century pietism is such a strange alliance of fundamentally orthodox Christianity with ancient heterodoxies and fantasies thinkable. What for Faust is a decisive step away from Christian belief was for the youthful Goethe of the Frankfort interim months a decisive step towards it.

Faust's rejection of all established academic learning is indeed symbolic for Goethe's own Storm and Stress revolt against Enlightenment rationalism, but the impulses underlying that revolt were infinitely more vigorous, clear sighted, and independent than those that had led him two or three years earlier to dabble indiscriminately in occultism and pietism. All the indications are that, in adopting a detached and critical attitude towards pietism, as he did from summer, 1770, onward, Goethe also adopted a detached and sceptical attitude towards occultism, no longer devoting much of his time or energy to it, but waging the battle against Enlightenment mentality with the weapons of his own bold, fundamentally modern, and by no means unenlightened intellect. * * * In fact, such evidence as we have suggests that occultism was only a brief phase in Goethe's development, that it was nearly over, leaving few traces behind it, by the time that his so important Storm and Stress epoch properly began, and that even in 1769 and early 1770 he was interested in it rather than swept off his feet by it, retaining his critical faculties and his intellectual independence in face of it. * * * For Goethe, so far as we can judge, the only way of taking the cabbalistic writings seriously was to take them figuratively, not literally; that was why he could ridicule them mercilessly in the very months during which he is known to have been doing some of his work on the Urfaust, in the farcical drama Satyros of 1773. It is unlikely that, with such an attitude, he ever studied the cabbalists anything like as systematically and laboriously as many critics suppose him to have done. By 1771 he must have been fully conscious of the difference between his own comparatively sophisticated, subjective, imaginative, and symbolical conception of "spirits" in nature, and the naive, mentally undisciplined and quite literally understood animism which runs riot in cabbalistic writings and which was the one element in those writings that attracted him enough for him to be able to borrow it and adapt it to his own poetic purposes in the early stages of his work on Faust.

When Faust opens his book of magic he does not, as we might well expect him to do, proceed immediately to invoke the Erdgeist. Instead he sinks into a long, intensive contemplation of the Sign of the Makrokosmus, about which no more is heard. Poetically this Makrokosmus passage is one of the finest in Faust, but it is widely regarded as only obscuring the purport of the play, without in any way furthering the action, and the question arises, how it comes to be there at all. Here too the favorite higher critical hypothesis of a later plan having been negligently superimposed upon an earlier one with which it is incompatible has been resorted to. * * *

* * * It is felt that there was not much point in Goethe's introducing two symbols for the pantheistic idea of nature, which differ from one another apparently only in degree (that is to say, in their magnitude and scope), where one might have served his purpose just as well or better. For that they are both pantheistic symbols is

evident from their names and from the way in which they are presented; about that there can be no disagreement. What we have to
decide is how Goethe came thus to duplicate the pantheistic principle here. Is one or the other symbol merely an accidental excres-
cence due either to his having temporarily lost control of his material, * * * or to his conception of nature having undergone a
change * * *? Or did he * * * simply wish to indicate within the
pantheistic framework a descending scale of dignity and power? The
far likelier possibility, which remains to be considered, is that the
Makrokosmus and the Erdgeist are meant to differ from one
another not only in degree, but also and primarily in kind, that the
relationship between them is one of contrast, of antithesis. This
view has also occasionally been maintained; but it has found little
support. In maintaining that the two symbols are indeed intended
antithetically and that therefore both are necessary, and the one is
only fully intelligible in the light of the other, we must from the
outset admit that Goethe has not brought this antithesis out clearly
enough and that it can easily be overlooked. The very names that he
employs suggest a difference of degree, of greater and less (as earth
is obviously less than the whole universe), rather than one of kind.
Verbally considered, the opposite of the Makrokosmus would be Man
as microcosm, and that of the Erdgeist would be the "Himmelsgeist"
(the Spirit of Heaven)—presumably the transcendent God; but of
these palpable antitheses there is no real trace in the invocation
scene with its consistently pantheistic postulates. Nevertheless it
will be seen that everything does indeed here turn on a genuine, all-
important, though not clearly enough worked out, antithesis.

* * *

What is found at every hand in the old cabbalistic writings and
does seem to correspond far more closely to Goethe's Erdgeist than
their peripheral and shadowy ideas of an *archaeus terrae* or *anima
terrae*[1] is the *anima mundi* or *spiritus mundi*, the World Soul or
World Spirit, "world" in this context being conceived of always as
signifying not just earth alone, but the whole universe. The
difficulty, however, is that Goethe, by distinguishing between his
spirit and the Makrokosmus, and by explicitly designating it as the
"Geist der Erde," has made it clear that it is something other than
the World Spirit as such, or that it is the World Spirit with a difference, in some special sense. For the World Spirit in the usually
accepted sense would obviously correspond to the Makrokosmus.

* * *

Whatever share such cabbalistic conceptions as the *archaeus
terrae* and *anima terrae* may have had in suggesting the name of the
Erdgeist to Goethe, it is essentially * * * something that Goethe
himself freely invented, and—it may be added—something that he
invented specially for the purposes of his Faust drama and would

1. See note following line 446 of *Faust*.

probably otherwise never have thought of. The word he uses for his own personal purposes is "Weltgeist" or "Weltseele" (World Spirit or World Soul); only once does he refer to the "Erdgeist" outside *Faust*. The real meaning of the Erdgeist, wherever else it is to be found, is certainly not to be found in the cabbalistic writings, which were for Goethe ultimately only material to be freely moulded and transformed by his own imagination in keeping with his own experiences and reflexions. He did not indeed invent the actual German word "Erdgeist" or "Erdengeist," but he gave to it a meaning which it had never had before. * * * The technical terminology of the cabbalists was always Latin or Greek, but the natural connotation of the German word "Erdgeist" from the cabbalistic point of view and on the analogy of cabbalistic ways of thinking would have been, as we have found, a personification either of Earth as one of the four elements or of Earth as one of the heavenly bodies. We shall see, however, that neither of these conceptions has any relevancy to the most important aspects of Goethe's Erdgeist, which turn not upon cosmogonic, but upon ethical and psychological issues.

In *Faust, Part I*, as Goethe completed it after 1797, no causal relationship is indicated between the conjuration of the Erdgeist and that most important motif dictated by the intrinsic character of the legend and idea of Faust, the first appearance before him of Mephisto. It is unthinkable, however, that when Goethe first wrote the conjuration scene he did not envisage some such causal relationship, that the invocation of the Erdgeist was not specially intended and designed to lead up to and in some way to motivate Mephisto's first appearance. Mephisto was originally to have come to Faust *as a result of* his having conjured up the Erdgeist; that is clearly enough indicated by Faust's own statement that Mephisto has been "chained to him as a companion by the great and glorious Spirit." That conjuration was to be the great, decisive deed by which Faust is launched upon his specifically Faustian destiny, and therefore everything depends upon the frame of mind in which he performs that deed, whether or not he performs it as an absolutely free agent, with his eyes open and his head erect and with a full sense of responsibility and of his own powers.

If he sees in the Erdgeist nothing but a kind of inferior, smaller-scale substitute for the Makrokosmus, a second best that he must put up with, because the genuine Makrokosmus is too mighty for him, then his frame of mind in invoking it can only be one of resignation, frustration, discouragement and defeat, and his deed is determined less by his own will than by external agencies; he is doing not what he would really have preferred to do, if he had the choice, but what the hampering circumstances in which he finds himself alone allow him to do. * * * But is it appropriate that Faust, whose most essential characteristic it is never to content himself with anything, should, on the first occasion when he appears before us, and in the moment that is to decide his destiny for all eternity, be shown to us as "ready to content himself" with a mere second best? If nothing more than that is involved in his appeal to the Erdgeist, then he is less aspiring and venturesome than the older Faust of the popular dramatic tradition, who is always represented in the opening scene as being faced with a choice and freely making that choice, not as simply sliding into his destiny resignedly from frustration to frustration. Marlowe took over a primitive allegorical device from the old moralities to project this existential choice of Faust's into concrete, visible action upon the stage; Faust's Good Angel appears on one side of him, warning him against the pursuit of magic, while on the other side his Bad Angel encourages him in it, and it is the Bad Angel whose advice he follows. This feature in Marlowe's drama recurs regularly in the German Faust puppet-plays and must have been known to Goethe from them. It was not, of course, a device that he could use unmodified in his own Faust drama, which was evidently conceived from the first not on orthodox Christian, but on pantheistic lines, in keeping with the bent of his own mind since 1771 and with the dominant tendency amongst the advanced minds of his generation, and in which Faust was not unambiguously to choose "evil" as such. But some sort of corresponding existential choice Goethe's Faust too had, *mutatis mutandis*, to make, and the possibility suggests itself that the sign of the Makrokosmus and the Geist der Erde may be so to speak pantheistic equivalents or substitutes for the Christian Good and Bad Angels of the Marlovian tradition or may at least fulfil a similar dramatic function; that the pantheistic principle may have been duplicated here, in order that Faust may be faced with two alternatives to choose between. This can, however, only be so, if there is some fundamental *qualitative* difference between the two, compared with which their merely *quantitative* difference in magnitude and cosmic status counts for very little, so that Faust, in turning from the Makrokosmus to the Erdgeist, is not resigning himself and making the best of a bad job, but spontaneously and actively giving the preference to the Erdgeist and deciding in favour of it, in fact making the momentous existential choice which is to be expected of him. We should remember here that Goethe had by October, 1771, already largely emancipated himself from traditional morality; for he wrote in that month, in his "Speech for Shakespeare's Day": "What we call evil is only the other side of good." It is therefore out of the question that the Makrokosmus should be simply "good" and the Erdgeist simply "evil"; but there may nevertheless be a qualitative antithesis between them corresponding at a considerable remove and in an emancipated, heterodox way to the primitive old antithesis of good and evil. Are there any legitimate grounds for regarding the Erdgeist not indeed as an Evil Spirit in the traditional sense of the word, but still as sinister, ambivalent, ruthless and dangerous, so that in turning to it Faust is taking an imprudent, temerarious, ominous, reprehensible step, as he would not be doing, if he adhered to the Makrokosmus instead? * * *

The best point of departure in investigating these problems is the passage in which Faust turns away from the Sign of the Makrokosmus and addresses himself to the Erdgeist. This is indeed the key passage of the entire invocation scene, the pivotal point on which everything else turns * * *. Faust breaks off his contemplation of the Sign of the Makrokosmus with the words:

> What glorious show! Yet but a show, alas!
> How, boundless Nature, seize you in my clasp?
> You breasts where, all life's sources twain,
> Both heaven and earth are pressed,
> Where thrusts itself my shriveled breast,
> You brim, you quench, yet I must thirst in vain?

> [*Moodily he turns up another page and perceives the sign of the* EARTH SPIRIT.]

> Not so this sign affects my soul, not so!
> You, Spirit of the Earth, are nigher,
> I sense my powers rising higher,
> Already with new wine I am aglow. [lines 454–63]

There is nothing to be detected in these verses of that resigned acceptance of a second best, which they are commonly interpreted as expressing, nor does Faust anywhere in the course of them suggest that the Sign of the Makrokosmus is too mighty for him. All he says is that it cannot give him what he desires, and that he must therefore seek that elsewhere. What it can give him is a "show," by which we are here to understand a purely spiritual, inward vision, and that spectacle Faust has received to the full in his contemplation of it. There is no suggestion that it could have given anything else or anything more, if Faust had been mightier than he is. He has exhausted its possibilities and turns away from it not resignedly, but "angrily." It is not Faust who proves unequal to the Sign of the Makrokosmus and is rejected by it; on the contrary, the Sign of the Makrokosmus proves unequal to Faust and is rejected by him. Beautiful though the inward vision that it affords him is, it still does not give him that intimate, sensuous, tactile union with the overflowing breasts of "boundless Nature" after which he yearns. It is important to note here that the question is throughout only of the Sign of the Makrokosmus, not of the Markokosmus itself or of a Spirit of the Makrokosmus. There is no indication that the spiritual principle embodied in the Sign of the Makrokosmus could have manifested itself in any other more palpable and objective way than in Faust's inward vision, which is nothing less than a kind of *unio mystica*,[2] such as the contemplative ascetics experience. The way of the ascetic, who austerely renounces all sensual gratification, all entanglement in the particular and many, in order to devote himself to undistracted contemplation of the One-and-All, is open to Faust if he chooses to take it, but he does not choose to do so. To be so strongly endowed with the inward, visionary gifts of the mystic as Faust proves himself to be in his contemplation of the Sign of the Makrokosmus is to have, in some measure at least, a vocation to the ascetic life; and then to resolve in spite of that to plunge quite unrestrainedly into the rough-and-tumble of worldly existence, as Faust does when he turns to the Erdgeist, is to fly in the face of that partial vocation and to ask for trouble. Faust can only do this because he feels an equally strong or rather an even stronger urge or "vocation" (if one may call it that) to the worldly life with its excitement, adventures, and sensual gratifications. Faust is in fact torn between these two urges or vocations, the one spiritual and ascetic, the other worldly and sensual. Or as Goethe was to formulate it later in much quoted words, "Two souls . . . are dwelling in [his] breast" [line 1112], and it is to the loftier of these two souls that the Sign of the Makrokosmus, to the lower that the Erdgeist appeals. Here at the outset, in turning to the Erdgeist, he decides in favour of the worldly, sensual side of his nature. When the Spirit appears Faust does indeed prove unequal to it and is rejected by it, but that is almost the exact opposite of the experience that he had gone through with the Sign of the Makrokosmus.

* * *

There is one fairly obvious contrast between the Sign of the Makrokosmus and the Erdgeist which has often been pointed out * * * and is widely acknowledged: the former embodies the principle of contemplation and evokes the contemplative element in Faust's nature, the latter embodies the principle of activity and evokes the active element in Faust's nature. In fact, we see under these symbols the *vita contemplativa* confronted with the *vita activa* * * *. Goethe and most of his eminent contemporaries, particularly Fichte,[3] return again and again to this theme, insisting almost unanimously on the higher value of action as against a contemplative attitude towards existence. This is indeed a central theme of Goethe's Faust drama, for his Faust only is Faust in so far as he is a man of action in the sense of being committed to the principle of activity. But he has first to become a man of action, and only in doing so does he really become Faust in the essential meaning of the name. Previously, throughout his long years spent amongst books as a scholar and professor, he has led a contemplative life, and it is in the opening monologue, above all in the passage now

2. The medieval Christian mystical doctrine of spiritual union with God.

3. Johann Gottlieb Fichte (1762–1814), German philosopher of idealism.

before us, where he decides in favour of the Erdgeist and against the Sign of the Makrokosmus, that he breaks violently with his past and his own former contemplative self, dedicating himself to the life of action that is the specifically Faustian mode of existence.
* * *

One of the grounds for regarding the Sign of the Makrokosmus as representing the contemplative principle is that, after initially arousing in Faust—much as the Sign of the Erdgeist does—an "enchantment [that] at the sight of this/Suffuses *every sense*" [lines 430–31], with a glowing, youthful feeling of life in all his nerves and veins, it almost at once tranquillizes this "tumult in [his] breast" [line 435] and suspends the activities of all his senses except that of sight, for which Goethe here employs the word specially associated in the German language with mystical contemplation and inward vision, "Schauen." This gives more point to the lament, "What glorious show [*Schauspiel*]! Yet but a show, alas!" [line 454] for the decisive component in the word *Schau-spiel* is also *Schauen*. Faust's vision of the Makrokosmus, which he thus dismisses as "ein Schauspiel nur," is characterized by perfect harmony, by the absence of all violence, effort, or suffering.

> How all one common weft contrives,
> Each in the other works and thrives!
> How heavenly forces rising and descending
> Pass golden ewers in exchange unending,
> On wings with blessing fragrant
> From Heaven the earth pervading,
> Fill all the world with harmonies vagrant! [lines 447–53]

A certain cool clarity distinguishes this vision, which, based in part on Jacob's Ladder, gives so to speak a bird's-eye view of the cosmic processes from some lofty and distant vantage-point, *sub specie aeternitatis*, far from the heat of the *mêlée* and the stress of the moment, where all agitation, striving and conflict no longer count in the timeless harmony of pure being, where the disorder of earthly, fleshly, human existence is overarched and counterpoised by a higher spiritual order analogous to that of Christian theism with its Heaven and angels. * * * Faust has here already found an answer, and in its own way a valid answer, to his question, "what it is that holds the world together at the innermost core?"—if he could accept it. But his will refuses to accept it, his nature is incapable of accepting it, and in this non-acceptance, which is equally determined by necessity and free choice, lies at once his greatness and what may be called his tragic guilt, his "hubris."

The Erdgeist embodies a vision of existence seen not from above and afar, but from close up and at the heart of the turmoil; not from the perspective of eternity, but from that of the moment, where passion, pleasure, and pain still assert themselves in full intensity, with nothing to mitigate or counteract them. It impresses itself not only on sight, in isolation the sense of distance, detachment and serenity, but upon the other senses too, above all that of touch, the sense of nearness, involvement and precipitancy. * * * Faust demands, instead of a "spectacle" for his eyes only, something that he can also "grasp," something that is "nearer" to him. He feels that he has found this in the Sign of the Erdgeist, which produces an effect upon him exactly opposed to that produced by the Sign of the Makrokosmus, intensifying his inner tumult instead of tranquillizing it, so that he cries:

> I feel emboldened now to venture forth,
> To bear the bliss, the sorrow of this earth,
> Do battle with its tempests breaking,
> Brave crunching shipwreck without quaking. [lines 464–67]

It is by uttering these words that Faust evokes the Erdgeist. They are not a formal magical incantation, but they have the efficacy of one, because they are so fully attuned to the Spirit's nature. "Give me an answer, if you hear" [line 429], Faust had called a little before to the spirits in general, and these are words which the Erdgeist must hear and answer. It makes its presence felt by causing the light of the moon and of Faust's lamp to be extinguished, and red rays to emanate from his head. A mysterious haze spreads in the room, a tremor descends from the vaulted ceiling and communicates itself to Faust's frame. All that remains for him to do, in order to make the already present Spirit manifest itself visibly, is to speak in undertones the incantatory formula given in the book, and this he does, "were [his] life at stake" [line 481]. That is the nearest he comes to practising magic in the conventional sense, and Goethe makes as little of it as possible. The Spirit itself sums up its essential character in a lyrical passage that is a pendant to Faust's Makrokosmus vision:

> In tides of living, in doing's storm,
> Up, down, I wave,
> Waft to and fro,
> Birth and grave,
> And endless flow,
> A changeful plaiting,
> Fiery begetting,
> Thus at Time's whirring loom I weave and warp
> And broider at the Godhead's living garb. [lines 501–9]

The insistence here is upon life, activity, movement, change, time, transiency, as opposed to the harmony, stability, and permanency of pure being which characterized the hymn to the Makrokosmus. Where the earlier vision had been static and serene, the later one is dynamic and turbulent. This is at once perceptible in the contrasted rhythmical character of the two passages. But for such terms as "all," "all the world," and the actual name "Makrokosmus" the earlier vision of nature permeated by celestial powers from above might almost be thought to presuppose the transcendental Creator-God of Christian tradition, rather than the immanent deity of pantheism, and certainly stands near to that tradition in spite of its impersonal character. No such doubts can arise about the deity whose very flesh, whose "living garb" is wrought by the Erdgeist at the humming loom of time.

The vision of the Makrokosmus leaves Faust no scope or incentive for the assertion of his own individuality: in face of such perfect harmony there is nothing for him to do but to remain absorbed in passive, depersonalized wonder and awe, as one who recognizes that anything splendid *he* might originate, aspire after, or perform has been forestalled by the divine cosmic order. The vision of the Erdgeist, on the other hand, arouses in him a maximum of individualistic energy and aspiration. * * *

* * * "The first vocation of Man is to be active," writes Goethe in *Wilhelm Meisters Lehrjahre*; and again: "The highest thing of all is the spirit which stirs us to activity." Many parallels to this sentiment could be cited from all phases of his development. The Erdgeist is "the spirit which stirs us to activity," and Faust's decision in favor of it is one which we can be sure Goethe sympathized with and approved of. He had himself, in his own way, come to a similar decision during his Strassburg years. There are difficulties indeed about the idea of Faust as a "man of action," since in practice he really performs comparatively little in the way of definite deeds. But he is dominated by a restless inner urge towards activity, for which Goethe regularly uses the word "striving"; that word, more than any other, sums up his specifically Faustian character. The important point that is not always taken into consideration here is, however, that Goethe sees in activity not only the first and highest vocation of man, but also something problematic. In his *Maxims and Reflections* he writes: "The doer is always without a conscience; no one has a conscience except he who contemplates"; and again: "Unconditional activity, of any kind whatsoever, leads in the long run to bankruptcy." He expresses these views even more forcibly in one of the drafts for *Poetry and Truth*: "There is a permanent nexus between the deed and remorse, between activity and care." Nor is this sense of the dangers of the active, self-assertive, individualistic principle confined to Goethe's middle and later years, as we might at first expect it to be. It is implied in the remarkable Storm and Stress definition of tragedy which he gives as early as October, 1771, when he says of Shakespeare: "all his plays turn upon that mysterious point where our individuality, the supposed freedom of our will, comes into conflict with the necessary course of the Whole." We may fairly assume that his own Faust drama was intended to turn upon this same "secret point." An individualism

that knows nothing of the grave dangers of individualism is only a vague, rhetorical gesture. We can legitimately recognise a certain analogy between the Sign of the Makrokosmus and the "necessary course of the whole," between the Erdgeist and "our individuality, the supposed freedom of our will." In so far as the Erdgeist embodies the principle of activity, it is indifferent to ethical distinctions and takes life and death in its stride. In choosing it Faust is inevitably estranging himself from his own conscience and heading sooner or later for "bankruptcy."

One way in which Goethe made it clear that there is something sinister about the Erdgeist was by a stage direction running: "A reddish flame flickers, the Spirit appears in the flame *in a repulsive form*." This revealing final phrase Goethe suppressed, however, in preparing the text of *Faust, ein Fragment* for publication in 1790. He retained indeed the words "appalling vision!" with which Faust reacts to the manifestation of the Spirit, but explicitly declared in a letter of June, 1819, to Graf Brühl, who was planning a stage production of *Faust I*, that the word "appalling" here was to be regarded only as expressing Faust's own feeling and not as describing the actual lineaments of the Spirit, and went on to say that "nothing grotesque and repulsive ought to appear here." In the same letter he said that he had himself thought of representing the Erdgeist on the stage by some kind of magic lantern device with the head of the Zeus Otricoli enlarged to gigantic proportions, and in a rough sketch of the Invocation scene made about 1811 he shows it with the magnified head of an Apollo. But these were the years in which he had grown out of touch with the original conception of the Erdgeist and would sometimes—for example in a scenario of November, 1812—refer to it simply as the "Weltgeist." For the understanding of that original conception the deleted phrase "in widerlicher Gestalt" is of considerable importance.

One of the chief clues to the true point of the Erdgeist is its actual name, which we have become used to and take for granted, but which was calculated to disconcert Goethe's contemporaries. The metaphysical and emotional associations of the word "earth" (*Erde*) are very different from those of the word "world" (*Welt*), and this distinction is very strongly felt in the German language. The conception of a Spirit of Earth was novel, paradoxical and startling; it could not be seen as simply identical with that of the World Spirit. It made a deep impression when it was first put before the reading public with the appearance of *Faust, ein Fragment* in 1790, and many writers took it over, each interpreting it in his own way. There was a tendency, most strikingly represented by Schiller and Novalis, to assume that the *Erdgeist* must be an evil spirit, undoubtedly because "earth" was symbolically associated with the baser side of human nature. This is closely connected with one of the most important connotations of the word "earth" and its derivatives, when it is thought of as standing for *this* world as opposed to any other world, particularly to the other world of Christian tradition, but also to the purely spiritual, "higher" world postulated by idealistic philosophy with its heroic ethical standards and its aesthetic doctrines of a beauty which is all harmony, tranquillity, nobility, dignity, and perfection. * * * The youthful Goethe was one of the most important initiators of this revolution in our attitude towards the earth and earthliness. He appears in his Storm and Stress years particularly as an ecstatic earth-worshipper, infecting many contemporaries with his chthonic sentiments and outraging others.

* * *

* * * It is likely that Goethe coined the name "Erdgeist," exactly as he coined so many other earth-compounds during the same years, and out of the same impulse, to give emphatic expression to his this-worldliness, and that it therefore had in its origins, unlike the Sign of the Makrokosmus, very much less to do with the cosmogonies and demonologies of the cabbalists than is universally assumed. The conceptions of the heavenly body, earth, as distinguished from the other heavenly bodies, and of the element of earth, as distinguished from the other three elements are, as we have seen, the only ones that could play any part in the old cabbalistic systems. But both these conceptions of earth are irrelevant to the essential character and purport of the Spirit that appears before Faust, and help us very little to a proper understanding of it. That Spirit would seem to stand rather for earth as opposed to "Heaven," that is to say for "This World" as opposed to the "Other World"—the Other World connoting here not only the specifically Christian Heaven, but also quite as much or perhaps even more the purely spiritual "higher" sphere beyond time and space postulated by idealistic philosophy.

* * *

At this point it becomes possible for us to recognize more clearly why Goethe duplicated the pantheistic principle in the opening scene of the *Urfaust*. There is nature pantheism and nature pantheism, and the kind of devotion to nature that had become current from the early years of the eighteenth century onward had been decidedly contemplative, high-minded and fastidious, tending to avoid any open breach with Christian theism or with traditional philosophical and religious ethics. The nature it was prepared to exalt was an idealized, moralized, humanized, and beautified nature, as distinguished from mere vulgar, physical, empirical nature, which it tended to look down upon or to hide from sight beneath a veil of humanitarianism and propriety. It was not with such an ethereal-ized and bowdlerized nature as this that Goethe wanted his Faust to enter into communion, but with nature as she really is, in all her ruthlessness and all her disconcerting aspects. Though unfortunately it does not come out as clearly as it was meant to do, that is the

point of the contemplation of the Sign of the Makrokosmus preceding the invocation of the Erdgeist. It was not just a matter of
Faust's seeking a pantheistic relationship to nature in a quite
unspecified way. That would, according to the postulates of the age,
have been a perfectly innocuous, indeed an unambiguously high-
minded thing to do, and Faust could have done it and still
remained a respectable professor; it would not have made a Faust of
him, not have involved him in companionship with the devil. It was
a matter of his deciding in favor of a particular conception of
nature, of a this-worldly and realistic, as opposed to an other-
worldly and idealistic way of seeing her. That is why the Spirit that
appears before him is not just the World Spirit of philosophical and
mystical tradition, but the Spirit of *Earth*, of *this*-worldliness, and it
is also why it appears "in appalling shape."

Goethe's *Faust* then, like all other great works of the world's literature, turns not upon some hypersubtle, abstract, and abstruse
metaphysical issue comprehensible only to professional philosophers, or upon some obscure, esoteric point of cabbalistic lore, but
upon one of the central problems of universal human nature, envisaged, admittedly, in the light of and in terms of the mentality of
Goethe's own age. It turns upon the antithesis between this-worldliness and other-worldliness, between realism and idealism, between
the dynamic and the static, between what Mephisto in his conversation with the young student calls "the golden tree of life [and]
gray theory." But though there can be no doubt that Goethe's own
sympathy when he wrote the *Urfaust* was with the this-worldly,
realistic principle, he was by no means undividedly committed to it;
even at that early stage he knew that there is much to be said for
the other side, and was at pains to indicate that both are justified
and necessary and cannot exist independently of one another, that
the relationship between them is ultimately not just one of blind
opposition, but of polarity. * * * The sheer poetic quality of the
Makrokosmus passage shows that there is in a way as much, or
almost as much of Goethe himself in it as there is in the Erdgeist
passage. * * * Later Goethe was to see in all existence a rhythmical alternation of such states of expansion and contraction, as in the
motion of the lungs and the heart.

* * *

From this it is only one step to recognizing that there is behind
Faust, in very rarified and trasmuted form, something of that primitive conflict between good and evil, which, however sophisticated
and emancipated we may be, still tends to interest us more and to
have more reality for us than all other conflicts. In this connexion
Goethe made an illuminating remark in one of his draft notes for
the seventh book *Poetry and Truth*: "The conflict between good
and evil cannot be represented aesthetically: for one must add
something to the evil principle and take something away from the

good principle, in order to bring them into equilibrium with one another." This is exactly what he himself has done in the opening scene of the *Urfaust* and does indeed in most of his major works. For although the Erdgeist is quite certainly not the principle of evil in an absolute sense, it is so relatively, by comparison with the Sign of the Makrokosmus. In order to establish between the two that parity or "equilibrium" which he needs for his aesthetic purposes, Goethe evokes the Sign of the Makrokosmus less amply, vividly, and circumstantially, with a marked *diminuendo*, the Erdgeist with far more sheer weight and in a prolonged, overpowering *crescendo*. It may not be a "good" spirit, but to make up for that it is a "great" and "glorious" one, which interests and excites us and spurs us on to audacious enterprises and ambitions, as the benign, orderly Sign of the Makrokosmus does not. Having chosen it, Faust finds out too late that he has after all chosen evil, for it gives him Mephisto as his companion.

* * *

As the incarnation of nature, the Erdgeist is essentially ambivalent. It appears to Faust "in a repulsive form," but remains in his memory as "glorious"; it rejects him with scorn, but it seems to him in retrospect to have "understood his heart and soul"; it overwhelms him with its supremacy, so that he recoils from it like "a fearful writhing worm" [line 498] and fails dismally in his efforts to assert himself as its equal, and yet he feels that, as "God's likeness" [line 515], he should be able to claim equality, perhaps even superiority to it, and cries: "Yet like—not even thee?" [line 517]. In this phrase, * * * Goethe is drawing on biblical tradition. It is not as an exceptional individual of genius, but simply as an ordinary human being, "made in God's likeness" [line 516], that Faust might fairly have been able to claim some ascendancy over the Erdgeist. But that claim resides above all in the acknowledgment of ethical responsibility, through which alone man distinguishes himself from nature, and Faust has forfeited it by venturing beyond the "limits of humanity" and trying to raise himself as a "superman" to the level of the spirits, that is to say, beyond good and evil. In aspiring above humanity he has sunk below it, and it is now too late for him to insist that he was "made in God's likeness." For the rest, the word, "I am Faust, your match, I am the same!" [line 500] and "Yet like—not even thee," with which Faust tries to brave out his humiliation, are no more legitimate, objective evidence as to the real stature and rank of the Erdgeist than Brutus' words, "Away, slight man!" are as to the real stature and rank of Cassius. There can be no doubt the immense superhuman dignity and power of the Erdgeist; it does quite certainly represent the whole of nature, envisaged from the this-worldy angle, and not just some obscure, minor, cabbalistic conception * * *. But it is ambivalent, as nature itself is. It has to be ambivalent, in order that it may serve so to speak as a liaison officer or intermediary between God and the Devil. For that is what Goethe needed it for. The same conception is found in his conversation of September 8, 1815, with Boisserée[4]: "Nature is an organ on which God plays, while the devil works the bellows."* * *

It is often maintained that the real reason why the Spirit rejects Faust is because he makes a grave mistake by responding to its revelation of its own being with the words:

> You who bestride the world from end to end,
> Spirit of deeds, how close I feel to thee! [lines 510–11]

* * * But such interpretations are too artificial. Faust's words do not betray any misunderstanding or underestimation of the Spirit. * * * The Spirit rejects Faust not because of any particular thing he says or does, but because of what he is, because of the entire situation. It is not a stickler for spiritual etiquette or terminological niceties. It sees that he is afraid and it sees through the spuriousness of his attempts to persuade it and himself that he has overcome his fear. It is too much for him, as it must be too much for any man or any superman.

When the Erdgeist vanishes, it cries to Faust: "Close to the Spirit you comprehend,/Not me" [lines 512–13]. In view of the distinctive way in which the word "spirit" is used throughout the scene, it is natural to assume that this phrase, "the spirit you comprehend," spoken itself by a Spirit, is not intended vaguely, non-committally, and metaphorically, but refers to some specific Spirit; and if so, the only Spirit it can reasonably be supposed to refer to is Mephistopheles. In fact these words seem to link up with Faust's declaration in the scene "Dreary Day. A Field" that Mephisto has been "chained to him as a depraved companion" by the "great and glorious Spirit." * * * Goethe's own text clearly enough indicates that this is just what we are intended to suppose. That he never managed to work the conception out and eventually abandoned it in favour of another quite different device for bringing Faust and Mephisto together is presumptive evidence that he himself had great difficulties with it. We need therefore not be surprised at its causing us difficulties too. But it is likely to have been on some such lines as these: The Erdgeist is indeed daemonic, ruthless, destructive, beyond good and evil, and consequently also sinister, but there is nothing base about it. It is not a person with a consciousness or a conscience or a sense of responsibility; it is nature, and does what it has to do in magnificent indifference. * * * In all its contradictions it still remains at one with itself. No human being can do this

4. Supliz Boisserée (1783–1854), who together with his brother Melchior (1786–1851) researched and collected old German and Dutch paintings, in particular those of the Middle Ages. The enthusiasm of the brothers greatly stimulated Goethe's own interest in German Medieval art and architecture. (See Goethe's letter to Boisserée, p. 413, above.)

or be this, not even a man of Faust's stature. There is always, at least potentially, a baser side to his nature, which will insinuate itself into and degrade his most heroic and generous aspirations beyond good and evil, causing them to end in disaster and shame. It is to this potential baser side of Faust's nature that Mephisto corresponds, and that is why he resembles Mephisto and can "grasp" him, as he cannot resemble or grasp the Erdgeist. Goethe himself, in a conversation with Eckermann of May 3, 1827, praised the acumen of Ampère[5] in having observed that there was much of his own nature in Mephisto as well as in Faust, and it can reasonably be maintained that Mephisto is indeed Faust's grosser *alter ego*, to whose visitation he has exposed himself by being able to invoke the Erdgeist, but unable to retain his hold upon it. Or one can conceive of it so, that the negative aspects of the Erdgeist, of this-worldliness and unconditional activity, have become embodied in Mephisto.

* * *

EMIL STAIGER

[On the "Great Lacuna" and the Pact Scene][†]

* * * The "great lacuna"[1] extends from line 606 through the second scene in the study beginning "And what to all of mankind is apportioned" [lines 1770 ff.], already contained in the *Fragment*. Here at last the pact between Faust and the devil had to be dealt with. But Goethe was in no hurry to do so. Neither in Frankfurt nor in Rome could he make the decision to compose this important section, and even now he seemed [in Weimar around 1800] to put off still further this unpleasant task. After being frightened away from the Earth Spirit, Faust should be ripe for Mephistopheles. To our amazement, however, the Easter chorus restores his balance. Consequently Goethe was obliged, during the Easter walk, to put him once again into that state of mind familiar to us from his first appearance. At this point Mephistopheles announces himself. But still the pact does not come about. For a second time Faust feels content. In a resigned yet peaceful manner, like St. Jerome in his cell,[2] Faust translates the New Testament; and the first scene in the study closes in a strangely inconclusive way. At this point Goethe planned the superfluous academic disputation, in which

5. Jean-Jacques Antoine Ampère (1800–1864), an important french Romantic critic, had written a review of Goethe's dramatic works which appeared on April 29 and May 20, 1826, in *Le Globe*.
† From *Goethe*, Vol. II (Atlantis Verlag: Zürich and Freiburg, 1956), pp. 334–56. Reprinted by permission of Atlantis Verlag. Translated by Dolores Sig-

nori and Cyrus Hamlin.
1. So called by Goethe in his letter to Schiller of April 4, 1801.
2. St. Jerome (340?–420), a Latin Biblical scholar and Doctor of the Church, responsible for the preparation of the Vulgate, who is often represented at work in his study or cell.

Faust, with his thesis of the creative mirror, presumably was for a third time to think himself into the right frame of mind. Not until the second study scene (or the third, if we consider "Night" to be a study scene) does the long-awaited central event of the legend take place. All this is remarkably inexpedient, confusing, and explicable only because Goethe did not want to approach the matter directly, as this motif above all caused the most serious difficulties. We shall attempt to demonstrate them. Before doing so, however, we must consider the intervening scenes, perhaps unnecessary and yet magnificent, beginning with the monologue which follows the Wagner scene and flows into the Easter choruses [lines 606–807].

Goethe is evidently trying to conform as closely as possible to the lines which he wrote decades earlier. By recapitulation he attempts to put himself back into that unhappy frame of mind. "I, made in God's likeness" [lines 515–16], "worm" [line 498], the "fumigated" [line 404] paper: these quotations are intended to blind us to the gap between the words of youthful ill-humor and those of the fifty-year-old. But this gap cannot be concealed. The following lines give it away already:

> That fleeting moment of high bliss,
> I felt myself so small, so great; [lines 626–27]

The moment has only just passed; "that," in a touchingly naive way, reveals the passage of a quarter-century. Then thoughts press forward which only a mature man experienced in life and work would be able to grasp. The hero of the *Urfaust* was intended to be an adult man; but he was not yet so. His excessive desires give the lie to his presumed age. Now a more suitable reason for dissatisfaction is granted him; the repetition of his protest against all the useless objects piled up in his study assumes a more appropriate form. In the *Urfaust* one can perceive only the impatience of a youth eager for a life in the open air, who wishes once and for all to be himself and to be free of all the burdens of tradition. Now arises the question of the nonsense as well as the sense of such tradition, the problem of how to appropriate and revive what is past; and into Faust's criticism of the alchemical instruments is incorporated Goethe's morphological views concerning the "open secret" [line 10093] of natural transformations.[3] But the following passage surprises us most of all:

> Where fancy in audacious flight expanded
> To the Eternal once its buoyant hope,
> Now it contents itself with little scope,
> As ship on ship in whirls of time is stranded.
> Deep in the heart, grey Care anon will settle,
> In secret plant her stinging nettle,

---

3. Staiger alludes to Mephistopheles' speech in Act IV about the war between the angels and the devils, which is couched in naturalistic geological terms.

With restless rocking spoil repose and joy,
Ever new masks for her disguise employ;
And be it wife and child or land and corn,
Be it knife, poison, fire or water,
At blows that never fall you falter,
And what you never lose, you must forever mourn.

[lines 640-51]

"Fancy" is the privilege of youth. In more mature years a free imagination is no less active, but then, as we are no longer disposed to believe in an endless future, since our sphere is fixed and filled with various riches, freedom is transformed to "Care," into presentiments of loss and premonitions of danger. Life's skies are darkened by the demonic force against which Goethe already struggled in *Egmont*,[4] which he tried to outwit by silence and to endure with patience and courage, yet which he could never conquer, the demon which will later breathe upon the face of the hundred-year-old Faust and threaten him in his final moments—it is the darker side of man's poetic power, the price we pay for our most unique and exalted gift.

Such torments do not stem from an inappropriate demand. They are bound in with the eternally established limits of humanity and are therefore, at times, reason enough for wanting to put an end to life. The Faust of Chamisso[5] (1803) commits suicide in a similar situation; the ringing of the bells and the chorus of angels hold Goethe's magus back. Some have maintained that Mephistopheles causes the heavenly music to resound, but such a thought is absurd. Naturally he knows that Faust has "left untasted/A certain brownish elixir" [lines 1579-80]. Yet what he knows he need not have himself assisted with. On a later occasion he boasts:

And but for me you would have long
On tiptoes left this vale of tears. [lines 3270-71]

These lines are, however, already contained in the *Fragment* of 1790, and can refer only to the "Witch's Kitchen," not to the Easter night, which could scarcely have been anticipated then.

Angels sing; that suffices. The women and disciples join in. It would be narrow-minded to ask whether we are to think of real angels or of a concert in a church, and, if they are real angels, how then it is possible that Faust does not believe the holy message. What happens at this point is no other than a particularly magnificent example of that procedure which we encounter time and again at decisive points in Goethe's work: the rebirth, the renewal of life out of the depths of its origin. Above and beyond all the doubt and

4. In Goethe's play *Egmont* (1788), in a conversation with his secretary (Act II) the hero speaks of "invisible spirits" who steer the carriage of destiny drawn by the horses of time in which each individual rides. Goethe later cited this passage in reference to his own destiny at the end of his autobiography, *Poetry and Truth*.
5. Adelbert von Chamisso (1781-1838) attempted a dramatization of Faust in 1803.

impasses of logical thought triumphs an understanding of the whole, which is inexplicable and beyond proof, a knowledge which is beyond reason and which mocks all sense of tragic consequence. * * * It is based on forgetting. To forget that which we have achieved late and in full consciousness strengthens the recollection of a happiness in which we could not yet distinguish ourselves as individuals from that eternal force which the Easter chorus calls the "urge to become" [*Werdelust*, line 789]. This recollection may extend back to an original condition, to a state which is simultaneously an embracing and a being embraced,[6] which terminates with the mind's awakening. Similar recollections of childhood and youth are familiar to everyone, above all to Goethe, for whom the comfort of having been hidden in the womb was never exhausted during his lifetime.

Such a cure is now experienced by Faust. It is expressly stated that this cure does not stem from belief in the dogma of Christ's resurrection, which for Goethe, too, had no meaning. Of supreme significance, however, are the flattering insinuations of youthful, religious feelings, the childlike inner fervor which triumphs over all care, in the blissfully self-transcending rhymes of the choruses of angels, women and disciples. And it is highly significant that this wonder is brought about by a song of Easter, the springtime festival of renewal, of eternal life risen out of the grave of winter.

Faust's entanglement with death is resolved in genuinely Goethean fashion. Yet we have thereby been diverted from the poem's immediate aim. In the "Easter Walk," Faust's inner receptivity for the pact with Mephistopheles must be reestablished. Goethe begins with a picture of bourgeois springtime cheerfulness. Good form in commentaries on *Faust* demands that one belabor its philistine characteristics: the rather silly banter of the girls, the students, and the soldiers, the pomposity of the citizens and their complacency, which is only intensified by distant rumors of war. This ambience of course only serves as a foil for Faust in his lonely struggle and thus is denied all greatness and all more serious controversy. Yet no satirical tone may be perceived, at the most a faint irony which is still friendly, indeed animated by a sense of genuine pleasure. * * *

With the same stroke the poet acquaints us with the milieu in which Gretchen's tragedy will take place. Among the townspeople there are also doubtless girls like Bärbelchen, Lieschen, and Gretchen to be found. On St. Andrew's Eve one of them saw her future lover in person.[7] According to a note by Goethe, this was supposed to happen to Gretchen. The brisk song of the soldiers also prepares us for Valentine.

As it fades away in the distance, Faust and Wagner come on-

6. Staiger here alludes to a phrase from Goethe's hymn "Ganymed," line 29, in which the individual soul embraces the all and is simultaneously embraced by it.
7. See note to line 878 of *Faust*.

stage. Wagner is still the ridiculous scholarly pedant, but nevertheless a bit elevated; Faust is satisfied and in a tender mood due to the echoes of the blissful Easter song. He can understand that joy which abandons itself equally to large and small things, and he sums up the crowd's feeling in the following words: "Here I am Man,—and free to be!" [line 940]. Coming from him this probably means that, even as a great scholar, he recognizes the fulfillment of human nature in pleasure and joy, in the harmony of a merry heart and the cheerfulness of nature; and only to this extent does he not act completely out of character when he silently excludes himself and remains alone in the midst of admiring farmers and townsfolk. This loneliness is made emphatic in his account of his deeds as a medical doctor. Goethe appears once again to lose sight of the plot. He depicts recollections of his youth, which are the same as those contained in the eighth book of Goethe's *Poetry and Truth*. Of course, he could not have made better use of them anywhere but here; they are, however, inappropriate insofar as Faust himself now presents the practice of alchemy as fraudulent and thereby once again accidentally speaks the mind of the older poet. Yet what do such reservations matter when, immediately afterward, he begins his marvelous speech of longing:

> Observe how in the flaming evening sun
> Those green-embowered cabins glitter.
> He yields and sinks, the day is lived and done,
> He hastes beyond, new life to breed and nourish.
> Oh, that I have no buoyant wings to flourish,
> To strive and follow, on and on! [lines 1070–75]

These lines are directed to the desire, "Why, if a magic cape were only mine" [line 1122], which is occasioned by Wagner's warning; this in turn prepares us for the appearance of the poodle. We are to understand that Faust's supernatural craving attracts Mephistopheles. Already in the "Prologue in Heaven" the devil rejoices at the foolishness of wanting to enjoy at once what is close at hand and what is distant. He now perceives the same desire in Faust, who speaks of having two souls, one of which clings to the earth while the other attempts to flee to "fields of lofty forebears" [line 1117], the "silver shapes of an anterior age" [line 3238], as they are called in "Forest and Cave," in which we are confronted by the pure spirit, cleansed of the transient. To that extent the Easter walk, of course, leads once again to the thought which in the *Urfaust* is already indicated by the comparison of the Macrocosmos and the Earth Spirit. Yet how much more humane and mild are the forms the conflict now assumes, just when it is to be felt more strongly than ever before. Faust no longer believes himself pursued by a unique curse. "It is innate in us all" [line 1092] to see oneself thus projected as he does. He stands at evening in the German landscape as Goethe once did at the edge of the sea, when a frigate in full sail "passed between Capri and Cape Minerva and finally disappeared. If a man were to watch a loved one sail away in this fashion, he would die of longing."[8] Such longing is scarcely expressed during the 1790s; it is not productive for his Classical style. Yet *Faust*, which does not belong to that style, provides free access for it. Now it can stream forth uninhibitedly, yet is so blissful in itself, so full of melodic delight, that Faust has no reason to doubt and to deplore his instincts. It is astonishing that, as in the angelic chorus, what is close at hand does not get lost in what is distant, that not the mortal eye, to be sure, but the power of fantasy preserves within a boundless expanse the feeling for all things, with "each hill ablaze" [line 1078], "golden rivers" [line 1079], and the "sun-warmed bays" [line 1682], the eagle, the crane, plains and seas. * * * A soul open to the infinite transforms in its exaltation the expansive multiplicity of nature into music. * * * Beauty's gentle pain—the poignant sense that only what is limited can be beautiful —breaks through at this point; here for once beauty is affirmed as an element of earthly things a boundless inner feeling, a stream of emotions which flows into eternity.

Such an interpretation is hard to reconcile with the intention of the scene, which is to introduce Mephistopheles. Yet time and again in *Faust* we find ourselves faced with choosing whether to maintain a view of the whole and to deal with particulars, either carelessly or ruthlessly, so that they are accommodated to the whole, or to immerse ourselves affectionately in each episode and then acknowledge that it does not precisely fit into the plan of the whole. Dissonances of structure do not disturb us because most of the individual episodes are so beautiful. Every reader, however, is capable of comprehending aesthetically the verse and the thought, motif and rhythm, as discrete entities and can only truly penetrate the separate parts. Reason, which persuaded the poet to ignore several contradictions and which since then has achieved the cheapest triumphs in *Faust* scholarship, is always ready to reassure us about the whole. With regard to this scene it would argue that Faust has again been presumptuous and has thus attracted the skeptical, negating spirit [of Mephistopheles], who does not hesitate to appear and to "weave" around the travellers "some future bondage, thread by stealthy thread" [lines 1158–59]. Since Goethe himself apparently wants to be understood in this way, no other way remains open to us. But an injustice would thereby be committed to the sublimity of lines 1070–99; and not until Faust's reply to Wagner's objection, not until Faust's call to the spirits of the air, do we recall the event which has been due for so long. The scene closes on a slightly parodic note with the leaps of the poodle and Wagner's unknowingly wise remarks; once again we approach the tone of the puppet play.

8. From the *Italian Journey*, March 3, 1787.

This tone dominates throughout the following scene, "Study I," which has more of a historical flavor than any other and which may be regarded as a burdensome task mastered brilliantly. The peaceful evening mood at the outset, and Faust's translation from the Bible (which recalls his historical proximity to Luther) has often been interpreted as an important stage of his development. We cannot share this opinion. Only one thing matters here, to present the transformation of the poodle into Mephistopheles in the most effective, balladesque manner, suitable to the substance of the legend and in the style of popular theater.

> Then reason reasserts its forces,
> New hope begins to stir and flow;
> One yearns again to trace life's courses,
> Alas—life's springs one yearns to know. [lines 1198–1201]

This is a staged feeling, not at all derived from the depths of the heart. The unusual use of the word "one," reminiscent of lyrics of the Enlightenment, has a chilly effect. And the metrical counterpoint is worked out almost too clearly. The exegesis of the Logos from the Gospel of John could also be considered simply an allusion to the Earth Spirit regarded as the "genuis of the world and deeds."[9] Yet the thought is not developed. It suffices here that the Bible incites the dog to bark and howl. The conjuring ceremony rightly takes shape as a mock-solemn prank. We are reminded that the time was not long past when a single cry of "Faust" would cause the German theater public to laugh. A light, atavistic horror is nevertheless brought to bear as well. If there are interpreters who even here wish to belabor profundities, we acknowledge them cheerfully. It goes without saying that each line is determined by magical tradition. But what does it matter, since Goethe handles these symbols with apparent gallows humor, without bothering about the meaning since it had palled on him decades ago? Consistent with the established model of all broad farce in poetry, the inappropriate seriousness is gradually intensified. The artistic device of requiring the actors to narrate what happens on stage, an epic technique already used in the "Zauberlehrling,"[1] contributes its share to setting the scene with the greatest visual effectiveness. The poodle swells into a hippopotamus, into an elephant, and fills the room. The symbol of Christ and even, very nearly, the flowing light of the Trinity are incorporated into the farce. The tension suddenly snaps. Mephistopheles steps forth from behind the oven as a travelling scholar and says, "Why all the fuss? What's milord's pleasure, pray?" [line 1322]. This sentence alone cancels out all the magical-religious excitement. The devil is not so terrifying as pious belief would picture him. He can be talked to; he is polite enough to

---

9. See the "*Faust* Plan of 1800," above, and the essay by Wolfgang Binder, below.

1. "The Sorcerer's Apprentice," a ballad written by Goethe in 1797.

appear before the professor as a subordinate academic. We return from the mystery play, which has been put on for our entertainment, to the stage of the worldly and the human.

And so Mephistopheles is finally there, confronted by the man on whom he places his hopes. For the moment, however, he is content to offer a modest self-portrait. He introduces himself as a nihilist, as part of the original darkness, as the enemy of the living and of the light. Again we do not feel called upon to investigate the background of these demonological speeches. In the "spirit which perpetually denies" [line 1338] which after the "Prologue in Heaven" has to "play the Deuce, to stir, and to entice" [line 343], everything important to Goethe in 1800 is summed up. The mythical-magical elements provided only welcome coloring.

But with that the magic show is over. With a considerable expense of "commanded poesy" Goethe has paid his initial unavoidable debt to the legend. Now once again he takes a breather and lets the devil depart without even looking for a valid reason. Is Faust at the moment too composed for Mephistopheles to dare submit his plan to him? Why then did Goethe not draft the scene differently from the outset? Faust has spoken of a pact. Does Mephisto first have to ask Lucifer for full authority as in Marlowe's play? Here there *is* no longer any Lucifer. Goethe may have preserved the interruption in order to secure space for the disputation. That could well be the most valid explanation. But it too only affirms that the crucial scene is postponed yet longer. In any case we find our expectations once again deceived, but, as so often, we are compensated with princely generosity: the spirits which Mephisto conjures up to sing Faust to sleep begin a song filled with imagery and which has an indescribably pleasing sound. One hardly dares marvel at this song, since it occurs in the context of frivolous tricks of the devil. And Goethe could well have intended a certain restraint. The decorative and flattering effect of the rhymes is carried to the farthest extreme. Erotic and Bacchantic colors play together in a confusing manner. * * * The song of the spirits retains a totally un-Classical, operatic magic, but on the other hand, it is also strangely spiritualized:

> . . . the arbor
> Where thought-rapt lover
> Lifelong trusting
> Pledges to lover. [lines 1466–69]

"Thought-rapt lover"—how heavy with meaning the phantasmagoria seems to become with these words.

> Heavenly offspring's
> Graces uplifting,
> Swaying and turning,
> Drifting they wander, [lines 1457–60]

At this point hints of Goethe's late style may already be per-ceived, in which both sensuous and spiritual elements are intensified so that classical fusion gives way to a highly characteristic tension between enchantment and significance. If the chorus of spirits was included on its own among Goethe's poems, it would long ago have come to be treasured as a magnificent lyric. As it stands, there is an odious Mephistophelian tone about it; and Goethe himself would not wish it to ensnare us all too much.

Now finally the *second "Study" scene!* We already know that with the line, "And what to all of mankind is apportioned" [line 1770], Goethe makes the connection with the *Fragment* of 1790, and we should not therefore be surprised if what follows does not seem to be from the same mold. Still other passages present prob-lems. The scene begins so abruptly and the conversation attains a peak of such passionate misery so quickly that it is difficult for us to accept the fact that Faust is seeing Mephisto again for the first time since, as he believes, "in a cheating dream the Devil has intruded" [line 1528]. The chorus of spirits is also strange. From its subject matter we can surmise only a plaintive, admonishing commentary on Faust's curse by the poet. Mephistopheles, however, claims the "little ones" as "his own" and glosses their speech with a meaning contrary to the wording. Is he lying? Something is not right. For after the words "they bid you aspire" [line 1634] he carries on in an entirely different key without any transition. Indeed earlier edi-tions at this point leave a space for a line in between. Thus several points suggest that the central scene is laborously assembled from various fragments. It provides considerable difficulty for interpreta-tion.

At last, then, Goethe steers ahead full sail toward that state of mind in Faust, so unwelcome and so often avoided and yet abso-lutely necessary for the contract with Mephistopheles. We are brought back to the stage of the second monologue. Again it is a question of establishing despair in a more credibly human manner. "Abstain! it calls, thou shalt abstain" [line 1549]. * * *

> The god who dwells within my breast
> Can stir me to the inmost kernel;
> Enthroned, of powers beyond all mine possessed,
> He cannot alter anything external. [lines 1566–69]

That points back to the Easter walk:

> To spirit wings will scarce be joined, alas,
> Corporeal wings wherewith to fly. [lines 1090–91]

The breadth of the spirit, the constriction of the body—it is the old Faustian song. Yet this time it will not fade away in mild resig-nation. It builds up to the grandiose curse against man's exalted self-consciousness, the splendor of his appearance, his dreams, his fame, his possessions and every kind of pleasure, against hope, faith and patience. This is no virtuoso performance. * * * It is the denial of the whole, something of which only that man is capable who really has grasped the whole. And thus the time for Mephisto's offer has arrived. The words are spoken which every reader of a Faust poem expects:

> I shall be at your service by this bond
> Without relief or respite here on earth;
> And if and when we meet again beyond,
> You are to give me equal worth. [lines 1656–59]

At this point all the problems appear once again to have arisen which we believed to have been already settled in the "Prologue in Heaven." In each scene there is talk of Faust's eternal damnation. This cannot be denied, but the question remains as to how seriously it is to be taken. On the twenty-third of June 1797 Schiller wrote to Goethe, "The demands on *Faust* are both philosophical and poetical."[2] The poetic and philosophical demands here come into conflict. The proposal which Mephistopheles makes is poetic, and in the spirit of the tradition, and may not be evaded in this form. The meaning which Goethe gives to the tradition is philosophical, but is *suspended* in mid-air and can have no decisive consequences. And indeed it has no consequences. Faust, to be sure, does not deny the afterlife; yet he does not worry about it, just as Goethe himself worried little about it at the turn of the century. It is conceivable that the ritual would nonetheless be carried out according to the legend and that Faust, agreeing with the devil's offer, would be solemnly committed to the pact. Yet not even this occurs. No pact whatsoever is concluded. Goethe has paid his compliment to the legacy of tradition and does not revert to it again. Mephisto extols his arts. Faust has doubts about their desirability. He too is firmly convinced of the transitoriness of all earthly pleasures, but nevertheless he declares himself ready to sacrifice his better self for this transitory pleasure, which has begun to disappear at the very moment it is enjoyed [lines 1675–87]. To such an extent is his past existence a "burden" [line 1570] for him. Mephisto regards him mockingly, promises him complete satisfaction and thereby provokes him to the decision to attempt it on a trial basis. The pact is replaced by a wager.

With this new idea the difficulties of the legend are resolved; now one can almost tell what Goethe means to say. But what does the wager consist of? The well-known lines read:

FAUST. Should ever I take ease upon a bed of leisure,
  May the same moment mark my end!
  When first by flattery you lull me
  Into a smug complacency,
  When with indulgence you can gull me,

2. See Schiller's letter to Goethe, p. 408, above.

Let that day be the last for me!
This is my wager!
MEPHISTOPHELES. Done!
FAUST.   And beat for beat!
If the swift moment I entreat:
Tarry a while! you are so fair!
Then forge the shackles to my feet,
Then I will gladly perish there!
Then let them toll the passing-bell,
Then of your servitude be free,
The clock may stop, its hands fall still,
And time be over then for me!
MEPHISTOPHELES. Reflect upon it—we shall not forget it.
[lines 1692–1707]

In dramatic terms it may be understood that Faust holds out his
hand with the words "This is my wager", Mephistopheles seizes it
—"Done!"—and Faust, with the words "And beat for beat," places
his left hand on top of Mephistopheles' right, Mephisto's left follows, and not until "Reflect upon it" do Mephisto and Faust release
their hands. Faust's entire speech, therefore, is included in the
wager.

The key word, "moment," is spoken, * * * a concept which
strikes the essence of Goethe's concern in the period after his Italian journey, the peak of his career. And even in the poem "Legacy"
(1829) one still reads:

> Enjoy with moderation its fullness and blessing;
> Let reason be ever present
> Where life takes delight in life.
> At such times the past lives on,
> And the future lives in anticipation,
> And the moment is eternity.

The word preserves its import in Goethe's last years. We cannot
believe that in *Faust* he used it only by chance, unconscious of its
full significance. Then the point lies precisely in the fact that Faust
himself is excluded from knowing the high and noble meaning of
the concept. In that "moment" which *he* has in mind the past has
no permanence and the future has no preceding existence. He does
not speak of organic time, * * * of time in which each individual
moment is at once means and end, and in which incessant progress
and self-contained repose are united in the concept of a phase:
Faust's moment is the kind which does not pass. A noble person
may and should allow himself to exploit such a moment, to take
such a risk with Mephisto. If only this did not cause such an important misunderstanding! For as the wager is formulated, Faust condemns not only the "bed of leisure," but also that happiness which,
according to the unforgettable words in Goethe's study of Winckelmann,[3] alone compensates for the entire, overwhelming extrava-

---

3. *Winckelmann   and   His   Century*   the famous art historian of the mid-
(1805), an appreciation by Goethe of   eighteenth century.

gance of the universe. "To please oneself" is not objectionable; and it is only natural—even if hopeless—to say to each transcendent moment and to each meaningful stage of life: "Tarry a while! you are so fair!" [line 1700]. "For what purpose"—thus we read in the chapter "Antiquity" of the Winckelmann essay—"what purpose has the entire extravagance of suns and planets and moons, of stars and the Milky Way, of comets and cloud patches, of worlds realized and being realized, if ultimately a happy man does not unconsciously rejoice at his existence?"

The enormous ambiguity of the wager thereby becomes clear to us. Goethe succeeded in his person, in his life, and in his work in uniting, within a higher existence embracing all contraries, the presence of antiquity at rest within itself with the resoluteness of the Christian world, the sphere of nature with the straight lines of progress. * * *

How different is Faust! His greatness lies in the fact that he never shuns the incessant progress of the intellect; his fate, in the fact that as a mental traveler he is never content with himself and does not know happiness and peace at any point along the way. If he were to attain Goethean maturity, he would win and lose the wager at the same time. He wins, if one is prepared to understand the word "moment" as the insignificant present. To this moment he will never say: "Tarry a while! you are so fair!" [line 1700]. He loses, if "moment" is to be considered in the broader sense. Correspondingly he will be half right and half wrong if during his lifetime he never attains a more exalted insight and persists, disgruntled, in abusing every moment, no matter what it is.

Goethe's letter to Schubarth supports this interpretation of the wager. Schubarth had surmised that the knot of the action was "tied to such an extent that, while Mephistopheles wins his wager, Faust at the same time must approach clarity." Goethe answered on November 3, 1820: "You have sensed the outcome correctly. Mephistopheles can only half win his wager, and if half the blame falls on Faust, then the old gent's [line 350] right to pardon can step right in to achieve a most cheerful conclusion to the play."

* * * As a rule, the broader German public emphasizes Faust's greatness and believes his restless advance to be generally admirable. The whole tradition of the "Faustian man" is founded upon this opinion; and, during the last century, officious people were never at a loss for a Faust quotation, whenever it was needed to celebrate incessant endeavor, striving and accomplishment. Faust became the hero of the Bismarck era, the symbol of the German soul. Certainly even Goethe would have made little objection to that. Yet, as he had done once before, he would again have distanced himself from his hero, like the Lord in the "Prologue in Heaven," recognizing his striving as naturally and spiritually justifiable behavior, but on the other hand condemning his eternal unrest, his curse upon every

kind of happiness and fulfillment, as inhuman pathos, as tragic madness.

Stylistic criticism of the work is intimately connected with such problems. The hazy and foggy path of nordic fancy here, the doggerel, the operatic or balladesque rhyme, dispenses, as does Faust himself, with a full awareness of the present. This too is "German," and Goethe with overwhelming success allows it as appropriate to the meaning of the work, showing a mastery and freedom by which we can truly measure how much he too is a born "German" and is exposed to all "German" temptations. Yet always alert is his knowledge (indeed more than knowledge, a feeling housed in the depths of his heart) that life like art misses its highest goal and an injustice is done to nature and to man, that only through restraint and renunciation can the Yes blossom for that whole which expects from us and grants to us the "font of living grace" [line 345]. Thus the peevish comments in Goethe's letters and those ironic evasions which so estrange many readers are no less genuine than the more gloomy and rash adventures of the spirit and of unfettered poesy. Here we confront Goethe's infinitely delicate and highly complicated mode of being and must not submit to the temptation to gloss over the contrasting colors of the picture for the sake of an aesthetic or intellectual consistency which we are inclined to presuppose in the poetry.

The wager is concluded. In order to disguise the absence of the pact and to satisfy the poetic demand for such a pact with the devil, Mephistopheles has to ask Faust for a few lines written in blood. What they contain we do not learn. It appears as if a prepared paper were laid before Faust. Yet this cannot be the case, as the conversation has taken an unexpected turn. We shall not enlarge upon the matter. It is theater, "hocus-pocus" [line 1739], as Faust himself says, and as Goethe on similar occasions also used to say. A few lines are added in which Faust once again acknowledges his fierce intention of becoming base and of pandering to sensual pleasures, untroubled by the sufferings which grow out of the unlimited intensification of burning passions. So it continues to the break between lines 1768 and 1769:

> Henceforth my soul, for knowledge crazed no more,
> Against no kind of suffering shall be cautioned.

These lines are still spoken in the spirit of the wager, or rather are consistent with the wording of the wager, but they are consistent, also, with the two rhymed lines which follow immediately and which, like the rest of the scene, had been contained in the *Fragment* of 1790 and, by their completely different train of thought, turn us back twenty years in Goethe's development.

> And what to all of mankind is apportioned
> I mean to savor in my own self's core,

> Grasp with my mind both highest and most low,
> Weigh down my spirit with their weal and woe,
> And thus my selfhood to their own distend,
> And be, as they are, shattered in the end. [lines 1770–75]

Here there is no longer talk of despairing self-abasement. Here speaks a Faust who wants to gather within his person everything that the human race has ever felt and thought and who wants to "enjoy" what is highest and deepest. "Enjoyment" forms yet another contrast to mere knowing, yet no longer in the sense of "common enjoyment," but rather, just the opposite, in the sense of "most intensive experience." * * *

Those who stress the unity of *Faust* maintain that this is a characteristic change. As happens again and again, here, too, better qualities prevail in Faust, much to the annoyance and embarrassment of Mephisto. Yet this interpretation cannot be maintained. Too many passages speak to the contrary. It no longer at all appears as though something had already been arranged. Mephisto once again attempts to excite Faust to make an excursion into the world. Faust, as if he had not long ago declared his willingness, poses the naive question, "How do we set about it?" [line 1834]. And in the concluding monologue Mephisto reveals a program which runs directly counter to all the arrangments just made. The wager is laid out with a view to Faust's attaining peace through enjoyment. Now the devil cannot rest until he prevents his own success:

> Through dissipation I will drag him,
> Through shallow insignificance,
> I'll have him sticking, writhing, flagging,
> And for his parched incontinence
> Have food and drink suspended at lip level;
> In vain will he be yearning for relief,
> And had he not surrendered to the devil,
> He still must needs have come to grief! [lines 1860–67]

The sophistical turns of phrase, which are resorted to even here, are familiar to us. The alliance has been a trap. Faust's soul is lost precisely at the moment he wins the wager. The following line (1855) refers to this: "And I shall have you dead to rights."

"Dead to rights" means, to be sure, without having to fulfil the condition of the contract. Other excuses have also been looked for. There is no end to scholarly conjecture and quibbling. Yet each explanation that helps with one problem embroils us in countless new contradictions. Nothing remains but to admit: In a house which was constructed according to a later rejected design, here is another small wing left standing, evidently for the sole reason that Goethe did not want to revise the lines already printed. It is not difficult to locate the earlier plan in the context of the drama's inner development. Faust would like to win "mankind's loftiest plane" [line 1804]. He is a man of the same sort as Prometheus, Mahomet and Caesar, a Titan in the style of the *Sturm und Drang*. Even before moving to Weimar, Goethe was critical of such titanism, by which he also felt tempted. Both criticism and temptation are intensified during the second half of the 1770s, after the poet achieved a public reputation. We possess two letters from this period which remind us of the pact scene. On March 6, 1776, Goethe writes to Lavater,[4] "I have now completely embarked on the waves of the world—and have fully decided to make discoveries, win, struggle, go astray, or to blow myself up with all my cargo." On November 6, to his mother: "Besides, I have everything a man can wish for himself, and yet, I must admit, I am not at rest; man's driving force is infinite until he has driven himself out." On January 8, 1777, again to Lavater: "In the life I lead these days, all my distant friends fade into a kind of mist. Whether it lasts or not, I have at least wholeheartedly enjoyed this topsy-turvy bit of life. Annoyance, hope, love, toil, need, adventure, bordeom, hatred, absurdities, foolishness, joy, the expected and the unforeseen, the shallow and the profound—all just as the dice fall, with festivities, dances, bells, silk and tinsel—a wonderful kind of life." * * *

An overwhelming discovery! And it is not only a matter of the nexus of meaning in a single scene, for this scene is to shed its light upon all those which follow, "Auerbach's Tavern," "Witch's Kitchen," the entire Gretchen tragedy, "Forest and Cave," and the "Walpurgis Night." Yet which of the two beams of light applies to what follows? If we keep to the older material, we must deal with the fact that Faust, despite what Mephisto says, somehow finds happiness and satisfaction. If we keep to the first half of the scene, then we will be worried as to whether Faust will let himself be seduced and say to any moment: "Tarry a while! you are so fair!" [line 1700]. Most commentators read the work with this kind of worry. "Witch's Kitchen" and "Forest and Cave" originated, however, before the wager, and "Auerbach's Tavern" and the Gretchen tragedy even before the latter part of the scene was written. Nevertheless, it would be more logical to rely on that part of it which appeared in the *Fragment* of 1790. It is substantially closer to the *Urfaust*. But of course now it is no longer comparable to the clearly described wager; one simply reads over it and works out the sense of what follows as best one can. Ultimately one is comforted to know that indeed only the ambivalence of the moment subsequently reappears. Eternally restless striving is as false as mere tenacity. Mephistopheles undermines human nature both when he incites restlessness and when he brings Faust "to good things savored at . . . ease" [line 1691].

---

4. Johann Caspar Lavater (1741–1801), Swiss physiognomist with whom Goethe had then recently come into contact.

The Gretchen Tragedy

BARKER FAIRLEY

[The Gretchen Tragedy and the Young Goethe]†

The series of episodes constituting the main body of *Faust* was complicated at the start by the circumstance that the first major episode, the Gretchen tragedy, was almost certainly composed without regard to a series and without regard to the philosophical needs of the argument. At least it would be difficult to maintain that this episode was written with an eye to its place in the development of the poem or with any thought of what was to come after. On the contrary, everything points to the conclusion that the Gretchen tragedy was written for its own sake, in disregard of the poem's needs, and that if it now takes its appropriate place in the larger context, this is more by good luck than by good management.

What management there was lies chiefly in extensions of the text made at a later date, when Goethe was putting *Part I* in shape. The task was not attempted till 1788–90 and not completed till after 1797; the Gretchen tragedy was written in the Frankfurt years, probably in 1775. * * *

No matter which of the two versions we read, the difference between this part of the poem and the rest is one that every reader feels. * * * The difference is that while Act V keeps our minds on the whole poem all the time, it is almost impossible to read the Gretchen part and not for the time being forget the rest. The philosophical argument which precedes it is completely wiped out in our passionate absorption in Gretchen and her fate. So much so that it is only with difficulty that we feel our way back into the main stream again.

* * * The Gretchen tragedy makes its own demands and takes possession of us, so that we read it as a thing existing in its own right with little or no thought of Faust's wager or anything else. This is a part of the poem that has impressed itself quite separately on the popular imagination, almost as if it were the whole. More especially in countries outside of Germany, and thanks partly, but

† From Barker Fairley, *Goethe's Faust: Six Essays*, pp. 44–65, copyright © 1953 by Oxford University Press. Reprinted by permission of The Clarendon Press, Oxford.

not wholly, to Gounod's opera, the Gretchen tragedy is the Faust tragedy pure and simple, and the remainder is forgotten or only half remembered. It is likely enough that, when Goethe had finished writing the prison scene, he too only half remembered where it all started and was himself at a loss. At any rate he put his manuscript away for nearly fifteen years, and this may well have been the initial reason.

In thus running off his course into what looks like a bourgeois drama of the sexes with little or no philosophy in it, Goethe was drawn by forces that we can readily understand. Having chosen a theme so rich in native associations, the Faust legend more perhaps than any being the German legend, and having chosen to write in what he undoubtedly felt to be the most indigenous of German metres, the *Knittelvers* of Hans Sachs,[1] it is quite understandable that Goethe should have been drawn into a folk-theme for its own sake and should have developed it accordingly. Herder[2] had recently fired him with enthusiasm for popular literature; under Herder's inspiration he had collected folk-ballads in the Alsatian villages, some of them very close in theme to Gretchen; and this must surely have been his channel of approach, not, then, in terms of social justice or injustice, but in sheer enthusiasm for the one and only subject that a poet who had sat at Herder's feet in the German seventeen-seventies might dream of. The result is what we know—a piece of writing so steeped in popular associations that there is nothing in German to rival it. * * *

But there is more here than folk-associations. The enthusiasm for popular literature as against cultured which took such a strong hold of Goethe's generation was only part of a larger enthusiasm for the irrational in general. After a period of European letters in which the emotions were made little of, the pendulum swung violently over and poets began to idealize them, as we see Goethe doing almost exclusively in the years before Weimar. * * *

It can only be because it came into existence in this way, as the creation of a poet preoccupied with and even ideally in love with emotion and with passion, that we can understand the spirit of purity in which it was written and which every sensitive reader feels. If we surrender to these inspired pages we do not find ourselves in the dubious atmosphere of sin and society, but for want of a better word in what we can only call a world of innocence, which somehow remains innocent even in its tragedy, even in its collapse. Gretchen's innocence, one is tempted to say, is something she cannot lose, because she is made of it. * * *

Something of the same applies even to Faust who, as we shall see, takes colour from Gretchen in these scenes and in any case is

1. See note 5, p. 451, above.
2. Johann Gottfried Herder (1744–1803), leading critical theorist of the *Sturm und Drang* movement, renowned for his research into the German language and the heritage of a nation as revealed in its folksongs.

very unimpressive as a seducer beside the many we could name.
Indeed this aspect of the affair is as nearly as possible eliminated in
the brief conversations he has with Gretchen, thanks largely to
Mephistopheles, who relieves him of it. * * *

* * * By having Mephistopheles as an accomplice and pander,
who does all or most of the managing, Faust is, as it were, released
from his adverse role as seducer of Gretchen to indulge his affinity,
his kinship, with her and even become her champion. For it will be
evident to anyone who reads or re-reads the scene in which Faust
soliloquizes Gretchen's room that his instinctive or deeper relation
to her is not the one dramatically assigned to him but rather that of
a worshipper in a not quite compatible sense. No doubt we can, if
we choose, cast Faust in the single role of idealistic seducer, but it
is an ugly role and hardly the one Goethe intended for him. * * *

* * * Looking at the Gretchen tragedy as a whole, we can say
that Faust extricates himself from his destructive role by thrusting
Mephistopheles into it and standing beside Gretchen against him.
Thus, while the alignment in terms of plot is Faust and Mephistopheles against Gretchen, at the deeper level it is Faust and
Gretchen against Mephistopheles. The discrepancy which half
emerges in the passage just quoted comes out fully in the scene
"Dreary Day. Field," in which Faust denounces Mephistopheles out-
right as the destroyer, speaking as if he had had no part in what had
happened and going to such lengths in his denunciation that Mephistopheles is driven to ask who it was that seduced Gretchen, himself
or Faust—"Who was it that plunged her to ruin? I or you?"—but
this has no effect on Faust, who continues as before—"Murder and
death of a world upon your head, monster!" Later in the prison
scene Faust almost recognizes his dual part when he says to
Gretchen that from being her murderer he has become her rescuer.
But this somewhat perplexing thought was omitted in the final
version.

* * *

If we accept the view that Goethe approached this piece of writing through an initial fellow-feeling with Gretchen rather than
through dynamic thoughts about Faust, much is explained or clarified. The movement of the Faust poem from an ideological to a
folk theme is more intelligible if we associate the movement primarily with Gretchen, since she is purely and simply a folk figure,
whereas Faust, while he is part of a popular legend to begin with, is
not treated by Goethe quite in this spirit, but is lifted out of his old
associations to become the spokesman of a new philosophy. With
Gretchen as the dominant figure we also understand better why
there should be so little development of Faust's thought after the
bold lead given in the preceding scenes. What we find in the early
Gretchen tragedy is a Faust unimpressively reduced to third place,
Gretchen being sketched in simple and perfect strokes which absorb

most, if not all, of our attention, while any initiative Faust may have had passes largely into the hands of Mephistopheles. Faust's two attempts to assert himself in a speech or monologue are both a little flat after his tremendous beginnings. That is to say, in neither case does he manage to assert his Faustian impulse, and to this extent he falls short. The first case is when he soliloquizes in Gretchen's room, where he completely loses himself, Werther-like, in her world; and the second is when Gretchen catechizes him and he voices his sense of the divine, not with the self-assertion that we expect of him, but rather in self-surrender: "For who may name Him?" [line 3432]. It is not till virtually the last scene but one, "Dreary Day. Field," in which Faust and Mephistopheles quarrel violently, that we feel we are in the presence of a Faust not subordinate to Gretchen but himself again in all his vigour. In the prison scene he is returned to his passive and now helpless role.

If the Gretchen tragedy is not always initially read in this light with Gretchen, not Faust, as protagonist, it is not surprising. The reader who comes to it, as most readers do, in the course of reading the whole poem, naturally reads it from Faust's point of view, because Faust's importance as the poem's chief spokesman is already fully established and we do not question it. Moreover, the scenes added later tend in no small measure to enlarge Faust at Gretchen's expense. But if we read the Gretchen scenes in their first writing we shall have little difficulty in discovering the primacy of Gretchen and in recognizing the continuance of this primacy in the final version.

Reading the Gretchen scenes in this spirit—a spirit of love and enthusiasm for the figure of Gretchen and for the emotional life with which Goethe and his age surrounded her—we may ask ourselves why he should have involved her in a plot that destroyed her.
* * *

* * *

* * * The prison scene with which the tragedy ends is almost wholly devoted to the exploration of Gretchen's agony, with only a brief glimpse or two, caught through her mind and imagination, of what awaits her. And this holds good for the revised version, equally. It is Gretchen's scene from first to last with the other two as little more than onlookers. And it rises to such a pitch of absorption in her inner condition that the world outside loses its reality. If we were drawn or half drawn by earlier scenes into Gretchen's environment, here we are swept out of it again. All we experience is the quintessence of anguish.

This must not be taken as meaning that we do not judge the Gretchen tragedy morally, though the temptation is there. No doubt it is comfortable to say, as many have said, that this piece of literature is so beautiful, so sustained and intense in its beauty, that we are disarmed, or that in the face of such a poetic miracle words are beyond us. But the notion of art without morality is very difficult to conceive, especially when it is Goethe's art and, more especially still, when it is Goethe's *Faust*, a poem bearing always on the conduct and control of life. If we try to dispose of the Gretchen tragedy as beauty transcending judgment or as poetry outsoaring ethics, we are scarcely reading it in Goethe's spirit and certainly not in the spirit of *Faust*.

* * *

Here again it would be incorrect to say that Goethe wrote by plan, that he saw the moral and then wrote his tragedy in the light of it. Rather he wrote the tragedy out of the extremity of what he felt, at once loving his emotions and disburdening himself of them, and the moral followed of itself from the tragedy that he could not help writing. * * * In *Faust* no judgment is pronounced, whether in the text or by way of comment on it, unless we find it in the reference in *Part II* to the "unbridled blood" [line 10202] which Faust disagreeably recalls. But this is too remote a reference to be effective.

However, what the poem fails to tell us explicitly it tells us implicitly by passing on to new and ultimately higher levels of activity, which throw the Gretchen tragedy into relief and in this sense pass judgment on it. In saying this it will not be claimed that the Gretchen tragedy merges perfectly into the body of the poem; its separateness will be felt in varying degrees by everyone. But if we read it deeply enough as pertaining not merely to an action but to the state of mind, the immature state of mind, generating the action, we shall have little difficulty, philosophically, in fitting it in.

Poetically the fitting is harder, not so much in the preparatory context where there is a sufficient approach to Gretchen's world, in "Outside the City Gate" and elsewhere, to make the transition easy, but rather in the join at the other end, where the context is not very helpful. The Gretchen tragedy, it will be remembered, terminates *Part I* and the continuation of the text is in the opening of *Part II*. At this point it is well to remember that, while as readers we only have to turn a page or reach for another volume, Goethe waited fifty years. The prison scene in its prose form was written not later than 1775, the opening part of *Part II* not before 1825. No wonder there is a gulf. Yet the tragedy is not forgotten. Faust is presented to us as recovering from the shock of it on an evidently Alpine pasture with nature spirits in attendance on him, and the chief spirit Ariel bids them 'ease his cruel suffering, remove the bitter burning arrows of reproach, purge his heart of horror':

> Soothe now the wearied heart's contention dire,
> Withdraw the searing arrows of remorse,
> Of horrors suffered cleanse his soul entire. [lines 4623–25]

* * *

GEORG LUKACS

[A Marxist Interpretation of the Gretchen Tragedy]†

The *Urfaust* and the *Fragment* of 1790 are still dominated by the Gretchen tragedy. And however the proportions change in the later, completed version, it is this tragedy which preponderates in the popular imagination. In the broad, mass effect of *Faust*, the Gretchen tragedy, along with the tragedy of immediate knowledge and that of the pact with the devil, is dominant even today. In large measure this is justified. For the immediate poetic impression of the "little world," in which what pertains to the species forms only a backdrop and determines only the peculiar form of typical characterization and the direction of the plot, is inevitably bound to be stronger than the impression made by the rigorously objectified philosophic and poetic profundity of the "great world" in *Part II*.

Whatever the clarity or vagueness with which the youthful Goethe envisaged the outline of the entire poem, there is no doubt that, even then, he was most affected poetically by the tragedy of Gretchen. And this is understandable. For this was something young Goethe could adequately enlarge on. Indeed, it was a central theme not only of his own early writings, but of all German literature of this epoch.

In *Dichtung und Wahrheit*, Goethe mentions that the friend of his youth, Heinrich Leopold Wagner,[1] plagiarized him by making use of what he had related concerning the Gretchen tragedy. Now, to what extent can this really be considered plagiarism? Wagner presents the tragic fate of a girl seduced in accordance with the spirit of the age: as a glaring example of class oppression of the bourgeoisie and petty bourgeoisie by the nobility. * * *

The popularity of this theme is by no means accidental. It also plays a considerable role in the English and French literature of the Enlightenment from Richardson to the *Figaro* of Beaumarchais.[2] In the class conflict between nobility and bourgeoisie, individual cases of flagrant injustice were necessarily bound to be placed in the foreground, so long as the oppressed class was not yet sufficiently developed. * * * The seduction of bourgeois girls by aristocrats and the resultant tragedies understandably form an important part of this still insufficiently developed revolt against feudal domination. And

† "The Tragedy of Gretchen," by Georg Lukacs. Reprinted from *Goethe and His Age*, by Georg Lukacs, translated by Robert Anchor, pp. 217–34, Copyright © 1968 by The Merlin Press Ltd., London. Reprinted by permission of the publisher, Grosset & Dunlap, Inc.
1. Heinrich Leopold Wagner (1747–79), German dramatist and friend from Goethe's youth in Frankfurt and Strassburg.

2. Samuel Richardson (1689–1761), English author of epistolary novels; Pierre Augustin Caron de Beaumarchais (1732–99), French dramatist, author of *Le Mariage de Figaro* (1784). Both Richardson and Beaumarchais were important for their implicit criticism of the social mores and social order of their own day. Beaumarchais' Figaro has often been interpreted as a proto-revolutionary figure.

it is obvious that all these tendencies were bound to appear even more in the foreground in Germany, where the bourgeoisie was weaker than in France.

From the social standpoint, then, the tragedy of the bourgeois maiden seduced is only one of many abuses perpetrated by degenerate feudalism. From the standpoint of poetic creation, however, this theme has advantages such that it became, not by chance, the principal dramatic theme of the German Enlightenment. Above all, in a palpable and terse manner, it concentrates, in a typical individual case which is easy to relive imaginatively, the most repugnant features of the oppression, features apt to rouse spontaneously to indignation the whole bourgeoisie (even its least developed elements). * * * It is precisely this theme, moreover, which presents, with the greatest efficacy, the antithesis of the first importance: that of the two moralities—the moral depravity, the moral nihilism of the nobility and the wholesome moral sensibility of the bourgeoisie. Finally, the weakness of the bourgeois, their impotence in the face of the nobility can be presented in a perfectly truthful manner in this theme; yet it is able to give expression successfully to their passive and authentic heroism which is neither violent nor affected. * * *

The poetry of Goethe's youth also forms part of this current, but, right from the beginning, Goethe has a unique position and unique formulation of the problem. He presents something broader and deeper than do his contemporaries: he gives a critique of the love relationship in bourgeois society in general. Engels[3] describes in detail how the social earthquake which gave the bourgeoisie its leading economic position also brought forth the modern forms of love and marriage, but, at the same time—with the same socio-economic necessity—made their realization in life very rare exceptions. It is this internal contradiction of bourgeois society that forms the point of departure for the creative work of young Goethe. And it does so, in accordance with his whole tendency, from the standpoint of the full development of the personality, which also belongs to that complex of problems that the emergence of capitalism and the ripening of the bourgeois revolutions put on the agenda; problems of which, however, the economic and social structure of this same bourgeois society also prevents even an approximate solution. The love tragedies of young Goethe present, in deeply experienced individual destinies, different combinations of both these groups of social contradictions. The problem of the class conflict as it bears on sexual relations, a problem brought to the fore by his contemporaries, remains an important factor for him also, but, nonetheless, only one factor of this totality.

3. Friedrich Engels (1820–95), German socialist writer, friend and collaborator of Karl Marx. Lukacs is citing Engels' book *The Origin of the Family, Private Property, and the State* (1884).

The rare realization of the unity of individual love and marriage among the ruling classes of bourgeois society—Engels never tires of repeating that this problem is quite different from the plebeian strata and especially for the proletariat—has economic and social foundations. But this realization occurs in individual cases only through crises and tragedy. The conflicting social tendencies fight out their battles in the emotional life, the thought, and the social activity of men. The most primitive form of these contradictions is that between emerging passionate love and the economic and social well-being of the individual. Stated crudely, it is the problem of whether love and marriage are or are not advantageous to his "'career"—where the "career" may be of the most varied kinds, from the brutal material pursuit of success to the inner unfolding of the personality, from the most base and narrow egoism to really tragic conflicts.

* * *

* * * We know how Goethe conceived the development of man's potentialities. This development is impossible without love. The ascetic is an incomplete human being. The passion of individual love, precisely because it is both the most elementary, the most natural of all passions, and also, in its present individualized form, the finest fruit of culture, represents the most genuine fulfilment of the human personality, so long as its development is regarded as a "microcosm," as an end in itself. It can attain to this fulfilment only when the passion of love becomes a sweeping current into which flow, in their supreme perfection, the noblest spiritual and moral strivings of the individual; when the power of love, which unifies the personality, effectually raises everything in man to the highest level attainable.

* * *

This ideal of a harmonious love which promotes the highest harmonious development of the personality grew out of the ground of bourgeois society. But the realization of this ideal is obstructed by the development of the very social reality that engendered it. And this is directly due not only to economic and social factors, such as the economic drawbacks of a marital union, nor only to external differences in class and internal differences in culture which are difficult to bridge: the immanent logic of personality development also sets limits to the realization of this ideal in bourgeois society.

From this point of view, the impossibility of a real equality of man and woman in bourgeois society appears in the most varied forms, from the most brutal to the most spiritual. Without love, the self-perfection of the personality is impossible, or at least very incomplete. But in a society divided into classes, this self-perfection, to which the deep spiritual and sensual comradeship between man and woman belongs, necessitates a solitary development whereby the man imposes on himself an unfettered and unattached existence without family, without wife and children. This is true at least at the beginning of his quest, at the stage of (inevitable) erring, until he finds the course of action proper to him—mastery in his command of the given realities of the world and of his own potentialities.

In a society divided into classes, therefore, a premature union, even one founded on the deepest and most genuine love, can become the starting-point of irresolvable tragic conflicts. If it endures, the young man involved in the union will be the victim; if, under the pressure of his fettered possibilities for development, he breaks away, then the girl must be sacrificed.

These are the contours of young Goethe's tragedies of love. Because of his deep human decency and ever alert sense of responsibility, swift renunciation became the recurring leitmotif of his youth. Precisely because he became aware of this conflict at a very early age, the inevitable parting already cast its shadow on his intense, most enriching, and happiest love. At the age of eighteen, at the height of his intense passion for Käthe Schönkopf, Goethe writes to his friend, Behrisch:[4] "I often say to myself: if she were yours now, could anyone but death contest your claim to her or deprive you of her embrace? Imagine what I feel, everything I think about—and when I come to the end, I pray God not to give her to me."

Here we have the archetype of all young Goethe's subsequent love tragedies, from Friederike Brion to Lili Schönemann, in which material factors in general could play no role. * * *

The tragedy of Gretchen is the most typical of all these dramas. We have already pointed out that in Faust, as in Gretchen, Goethe gives expression not only to the passion of love itself, but also to all its stages of development, from its frivolous and half-conscious beginnings to the deepest tragedy. All the great tendencies of evolution are concentrated in the person of Faust. When, turning to life, he approaches Gretchen, the sad burden weighs on him of the scarcely surmounted tragedy of immediate knowledge and his pact with the devil. And, at the height his ecstasy with Gretchen, enraptured by the charm of her person and her nearness, there is at work in him the invincible aspiration: to go further, higher! Faust knows, even if he does not wish to admit it to himself, that he cannot long stay in the "little world" of Gretchen. * * *

Hence, his love for Gretchen is also tragic for Faust himself. The tragic intensification manifests itself most clearly in the fact that the opposed forces which produce the conflict no longer assume the form of distinctly different characters as in Goethe's other youthful dramas. It is from within rather that Faust's upward striving and his relationship with Gretchen mutually reinforce and at the same time

4. Ernst Wolfgang Behrisch (1738–1809), a friend from Goethe's youth in Leipzig, remembered with affection in Goethe's autobiography, *Poetry and Truth*, and in his conversations with Eckermann.

destroy each other. The scene that we have already examined, which forms a turning-point in the destiny of Faust's love, shows this irresolvable tragic connection. Faust flees Gretchen in order to save her; flight and solitude give a new and unexpected uplift to his spirit, to his world-view. But it is precisely his love for Gretchen which bears him aloft, so that his flight is rendered futile—not, of course, without the assistance of Mephistopheles, too. Thus the highest and most spiritualized stage of Faust's love becomes fateful for the destiny of Gretchen. That Faust is fully aware of his destiny mitigates nothing; his awareness is only a subjective consciousness of the irresolvable character of the situation. Even at the height of natural-philosophical fervour Faust's *Weltanschauung* is unable to answer Mephistopheles' cynicism: it is unable to resolve the moral dilemma:

> What use her love's celestial graces?
> As I grow warm in her embraces
> Do I not always sense her doom?
> Am I not a fugitive, the homeless rover,
> The man-beast void of goal or bliss,
> Who roars in cataracts from cliff to boulder
> In avid frenzy for the precipice? . . .
> Let it be now, what needs must be!
> May then her destiny collapse on me
> And she be joined in my perdition. [lines 3345–65]

We find the same high level of typicality in Gretchen. * * * All the spiritual and moral prejudices and weaknesses of a girl from the lower middle class are present in her. But, at the same time, her feelings are absolute and intact, her devotion is unconditional, and she possesses courage, selflessness, and clarity of feeling with respect to persons and even ideas.

It is true that objectively the—very complex—factor which leads to separation manifests itself just here. It is important that, after the peripeteia in "Forest and Cave," Faust also seeks an ideological *rapport* with Gretchen. And if, in his discourse on God since become famous, he goes a long way in adapting his (and Goethe's) wholly immanent pantheism to the religious mentality of Gretchen, this is not the mere mimicry of a lover who wishes to bring about at any price a psychological and spiritual union, but rather a tendency often manifest in Goethe himself, to make his Spinozism[5] unpolemical, to show a far-reaching tolerance in the presence of sincere faith if only it is faith in something and not nihilistic indifference. This is why Gretchen's words

> All well and good; the turn of phrase
> Is something different, but I presume
> What Parson says means much the same. [lines 3459–61]

5. An allusion to Goethe's abiding interest in the philosophy of Benedict de Spinoza (1632–77), which in the later eighteenth century was frequently associated with pantheistic doctrines.

have a double meaning. At the moment of ecstasy, the two of them achieve a psychological and spiritual *rapport* on the subjective level; objectively, however, and without their being aware of it, the abyss which will separate them is already opening up here. Whence the complicated dialectic involving, on the one hand, deep sincerity and mutual self-revelation, and on the other, deception and self-deception which, in a society divided into classes, are characteristic of love, even in its most exalted form. Accordingly, * * * at the height of the tragic involvement, when Gretchen is already in prison, Faust says: "And all her crime was but a trusting heart" [line 4408].

But the fact that Gretchen does not understand Faust's philosophy, or else misinterprets it on her lower level of culture, also has two aspects in which the justification and the tragedy of her situation find expression. When she reproaches him with the words: "You have no Christianity" [line 3468], this is intellectually, no doubt, the uncomprehending reproach of a petty bourgeois girl; but, from a human and moral standpoint, it refers to the decisive tragic point in the highest development of Faust's personality: to his indissoluble, liaison with Mephistopheles. And Faust can only confront it with embarrassed and evasive excuses, for he is aware, and has just admitted to himself in the scene, "Forest and Cave," that Mephistopheles has become indispensable to him. The impossibility here of breaking through the barrier of unintended tragic insincerity lies, then, not in the intellectual difference between Faust and Gretchen, nor in the inability of Gretchen to understand Faust completely, but rather in the involvement of the Mephistophelian in even the highest human aspirations.

This is why—despite the depth of Faust's love, his pity and compassion—Mephistopheles is in very large measure (relatively) right when, confronted with the highest ideological and moral uplift of Faust's love, he merely points cynically to the consequences of the bed and rejoices in it. Both the function and the limitations of Mephistopheles clearly manifest themselves here. The essence of Gretchen is inaccessible to him; nor does he understand the core of Faust's real inner conflicts—but the course of this tragedy is nonetheless paved all along with the stones of his "wisdom." Because Gretchen is inaccessible to Mephisto, her love is also completely unproblematical. And her tragedy unfolds with the same necessity from this sraight and narrow character of her undoubting and unreflecting love as does the tragedy of Faust from the fact that he is torn between his desire to immerse himself in his life-work and the ecstatic happiness of his love.

The greatness of Goethe's typification consists, therefore, not only in the general truthfulness to life of all the elements of this evolution up to its tragic climax, but also in the fact that its unfolding, the antagonistic mixture of high and low motifs, always remains deeply typical. The result is that the entire history of the love, from its—half fortuitous—origins to its—inevitably tragic—break-up is expressed here in all its important stages of development. This is why Gretchen, like the other heroines of "Storm and Stress," has to be a girl from the lower social strata who is seduced and whose seduction leads to her downfall. But Goethe's depiction of this downfall, which contains all the social motifs of "Storm and Stress," goes deeper. Not only is the development which leads to this downfall more complete, but it is also more abundant in dramatic contradictions. For "Storm and Stress" there were only two possibilities: either frivolous, casual seduction and abandonment after the satisfaction of lust, or true love which remains constant as love, but proves unavailing against the irresistible might of class stratification. The Gretchen tragedy unites both series of motifs on Goethe's own higher level. Faust loves Gretchen right to the end. But—as his passion increases—he is nonetheless inwardly untrue to her, because the elements of his development which transcend her gain strength along with the strengthening of his passion for her and its fulfilment. And Gretchen not only sacrifices for her love her honour and existence, her mother and brother, but—in the prison scene—despite all her passionate attraction to Faust, who appears unexpectedly at the moment of her greatest need as lover and rescuer, she also senses the end of his love.

> Where is your love abiding,
> In hiding?
> Who took it away? [lines 4495–97]

As if I had to brace myself, as if you too
Repulsed me, spurning my caress;
Yet it is you, as ever kind and dear. [lines 4533–35]

Into the tragic fluctuations of this omnipotent passion with its irreconcilable abysses; into this psychological-spiritual development of love enters Mephistopheles. Tearing it apart he presses for a decision on the terrestrial, practical rescue of Gretchen. At this point, Gretchen makes her final decision: she will not be rescued by a Faust to whom Mephistopheles is indispensable. This is why the voice from above can proclaim: "Redeemed!"

The Dramatic Structure
of *Faust*

L. A. WILLOUGHBY

Goethe's *Faust:* A Morphological Approach†

When in January 1825 Goethe received a duty-call from one of the many young Englishmen then living in Weimar, he enquired of him in the course of conversation what he had read of German literature. "*Egmont* and *Tasso*, with much pleasure," came the answer, "and just now I am reading *Faust*." Then, with an understatement characteristically English, he continued: "But I find it just a little difficult." At this Goethe chuckled. "Indeed," he said, "I would scarcely have advised you to go on to *Faust!* It's crazy stuff, and transcends all ordinary forms of feeling. But since you've embarked on it of your own accord without first consulting me, it's for you to see how you get through it."

"Wie Sie *durchkommen!*" The very word, with its sinister implications of getting through—or not getting through—examinations, is bound to leave on the reader's mind a sense of impending trials if not necessarily of disaster. And there are surely few works of literature which present the critic with such problems as does Goethe's *Faust*. Even its creator allowed that it was almost as "incommensurable" as Nature herself. There it stands, a mixture of tender lyricism and stark tragedy, of magic opera and realistic drama, of cosmic philosophy and unconscious symbolism, stubbornly resistant to traditional canons of literary criticism. Whether we come to it from Shakespeare or from the Greeks, from Racine or from Ibsen, measuring it by forms alien to its own, or whether we apply to it preconceived notions of what a drama or a tragedy ought to be, it remains equally intractable, defying every attempt to place it within accepted categories, one of the gigantic monuments of world-literature, refusing sphinx-like to disclose the secret of its "law."

Nor, at first sight, is Goethe himself very helpful in offering us a clue to its riddle. It is of no use at all, if we are to believe what he

† From *Goethe: Poet and Thinker*, by Elizabeth Wilkinson and L. A. Willoughby, pp. 95-117. Published by Edward Arnold (Publishers) Ltd., 1962. Reprinted by permission of Edward Arnold (Publishers) Ltd.

once said in the presence of Eckermann, trying to find some central "idea" which would explain everything and might serve the student as a thread to guide him through all the intricacies of its labyrinth. The words with which Goethe repudiates and ridicules attempts to either read out, or read in, any such "idea" are unambiguous: "And what a fine thing it would have turned out to be if I had tried to string a life as rich, motley, and as utterly diverse, as that I have displayed in *Faust*, on the thin and meagre thread of a single idea running through the whole."

Must the reader, then, be content just to enjoy the various parts of this vast poem singly, each for itself and without reference to the whole? Not if we are to appeal to Goethe's own authority elsewhere. For in the second of his more important pronouncements on *Faust*, that long conversation with the historian, Luden,[1] in 1806 which at first sight so blatantly contradicts, but in reality so perfectly supplements, the statements recorded by Eckermann, he expressly rejected the suggestion that the play might, perhaps, best be appreciated piecemeal. "But that's a paltry, a fragmentary, sort of interest," he retorted. "*Faust* does after all possess interest of a higher kind—the idea, that is to say, which inspired the poet and binds all the individual parts of the poem into a whole, furnishing the law for each and every one, and apportioning to each its due and proper importance."

The "idea" of *Faust*! Is it not strange that, at a time when nothing of it had as yet appeared in print except the *Fragment* of 1790, he should have insisted to Luden that there resides in it an idea so dominant and so unifying that it ought to be apparent even from the as yet unfinished torso? And that then, almost twenty years after the publication of *Faust, Part I*, and with *Part II* nearing completion, he should have so categorically denied it any such idea at all? Is this just another of those many contradictions Goethe's critics are always ready to find in him? Or is it not rather one of those cases where—to quote from another conversation with Eckermann—"the imperfections and inadequacy of language have caused the spread of errors and false opinions which at a later date are not so easy to overcome"? For the word "idea" is in fact used in a different sense in each of the two contexts, and the exact shade of meaning can only be determined by attention to the verbal *milieu*. In the conversation with Eckermann the attenuated abstractions of philosophical interpretation are being contrasted with the living plentitude of poetry itself. The word "idea" is there equated with "abstraction," "abstract thought," "profound thought," and opposed to such words as "perception" and "impression." In the conversation with Luden, by contrast, the word "idea" is roughly equivalent to "centre.'" * * * And the words in its immediate

1. Heinrich Luden (1780–1847), German historian.

vicinity which, so to speak, determine the climate of its meaning are not derived from the sphere of abstract thought at all, but from that of organic growth: Goethe speaks of "organic parts" makes use of the verb "grow" and is obviously preoccupied with his notion of living form, with the reciprocal relation of the parts to the whole and the whole to the parts. The unifying principle he here has in mind is not a philosophical "idea" at all, not one which can be abstracted from the poetic structure and formulated in other terms. It is rather the principle which is active in the living processes of the poem itself, the formative tendency which organises all the parts, however diverse, into a meaningful whole. "Idea" here signifies "organic centre," "nodal point," or "focal point"—Goethe at various times employs all three words—the point from which all the parts radiate and "out of which, mutually replenishing and completing each other, they have all grown and could well go on growing." "The poetic tendency of the individual part," he insists, "points at all times to a necessary connection, that is, to a common centre, to a primary idea." Luden's fears that the "fragments" he had learnt to love might get lost in the completed whole seemed to Goethe quite incomprehensible. To him the work was like a living, growing, thing whose green foliage would only appear in its true significance once the plant was ready to blossom and bring forth fruit. "But how could the fragments," he protested, "ever get lost in a whole from which they have themselves been taken? They will appear in that same whole as organic parts, and then, and only then, will they assume their true significance."

It is not surprising that in his conversation with Luden Goethe should have made use of the language of morphology. For he was at the time intensively, if not exclusively, preoccupied with his scientific work. But long before he turned to natural science at all, long before he formulated those pregnant maxims concerning the relationship between art and nature—"What is beauty but a manifestation of hidden laws of nature" or "A work of art ought to be treated like a work of nature"—long before this, in his early Strassburg days, he had, following Shaftesbury,[2] spoken of works of art in terms of works of nature. The dithyrambic ardour of his song of praise to the great Gothic minster—he likens it to a giant tree, in the innumerable branches and leaves of which the birds of the morning have their nest, the whole vast structure proclaiming the glory of God—should not blind us to the fact that there is embodied within it a concept to which he would much later give biological precision: the notion that in a living organism all the parts, down to the smallest of them—the tiniest little fibre, as he puts it

2. Anthony Ashley Cooper, Third Earl of Shaftesbury (1671–1713), English statesman and philosopher, whose theory of the artist as a creator figure like Prometheus was very influential in the eighteenth century.

here—are subordinated to the dominant principle governing the whole. "As in the works of eternal nature, down to the tiniest filament, everything is form, everything purposeful for the whole."

Nor, even at this early stage, was he under any illusion that the language of plant-growth could afford more than an illuminating analogy. True, he did not, and probably could not, transpose these biological notions into terms of architecture. He was after all not an architect. But he *was* a dramatist. And he could and did transpose them into terms of the theatre, exhorting his fellow *Stürmer und Dränger* to concentrate on scenography, on pasteboard and canvas, boards and battens, grease-paint, lights and tinsel, and leave Nature where she belongs. And into terms of language too, defying even the severest critic "to separate the merely translated passages [in his *Clavigo*[3]] from the whole without tearing it to pieces, without inflicting, and not just on the plot alone, but on the very structure of the play itself, a deadly wound."

If *Clavigo*, a work based on the *Mémoirs* of Beaumarchais and exhibiting a surface regularity of form, a conventional structure in the French dramatic style—if such an obvious "Komposition," as it seems to us, was nevertheless thought by him to have a "Lebensorganisation" too vulnerable to tamper with, how much more must this hold of *Faust*, which "grew" out of the Gothic germ of the *Ur-Faust* until it finally unfolded into the Baroque exuberance of *Part II*. The critic—if not the reader or spectator, who may well feel it intuitively—is faced with a formidable task if he would try to articulate its formative principle, or follow Goethe's hint when he remarked to Luden that "great scholars and gifted individuals had not considered it beneath them to search for its *Mittelpunkt*, or nodal point." How is he to communicate the "law" of its growth without abstracting it from the living material of which the play is made, without himself forgetting, or leading his readers to forget, that this living material is the poet's words; words not just thought of as black marks on a page, nor as sounds without sense, but words having meaning—and yet at the same time nothing but words. For what we are looking for is, as Goethe says, not "some mystic something which lies behind or beyond" them, but a significance inherent within them. And not just the significance inherent in any one quotable statement, such as

> "Whoever strives in ceaseless toil
> Him we may grant redemption." [lines 11936–37]

> Wisdom's last verdict goes to say:
> He only earns both freedom and existence
> Who must reconquer them each day. [lines 11574–76]

or even in a selection of such statements, but a significance inherent

---

3. A tragedy by Goethe (1774) in which he used material from *Quatrième mémoire* (1774) of Beaumarchais.

in the whole complex of words that go to make up the 12,111 lines of the play. In order to avoid equating the import of *Faust* with that of any lines snatched out of context, or—worse still—reducing its mystery to philosophy by "atomising it into everyday prose," as Goethe puts it, it may be salutary to remind ourselves, and especially with a work of such obvious and multifarious depths, that a true artist hides these depths on the surface. Provided that soundings are taken at the right points, we should eventually encounter the mythical, religious or philosophical import, and in a way which keeps us more closely in touch with the *poetic* world of the play than if we had started our investigations from a point outside it altogether, from the theological premises of Faust's salvation, for instance, or from the occult sources on which Goethe drew. For, to revert to Goethe's own organic metaphor: If it is true that art, like nature, "has neither core/Nor shell,/It is everything all at once," then to explore the relations between words on the outer "covering" must lead us to the most inward systems of the whole organism. Nor should we be unduly perturbed if the first stages of our search into the intercommunication between the parts—into the "anastomosis" of the organism, as Goethe calls it—should seem almost mechanical. He himself was quite content to do likewise * * *. "There is no surer way," he wrote, "of becoming intimate with the essentially *poetic* spirit of the poet than by a comparison of parallel passages." And for a start we may well extend his comparative method to occurrences of individual words.

The path has been made easy for us by the *Wortindex zu Goethes Faust* compiled in 1940 at the University of Wisconsin. Let us select from it the word *Welt*. Not indeed at random, but because our general impression of the play tells us that it may well be a key-word. It would clearly be impracticable—even undesirable, an excess of critical zeal—to pursue all the ramifications of its 109 occurrences. But what a sense of interconnection and interweaving we get by following up just a few! From the cosmic panorama of the Prologue in Heaven, the "suns and worlds" hymned by the Archangels, through Mephisto's scornful gibes at man, "the little god of this world," on to Faust's ardent longing to discover "what holds the world together at its inmost centre" and his bitter rejection of the narrow "world" he has made for himself within the four walls of his study: "This is your world! Call this a world" [line 409]. Or there is the fine frenzy of his impulse to venture forth from this into the "real" world, the world of warm humanity, his unrealistic readiness to take upon himself the burden of all its "weal and woe"; and, in pointed and ironic contrast to such a superhuman ideal, his egotistical urge "through the world send all [his] senses casting" [line 3062]. If we were to cut our enquiry short at this point, we might be tempted to think that the play turns on a tension between two worlds only: between the world of sense, to which Faust clings "with organs," and the ideal world he is constantly building up within his soul, and which is the butt of so much of Mephisto's deflating irony. But this would be to confuse the work as a whole with the experience of one of its characters, and to string its "life, so rich and colorful, so highly various . . . upon the narrow thread of a single, pervasive idea." For it is Faust who feels this tension between the two souls warring within his breast"—and feels it chiefly in *Part I*. The picture of "worlds" offered us by his creator is much more varied and complex than this. There is Mephisto's mocking disdain of a "clumsy world" of solid ordered reality, to which he opposes the—from his point of view—desirable state of chaos from which he himself derives, and which it is his whole aim to restore. There is the "fair world" of the Invisible Choir of Spirits, the fair world of illusions—but necessary illusions—which the mind of man is capable of building, and which is as vulnerable to the "clearsightedness" of human despair and disillusion as to Mephistophelian negation. There is the tom-cat's satiric denunciation of worldly institutions in the Witch's Kitchen, a "world" as hollow and brittle as a sphere of glass:

> The world's a ball,
> Will rise and fall,
> Roll far and wide;
> Like glass its tune,
> Can break as soon!
> It's hollow inside. [lines 2402–7]

In the mouth of a Frau Marthe this "common" world becomes as trivial as she is herself; when a pedant such as Wagner speaks of it, there is something pathetic about the distance it assumes, a "world" seen, if at all, only on high days and holidays, and then only as it were through a spy-glass—"By spy-glass from afar, on rare occasion" [line 532]. This scholar's distrust of the "world" of men and affairs is one of the things his famulus shares with Faust:

> I never had a vein for worldliness.
> In company I feel so small;
> I'll never be at ease at all. [lines 2058–60]

In Gretchen's "world," by contrast, Faust feels unexpectedly and reassuringly at home. It has all the closeness and cosiness of her warm domesticity. She is "encompassed in her little world" [line 3355], and he, "the wanderer on the face of the earth," becomes its be-all and end-all, its boundaries co-extensive with his presence. Yet, small though it may be, it is through entry into this "world" of hers that Faust embarks on the adventure of *experience*, and learns more about life than through all his learning in the "world of learning." It is here, as he destroys her little world, that he has his first taste of guilt and suffering, and realises that the tragedy of one single individual can symbolize the tragedy of all mankind:

"Murder and death of *a world* upon your head, monster!" is his anguished answer to Mephisto's cynical "She is not the first." Now indeed he bears upon himself "the weal and woe of all mankind" —not as before in the god-like presumption of his imagination, but through the concrete reality of a particular case. Whilst Gretchen, for her part, feels the "little world" in which she so safely dwelt widen to embrace the whole world of suffering as she anticipates her execution and hears no answer to her cry of pain:

> All napes shrink back from the winking blade
> That will glint and find me.
> Mute lies the world like the grave! [lines 4593–95]

Then from the "little world" of the first part we move into the "great world" of the second, into the world of the past and the future, into the medieval world and the world of antiquity, the world of nature and the world of science, the beginnings of natural creation and audacious attempts to short-circuit these in the laboratory—until we even catch a glimpse of the "world" beyond the grave. A whole book might be written on the use of this word in *Faust*, and it would reflect not only the course of the action—"from Heaven through the World to Hell"—not only the characteristic *Weltanschauung* of many of the minor as well as the major figures in the play, but the interplay of the different "worlds," the different structures of reality, which may well exist within one and the same person at different times, or in different moods and situations. What we are offered here is not only a view of the intersection and interlocking of these many worlds but insight into the modifications and metamorphoses they undergo through their action and reaction upon each other—a realization, through the vehicle of poetry and dramatic action, of the truth that our "worlds" are many and that we make them ourselves, and that those we make now are influenced by those that have been made in the past. Through exploration of the expansion and development of this one cell, the word *Welt*, we gain intimate knowledge of the movement and growth of the whole vast organism—so that when we light again on Mephisto's words,

> It's long been dear to human bosoms
> To swap the universe for cozy microcosms. [lines 4044–45]

it strikes us with new resonance and is pregnant with our experience of all the "worlds" we have encountered whether in the poetry or the dramatic action.

At whatever significant point we strike this verbal surface—at *Brust* (breast), *Fels* (rock), *Feuer* (fire), *Gefühl* (feeling), *Geist* (spirit), *Herz* (heart), *Kraft* (power), *Kreis* (circle), *Schlüssel* (key), *Weg* (path)—we are able to follow up a similar pattern of meaning. Each makes its own pattern, but interlocks with and sup-

ports the others, enriching and modifying them. Take "breast" for
instance, and its synonym "bosom." It is a word which falls naturally from Faust's lips as a symbol of the endless fertility of nature:

> How, boundless Nature, seize you in my clasp?
> You breasts where, all life's sources twain [lines 455–56]

His own breast, on the other hand, his "shriveled breast," is symp-
tom and symbol of the sterile emptiness of his own study-world. In
the mouth of Mephisto the word takes colour from his habitual
tinge of mockery, as he admonishes the student to "cling to the
breasts of Wisdom" so that each day he may experience a greater
lust for it:

> So you will suck the breasts of learning
> With rising appetite and yearning. [lines 1892–93]

The erotic overtones are obvious here. And when, in order to excite,
but at the same time deride, Faust's lust for Gretchen, this Mephis-
to-Satan, Hebrew devil that he is, quotes from the Song of Songs,
breasts though evoked only by the simile of the "twin roes feeding
among the lilies" (or "roses," as Luther has it)—becomes offen-
sively lascivious:

> . . . I've often envied you, my friend,
> That pair of twins beneath the roses penned. [lines 3336–37]

All the finely calibrated nuances of sensuality and fertility, of eroti-
cism and spirituality, are made manifest in and through this image.
And all of them are united in one single occurrence when Faust,
moved by the mysterious enchantment of love's first stirrings, imagines Gretchen lying in her cot as a little child.

> Here came, its bosom gently heaving
> With tender life, the child in bloom, [lines 2713–14]

But he has drunk deep of the witch's potion and, spurred on by
Mephisto, he is soon all desire for complete union with his beloved:

> Must I forgo the bliss
> Of knowing at your bosom an hour's rest
> Thrusting together soul to soul and breast to breast?
> [lines 3502–4]

Yet, though Mephisto may think he has succeeded in severing
divine from mundane love in Faust's heart, the sensual-erotic from
the spiritual-tender, Faust's coupling of "breast" and "soul" in the
same breath is in itself an indication of Mephisto's impending dis-
comfiture. And from the way in which Gretchen herself uses this
word we may follow the whole course of her overpowering love.
More direct in the expression of her emotions, she had in the Ur-
Faust voiced the intensity of her longing by fusing and confusing

physical desire with the maternal urge to envelop the beloved in the security of the womb:

> My womb, Lord! how
> It longs for him. [lines 1098–99]

With the substitution of "bosom" for "womb" at this point in the completed play, Goethe weaves this single thread more firmly still into the texture of the whole, making Gretchen in prison echo, not only her own words, but Faust's "at your bosom an hour's rest" and unite desire and trust in the completeness of her love:

> To his arms I shall fly,
> At his bosom lie! [lines 4464–65]

The pattern made by "breast"/"bosom" reaches its climax in *Part I* with Gretchen's pathetic description of the churchyard where she will lie with her loved ones, her baby at her breast—but no lover at her side!

> And the little one at my right breast.
> There's no one else will lie by me!—[lines 4528–29]

Each of these verbal "filaments" has a "purpose for the whole." Each has a definite function to perform in the aesthetic effect of the whole. Nor can the importance of its function be judged by the number of times it occurs. "Bolt," for instance, only occurs nine times; but almost always at a strategic point, and each time with increasing weight of remembered or anticipatory significance. It first appears as a metaphor, to express Faust's despair that none of his instruments, neither of his learning nor of his craft, can 'raise the bolts' which bar the door to Absolute Truth and prevent him discovering "the inmost force/That bonds the very universe" [lines 382–83]. Truth cannot be compelled, he finds, neither by natural nor by supernatural means. Yet it only needs a tiny human hand to "leave the bolt undone" on a door which admits him to love and guilt for him to be afforded a glimpse into life's deepest mysteries:

> I'd gladly leave my door unbolted tonight [line 3506]

The two poles, of uncommitted sensuality and tragic human relationship, between which Faust is flung, back and forth, are exemplified through this word *Riegel*. On the one hand, there is its appearance in the ribald song of the student—

> Unbolt the door, in dark of night;
> Unbolt the door, the lover cries;
> Bolt up the door, at dawn's first light. [lines 2105–7]

which anticipates, at the stock level of Mephistophelian comprehension, Gretchen's impending surrender. But, at the other pole, it can be expressive—and even on such devilish lips—of human helplessness in the face of deeds irrevocable, and crimes committed:

I cannot lose the avenger's bonds, nor undo his bolts. ["Dreary Day. Field"]

It is often said that the connection between the two parts of *Faust* is extremely tenuous—hardly more, in fact, than the persistence of the two protagonists and the sporadic reappearance of some of the other characters. The deliberate counterpointing of scene against scene—and not just of the obvious ones, such as Classical versus Northern "Walpurgis Night," or the "un-bolting" of Faust's long abandoned "Narrow, high-vaulted Gothic chamber," this time to reveal a "Laboratorium" beyond; the double academic promotion —of student to famulus, and famulus to professor; Faust's second restoration to life—this time by a chorus of nature-spirits instead of Easter bells and angel-choirs; the return at the end to regions approximating to those heavenly regions from which we started out —all this would be enough to refute such a charge even as regards outer structure alone. But if we keep close to the linguistic surface, we find that the "intercommunication" between the two parts is more subtle still, more intricate—and more "inward" than this. When, for instance, on the second stage of Faust's search for "Woman Eternal," he and his Northern companion set foot on Classical soil, Mephisto—true to type—"sniffs around" (*umherspürend* is the stage-direction here) in Helena's habitat exactly as he had done in Gretchen's bedroom (*herumspürend* was the stage-direction there.) Already disconcerted by the unashamed nakedness, sensing his powerlessness over these serene figures of antiquity, casting a nostalgic glance back at the obscene antics of those Northern witches whom he could command at will, he lets an apprehensive eye linger upon the Sphinxes, symbols of fertility and the repository of esoteric wisdom, and—half-attracted, half-repelled—evokes, without actually using the word, all the accumulated connotations of "breast":

> Your upper parts entice, naught were fairer,
> But down below, the beast excites my terror. [lines 7146–47]

It is clear from this single example that a morphological investigation, though it may start mechanically, cannot for long proceed mechanically: the word *breast* itself did not occur, but the notion was present. It may indeed be a salutary corrective to over-zealous probings after philosophical significance to sit back and just let eye or ear register recurrences of the same word. In this way hidden connections may well be uncovered, and meanings poetic and dramatic, as distinct from merely discursive, thus brought to light. But words are related, not by outer form and appearance alone, but by their meanings as well. And it is the mind that must be on the alert for these. Suppose, for instance, that we would look in *Part I* for some antecedent of that Wanderer who appears so casually, and to no apparent dramatic purpose, in Act V of *Part II*. This figure appears so completely out of the blue that we have even been told he can only be accounted for by going outside the world of play altogether and seeking his origins in Goethe's own early life. But surely there is an antecedent in Faust's life too. And a close one at that. Yet it is not really to be found in any of the three early occurrences of the word *Wanderer* itself, though each one of them is in its own way a poetic anticipation of this figure and his fate. In the first of these, Faust feels himself no more than a worm trodden under foot by the casual step of a wanderer. In the second, the wanderer himself is threatened on every side by the exuberant and inimical forces of nature. In the third, moral evil—in the shape of Mephisto's casual and callous dismissal of Gretchen's suffering—rears its head so alarmingly that Faust prays for a return of the time when he was "a wanderer without grief or guilt" and the devil just a dog playing round his feet. But closer than any of these—and a dramatic as well as a poetic anticipation of the whole scene in which the innocent old couple, and their no less innocent guest, are destroyed when Mephisto exceeds his master's injunctions—are those lines in "Forest and Cave" in which Faust describes himself as "fugitive, the homeless rover,/The man-beast void of goal or bliss." He is indeed a "wanderer" upon the face of the earth, though only synonyms of the word occur, and a wanderer who, with all the frenzy of a natural force, will destroy Gretchen's "Ruh," her peace of mind and her whole little world, symbolized here by the "small cabin on an alpine meadow." In the old couple, Philemon and Baucis, the aged Faust sees the Darby and Joan he and Gretchen might have become. He hates their "Hütte," not just because it is a hindrance to his engineering plans, but because it is a reminder of his first great guilt. And so the cottage must go; and though, like Ahab, he is but half-responsible for the death of its inhabitants, what *we* witness through the brief appearance of these three figures, and their rapid destruction, is a symbolic re-enactment of aspects of Faust he had long ago destroyed in himself, aspects relating to innocent wandering and the haven of domesticity.

Here we see a word, image, metaphor, from *Part I* turning into a full-blown dramatic personage in *Part II*. It is by no means the only time this happens in Goethe's works. And it is not the only time it happens here. There is, for instance, Homunculus, the synthetic man produced in his retort by a Wagner turned scientist. He is a dramatic illustration of Goethe's conviction that a living whole is more than the sum of its parts. Though very much "all there," he still feels the need to "originate," to come into being by going back to the origins of life and passing through all the forms of living creatures; and it is he who exhorts his maker to remember, when trying to put living elements together, that the "how" is more important than the "what," the form that the substance:

> The How needs even more thought than the What. [line 6992]

If now we turn back to *Part I*, we can easily discover the origins of this engaging little creature in those lines in which Mephisto entertains the student by gibing at the scientist's claim to have discovered the essence of a thing by dissecting it:

> Who would know and describe a living thing,
> Seeks first to expel the spirit within,
> Then he stands there, the parts held in his grasp,
> Lost just the spiritual bond, alas! [lines 1936–39]

And then there is Frau Sorge, the only one of those four weird women who at the end of *Part II* is able to penetrate into Faust's consciousness—and his conscience. She too is an old acquaintance. We have known her since Faust, in his first extremity of despair, vividly evoked her power to gnaw and nag at a man's peace of mind. No sooner does she take up her abode in his heart than she works in myriad guises to destroy him with needless fears:

> Deep in the heart, gray Care anon will settle,
> In secret plant her stinging nettle,
> With restless rocking spoil repose and joy. [lines 644–46]

Here already is the germ of a later personification. And it is already clear that it will be a woman—for she is constantly putting on a new face!

> Ever new masks for her disguise employ. [line 647]

And is not the image of womanly beauty which Faust glimpses in the mirror of the Witch's Kitchen already half-way to being transformed into the Helen of *Part II* when Mephisto whispers lasciviously into his ear,

> No fear—with this behind your shirt
> You'll soon see Helen of Troy in every skirt! [lines 2603–4]

Whatever Shaftesbury and the neo-Platonists may have meant by "inward form," what Goethe meant by it was not some "mysterious something" lodged within, but the growing awareness by eye, ear and mind of the significance of such connections and cross-connections.[4] He knew this as certainly when he was twenty-five and writing about works of art, as when at seventy he rebuked those "physicists" and natural philosophers who, with Haller, postulated

4. An allusion to the traditional neo-Platonic notion of beauty in art as a manifestation of an inner spiritual value which the work appears to embody.

an inner essence in nature which is inaccessible to the human mind:

> *"To the inside of Nature"*—
> Oh you philistine!—
> *"No created soul can penetrate."*

"I've been hearing that for these past sixty years," cries Goethe in a playfully serious little poem, "and calling down curses upon it—though surreptitiously of course." And to such philistine heresy he opposes his own belief that at point after point on the surface of nature we have already penetrated to what is within:

> We think: from place to place
> We are in the inside.

So far we have been taking as *our* points of departure on the surface of *Faust* small verbal units—even though some of them may eventually have been bodied forth as symbolic figures. Let us now consider larger units; not indeed as large as a whole character or a move in the action, but sizable enough to mediate between such dramatic and theatrical elements and the fine-structure of the poetry. Gretchen's four songs serve this purpose very well indeed. In the meagre verbal texture of the *Ur-Faust* they had stood out as pillars of an action which comprised little more than a love-tragedy, and in that narrower context it is illuminating to consider them from an architectonic point of view. They there provided those turning-points of high tension around which the dramatic action—often left to the imagination—revolved. And in them the action itself was distilled into poignant lyrical—or, perhaps more accurately, ballad-like—expression. But once these same songs have taken their rightful place in the far wider action of the whole *Faust,* once they have grown into the dense and intricate poetic weave out of which this action is made, their ramifications multiply, and extend far beyond the little world bounded by Gretchen's love and passion. In the *Ur-Faust,* "The King in Thule," so fashioned by Goethe that it might well have been among the store of folk-songs Gretchen knew, springs unbidden to her lips—a good example of Goethe's knowledge of "the psychopathology of everyday life"[5] perfectly expressing her as yet barely conscious desire for the handsome stranger and the ingrained longing of every woman for a fidelity which will last beyond the grave. Its repercussions here are limited to this psychological moment and its dramatc implications. But in the completed work it anticipates her own fidelity beyond the grave and her intercession with the *Mater Gloriosa* on behalf of her erring lover. The next song she sings is far from having the appearance of a ready-made *Volkslied.* She is now all too conscious of the nature of her desires, and there is no question of "My peace is gone" springing inadvertently to her lips. Love has made her creative in her own small

5. The title of a well-known work by Sigmund Freud which appeared in 1904.

way, and what she now sings is a unique utterance of personal experience, of the profound disturbance of newly awakened desire. And
in the *Ur-Faust* it is no more than this. If she feels that the world is
like a grave when Faust is not there to fill it, this is no more than a
metaphor:

> My peace is gone,
> My heart is sore;
> Can find it never
> And never more. [lines 3378–81]

Only by implication does it point forward to her own tragic end, to
the grave in which she will lie alone. But when Goethe came to complete *Part I* he made this connection explicit. As in her tortured
imagination she feels the blade about to strike her neck, the dreadful silence of the whole world, the lack of answering resonance to
her pain, is what appals her. And, in a different sense now, "the
world" is again like "the grave":

> Mute lies the world like the grave! [line 4595]

Nor did he forget this "filament" when he came to complete *Part
II*. The "peace" she felt she had lost for ever with the invasion of
her world by unsuspected forces, and in neither *Ur-Faust* nor *Part
I* ever did recover, she does finally regain when, after Faust's own
"entombment," the double designation, in Latin and in the ver-
nacular, perfectly exemplifying Goethe's abiding conviction that the
universal is only to be found, and can only be shown forth, in and
through the particular. And in this transfigured form she can ever
bear to recall the anguished accents of her third "song," the prayer
which in extremity she had addressed to the *Mater Dolorosa*:

> Incline,
> Thou rich in grief, oh shine
> Thy grace upon my wretchedness! [lines 3587–89]

Nestling close to the *Mater Gloriosa*, she varies both words and
rhythm, as she awaits in bliss and blessedness the return of her
erring lover—who now, in this order of being, is no longer "blem-
ished," no longer subject to the refraction of light by the solidity of
earthly bodies, neither to the play of colour they produce nor to the
shadows they cast, nor indeed to any of the polarities which are the
condition of our mortal existence:

> Incline
> Thou past comparing,
> Thou radiance bearing,
> Thy grace upon my happiness.
> The early-cherished,
> No longer blemished,
> Returns to bliss. [lines 12069–75]

The fourth song she sang, when awaiting execution for the murder of her child,

> My mother, the whore
> Who smothered me,
> My father, the knave
> Who swallowed me! [lines 4412–15]

is an actual folk-song from a fairy-tale. In its bare juxtaposition of images, its absence of logical or causal relations, it expresses as directly as Ophelia's bawdy[6] the sexual phantasies and projections of a mind unhinged. It is with such literary antecedents, or with Goethe's astonishing insight into the unconscious workings of the mind—the essential rightness of Gretchen's projection of her own "whoring" on to her mother, her identification of herself with the child she had killed—that the critic will be concerned if he is treating of the *Ur-Faust* alone. But if he is treating of *Faust* as a whole he must go on to the intercession of the three "Great Sinners," the three Marys, for the soul of Gretchen—and, indirectly, for the soul of Faust—and to ancient associations between sin and holiness. It was a theme to which Goethe had already given universal expression in his two Eastern ballads: "Der Gott und die Bajadere," in which the god descends to the whore and raises her up to him in glory; and "Paria,"[7] a trilogy in which there is enacted the creation of a god whose sole care will be for sinners and outcasts. And in the context of his last and greatest work, the song he had some sixty years before drawn from the fairy-tale world of magic and madness, is assimilated into the overall tone of compassion which encompasses this mystery-play—for all the satire and irony which pervades so much of its action and its style. No wonder Goethe told Luden he need have no fear that the "fragments" he had learned to love in the *Fragment* of 1970 would be lost in the vastness of the completed whole!

There remains the question of the "center" with which we started. It is, I am well aware, an enterprise full of hazards to vie, not only with those "great scholars and gifted individuals" who had, according to Goethe, been trying to discover it from the moment the "torso" appeared, but with the many who have gone on doing so ever since. But it is a task not therefore to be shirked; and the critic may console himself as he tackles it with the thought that it is an occupational risk—is indeed the very nature of his calling—not to be right. And, fortunately, he may even succeed in illuminating something when he is wrong. I shall in any case cover my retreat by suggesting that the specific scene I have in mind is not necessarily *the* "Mittelpunkt," but certainly one of those nodal points at which Goethe located the sudden "contraction" of all the plant-processes, the

---

6. See note to lines 3682 ff. of *Faust*.
7. "The God and the Dancing-Girl" (1797) and "Paria" (1823) are ballads based on Indian legends.

intense concentration of the sap, the systole before, in a comple-
mentary rhythm of diastolic expansion, the plant proceeds to the
next stage of its life-cycle. There may, perhaps, be a shade of contrariness in singling out for such function "Forest and Cave," a scene
which one distinguished scholar even went so far as to describe as
superfluous—"disturbing, misleading and best left out on the stage"
—partly on the grounds that Goethe himself did not seem to know
exactly where it belonged, placing it in the *Fragment* after Gretch-
en's surrender, and shifting it back later to a position immediately
before it. But my apparent perversity has the double advantage of
throwing into sharp relief the kind of law which governs the form
of this "monstrous" and unique dramatic structure, and of vindicat-
ing the usefulness of a morphological approach.

If we consider this scene simply as one of the "peaceful pauses"
in the action—and there are many—it could indeed be left out in
any kind of theatre which is solely concerned with the onward
march of dramatic events. But there is a long tradition of poetic
drama which makes use of monologue, or of chorus, as the vehicle
of essential aspects of meaning, and in which these are therefore
inherent elements of the dramatic form. And "Forest and Cave"
consists of far more than the contemplative monologue with which
it opens, important as this is in itself. Whether here, or in Faust's
subsequent dialogue with his now hated companion, we find all the
threads of the earlier action gathered together, and the shuttle
poised for a moment, before it is thrown forward again with new,
and now tragic, impulse to complete the pattern. The very first line
of the scene,

> You gave me, lofty spirit, gave me all
> I pleaded for, [lines 3217–18]

challenges the critic to test the validity of a morphological approach
to the verbal fabric of this play. For the identity of this "lofty
spirit" has been something of a crux. It can scarcely be the "Erdgeist," some commentators have declared, since that spirit certainly
did not grant Faust all he asked for; on the contrary, it rejected
him, reducing him to suicidal despair with the words,

> Close to the spirit you comprehend,
> Not me! [lines 512–13]

Against such an argument, there is of course the awkward fact that
no spirit other than the "Erdgeist" had ever appeared to Faust as a
"creature of the flames" and that Faust, when he now addresses the
"lofty spirit," recalls that this spirit had in fact—and "not in vain"
either—turned his face towards him "in the fire." But scholars
attached to the theory that the two are not identical could of course
counter this by saying that much in this play happens off-stage; or
else fall back on the stock "argument from the creative process,"

and warn us that anything which took a lifetime to compose cannot possibly be free of contradictions. But if we reject unverifiable hypotheses about the operations of a mind long dead in favour of close examination of the work we still have, we cannot fail to be struck by the close verbal parallels between the two scenes. Faust's motive for calling up the Earth-Spirit at all was profound discontent with what the Spirit of the Macrocosm had to offer. It was a spectacle so grand that it made him feel "like a god," the "equal of spirits," and "close to the mirror of eternal truth." But sublime though it was, it was a spectacle and nothing more:

> What glorious show! Yet but a show, alas! [line 454]

Recalling its cold remoteness now, he contrasts it with the rich insight into the processes of Nature which has been afforded him since, and tells the "lofty spirit":

> Not merely
> A coldly wondering visit did you grant,
> But suffered me into her inner depth
> To gaze as in the bosom of a friend. [lines 3221–24]

Instead of the cosmic play, at which he could never be more than a mere onlooker, he had longed for the closeness of participation, and therefore conjured a spirit closer to earth and, as he thought, more akin to himself:

> You, Spirit of the Earth, are nigher, [line 461]

or again,

> Spirit of deeds, how close I feel to thee! [line 511]

only to find that it rejected his claims of equality by scornfully referring him to a spirit he might be capable of comprehending. Now, in "Forest and Cave," having dilated, in ecstatic terms strongly reminiscent of the "Erdgeist" scene, on his power to enjoy and participate in the living processes of nature, he breaks off sharply. There is a turn in his monologue here—a turn, from the gifts which bring him ever nearer to the gods, to the thought of the now hated, if indispensable, companion who is apparently the inevitable concomitant of such gifts—a turn which parallels exactly his former deflation by the Earth-Spirit, and makes it clear beyond all doubt that the spirit to whom he was then contemptuously referred is in fact the Mephistopheles whom he now admits to having received from the Spirit he still feels inclined to address as Sublime:

> Unto this ecstasy
> That takes me near and nearer to the gods,
> You joined me that companion, whom already
> I cannot miss. [lines 3241–44]

And when this companion, this Spirit of Negation, now enters the scene, he does not miss the opportunity of pricking the bubble of Faust's "presumption" again, of deflating his recurrent impulse—which is indeed his saving grace—to remember that he is "made in the image of God." And he pricks it in terms not at all unlike those of the Earth-Spirit:

> EARTH SPIRIT. Where's the soul's call you hurled?
>   Where is the breast that wrought in it a world,
>   That bore and nursed it, that with joyous tremble
>   Swelled up to soar, us spirits to resemble? [lines 490–93]
> MEPHISTOPHELES. A truly transcendental binge!
>   By night and dew lie on a mountain range,
>   Of earth and sky essay ecstatic capture,
>   Swell up to girth divine with mystic rapture . . . [lines 3282–85]

One could almost believe he had been listening-in on that early dis-comfiture—as indeed he probably had!—and is now parodying that whole scene.

Such close linguistic parallels are the "unveränderliches Factum"[8] from which the critic must start if he would broach the apparent contradiction between the Earth-Spirit's rejection of him and Faust's subsequent assertion that he has, notwithstanding, granted him all he asked. This is the world "as the poet has made it," and its logic takes precedence over the logic of any of the "worlds" in the occult sources on which he drew. It matters not a whit if in the hierarchy of spirits there an Earth-Spirit would have been precluded from sending Mephistopheles to Faust. Here, in Goethe's play, that is what he does. And it is up to us to try to understand in what sense this "lofty spirit" may be said to have granted Faust's wishes. Surely in the sense that what he had longed for was participation in reality *as known under earthly conditions*, that is, in terms of polarity. The Spirit he summoned because the spectacle of the macrocosm left him unsatisfied was a spirit who was in the thick of life, "weaving the living garment of God," and weav-ing it in terms of interdependent opposites:

> In tides of living, in doing's storm,
>   Up, down, I wave,
>   Waft to and fro,
>   Birth and grave,
>   An endless flow,
>   A changeful plaiting,
>   Fiery begetting, . . . [lines 501–7]

Nor is there any question of Faust being unaware of the essentially "polar" nature of the Spirit he summoned. It was precisely because he felt a rising courage to bear the woe as well as the weal of the

8. "Unalterable fact", a phrase drawn   dated December 31, 1809.
from a letter by Goethe to Reinhard

world [line 465] that he summoned it at all. And it is precisely this polarity that he insists on again when he makes his wager with Mephisto. The devil's traditional temptations, of unlimited knowledge and unlimited pleasure, are rejected with contumely. What this "servant of the Lord" demands are pleasures which will never satisfy, which will turn in the moment of satiety to new desire [lines 1675–87]. And when Mephisto still fails to grasp either the direction or the compass of his mind's intent, he rounds on him with "I tell you it's not a question of *pleasure* at all." In a speech compounded of oxymora and antitheses, he then announces that from now on he is dedicated to the reeling tumult of existence, to its pain no less than its pleasure:

> Frenzy I choose, most agonizing lust,
> Enamored enmity, restorative disgust.
> Henceforth my soul for knowledge crazed no more,
> Against no kind of suffering shall be cautioned,
> And what to all of mankind is apportioned
> I mean to savor in my own self's core,
> Grasp with my mind both highest and most low,
> Weigh down my spirit with their weal and woe,
> And thus my selfhood to their own distend,
> And be, as they are, shattered in the end. [lines 1766–75]

If now, in "Forest and Cave," he recalls with bitterness, and in the compression of a chiasmus,[9] those terms on which he had so impatiently and impulsively insisted when making the pact—

> Thus reel I from desire to fulfillment,
> And in fulfillment languish for desire [lines 3249–50]

—this, at least, is not one of those "contradictions" which critics have always been ready to find in the work and which Goethe so vehemently denied were there: "In poetry there are no contradictions. These occur only in the world of actuality, not in the world of poetry." This change in Faust is one of the contradictions that are to be found in plenty in "the real world" and form part of life itself. It is a change which has come about because he has now felt in his very flesh all that the generous presumption of his earlier demand implies when realized in a concrete situation. He now knows—and to the end of his days he will not cease to make discoveries of a similar kind—the difference between knowledge glimpsed through the imagination and knowledge bought through bitter experience. And it is out of a hard-won realization that man's finest endeavours of mind and will are inseparable from his power to do evil and know pain that, in his monologue in "Forest and Cave," he can fall from the sustained soaring of the first twenty odd lines to a heavy but realistic acceptance of human imperfection:

9. From the Greek meaning "cross": a rhetorical term describing a passage made up of two balanced parts which have their syntactic elements reversed.

> Ah, nothing perfect is vouchsafed to man,
> I sense it now. [lines 3240–41]

Rarely can the particle *now* have had to bear such weight of experience as it is here given by the caesura.

But the threads of this scene run further back still, beyond the pact or the conjuring of the "Erdgeist," to the Prologue in Heaven. It was with a synonym of *companion* that the Lord there announced why he gave the Devil to man—

> Man all too easily grows lax and mellow,
> He soon elects repose at any price;
> And so I like to pair him with a fellow
> To play the Deuce, to stir, and to entice. [lines 340–43]

—and it was in words not unlike those of the Earth-Spirit that the Archangels spoke of the polarities existing in the fair but turbulent life on earth:

> The earth's resplendence spins and ranges
> Past understanding swift in flight,
> And paradisiac lucence changes
> With awe-inspiring depths of night; [lines 251–54]

The fact that this Prologue was written some ten years *after* "Forest and Cave" is no objection to the view that the threads run *backwards*, any more than it is relevant when considering the present function of the scene to recall that Goethe had doubts and hesitations about where it ought to go. He certainly often spoke of his works "growing" in his mind; but he was as aware of the limitations of the plant-analogy when he used it of the creative process as he was when he used it of the finished products. The last letter of his life, in which he talked about the completion of *Faust* in the larger context of mental processes in general, makes it abundantly clear that for him the "growth" of the human mind, or the "creation" of a work of art, implied not only those unconscious and half-conscious activities which proceed under their own momentum, but "taking thought" and reflection too, the fully conscious acts of selection, adjustment and revision. The time when he conceived and wrote "Forest and Cave"—during his first and momentous visit to Italy—may certainly be regarded as a "nodal point" in his own growth, a moment of rejuvenation and rebirth, as he repeatedly called it, a "Mittelpunkt" from which he looked backwards and forwards, taking stock of himself and making decisions for the future. It is not at all improbable that in the case of *Faust*, a work which accompanied him through so much of his life, this phase of contraction and intensification should have brought forth a scene which may likewise be regarded as a "Mittelpunkt." But however that may be, of one thing we can be certain in the light of Goethe's many utterances about the way he made his poetry: whenever he took up

ity and development between the two parts, with unexpected balances in the sequence of scenes.

In sum, the unity is not a mechanical construct, it stands in analogy to a musical composition, a vast symphony of greatly varied movements and developments presided over by a master in full control who knows where he came from, where he is going to, and exactly and deliberately how he plans to get there. Just as subsequent critical analysis of a large-scale musical composition will even reveal various mathematical symmetries and continuities (which will never be mechanical, which the composer may possibly have arrived at consciously but just as possibly intuitively through a guiding sense of balance), just so the *Faust* has a more closely knit composition than we may be willing at this stage to attribute to the conscious formal will of its author.

* * * A truly simple observation of the light symbolism in its broadest formal perspectives has apparently escaped the attention of the critics. The earthy action of *Part I* begins at night, "Night," in a "high-vaulted, narrow Gothic chamber," which Faust promptly calls a "prison," and it ends in the darkness before dawn with the scene entitled "Prison." *Part II* begins with a scene entitled "Charming Landscape," a pleasant region that is promptly shown to be in the mountains just before dawn and at sunrise (with Faust again confirming the validity of life on earth with all its limitations), and it ends, not at midnight with the death of Faust, but on the way upward through the "Mountain Gorges," the mountain defiles, past the holy anchorites of ever higher and wider perspective, when the angels carry the immortal parts of Faust, to which, as they observe, there still persistently clings "ein Erdenrest," a remnant of the earthly [line 11954]:

> No Angel divorces
> Twin-natures single grown,
> nor extricates them. [lines 11961–63]

Only with the Doctor Marianus do we have the transition out of the earthly to the heavenly. In sum: *Part I* is encompassed by confinement, cut off from perspective, *Part II* is encompassed by mountain vistas, by widening perspectives. Only *after* a full earthly life and widest earthly perspectives can come the transition, the transcendence to higher spheres.

At all four points we have a darkness before dawn, a "death" before resurrection:

1. Suicide, "The last drink" [line 735], versus "Christ is arisen" [line 757].
2. "She is condemned," versus "redeemed" [line 4611].
3. Faust's collapse after the catastrophe, over against his recovery in the symbolic passage of time: "Of horrors suffered

cleanse his soul entire" [line 4625], "Return him to the sacred light" [line 4633].

4. "The final moment, worthless, stale and void" [line 11589], versus

> Pure spirits's peer, from evil coil
> He was vouchsafed exemption. [lines 11934–35]

When Goethe at the second point, for the completed first part, added the word which was lacking in the *Urfaust*, he did so not for any sentimental reason, as has been asserted or implied, he did so for compelling reasons of form and symbol from the broad perspectives of the total drama, its larger patterns and harmonies.

* * *

For another aspect of form let us see how the drama begins at its very beginning, namely with the lyric "Dedication" in which the poet speaks with his own voice and tells us of his own attitude toward his creation. * * *

We should first look at what the poet says here. He is about to resume his work on the drama. Years have elapsed since he began it; many of those dear friends among whom and for whom he first wrote it are gone now or widely scattered. Those who will hear its continuation are later comers, strangers, whose very applause is frightening.

And yet, as the poem begins, the wavering forms of his youthful creation rise up before him once more. They come from so remotely in the past that he doubts whether he can continue with the task of giving them poetic realization. But at once he sees that it is not up to him to decide whether or not he will continue; they take possession of him:

> You press me! Well, I yield to your petition, [line 5]

and he feels himself transported out of the present back into his youth.

Then, in conclusion, he notices that something strange is happening to him: with this invasion of his present by his remote past, with the emotions that this engenders in him, with the breaking down of the barriers that it achieves, his sense of present presence is lost. That which he is and has, seems remote and unreal; that which has long since disappeared, becomes reality.

The chief poetic motifs in the "Dedication," then, are: the mystery of creativity, the mystery of time, the mystery of the different kinds of reality, the mystery of the creative individual whose "real" environmental configuration can be made unreal by an imaginative, mentally created and projected configuration. This, once brought into being, has a life of its own and can at any time, unsummoned, rise up out of the past and demand its creative due.

Therewith we have, at the very beginning, a first statement of the great themes that run through the whole of *Faust* and give it symbolic coherence and continuity. Again and again, in ever varying form and action and situation, we shall find the poet exploring the great mysteries of time, of place, of creativity, of the reality and unreality of man's life on earth between birth and death, and beyond in that great arc of the cycle that lies outside his ken. If we notice these recurrences and developments of primary themes as we progress through the work, we shall be better prepared to understand Faust's entrance into the realm of memory for the recovery of the greater past, and to understand the great voyage through time and place that becomes all-encompassing in the second and third acts of *Part II*.

In the very next part, the "Prelude in the Theater," the poet varies the handling of these great themes to the point of making a jest about them. The dialogue moves along so gaily and divertingly that the jest may be at the expense of the viewer and critic if he is not alert to it. * * * In this scene the director, the comedian, and the poet are talking together, as the spectators are filing in and some of them are already seated. And what are they talking about? About the play that is to be presented. The director wants a great box-office success; he represents showmanship. The comedian wants a good acting vehicle; he represents entertainment. And the poet uncompromisingly insists on making it a literary work of art; he represents creativity. So entertaining is the dialogue, so eloquent the poet's declaration of the integrity of the work of art and the nature of the creative processes, that only in the end do we realize with a shock that though the audience is assembled, the drama is not yet written, far less rehearsed and staged, and yet the director, unperturbed, puts an end to the discussion, commands the poet to commandeer his poetry, the stage hands to produce their most splendid effects, and the actor by his magic to transmute the stage of boards into the stage of the world.

We shall know for a certainty as we go along that this anachronism was not caused by any lapse or inattention on Goethe's part. At a number of points he deliberately introduces anachronisms (and also anachorisms), with humorous intent on the surface though with large intent in the thematic continuity of the whole. By the time we reach the second part, particularly the second act, we shall know what all this jocoserious play with time is leading to.

There is yet a third preliminary part, the "Prologue in Heaven." Here we leave these single and limited and conflicting points of view, and see the drama and its show-place, the earth, *sub specie aeternitatis*, first in the song of the archangels, and then more specifically directed toward Faust in the words of the Lord, with the dissenting reedy voice of Mephistopheles in comic contrast to the heavenly harmonies. The great theme of this scene, raised to an ultimate beyond the limitations of place and time, is announced by the archangels at the beginning and confirmed by the Lord in his last words. It is the theme of creativity, continuing creativity as the ultimate meaning of the universe, embracing all in its divine purpose, even Mephistopheles who has an unintentionally creative function in spurring man on to constant striving, constant overcoming of his past errors, constant rising to higher things. We are thus early prepared for Faust at the last choosing a life of creativity (under the oldest and most persistent symbol of creativity, that of separating the land from the waters), and for the angels at the end restating the intent of the whole: "Whoever strives in ceaseless toil, him we may grant redemption" [lines 11936–37], with love coming down from above to welcome him.

There is also something else of great importance that the poet wishes to convey to us by implication in the course of these preliminary scenes. This becomes all the clearer when we turn to the next scene and find Faust himself coming to word and telling us his attitude toward his own and the human dilemma. We suddenly realize that what Goethe has been giving us is a series of quite different points of view of the action that is to follow: first his own as the poet's, then the director's the dramatist's, the actor's, then the Archangels', the Lord's, and Mephistopheles', with each of them, except the Lord's, limited in its perspectives, true so far as it goes, but incapable of comprehending the whole. Hereby Goethe establishes for the drama the principle of *multiple points of view*, each of them more or less important but only all of them together leading to a comprehension of the total intent. Mephisto, in the Prologue and so often thereafter, is "right," brilliantly and wittily right, but his rightness is of a lower order than Faust's and more especially than the Lord's. Faust's assistant, Wagner, is also "right," in his limited way, so is the Earth Spirit, or Margarete, or the Emperor, or Thales, or Anaxagoras, or Homunculus, or Euphorion. To each his due, no more than his due, no one alone will lead us to the play's full meaning or the author's full intent. Only in the combination of them all, only in their multiplicity (intended to stand for and poetically reflect the rich variety and bewildering diversity of life itself) do we come to some approximation of the ultimate meaning, and understanding of the "important action that points to a still more important action," to quote Goethe's definition of a symbolic drama.

Even this, all together, does not exhaust the formal import of these three preliminary parts. Let us continue viewing them together, as we did for the purpose of establishing the principle of multiple points of view. What do we see? A lighter, more relaxed, even comic scene between two intense and serious scenes. If we go on, what do we have between the two first great monologues of Faust? We have the lighter, more relaxed, comic Wagner interlude (with Faust, like the "Poet," remaining in an eloquent state of high seriousness).

Let us go on. Between this double monologue of Faust and the two study scenes to follow, what do we have? The light, gay, relaxed scene, "Outside the City Gate," of Faust's and Wagner's Easter walk amid the festive populace, with Faust again turning serious, and here making one of the profound thematic statements about himself and the condition of man, in the middle of which stand his reflections on the "two souls," reflections consistently misinterpreted through the introduction of alien points of view and through a lapse in the observation of the exact syntax.

And so it continues. After the study scenes comes the double interlude of "Auerbach's Tavern" and "Witch's Kitchen," one closing the previous action, the other opening the coming action, both serving deeper dramatic purposes, the former a more profound one that would seem possible under a separatist, fragmentist reading. Having two scenes here tying together a larger group of scenes before and after, warns us that we cannot simply speak of a tripartite sequence, as we might be tempted to do from the first instances. We had better speak more generally of the principle of the interlude, and indeed as we go through the *Faust*, we shall see that this is one of the chief compositional principles of the drama, bringing together not only single scenes, not only groups of scenes, but even the two parts of the drama.

* * *

For a larger group of scenes connected and divided by an interlude, let us look at the Gretchen tragedy as it develops up to the "Walpurgis Night," that is, from the scene "Street" where Faust first sees Margarete through the scene "Cathedral" where she finally collapses in tragic misery. The three scenes of the catastrophe follow after the "Walpurgis Night" and the "Walpurgis Night's Dream." The middle scene is the serious interlude, "Forest and Cave." Its pivotal position has always been recognized, easily recognized, though its relation to the six scenes immediately before it and immediately after it has never been examined. No one has even so much as counted them or noticed the fine balance that exits. Here we shall perceive something as artistically remarkable as it is unexpected, a tightening of the composition, the establishment of a beautiful symmetry that raises the final version far above the level of the *Urfaust*, though even there it is already adumbrated. Let us look at this group of scenes.

In the first scene, "Street," Margarete comes from church, from confession, innocent and absolved from her small sins. In the last scene, "Cathedral," she is again in church, laden with guilt, with the dreadful "Dies irae" resounding and the voice of the "Evil Spirit" driving her to despair and collapse.

In the second scene, "Evening. A clean little room," we find her in the serenity and security of her own home and room, with the serenity and security for the first time invaded by Faust and Mephistopheles. In the second from last scene, "Night. Street in Front of Gretchen's Door," we find her at home, all serenity and security shattered, with the last remaining relative, her brother, turned against her, and even he killed by the last invasion of Faust and Mephisto.

In the third scene, "On a Walk," we have the comic episode, as narrated by Mephistopheles, of the official external church taking unto itself the jewels of Margarete, naturally for her own good. In the scene third from last, the "By the City Wall," before the image of the Mater Dolorosa, we see her turning, in her tragic agony, to the true spiritual church as her last and best refuge.

In the fourth scene, "The Neighbor's House," we meet the fitting feminine instrument through which Mephistopheles can attain Faust's desire in the worst way, namely Martha, an exemplar of the negative corruptive feminine. Another example of the negative corruptive feminine comes in the scene fourth from last, "At the Well," with Lieschen's gossip about Bärbelchen and a report of the vicious actions against her. Gretchen sadly reflects on her earlier consent to such conventional cruelty before she herself was stricken, even as earlier she had taken the second gift of jewels to Martha, well knowing that from her she would get desired rather than good advice.

In the fifth scene, another "Street," with dialogue between Faust and Mephistopheles, Faust hears that all is arranged for him to meet Margarete if he will only bear witness to Martha on the death of her husband in Padua. He at first rejects this device as obliging him to bear false witness, but then with the haste of impatience succumbs to Mephisto's evil design, "You're right, the more so since I have no choice" [line 3072]. In the scene "Marthe's Garden," fifth from last, Margarete, deeply troubled, especially by the presence of his ominous associate, probes Faust on the state of his religion, Faust is evasive on specifics and veils himself behind an eloquent general statement on the Divinity and the universality of His worship. He is also evasive about Mephisto, and all the time he has with him the sleeping potion which he persuades Margarete to administer to her mother, a potion which by Mephisto's evil design is something more deadly.

The sixth scene, "Garden" (with the appended "Garden Pavilion"), leads to Margarete's first acknowledgment of love. The scene sixth from the last, "Gretchen's Chamber" ("My peace is gone"), gives lyric expression to Gretchen's final surrender to love.

The pivotal scene in the midst of this symmetrically spreading sequence, this rising and falling action, the "Forest and Cave," also makes the transition from the bright to the dark side, from Faust's prayer of thanksgiving to the exalted spirit who has brought him to harmony with nature and all its living creatures, an imperilled harmony, as he adds, with the thought of the sinister companion attached to him who fans his emotions to a consuming fire. Mephisto on his arrival finds it relatively easy to plunge Faust back into his emotional turmoil, back on the course which he realizes helplessly will lead to destruction.

* * * In both *Parts I* and *II* there is, on closer and more careful examination, an articulation of scenes into groups, sometimes, as here, centering about a point, at other times in parallel series, never mechanical or routinely repetitive, never forcing a symmetry, always the work of a presiding genius for whom form is the direct outcome and expression of function.

* * *

However, another sequence, another repeated pattern is even more instructive in showing the contrast between the poet's intent and the critics' apprehension. It is the recurrent motif of *macrocosm* and *microcosm*, sometimes clearly expressed, sometimes obscurely and indirectly, frequently with the twist and perversion that Mephistopheles in his special animosity can give the term. Where the modern critic fails is in the realization that the term *microcosm*, small world, had a single specific meaning on through the age of Goethe and that the vaguer usage of small world, any kind of small world, is of later origin when the traditional symbolic complex was forgotten or disregarded.

For the *Faust*, as for the centuries before it, the one valid meaning of the word *microcosm* is *man*. The concept of the microcosm is built on the old postulate that man's increasing understanding of the macrocosm, the universe and its phenomena, implies a development of man's inner self toward a harmonious correspondence to the whole of nature. Only man of all creatures has this microcosmic potentiality; out of this, his unique position, flows the concept of the dignity of man. * * * Faust's words on viewing the sign of the macrocosm [lines 430–453] suffice to introduce us to this creative view of harmonious correspondence. The whole concept irritates and outrages Mephistopheles, particularly because the creativity of man is so clearly implicit in it, and from the Prologue onward he continues his perversion and mockery of it:

Earth's little god [line 281]
. . . of Heaven's light a glitter; . . . reason [lines 284, 285]

. . . your Man, that microcosmic fool. [line 1347]

Associate yourself with a poetaster,
And let that worthy muse and roam
And all the noble virtues cluster
Upon your venerable dome, . . .
I should myself be glad to meet him,
"Sir Microcosm" I would greet him. [lines 1789–92, 1801–2]

These are the more obvious of his references to man as a micro-cosm, though, continuingly through the rest of the drama, his more or less veiled scorn of man's higher pretensions conveys his hostility. However, his real perversion of the term, a perversion anticipating modern usage, comes near the end of the last Study scene, after the new student has left and Faust returns ready for departure. On his question where they are going, Mephistopheles answers:

> Wherever you choose.
> The small world, then the great we shall peruse.
> Ah, with what profit, with what flee
> You'll take this seminar for free. [lines 2051–54]

* * * Mephisto by his perversion of the terms announces the per-versions of the concept of microcosm that we are to witness in the next two scenes, the "Auerbach's Tavern in Leipzig" and the "Witch's Kitchen."

His perversion of the concept of the dignity of man, man as a microcosm, is developed in its full destructive negativism in these two scenes where he is master of ceremonies. The potentiality of man, indicated in the Prologue and in the whole implicit philoso-phy of rising upward toward divinity (higher than the angels), has its necessary complement in the potentiality of man to sink lower than the animals. Such are the implications of man's freedom, man's freedom of choice. Just as the dignity of man is a potential state, so the indignity of man is equally potential, equally possible.

In "Auerbach's Tavern" we meet a group of four boon compan-ions who have exercised this freedom of choice. Their God-given intellects and their education to reason they have chosen to befud-dle in drink. Through all their self-stultification they retain the illu-sion that they are still in brilliant possession of their wits; the "wit-ticisms" they exchange seem to them the acme of scintillating social intercourse, and their "humorous" social song about the passionate poisoned rat indicates that they have reached their proper level, a level on which the newly entered Lord of the Flies joins them in his "Song of the Flea," a favorite basso aria to our day.

* * *

The "Witch's Kitchen" is Goethe's virtuoso piece of surrealism, Breughelesque in its cast and setting, almost unprecedented in its verbal calisthenics, with sense gliding over into nonsense and fluc-tuating indeterminately between the two, with free association and every other kind of non-sensical continuity substituting for coherent sequence. This goes on, depth beyond depth, to the culminating nonsense of the witch's "one-times-one," in which the crowning irony is that this *can* be explicated by magic square or cabalistic cal-culation, with the end result that when one has that explication, one has nothing at all.

But the monkeys in the scene are the ultimate symbolic reposito-ries of the triumph of un-reason and non-sense. They can verbalize, quite free of any brain control, with rhyme taking the place of reason and free association that of responsible con-sequence. In places sense seems to emerge, but it is arsyversy sense, as in the male monkey's formula for getting rich, with its displacement of cause and effect, or as in the play with the globe where rhyme and set phrase determine the "order," though in the crown sequence the rhyme does accidentally lead to the sensible statement that rhyme can sometimes accidentally lead to sense:

> If haply point
> Is joined to point
> With luck it's meaning! [lines 2458–60]

If Mephisto had been right in his monologue in counting on Faust's abandonment of reason and knowledge, he might have been able to draw him into this chaos of unreason and word wandering. Being a "son of chaos" Mephisto is in his element. But Faust, being a "servant" of the Lord, remains in full control of his reason and of his critical detachment from unreason, as his first words clearly indicate. But even more than that, he goes on to exercise his microcosmic potentiality in creatively making cosmos emerge out of chaos. In the midst of this subhuman, scurrilous parody of human activity and speech he has emerge out of the magic mirror the image of womankind perfected.

Even a moderately careful examination of his description of the vision of her outstretched body in a landscape, like the Giorgione Venus [lines 2429–40],[1] especially an awareness of its imagery in rela-tion to the imagery of those other passages throughout the drama where the principle of the feminine, the womanly creative, comes to the fore, makes it clear that we must take this vision on Faust's own terms and not on those of Mephisto as expressed immediately there-after and then at the conclusion of the scene. * * * Even Mephis-to's perversion is unable to avoid the allusion to Helen, and if we read only the later poetic passages of Faust's vision of Helen in con-junction with the present passage, even this alone will suffice to put it in its proper context, though the full richness of its connotative filiations go well beyond this.

* * * We cannot hope to see the full import of these themes and motifs, together with their accompanying symbolic network, unless we see them in the context of the total drama beginning with and including the "Dedication." The motifs of the mystery of place and time here announced rise to a point of highest importance in the second and third acts of *Part II*. * * * The crowning motif of the drama is that of human creativity, so strongly emphasized in all three preliminary parts, then continuingly throughout the drama by

1. See note to line 2440 of *Faust*.

Faust himself and by his opposite pole, Mephistopheles, the anti-creative negativist, so well characterized by the Lord in the Prologue and so frankly by himself:

> [I am] the spirit which perpetually denies!
> And justly so; for all that which is wrought
> Deserves that it should come to naught;
> Hence it were best if nothing were engendered.
>
> [lines 1338–41]

His preceding and following words add all the necessary background and details on his anticreative role. Man's microcosmic role is most fully realized when he rises to creativity and, with all his human limitations, endeavors to turn at least one small corner of chaos into cosmos. Thus the theory of artistic creativity, when it comes to be formulated, revolves around the precept that the artist, the poet, must be like God, creating a universe within himself within his work. For the final creative act of Faust Goethe uses the oldest symbol of creativity, of cosmos arising out of chaos, namely the separation of the land from the waters, first formulated by the divine act of Genesis, confirmed in poetic tradition, notably by Milton, and developed by Faust to his ultimate vision of gaining a new land for a new start of a free people on a free soil.

Let us turn now to another structural feature * * *. If we look carefully at the first monologue of Faust, see what is actually there, the larger formal import of the scene will also become clear. It is meaningful that in the first great sequence of scenes in which Faust himself appears the theme of time should be announced in the title and the theme of place in the first stage directions. The time, the action, and Faust's own attitude proceed from the late despairful Saturday night of Easter-tide, under the sign of death, past the mortal crisis at midnight, to the joyful announcement of the angelic choir that Christ has arisen from the dead—an arc of development through which Faust himself passes and which he himself in the next scene, the Easter Walk, extends symbolically to the whole populace, and the whole earth [lines 921–22].

The place is indicated as follows: "In a high-vaulted, narrow Gothic chamber, Faust restless in his chair at the desk." The room dates from the past, his father's past, as we soon hear. It is spacious, upward but narrow, confining to either side. The way is open to transcendence but not to immanence, and Faust himself in the same passage of the Easter Walk confirms the parallel of the liberation of Christ from the grave, of spring from the icy bonds of winter, of mankind from its confining chambers, and of himself in a sympathetic relationship to this general Easter spirit of rejoicing as a man among men.

Before he reaches this point, however, he has a perilous arc of darkness to traverse. Here actually in these first few hundred lines of the Faust action we have in prefiguration and epitome the greater arc of the total drama from the dark night of despair, through first insights, relating past with future, to the ultimate vision of the meaning of man's life on earth and beyond. We can, therefore, with some justice think of this initial section as a kind of monodrama with interludes.

We need not review the whole of this familiar scene but we do need to look more closely at the concluding parts of it. Here Faust embarks upon a second perilous adventure, now that magic has failed him, the venture that seeks forcible release from earthly limitations and attainment of pure intellectual insight by means of suicide. He is already tending that way when he develops the theme of "image of God," by splitting the divinity from its incorporation: the exaltation of feeling oneself "more than cherub" [line 618] (a cherub after all is only a specialized power rather than a microcosm), then quickly the depression at being hurled back into the realm of human incertitude [line 629].

As he continues, the mention of his father and his heritage establishes the first still tenuous, still disparaged link to his own past that is to furnish the gradually emerging counter-theme to his new bold venture into the uncharted future. The vial with the potent poison also comes by inheritance and suggests a way over uncharted seas to a new shore, or (with heightened imagery) on a chariot of fire to new spheres of purer activity. With that he is ready to turn his back on the earthly sun (how differently he does so later) and courageously venture through that darksome portal before which most men quail, even at the risk of dissolving into nothingness.

The crystal cup he takes down is also a heritage, but the images it summons up in him are those remembered from a happy childhood and youth when the cup filled with wine went from guest to guest about his father's festive table: the guests before they could drink had to improvise the appropriate verses to go with the emblems engraved upon it. Faust pours into the cup the more potent drink from the vial and raises it in festive greeting to the new morn.

But this is not only the new morning through the portals to death, it is also the old traditional morning from the tomb back through the portals to the new life in Christ's resurrection. And at once, after this last moment of dead midnight Saturday, the first moments of Easter morning are announced by the sound of bells and the song of the angels, "Christ is arisen."

The musical beauty of these Easter choruses must not cause us to overlook their content and intent. They meaningfully accompany the successive closing stages of Faust's monologue. This first chorus of angels tells us that Christ's resurrection brings joy to mortal man who is surrounded by his heritage of destructive insidious shortcomings. Faust's own heritage of recollected Easter morns from childhood onward is a force strong enough to draw the cup away from his lips. The first conscious associations Easter summons up in him, questioningly, are those of consolation, of assurance of a new covenant.

The choir of women tells of the preparation of Christ's body for the tomb which He has now left and the choir of angels confirms the glad tidings of Christ's great love that carried Him victorious through these sorrows and bliss-filled trials. Faust's heart is melted at the message; even though the faith of his youth is not restored, the whole meaning of his youthful faith comes over him so powerfully that his past takes control of his present and his future. His urge toward transcendence by an act of violence now seems incongruous when the message comes to him of Christ's loving immanence, of His resumption of His human body in His resurrection. In unwonted humility and gentleness Faust abjures the superhuman spheres [line 767] and concludes with quiet finality: "to Earth I am restored!" [line 784].

The final choruses reecho this deep human conflict between the urge to transcendence and the realization that the sphere of man's activity is on earth. After the joy of Christ's resurrection comes sadness for His disciples in His ascension to higher spheres of creative joy and their feeling of foresakeness in the sorrow and yearning of earth. The final chorus of angels brings the resolution of the conflict: that man's creative activity on earth, in praise of God, in love and help to his fellow man, in spreading of the gospel of promise over the earth, will bring the Master to dwell among them and make His presence near. Though the Savior's transcendence has seemed to remove Him, He again becomes immanent through the Pentecostal experience.

It conforms to the design of the whole that this brief monodrama should, like the great drama as a whole, end with an angelic choir proclaiming the validity of the earthly, transitory, and human as a symbol of the great divine creativity, however grave the earthly and human shortcomings may be, however shadowy their anticipations of heavenly glory. And it is significant that in both instances Faust's commitment to earth should be the necessary prelude to the transcendence to higher spheres. In the next scene Faust again, but only in passing, yields to the yearning for transcendence [lines 1074–99] but then goes on in the passage on his two souls to counterbalance it with the strong earthly urge [lines 1112–17]. Much later in the drama we shall come upon an equally strong will to transcendence in Faust's son, Euphorion, though here, tragically, unmitigated by the perspectives of heritage and experience, so that Euphorion commits the act of violence from which Faust refrained and finds himself not in higher spheres of pure activity but in the darksome loneliness of the underworld.

* * *

Thus once more we have an instance of a scene illuminating and being illuminated by the larger context. * * * When we see the close parallels that exist between the monodrama and the drama as a whole, particularly in the endings with Faust's commitment to earth and especially the message conveyed by the two sets of choruses, we must come to the conclusion that the ending of the whole is exactly the kind of an ending the poet had planned at an early stage. At the very latest his writing of the Easter choruses in the first years of the new century foreshadowed the ending he would give to the whole, inevitably, for no other kind of ending would have fitted into the structures of the whole.

We can, with caution, go one step farther. Faust's last monologues in the scenes "Midnight" and "Great Outer Precinct of the Palace," proceeding undeterred first amid the oppressive negativism of Care and then amid the grotesque negating activities of Mephistopheles and his Lemures, is, in a sense, also a monodrama with interludes in which Faust once more and finally faces all the issues in parallel and contrast to the first monodrama, from:

> So I resorted to Magic's art [line 377]

versus

> Could I but clear my path at every turning
> Of spells, [lines 11404–5]

through

> I feel emboldened now to venture forth,
> To bear the bliss, the sorrow of this earth [lines 464–65]

and more decisively

> I know full well the earthly sphere of men . . .
> Let him stand firm and gaze about alert;
> To able man this world is not inert [lines 11441, 45–46]

to the early foolhardy

> I am ready, I feel free
> To cleave the ether on a novel flight,
> To novel spheres of pure activity . . .
> Resolve serenely to essay no less—
> Be it at risk of ebbing into nothingness. [lines 703–5, 718–19]

countered here by

> . . . to Earth I am restored! [line 784]

and near the end by:

> The yonder view is blocked to mortal ken;
> A fool who squints beyond with blinking eyes,
> Imagining his like above the skies;
> Let him stand firm and gaze about alert. [lines 11442–45]

with final confirmation in Faust's final words:

My path on earth, the trace I leave within it
Eons untold cannot impair.
Foretasting such high happiness to come,
I savor now my striving's crown and sum. [lines 11583–86]

Thus we have a monodrama at the beginning of the earthly action and a monodrama at the end of the earthly action, each of them with discordant intrusions, each of them leading to the Christian choruses conveying the message of resurrection, grace for those who strive, and salvation. From this view it is as though we had two small arcs of action flanking the great arc of action, epitomizing it in miniature and indicating its larger configurations. Before the earthly action and after the earthly action the vistas lead from eternity to eternity, with the final reflections of the Chorus Mysticus on the symbolic validity of earthly endeavor, if in the service of the Lord under the aspect of the humanly creative.

* * * [But] this drama does not circle back on itself and end where it began; it moves on, in the Lord's words, from the "darksome urge" to an emerging "consciousness of the right way," through a labyrinth of errors, to a final creative act. In our first observation of intrinsic form in this paper we noticed the fourfold movement from death to resurrection. The movement at the end must therefore be the ultimate carrying out of the direction of the beginning and of the two middle parts; if there were a reversal for the sake of symmetry, then the form would be discrepant with the content and therefore artistically bad. What we do have at the end is a threefold movement as we have at the beginning: the poet's reflections at the beginning revolve around the themes of time, reality, and creativity; so do Faust's last reflections. There follows in the one case the comic variant on these themes in the "Prelude in the Theater," in the other case the grotesque comic interlude of the "Entombment." * * * And finally in both cases we rise beyond earthly time and place in the "Prologue in Heaven" and the "Mountain Gorges" and look down upon them *sub specie aeternitatis*, with the words of the Archangels, the Lord, and the Chorus Mysticus devoted to what remains on earth as it is in heaven, the striving toward creativity in the one and its accomplishment in the other. On this vast landscape then is constructed the great edifice of the Faust drama, with the arcs of the monodramas at beginning and end indicating to us and clarifying for us the vastly larger and more complicated structure of the whole, the polydrama. Miniature form anticipates total form; miniature form recapitulates total form.

* * *

* * * The various means of articulation and construction used in the drama are of a variety and complexity well beyond the usual group of formal devices employed in the literary work of art. The formal aspects of the drama have in their full complexity not been properly observed, firstly because the conventional kinds of dramatic form were predicated for the drama and then not found, with the result that the work was dismissed as formless. In the few instances where truly present factors of form were found, they were seen in isolation, thought to be of only limited relevance, and then the work was dismissed as fragmentary or discontinuous. Only when all the main factors of form are brought together: the continuous fabric of theme, motif, symbol, with its patterns of repetition and variation, then the structural principle of the interlude, then the architectonic relationship of monodrama and polydrama, then the succession of symbolic prototypes that give to the protagonist the world scope called for by a drama of these dimensions, and added to all this the wealth of other factors, large and small, that give relation and relevance of the parts to one another, so that no part can rightly be understood outside the context of the whole—only when all of these come together, do we attain to some insight into the form of *Faust*.

WOLFGANG BINDER

Goethe's Classical Conception of *Faust*†

DEDICATED TO EMIL STAIGER ON FEBRUARY 8, 1968, IN GRATEFUL FRIENDSHIP

When the first scenes of *Faust* appeared in print in 1790 they evoked curiously conflicting reactions. In contrast to *Iphigenie* or *Tasso*,[1] this work seemed accessible to a direct sympathetic response; yet for the reflective understanding it presented apparent difficulties. In both ways, however, it attracted the reader and provoked him, at times to explore the difficulties of the text, at times to master them.

Part I of the tragedy confirmed and reinforced this impression, but *Part II* appeared at first to deny access completely. Today, however, while we profess to have adequate sense of the work and a whole body of literature on *Faust* at our disposal, we still resemble the first readers, in that we feel at home within this poetic work as in few others, yet the interpretation of it poses riddle upon riddle for us. * * *

We first encounter the question regarding the unity of the work in Goethe's well-known conversation with the historian Luden in 1806.[2] Luden there relates how he became involved in a quarrel

† From *Deutsche Vierteljahrsschrift für Literaturwissenschaft und Geistesgeschichte*, Vol. 42, 1968, published by J. B. Metzlersche Verlagsbuchhandlung. Reprinted by permission of Wolfgang Binder. Translated by Cyrus Hamlin and Dolores Signori.

1. Goethe's plays *Iphigenie* and *Tasso* were also published in 1790.
2. See note 1, p. 532, above. According to Goethe's diary this conversation with Luden took place on August 10, 1806.

with friends, pupils of Fichte and Schelling concerning the interpretation of the *Faust Fragment* which was known at that time. These friends thought they detected a speculative symbolism in it which pointed to a comprehensive idea for the whole. Luden himself was content to enjoy the beauty of individual aspects of the work, and as a historian he attributed various inconsistencies to the history of the work's composition, already quite lengthy at that time. Thus we have the systematic and historical approaches, an antithesis which recurs in Friedrich Theodor Vischer's satirical classification of *Faust* scholars into "Sinnhuber" (sense-mongers) and "Stoffhuber" (stuff-mongers)[3] and which has continued to our time in controversies between *Faust* interpretations which emphasize philosophical coherence and those concerned with philology and the history of composition. As in Homeric scholarship, critics now appear to have grown tired of this hundred-year-old war; interest has turned to questions of verbal form, symbolism, the use of myth and its psychic structures. Yet these inquiries have not produced a peace treaty, nor have they aspired to one, because they concern phenomena which have little to do with the question of the work as a whole and its problematic unity.

The following reflections hark back to that unresolved controversy and explore, at least for *Faust I*, the possibility of a solution. Due to the limits which are drawn between the unitarian and the genetic approach it will be necessary to find a new point of departure.

Those who wish to understand the work as a unity can appeal to Goethe, who basically wanted it so understood. But as soon as they undertake to verify in the text the unity of the *Faust* idea which they profess to see, they run up against undeniable contradictions which only the process of composition can explain. If they are not willing to acknowledge this, * * * then violence to the text and misinterpretations cannot be avoided. It is precisely with these contradictions that historical-genetic criticism commences. This, too, can appeal to Goethe, who, though unwillingly, yet on occasion admitted that this development did bear some influence on the style and conception of the work. * * *

Meanwhile the need for understanding the unity of the work is no less dispelled than the duty of sorting out historical facts, and nothing is gained by a decision, whether it be for the latter or the former. Our question concerning Goethe's classical *Faust* conception[4] could indicate a way out of this dilemma, for a conception implies a unifying idea and a classical conception counts upon the existence of other, earlier and later conceptions, which perhaps

---

3. Friedrich Theodor Vischer (1807–87) speaks of *Sinnhuber* and *Stoffhuber* in his massive work of criticism *Goethes Faust, Neue Beiträge zur Kritik des Gedichts* (New Contributions Toward the Criticism of the Poem) (1875).

4. "Classical" refers to the era of composition from 1797 to 1801, when *Part I* was completed.

contradict it. But this combination of aspects is attained by limiting our discussion to a specific stage of composition.

If we want to advance beyond this, it will be necessary to refer to structures of the poetic outlook and form, within the limits of which Goethe sketched this as he did every concept of his work; they may be inferred from his vocabulary, his imagery, and his mode of thought. For only at these levels do historical and systematic relevance coincide: they develop as the poet develops, but they contain an identical core out of which they develop. Considered in this way, the different conceptions of *Faust*—the earliest, the Italian, the classical in the era of his friendship with Schiller, and even the final one[5]—may be understood as metamorphoses of one basic type. One might thus avoid the notion of a discontinuous process and a constant change of plans, such as the historical interpretation believed it could observe, and also the phantom of a unified conception extending from the *Urfaust* through *Part II*, as if interruptions of years and decades would have allowed the author to pick up the thread of his work at any point. Instead, a picture of the development of *Faust* would result in which each conception so absorbs the previous one as to interpret or re-interpret it in such a way that what hitherto had been the total plan can be maintained as an element of the new plan. In that conversation with Luden Goethe himself seems to infer something of this sort when he says concerning the "fragments" (i.e., the fragment from Rome), "they will appear within the whole as organic parts and thus first receive their true meaning."

That he calls precisely these *Fragment* scenes "organic parts" of the whole—they are the most unmanageable parts—is surprising, to be sure, but understandable in view of the time of the conversation, which took place in the period of his fully developed organological thought. * * * Within the history of the *Faust* conceptions there is in the first place no single anonymous principle of composition at work which enforces their "formulation, re-formulation," but rather a recurring intellectual decision by the author, who, within the broadened horizon of his forms of perception, each time conceives the drama anew *from the ground up*, while yet making use of, or at least sparing the earlier drama.

Faust 1797

The content of the classical conception, insofar as such a one is considered, remains controversial; its date is ordinarily associated with the recommencement of work on *Faust* in the summer of 1797. This supposition seems natural but does not hold up under closer examination. According to all available information, the "plan" and "scheme" or "summary" with which Goethe began served only to

5. Stages of composition for *Faust*: i.e., 1770s, 1788, 1797–1801, 1825–31.

organize the material. The "Prologue in Heaven" and the comple-
mentary epilogue as intended at that time—both date from this
period—invest the earthly drama with a higher significance, yet conceal its guiding idea, which could only become apparent within the
framework of the wager; and the pact scene was written in 1799 at
the earliest. Finally, Goethe nowhere indicates that he had already
found his idea; on the contrary, various evidence indicates that he
was still in search of it. In order to consider this question more
closely let us put aside for the moment the problem of conception
and reconstruct the external situation of the author at the beginning of this period of work, which is initially the result of the two
previous stages on which the third rests.

A Faust drama, which breaks off before it has really begun, and a
completed Gretchen tragedy, which has forced its way into the play
contrary to the legend and to the poet's intention and which
appears to be unaware of the bold magician of the beginning—this
heterogeneous content of the *Urfaust* could indicate a rather plan-
less procedure, which would conform to reports about the work
habits of the young author. * * *

Quite different was the situation in Rome in 1788. The *Urfaust*
torso is still to be completed, Goethe sketches a plan, which has not
been preserved, and writes a scene [lines 1770 ff.] which leads
directly to the center and provides the missing connection between
Faust and the Devil. This scene contents itself with a free alliance
without a formal written promise, evidently because the pact of the
legend was not to be used, since it prejudiced Faust's fate, and the
wager, which leaves the conclusion open without relinquishing
the ritual of the written promise, had not yet been discovered.
This interim solution corresponded to the nature of the Roman conception, which will be discussed later, yet remained dramaturgically
unsatisfactory, since *Faust I* would reduce the scene to an inorganic
epilogue to the conclusion of the pact. Such presuppositions could
only restrict the work; thus after writing two additional scenes
Goethe broke off and allowed the work to be published as a fragment.

In 1797 he is faced with the same necessity of completing the
play. After establishing his plan and his outline, he begins this time
not in the middle, with the yet unmastered written promise of the
Devil, which would require that Faust "spell out just what the bar-
gain turns upon" [line 1654], but instead at the outermost edge.
Goethe writes or sketches the "Dedication," "Prelude in the Theater," and "Prologue in Heaven," and, in addition, as counterparts to
the first pieces, the poems "Notification" and "Farewell";[6] he also
considers an epilogue in Heaven. Hardly comprehensible, to be sure,

6. The poems "Abkündigung" and "Ab-   *Faust* but subsequently omitted.
schied" (April, 1800) were composed for

was the fact that, at a time when most of the play is still to be written, he began the stanzas of his "Farewell" with these lines.

> But now concluded is my tragedy,
> Which I achieved in trepidation.

But this is the case, and it may perhaps be explained only by assuming that Goethe is here indulging in strategy to gain control of his work once again. Along with the "Dedication," in which he once more claims his work as his own, he anticipates its conclusion; he leaps across the entire stretch of time which still lies ahead of him and assures himself about his task by considering its end. He makes use of similar strategy when he has the printed *Fragment* transcribed again, in order to have the feel of a manuscript, and again, decades later, when he has several quires of white paper representing the yet unwritten fourth act bound into his manuscript book, in order, as he says, "to come to the aid of the spiritual with all manner of devices."[7]

The outcome and limits of the new beginning of 1797 can thus be clearly recognized. Goethe had composed a plan of the material, which outlines the scenes or the spheres of action, and a lyrical-dramatic frame poem, which places three concentric rings around the play. The latter approaches the Faust theme from the outside in and touches it at its inner limit with the ring formed by the prologue and planned epilogue, which presumably represent the old idea: God relinquishes Faust, the man, to the temptation of the Devil; for he knows that as man too is part of the creation, which is good, he will not lose himself entirely and will remain worthy of being saved. This, to be sure, is a general idea which elucidates the meaning of the whole but not, however, a concrete draft which indicates the stages of action for the earthly drama. Were it the latter, it would have to mediate step by step between the abundance of material on the one hand and the central idea on the other. It would have to provide a meaningful structure which permitted the organization of the material in light of the idea and the realization of the idea within the arrangement of the material. For the present such a structure is not apparent, and without it one cannot very well speak of a conception.

In his first letters on *Faust*[8] Schiller, although he has before him only the *Fragment*, refers to this very point. The play, he says, requires according to its design a "symbolic treatment," and the imagination of the author will have to accommodate itself "to serve a rational idea." This is, as it were, a demand from above. If, however, this idea is to be "carried out," that is, realized in action and in characters, then it requires also a "totality of material"—the demand from below. At this point Goethe is not aware that he has

---

7. From Goethe's conversation with Eckermann of February 17, 1831; see above.

8. From Schiller's letters to Goethe of June 23 and 26, 1797; see above.

already begun to fulfill both demands. And now follows an important postscript: for "a mass that springs up to such a height" he
cannot find a "poetic framework" which will hold it together. A
poetic framework which would make the totality of material serve
the unifying rational idea is nothing other than that organizing
structure for the meaning which we are here concerned with.

Goethe accepts Schiller's demands completely, yet his reply indicates that he has not yet found such a framework nor is he—at least
he gives this impression—seriously looking for one.[9] He writes that
he proposes "rather to touch upon than to fulfill" Schiller's highest
demands. With ironic pleasure he indulges in the well-known
expressions and comparisons: "barbaric composition," "tragelaph,"
"species of fungus," "airy phantom," "witch's produce." He also
makes a very informative observation, namely that in this work the
"new theory of the epic poem" will prove useful to him, that is, the
theory he had developed with Schiller during the preceding weeks,
according to which the epic is not like the drama, which is so
arranged that its parts are joined for the sake of the ending, but
rather is arranged for an autonomy of parts and an inner truth, so
that it fulfills its aim at each point in its development. In accord
with this theory the "Notification" explains:

> The life of man is a similar poem:
> It has a beginning, has an ending,
> But yet it fails to be a whole.

Actually the draft of these lines reads, instead of "a similar poem,"
as follows: "The life of man is an epic poem."

No matter how one considers the revived *Faust* poem, the wide-
spread opinion that 1797 is the year of the definitive conception
does not hold true. Goethe had not yet found it, but it is also
apparent that—contrary to the tenor of his letters—he is convinced
that it must be sought. We find evidence for this in the "Prelude in
the Theater." For in this scene both Schiller's "demands" as well as
Goethe's restrictions are reiterated so fully that one cannot overlook
the connection with the correspondence of the first days.

First of all, Goethe's arguments. On the twenty-seventh of June
he writes that he will see to it "that the parts are pleasing and
entertaining, and that they inspire thought." The director asks:

> How can we see that all is fresh and new
> And, with significance, engaging too? [lines 47–48]

That is, *delectare* and *podesse*, to please and to instruct. In addition, the epic autonomy of the parts, to which the director's words
"a piece . . . in pieces" [line 99] conform; and his "ragout" belongs
to the species of the "fungus" and similar expressions. Schiller's

9. See Goethe's letters to Schiller of
June 24 and 27, 1797, above. In addition, see the letters of July 1 and 5, December 6 and 25, 1797.

"totality of material" is heard in the phrase "creation's fullest circle" [line 240]. His demand for a "symbolic treatment" is picked up by the poet and made his own:

> Who calls the single to the common ritual,
> Where it resounds in glorious harmonies? [lines 148–49]

And the preceding verses allude to a "poetic framework," that is, an organizing structure for the meaning:

> Who parts the sequence, changeless and perpetual,
> Enliveningly into rhythmic ease. [lines 146–47]

Scarcely a single aspect of the letters is ignored. The dialogue with Schiller, consciously or not, is part of the work for the "Prelude"; whereby we hope to support the assumption that the "Prelude" must have been written at this time. Especially attractive is the idea that Schiller's "highest demands" are being put into the mouth of the poet, while Goethe's own, more trivial requirements suffice for the theater manager. Should we not regard this as a small token of tribute to his friend?

The First Paralipomenon

By 1801 *Part I* is almost complete, sections and sketches for *Part II* are already at hand, the play now has its inner form. When and how did Goethe arrive at his new conception?

The poem gives us only an indirect answer. A direct answer, however, is provided by a paper where Goethe with clipped phrases hastily sketched his basic thoughts for *Faust*. This first Paralipomenon—so named because it bears the number one in the Weimar edition of Goethe's works[1]—has always been considered important, though its full worth has not been completely assessed. For among the almost two thousand statements which Goethe made about *Faust* * * * it is the only one which offers an explanation of the work as a whole in the words of the author. It is, of course, an explanation in a nutshell, comprehensible only in conjunction with those forms of Goethe's perception which were considered earlier. * * *

The paper bears no date, its origin is still disputed; some have even argued that it dates back to the *Urfaust* or the *Fragment*. * * * By far the simplest way of dating the manuscript is to consider that it mentions both the first and the second part of the tragedy. Only in 1799 at the earliest, when the play was expanded beyond expectations, could Goethe have conceived of a division into two parts; this becomes apparent from various letters by both

---

1. For the German text of the plan see the Weimar edition of Goethe's works (1887), Vol. XIV, p. 287. The following analysis refers to the English translation of the "*Faust* Plan of 1800" (above).

Goethe and Schiller to several addressees.[2] * * * We shall thus content ourselves with a date around the turn of the century.

Still another point must be borne in mind. This hasty draft does not follow a definite principle of organization, as do other schemata by Goethe, but strings together extremely heterogeneous notes. First the quintessence of the three opening scenes is established. The third scene, the Wagner scene, leads to reflections about form and content which seem to achieve their own autonomy and remove themselves from the *Faust* text, yet which still are linked to it in the plan for a new scene or for a different version of the old one. Then two persons—Wagner and the student—are confronted. The words crossed out in the next line are intended to characterize Faust. Considered in conjunction with the concept of "enjoyment," these words provide a survey of his entire development, which seems to have been important enough for Goethe to outline it with supplementary notes. Finally, mention is made again of a single scene, the epilogue, the indicated setting for which differs both from the 1797 plan for an epilogue and from the epilogue as we now have it. Mephisto is not characterized at all.

These are ideas on the spur of the moment, which we literally "catch up as they come into being." Despite this they are not at all negligible, and they constitute at an embryonic stage, yet clearly recognizable, that adequate conception for *Faust* which we seek.
* * *

Let us concentrate on the concluding section of the draft and attempt first to determine the order of its composition. From the words "Life's Deeds Essence" the following lines were developed:

> Enjoyment of Life by the person Part I
> Enjoyment of Deeds second

But the formula "Enjoyment of Deeds" must have seemed too narrow to embrace the various experiences of Faust in *Part II*. Goethe then added a third stage:

> Enjoyment of Creation.   Epilogue in Chaos.

(We shall consider later whether this enjoyment of creation is meant to be the theme of the epilogue.) Then follow additional notes, first concepts of direction: enjoyment of life "viewed from without," enjoyment of deeds "directed outwards," enjoyment of creation "from within," then a restriction of the enjoyment of life: "in a stupor Passion." From these it seems apparent that the divisions are still too summary. Between the enjoyments of activity and creation, Goethe then inserts their counterpart:

> Enjoyment with Consciousness.   Beauty.

That is aesthetic enjoyment. At this point we would expect a note such as: directed inwards. Its absence, together with the arrange-

2. See Goethe's letter to Cotta of January 2, 1799, Schiller's letter to Cotta of March 24, 1800, and Schiller's letter to Goethe of September 13, 1800.

ment of the lines, proves the sequence assumed here; this addition could only have been forgotten at the conclusion of writing down the draft. Finally the "Epilogue in Chaos" is more precisely indicated: "on the way to Hell." * * *

The last lines of the draft thus describe a scheme of stages which, with the help of the key concept of enjoyment and *ad hoc* analogues to the "enjoyment of life," outline Faust's entire career. Since the plan anticipates as yet still distant, unwritten parts of the play, only a very little of it can be tested against sections of the text available at this stage and critical comments on them by the author around 1800. We must limit discussion to the intrinsic meaning of these notes and traces of them in *Faust II*.

We find an initial allusion to this meaning in the word "person." If the dramatic person only were meant, i.e., the main character of the play, Goethe would presumably have inserted the name. More in keeping with his Classical language, it may mean "individuality" or "entelechy," as in the line; ". . . in merit not alone,/But in our loyalty we live as persons still" [lines 9983–84]. Thus the stages of enjoyment would be codes indicating transformations through which Faust's entelechy was to unfold. This problem will be considered shortly.

Coordination with stages of the action in the drama presents no difficulty. In the scenes from "Auerbach's Tavern" through the "Witch's Kitchen" and the Gretchen tragedy to the "Walpurgis Night," Faust surrenders himself to the various pleasures afforded by the enjoyment of life. At the emperor's court he expects to accomplish spectacular deeds and to enjoy their effects in the light of "honor, fame, power and sovereignty": the enjoyment of deeds.[3] It goes without saying that "enjoyment of beauty" refers to Helena, the archetype of beauty, and everything that leads up to her. "Enjoyment of creation" would correspondingly indicate Faust's project to win land from the sea, the plan for which originated at the time of Goethe's friendship with Schiller. * * * Faust's creation is the new land from the floor of the sea and his enjoyment of it— an enjoyment "from within," since he is blinded—is the "high happiness" which he achieves by anticipation at the moment of his death. He explained his project explicity to Mephisto with these words:

> Earn for yourself the choice, delicious boast
> To look the imperious ocean from the coast. [lines 10228–29]

We observe in this an intentional analogy to the third day of creation in the Book of Genesis. * * *

Finally there is the "Epilogue in Chaos on the way to Hell." Most interpreters associate this with the "enjoyment of creation," since it would correspond to the distinction between *Part I* and *Part*

3. See the "Outline of the Contents for *Part II*" (1816), above.

II and since chaos and creation ought to be related. Though this reasoning may seem plausible, the assmption itself is totally unrealistic. For, if we also take into account the "Prologue in Heaven," the speaker of such an epilogue could only be Mephisto, perhaps engaged in his battle with the angels, a scene which was planned as early as 1781—even in *Faust II* the "gruesome Hell-mouth" still opens at the side of the stage, though admittedly without "chaos" [line 11643]—but Faust is dead, the case concerning his earthly career is closed, his liberated entelechy may well experience enjoyment of creation, but only the living Faust could tell about it. We must therefore separate the two concepts, and the manuscript makes this possible. For it followed from "Life's Deeds Essence" that at first Goethe thought only of two stages; "enjoyment of deeds" was a formula embracing the whole of *Part II* and included also those parts which he subsequently distinguished under the heading "enjoyment of creation." This accords with the fact that, in contrast to the terms which correspond to it, "from within" is separated from "Epilogue" by a period. This eliminates the incongruity in the last line.

Enjoyment and Striving

We have been able to locate Goethe's outline within the larger sequence of the *Faust* plot. We have likewise determined in each case what the key word "enjoyment" referred to. Yet, if we look to this concept for a principle which will make Faust's transformations basically comprehensible for us, we get into difficulty. For wherever enjoyment, at least in the sense of the word which is familiar to us, appears as the purpose of life, the question immediately arises as to its moral value. * * *

Faust strives incessantly to give his life an absolute value as the existence of an individual person. Goethe's plan calls this value "enjoyment"; within its scope the "person" of Faust is thus thematized. * * * The word "enjoyment" occurs frequently in Goethe's language and in all periods of his career, sometimes in the superficial sense of amusement, most often in the specific sense of appropriation and participation. * * * The core of this concept lies in the notion that only through enjoyment can man, who is locked within his selfhood, attain that which exists outside himself, take possession of it, and at the same time unite himself with it.

> And what to all of mankind is apportioned
> I mean to savor in my own self's core.

Thus says Faust [lines 1770–71], whereby he uses the term "grasp" [line 1772] as a significant synonym for this universal enjoyment and also includes within it that "sorrow" [line 1773] which is the dark side of the human condition. Through enjoyment the self realizes itself within the world. * * *

As a consequence of Goethe's tendency to think in polarities, his concepts often presuppose opposing concepts which, though unstated, must also be taken into account. Such is the case here. In letters from the spring of 1801, at the time of the Paralipomenon and during a period of continuous work on *Faust*, the question often arises concerning "that which perseveres in man"—intended are the permanent substrata of human nature—that which allows the phenomena of cultural history to be brought into a comprehensible order. Goethe believes he has worked out "four basic conditions": "striving" and "enjoyment," which are the "two extremes of human activity," and their negative counterparts, "resignation" and "habit." This striving, the opposing concept which we seek, is, like enjoyment, not determined in an *a priori* moral way. Goethe understands it * * * as the urge of entelechy to expand itself so as to embrace the world whether it expresses itself in thought, action, artistic creation or whatever. He thus conceives of two basic forms of existence which constantly refer to one another: the one which strives, always going beyond itself, lives in what it seeks and wherever it looks for itself; the one which enjoys has found its fulfilled state of being and, even if only for a moment, is certain of this state. Time is associated with striving, the eternal moment with enjoyment.

This relationship, however informative it may be about Goethe's way of thinking, concerns us for practical reasons. The concept of striving naturally plays a significant role in the interpretations of *Faust*, but enjoyment is seldom mentioned and then, since a conventional moralistic view is involved, only with a certain reserve. The plan of *Faust*, which makes this point specifically, must appear by this consideration as perhaps an interesting experiment but nonetheless a digression by Goethe. If one recognizes, however, that the stages of enjoyment which it mentions presuppose the paths of striving which will come to dominate in the course of the drama, then the plan acquires a far more concrete relation to the play. This must be tested against the text of *Faust*. If it can be shown that the concept of enjoyment plays a decisive role for its meaning, then the connection between the two concepts is affirmed from two sides.

First it becomes apparent that the word appears frequently, approximately forty times, often in important passages and almost always with the significance discussed above, but it occurs in this sense only in scenes composed later than the *Fragment*. The question why this meaning is not known to the *Urfaust*, even though the young Goethe knew the word in this sense, will be considered later on. We do find the word, however, when we look back to one scene in the *Urfaust*: in the confrontation with the Earth Spirit Faust was "self-relishing in heaven's radiant clarity" [line 616], he believes "through creation, to enjoy God-like estate" [lines 620–21], he even speaks of "the voluptuous enjoyment" of prayer [line

774]. Such phrases express not only feeling but also possession; feeling grasps and possesses, if only for a fleeting moment, a god-like state of being and thereby its own selfhood. These are the earliest examples of the concept in the play; from here on to the end of *Part II* there is an unbroken sequence of such instances.

Let us consider in addition a passage from the *Fragment*: the monologue in "Forest and Cave" closes with these lines:

> Thus reel I from desire to enjoyment,
> And in enjoyment languish for desire. [lines 3249–50]

Desire is extinguished in enjoyment, when enjoyment is exhausted it awakens anew—* * * this is the usual interpretation of these lines. But even the wording here raises doubts. How can Faust, in experiencing an enjoyment which soothes desire, yet languish for desire, and why does he call the step from desire to enjoyment a "reeling," as if he were oscillating between the two? A glance at the monologue as a whole provides the solution to this puzzle. In the second section Faust complains about "a raging fire" of desire [line 3247], which Mephisto fans within his breast "for that fair image with his busy spite" [line 3248]; in the first section he thanks the "lofty spirit" [line 3217] for a threefold blessing: his blissful vision of nature, his own inner self and the "silver shapes of an anterior age" [line 3238]. And here the word "enjoyment" appears again: "you gave me splendored Nature for my kingdom,/And strength to feel her, to enjoy her" [lines 3220–21]. The concluding lines of the monologue thus refer to this enjoyment of deepest feeling and sharing. They summarize the entire monologue, not only the words about Mephisto's demonic power of seduction. And Mephisto also understands these lines as a relapse into desire:

> A truly transcendental binge!
> By night and dew lie on a mountain range,
> Of earth and sky essay ecstatic capture, . . .
> In pride of potency I don't know what bestowing,[4] . . .
> Then the transcendent act of knowing—
> I won't say how to end. [lines 3282–83]

Sensual abandonment of the self and intellectual recovery of the self, this is the meaning of desire and enjoyment; Faust "reels" back and forth between both of these. We shall return to this basic motif in the scenes composed when Goethe was in Rome (1788).

Meanwhile there are two passages which directly touch upon the plan of 1800. Wager and death are seen to be allied in the words: "If the swift moment I entreat:/Tarry a while . . ." [lines 1699–1700]. In addition to the motif of the moment, however, a second is added. The crucial passage of the wager reads:

4. The word "bestowing" in the original is *geniessen*, "to enjoy."

When with indulgence you can gull me,
Let that day be the last for me!
This is my wager!
Done!
And beat for beat!
If the swift moment I entreat: . . . [lines 1696–1700]

Yet Faust's last words read:

Foretasting such high happiness to come,
I now enjoy my striving's crown and sum. [lines 11585–86]

Enjoyment and the moment, linked in both instances, yet rejected
in the wager and affirmed in death—this change is the result of
Faust's journey through the world. The plan explains this change by
defining the journey through the world as sequential stages of enjoyment, thereby re-interpreting step for step its meaning and temporal
reference—out of a pleasure which betrays time develops a pleasure
which fulfills time; and so, naturally, the end proceeds out of the
beginning, as the blossom grows out of the root. The context and
the purpose of the plan are thus determined; it can only have been
conceived with reference to these two central passages of *Faust*.
Both the pact scene and the scene "Great Courtyard of the Palace"
must have been written around 1800. This coincides with the date
proposed earlier for the Paralipomenon.

It is now possible to resolve the question concerning the organizing principle for the meaning of *Faust* which resulted from the
situation when Goethe began work again in the summer of 1797.
We have been discussing degrees of enjoyment. Such a distinction
of degrees is characteristic of the philosophy of sentiment and life
at that time. Unique to Goethe is the particular form of his grad-
ualism, which is clarified by the directional concepts; "from without
—directed outwards—<directed inwards>—from within." These
concepts occur together side by side in his verse and his prose, especially when there is a polarity between "within" and "without"—
subject and object, self and world, man and nature, individual and
society, etc.—which is mediated through the extension of the one
into the other. The primal instance (*Urphänomen*) for such mediation is enjoyment. Its metamorphoses may thus be interpreted as
follows: after the "enjoyment of life viewed from without," wherein
the senses snatch up the substance of experience and, * * * as it were,
"devour" it, occurs the "enjoyment of deeds directed outwards," in
which the self asserts itself outward into the world and engages
itself in its deeds. The next two stages repeat this game in intellectually intensified form: in the "enjoyment of beauty <directed
inwards>" the subject fulfills itself through the intuition of those
"secret laws of nature" which would remain eternally concealed

from us were it not for the manifestation of the beautiful,[5] while in the "enjoyment of creation from within" the subject experiences the creative realization of its inner self in the manifestation of an external work. One recognizes here the universally valid image in Goethe's thought of inhaling and exhaling, of systole and diastole, in whose twofold polarity we perceive the second of the "driving-wheels of all nature," the law of intensification. The plan conceives of Faust's path as a spiral movement, such as Goethe believed to be perceptible everywhere in the processes of nature, of history and of individual existence. Here we have clearly returned to the sphere of those forms of perception which were discussed at the outset. Goethe fulfills Schiller's demand for a "poetic framework," but he forges this framework with his own tool.

We also find ourselves in the sphere of the Classical Goethe, who thinks in symbols, proceeds genetically, and regards the highest form of humanity as attainable. Between Faust's wager and death, we said, the meaning of enjoyment transforms itself into its opposite. Such a change could be brought about through a fundamental decision by the hero or an anonymous dialectic of events. Goethe joins these poles together through a process of organic transitions, which reveals a basic law, yet remains at the same time humanly comprehensible and exhausts symbolically a circle of human possibilities. Thereby, however, a system of perfection is created, which leads Faust to the height of the human condition, without accounting for its darker sides. The demonic world which undermines reality in *Faust II*, Faust's petrification in senile avarice before his final transformation through Care, above all the comprehensive irony of presentation and interpretation—all this lies beyond the scope of the plan. However easily the formulas of the plan may be applied to the mass of material in the second part, to apply along with them its perfectionism would be to revert to the *Faust* interpretation of later idealism. The first Paralipomenon derives from the time of Goethe's friendship with Schiller. At that time Goethe still believed in the metamorphosis of man and his self-realization in that goal which entelechy due to its origin carries within itself.

The Classical Conception of Faust

We have located the structural idea of the plan in relation to the text of *Faust* and the history of its composition. To speak of a conception, however, would be premature. Still lacking are the events leading up to the wager—how does the pact with the devil come about?—Only the work as a whole, as it already existed or was conceived around 1800, allows such a conception to be discerned. * * *

---

5. Binder here alludes to Goethe's maxim No. 183 (critical edition of the *Maximen und Reflexionen*, 1907, edited by Hecker): "The beautiful is a mani-festation of secret laws of nature, which, if the beautiful did not manifest itself, would have remained eternally concealed from us."

In the situation depicted in the "great lacuna" two ways seem to be open to Faust. First, to retreat idealistically into his own self—that is, to flee into freedom' of thought and to renounce a reality whose "No!" seems insurmountable. Such presumably would be the decision of a hero in a drama by Schiller. For a Goethean hero this course is not accessible; but only the second way, which is more realistic, namely to endeavor nonetheless to deal with this external realm which closes itself off. Yet, since in the sphere of finite existence an infinite striving cannot achieve a corresponding enjoyment —that has been sufficiently demonstrated, we could even make a bet about it with the devil—there remains only the attempt to begin down below, at the level of the most common sensual enjoyment.

Faust's journey through the world is, strictly speaking, the journey out of the study into the world. In a higher sense it is the path out of the self into the world, out of the subject of an infinite inner realm into a concrete outer reality. In the mediation between what is without and within, which now commences—enjoyment of life viewed from without, enjoyment of deeds directed outwards, enjoyment of beauty directed inwards, enjoyment of creation from within —entelechy realizes itself in that which exists, not in a divine, but in a human manner. Only through that human enjoyment which is analogous to divine fruition (*fruitio divina*), is it established that entelechy can attain the highest state of its existence. Thus the devil loses the wager; for the enjoyment with which Mephisto sought to deceive Faust has no more in common with such "enjoyment" than the word they share. All the same, in the highest meaning of the word, that issue which constituted the motive for the wager remains present to mind. Mephisto has lost the wager, but Faust has not won it. That which eludes a legal decision can therefore be submitted to the power of grace. If we bear in mind the forms of Goethe's intuition, this design must underlie his classical concepton of *Faust*. This also concludes the sequence of changing conceptions which we have discussed. * * *

The Universal Plan

* * * Of interest in the *Faust* poem is the pure form of a self-becoming which manifests itself there; for not only the course of the human entelechy, but also quite different processes in nature and history conform to its law, insofar as it does not involve merely a succession in time but rather the temporal fulfillment of a timeless meaning. Here we appear to have grasped an image in which the various forms of Goethe's intuition, to which we have referred several times, express themselves directly. * * *

The pure form of the process is thus: in accord with an entelechistic impulse, an original unity, which exists but is concealed, seeks to manifest its existence as a phenomenon. In order to do so it must differentiate itself from within itself. It divides and separates into two poles of visible reality; through the reciprocal mediation and permeation of these poles, beginning at the lowest level, it now develops stages of a concrete existence; and thus, by degrees, it fulfills its determined reality. At the end of its way it exists in actuality, where before it was directed towards that end in potentiality.

* * *

Analogies in Faust II

This is the form in which the classical conception of *Faust* becomes a model for entire sections of the second part: figures, groups, incidents, and significant movement repeat in a purely formal manner Faust's way, or at least parts of it. We shall limit ourselves to three examples close at hand.

Homunculus, like Faust, exists in a pure inwardness of intellect, striving universally, yet strictly separated from the outer realm; the symbolism of the glass in which he is enclosed corresponds to that of Faust's study as prison. He desires, however, to "come to be" [line 8133]; his entelechy wishes to realize itself. For this to occur the division between inner and outer must fall. Faust crosses the threshold into the world. Homunculus smashes his glass against the scallop-shell chariot of Galatea, the sea is illumined by millions of the smallest organisms, which have been called to life by the self-dissipating intellectual substance of his entelechy. Once again the process of becoming commences from the lowest level; there is only one path which leads to man: "to begin creation from the start" [line 8321] and to work one's way "through thousand, countless thousand forms" [line 8325]. The symbol of Homunculus repeats that "long prelude of creatures and shapes,"[6] which nature provides in order that man may be attained. If Faust symbolizes the way of man, then Homunculus symbolizes the way to man; man and mannikin [line 6784], *homo* and *Homunculus*, are reflected in each other.

The appearances of Helena in the drama have a similar significance. Through the power acquired from the Mothers to achieve the vision of archetypes, Faust fetches Helena from the indifferent "Nothing" [line 6256] of shadow existence, yet once again only into the inwardness of his intellect, for the Paris-Helena scene is the materialization of an occurrence in Faust's inner self. "It's your own work, this ghostly mask, you dunce!" says Mephisto [line 6546]. Under the illusion that he sees something real, however, Faust touches Helena, in order to draw her immediately and completely into reality and thus secure for himself command of both the inner and the outer, "the greater double realm" [line 6555]. Faust's plan

6. From Goethe's letter to Friedrich Wilhelm Riemer, November 23, 1806.

has to miscarry, realization is denied to unconditional desire: an explosion knocks him to the ground, the spirits disappear. This moment corresponds, purely structurally, to the attempt of Faust as magus to grasp the world of spirits and his collapse in the confrontation with the Earth Spirit. And then begins, once again from the lowest level, the self-development of Helena. For all the figures of the "Classical Walpurgis Night," the Sphinxes, Griffins, Ants, Lamiae, Sirens, and whatever else allows itself to rendezvous in this night, are, according to a note by Goethe,[7] early forms of Helena, "antecedents" in more than merely a dramatic sense: the ugly and the amorphous must serve time by stages before the pure figure of beauty can appear, first as Galatea, then, in more intensified form, as Helena.

The story of the emperor provides a third example. He too begins in an undetermined indifference; he wants to be pre-eminent, yet he also wants to experience enjoyment with everyone else as one among many. Enjoyment, however, "makes common" (*gemein*), as Faust remarks [line 10259], where, according to older usage, the word "common" means "general" (*allgemein*). Then an opponent appears, and for the first time the emperor becomes aware of who he is:

> A rival Emperor profits me—I feel
> My sovereignty's never been more real. [lines 10407–8]

Here is the separation. Then in the fourfold sweep of battle back and forth the symbolic union of the inner and the outer occurs: enemies push their way in, a counter-attack draws the emperor's forces out, the enemy pushes ahead anew, this time penetrating to the inner realm of the emperor's army, finally the victory, which, in a literal sense, goes forth from within: the mountain opens, the elements issue forth and, as magical auxiliary troops, inundate the fleeing enemy.

There is no need to cite further examples. Unity, separation, mediation by stages of what is separated: this scheme occurs in both large and small every step of the way, and *Faust II* is full of fourfold sequences which bear a physiognomical resemblance to the stages of Faust's development, often *per contrarium* or ironically. Its symbolism is by no means exhausted through such structural relationships. Yet the interpretation of symbolism with regard to the specific content of the drama, which today constitutes the forefront of criticism, not only allows but also demands the analysis of pure symbolic structures, which in many instances corroborates, in others corrects the results of such criticism.

What is the significance of Goethe's procedure? Archetypes present themselves only in series of metamorphoses; for they do not

---

7. For the note to line 7271 see the Weimar edition, Vol. XV, 2, p. 48. For "antecedents" (*Antezedentien*) see Paralipomenon 157 in the same volume.

exist alongside their metamorphoses, but are the element common to all of them, thus can only manifest themselves as archetypes in the diachronic sequence of related phenomena. For this reason the symbolic view of Faust and his path insists upon a totality to this sequence; developments of similar structure must step out of his way, in order that the "idea" itself may finally be perceived. Since this idea stipulates the same law of being for all the spheres of reality in which Faust as the representative of man participates, i.e., nature, history, art and society, the form of "repeated mirror images"[8] is the most appropriate procedure for bringing them into poetic view.

Thus the Classical conception of *Faust* finally offers an approach to the inner meaning of the second part. Faust was an image for the humanity of man; but the drama in its entirety is more: it designs a universal image of being.

8. See Goethe's letter to K. J. L. Iken of September 23, 1817, above.

The Problematics of Part II

WILHELM EMRICH

The Enigma of *Faust, Part II*: A Tentative Solution†

When Goethe had completed the second part of his *Faust*, he did a very remarkable thing. He sealed the manuscript and refused to have it printed. It was to be published only after his death. In the last letter Goethe ever wrote, he gave the following reply to his friend Wilhelm von Humboldt's request to be allowed access to the manuscript:

> It would naturally be an infinite joy to me if during my life-time, too, I could dedicate these serious jests to my valued friends everywhere. I have always been grateful for their interest and should like to hear their response. But the present age is so sense-less and confused that I know I should only be poorly rewarded for my many years of sincere effort at erecting this strange build-ing. It would be driven like a wrack on the shore and lie there, getting gradually covered by the sands of time. The world is ruled today by bewildering wrong counsel, urging bewildered wrong action.

* * * A survey of *Faust* studies published since 1900 containing no fewer than 512 entries, which appeared in 1939, bore the very apt title *The Argument about Faust II*. We have to admit the deplorable fact that dispute and uncertainty still mark the position of the second part of the greatest of German poetic works. One opinion clashes with another, positive appreciations contend with negative judgments. The question, and it is one of urgent concern, is this: Is an approach possible to the inner meaning of this work? Can the enigma of *Faust, Part II*, be solved? Can we, as it were, see the work with Goethe's eyes and thus come to understand from within the poetic mystery of this strange creation?

First, it may be useful to point out a curious fact, to which most people are apt to pay too little attention. We are all in the habit of going straight on from the first to the second part of *Faust*. After Faust's wager with Mephisto, we expect that Faust will have to

† From *The Literary Revolution and Modern Society and Other Essays*, tr. Alexander and Elizabeth Henderson.

undergo further temptations at Mephisto's hands, that he will * * *
now withstand and conquer Mephisto's allurements in the great
world of politics or in his encounter with Helena. That would have
been the natural continuation corresponding to the design of *Part
I* * * *. Surprisingly, however, we find Goethe foregoing such a
continuation, and not by any means for reasons of senile debility, but
deliberately and with full intent. Originally he meant to continue
the work exactly in this sense desired by all the critics, but in
1825 he struck out all the scenes he had already written—and some
of them were magnificent—and deliberately gave the work an
entirely new character. According to the original drafts, for instance, Faust's sleep in the alpine meadow at the beginning of
Part II was not to be a sleep of "forgetting," in which his sin
against Gretchen is, one might say, temporarily wiped out and forgotten; on the contrary, it was to open the door to new temptations. "Spectral choruses of fame and glorious deeds" were, by
means of "visible symbols and pleasing songs" to "dazzle him with
the delights of fame, glory, power, and domination." Faust, that is to
say, was in fact to become a man of active politics. Mephisto was to
try to lure him with new temptations. Fame, glory, power, and
domination are the outstanding and dangerous seductions of political life, and over them Faust was to win an inner victory. The further action was planned quite consistently. Mephisto joins Faust
and gives him an "amusing and exciting description of the Augsburg Diet."[1] At Augsburg, Faust was to "revert to his former
abstruse speculations and demands on himself." In a great discussion with the Emperor, he was to press for "higher claims and
higher means." He was to make his entry as a world reformer, to
proclaim an ideal of government, and try to win the Emperor for it.
But the Emperor, the drafts continue, does not understand him,
relates everything to worldly, material things and, bored, begins to
yawn. At this critical moment Mephisto steps up and, disguised as
Faust,

> argues and swaggers and blusters right and left, backward and
> forward, into the world and out of it, so much so that the
> Emperor is beside himself with amazement and assures the sur-
> rounding gentlemen of his court that this is an extraordinarily
> learned man, whom he could listen to for days and weeks without
> tiring of it. . . . He, as Emperor, had to admit never to have
> found such a wealth of ideas, knowledge of human nature and
> profound experience combined in any single person, not even in
> the wisest of his counsellors.

This would, in fact, have meant continuing in the vein of *Part I*.
Exactly as in *Part I*, Faust was to develop ambitious plans, and
exactly as in *Part I* he was to have been disillusioned by Mephisto
and driven to despair when all his ideals were distorted and debased
by Mephisto. The conjuration of Helena, too, was originally

1. See note following line 4722 of *Faust*.

planned in this sense. Disguised as Faust, Mephisto was to have conjured up the ghosts, among them Helena, while in the background the real Faust watched this perversion of his ideals with horror and lay in a dead faint at the tumultuous ending. "There is a suspicion of trickery [Mephisto as Faust]. Nobody is at ease about the whole thing."

* * *

* * * The Faust of *Part I* was a subjective, passionate, even barbaric individual, always alternating between high-flying ideals and despair; the Faust of *Part II* was a man more pure, objective, superior, noble, and dignified. In Goethe's own words, he had, indeed, to extinguish the "subjective, more self-conscious and more passionate individual" Faust of *Part I*, and to "destroy" him by means of the sleep of forgetfulness in the Alps "in order to kindle new life from this apparent death." Faust, the individual, goes under, and in his place rises the supra-individual, timeless, superior, objective type of man. For this reason Goethe did not make Faust enter into a discussion with the Emperor after the cleansing sleep—Mephisto is now left to do that. Instead, Faust, after his sleep, makes his reappearance in a fancy-dress parade, unrecognizably disguised as Plutus. Of Plutus we are told: "There's nothing more for him to strive for,/ His eyes watch out for what's amiss" [lines 5556–57]. Faust, who strives eternally, has "nothing more to strive for." We seem to be faced with a complete transformation, indeed a reversal of Faust's whole character. This radical transformation of Faust's character has been overlooked in nearly the whole of the Faust literature, yet it is only when we have grasped it that we can really understand Goethe's abrupt change of direction in moving on to *Part II*. Faust has nothing more to strive for. He is "Plutus," that is to say, inwardly so rich and so perfect within himself that he can do without the subjective passion of ever unsatisfied striving. Like a spirit superior to the world, he takes a bird's-eye view of the whole political bustle at the Court. "His eyes watch out for what's amiss"; he is the one who helps, saves, watches out for mistakes and weaknesses. He has, furthermore, lost all subjectivity, self-consciousness, individuality. He has become a type. His appearance, we are told, is "open" and cannot be described, for the good reason that it is the timeless combination of all human appearances [line 5562]. He is supra-individual, and in a gay mood Goethe talks of his moon face glowing with fresh, all-round health, and no longer showing any sign of anything passionate, characteristic, personal, or instinctive:

> We saw the healthful, rounded face,
> The swelling lips, the cheeks full-blown
> That by the splendid turban shone;
> The robe's luxurious caress!
> And what of his august address?
> Renown and reign is what I sense. [lines 5563–68]

No less than twice in the second part, Faust is granted the grace of a sleep of renewal. And yet a third time, in Act II, during the search for Helena, he is advised to lie down and sleep:

> 'Twere best of all for thee
> Here to be bedding,
> Cool mould restore thee,
> Weariness shedding,
> Savor the heart's rest
> That everywhere flees thee;
> Our wafting and purling
> And whispering ease thee. [lines 7263–70]

Faust—once so restless, impetuous, titantic, and active—now sleeps. He partakes of the organic, healing, recuperative power of sleep. This is how Goethe, in his concern with polarity, with the wholeness of man, compensates the one-sidedness in Faust's original nature and turns him into a universal type. This fact is most often overlooked even today, when references to so-called Faustian man imply the predicament of this one-sidedly active, Faustian man. Goethe himself overcame and compensated this bias in the second part by Faust's passive attitude, organically anchored in nature and sleep. Another important point is that the characterization in the second part is that of a mask. Faust's original character, as such, remains unaltered. In the initial monologue of *Part II* he speaks of "ever striving for the highest life," and in Act V there is again a strong emphasis on striving, on never being satisfied, for example, in the scene with one of the Gray Sisters, Care. Similarly, at the end of Act I Faust reverts to a passionate attitude toward Helena, which is overcome only in the third act, when he faces her in sovereign detachment as a lover and master who has tamed passion within himself, as symbolized in the taming of Lynceus. The Plutus mask is, as it were, an ultimate aim that Faust, the man, has not yet achieved but which he assumes as a counter-image, and through this polarity reaches balance at a higher level. The effect of this is not to destroy the unity of *Faust*, but to create it. For this unity does not consist in linear action and identity of characters, but in the law of polarity and intensification, which, among other things, also determines the relationship between the first and the second part.

But it is not only Faust who is altered in this sense; the whole setting, atmosphere, and action are transposed to an objective, more dispassionate, and lighter level, as Goethe says. No longer, as in *Part I*, is the drama dominated by philosophical and impassioned dialogues, but existence itself unrolls as a play, and a play, to be precise, in which life's so-called "basic phenomena," the eternal fundamental manifestations of existence, are revealed and displayed in masquerades and opera-like revues. Faust-Plutus himself leads the parade in the first act, when fire threatens to break out, and in this sense he is the ruler dominating the world. He no longer discusses political problems with the Emperor, but reveals to our astonished eyes the eternal, ever-recurring fundamental laws of all political and social life. * * *

As existence itself thus unrolls before us in its eternal principles, Mephisto, too, assumes a different function. Goethe carefully discarded all drafts that could be interpreted as temptation of Faust by Mephisto. Faust is no longer tempted by Mephisto—at least not in the first three acts. Even Helena, as we shall see, is no longer a temptation for Faust, but on the contrary represents the highest form of existence, that is, the pure prototype of all that is beautiful, artistic, poetic. She combines in herself everything that Goethe, the poet, himself loved and revered in classical art. Faust is to be led to Helena in a positive sense. Helena is no longer a temptress. For this reason, even in the first act, Faust, in the Plutus mask, is shown as the "poet," "driven" by the genius of poetry in the person of the Boy Charioteer. In some extant variants, Goethe quite openly calls Faust-Plutus a poet, and in the final text Faust speaks of the genius of poetry as his beloved son. Faust, then, is the father of poetry; the name Boy Charioteer may be explained by the simple fact that Goethe often mentioned in conversation how the genius of poetry—or higher demons and good spirits—had once more today happily guided and directed him. In other words, Faust and the Boy Charioteer here impersonate Goethe's own existence and awareness as a poet, and all the treasure of poetry to which man's spirit and love gain him access.

But how does Mephisto fare in all this? There is a remarkable sketch for the Helena interlude, dating from 1800, where Mephisto appears in the Rhine Valley as Helena's Egyptian maid servant and says to her:

> And the sacred human rights,
> Are the same for slave and master,
> I don't have to take your orders,
> I can snap my fingers at you,
> You don't own me any more.
> I am Christian, have been baptized.

This is odd. Mephisto calls himself a Christian, talks of human rights that entitled him to refuse obedience to Helena. In addition, he is an Egyptian woman. What does this mean? The passage is really quite clear. Mephisto stands for everything that is non-classical, anticlassical, opposed to Helena's world of classical beauty and art. Egypt means the world *before* classical antiquity, Christianity the world *after* classical antiquity. And the modern world means the ideas of the French Revolution, the sacred human rights, which at that time, around 1800, were of highly topical interest for Goethe. Thus Mephisto becomes Helena's real counterpart,

whereas Faust is to be led toward her. Accordingly, Mephisto's character undergoes a complete change. When, around 1825, Goethe
began to reshape the Helena interlude and the whole of the second
part of *Faust*, a work he completed in the following years, the
"modern world" is represented for him no longer by the French
Revolution, but by Romanticism, to which at that time he was in
critical opposition. Mephisto, therefore, now defends the romantic
world of sentiments, the soulful modern attitude of inwardness,
against the plastic, objective, architectural beauty of classical antiquity. That is why in the third act Mephisto praises romantic music as
against the classical chorus:

> Listen, strings in sweet collusion . . .
> Ancient deities' confusion
> Put to rest, it had its day.
> Rest, old tales, for none will miss you,
> We demand a higher art:
> From the living heart must issue
> What would work upon the heart. [lines 9679–86]

Mephisto, the cynical mocker of Part I, suddenly praises the
inwardness of Romanticism, of sentimental education. The appeal to
the heart in modern music and sentiments is played off against
antiquity. In so doing, Mephisto indeed turns upon the ancient
polytheism. As Goethe and his age saw it, Romanticism really
meant all post-classical poetry and art, this is, all art from the migra-
tion of the nations onward until the present time. * * * Christianity, with its other-worldly orientation, is supposed to have imparted
a profound inwardness and spirituality to art. In the Helena Act,
Goethe's concern is to reconcile modern Christian art with classical art in the encounter between Faust and Helena. This is
why Mephisto, as the spokesman of modern poetry, has important
positive traits. It is true that he persists in the anti-classical world,
but in the classical mask of Phorcyas he approaches the Greek
world and accepts the invitation of the classical tree nymph, Dryas,
to turn his mind no longer to his home, the German North on the
Blocksberg, but to revere the greatness and originality of antiquity
as exemplified in the grandiose ugliness of the Phorcyads. Thus
Mephisto can pay tribute to Helena with genuine feeling:

> Issue forth from fleeting vapors, sun exalted this day . . .
> Now you face us in your grandeur, in your beauty once again . . .
> [lines 8909–17]

And when Helena disappears, he even advises Faust to hold on to
her veil:

> It is the goddess, whom you lost, no more,
> Yet godly still. . . . rise aloft,
> It bears you swiftly over all that is base
> Across the ether, for as long as you may endure. [lines 9949–53]

Mephisto has thus undergone a tremendous transformation, no less astonishing than Faust's own. Mephisto, of all people, admonishes Faust to rise above all mean things and to hold on to the divine part of Helena. Even in the second act, in the "Classical Walpurgis Night," he shows himself in a similar mood. There Mephisto appears as the prim and prudish modern Christian moralizer against the shameless nudity of antiquity:

Quite à la mode these moot points should be mastered
And fashionably-triply overplastered . . . [lines 7088–89]

As Phorcyas he defends the genius of Romanticism, even the latest romantic sculpture, "the most daring chisel of the newest age," by means of which he is to hold his own as Helena's peer in the temple of classical art, and thus to reconcile the antique and the modern:

With gods and goddesses then may it fall
To us to stand within the temple hall.

And throughout the third act he keeps moralizing, reminding Helena of all her misdeeds and severely castigating her immoral way of life. His role as Faust's tempter, even his wager with Faust, seem completely forgotten. This is most obvious at the climax of Act III, when Faust meets Helena and enjoys and celebrates the "moment":

Now seeks the mind no forth or back from this,
Alone the present moment—Helena is our bliss . . .
Being is duty, fleet as it may be. [lines 9381–82, 9418]

With this enjoyment of the present moment, one would think, Faust has already lost his wager. But what does Mephisto do? Instead of taking advantage of this moment to catch out Faust and finally bind him to himself, he "disturbs" this supreme, spiritual, and sensual moment of love by entering violently with these words:

Spelling-books of love construing,
Playfully bemused in wooing,
Vainly cooing, idly suing,
But there is no time, I say.
Blind to distant lightening's flaring,
Listen to the trumpet blaring. [lines 9419–24]

There is no word of the wager. Why not? Because Goethe's concern has shifted to something different, to the pure, spontaneous deployment of the basic phenomena of beauty, art, nature, history, existence itself. Mephisto, too, must serve his role in this phenomenological primary series of existential elements. He becomes a partial manifestation of these basic phenomena. It is only in the last two acts, especially in the fifth, that the problems of *Part I* come to the fore again, the problem of the wager and the original characterization of Faust and Mephisto.

So much, then, for clearing our view as to what is radically new, especially in the first three acts of *Part II*, that is, those most difficult and most incomprehensible to most readers. The next question is how Goethe treats the basic phenomena of existence in these first three acts.

Goethe himself felt these first three acts to have an inner unity. The first one he wrote was the Helena act, the third, as the climax of the drama; the first two he described as "antecedents" to the Helena act, that is, necesary prior stages that prepare for Helena's appearance.

Helena was for him the essence of beauty and art, and beyond that also the symbol of man's creative, productive powers, of timeless, classical culture. The question that preoccupied him was this: How can man, amid the upheavals and fatalities of history, find his way once more to a great, creative achievement, to a classically supreme culture? He wants to show all the paths that lead to it, but also all the wrong turnings that lead away from it and prevent great and timeless creation.

The first act shows the path that leads to Helena from without. Helena is conjured up at the Emperor's Court. The problem here is how to arrive at a timeless, creative culture within the framework of human society and politics. The attempt to reach it from without fails. The conjuring up of Helena at the Emperor's Court ends in catastrophe.

The second act shows the path that leads to Helena from within. It is the organic, natural, genetic way. Access to Helena is sought from her own origins. The attempt succeeds.

Let us now retrace both paths. The first act, which represents the path to Helena from without, turns on the following question: What are the conditions and basic phenomena on which human society rests, and how are creative activity, beauty, and art possible in human society? The masquerade, in which Faust appears in the guise of poet and Plutus, shows in the first place the socially fashionable precursors of art.

> Let the motley fancies flower
> For the fashion of the hour. [lines 5144–45]

The problem of "fashion" was one that often preoccupied Goethe in the course of his life. He always saw fashion as an important preliminary to art and gave it much thought. For him, the problem was also in a very profound way connected with the nature of woman, to whom he attributed an educational potential and preparation for the artist. Woman develops in the artist a sense for beautiful forms, a sense of taste, proportions, and propriety, all of which Goethe always considered as important preliminaries to genuine, mature art, though only in social terms, not as inner essentials of art. This is how we should interpret the Garden Girls' words:

Flower girls appeal, admit it,
Charmingly to eyes and hearts;
For a bond of nature fitted
Female temper for the arts. [lines 5104–7]

In the dispute betweeen the natural and the "fabricated" flowers, furthermore, we find an intimation that the art of fashion merely tends to imitate nature and thereby to render it artificial. But a deeper problem, too, is touched upon here: the fabricated flowers "blossom all the year," that is, contrary to natural blossoms, they are endowed with timeless duration. This first scene of the masquerade concludes with the significant ideal that in art everything is to be found simultaneously, "Buds and leaves, and flower and fruit." [line 5177] Whereas in nature everything proceeds in a time sequence, art has the capacity suddenly to bring together in a unity all the stages of development and thus, indeed, to make the "basic phenomenon" of plants, all the stages of their development, visible in timeless duration: "All the blossom must fade before fruit can ripen,/Blossoms and fruit at once only the Muses give," we find in one of Goethe's poems. For Goethe, finally, the supreme artist is he who does not simply copy nature, but shapes his creations as organically and inevitably as nature, that is, who has learned nature's laws of development.

After this opening scene, in which art and society are confronted in their external relationship, the inner construction of society itself is displayed in concise allegories. The Woodcutters create the conditions of human civilization. They clear the virgin forests, create space, build houses; they represent rough, rugged labor. Next come the Pulcinelli, who take care of communications, "eel-like gliding," followed by the Parasites, who skim cream off everything. The Drunken Man and the concluding Chorus represent the climax of work: sociable feasting. Then, by way of polarity, poetry intervenes, and poetry, moreover, in its dated fashionable forms, or as we would say today, the "isms" of poetry—the fashions of naturalism, classicism, romanticism, and so on. The last word among the poets is given to the Satirist, because he alone can recognize and scornfully pillory this debilitating social bondage of poetry. After that, the inner construction of society continues. The Graces represent the original forms of exchange, of social relations: giving, receiving, thanking. It is on these three attitudes that the whole of economic life rests, and equally all social intercourse among men. Next, the Fates guide the threads of individual life so as to keep them in order in the skein of human interrelationships. They are followed by the real plagues of professional and social life, the Furies of gossip, defamation, slander, and vindictiveness. The scene comes to a climax with the cortege of the "Goddess of all active forces" [line 5456], which is meant to illustrate how it is possible at all to develop any genuine, fruitful, creative activity within the framework of society. Every active individual in society is always torn between fear and hope. Fear of defamation and slander, of the envy of others, poisons his actions, while his hope of improvement and his excessive trustfulness equally imperil his activity. Both—fear and hope—are therefore two of mankind's greatest enemies. Only wisdom can master and bind them, so that they can do no damage. But even when done, the work is still in danger: Mephisto, in the mask of Zoilo-Thersites,[2] belittles and decries the successful achievement.

Thus Goethe, as it were, here indicates the external premises, conditions, and limits subject to which human activity proceeds always and in all human societies, whether in the setting of a small village, a town, a professional association, or a government. After this prelude the real theme begins. Genius himself appears, the Boy Charioteer who alone can lead Faust to Helena. Something unexpected, magical, miraculous, something higher enters society:

> Storms up with tempestuous snort.
> All make way! I shudder! [lines 5519–20]

A sacred shudder overcomes the herald when these "airy specters" are borne through the crowd in their chariot, but without dividing the crowd, because they are bodiless and eternal. This Boy Charioteer who drives the poet Faust-Plutus, is, as was noted before, the genius of poetry itself. * * * Originally, the Boy Charioteer was called Euphorion, that is, he was identical with Faust's and Helena's son in the third act. Goethe crossed out this name in the manuscript and wrote Boy Charioteer instead, probably for the mere formal reason that it would be asking a bit much of the public to accept in Act I a character who is born only in Act III. But in essence the two characters are identical. They represent the timeless, ever recurring genius of poetry. * * * Euphorion leaps higher and higher, eventually flies off into the infinite and falls to the ground. And just as Euphorion radiates flaming gold brought up from the depths as a symbol of the spirit's genius, so the Boy Charioteer digs into a mysterious gold chest and scatters the same flaming gold among the crowd, who greedily snap it up, but see in it no more than material wealth and thus get their fingers burned. To only a few does the little flame of genius, of poetic gift, remain and glow on. Thus the Boy Charioteer is not at ease in this confused human society, amid this avid, restless grabbing for external happiness, and departs into solitude, where alone the true genius of poetry can breathe and work.

And now comes the most powerful, the most awesome and most profound scene of the whole masquerade. Faust has the mysterious chest of flaming gold placed on the ground and draws a circle around it to protect it from the greedy grasp of the crowd. But

2. See note to line 5457 of *Faust*.

the Emperor, disguised as Pan, the symbol of the whole world, breaks through the circle and stretches out his hand for the treasures in the chest, which include crowns, chairs, and rings—the symbols of political power. At that moment he catches fire. The "world's great All" and his entire court are in danger of burning as a result of their hunger for gold, until the poet Faust-Plutus quenches the fire.

* * *In the fragmentary sketches for the Walpurgis Night on the Blocksberg, in *Part I*, Goethe describes a gigantic, infernal Diet, at which the whole world pays tribute to Satan—kings, ministers, writers, men and women alike. The devil seduces them with flaming gold, which appears in two forms: first as greed for money, as Mammon, whose golden glow casts an eery, lurid light upon the whole mountain, and second as desire for sexual love, for earthly immortality through biological procreation. Gold represents man's elementary power of life and love, which in the first instance is neither good nor evil. If man merely wants to possess this power, to degrade it for his own enjoyment alone, it becomes the source of all evil, avarice, and selfish sexuality, the true elements of evil. But if man uses this power serenely and spontaneously, in a selfless striving for the divine, it becomes the source of genius, of all that is beautiful and good, the genuine power of creation. Thus, in the hands of the Boy Charioteer, gold is the real creative power of genius. But in the hands of Mephisto, who in this masquerade appears as a Starveling, a thin old miser wanting to possess everything in contrast to the inwardly rich and generously giving, selfless poet Plutus, gold becomes the symbol of base sexuality. Mephisto as avarice degrades and distorts this supreme power of love and the spirit into baseness and evil. Correspondingly the Emperor, disguised as Pan, with his greed for crowns and chains and rings— that is, for power—unleashes the world catastrophe, the downfall of political and social life.

At the same time, however, the Emperor's contact with the liquid gold, this primordial power of life, had not only a negative, but also a positive significance. It gave him a glimpse of the elementary laws and secret foundations of political life. In the scene that immediately follows the masquerade, the Emperor describes a strange occurrence. When the flames pressed in upon him, he felt as though he were in Pluto's realm, in the underworld. Even there he was a prince and the ruler of the fire.

> Far off through twisted fiery trunks and steeples
> I saw the endless moving files of peoples. [lines 5997–98]

All the peoples paid homage to him. He stood at the center of human history. He, therefore, becomes master over this primordial force of life, this flaming liquid gold; he is not conquered by it, but withstands it and uses it selflessly and correctly. He thereby also overcomes everything negative in political life, and in a very positive way takes his sovereign, serene, and superior place in the whole of the earth's existence. For the text goes on to describe how the Emperor could similarly become master over water, air, and land, ruler of all the four elements, of the whole cosmos, if only he had the courage to face these primordial forces without fear, to leap into them regardless of his own safety:

> You sampled now the fire's obedient ravage:
> Next plunge into the sea at its most savage,
> . . . Gold dragons sport, prismatic scales and claws,
> There gapes a shark, you laugh into his jaws. [lines 6005–18]

Death and rebirth, ruin and renewal of earthly existence—life's extremes are here put before us by Goethe in magnificent and striking symbolism.

Goethe, therefore, did not evade taking issue with the so-called great world, but instead projected it onto an infinitely more profound, timeless plane. He explores the source and origin of all evil, of catastrophes and war. Say the Gnomes:

> And yet the gold that we unseal
> Is what they use to pimp and steal,
> Our iron arms the haughty man,
> Though wholesale murder be his plan.
> Who these commandments takes in vain
> Holds all the others in disdain.
> All this is not our fault, you see,
> So bear with it, for so do we. [lines 5856–63]

Goethe is here seeking to apprehend symbolically the essential, eternal causes of war.

All this becomes even clearer in the following scene. Mephisto gives the Emperor not genuine gold, but paper money in lieu of the treasure of gold in the earth. It is a description of a modern inflation, a huge economic fraud. The genuine is replaced by an illusion. This, for Goethe, was the real trouble with modern economic and political life.

Having reduced social and political life to eternal phenomena, Goethe similarly lets Faust conjure up Helena from eternity itself. Faust descends to the Mothers, who dwell outside time and space, where the eternal prototypes of all things, also of Helena, are to be found. What gives him access to the Mothers is a key of flaming gold, once more the element that symbolizes the supreme power of life and the spirit.

But again the desire to possess Helena prevents her being truly won. When Faust passionately wants to embrace Helena, catastrophe ensues. With an explosion, the spirits dissolve in vapor. Faust falls to the ground in a dead faint. Beauty cannot be transplanted from eternity into this world suddenly and without an intermediary, and every attempt to do so is bound to fail. Goethe furthermore illustrates how beauty and art must inevitably be misunderstood in mere social life. Everyone wants to draw art down to himself, instead of rising toward it by strenuous effort. Thus the men want only to possess Helena; the women, the beautiful Paris. No genuine access to art has as yet been found.

After this catastrophe of the first act, there follows Faust's inner, natural path to Helena. Act II is that of genesis, of Helena's birth. In the very first scene Faust, in his study, dreams of Helena's conception and birth. This inescapably implies also the birth of creative genius itself. Goethe here approaches the tremendous problem of the origin of genius. How does genius come into being? How can it become a living, creative force? This is why Goethe causes genius to be generated, produced before our eyes, and Helena's birth to be seen and interpreted; and he does so in the shape of Homunculus, the subject of so much speculation. Homunculus has all the features of the Boy Charioteer and Euphorion. Again, he is half-boy, half-girl, a glowing flame. Goethe himself called him a genius, a creatively active *Daimonion*[3] with a tendency toward the beautiful. But unlike the Boy Charioteer, he does not come to Faust out of the air, as it were, into which he again dissolves. The problem, rather, is this: how can this genius be born, how can he enter into real life and engage in creative activity? This problem governs the whole of Act II. This act begins with the illusory, artificial production of Homunculus in the glass phial and ends with his genuine, organic birth and origin in the waters of the Aegean Sea, as a result of the glass phial being shattered on the chariot of the goddess of love and the spiritual flame being united with the elements of life.

In Faust's northern laboratory, the Boy Charioteer is only half born, only artificially generated. He is merely spiritual, possesses no body. One might say: pure intellect without connection with life. In the drafts he appears as an erudite know-it-all, a historical, world-almanac imp who surveys all of world history from Adam to the present, rattling off the facts of world history during the air trip to Greece until Faust and Mephisto are quite overwhelmed. He is purely artificial spirit devoid of creative, vital force.

> He has, so I have heard him say,
> Been born but half in some prodigious way.
> Of intellectual traits he has no dearth,
> But sorely lacks the solid clay of earth.
> So far the glass is all that keeps him weighted,
> But he would gladly soon be corporated.
> A genuine spinster's progeny,
> You are before you ought to be! [lines 8247–54]

The paradox of the spirit that has existed in all eternity, but must in fact first be generated, if truly perfect artistic creation is to be

3. From the Greek *daimōn* (divine power, fate, god).

possible, is here illustrated in magnificent symbolism. * * * It was always the same great problem that preoccupied Goethe, the problem of how the spirit, the idea, can assume living, active and artistic *shape*. The birth of Helena and the birth of this genius are * * * one and the same thing. Goethe therefore deliberately deleted Faust's bringing Helena from Hades as redundant, once he had shown the full birth of Homunculus at the end of Act II and once he had brought this act to its conclusion in a triumphal hymn to the god Eros and the four elements fire, water, air, and earth, from which stems all life.

With this the theme of the whole second act has assumed, from within, vast dimensions beyond all measure. Goethe is not really concerned with the historical figure of Helena, but with the creation of being as such, that is, with the representation of the ultimate sources and origins of the cosmos. And in fact the third act does illustrate the genesis of the earth, of life, of the gods, of history and its ever recurring wars, of art, and so on, in a seemingly confusing abundance of mythological figures and events—that is, their symbolic genesis, not, of course, their real one. How can something great, something eternal be forever repeatedly generated on earth—that is the great, overriding question in this most stupendously daring feat of poetry known to mankind.

It is not possible to discuss here all the lines and interpretations of this work, whose composition is really marvellously clear. Only the most important points will be mentioned. The central feature of the "Classical Walpurgis Night" is the great volcanic earthquake, which symbolizes human revolts, wars, and party strife. Political unrest of this kind is what really disrupts any organic construction and any genuine creative development, and therefore it has to be overcome. This earthquake throws up the mysterious gold, which at once becomes the subject of violent party strife between the Pygmies and the Cranes, that is, the democrats and the aristocrats. * * * This party strife can be traced through considerable parts of the "Classical Walpurgis Night." It is for Goethe a constantly recurring basic phenomenon in history. It is in the background of the battle of Pharsalus that is conjured up at the beginning, the battle between the dictator Caesar and Pompey, the representative of the old freedom; it is a sort of permanent battle that rages through the Middle Ages between the Guelfs and the Ghilbellines[4] and broke out anew in the French Revolution. Even the dispute between the classics and the romantics, which is another feature of the "Classical Walpurgis Night," is seen by Goethe as a recurrence of this, for him, ultimately senseless party strife. In Act IV we read:

> When all is said, it's party hate
> Works best in every devil's fête,
> Down to the very utmost horrors;

4. See note to line 4845 of *Faust*.

With sounds now hideously panic,
Now shrill and stridently satanic,
It spreads alarm through vale and forest. [lines 10777–82]

A meteor, suddenly falling from heaven, puts an end to all these party squabbles by destroying friend and foe alike. The meteor always served Goethe as a symbol for a demonic and dreadful event, as in the case of Napoleon. A revolt "from below and above" upsets everything. And yet—and this gives a clear indication of Goethe's own attitude—this whole political and historical upheaval and unrest are only deception and appearance. "Be still! 'Twas but imagined so," says Thales [line 7946]. No genuine creative reality can be attributed to it at all. It is a repulsive, senseless confusion, as indeed for Goethe all historical struggles were more or less lunatic disturbances of the ever identical, organically developing power of nature and the spirit—disturbances resting on fanaticism, dogmatism, and barbarity.

Helena is found by another path. In the midst of all the turmoil, Faust is told to go to sleep by the waters of Peneus. He finds the organic, natural way to Helena, by traversing all the prior stages, all the transformations from the elemental through the human to the divine. But the gold, which gave rise to the dispute, is returned to the sea and thus to its pure, divine origin. During this pageant of the sea at the end of Act II, time stands still: "The Moon delaying in the Zenith," say the stage directions [before line 8035]. History holds her breath. All is ready for the eternal to emerge. During all the millennia of wars raging on the surface, the goddess of love and beauty has eternally guarded in mysterious caves the beautiful and the great. Now it must be won anew. And it is won by the fusion of the divine and the elemental. Ocean nymphs, in whom the divine and the elemental are combined in marvelous purity, go to fetch the gods, the Cabiri from Samothrace, in whom Goethe illustrates step-by-step the genesis of the divine. Then the divine appears in human shape, in the Greek sculptures. But even these "forms of Gods" must be melted down again to make room for eternal transformations and re-creation on earth. At the appearance of the goddess of love and beauty herself, the genius Homunculus smashes his glass. The spiritual is wedded to life. And an endless chain of creative birth and rebirth will begin on earth, sparked off by the ever recurring encounter of the divine and the human. That is the meaning of the second act. Only now can Helena herself appear, the personification of beauty and art. Now the truly great is born.

Act III brings Faust's encounter with Helena. This encounter, too, has a wider meaning. How is a rebirth, a new classicism possible in modern Europe? That is the problem of the third act. Helena is taken into the modern, Christian world, into a Gothic castle. Her encounter with Faust gives birth to modern poetry. Helena discovers the musical, sonorous rhyme, which was absent in ancient poetry. She is introduced to the more profound, more heartfelt depths of Christian poetry. The birth of Euphorion marks also the birth of romantic, operatic music. Greek polytheism is left behind, Nordic tribes take possession of Greece, but not in the sense of military conquest:

> These thrones are changing into arbors,
> Arcadian-free shall be our bliss! [lines 9572–73]

Politics give way to a higher culture in which man finds the way back to his pure, natural, god-like origins:

> And [one] stands amazed—the question still remaining
> If these are gods or mortal men?
> So was Apollo shaped to shepherd likeness
> That of their fairest, one resembled him;
> Where Nature works within her own pure cycle,
> All worlds link up without an interim.
> In this way did she bless me, did she bless you,
> Let all the past be put behind and gone;
> Oh feel yourself the highest godhead's issue,
> To that first world you appertain alone. [lines 9556–65]

Man is reborn in the knowledge that he is one with the highest god. He stands once more at the pure origin of existence, even in the midst of the present's confusion. Thus this Helena act, which retraces three thousand years of European development in a symbolic flash, represents the reconciliation of classical and Christian culture. It stands for Goethe's own classicism, in which Christianity and antiquity are fused in miraculous unity. But Goethe knows that this classicism is nothing rigid and unique. It will have to dissolve and give way to a new, creative transformation. This is why the Helena act leads up to the profound conclusion of disassociating the elements from which this supreme form of classicism has developed. Euphorion's flame of genius ascends to heaven, to eternity, but he leaves behind his garment, that is, the external styles and forms of poetry, which give rise to new literary schools:

> The flame is vanished, to be sure,
> But leaves the world in no distress.
> Enough remains to consecrate the poet,
> Stir guildsmen's greed, collegial pettiness;
> And, ready talent lacking to bestow it,
> I can at least lend out the dress. [lines 9956–61]

In other words, the costume, the external forms of poetry, will be copied in later years and thus give rise to new schools of art. Helena herself, however, beauty as such, remains in Hades as an immortal personality. Individuality, the name, is preserved. The personality of beauty has become immortal. But the natural elements that were its ingredients are impersonal. They revert to nature, Leader of the Chorus:

> He who has earned no name, nor strives for noble things
> Belongs but to the elements, so get you gone!
> I yearn to join my Queen; in merit not alone,
> But in our loyalty we live as persons still. [lines 9981–84]

The girls' return to nature is symbolized by Goethe by means of their transformation into the elements, into fire, water, air, and earth, those same elements out of which beauty was born at the end of Act II. Now, at the vintage feast, a bacchanalian riot breaks out. Chaos once more prevails.

> The cloven talons trample down all chaste decorum,
> Senses all are whirled a-stagger, stunned to deafness dread the ear.
> [lines 10034–35]

The classical form is smashed. But the Helena drama closes with the hope of rebirth:

> For to garner fresher vintage, older skins are swiftly drained!
> [line 10038]

Or, at Euphorion's death:

> Yet afresh new anthems sow them,
> Stand in mourning bowed no more:
> For the soil again will grow them
> As it ever has before. [lines 9935–38]

The great circle is completed. The birth and end of a classical culture have been retracted under all conceivable aspects in timeless types and forms, and we are shown the possibility of the birth of a new classical art from the same elements.

And here, by and large, is the answer to the enigma of *Faust, Part II.* The two following acts can be understood in their own terms. They treat the ultimate questions of faith, of the question of man's conquest of death, of the question of redemption. Goethe tried to solve these questions in a universal sense, so universal indeed that it cannot easily, or at all, be reduced to a formula. Christian and humanistic elements are inextricably interwoven. Man's innate ceaseless striving is rewarded, even if it led him through profound guilt and error. This seems to be humanistic, to speak of trust in man's own creative powers, his powers for good. But Goethe also explicitly stresses the limits of these human powers. Man cannot be redeemed by his own effort. He needs grace and love from above. This is Christian. That is why, quite logically, the work ends in Christian symbols and sacred ceremonies. It is not possible here to enter in detail into the strange combination of Catholic, Protestant, and humanistic elements in Goethe. It would demonstrate that in Goethe the Western world reached a synthesis of nearly all the religious, philosophical, and cultural currents, such as can hardly be found in such far-reaching unity and compactness, either before or after him.

And this brings us to the important final question, namely, what is the significance of *Faust, Part II*, for our own age? It will have become clear that Goethe did not evade political questions and catastrophes, but that he sought to define and master them on the basis of fundamental premises. Goethe sought out the very origin of evil, of wars, revolutions, and party strife. Nevertheless, he also took a very realistic view of human society, its economic and other crises. We may recall, for instance, the description of inflation in Act I. And Act V shows us the destructive, murderous power of technology in all its frightfulness, when Faust's civilizing activity on the seashore involves the destruction of godly, pure humanity in the shape of Philemon and Baucis:

> Human victims bled and fevered,
> Anguish on the night-air borne,
> Fiery torrents pouring seaward
> Scored a channel by the morn. [lines 11127–30]

The whole horror of the technological age is presaged in these lines.

But Goethe considered also the reversal of the dialectical process. Genius is born and becomes creative only when it steps out of itself, when, "moved by the impulse of love," it smashes its artificial glass phial and is prepared unreservedly to sacrifice itself, to give itself up even at the risk of death to the overwhelming powers of existence, the elements—to face them, enter into them. * * *

All the catastrophes, all evils in the world are caused by man pressing into finite limits the divine spark that burns within him, which Goethe expressed by the symbol of the flaming gold, by man selfishly and greedily wanting to possess it, making it subservient to empirical, purposeful thought. All disaster then stems from Mammon and from the perversion of divine love into mere possessive lust. But evil can again be turned into good, if man serenely and freely sacrifices himself, conscious of the power of love at work within him as the divine flame, the spirit. The man is promised rebirth, and indeed, like the Emperor after the "jugglery of flame," even genuine, true domination over the elements that earlier threatened to destroy him.

This work of Goethe's also contains a hidden criticism of our own writers and poets. They will never rise to being critical of their age, that is, superior to it, until they try to realize in their consciousness those truths that Goethe expressed in this work. For poetic criticism, caught in its own subject by merely retracing its contradictions, must indeed rightly reject every "way out" as a lie and must remain in a state of despair like the "trapped, passionate individual" Faust: "And despair alone is duty." But poetic criticism can become genuinely "radical" only by pushing its questions and creative forms down to the very "roots," to power, love, and spirit. Only such sovereign awareness can fearlessly retrace the basic phenomena of human reality and thus break out of the infernal circle of our empirical thought and once more transform the searing flame of gold, around which the battle still rages today, into the pure flame of love and spirit. Then our activity will again find the way to new creation, as Goethe presaged around the turn of the century, in January 1800, in "Palaeophron and Neoterpe" (lines 178 ff.)—in words that seem addressed directly to outselves:

> Men and women, listen to my words of truth.
> What makes people happy is activity,
> Achieving useful things and able to transform
> The evil into good by its divine effect.
> Get up, then, at the break of day, and though you may
> Find yesterday's constructions crumbled overnight
> Set to like busy ants and clear the ruins out.
> Devise your plans anew, employ new ways and means.
> If then the world itself be out of joint and race
> To its destruction of its own accord, you shall
> Rebuild it once again, for everlasting joy.

HERMAN MEYER

"These Very Serious Jests"†

When in ten thousand years' time some remains of that archaic cultural period in which Goethe and we have lived are dug up, perhaps it will happen that by chance no text of Goethe's *Faust II* will see the light of day, but instead a number of texts of a more or less learned nature, let's say tentatively a few dozen books and essays, which will then give indirect information about that lost work. What impression will our latter-day descendants derive from those rudiments of our "Faust literature"? Naturally it will depend upon what selection chance will have made. But it is highly probable that from those learned testimonies the following picture of *Faust II* will be reconstructed: a work of the highest poetic stature and the deepest seriousness also, because of its rigid seriousness, a rather forbidding work. If by chance a scrap of Goethe's last letter is also dug up, in which, five days before his death, he describes a particular poetic work as "these very serious jests," it will not easily be guessed that this refers to the very same *Faust II*.

It would seem timely to consider Goethe's term *jest* more seri-

† From *Poesie und Wissenschaft*, Vol. 19 (Heidelberg: Lothar Stiehm Verlag, 1970). Reprinted by permission of Lothar Stiehm Verlag. Translated by Dolores Signori and Cyrus Hamlin.

ously than has hitherto been the case in Faust criticism, and to regard the element of the jestful not only as derivative and as a constellatory condition, but also and above all as an unmediated and original quality. Let us attempt first of all to put the phrase cited from Goethe's letter in perspective. A few months earlier, Goethe had attempted to comfort his friend Sulpiz Boisserée, who was justifiably discouraged by the news that the second part of *Faust*, according to Goethe's firm resolution, would not be appearing "forthwith," nor, as Goethe cautiously indicated, during his lifetime: "As I sealed up my completed *Faust*, I was not entirely content to do so; for it occurred to me that my most valuable friends, those who are generally in agreement with my views, should not have the pleasure forthwith of enjoying for a few hours these very seriously intended jests and thereby perceiving what had gone around in my head and mind for years until finally assuming this form." Those are remarkable words. From a sense of delicacy for the feelings of his friend, and probably also to protect his own feelings, Goethe speaks about this decision of denial, which surely did not come easily to him, in a curiously light tone, which would sound highly disrespectful if it came from another: "to have pleasure"; "to enjoy for a few hours"; and even, concerning the great poetic work of his late years, "these seriously intended jests." Does this jest-like understatement perhaps exempt us from the responsibility of taking these last words at all seriously?

* * *

* * * In all its variations the term [*jest*] has an evident consistency. At the same time, however, it is striking that its range of meaning is not very firmly circumscribed. The word *jest* has become less fixed as a literary *terminus technicus* than such words as *wit*, *irony*, *humor*, and the *comic*. The term maintains a certain generality which includes potentially those more specific meanings that can be actualized accordingly. In regard to *Faust II* we must not lose sight of this quality of Goethe's term *jest*.

* * *

But now to the work itself! We cannot of course be satisfied with simply selecting from the whole of the poem a series of pleasant passages of a comical-ironic-humoristic nature and displaying them here in an agreeable fashion, however entertaining this social game might be. Rather our questions and observations are directed toward the fundamental and basic character of the jest, which, in a fraternal alliance with seriousness, serves as a ferment for the entire work and co-organizes its structure. I cannot refrain from expressing my own conviction: It is essential to the nature of this work and determinative of its structure that jest (extending upwards from low comedy to the most refined heights, for which only the word brightness is applicable) and seriousness (extending downwards into the deepest and sometimes the darkest spiritual basis) are combined within it into a higher unity, for which poetics has no appropriate term and which is most effectively denoted by the word *oxymoron* as Goethe used it. Admittedly, these are joined in a higher unity within the work as a whole, not in each of its single parts. In these parts the relationship of seriousness and jest is infinitely variable: it can be a matter of abrupt juxtaposition, colorful mixture, intimate entanglement, or homogeneous fusion of both. All these variations, however, contribute each in its own way to that higher unity of the whole. * * *

Where to begin, where to stop? For the present I do not, or not very much, wish to speak of those parts and passages whose jestful character is so boundlessly evident that it cannot fail to be clear even to the dullest reader of *Faust*. I would rather like to assume silently that this reservoir of jest is present to our consciousness. Think, for example, of the overwhelming merriment of many scenes involving Mephisto: his conversation with the Baccalaureus; his metamorphosis into the guise of Phorcyas; the basic humor of the phallic element in his appearance as Avarice personified in the Carnival; and the Breughelesque battle between the angels and the sturdy, robust devils in the scene "Entombment." Let us rather turn in preference to those areas where the jest-serious question is sharply ambiguous. * * *

Firstly, therefore: the flashes of individual verbal wit. In the state council the chancellor warns vehemently against Mephisto's "gold bait" [line 4941], that is, his promise to extract buried treasure from the ground by means of special skills: "That scheme sounds neither sound to me nor pious" [line 4942]. Thereupon the Marshal says:

> For means to make our style at Court more regal
> I should be glad to be a shade illegal [lines 4943–44]

His opportunism is concealed in double entendre. The word *be* (*haben* in the German) has a twofold grammatical function: I want to *be* wrong (i.e., be in the wrong), even if I thereby *do* a wrong (i.e., by procuring gold in a disreputable way). Does the speaker himself intend this or is it the attentive reader who supplies the ambiguity? A question which is both fundamental and open. In the following example, ambiguity is clearly divided between two persons. Wagner, eager for the success of his "glorious work," the creation of Homunculus, considers Mephisto's entrance an intrusion and admonishes him to be quiet: "A man is being made" [line 6835]. In Wagner's mouth this making [*machen*] means specifically an artificial creation; he looks with suspicion upon the "tricks" of procreation. Mephistopheles, however, intentionally misunderstands such "making" to be a vulgar name for "procreation" (compare the idiom *ein Kind machen*, to "make" a child) and instantly imagines the drastic grotesque situation of lovers in the sooty chimney of the laboratory:

> A man? And what young pair in passion
> Did you imprison in the flue? [lines 6836–37]

Here therefore the burden of supplying the ambiguity is removed from the reader. The touch of ambiguity differs again when the offspring in the retort hovers in his phial over Faust, who is stretched out asleep, and espies and comments on Faust's Correggio-like dream of Leda.[1] His first word: "Momentous!" [line 6903] is a ceremonious favorite of the aged Goethe himself, Correggio can be content. Then:

> Fair-environed!—Limpid waters
> In a dense grove, young nymphs their garments shedding;
> Sweet sight! Now sweeter still. [lines 6903–5]

Each reader has the right to perceive here only a highly serious enthusiasm for art. On the other hand, to introduce a human, indeed all-too-human, element into such enthusiasm for art is an exquisite touch! It is the phrase of a lady's man, "Now sweeter still," which comes from the mouth of this little *voyeur*, who in body has yet to "come to be" [line 8246] and who is all too lacking in "the solid clay of earth" [line 8250]. Through such double attention the sublime charm of the Leda vision is not diminished in the least, but indeed enriched by a cheerful component which, moreover, stands in perfect harmony with the intensely aesthetic sensuality of Correggio's magnificent painting of Leda. Again: Correggio can be content, more so perhaps than many a serious interpreter of *Faust*, for whom such an explanation would be a disrespectful outrage.

* * *

In proceeding from the smaller to the larger our attention is demanded by the abundance of individual tones of speech which are distributed among the figures in the drama. Many figures remain in our consciousness or at least in our sensory recollection primarily due to their vocal pitch (Homunculus' thin little voice), some almost exclusively *as* sensory pitch: the rumble of Seismos, the growling of old Nereus. The concept of "tone," however, must also be understood more intellectually. Here the distribution of seriousness and jest among the figures offers an extremely rich area for observation. How fundamentally different is the individual figure of Faust from the multi-layered work, which bears his name! Faust, the rigorous and absolutistic superior man, is a fundamentally humorless figure, perhaps the most humorless figure in the entire drama. Never at any time does he make use of the relativistic optic plurality in which this poetic work excels. How different, in contrast

1. See note to line 2440 of *Faust*.

to him, is his more supple opponent. Mephistopheles is by no means, as has been maintained, marked by a uniform tone of cynicism. Rather, as a virtuoso of language he can assume many roles. His sympathetic common sense sounds almost good-natured when he sums up the result of his conversation with the Baccalaureus:

> Young must, for all its most outlandish antics,
> Still makes some sort of wine at last. [lines 6813–14]

Goethe lends to Mephistopheles' words a ring which is native to the Main-Franconia[2] area. In general it has been correctly observed that in many situations Goethe himself speaks through him in a true-to-life accent. Mephistopheles sits comfortably in many saddles and, if need be, even in that of the exalted Faustian language of enthusiasm.

> You all can feel the secret virtue
> Of Nature constantly at work,
> As rising effluents alert you
> To powers that deep within her lurk. [lines 4985–88]

If this were an anonymous fragment we would hardly guess that here not Faust but Mephistopheles is speaking! He borrows such a high idealistic tone entirely for a base realistic purpose, however, to soften the minds of the Court for his deception with the paper money; and immediately afterwards he can with the same intention be quite different, with an extremely firm bite:

> When every limb will twitch and tweak,
> Uncanny signs disturb the mind,
> There resolutely delve and seek,
> There lies the fiddler, lures the find. [lines 4989–92]

Quasi-Faustian and genuine-Mephistophelian diction clash abruptly in his speech. His high-flown statements often acquire an ambivalent character in this game of quick changes. Are we to understand his words to express deeper wisdom off the top of his head, or are these only tricks whose illusory quality he disguises in a feigned cloak of profundity? The question is perhaps not so serious with regard to his sham in the state council, but it becomes terrifyingly delicate when we apply it to that "higher secret" which he, ostensibly unwillingly, reveals to Faust: the realm of the Mothers.

> Goddesses sit enthroned in reverend loneliness,
> Space is as naught about them, time is less; [lines 6213–14]

> No road! Into the unacceded,
> The inaccessible; toward the never-pleaded,
> The never-pleadable. [lines 6222 ff.]

Is there here, too, a hidden parodistic tone? Does Mephistopheles actually announce a higher mystery, however well or ill this

---

2. Goethe's native region, which includes the middle region of the Rhine, the territory on both banks of the River Main, and Hesse.

role becomes him, or are these "mothers" the product of his incentive fabling mind, a jesting pseudo-mythos, with which he hypnotizes Faust? And supposing that were so: what is to be made of such lines as

> Formation, transformation,
> The eternal mind's eternal recreation. [lines 6287–88]

Are we not allowed to understand these words of Mephisto as a serious statement of Goethean wisdom, even if embedded in a context of a jesting illusory nature? * * *

The phenomenon, again somewhat more complex, to which we now turn is the interweaving of jest and seriousness in the rhythmic succession of entire groups of scenes. Let us advance at once from the more apparent to the more problematic and consider first in this regard the scene sequence "Dark Gallery"—"Brightly Lit Ballrooms"—"Hall of Chivalry." The degree of scenic illumination apparently has much to do with the rhythm of this sequence. The darkness which surrounds the whispering evocation of the "Mothers" is followed by the superficial bustle of the court and the low comedy of Mephisto's practical jokes in a stark contrast of bright illumination. In "dim illumination" (according to the stage direction) there then ensue Faust's return from the realm of the Mothers (however real or illusory) and the magic conjuring of the phantoms of Helena and Paris. The motif of the play within the play, a magical stage upon the stage, decidedly favors the twofold optics which appear repeatedly in the twilight scene. The impassioned *engagement* with which Faust expresses to the shade of Helena his "desire, love, worship, adoration, frenzy!" [line 6500] comes still more strongly into relief through contrast with the courtiers' disengaged attitude, in which naïve banality and mundane arrogance are charmingly mixed. On both sides now an equal disinterest in the theatrical and illusory quality of the play within the play lends a note at times of farcical, at times of highly serious jesting. The foolish treasurer, as the custodian of propriety, complains that Paris is disrespectful "in the presence of the emperor" and has to be corrected by a lady in waiting [lines 6468–69]. This simple comic device mirrors charmingly the shrill tragicomic quality of Faust's conduct; he increasingly forgets his role and interferes in the "ghostly mask" [line 6564] with catastrophic results. The destruction of illusion by Mephistopheles' admonition, "Don't blow your part, man! Will you curb your fancy!" [line 6501] is akin to "romantic irony." * * * An exquisite counterpart to Faust's passionate engagement is offered meanwhile in the cautious skepticism of the "Savant," who can only involve himself in plain reality indirectly through booklearning and pedantically strict deduction:

> I must say, though I see her from close in,
> I have my doubts that she is genuine.

The present tends to court exaggeration,
That's why I rather trust documentation.
There I do read she was the special joy
Of every grizzlebearded man in Troy.
The situation fits here to a tee:
I am not young and yet she pleases me. [lines 6533–40]

* * *

Seriousness and jest are more covertly interlaced in the sequence
of scenes in the third act which culminates in the love duet
between Faust and Helena. As regards this latter, I dare not attempt to resketch in a few words this instance of the most exalted and
charming poesy, in which the union of Classical and Romantic is
perfected and embodied; it is to be recalled that important exposi-
tors of Faust have most admirably proved their skill at interpretation and representation in regard to the scene presenting the discovery of rhyme. Hence let us only briefly call to mind its pragmatic
context. The couplets spoken by the watchman Lynceus have
touched the Greek Helena as something unfamiliar and pleasantly
novel. She asks Faust for instruction, whereupon he rehearses with
her the art of rhyme in the form of an exchange. In each case Faust
speaks all of the first line of the rhymed couplet and part of the
second, whereupon Helena alertly adds the missing syllables and
establishes the rhyme:

HELENA. Tell, then, how can I speak with such fair art?
FAUST. It's easy, it must well up from the heart,
    And when the breast with longing overbuoys,
    One looks about and asks—
HELENA.   who shares our joys.
FAUST. Now seeks the mind no forth or back from this,
    Alone the present moment—
HELENA.   is our bliss. [lines 9377–84]

A profound love-duet and at the same time roguish didactics of the
gradus ad Parnassum, light and bright, which transcend all the gravity of earth. It would be foolish pedantry if we attempted to determine the measure or degree of jesting here. Yet it may be useful for
an intuitive understanding of the atmosphere which pervades it if
we call to mind the course of action and poetic form which leads
up to this high point. Concerning the poetic aspect in a narrower
sense, just this word: in the course of the section "Inner Courtyard
of a Castle" the "Classical" and "Romantic" verse forms themselves are put into action; as actors in that winged drama which
achieves its climax in the game of inventing rhyme. After the Classical meters of the chorus and chorus leader comes Faust's speech in
"Romantic" blank verse, which Helena immediately adopts with
affectionate presence of mind; then the romantic element is intensified in Lynceus' rhymed stanzas, which solicit Helena's inquisitive
question, thus leading to the love-duet on the discovery of rhyme.

As regards the content of the Lynceus scene, I wish to draw attention to the secretive interplay of the human, almost all-too-human, motif of cunning rivalry between Faust and Lynceus in their relationship to Helena. Faust, with an exaggeratedly pejorative tone, calls Lynceus "a servant," and has him put in chains for neglect of duty. In reality Lynceus is hardly a "servant" but rather, despite his vassalage, a noble warlord, as the context reveals further on. Faust has in effect already condemned him to death, and only Helena has the right to pardon him. But this judgment was too hasty. Helena sets back the execution of justice. Faust has only been the plaintiff, she herself is the judge, and with sound common sense she observes the legal maxim *audi et alteram partem*.[3] The magic of Lynceus' rhymed verses:

> Keep me kneeling, keep me gazing,
> Whether dying, whether living,
> All my soul is freely given
> Her, by Heaven sent, amazing, [lines 9218–21]

does not fail to affect his judge. This man, as she understands it, has in no way forfeited his life; as one who is "god-bewitched," he is innocent. Really at fault is her own infatuating beauty. Through this sentence Helena has in the most urbane manner seized the reins herself and put the presumptuous judge in his place. For Faust this is truly a bewildering situation, yet this bewilderment is not expressed naïvely, but rather concealed in a splendid vestment of language. The rhetorical stylistic figures of speech—paronomasia, metaphors and paradoxes—of his courtly speech of love in high-medieval style are no less reminiscent of the convoluted love-sophistries of Reinmar or Gottfried than are Lynceus' songs of Heinrich von Morungen:[4]

> In wonderment, oh Queen, I see at once
> Unerring markswoman, and here her prey;
> I see the bow from which the arrow sped
> And this one drooping. Arrow follows arrow
> Striking myself. [lines 9258–62]

His courtesy seeks even to surpass Lynceus' servitude of love, especially through the verbal gestures with which he presents himself and all that is his to her: "Fundamentally I am giving you nothing, for it is already yours anyway."

> What choice have I but to consign myself
> And all I owned in fancy unto thee?
> Let me in chosen fealty at your feet
> Acknowledge you as mistress unto whom
> By her mere advent fell estate and throne. [lines 9268–72]

3. "I also heard the other side." In other words, Helena reverses Faust's judgment by offering contrary evidence.
4. Reinmar von Hagenau (1190–1210) and Heinrich von Morungen (died 1222) were both minnesingers (medieval courtly love poets); Gottfried von Strassburg (fl.1210) was a German poet famous for his courtly, chivalric epic *Tristan*.

Once again, however, Lynceus begins to speak, and places his splendid treasures, emeralds, pearls, and rubies, at Helena's feet, whereby he employs basically the same sophistic argument as Faust and even carries it one degree further:

> All wilted what I held with pride,
> As meadow grasses mowed and dried:
> Deign to return with one gay glance
> Its former worth to it at once! [lines 9329–32]

Faust cannot tolerate that, and reduces Lynceus to silence with a surly, authoritative remark:

> All that the castle harbors in its depth
> Is hers already. Proffering her particulars
> Is useless. [lines 9335 ff.]

He then commands that the immense treasures of the castle be presented to Helena. To be sure, the powerful prince has managed to carry the day in his verbal tournament with the vassal, but the latter cannot deny himself a final word, which strikingly diminishes the triumph:

> Master's bidding needs small wit,
> Servant makes light work of it:
> Does not flesh and treasure all
> Own this sovereign beauty's thrall? [lines 9346–49]

All the same, the battle is won, the union in the love-duet can follow. Its fragile nature is accentuated by the twofold ironic breaking in which it forthwith, indeed already simultaneously, appears. The Trojan maidens, who interrupt the love-duet halfway with their choral song have not the least understanding of the more profound import of this union of the Classical with the Romantic, particularly not of the "Romantic" components of inwardness ("heart," "breast," "desire"), and they comment on the event from their perspective of heathen antiquity, in which native archaism and modish, erotic impartiality are strongly blended:

> Ladies to men's love accustomed
> Are not hesitant choosers,
> Rather expert judges.
> Be it shepherds, gold of ringlet,
> Be it fauns of swarthy bristle,
> As occasion may afford,
> To their limbs' luxuriance
> Equal claim they grant in full. [lines 9393–9400]

The intentional unsuitability of this view (even if it is unconscious on the part of the naïve maidens) is then joined by an equally distorted, indeed contrary, perspective, when Phorcyas-Mephisto as an insolent mischief-maker cruelly interrupts the then resumed love-duet and draws the sublime euphony of the rhyme-play into the mire of his coarse-sounding parody:

> Spelling-books of love construing,
> Playfully bemused in wooing,
> Vainly cooing, idly suing,
> But there is no time, I say. [lines 9419–22]

* * * From here let us pursue the question: How far and how deeply can jest reside in the most profound seriousness? We must feel our way toward the farthest limit of our theme. At the beginning of the scene "Deep Night," Lynceus the watchman sings his song "To seeing born,/To scanning called" [lines 11288–89]. Goethe's last great lyric is a blessed and glorifying song in praise of vision and of everything visible, the earth and the entire cosmos, in a manner which could not be more profound, more sublime, more comprehensive. "In all I behold/Ever-comely design," [lines 11296–97]. But at what moment is this praise announced? It impedes the advance of the most gruesome event of the entire Faust poem, at which the blood congeals in our veins: Faust's crime against Philemon and Baucis. Lynceus' song as it continues turns into a "crooning whimper" [line 11338], where he describes the burning of the hut teichoscopically.[5] But the antithesis of the context is not thereby exhausted. Even a moderately clever spectator or reader who has paid attention knows full well about the imminent disaster when Lynceus begins to sing. Faust has decided with regard to both the old people that Mephistopheles should "clear them from my sight" (11275); Mephistopheles has passed the order to his three henchmen, whose soldierly coarseness Faust knows all too well, as we do also; and as if that were not enough Mephistopheles has predicted the result *ad spectatores*:

> What passes here is far from new;
> There once was Naboth's vineyard, too. [lines 11286–87]

Lynceus' song follows immediately afterwards, closing with the lines:

> You fortunate eyes,
> All you ever did see,
> Whatever its guise,
> Was so lovely to me! [lines 11300–303]

From a superficial and sober viewpoint one may remark that for the spectator to know more than the character in the play is a normal instance of dramatic irony, even though here a particularly keen example. Perhaps it is preferable to speak of "very serious jests,"

---

5. From the Greek, meaning "observed from a wall," in reference to the old men of Troy watching the battle in Homer's *Iliad*, Book III. In drama this occurs when a character describes something which he is witnessing as it happens offstage.

whereby strong emphasis must be placed on the first two words. Through the jest the seriousness is enormously deepened. The import and value of the song of praise is not undermined by the ironic configuration; and, on the other hand, through the perspective opened by the song of praise, the crime becomes all the more darkly revealed. Had the song of praise not been sung, the shudder which seizes us at the consummation of the disastrous deed would be somewhat less severe.

* * *

We come finally to our problem, which has already been postponed too long, and which, whether a genuine or a false problem, is in any case central to research on Faust: Does Faust win or lose the wager with Mephistopheles? * * * If one considers scholarly opinions, there emerges, as it is customary to say, a bewildering picture. A cataloguer of doctrines in the scholarship of *Faust II* once drew up a schematic list which I do not wish to withhold from you:

1. Faust wins:
   a. Faust wins in the literal sense and in the higher sense: 21 scholars, of whom only 1 is undecided.
   b. Faust wins not in the literal sense but in the higher sense: 10 scholars, but in compensation no cases of indecision.
2. Faust loses: 13 scholars, but 1 in a certain sense only halfway, for later he crosses over into the camp of those asserting that Faust wins; and 3 undecided.
3. Faust half wins and half loses: only 1 instance and that undecided, to which, of course (this is my comment), Goethe's name may be added, at least the Goethe of 1830 who wrote, "Mephistopheles can win his wager only in part . . ."
4. Nobody wins; the wager is invalid:
   a. because Mephistopheles has broken the contract: 2 scholars.
   b. because presuppositions prove to be false: 2 scholars, of whom 1 is undecided.

It is scarcely our cataloguer's fault that this tabulation resembles a caricature of serious research, like a jest which is not even serious, but rather involuntary.

* * *

Let me explain finally what I have in mind. I am convinced (and have arrived at my conviction only gradually and, as is natural, by overcoming inner opposition) that this disastrous confusion rests largely on the fact that here all too often inquiry has been made in a basically "spoilsport-like" manner. I mean this quite literally. The game is spoiled by looking and arguing past the sense of autonomous play in the poetic. Let us call to mind the awesome yet magnificently tragicomic aspect of Faust's death scene in the large outer courtyard of the palace. The testamentary last speech of the blinded Faust is accompanied by the roguish gestures of the shoveling Lemures, digging not a canal, as Faust, preoccupied with his illusion, believes the clanking of spades to signify, but a narrow house, his grave. Elements of the sublime and of buffoonery clash harshly with one another. * * *

Within this framework Faust's last words are spoken, which, as is maintained, must determine whether the wager is won or lost. We may recall the much discussed emendation which Goethe intro-duced presumably just before his death. Until then the much shorter concluding speech had read:

> I may entreat the fleeting moment:
> Oh tarry yet, thou art so fair!
> My path on earth, the trace I leave within it
> Eons untold cannot impair.

In the final version the speech concludes, as is well known, in a more conditional manner which looks to the future:

> Such teeming would I see upon this land,
> On acres free among free people stand.
> I might entreat the fleeting minute:
> Oh tarry yet, thou art so fair!
> My path on earth, the trace I leave within it
> Eons untold cannot impair.
> Foretasting such high happiness to come,
> I savor now my striving's crown and sum. [lines 11579–86]

In the scholarly "war of all against all" those who place essential importance upon the change of "I may" to "I should" are again and again severely reproached. That is considered to be subtlety and sophistry. So be it; from the perspective of mere seriousness this view may even be correct. It should be considered, however, whether we may here have before us one of the central and choice instances which Goethe had in mind when he coined the expression "very serious jests." With profound artistic wisdom Goethe realizes through his use of the subjunctive the intention, already present though more obscure in the earlier draft, to leave the problem of the outcome of the wager essentially open. The reader is given free scope to reflect on this problem and to consider the possible answers; any further specification constitutes a restriction which is basically unfair to the enigmatic profundity of the course of Faust's life and death. In order to make this wisdom poetically concrete, Goethe employs a verbal device which is highly cheerful. He actual-izes the humorous ambiguity which is potentially contained in the conditional subjunctive. * * *

It is possible that some readers will interpret and condemn my repeated emphasis on indeterminateness and the lack of a specific point of view as agnosticism. It is not quite intended in this way. What I mean is that we have reason to impose discretion on one another in interpreting this text. To eliminate excessively senseless questions should only serve to clarify the horizon within which questions can be raised in a meaningful way. To this end the multiple perspective of the serious jest must constantly be kept in mind. And last of all just this. The serious jest does not signify a tired skepticism. It is the legitimate possibility for realizing a metaphysical poetry of wisdom in a post-Enlightenment age, in which the relation of religious faith to heaven and hell has changed irreversably. There is still faith, not in the strict sense, but in reserving freedom for personal decisions and interpretations. In such an age, the creation of and response to the most sublime poetry of wisdom requires courage and, more precisely (in a Goethean non-pejorative sense), presumption. In the summer of 1828, in the midst of planning and creating *Faust II*, Goethe wrote to his friend Zelter: "If this thing does not continuously point to a presumptuous condition, if it also does not require that the reader rise above himself, then it is worth nothing." I know of no words which paraphrase more precisely the demand which this great poem makes of us. A preacher provides a lesson for his sermon right at the beginning; let me offer one at the end. It is the introductory line of one of the most beautiful poems of the West-Easterly Divan:[6] "To write poetry is presumptous."

HANS EICHNER

The Eternal Feminine: An Aspect of Goethe's Ethics†

In his well-known book on Goethe,[1] Emil Staiger declares that an insurmountable sense of awe makes it impossible for him to attempt an interpretation of the final two lines of *Faust*. Other commentators have been less reticent, but the implications of these lines seem to be inexhaustible, and it is the purpose of this paper to take a closer look at them.

It may be helpful to begin by reminding ourselves of the context in which the lines are placed. At the age of one hundred, Faust has died. In the final scene of the play, which has a very elaborate setting for which Goethe drew on a group of frescos in the Campo Santo at Pisa,[2] we are looking into a steep valley covered with dense forests and populated by hermits. Hovering above the valley, a group of angels is carrying Faust's soul towards heaven, and above them there is a "choir of penitent women." Three of the penitents are identified, not without a touch of whimsy: they are the magna

6 Goethe's *West-östlicher Divan*, published in 1819, is a collection of love poems modeled on the work of the medieval Persian lyric poet Shamsuddin Mohammed Hafiz (ca. 1325–89).
† From *Transactions of the Royal So-*

ciety of Canada, Series IV, Vol. IX (1971), pp. 235–44. Reprinted by permission of The Royal Society of Canada.
1. *Goethe* (Zürich, 1959), Vol. III, p. 466.
2. See note to line 11603 of *Faust*.

peccatrix who anointed Christ in the house of the Pharisee; the Samaritan woman who was told by Christ that she had had five husbands and now lived in sin with a sixth man; and the Egyptian Mary of the Acta Sanctorum. The penitents, whose sins have long been forgiven, plead with the Virgin Mary on behalf of Gretchen, who is accepted by the Virgin and told to rise with her to higher spheres: Faust would feel her presence there and follow. A saint identified as Doctor Marianus prays to Mary, and then the famous final lines are intoned by the Chorus mysticus:

> Alles Vergängliche
> Ist nur ein Gleichnis;
> Das Unzulängliche,
> Hier wird's Ereignis;
> Das Unbeschreibliche,
> Hier ist's getan;
> Das Ewig-Weibliche
> Zieht uns hinan.

As the published English versions show, this final passage is quite untranslatable. A paraphrase might run as follows: "All that is transitory is merely symbolical; here (that is to say, in the scene before you) the inaccessible[3] is (symbolically) portrayed and the inexpressible is (symbolically) made manifest. The eternal feminine (i.e., the eternal principle symbolized by woman) draws us to higher spheres."

What is said at the beginning of our passage—that transitory things have only symbolic significance—was almost a commonplace in the Age of Goethe and need not concern us today. It is only the last two lines that I wish to examine. To a limited extent, they are almost self-explanatory: it is Gretchen, we know, whom Faust is to follow on her way to higher spheres. But neither Gretchen nor, for that matter, the three penitents who interceded on her behalf, and at least one of whom was a prostitute, can in themselves be meant by the "Eternal Feminine." One could, as Douglas Yates, in agreement with many other commentators, has done, take one's cue from the dominant presence of the Virgin Mary in the final scene and identify "das Ewig-Weibliche" with the redeeming power of Love, revealed to Man in its most perfect form as Woman. As Yates comments, "The possibilities of Love, which Earth can never fulfil, become realities in the higher life which follows; the Spirit [of Love], which Woman interprets to us here, still draws us upward."[4] This interpretation has the virtue of simplicity and is supported by its immediate context. But *Faust* is not primarily a play about divine love, and the last lines of a play have such a privileged position that no interpretation is satisfactory unless it explains

3. For the translation of "unzulänglich" as "inaccessible," see Staiger, p. 466.
4. J. W. v. Goethe, *Faust. A Tragedy in Two Parts*, translated by Bayard Taylor, with notes by Douglas Yates (World's Classics, vol. 380; London, [1963]), p. 447.

them in terms of the play's *total* context. I feel therefore that the final sentence of Faust must contain a further meaning, which I propose to seek by way of a long digression.

Among the maxims Goethe published in *Über Kunst und Altertum* we find the following analysis of the human predicament: "Der Handelnde ist immer gewissenslos; es hat niemand Gewissen als der Betrachtende"—"He who acts is always without scruples; only he who contemplates has a conscience."[5] Because we can never completely foresee the consequences of our actions, Goethe suggests, we can never act with a good conscience: guilt is always just around the corner. But inaction presents no escape from this dilemma and would be self-defeating. As we are told in *Wilhelm Meister*, "You can never get to know yourself through contemplation, but only through action; try to do your duty, and you will soon know who you are."

Needless to say, Goethe did not propose that we should act blindly. Ideally, thought and action should be combined. "To act is easy," Wilhelm Meister is told, "to think is hard; to act as your thought dictates is disagreeable." But the union of thought and action, postulated in this aphorism as an ideal, can never be completely realized, and Goethe's characters have two typical ways of falling short of it. On the one hand, there are those who become involved in the business of living, who take the risks of action or of intense emotional involvement, and who often enough, as a consequence, do great harm to others or to themselves; and, on the other hand, we find those whose primary concern is to keep themselves pure and to become models of moral virtue. Some of the former, even when they are presented as admirable, are peculiarly inaccessible to pangs of conscience—they shake off feelings of guilt as a duck shakes off water; most of the latter, even though they shine like beacons in a grey, troubled world, are in a peculiar way sterile. The former, in Goethe's mature work, almost without exception are men, and the latter women: the ideal of purity is seen as eternally feminine, the ideal of significant action as masculine.

In Goethe's earlier works the polarity exists without sexual differentiation. There are men of action, such as Götz von Berlichingen, but we would look in vain for women embodying an ideal of contemplative purity that contrasts with resolute male activity. The girls in the early works—Gretchen in the first fragmentary draft of *Faust*, Marie in *Götz*, Lotte in *Werther*, Klärchen in *Egmont*, lovable and unforgettable though they are, would all, given a kindlier fate, have turned into reliable and efficient, but quite unspectacular, good German mothers and housewives.[6] After Goethe's move to Weimar and his encounter with Frau von Stein, an entirely new type of woman begins to emerge in Goethe's *oeuvre*. Just as there is

5. Goethe, *Werke*, Hamburger Ausgabe, Vol. 12, p. 399.
6. These female characters occur in Goethe's earlier works as follows: the drama *Götz von Berlichingen* (1772), the novel *The Sorrows of Young Werther* (1774), and the drama *Egmont* (1788).

618 · *Hans Eichner*

a group of girls and young women who have a vague family resemblance in his early works—Gretchen, Marie, Lotte, Klärchen—there is an entirely different group of women who resemble one another in the later works: Iphigenie in the play that bears her name, Natalie and Makarie in the two parts of *Wilhelm Meister*, Eugenie in *The Illegitimate Daughter*, and Ottilie in *Elective Affinities*.[7] The first group is as homespun as their names; those in the second, as *their* names suggest, are not made of the common clay, and their names link them almost in a kind of rhyming pattern—Iphigenie, Natalie, Eugenie, Ottilie, Makarie. If the man of action is always devoid of scruples, these women emphatically have a conscience: they are all embodiments of an ideal of moral purity—the ideal of "das Ewig-Weibliche."

Since space is limited, I shall concentrate on Goethe's treatment of the theme in *Iphigenie* and the two parts of *Wilhelm Meister*, regretfully leaving aside the highly interesting and complex cases of Ottilie and Eugenie.

When Goethe wrote *Iphigenie*, he radically changed the traditional Greek plot.[8] With Euripides, Apollo sends Orestes to Tauris with instructions to bring back a sacred image of Diana; Orestes succeeds in doing so, and in rescuing his sister, through an act of deception in which Iphigenia is implicated. In Goethe's play Apollo gives Orestes ambiguous instructions: he and his friend Pylades are told to bring back "the sister." They think of course that Apollo's sister—i.e., the image of Diana—is meant, but it turns out in the end that the reference is to Orestes' sister, Iphigenie; and hence the play can be brought to a happy end without involving Iphigenie in treachery. There is some loss in dramatic excitement, but we are rewarded for this loss by a serious treatment of an important moral issue. Goethe's Pylades is the typical man of action: brave, loyal, full of good intentions, but not very scrupulous in his choice of means. He works out the plan by which he and Orestes can be saved and the image stolen—a plan which requires for its execution that Iphigenie must lie to Thoas, the King of Tauris. The turning point of Goethe's play comes when Iphigenie is told the part she has to play. Pylades tries to persuade her to lie to the king; he argues that the world is such that we cannot afford to insist on moral perfection.

> You led a life apart, safe in your temple;
> We learnt to be less strict with ourselves,
> And you will learn it too. All men are caught
> And tangled in the web of circumstance

7. These female characters appear in Goethe's later works as follows: the drama *Iphigenie in Tauris* (1788); the novels *Wilhelm Meister's Apprenticeship* (1795–96) and *Wilhelm Meister's Travels* (1821), the tragedy *The Illegitimate Daughter* (1804), and the novel *Elective Affinities* (1809).

8. Goethe's play *Iphigenie in Taurus* (1788), which is described in what follows, was adapted from the drama of Euripides with the same title.

And no man keeps himself from blame and lives.
It is not our task to judge ourselves,
But to perform what our lot demands,
For no-one knows the value of his deeds.
Besides, you have no choice. [*Iphigenie*, lines 1653–64]

But Iphigenie decides that she must not deceive the king who has befriended her: she feels that she must keep herself pure at all cost, and she refuses to believe that the world is such that one has no choice but to become guilty or perish. Her convictions are borne out when, having revealed the plot to the king, she is forgiven and allowed to depart with Orestes and Pylades.

The maxim with which Iphigenie replies to the urgings of Pylades—"the heart is only at ease with itself if it preserves its complete purity"—might equally well be claimed by Natalie, the exemplar of moral purity in *Wilhelm Meister's Apprenticeship*; but here—as Goethe's novel projects a less optimistic world view than his play—matters are more complicated.[9] It has always been recognized that Goethe intended Natalie to represent an ideal. She is admired by everybody in the novel, and she is the great prize Wilhelm gains at the end of his apprenticeship. Yet the picture Goethe drew of Natalie is somewhat anaemic. We hear of her constant devotion to duty, but her activities are confined to the narrow circle open to a young noblewoman in eighteenth-century Germany—a circle so narrow that in it you could indeed act and yet afford a tender conscience. For the most part, Natalie is characterized by negatives—for instance, by her lack of passionate involvement even with Wilhelm, whom she is to marry. The novelist does not seem to have very much to say about her—and his silence is eloquent. The story of Wilhelm and Natalie is the only love story I have ever read that culminates in an engagement in which the lovers do not kiss each other—and there is worse to follow. The wedding takes place after the end of the first part of the novel, the *Apprenticeship*, and before the beginning of the second part, *Wilhelm Meister's Travels*, and we can only infer from circumstantial evidence that the wedding took place at all. When we meet the fortunate husband again, he has left home, on the instruction of the secret society to which he belongs; and, unlike other women in the novel, Natalie never bears her husband a child: she seems to be just as much a priestess of Diana as Iphigenie.

What we are to make of all this is a matter of dispute. The majority opinion among the critics is that Goethe simply failed to realize his intentions—an opinion which I do not share. I find it significant that Natalie's brother, Lothario, occupies the same position of supremacy among the men in the novel that Natalie occu-

9. Cf. Karl Schlechta, *Goethes Wilhelm Meister* (Frankfurt am Main, 1953); and Hans Eichner, "Zur Deutung von 'Wilhelm Meisters Lehrjahren,'" *Jahrbuch des Freien Deutschen Hochstifts*, 1966, pp. 165–96.

pies among the women. The portrait Goethe draws of him is equally odd: he is obviously portrayed in the novel as a man of action, but we are told far more about his love affairs than about his practical activities, and these love affairs show beyond doubt that he does not have a very finely honed conscience. We can of course conclude that Goethe made a mess of the portrayal of both brother and sister, but it seems far more natural to assume that he knew what he was doing: he created a perfectly matching pair. The brother, Lothario, is held up for our admiration as a practical and resolute man of action, and we learn from his characterization that such a man is unlikely to be squeamish. Natalie is held up for our admiration as a model of moral purity, and her characterization teaches us that such absolute purity can be maintained only at the cost of avoiding all serious involvement with the world: he who acts cannot afford a conscience.

Finally, there is Makarie in the novel of Goethe's old age, *Wilhelm Meister's Travels*. This is a very loosely constructed and episodic work with hardly any coherent plot. Some aspects of contemporary German society and some aspects of experimental colonies in America are explored, and a number of interpolated love stories illustrate, not without a touch of monotony, that intense emotional involvement leads to trouble, from which only renunciation can save us. Thus, *Wilhelm Meister's Travels* would be a trite and preachy work were it not that the rich and sometimes highly emotive concrete details of the novel pull against its soberly moralistic and abstract message. Caught in the web of circumstance, intensely involved and sometimes blinded by passion, the young lovers in the novel as often as not do the wrong things, but they are intensely, movingly, and beautifully *alive*. They represent one end of the spectrum of human possibilities that the novel projects. At the *other* end there is Makarie, in whom that chain of representatives of the "noblest femininity," Iphigenie, Natalie, Eugenie, Ottilie, culminates; she is hardly the most attractive or convincing, but the most instructive representative of her type. She alone, among the long array of saintly women, leads a life of almost pure contemplation. She lives in considerable isolation on a country estate, leading a life without external events—a life whose story cannot be told as there is no story. Her existence is not useless. On the contrary, to repeat a phrase I have used before, she shines like a beacon in a dark world, like a motionless lighthouse by which others, the travellers whose lives do have a story, can set their course. When those involved in feeling and action turn to her in their need, they are never dismissed without advice and consolation. She is an ideal, a model of selflessness and of purity of heart. Yet—such is the realism of Goethe's prose world—this embodiment of *das Ewig-Weibliche* suffers from migraine headaches and is cast in the unenviable role of old spinster and maiden aunt.

We are skirting an age-old moral paradox. In a world dominated by greed, selfishness, and blind passion, selfless service to others is a necessary moral ideal; but as a model of universal conduct, it is self-contradictory: if we all take in each other's washing, we are back where we were to begin with. A woman like Makarie serves as an unfailing source of inspiration—yet if we were all like her, life would come to a standstill. Iphigenie is a priestess of the goddess of chastity; Natalie is childless and a perennial grass widow; Eugenie enters a marriage that is not to be consummated; Ottilie withdraws from life and dies a saint; Makarie is an old maid: the price paid for a blameless life is sterility.

This is the point where our digression at long last leads us back to our starting-point. The two major works Goethe completed in his old age, *Faust* and *Wilhelm Meister*, complement each other. The sequence of saintly women we have glanced at shows us one path man can follow in his search for perfection, but shows it to us in all its devastating, and yet inevitable, one-sidedness. Faust, as we shall see in a moment, shows us the other way, the way of action, which exacts an equally heavy price: we are all like Philoctetes; if we would have the bow that never fails, we must endure the wound that will not heal.[1]

As I am sure you know, Goethe's *Faust* begins with a conversation between the Lord and Mephistopheles concerning the nature of man, in which the Lord declares that, as long as man keeps striving, he will always go wrong (he who acts is always without scruples):

> Man ever errs the while he strives. [line 317]

But the real danger, the Lord adds, lies not in the wrong man may do, but in that he may decide not to do anything at all; in fact, he explains, it is the particular function of the devil to see to it that man does not relapse into inactivity:

> Man all too easily grows lax and mellow,
> He soon elects repose at any price;
> And so I like to pair him with a fellow
> To play the deuce, to stir, and to entice. [lines 340–43]

The Lord then points to Faust as his loyal servant and permits Mephistopheles to try to corrupt him.

Such corruption can take two forms. Faust might decide deliberately to do evil instead of good, or he could decide to do nothing at all; but as the first possibility is never seriously taken up in the play —Goethe was never very much interested in the problem of deliberate evil—we are really left only with the second alternative. The question whether Faust *will* desist from activity and involvement—

1. The legend of Philoctetes, hero of the war against Troy, is the subject of a play by Sophocles. Philoctetes received the bow of Hercules at the time of Hercules' death but was bitten in the leg by a poisonous snake and became a cripple.

be it as a result of exhaustion, despair, remorse, or the realization that all action is reckless—must now form the framework within which the whole story moves.

We first meet Faust in his study, where he has presumably led a life of learning and contemplation. By the time the action begins, this stage of his life, however, is just about over. When he inspects the magic symbol of the macrocosm and rejects it—

> What glorious show! Yet but a show, alas! [line 454]

he has done with contemplation, and he turns expectantly to the Earth Spirit, a spirit explicitly symbolizing intense involvement and ceaseless action.

As action always involves the danger of wrong-doing, Faust promptly has his first encounter with the power that inhibits action, *Sorge*, that is to say, care, worry, excessive scrupulousness—the power which Horace had personified and demonized in one of his odes as *atra cura*,[2] and which Goethe himself, as we shall see, was to personify as an evil demon towards the end of *Faust*. At this early stage *die Sorge* is the subject of an important monologue, which, however, I will not quote. Two scenes later, Faust re-confirms his decision to turn his back on a life of contemplation when he tries to translate the Gospel according to St. John, is stumped by the word "logos" in the first sentence, and boldly *mis*translates the sentence as "In the beginning was the deed."[3] In the next scene, he concludes the wager with the devil which Goethe substituted for the traditional pact and declares that he will never cease from activity. But Faust is not merely concerned with action, but with *every* kind of involvement. He longs to experience all that is given to man to experience:

> Henceforth my soul, for knowledge sick no more,
> Against no kind of suffering shall be cautioned,
> And what to all of mankind is apportioned
> I mean to savor in my own self's core. [lines 1768–71]

It is quite consistent, therefore, that Faust's first involvement should be one of love, especially if you remember the striking contrast between the involved lovers in *Wilhelm Meister* and the uninvolved Makarie. In accordance with the general pattern we have discovered, involvement leads to guilt, and just as Faust's intensity of involvement is exceptional, so is the degree of his recklessness: he seduces Gretchen, kills her brother, deserts her, and thus, ultimately, destroys her. In a brief scene a group of nature spirits then frees him of all remorse.

2. Black Care. See Horace, *Odes*, III.1.40.
3. See, however, E. M. Wilkinson, "Faust in der Logosszene—willkürlicher Übersetzer oder geschulter Exeget?" in *Dichtung Sprache Gesellschaft. Transactions of the IVth International Congress* of Germanists, ed. Victor Lange and Hans-Gert Roloff (Frankfurt, 1971; Princeton, 1970), pp. 115–24, esp. p. 115, where it is pointed out that the New Testament usage of *logos* has been influenced by the Hebrew *dabar*, which does mean both "word" and "deed."

It has always annoyed moralists that Faust is let off so lightly, but a critic who takes offence at this scene must take offence at the whole of *Faust*. It is, Goethe tells us, human nature to err; those saintly figures like Ottilie whose law of being is purity are destroyed if they have offended against their own nature, but the man of action and involvement is ruled by a different law; remorse is a luxury *he* cannot afford. Having erred, he must not allow his conscience (worry about the past) or *Sorge* (worry about the future) to inhibit him and to wreck his life, but must start all over again and try to do better. (It is worth remembering that when Gretchen is overcome by remorse in the cathedral scene of *Part I*, her pangs of conscience are personified by a spirit explicitly called "ein böser Geist," an evil spirit—first cousin, we may add, to *Sorge*.)

Thus it makes perfectly good sense that Faust is quickly regenerated at the beginning of *Part II*. He now resumes his quest of intense experience, but has outgrown sensual involvement and turns to the aesthetic realm. His encounter with the world of art, culminating in his union with Helena, fills the first three acts of *Part II* —a very important section of the play, but one that we must pass over in silence. Once separated from Helena, Faust at long last really turns to involvement in *action* rather than love or beauty— and he does so in the same grand, excessive manner in which he has done everything else. The earth, he now tells Mephistopheles, has room for great deeds; he means to astonish the world—he wants to acquire power and property. Faust now pursues this aim as we would expect him to, not very choosy in his means, recklessly, without counting the consequences. With the aid of Mephistopheles he wins a battle for an incompetent emperor and is rewarded with a strip of coastland. Building dikes and acquiring a fleet, he achieves power and riches, in the way in which such things *are* achieved in this world: by violence, oppression, and exploitation, though, as the dirty work is done for him by Mephistopheles, Faust can close his eyes to what is going on. Finally, he becomes responsible for the death of an innocent aged couple, Philemon and Baucis, and this time no nature spirits come to his rescue to salve his conscience. As their cottage burns to the ground, the smoke materalizes in the shape of the familiar evil demon, Care, who assails Faust in a battle of life and death. Faust now realizes that all action is unscrupulous, that his own entanglement in the web of life has time and again led to evil. If this awareness is to inhibit him, that is to say, if Care is to gain power over him, he will henceforth be unable to act, his spirit will be broken, and Mephistopheles will have triumphed. The demon of Care unfolds this prospect in all its horror, in one of those masterly speeches that give Goethe's dramatic poem its undying appeal; but Faust, unrepentant, will have nothing to do with her. He emerges from the encounter victorious, and promptly plans new activities on an even larger scale—a great project of swamp drainage that is to provide room for a whole people. There is no guarantee that, if he were to live, his great project would not again depend for its execution on slave labour and exploitation; but it is at this point—his spirit unbroken, once again planning great deeds —that Faust dies.

The many critics who have accused Goethe of reckless optimism have not read him very closely. In his world, as we have seen, there are two incompatible ideals of conduct, each of them to be followed only at such a cost that perhaps I should not call them ideals. On the one hand, there is the ideal of purity, represented in Goethe's works exclusively by women, the Eternal Feminine; on the other hand, there is the ideal of ceaseless activity and involvement, shown up in all its dubious virtue, and yet glorified, in the figure of Faust. All sorts of compromises are open to us of course—the compromises of those who blow neither hot nor cold—but the compromisers can never rise above harmonious mediocrity. But is no genuine synthesis ever to be hoped for, not even at a future, more advanced stage in the development of man, or perhaps even in a better life after death? Can the man of action never acquire true wisdom without ceasing to be what he is? And must not the man of action be guided, in his intentions at least, by that ideal of purity which Goethe saw as eternally feminine, if he is to be more than a ruth-less condottiere and a Nietzschean blond beast? The answer to all these questions, as the end of *Faust* shows, is "Yes." In the last scene of the play, a hope is held out to us. The long series of saintly women we have studied ends with Makarie only on this earth, in the here-and-now. As Faust's soul shakes off the dust and ashes of mortality, the Virgin Mary hovers above, the Eternal Feminine without this world's limitations, the symbol of a purity that, by a miracle, is not sterile: Virgin and Mother. The Eternal Feminine in the last lines no doubt refers to divine forgiveness, and, in a half-hearted way, it must also refer to Gretchen, who precedes Faust in his ascent to higher regions; but most meaningfully, it refers to the ideal of purity that must inspire, though it must not inhibit, even the man of action, and that, to Goethe, always appeared in femi-nine guise:

> All in transition
> Is but reflection;
> What is deficient
> Here becomes action;
> Human discernment
> Here is passed by;
> Woman Eternal
> Draw us on high. [lines 12104–11]

Selected Bibliography

Books and articles included in this edition are omitted from this bibliography. Items are listed chronologically in all sections except the last, which is alphabetical.

EDITIONS OF *FAUST* PREPARED BY GOETHE

Faust. Ein Fragment. In Goethe, *Schriften.* Vol. 7, pp. 1–168. Leipzig, 1790.
Faust, der Tragödie I. Teil. In Goethe, *Werke.* Vol. 8, pp. 1–234. Tübingen, 1808.
Helena. Klassisch-romantische Phantasmagorie. Zwischenspiel zu Faust [i.e., Part Two, Act III]. In Goethe, *Werke (Ausgabe letzter Hand).* Vol. 4, pp. 229–307. Stuttgart, 1827.
Faust I and *Faust II,* lines 4613–6036. In Goethe, *Werke (Ausgabe letzter Hand).* Vol. 12, pp. 1–247, 249–313. Stuttgart, 1828.
Faust, der Tragödie zweiter Teil. In Goethe, *Nachgelassene Werke.* Vol. 1. Stuttgart, 1832. (= *Ausgabe letzter Hand,* vol. 41.)

SCHOLARLY-CRITICAL EDITIONS

Faust I, Faust II, and *Faust II, Lesarten.* In Goethe, *Werke (Weimarer Ausgabe).* Edited by *Erich Schmidt.* Section I, Vols. 14 and 15, Part 1 and Part 2. Weimar, 1887–88.
Goethes Faust in ursprünglicher Gestalt, nach der Göchhausenschen Abschrift [the *Ur-Faust*]. Edited by Erich Schmidt. Weimar, 1887.
Faust. In Goethe, *Werke.* Published by the German Academy of Sciences in Berlin. Vol. I, *Urfaust* and *Faust, ein Fragment,* with a facsimile of the MS. of the *Urfaust.* Berlin, 1954. Vol. II, *Der Tragödie 1. Teil.* Edited by Ernst Grumach and Inge Jensen. Berlin, 1958. Supplementary volume, *Urfaust, Faust, ein Fragment,* and *Faust I* printed in parallel columns. Berlin, 1958.

EDITIONS WITH COMMENTARY

Faust. In Goethe, *Werke.* Vol. 12. Edited by H. Düntzer. *Deutsche National Literatur.* Edited by J. Kürschner. Vol. 93. Berlin, 1882.
Goethe's Faust. Edited by Calvin Thomas. Vol. I, *The First Part.* Boston, 1892. Vol. II, *The Second Part.* Boston, 1897.
Faust I and *II.* In *Goethes Sämtliche Werke (Jubiläums Ausgabe).* Edited by Erich Schmidt. Vols. 13 and 14. Stuttgart, 1903, 1906.
Faust. Edited by Georg Witkowski. 2 vols. Leipzig, 1907; 10th ed., Leiden, 1949.
Faust and *Urfaust.* Annotated by Ernst Beutler. *Sammlung Dietrich.* Vol. 25. Leipzig, 1939.
Faust. Eine Tragödie. In *Goethes Werke. Hamburger Ausgabe.* Vol. 3. Edited by Erich Trunz. Hamburg, 1949.
Die Faustdichtungen. In Goethe, *Artemis-Gedenkausgabe.* Vol. 5. Edited by Ernst Beutler. Zürich, 1950.
Goethe's Faust. Edited by R-M. S. Heffner, H. Rehder, W. F. Twaddell. Vol I, *Part I: Text and Notes.* Boston, 1954. Vol. II, *Part II.* Boston, 1955.
Faust. In Goethe. *Poetische Werke (Berliner Ausgabe).* Vol. VIII. Edited by Gotthard Erler. Berlin, 1965.

ENGLISH TRANSLATIONS OF *FAUST*

Faust. A Tragedy. By Johann Wolfgang Goethe. *The First Part* and *The Second Part.* Translated in the Original Metres by Bayard Taylor. Boston, 1871.
Goethe's Faust in Two Parts. Translated by Anna Swanwick. London, 1879.
Faust. A Tragedy. The First Part. By Johann Wolfgang von Goethe. In a Modern Translation by Alice Raphael. New York, 1930.

J. Wolfgang von Goethe. *Faust, Parts I and II*. Translated from the German by George Madison Priest. New York, 1932.
Goethe's Faust [Part One]. A New American Translation by Carlyle F. MacIntyre. Norfolk, Conn., 1941.
Goethe. *Faust. Part One* and *Part Two*. Translated by Philip Wayne. 2 vols. Middlesex, Eng., 1949, 1959.
Goethe's Faust. Parts I and II. An abridged version translated by Louis MacNeice. Oxford, 1951.
Goethe's Faust. Part One and selections from Part Two. A new translation by Walter Kaufmann. Garden City, N.Y., 1961.
Goethe. *Faust. Parts I and II*. Translated by Charles E. Passage. Indianapolis, 1965.
Goethe's Faust. Translated by Barker Fairley. Toronto, 1970.

BIBLIOGRAPHIES, LEXICA, AND REFERENCE MATERIALS ON *FAUST*

Grundriss zur Geschichte der deutschen Dichtung. By Karl Goedeke and successors. [Subsection on *Faust* under "Goethe"]. 3rd ed. Vol. 4, section 3. Dresden, 1912. Vol. 4, section 5. Berlin, 1960.
Carl Kiesewetter. *Faust in der Geschichte und Tradition*. 2nd ed. Berlin, 1921.
P. M. Palmer and R. P. More. *The Sources of the Faust Tradition from Simon Magus to Lessing*. New York, 1936.
Ada M. Klett. *Der Streit um Faust II seit 1900*. Jena, 1939.
Wortindex zu "Faust." Edited by A. R. Hohlfeld, Martin Joos, and W. F. Twadell. Madison, Wis., 1940.
A. R. Hohlfeld. *Fifty Years with Goethe. Collected Studies*. Madison, Wis., 1953.
Stuart Atkins. *Forschungsbericht*: "*Faust*forschung und *Faust*deutung seit 1945," *Euphorion*, 53 (1959), 422–40.
Hans Schwerte. *Faust und das Faustische. Ein Kapitel deutscher Ideologie*. Stuttgart, 1962.
Historia von D. Johann Fausten. New edition of the Faust-Book of 1587. Edited with an introduction by Hans Henning. Halle, 1963.
Goethe-Bibliographie. Founded by H. Pyritz, continued by H. Nicolai and G. Burkhardt. Heidelberg, 1964.
Stuart Atkins. "The Interpretation of Goethe's *Faust* since 1958," *Orbis Litterarum*, 20 (1965), 239–67.
Faust-Bibliographie. Edited by Hans Henning. Published by the Research Center and Memorial of Classical German Literature in Weimar. 4 vols. (another forthcoming). Weimar, 1966–.

BOOKS IN ENGLISH ON *FAUST*

Atkins, Stuart. *Goethe's Faust: A Literary Analysis*. Cambridge, Mass., 1958.
Butler, E. M. *The Myth of the Magus*. Cambridge, 1948.
———. *The Fortunes of Faust*. Cambridge, 1952.
Dieckmann, Liselotte. *Goethe's Faust: A Critical Reading*. Landmarks in Literature. Englewood Cliffs, N.J., 1972.
Fairley, Barker. *Goethe's Faust: Six Essays*. Oxford, 1953; reprinted 1965.
Gillies, Alexander. *Goethe's Faust, an Interpretation*. Oxford, 1957.
Gray, Ronald. *Goethe the Alchemist*. Cambridge, 1952.
Jantz, Harold. *Goethe's Faust as a Renaissance Man*. Princeton, 1951.
———. *The Mothers in "Faust": The Myth of Time and Creativity*. Baltimore, 1969.
Mason, Eudo. *Goethe's Faust: Its Genesis and Purport*. Berkeley, 1967.
Salm, Peter. *The Poem as Plant: A Biological View of Goethe's Faust*. Cleveland, 1971.
Santayana, George. *Three Philosophical Poets: Lucretius, Dante and Goethe*. Cambridge, Mass., 1910.